John Hughes, John Breckinridge

Is the Roman Catholic religion, in any or in all its principles or doctrines, inimical to civil or religious liberty?

John Hughes, John Breckinridge

Is the Roman Catholic religion, in any or in all its principles or doctrines, inimical to civil or religious liberty?

ISBN/EAN: 9783741112522

Manufactured in Europe, USA, Canada, Australia, Japa

Cover: Foto ©Lupo / pixelio.de

Manufactured and distributed by brebook publishing software (www.brebook.com)

John Hughes, John Breckinridge

Is the Roman Catholic religion, in any or in all its principles or doctrines, inimical to civil or religious liberty?

A
DISCUSSION

OF THE QUESTION

IS THE ROMAN CATHOLIC RELIGION,

In any or in all its Principles or Doctrines,

INIMICAL TO CIVIL OR RELIGIOUS LIBERTY?

AND OF THE QUESTION,

IS THE PRESBYTERIAN RELIGION,

In any or in all its Principles or Doctrines,

INIMICAL TO CIVIL OR RELIGIOUS LIBERTY?

BY THE

REVEREND JOHN HUGHES,

OF THE ROMAN CATHOLIC CHURCH,

AND THE

REVEREND JOHN BRECKINRIDGE,

OF THE PRESBYTERIAN CHURCH.

BALTIMORE:
PUBLISHED BY JOHN MURPHY & CO.
No. 178 MARKET STREET.
PITTSBURG....GEORGE QUIGLEY.
Sold by Booksellers generally.
1867.

PREFACE.

THE following brief statement of the origin of this Discussion, and of the measures adopted for its publication, seems necessary. The question, "Is the Roman Catholic Religion, in any or in all its Principles or Doctrines, inimical to Civil or Religious Liberty?" was adopted, January, 1835, as a topic of debate in the Union Literary and Debating Institute. The object in view, was in accordance with the general design of the Institute—the improvement of its members. The Society, consisting of Roman Catholics and Protestants of various denominations, whilst it disclaimed all sectarian motive, entered on the discussion in that bold spirit of inquiry, conducted by candour, which characterized its debates, and without the slightest expectation that any but subscribing members would take part in the discussion.

So interesting and exciting, however, did this question prove, that after the debate had been continued three evenings, during which the Rev. Messrs. Hughes, M'Calla, and Breckinridge, Honorary Members of the Society, were the principal speakers, arrangements were made, by a Committee of the Society, for a continuance of the discussion, between the Rev. Messrs. Hughes and Breckinridge, for six evenings. It was further agreed, that at the expiration of the six evenings, the word "Presbyterian" should be substituted for the words "Roman Catholic," and an equal portion of time should be devoted to the new question.

According to the articles of agreement between Messrs. H. and B. and the Society, a Reporter was to be employed by the Society, and a report of the speeches furnished. The Society were disappointed as to the services of the Reporter on the first three evenings of the debate. The concluding speeches were also retained in the hands of the Reporter for some months after its close. In consequence of these difficulties, and others appertaining to the mode and extent of correction, an arrangement was entered into by the disputants to fill up the deficiency in the Report, and to correct the speeches, as each might think proper. The time necessary to re-write the Discussion, added to the previous delays, has protracted the publication to a whole year after the close of the oral debate.

These delays, though attended with some inconvenience to the Society, have, at least, given the disputants an opportunity of doing justice to themselves, respectively, in giving *their own* report of their speeches. The only disagreement between them now is, as to the amount of matter:—the one contending, that only one-third of the number of speeches delivered in the oral discussion are produced in their written report:—and the other maintaining, that each of the written speeches contains the matter of three, as they were spoken. It is not for us to decide, but to leave, as we do, the gentlemen themselves, and the public, to form their own opinion on this point. This misunderstanding, however, between the disputants, required the action of the Society, which was had in the annexed resolutions. In accordance with instructions from the Society, the Committee have disposed of the work to the present publishers, and we trust that the importance of the questions discussed, will cause it to meet with an extensive circulation.

The Letters, referred to in the subjoined resolutions, are appended, and will fully explain the views of the reverend gentlemen as to the publication.

In justice to the Society, it is necessary to state, that to have sanctioned a continuance of the debate for publication by them, would have so increased the size of the volume, as to have prevented the Committee from carrying out their views as to its immediate disposal.

THOMAS BROWN, M. D.
WILLIAM DICKSON,
Committee on Publication.

May 20*th*, 1836.

RESOLUTIONS

OF THE

UNION LITERARY AND DEBATING INSTITUTE,

Passed April 4th, 1836

Whereas, The Union Literary and Debating Institute has become involved, beyond the extent of its means, in consequence of providing a Reporter for the late Discussion between the Rev. Messrs. Breckinridge and Hughes: and *whereas,* the report of the stenographer, and the manuscripts furnished by him, were, after this expense incurred by the Institute, condemned as unsatisfactory and incorrect, and another mode, viz., rewriting the whole, agreed upon, and a satisfactory arrangement entered into to that effect: and *whereas,* another difficulty has now arisen relative to this affair, and the Institute can see no prospect of an event promised in the beginning, and are weekly at more expense and trouble on this account; therefore—

Resolved, That the Committee of Publication are hereby instructed, *forthwith,* to dispose of the manuscripts of the Discussion in their hands for *immediate publication,* and report final action on the next evening of meeting; and that all the letters which have passed between the parties be included in the publication.

Resolved, That both clergymen be permitted to continue the work, under the sanction of the Society, but at their own expense.

DEFINITIONS AND CONDITIONS.

DEFINITIONS.

I. RELIGIOUS DOCTRINES.

THOSE tenets of faith and morals which a denomination teaches as having been revealed by Almighty God.

II. RELIGIOUS LIBERTY.

The right of each individual to worship God according to the dictates of his own conscience, without injuring or invading the rights of others.

III. CIVIL LIBERTY.

The absolute rights of an individual restrained only for the preservation of order in society.

CONDITIONS.

1. That when the question, "Is the Roman Catholic Religion, in any or in all its Principles or Doctrines, opposed to Civil or Religious Liberty?" shall have been discussed, for any number of evenings not exceeding six, the question then shall be, "Is the Presbyterian Religion, in any or in all its Principles or Doctrines, opposed to Civil or Religious Liberty?" which shall be discussed for an equal number of evenings.
2. That, in both cases, it shall be the duty of the affirmative to prove, that what he calls a doctrine, is really such, before he can use it as an argument.

The decree of a General Council, the brief or bull of a

Pope, or the admitted doctrines by a Pope, shall be admitted as proof on the one side: the Westminster Confession of Faith, of the Presbyterian Church in America, shall be admitted as proof on the other side.

4. The discussion to take place before the Union Literary and Debating Institute, with one hundred Catholics and one hundred Presbyterians, to be invited by the reverend gentlemen.

5. All questions of order shall be decided by the President; and no person whatsoever to be permitted to take part in the debate, but the Reverend Messrs. Hughes and Breckinridge.

6. The President shall prevent any manifestation of approbation or disapprobation, and enforce perfect silence in the meeting.

7. That a stenographer shall be engaged by the Institute, to take an impartial report of the proceedings and debate, and that no unauthorized report be given by the Society.

JOHN HUGHES,
JOHN BRECKINRIDGE.

LETTERS, ETC.

Philadelphia, March 14th, 1836.

To the President of the Young Men's
    Literary and Debating Society.

Sir,

I HAVE had the honour, within a short time, of receiving a resolution from the Society over which you preside, requesting the respective parties, in the discussion which they are now preparing for the press, to condense the matter, as much as practicable, consistently with the end in view.

In reply to this communication, I am prepared promptly to say, that the wishes of the Society are entirely in accordance with my own; and that it will give me much pleasure to do all in my power, without a sacrifice of the object in view, to reduce the size, and hasten the appearance of the intended work.

It is well known to the Society, that it was esteemed by me a violation of my rights, and a departure from the original agreement among the several parties concerned, to adopt the present mode of preparing the debate for the press. It pleased the Society, however, to indulge Mr. Hughes, and I yielded my wishes to his. There were three methods of accomplishing the publication of the Discussion within our reach, viz.—1, the putting of the stenographer's report to press; 2, debating the whole anew; 3, writing it out anew, as the disputants might choose. The first and second were *declined* by Mr. Hughes; and the *third adopted*. I had preferred the first or second—but acquiesced in the *third;* and by mutual agreement between Mr. H. and myself, the Society approving, we have been, for some time, engaged in reducing the debate to manuscript form. In proof of this, I beg leave to refer the Society to the correspondence in the hands of your Secretary, and to the testimony of the *Publishing Committee.*

I have just been informed, however, by one of the members of that Committee, that Mr. Hughes *declines* the continuance of the Controversy, after the completion of the *third part* of the nights originally set apart for the debate. Upon what ground he ventures thus to abandon the Discussion, it is not *my* business to declare. Surely it cannot be with the approbation of the Society; and it must be at the entire sacrifice, if persisted in, of his cause, his honour, and my rights. I hereby, therefore, utterly protest against giving such a course the sanction of the Society, if, by such sanction, it be understood that it shall be expected, or required of me, *now* to close the Discussion; and I cast myself on the justice of your honourable body, claiming of them, very respectfully, the full protection of my equal rights. Nay, more, I may appeal to the magnanimity of the young gentlemen of the Society, as they must remember, that the very plan which Mr. Hughes now seeks to defeat, by a premature close, was accepted by me, in order to oblige the Society, and to indulge Mr. Hughes.

As, however, I am very desirous to bring this vexed question to an amicable termination, I offer to the Society, (for I can no longer permit myself to have any direct intercourse with Mr. Hughes,) the following propositions:—

I. I will agree to complete *six* evenings of the debate—*three* on *each question*, and then put the work to press. As the *written* speeches exceed those *spoken* in length, about *eight evenings* of the *former* might probably embrace the substance of what was spoken in *twelve;* and *six* might, with condensation, present the chief part of the Discussion.

In this event, I propose to pursue the subject hereafter on my own responsibility.

II. I will agree to publish *eight nights*, and for the *present, at least,* giving no additional matter—to the public—present the debate as in SUBSTANCE *complete*.

III. If Mr. Hughes declines both these propositions, I shall stand prepared to furnish my *part* of the entire debate, with the confident expectation that the Society will publish *all* that Mr. Hughes may have contributed; and, stating his withdrawal, publish the matter furnished by the other party.

IV. In the event of the Society's consenting to sustain Mr. Hughes, in the very extraordinary course proposed by him, which appears to me wholly impossible, I must seek another channel to the public; and, at the same time respectfully ask of the Society to refund to me the sums of $10, and of $150, advanced by me, (the first, as a donation, the second, as a loan, borrowed by me for that end,) to pay the stenographer. If *I* had *refused to abide* by the stenographer's report, then there might be some justice in my contributing so largely to pay him; as that refusal, by *preventing* the publication of the work, has dried up one chief source of your revenue. But so far was this from the fact, that my advance to the stenographer was made *after* I had failed to bring his work to press; and on the faith that the *present* arrangements would be enforced by the Society, so as to complete the debate, and secure its sale. Whereas, Mr. Hughes, who vilified the stenographer's report, paid *nothing* toward defraying the expense of it; and is now seeking to mutilate the matter, and, as I believe, to defeat the publication of the *manuscript*.

With much respect, I am, dear sir,
Your friend and servant,
JOHN BRECKINRIDGE.

March 22d, 1836.

To Messrs. BROWN AND DICKSON, *Committee, &c.*

GENTLEMEN,

I HAVE now finished the correction of my speeches, and my part of the Discussion. The matter is equivalent to more than eighteen hours' public speaking, and consequently it is time to stop. If the Society had, according to agreement, held a stenographer engaged, and thus taken down the arguments, *in the words of the speakers*, much trouble and labour would have been saved to all parties. But the first three nights of the Discussion were blanks, as to any report. Then came Mr. Stansbury, under the auspices of Mr. Breckinridge, to take notes of arguments, and fill up the supposed thoughts of the speakers in language, as near as might be to that which they employed. This did not give my arguments—except as Mr. Stansbury conceived them. Consequently, the report was imperfect;—the reporter was not employed at the expense of the Society, as appeared—1st, by the fact, that Mr. Breckinridge proposed to compensate him by a *public collection;* and 2d, by the fact, that he neglected the report, until after he had attended to business in Pittsburgh and Cincinnati. Hence, it follows, that the Society, having failed in that part of our understanding on which their claim to my speeches depended, could not have any right to expect them. But, least there should be the shadow of legitimate complaint, I have, by my own labour, supplied the defects of their mismanagement, and will hand them my part of the Discussion, authenticated by my signature, to be published for their benefit;—PROVIDED, that not a single page, in the printed copy, shall be allowed *more* to one side than to the other. If the aggregate number of pages, to be occupied by my speeches, should exceed that required by Mr. Breckinridge's manuscripts, I shall curtail. If his should exceed mine, he must curtail. I ask nothing but what is right; I shall submit to nothing that is wrong. I trust, gentlemen, that you, and the independent portion of the Society, will discover, in this proposal, that I ask nothing but that the *scales of justice be held even*. I am aware, that there may be, in the Society, a few little spirits, who, not having strength to burst the nutshell of bigotry in which they are confined, are accustomed to prefer what is *expedient* to what is *only just*. Now, I cling to justice.

If this just proposition should be defeated, then I shall hold myself as having done every thing honourable and fair to lay the merits of the Discussion before the public, and let the Society enjoy the benefits arising from it; but then, too, I shall use my manuscript as I think proper. The individual, or party defeating, or attempting to defeat the publication on this basis of justice and equality, must be responsible to the Society for the consequences. As to myself, I have not the slightest doubt but the public will see through the whole matter, and, with the exception of the little spirits in the nutshell, form a just judgment.

I have the honour to be, gentlemen,
Your obedient servant,
JOHN HUGHES.

Philadelphia, March 29th, 1836.

To the President of the Young Men's
Literary and Debating Society.

Sir,

Having been informed, that the young gentlemen of the Society have delayed the final decision of the painful question now pending, in regard to the publication of the debate, until this evening, I take the liberty of making an additional communication through you to the Society.

As no little time has passed since the debate began, and many changes have taken place in our arrangements, a rapid retrospect of the circumstances may not now be amiss. The following facts will not be disputed, it is supposed, by any member of the Society; or if disputed, are capable of ample proof.

1. Mr. Hughes *refused*, on the third night, to proceed without a *reporter*—yet *he* afterwards rejected the *reporter's work*.

2. Mr. Hughes selected the present method of preparing the debate for the press; and he pledged himself to complete it in this way; and he proposed no *limits* or *terms* at the *commencement* of this plan of preparation : on the contrary, he found fault with the former Publishing Committee for seeking to restrict him; and a new committee was appointed by the Society to carry the new plan into effect.

3. The Society did thus and otherwise sanction the present

plan, and agree to carry it into effect. And it was on the faith of Mr. Hughes's pledge, and theirs, that I gave up the stenographer's report, and adopted Mr. Hughes's plan. And it was on the faith of the same united pledge, that the debate should be completed, *sold*, and published, that I advanced a considerable sum of money to pay the Society's debt to the reporter.

4. Mr. Hughes first set the example of *enlarging* the form of the original debate; for when the first Publishing Committee opposed his *additions* to the report of the stenographer, he said he was to be the judge of how much or how little should be added. Acting on this principle, we began, *afterward*, to rewrite the whole, each having full liberty. When, therefore, Mr. Hughes complains of the dilation of the Discussion, he should remember that he is not only the *sharer*, but *author* of the practice.

5. Though more matter has been *written* than was *spoken* on the same number of nights, yet a considerable portion of the topics, presented in the oral debate, have, as yet, not been touched in the manuscript; as, for example, the *supremacy of the Pope;* the *doctrine of the Roman priesthood;* the *order of the Jesuits;* the *monastic institutions;* the *immoral tendency of the system of popery;* the *Inquisition;* the *papal conspiracy abroad against the liberties of our country, are all yet to be examined, and was all gone over in the debate.* This, Mr. Hughes well knows. Yet he seeks now to stop short, and exclude all that yet remains. Besides all this, there are allusions in the discussion of the second general question, to the discussion of the first, which *first* will not appear, if we arrest the debate here. How absurd will this appear; and to me, how palpably unjust? Mr. Hughes, contrary to the order of the debate, contrived to alternate, very absurdly, one speech on one question, and one speech on the other. And now we have each question half discussed; yet he insists on publishing *now,* and publishing *no more!*

In view of all these facts, I can hardly think it possible for your honourable body to do such violence to my rights, as *now* to force a close of the Discussion on me. Being, however, unfeignedly anxious to bring every part of the Discussion, as speedily as possible, before the American people, I have conceded much to the wishes of others, as will be seen in my last letter, to which I respectfully refer the Society.

That there may be no room left to complain of my terms, I here add, to the proposals of that communication, the following, viz:—

As Mr. Hughes *refuses* to go farther in the debate, let it be agreed, that, *for this reason,* we will *now* publish *four nights* of the manuscript debate: let me then complete my argument on the papal question, and publish it under the sanction of the Society, accompanied by an explicit avowal of the fact that Mr. Hughes declines to pursue the Discussion. I will publish the second part at my own risk, and ask no more than what is stated above. If Mr. Hughes asks more, his country must see why; and his best friends must blush for him, when he shall not only abruptly, and after all his pledges, withdraw from the Controversy, but even seek to silence me midway the question.

I feel well assured, sir, that the honourable young gentlemen, of all names and sects, over whom you preside, will esteem my wishes reasonable; and will unite to sustain me in my obvious rights.

But if not, then I must appeal to the American public; and reverting to the alternative, the painful alternative, stated in my former letter, I must seek shelter from injustice, before a larger and better tribunal, who love liberty, who will do justice; and before whom, if God give me help, I am resolved to spread out the *whole of the debate*, and the history, as well as the matter of it, if my stipulated rights should now be so seriously invaded.

With full confidence in the candour and justice of the Society, remain, dear sir, very respectfully,
Your friend and fellow-citizen,
JOHN BRECKINRIDGE.

P. S. I understand it has been alleged, that inasmuch as I called on the audience to aid in paying the fees of the stenographer, at the close of the debate, therefore, he was confessedly *my* reporter. It is well known, as I then avowed, that the *reason* of the call was the *poverty* of the *Society*, (which had no funds,) and the pressing wants of the reporter who expected to leave the city the next morning. Besides, it is fully known, that, for three nights, the Committee had failed to get a reporter; and Mr. Hughes *refused to* proceed *without* one. Then, at the *request* of the Committee, I wrote for Mr. Stansbury—the faithful reporter of the American Congress for some dozen years. And yet, after all, Mr. Hughes *rejects* his *reports*. *Then*, when we yield to his wishes, give up the reporter's manuscript, and begin, at his re-request, to write *anew*, he proceeds but *half* way through; when lo, again, and of a sudden, without consultation, or agreement with the other parties, he *resolves* to *stop*. Will the Society sustain such a course? It was on the faith of Mr. Hughes's repeated pledge, to complete the debate, and on the faith of the Society's pledge, to cause it to be completed, and sold, and published, that I advanced money to pay the debt of the Society. Will the Society now permit, nay, aid in a continuance to defeat the publication?

J. B.

Philadelphia, April 5th, 1836.

To Messrs. BROWN AND DICKSON.

GENTLEMEN,

I AM sure you must be weary, as I am, most heartily, of the *interminable* contests which have been going on about the publication of the debate. It seems apparent that Mr. Hughes will not, *on any terms,* publish the *entire debate;* and my friends have urgently solicited me to consent to publish the *four* nights, which will be complete, on my furnishing my reply to his sixth speech on the Presbyterian question. I hereby, then, signify *to you my consent to this course,* which I pray you to make known to the Society this evening.

In thus waiving my rights so entirely, I hope you will understand that it is intended as a testimony of my high respect for the Society which I am unwilling longer to embroil, even in doing me justice; and *that it is my purpose to go on, through the press on my own responsibility, to complete the Discussion.* For their desire, and their long continued efforts to issue the whole debate, I owe them my sincere thanks; and I am consoled by the thought, that the young gentlemen have had so practical a proof, that it is not Protestantism, but Popery, which *shuns* the *light.*

The only condition which I feel at liberty to make, is that the correspondence which relates to the publication of the debate, shall be published with it.

I know not, after this, what else Mr. Hughes can require of the Society, or of me, than that I should be *bound to write and debate no more on popery,* as the condition of his publishing any part of the debate.

I am, gentlemen, very respectfully,
Your friend and fellow-citizen,
JOHN BRECKINRIDGE.

Philadelphia, April 11th, 1836.

To THE PRESIDENT OF THE UNION LITERARY
AND DEBATING SOCIETY.

SIR,

IN certain letters of Mr. Breckinridge, which he wishes to have prefixed to the publication of our Debate, there are statements which are calculated to mislead those who are not acquainted with the facts of the case, and to which I have been indulged with the privilege of replying. In his letter of the 14th ult. he complains of the "present mode of preparing the Debate for the press." To this I reply, that owing to our not having a stenographer the first three nights of the discussion, and owing to the manner in which the remainder, or at least portions of it, continued in the hands of the stenographer for months after the debate closed, there was no other mode left in which to prepare it. After having attended the GENERAL ASSEMBLY, and the trial of Dr. Beecher, the reporter wrote to your Committee, on the 24th of June, that "his *next* business would be to *resume* the report," &c. By whose fault did this happen? Mr. Breckinridge says, there were "three methods:" 1. "Putting the stenographer's report to press." This is absurd. That report was but *three-fourths* of the discussion, and not the whole. It contained none of the citations of authorities, which were numerous. It merely referred to them, and left it to the speakers to fill up. Would it not have been absurd, then, to put it to press in this condition? His second method was, "debating the whole anew." This, indeed, would be a new method of preparing *the debate* for the press. The third was that which has been adopted. He says this was done to "indulge Mr. Hughes." The statement was incorrect;—it was done because no other, *in the circumstances of the case*, was practicable. I called on him through the Committee, and on the Committee themselves, to point out any other practicable method;—and when they could not, he, and they, and I, agreed, by mutual consent, to adopt the present mode. This is the simple history of the whole matter; and shows, that so far, if Mr. Breckinridge has any reason to complain, it is *not of me*, but of the Society—for not having a stenographer from the first, and not obliging him to attend to the business for which he was supposed to have been engaged, consecutively and in season.

2. He complains in the same letter, that I discontinued the debate after the completion of "the third part of the nights originally set apart for the Discussion. To this I reply, that each of the written speeches, one with another, contains as much matter as *three* of those that were spoken. Both parties spoke one hour and a half every evening; which, for the twelve evenings, makes, for each, eighteen hours speaking. In each half hour there must have been a waste of two or three minutes, by interruptions, looking for references, &c., which would take off more than an hour of the whole time, making it for each, less than seventeen hours. Now, let Mr. Breckinridge take his *twelve written speeches*, and attempt to deliver them, with that solemnity, and those graces of elocution, for which he is so distinguished, and he will find that twenty hours will not be sufficient. Consequently, the written speeches, though fewer in number, contain more than those that were spoken. But who began these long speeches? Mr. Breckinridge himself! Look at the speech with which he opened;— and according to which I was under the necessity of regulating

my reply. Here, therefore, is my reason for stopping—at the conclusion. Another reason was, that the Society had requested that the matter should be condensed as much as possible. A third reason was, that if the *two parts*, out of three which Mr. Breckinridge says are wanting, were added, it would swell the work to six or seven volumes, which would frighten any publisher in the city. It is on all these grounds that I have allowed Mr. Breckinridge to call it only the *third part* of the Discussion, knowing, that if he says he spoke *more in the time allowed for speaking*, than what he has written out, no one, who reflects a moment will put any belief in the assertion.

In his letter of the 29th of March, Mr. Breckinridge complains that, owing to the pretended abridgment of the Discussion, there are a great many subjects which he has not had an opportunity to introduce. To this I reply, that he had the privilege, in common with myself, of correcting the report in any manner, and to any extent he might think proper. If, then, instead of adhering to the original substance, he thought it more serviceable to fill up his space with new and apocryphal matter, he must not blame me for the consequences of his choice. He introduced, for instance, the subject on which the Rev. Murtoch O'Sullivan has been holding forth in Exeter Hall, viz., DENS'S THEOLOGY. I did not blame him for this; on the contrary, I approved it, by following his example in other instances.

But, besides, the very topics which he says he has been obliged to omit, are to be found in his speeches in tedious repetition. For the correctness of this statement, I refer to his speeches in connection, or rather, in contrast with his letter. He has introduced, into his written speeches, *whole columns* of printed matter from his own former writings, and from the writings of others; and this fact shows that he ought not to complain of want of space. He was uncontrolled in the choice of his matter and argument. The interchange of speeches on both questions at the same time, was merely to expedite the work according to the wish of the Society. From all this, it is evident, that the matter of the corrected, or written speeches, is fully as much as that of the entire Discussion; and, secondly, that the introduction of new topics was a matter of *choice*, and not of necessity, with Mr. Breckinridge.

He says, in his letter of the 29th, that, in reference to the lengthened speeches, I was not only "the sharer, but author of the practice." This is a mistake. The first speech—the rule for others, was HIS. It is true, that when the former Committee attempted to prescribe the length of my first speech *on the Presbyterian Question*, I resented their interference, because I would not consent to be deprived of any privilege which had been allowed to Mr. Breckinridge.

He says that I "refused on the third night, to go on without a reporter—and yet I afterwards rejected the reporter's work."

The first part of the statement proves that I wished the Discussion to be published. And the second is not correct. I never rejected the stenographer's work; but, as it was *avowedly incomplete*, I claimed to correct it; and, as no rule could be pointed out to obviate dispute about the correction, I suggested that he should correct his speeches, and I mine, as we pleased.

He says that, at the commencement, I "proposed no *limits* or terms." This is true; but it does not follow, that the Discussion should become endless on this account. The time employed by each speaker would determine the limits, and, by this rule, I maintain that the Discussion, as now presented, is larger than if every word uttered in debate had been taken down and preserved. If Mr. Breckinridge thinks that he has not done justice to the subject, he may write as long as he can find ink and paper; but I must be at liberty to follow him or not, as I may think proper. This matter is quite simple. I allow him page for page with myself; and if he require an appendix to help him out, then,—to borrow a phrase from his own letter,—"his country must see why; and his best friends must blush for him."

In his letter of April 5th, Mr. Breckinridge speaks of his having "waived his rights," &c. Sir, he has waived no rights. To every thing that has been done, he has been a free, voluntary party. I never dictated to him. I never submitted to his dictation. In the whole matter I never knew or felt but one principle, implied by the words *justice, honour, impartiality*—and, above all, "do unto others as you would that they should do unto you." But I knew my own rights, and have had both power and fortitude enough to resist and repel their invasion.

Mr. Breckinridge, in the same letter, sets forth, that it is not "Protestantism but Popery that shuns the light." If, by the phrase, "shuns the light," he means, that I have not wished to see the Discussion published, nothing can be more untrue. I entertain, after all, too high an opinion of Mr. B.'s sagacity and judgment, to suppose, for a moment, that he seriously entertains any such opinion. What *he* has said of the Catholic religion, has been often, and better said before. What *I* have said on the other side, will remove prejudice from every candid mind, and, as regards the genius of Presbyterianism, will exhibit the motives which should induce every lover of civil and religious liberty to watch its movements, and be prepared to resist its grasping spirit of sectarian domination over all other creeds. The question, on the other side, has been, not of "Protestantism," but of "*Presbyterianism*" alone. Against the Episcopalians, Methodists, Baptists, Friends, Lutherans, or other denominations of Protestants, I have said nothing.

In the same letter, Mr. Breckinridge says, "I know not, after this, what else Mr. Hughes can require of the Society, or of me, than that I should be bound to write and debate no more on

popery, as the condition of his publishing any part of the debate."
Now, I entreat the Society, not to "bind" the gentleman under
any such cruel obligation. By it, his *usefulness* to himself and
the country would be destroyed. But though I do not wish to
bind him in any sense, yet I cannot help expressing the opinion,
that to preach peace and good will among men, would be a holier
employment of his time. " Blessed are the peace-makers, for
they shall be called the children of God."

3. He refers, in his P. S. of the 29th of March, to the fact of
his having undertaken to remunerate the stenographer, not from
the funds, or by the credit of the Society, but from the pockets of
the guests—by a COLLECTION.

Now, let him give any explanation he may think proper of that
proceeding: it proves that the reporter had been employed by Mr.
Breckinridge, and looked to him for compensation. And here I
must refer to the position lately assumed by the Society, claiming as a *matter of justice*, an arbitrary right to indemnify themselves by virtue of an agreement *which they never fulfilled*. If
they had provided a stenographer, and he had taken down the
debate from beginning to end, in order, then, indeed, the report
should be theirs—because they would have fulfilled the conditions
on which alone their title, *in justice*, depended. But failing to do
this, they have thrown upon us the labour of reporting, *de novo*,
the whole debate. This debate was theirs, inasmuch as I am concerned, *because I intended to give it to them*, on the conditions of
a fair and impartial publication. But it was not theirs on any
other title; and it has been with deep regret that I have observed
the *Protestant* member of their Committee, in obedience to the advice of intrigue, setting up a pretension to detain my manuscript,
forcibly, unjustly, illegally. I had placed it in the hands of that
gentleman on deposit, until it should pass into the hands of the
publisher. I treated him with confidence by placing my manuscript in *his hands*, when I might have put it in the hands of his
Catholic colleague. I have been disappointed, and I regret it. If
I had ever violated my word of honour, in my whole intercourse
with the Society, or its Committees, there might have been some
pretext for this dishonourable proceeding to which I refer. But I
defy any member of the Society to point out a single instance in
which, so far depended on me, I did not comply with my engagement, and fulfil my promise. *Have the other parties done the
same?* It seems to have been a favourite object, with Mr. Breckinridge, *to make it appear* that I was *forced* to publish. To refute
this gratuitous and unworthy suspicion, I refer to the whole history
of my proceeding. I insisted that a stenographer should be in attendance. I took upon me to supply, by my own hand, the deficiencies and corrections of his report. I had the whole copied
at considerable expense. I had never refused to publish; but on

the contrary, desired it in thought, word, and deed. But I never should have given it to the Society, if the terms of publication had not been *fair, equitable,* and *impartial.* And to prove to the Society that I have given it, not only willingly, but FREELY, *I have had a copyright secured according to law.* This precaution was rendered necessary in order to remove all ground for the imputation which was attempted to be cast on my honour and integrity.

Thus, sir, whilst I acted honourably with the Society and its Committees,—refusing, with frankness, to do anything that I regarded as unfair,—but fulfilling, to the letter, whatever I had once promised,—I never left myself in their power. And when, by an attempted violation of my rights, a member of your Committee, in obedience to the voice of intrigue, would detain my property, I qualified myself to laugh the pretension to scorn, and to teach him that I proceed to publication, not by the coercion of petty artifice, but by the moral obligation of my own word, freely pledged, and FREELY redeemed.

I am an American citizen—not by *chance,*—but by *choice.* When circumstances seemed to make it a duty, I threw myself in the breach, to vindicate the principles of my fellow-citizens of the Catholic religion throughout the United States. I have done so; and, by carrying the war into the camp of the enemy, I have taught one of the ablest representatives of that Presbyterian combination, which is attempting to destroy the civil and religious reputation of Catholics, that if any denomination of Christians are to be *expelled* for the crime of persecution, it would be the lot of Presbyterianism—*to march first.* In doing this I have submitted to the sacrifice of much personal feelings, much labour, inconvenience, and anxiety. And the reason why I retained my just dominion over my manuscript, was, least if passed into other hands, it might never find its way to the public. If it belonged to the Society, the consequence would be, that, as *their property,* they would have a right to burn it if they thought proper. I have taken care that it should have a better destination.

But, sir, I am not only an American citizen, but also a Roman Catholic. I was born under the scourge of Protestant persecution, of which my fathers, in common with their Catholic countrymen, had been the victims for ages. Hence, I know the *value* of that civil and religious liberty which our happy government secures to all; and I regard, with feelings of abhorrence, those who would sacrilegiously attempt, directly or indirectly, immediately or remotely, to deprive any citizen of those inestimable blessings. God alone is the lord of conscience. As a Catholic, I trust I should be ready to renounce liberty, and even life, sooner than renounce one doctrine of the faith of the Church—for without faith it is impossible to please God. But what is faith without charity? And is not charity the love of God, as God;—and the love of our neighbours as ourselves? Let other men endeavour to serve God, and save their souls, in whatever religion they believe to be true—their rights are as sacred as mine.

Finally, sir, in taking leave of the Union Literary and Debating Institute, permit me to return my thanks for the personal courtesies, and honourable and impartial treatment, which I have experienced from the majority of its members, Protestants as well as Catholics. In my intercourse with them, I trust that, if I have manifested a reasonable measure of independence, I have never been deficient in courtesy and respect. I have never, by underhand measures, attempted to bias one member, or control one measure in your proceedings. As to the under-current of petty intrigue and prejudice, by which the best and most impartial measures of the Society have been sometimes turned aside, I, at this moment, think of those who have been engaged in the direction of its various courses, as persons to be only pitied and forgotten.

I am, with great respect,
Your friend and fellow-citizen,
JOHN HUGHES.

P. S. The following is the letter of Mr. Breckinridge, to which reference is made more than once in the progress of the Discussion. He knew I disliked personal contention with any one, and most of all with him, for reasons which I have not concealed. He knew that I had been *invited*, not to dispute, but *to deliver an address*, before the Society, on the subject referred to in his letter: and he had *privately* engaged Mr. M'Calla to attend. All this was before he left Philadelphia. He goes to New York, and after three or four days, writes me the following *modest, veracious*, but to me, extraordinary and unexpected letter. I give it as my apology and justification for the pain which my exposures of Presbyterianism must inflict on the feelings of many worthy persons of that denomination.
J. H.

New York, January 21st, 1835.

To THE REV. JOHN HUGHES.

SIR,

I HAVE just been informed that you are expected to address a Society to-morrow evening, on a question of which the following is the substance, viz.: "*Whether the Roman Catholic Religion is favourable to Civil and Religious Liberty?*"

I write a few lines, in order to say, that I will meet you, on the evening of the 29th instant, before the same Society, Providence permitting, on that question :—or, if that be not *agreeable* to you, in any other place where this vital question may be fully discussed before our fellow-citizens.

As I shall not be present, I request that you will yourself make the necessary suggestions to the Society to-morrow evening, and give me as early a reply as convenient. I can conceive of only one reason for your refusing, and I hope time has overcome that.

I remain, your obedient servant,
JOHN BRECKINRIDGE.

PART I.

―――

"*Is the Roman Catholic Religion, in any or in all its Principles or Doctrines, opposed to Civil or Religious Liberty?*"

DISCUSSION.

"Is the Roman Catholic Religion, in any or in all its principles or doctrines, opposed to civil or religious liberty?"

AFFIRMATIVE I.—MR. BRECKINRIDGE.

BEFORE I enter on the discussion of this important question, I wish to say to this society, that I hold in my hand a Roman Catholic paper, published in New York, called *"The New York Weekly Register and Catholic Diary,* No. 21, Vol. III., Feb. 21, 1835"—which purports, in a letter signed R. C. W., to give a true report of our preliminary discussion, held in this hall some evenings since.—This letter is a tissue of uncandid statements, and is most scabdalously and injuriously *false*. As a committee of this society has publicly corrected the representations made in a Protestant paper of this city, concerning a previous debate between the Rev. Mr. M'Calla and the Rev. Mr. Hughes, so I now demand, in the name of truth and equal rights, that a similar notice be taken of this base production:—and as the author has avowed in the course of his statement, that he waited on Mr. Hughes, and received from him *"a copy of the conditions on which the debate is to be conducted"*—so I have demanded of the Rev. gentleman the name of the author, as it must be known to him; and I shall hold him *responsible* for the letter and its contents until he gives it up.

[The Rev. Mr. Hughes said—I did not come here to listen to newspaper articles, but to debate the question before us; and no other business is in order.]

Mr. B.—I lay this publication on the table, and pronounce the author guilty of base and divers falsehoods, which I will prove by one hundred witnesses whenever he will venture to avow himself.—Till then, I hold Mr. Hughes responsible.

In advocating the affirmative of this question it is not meant to be asserted, that *all* the principles of the Romish religion are opposed to civil and religious liberty—but that many, very many of them are; and that the system of which they make a vital part is opposed both to civil and religious liberty.—Here it is worthy of remark, that the efforts of the gentleman to tie up the discussion by peculiar definitions drawn from his own views, are both unusual and highly characteristic of himself and the gentlemen with whom he is associated. A definition should be found in the terms of the question—and if terms are fixed, defining the limits of debate, they should be technically accurate, and entirely impartial. The definition offered by the gentleman on a former occasion was singular enough, and goes very far to show his whole system of belief as to the rights of man. He gravely proposed to you the adoption of the following definition of *civil liberty*, viz., "*the right of each individual to advance the good of the people, by every constitutional and honest means.*" Now, sir, this is the definition of a *duty*, and not of a *right*. But when you compare this definition with what the gentleman said in our preliminary discussion, you will see how the parts of the system explain each other. On that occasion he contended that the *majority* had in all *cases the right to rule;* and of course, as in Spain, the *majority* had a *right* to compel the *minority* to receive the Roman Catholic religion as the religion of the state, and the only religion to be tolerated. The minority here must submit. What rights had they? Why to promote the "*public good*"—viz., to be as "*good Catholics*" as possible; to help on the system as much as possible—their right is to *submit!*

[Here Mr. H. said,—I defined it to be the right of every individual to do all the good he could, in promoting public happiness.]

Mr. B.—I repeat it, this is a *duty*. But we are speaking of *rights*. The explanation alters not the case. If, as the gentleman said on the last evening, the *majority has the right to rule*—then if the majority did wrong, it followed that it was *right* to do *wrong*. And then, if the day should ever come, when Roman Catholics will compose the *majority* in *this* country, they may of *right* establish their religion by *law*. This is the broad and ruinous principle of the gentleman; and we see what it is, and where it leads. Hence his indifferentism as to the liberty of other lands;— and his views about other governments. Now I contend that there are certain rights which lie *aback* of all conventions among men. That, according to our ever memorable Declaration of Independence, there are certain inalienable imprescriptible rights derived from God, of which a man cannot deprive himself, or be deprived —such as no *majority* can deprive him of, and no possible state of society weaken or destroy.

I would give the following *constitutional* definition of liberty, (religious, especially as that enters peculiarly into this debate,) derived from the Constitutions of Pennsylvania, (1790); Kentucky, (1799); Ohio, (1802); Tennessee, (1796); Indiana, (1816); Illinois, (1818); Missouri, (1820); almost in identical terms. This definition is a compact among the citizens of these states. The Rev. gentleman is not a Pennsylvanian or an American if he *rejects* it; I will show he is not true to his holiness if he *adopt* it. It is this: "*All men have a natural and indefeasible right to worship Almighty God, according to the dictates of their own consciences; no man can of right be compelled to attend, erect, or support any place of worship, or to maintain any ministry against his consent; no human authority can in any case whatever control or interfere with the rights of conscience; and no preference shall ever be given by law to any religious establishments or modes of worship."* This is the right of *all* men, laity as well as clergy—everywhere; at Rome, as in North America—the indefeasible, natural right; that is, a right by the law of nature, or in better language, by the gift of the God of nature; and therefore a right coeval with the race of man, and not repealed but confirmed and illustrated by the gospel, to worship God according to the dictates of his own conscience. This right is indefeasible—that is, imprescriptible—not subject to alienation; it cannot be repealed, or abridged, or impaired, by power or numbers, nor divested by personal renunciation. It is a right indelibly impressed on each individual man by God himself; so that he cannot *make* himself, or *be* made less free than God has made him in this respect. It is an essential element of his free agency, and indispensable to his voluntary worship, which *alone* is worship in truth. It is *"according to the dictates of his own conscience;"* not that of the priesthood; and therefore each has a right to *inform* his conscience, by all means in his power; by reading the Bible, and, if he sees fit, by making it *the rule of his faith and practice.* Hence the translation, and printing, and free circulation of the Bible is lawful, is his unalienable right; and therefore all *restraints* upon the press as practised by the general councils of the Romish Church, in this and other respects, is an invasion of this natural and indefeasible right. (1)

According to this definition, churches established by law, by kings or pontiffs, and maintained by coercion, are an invasion of the natural liberties of man; and therefore the Romish hierarchy was an *usurpation* in the days of Luther, and *is so now*, wherever its power is felt, as in South America, in Spain, and in the temporal dominions of the Pope. All territorial precincts, such as parishes, dioceses, and the assigning by the authority of law of the inhabitants within them to the jurisdiction of an ecclesiastic, and the exaction of tithes, or other rateable stipends for ecclesiastical uses, upon pretence of ecclesiastical or temporal power, is an invasion of the rights of man; and therefore the government of the Pope, within his own dominions, and in the dominions of those sovereigns who acknowledge his pretensions, is an usurpation; and for the same reason all societies established by ecclesiastical authority, the object of which is to govern the *temporal affairs* by means of the *spiritual*, (THE JESUITS FOR EXAMPLE,) are irreconcilably repugnant to free institutions.

And our definition, (on which I dwelt more largely the last evening,) declares, that this right belongs to *all men*. It goes beyond the exigencies of a mere social compact. It is uttered in

(1) See Constitution of the United States, Amendments, Act 1st.

the *name of the human race*. It is an universal truth, everywhere, and at all times, *true*.

In its nature the proposition of this article is as liberal as it can be, but as a compact it necessarily excludes those who cannot *ex animo* assent to it; and hence Protestants and Roman Catholics cannot concur in it, not because of the illiberality of the rule, but on account of the scruples of Roman Catholics, who, as a matter of conscience, ascribe to the Pope lawful authority to invade a portion of their natural liberties; their conscience forbids them to assert their own freedom, or to allow to Protestants the measure of freedom which they claim. Hence the South Americans, notwithstanding their high notions of political liberty, in no instance have reckoned religious liberty among their *political* rights. They dared to throw off the yoke of the *King of Spain*, but not the yoke of the *Roman* Pontiff. The spirit of Luther *did not* pass in the direction of Spain: this shows why Spanish America is papistical and not free. It *did* pass in the direction of England; hence the United States are free. Had a Luther never lived, the United States might have been as Spanish America. The religion, or rather the *religious principle* of the American constitutions, is traceable under God to Luther, as an effect to its instrumental cause. This principle of the American constitutions is *Protestantism*. The liberties and intelligence, and the manifold blessings enjoyed by the citizens of the United States are its effects—which can properly be appreciated only by contrast with the condition of the vicious, ignorant, superstitious, and *priest-ridden* inhabitants of South America, Spain and Italy. The contrast shows also the natural tendencies of Romanism upon the civil and religious liberties of men.

There is a common *sophism* on this question, which consists in confounding the term *voluntary* with the term *free*. In this specious way a *voluntary slave*, (which is by no means a solecism,) may be proved to be a free man. A kindred sophism consists in confounding the freedom of government, or *constitutional* liberty, with individual or personal freedom. If a man were to be robbed of his property he would be esteemed poor; the manner by which he is divested of his property does not alter the *fact* or the *true character* of his condition. For the same reason, a man who renounces into the hands of another his *natural liberties* can with no more propriety be called a *free man*, than he could be if he were deprived of them by *the hand of arbitrary and irresistible power*. In truth a *voluntary slave* is more a slave than one who resists his oppressor, or who desires to throw off his chains. A voluntary slave is the lowest and most ignoble of all slaves. Suppose the people of Pennsylvania were, with one consent, to choose a governor or prince as their ruler, who should have *absolute power* to make and execute such laws as he saw proper. Could the government with propriety be called *free?* Yet the case supposes the people *voluntary* in making the change, and not constrained in submitting to it. They would voluntarily part with their natural liberties, but they would no more continue to be free, than a man who should voluntarily part with *all his property* would continue to be *rich.* Nor could the government with any propriety be called free, relatively to the governments of the other states, which are founded upon the principles of natural right.

For the same reason those who surrender voluntarily the natural rights of conscience, the rights of *free* worship to a *spiritual prince* or *pontiff*, do not continue to be free in these respects—nay, they cannot be said to be free in *any respect.* A man who is chained by one limb only is restrained of his natural freedom, as truly and almost as effectually, as to all useful purposes, as if he were chained by every limb. It is like a semi-paralysis of the body.

Now in view of the above definition and necessary inferences, which no true American can deny, it is apparent in how many respects the "doctrines" of the Church of Rome are directly opposed to human and especially to religious liberty.

With these great principles in view, I will proceed to specify more in detail the *proof* against the Roman Catholic religion.

What I said more fully at the preliminary meeting—and what the gentleman then scarcely pretended a reply to—I now *repeat—that as soon as a child is born into the world, the "indelible brand of slavery,"* as it has been justly called, is stamped upon him, by the Church of Rome, in what she calls *baptism.* The decrees and canons of the Council of Trent on this subject, eternize, in their self-styled—and *unchangeable* infallibility—the tyranny of Romanism. Thus, for example, the fourteenth canon on baptism is as follows—viz: "Whoever shall affirm that when these baptized children *grow up* they are to be asked whether they will confirm the promises made by their godfathers in their name, at their baptism; and that if they say they *will not,* they are to be left to their own *choice,* and not to be *compelled* in the mean time to lead a Christian life, by *any other punishment* than exclusion from the eucharist and the other sacraments, until they repent: let him be accursed."

Here it is evident that the doctrine of force is distinctly taught; and not *moral* force, but *physical;* for moral means, or ecclesiastical discipline, such as "*exclusion from the eucharist and other sacraments*"—is expressly stated in the above canon as not the *only* punishment meant. The Latin word also used in the original is COGENDOS, which every scholar knows, especially in such a connexion, means the application of coercion, superior power, force.

Besides: the *practice* of the church, in every country, where it has the power, and even at this day, is in accordance with this interpretation. Now here we say is a *doctrine* leading to a *practice* in the Church of Rome, which is directly and avowedly destructive of religious liberty.

Again; I referred on the last evening to the doctrine of the Church of Rome on *auricular confession,* as an invasion of personal liberty, and in the highest sense dangerous to the freedom and safety of states. In the fourteenth session of the Council of Trent, under the decrees on *penance,* it is thus written : " The universal church has always understood that a *full confession* of sins was instituted by the Lord, as a part of the sacrament of penance."— " It is plain that the priests cannot sustain the *office* of *judge,* if the cause be *unknown* to them ; nor inflict equitable *punishments,* if sins are only confessed in GENERAL ; and *not minutely and individually described.*"—" Those who do otherwise, and knowingly *conceal any sins,* present *nothing* to the divine goodness to *be forgiven by the priest."* Again, the sixth canon is as follows : "Whoever shall deny that sacramental confession was instituted by divine command, or that it is necessary to salvation ; or shall affirm that the practice of *secretly confessing to the priest alone,* as it has ever been observed from the beginning by the Catholic Church, and is still observed, is foreign to the institution and command of Christ, and is a human invention : let him be accursed."

Now we say this is usurping the peculiar prerogative of God. It is blasphemously setting up a *priest as judge* in God's stead, and *forcing* the poor subject, as the *condition* of *pardon,* to unveil the secrets of the heart *to a priest,* when this is due to God alone ! Never, perhaps, was such a device found out to rule with a rod of iron a subject world. No *secrets* from the priests, or *else no salvation !* and that, too, with the *priest alone !* Hence it is called *auricular.* Think of your daughter, your sister, your wife, thus secretly opening to a priest alone, all her feelings—on all subjects— as the medium of pardon. Think of the confessor of a prince ! think of that great *army of priests* located all over the world, prying into all the secret thoughts, feelings, acts, intentions, desires, of all their subjects. Think of the *power* it gives. Was there ever such a scheme of espionage : such a system of omnipresent police ? Can there be *liberty* under such a *regime ?* It is easy to be seen how, on this plan, a *priest* can restore stolen goods ; and why we poor *Protestants* neither *know* nor can *do* any thing like it ? They know all the secrets of all the villains, connected with their church ; and can, by a nod, compel restitution, or hand them over to hopeless perdition ! It may well be conceived also, what must be the habitual state of every priest's mind, being made, as it is, the receptacle of all the sins of all his people—*the common sewer of iniquity !* Now, under the operation of such a system, must not a *pure* priest or a *free* mind be almost a miracle ? Is not the destruction of all liberty necessarily involved in the application of such a system ? We commend this subject to the audience, and call for a reply from our reverend friend.

Without dwelling at present upon the other sacraments of the Church of Rome, as constructed and administered for the destruction of human liberty, *I draw my next argument from her tyrannical interference with the freedom of the press—of reading, &c.* The freedom of the press has justly been called the palladium of our independence. It is the glory, the pledge, and, under God, one of the chief securities of our liberties. Unlimited freedom of printing and reading has never been permitted by the Roman hierarchy, where she had power to prevent it. Speaking of printing, one has racily said, "Hereby tongues are known, knowledge groweth, judgment increaseth, books are dispersed, the Scriptures are seen, the doctors be read, stories be opened, times compared, truth discerned, falsehood detected, and with finger pointed, and all through the benefit of printing. Wherefore I suppose, that either *the Pope must abolish printing,* or he *must seek a new world to reign over; for else, as this world standeth, printing doubtless will abolish him.*"

The great Council of Lateran, held at Rome, A. D. 1515, under Leo X. session 10th, (1) thus enacted: "We ordain and decree that *no person shall presume to print, or cause to be printed any book or other writing whatsoever,* either in our city, (Rome,) or in any other cities and dioceses, unless it shall first have been carefully examined, if in this city by our vicar, and the master of the holy palace, or if in other cities and dioceses by the bishops or his deputy, *with the inquisitor of heretical pravity for the diocese,* in which the said impression is about to be made; and unless also it shall have received under their own hand, their written approval given without price, and without delay. Whosoever shall presume to do otherwise, besides the loss of the books, which shall be publicly burned, shall be bound by the sentence of excommunication." Caranza, from whom the above is extracted, more wisely than honestly omits several parts of this decree, such as, "That the transgressing printer was to pay 200 ducats, to help in building St. Peter's Cathedral at Rome;" "be suspended for a year from his trade," &c.

By authority of the Council of Trent, this decretal, and all others of a similar kind, are thus confirmed, viz. Rule I. "All books condemned by the supreme pontiffs or general councils, before the year 1515, and not comprised in the present index, are nevertheless to be considered as condemned." The *creed* also, as adopted by every Roman Catholic, requires all "to receive undoubtedly all things delivered, defined and declared by the sacred canons and general councils, and particularly by the holy Council of Trent." These decretals, &c. being thus confirmed by the *last* council, stand to this day, and bind every Roman Catholic on earth. That same *last* council, thus sealed with its *last* act the destruction of all liberty of printing, reading, and of thought itself, among all its subjects, viz. "Concerning the index of books, the most holy council in its second session under our most holy lord

(1) See Caranza, p 670.

Pius IV. entrusted it to certain select fathers, to consider what was needful to be done in the case of divers censures, *and books either suspected or pernicious*, and then report to the holy council; and having heard now, that their labours are completed, but yet seeing that on account of the variety and number of said books, the holy council cannot minutely, and with convenience, judge in the case; therefore it is decreed, that whatever may be determined by them, shall be laid before the most holy Pope of Rome, so that it may be completed, and published according to his judgment and authority." Here then is the decree of the council sanctioning the acts of the committee and Pope. Accordingly, the "committee on the index" proceeded to draw up a list of *"prohibited books,"* which makes a large volume; [here Mr. B. exhibited the book, adding, that there was another copy in the Philadelphia Library,] and they prefixed many "rules" to it, which received in full the sanction of the Pope; they were published by his authority, and have since been received by the church, and repeatedly sanctioned by subsequent Popes. The work, therefore, is binding on every Roman Catholic on earth; to *reject* it is *rebellion;* to *deny* its *existence* reckless *falsehood*. To show the oppressive character of this system, we give some of its *rules*, (they are ten in number.) The second rule is: "The books of heresiarchs, whether of those who broached or disseminated their heresies prior to the year above mentioned, or of those who have been, or are, the heads or leaders of heretics, as Luther, Zuingle, Calvin, Balthasar, Pacimontanus, Swenchfeld, and other similar ones, are *altogether forbidden*, whatever may be their names, titles or subjects."

The fourth is as follows: "Inasmuch as it is manifest from experience, that if the Holy Bible, translated into the vulgar tongue be indiscriminately allowed to every one, the temerity of men will cause more evil than good to arise from it; it is, on this point referred to the judgment of the bishops or inquisitors, who may, by the advice of the priest or confessor, *permit the reading of the Bible translated into the vulgar tongue by Catholic authors*, to those persons whose faith and piety they apprehend will be augmented and not injured by it; and this permission they must have in *writing:* but if any one shall have the *presumption* to read or possess it without such written permission, he shall not receive absolution until he have first delivered up such Bible to the ordinary. Booksellers, however, who shall sell, or otherwise dispose of Bibles in the vulgar tongue, to any person not having such permission, shall forfeit the value of the books, to be applied by the bishop to some pious use, and be subjected by the bishop to such other penalties as the bishop shall judge proper according to the quality of the offence. But regulars shall neither read nor purchase such Bibles without a special license from their superiors."

The fifth rule allows books of heretics containing but little of their own to be used by Catholics, *after having been corrected by their divines.* By the sixth rule, "*books of controversy, betwixt the Catholics and heretics of the present time, written in the vulgar tongue, are not to be indiscriminately allowed, but are to be subject to the same regulations as Bibles in the vulgar tongue.*"

The tenth rule is as follows: "*In the printing of books* or other writings, the rules shall be observed which were ordained in the tenth session of the Council of Lateran, under Leo X. Therefore, if any book is to be printed in the *city of Rome*, it shall first be examined by the Pope's vicar and the master of the sacred palace, or other persons chosen by our most holy father for that purpose. *In other places* the examination of any book or manuscript intended to be printed, shall be referred to the bishop, or some skilful person whom he shall nominate, and *the inquisitors of heretical pravity of the city or diocese in which the impression is executed.*"

"Moreover, *in every city and diocese*, the house or places where the art of printing is exercised, and also the shops of booksellers, shall be frequently visited by persons deputed for that purpose by the bishop or his vicar, conjointly with the inquisitor of heretical pravity, *so that nothing that is prohibited, may be printed, kept, or sold.*" "If any person shall *import* foreign books into any city, they shall be obliged to announce them to the deputies." "*Heirs* and testamentary executors shall make no use of the books of the deceased, nor in any way *transfer* them to others, until they have presented a catalogue of them to the deputies, and obtained *their license*, under pain of confiscation of the books."

"Finally, it is enjoined on all the faithful, that no one presume to keep or read any books contrary to these rules, or prohibited by this index. But if any one keep or read any books composed by heretics, or the writings of any authors suspected of heresy or false doctrine, *he shall instantly incur the sentence of excommunication*, and those who read or keep works interdicted on another account, besides the mortal sin committed, shall be severely punished at the will of the bishops."

Now if this be not restraint of human liberty, I know not what restraint is. Here the conscience, the intellect, and the means of knowledge—printing, selling, circulating, holding, importing, reading books, are, by the decree of an infallible council, and their authorized rules, trampled in the dust. But, in fine, look once more to the decrees of the Council of Trent on the editions of God's Holy Word itself. In the fourth session of that conventicle, is this open decree; "Moreover the same most holy council, considering that no small advantage will accrue to the church of God if, of all the Latin editions of the sacred book which are in circulation, some one shall be distinguished as that which ought to be regarded as authentic,—doth ordain and declare, that *the same old* and *vulgate edition*, which has been approved by its use in the church for so many ages, shall be held as authentic, in all public lectures, disputations, sermons, and expositions; and *that no one shall dare or presume to reject it under any pretence whatsoever.*" In order to restrain petulant minds, the Council further decrees, "that in matters *of faith and morals,* and whatever relates to the maintenance of Christian doctrine, no one, confiding in his own judgment, *shall dare to* wrest the sacred Scriptures to *his own sense of them, contrary to that which hath been held and still is held by Holy Mother Church, whose right it is to judge of the true meaning and interpretation of the sacred Word;* or contrary to the unanimous consent of the fathers; even though such interpretations should never be published. If any disobey, let him be denounced by the ordinaries, and punished according to law. Being desirous also, as is reasonable, of setting bounds to the printers, who, with unlimited boldness, supposing themselves at liberty to do as they please, print editions of the Holy Scripture with notes and expositions taken indifferently from any writer, without the permission of their ecclesiastical superiors, and that at a concealed or falsely designated press, and, which is worse, without the name of the author,—and also rashly expose books of this nature to sale in other countries; the holy council decrees and ordains, that for the future, the sacred Scriptures, and especially the old vulgate edition, shall be printed in the most correct manner possible; and no one shall be permitted to print, or cause to be printed, any books relating to religion, without the name of the author; neither shall any one hereafter sell such books, or even retain them in his possession, unless they have been first *examined and approved* by the ordinary, under *penalty of anathema,* and the *pecuniary fine adjudged by the last Council of Lateran.*"—Here the vulgate, or old Latin version, known by every scholar to *abound in errors,* including also the fables and falsehoods of the Apocrypha, and to the contempt of the original languages of the Bible, is *forcibly* made the *exclusive standard;* printers of all sorts, in all places, are forbidden to print the Bible, with notes—as in the former extract they were forbidden to print it in any way, without permission, under heavy pains and penalties, spiritual and temporal; and all persons are forbidden to *think for themselves.* Putting all these decrees together, there never was perhaps such a system of high-handed oppression.

In faithful keeping with these decrees, the index which I hold in my hand, on its thirtieth page, actually *forbids the reading of the Bible,* and not the *Protestant* Bible, (as my Rev. friend tried in the late controversy to make appear,) but the very Roman Bible, with all its parts, sanctioned by the church, *in every possible translation,* is prohibited; as follows: "Biblia Vulgari quocunque Idiomate conscripta." That is, THE BIBLE IN WHATEVER IDIOM WRITTEN, (*is prohibited.*) Finally, I have before me a decision fresh from Rome, viz. the Encyclical (circular) letter of the present reigning Pope, Gregory XVI., addressed to the faithful all over the world, and written at his coronation, dated August 5th, 1832. The following are extracts:

"*Towards this point tends that most vile, detestable, and never to be sufficiently execrated liberty of booksellers, namely, of publishing writings of whatsoever kind they please; a liberty which some persons dare with such violence of language to demand and promote.*"

"Far different was the discipline of the church in extirpating the infection of bad books, even in the days of the Apostles; who, we read, *publicly burned a vast quantity of books.*"

"Let it suffice to read over the laws passed on that point in the Fifth Council of Lateran, and the constitution which subsequently was published by our predecessor of happy memory, Leo X. Let not that which was happily invented for the increasing of the faith, and spread of good learning, be converted to a contrary purpose, and bring harm to the salvation of faithful Christians."

"This matter also occupied extremely the attention of the fathers of Trent, who *applied a remedy to so great an evil, by publishing a most salutary decree, for compiling an index of books, in which improper doctrine was contained.* Clement XIII., our predecessor of happy memory, in his encyclical letter on the suppression of noxious books, pronounces—"We must contend with energy such as the subject requires, and with all our might *exterminate the deadly mischief of so many books;* for the matter of error will never be effectually removed unless *the guilty elements of depravity be consumed in the flames.*"

"So that by this continual solicitude, *through all ages*, with which the Holy Apostolic See has ever striven, to condemn *suspected and noxious books, and to wrest them forcibly out of men's hands;* it is most clear how false, rash, and injurious to the said Apostolic See, and fruitful of enormous evils to the Christian public, is the doctrine of those, *who not only reject the censorship of books, as too severe and burdensome; but even proceed to that length of wickedness, as to assert, that it is contrary to the principles of equal justice; and dare deny to the church, the right of enacting and employing it.*"

Now perhaps my Reverend friend may say, these are only *opinions* of the Pope. Well—but the universal church has seemed for three years to approve them, and of course they become *law*. If not, does Mr. Hughes denounce and condemn them? Does he deny their truth, their wisdom, their righteousness, or their authority? Besides, will not *his reply be also an opinion?* Who are we to credit? the Pope or the priest? If *they differ,* where is *infallibility?* If *they differ,* who is to be *followed?* If *they differ,* the Pope is surely the more excathedra, impartial, authorized expounder of the doctrine and discipline of the church;—and especially as he quotes general councils to sustain him.

"Is the Roman Catholic Religion, in any or in all its principles or doctrines, opposed to civil or religious liberty?"

NEGATIVE I.—MR. HUGHES.

Mr. President:—The gentleman commences his argument by an attack on the *liberty of the press*. The article of which he complains, is a *true* statement of the *facts*, although it is inaccurate in a few details of a merely circumstantial character, the correction of which, would, in my opinion, tend rather to irritate than to soothe his wounded feelings. The Society were witnesses of what occurred, and of course competent to *specify* the pretended misstatements. If they cannot do this, it is unreasonable to require the reparation that is demanded. For this, neither is it necessary that the gentleman should be made acquainted with the name of the writer; and the gentleman's *demand* to have that name given up to him, is a pretty fair sample of what Presbyterians understand by civil and religious liberty.

If it be said that the paper called the Presbyterian, gave the correction of misrepresentation in regard to a previous debate—the answer is, that the cases are entirely dissimilar. There, the falsehoods were *specifically* attested by the Society,—here, they have not been pointed out; because they do not exist. There, they were acknowledged,—here, they are denied. There, the author of the acknowledged *falsification* of facts, was not *inquired after;*—here, though the falsification has not been specified, and cannot be proved, still the author is peremptorily demanded, as if the object were to inflict upon him a personal chastisement. Let the gentleman show wherein he has been injured, except by the statement of truth, and I pledge myself that he shall have reparation.

His next topic is my definition of civil liberty, which has been rejected as willingly by myself as by him. He has stated my *motives* for having offered it. They were, of course, such as the eyes of a Presbyterian can always discover in the breast of a Catholic. The public must judge whether their *baseness* is to be ascribed to their supposed origin, or to the medium through which they are made to pass, in the gentleman's analysis of my thoughts, which was never revealed to him. There has been nothing in my conduct to justify such insinuations; and I shall dismiss the topic with the single remark, that a mind conscious of its *own* rectitude, is slow to indulge in the gratuitous imputation of bad motives to others.

Before I proceed to lay down the principles involved in the discussion of the present question, I must briefly advert to some of those *assumptions*, which the gentlemen has selected *for the occasion*, and would dignify by the appellation of "principles." He has charged on me, as an error sanctioned by *Catholic authority*—"that the majority shall rule." Of course the true Presbyterian doctrine must be, that the *right* of ruling belongs to the minority. Now, I maintain, as a general principle of all free and popular government, the very doctrine which this gentleman has here condemned. I hold it to be self-evident;—and I say that the opposite doctrine is suited to the meridian of despotism all over the world. It is the majority that rules in this country, from the chief magistrate down to the township constable. In *Russia*, it is the minority. The gentleman's first principle, so called, is adverse to the fundamental principle of our republican government—and furnishes the very text by which kings and tyrants govern. Neither does it follow, as he pretends, that, admitting my principle, the majority would have "a right to do wrong." There is *no such* RIGHT, in either the majority or the minority. "*And then*," says he, "*if the day should ever come, when Roman Catholics will compose the majority in this country, they may*, OF RIGHT, *establish their religion by law*." Why, if the minority are to rule, as the gentleman seems to maintain, there is no reason why the Presbyterians might not do *now*, what it is pretended the Catholics could do "if ever they should come," &c. &c. In the first place, it is to be observed, that the right of the *majority to rule*, is circumscribed in a free government by the boundaries of civil jurisdiction. It means that the laws passed by the majority for the *civil* well-being of society, are to be obeyed by the minority, and by all. But it does not mean that the majority have any right to be tyrants, by *making* a religion, as when the Westminster Assembly met; or *daring* to rule for the minority in relation to another world, as well as this. The question of religion does not appertain to *state majorities:* it is a spiritual concern between man and his God. So that the consequence, which the gentleman pretends to derive from *my* principle, is the legitimate offspring of his own bad logic. The Catholics are but as one to twenty-six of the population; and if we suppose with the gentleman, that they should become a *majority*, and establish their religion by law, they would be still only imitating an example which the Presbyterians have set to all denominations, whenever *they* had the power. The history of his own sect furnishes the *true* shades to the *false* lights of his picture. Does it follow, from my principle, recognising the right of the majority to rule, that because the Presbyterians were the *majority* in Scotland and New England, they had therefore the right to take away the lives of men who differed from them in religious opinion? No: it only follows that they had the POWER—and we all know what use they made of it. Now it is singular that the gentleman should have entered, nay, forced himself, on this discussion, without having taken pains to clear up, *in his own mind,* the very important distinction between RIGHT and POWER.

Thus, the action of the majority-principle, is restricted by the sphere of the purely *civil* and *social* relations. It has nothing to do with those "natural and imprescriptible rights which lie *aback* of all conventions." These belong to another category, and shall be treated of in their proper place. That the gentleman should have confounded them with *civil* and *social rights,* is the more surprising, as the constitution has expressly EXCEPTED THEM from the operation of the principle, which that same constitution has sanctioned, for the regulation of social rights; and this exception the gentleman has quoted, without seeming to comprehend its meaning. *"All men have a* NATURAL *and* INDEFEASIBLE *right to worship Almighty God according to the dictates of their own consciences: no man can,* OF RIGHT, *be compelled to attend, erect, or support, any place of worship, or to maintain any ministry against his consent: no human authority can, in any case whatever, control or interfere with the rights of conscience, and no preference shall ever be given* BY LAW *to any religious establishment or any modes of worship."* Here are the rights which the constitution recognises, as *indefeasible* and *natural*—especially beyond the reach of the majority and minority. These, then, have no reference to the *civil* or *political* rights, secured by the national instrument in question, but to religious, spiritual rights, which are to be inviolable. And yet, it was for the exercise of this prerogative, under the faith of that constitution, that the CONVENT was burned down, and that a Presbyterian crusade is now proclaimed throughout the land against Catholic citizens. It was by the violation of these principles, that the same Presbyterians, in former days, shed the blood, and seized the property of other denominations of Christians, whenever they were possessed of political power to do so. And since the gentleman tells us, that these principles "are confirmed and illustrated by the Gospel:"—it follows, on his own showing, that for their knowledge of the gospel, Presbyterians are indebted to the CONSTITUTION, which took from them the *power* of oppressing men for conscience sake. Now, these are the imprescriptible rights of man. My argument leaves them precisely where the constitution places them : and when the gentleman represents me as advocating their infringement, on the ground that the "majority has the right to govern," he only furnishes another specimen of his vicious reasoning. They are inalienable : and therefore every Catholic, and every Protestant, worships God "according to the dictates of his own conscience," and not that of the priesthood, nor of the presbytery. The gentleman reckons among these *natural* rights, translations, printing, and the unbounded freedom of the press. By this we can discover how much attention he has *not* paid to the subject. Natural rights are rights derived from nature; common to all men ; and printing is as much a right as steam navigation, or the use of gunpowder. These are all *acquired rights*—and the freest government is that which puts the least restraint on their exercise. If printing be a natural right, why did the gentleman complain of its exercise in the New York Diary? He tells us that to circulate the Bible is a "natural and inalienable right;" I answer, that if each one has the right "to worship God according to the dictates of his own conscience," it is just as natural a right and as inalienable, not to circulate the Bible.

From the moment the gentleman read, without seeming to understand, the doctrines of the American Constitution, on both social and natural rights, he becomes, at once, inspired and oracular. Hence we find him breaking out in the following rhapsody, which contains about as much solemn nonsense as it is possible to express in so many words. The reader who is acquainted with the history of the Presbyterian Church, and knows how it trampled on *older rights*, in Geneva, Holland, Scotland, and England, graciously betrothing itself to the *Laws* of the State, "for better and for worse," will smile at the gravity with which the gentleman gives in the following catalogue of "usurpations on the natural rights of men."

"According to this definition, churches established by law, by kings or pontiffs, and maintained by coercion, are an invasion of the natural liberties of men." (This is a good hit at the present churches of England and Scotland, and Denmark and Sweden and Holland. All of them were established as the gentleman describes. But mark his logical conclusion.) "Therefore the Roman hierarchy was an *usurpation* in the days of Luther, and *is so now* wherever its power is felt, as in South America, Spain, and the temporal dominions of the Pope." (That is, the Presbyterians claim your property, and *therefore* you hold it by "usurpation.") "All territorial precincts, such as parishes," (or presbyterial boundaries by *geography*) "dioceses, and the assigning by the authority of law of the inhabitants within them to the jurisdiction of an ecclesiastic, and the exaction of tithes, or other rateable stipends for ecclesiastical uses, upon pretence of ecclesiastical or temporal power, is an invasion of the rights of man; and therefore the government of the Pope in his own dominions, and in the dominions of those sovereigns who acknowledge his pretensions, is an usurpation," (that is, Mr. Breckinridge being *judge*,) "and for the same reason, all societies established by ecclesiastical authority, the object of which is to govern the *temporal affairs* by means of the spiritual," (as the Presbyterian parsons are now doing,) "the Jesuits for example, are irreconcilably repugnant to free institutions." When the gentleman adduced the "Jesuits for example," he falsifies absolutely the object of their institution. For the rest, he wounds as many friends as foes.

In short, the gentleman might have been more concise, and told us at once, that ALL jurisdiction both in Church and State is a usurpation on the natural rights of men, save and except that which is exercised by CONGRESS and by the *General Assembly* of the PRESBYTERIAN CHURCH. As this conclusion is founded on false premises which have already been exposed, it would be wasting time if we were to enter on the exposition of its special absurdities. He proceeds to speak of something which he calls "this article," and says that "Roman Catholics cannot concur in it, who, as a matter of conscience, ascribe to the Pope lawful authority to invade a portion of their natural liberties; their conscience forbids them to assert their own freedom, or to allow to Protestants the measure of freedom which they claim." Without pretending to know what the "article" is to which the gentleman makes such pointed allusion, I shall reply to the *reason* which he assigns for his opinion. That reason is utterly FALSE. He calumniates Catholics when he says they ascribe any such "lawful authority" to the Pope, or that their "conscience forbids them" in the matter described. The gentleman thinks the South Americans are still slaves, because they did not throw off the profession of their religion at the same time when they asserted their political freedom. The same might be said of the North Americans for not having at the revolution burst the fetters of *their* ecclesiastical bondage. The only difference I can see, is, that in the one case, the people, if the gentleman will have it so, chose to be ridden by priests; in the other, they preferred to be ridden by *parsons* and their *families*. The people of South America have the lighter burden. The gentleman ascribes the freedom of the United States to Luther. I say that Faust, by inventing printing, contributed, under God, much more to it than Luther. "The condition of the vicious, ignorant, superstitious and priest-ridden inhabitants of South America, Spain, and Italy," is a very *appropriate* and *consoling* phrase on the lips of the Presbyterian parsonhood, when they are pressing on their own followers with a weight of spiritual and temporal domination, whose little finger is heavier than the loins of Catholic bondage in any country under the sun. The tithes in most Catholic countries are but a trifle, compared with the enormous amount of money which is extorted, for one object or another, from the *religious* portion of American Presbyterians. It is true the parsons do not send the constable to collect it, but they send forth what seems to answer the purpose just as well, a picture of the premonitory symptoms of "election and reprobation."

Next comes a "sophism," which the gentleman undertakes to expose for the good of posterity. It consists in confounding the term "VOLUNTARY" with the term "FREE." We must pass over his illustrations. If they have not the merit of being apposite or profound, they have, at least, that of being diversified and numerous. The whole meaning, however, breaks out in the *object* for which they were adduced, which is to show "that those who surrender *voluntarily* the *natural rights* of conscience, the rights of free worship to a spiritual prince or pontiff, do not continue to be free in these respects; nay, they cannot be said to be free in any respect." Now it is to be observed, in the first place, that the gentleman's notion of freedom would place the human mind in the position of the animal between two bundles of hay, where the inducements *should be as strong* on the one side as the other. Any deviation towards either might be "*voluntary*," but it would not, on that account, he tells us, be "*free.*" Secondly, according to his distinction all *laws*, in Pennsylvania and elsewhere, are compatible with "*voluntary* submission," but not with "*freedom.*" So that the sons of the commonwealth have the honour of being classed by him, in the *principle* of their subjection, with the "most ignoble of all slaves, *voluntary* slaves." Thirdly, if the gentleman, in striking out one distinction, had not overlooked another, he would not have confounded the rights of *society* with those which are *natural and personal* to every man. Fourthly, neither would he have talked of "*surrendering*" rights which cannot be surrendered. The rights of *conscience*, in their personal relation, are as inalienable as the rights of *memory:* and it is just as absurd to talk of "surrendering" the one as the other. As to the rights of "free worship," they are of that order which the Presbyterians denied to Catholics in Scotland when they made it DEATH to have SAID OR *heard mass* THREE TIMES, and denied to the Episcopalians, when they punished them by civil penalties for READING *the common prayer-book*, even in private families. These rights may be TAKEN AWAY by the power of bigotry and despotism united; but to talk of their being "surrendered," either "*freely*" or "*voluntarily*," is too absurd. Finally, supposing the thing possible, the charge stands as pointedly against those who "surrender" these rights to the spiritual junto, called the General Assembly, as if they were resigned to the "spiritual pontiff."

Having thus briefly exposed the absurdity of some of what the gentleman calls first principles, his inferences perish with the mistaken premises on which he thought them established. Before I advert to what he calls "the tyranny of Romanism," it is proper to lay down the *true* principles, by which the merits of the present discussion can alone be tested. The question is, whether the "religions" called the "Roman Catholic" and "Presbyterian" are opposed in *any* or *all* of their doctrines or principles to civil and religious liberty. The gentleman and myself have, by a written agreement, determined and fixed the meaning of the terms employed. If he had adhered to his engagement, and abided by his own definitions, the question would be extremely simple; but such an instance of good faith was more than my experience should have taught me to expect.

Accordingly, in the very first speech, we find him quitting the definition which he *could* understand, and plunging into the mysticism of universal ethics, far beyond his depth;—confounding all *rights, personal* and *social, human* and *divine*, in order to extract from the confusion, materials for the unhallowed purpose of Presbyterian zeal, which is, to excite odium against Catholic citizens, under pretence of advocating "civil and religious liberty."

Let us endeavour to introduce order into the chaos of his speculations. RIGHTS *are privileges either inherent in our nature, or derived from some extrinsic source. The former class are termed* NATURAL, INDEFEASIBLE, *imprescriptible* and *eternal.* The latter are classed under various heads;—those which are derived from God by revelation, are termed *divine rights;* those which result from the social compact, are called *civil* or *political rights;* when that compact secures us in the privilege of EXTERNALLY "worshipping Almighty God according to the dictates of our conscience," it guarantees our *religious rights.* The immunities of the standing which we hold in the ecclesiastical body to which we belong, are termed our *ecclesiastical rights.* Let us explain.

1. NATURAL RIGHT. If every man were living by himself, having no connexion with his fellow-beings, he would have a natural right to do whatever he chose, except only what God would have forbidden him. He might be a KING without subjects, or a SLAVE without a master. He might print treason and preach sedition. And the reason is, that *he* ALONE would be affected by his proceedings. But the moment he enters into society, the natural rights must be restrained. Let the society be composed but of three persons, he has no right to league with the *second,* in order, by calumniating, to oppress the *third.* In proportion as the interests of society would become more complex and diversified, in the same proportion the natural rights of each individual should have to yield to the paramount good of the whole. At one period of mankind it was a *natural right* for a brother to marry a sister —for a man to have several wives at the same time; at another period, society has prohibited the exercise of this right, and yet I trust the gentleman will not adopt the conclusions to which his pretended principles lead, and accuse society of being guilty of "tyranny" by invading the *natural rights* of man. When individuals offend against the rights of society, society robs them of the natural rights—FREEDOM, LIFE. Is this tyranny?

2. DIVINE RIGHT. This is the authority with which God has invested certain men and conditions of life, for some purpose of good. Thus, Moses, after his appointment, had the *right* to command the people of God. The Jewish priesthood had the *right* to offer sacrifices. The apostles had the *right* to establish Christianity, and their legitimate successors have the right to perpetuate it, both by the preaching of the word and the administration of the sacraments. These rights are peculiar to those *only,* to whom God has given them, and in *this* they differ from *natural rights,* which are common to all men. Now *rights* and *duties* are corelative: and therefore it was the *duty* of the people of God to obey Moses, and it is the *duty* of men to hear (and practice) the doctrines of Christianity from those who have the *right* to preach them. This right is not derived from *nature;* neither is it, nor

can it be, derived from civil authority. And consequently those who have not received the *divine* appointment to exercise it, do not possess it at all. The sphere, and direct object of this *right*, is spiritual. It is degraded by those who wield it for base, temporal purposes. "My kingdom is not of this world." The exercise of this *right* is no *usurpation*, except by those who do not receive it from God, and could not receive it from any other source.

3. POLITICAL, OR CIVIL RIGHTS, are "*that residuum of* NATURAL *liberty which is not required by the laws of society to be sacrificed to public convenience: or else those civil privileges, which society has engaged to provide in lieu of those natural liberties so given up by individuals.* This definition is from a Protestant jurist. It distinguishes properly between those *natural rights* which the laws of society do not require us to sacrifice, and those conventional rights which result from society itself. Hence the constitution of the United States guarantees the citizen in the enjoyment of the *former* as well as the latter division of those rights. It recognises the privilege of every man "to worship God according to the dictates of his own conscience" *as among the natural rights of man*. It pledges the faith of the nation to recognise no distinction between the professors of one creed and those of another; because it understands that religion is a matter between man and God. In this, it differs from *many* of the *civil constitutions* in Catholic states; and from ALL the civil constitutions that were ever drawn up or administered by CALVINISTS. In short, it secures unbounded "liberty of conscience." Again, it secures in lieu of the natural liberties, which it abridges, all the advantages of social assistance: which could not be realized except by the legal imposition of *personal* restraint.

The idea of "*compelling*" a man to believe this doctrine, or that, is an absurdity. Hence the privilege of believing, *as an act of the mind*, bids defiance to *all external power*. But the right to *practice* the doctrines that one believes, must be exercised in harmony with the rights of others. Thus, for example, the Presbyterians believe that God has commanded them to "*remove* all FALSE worship." Now, they can *believe* this in despite of the Constitution: they may even preach and publish that God has commanded them to "remove all false worship;" but the Constitution interposes between the *belief* and *practice* of the doctrine, and says, "whether God has *commanded* it or *not, you shall* NOT *do it.*" And why? Because what Presbyterians believe to be "*false* worship," other denominations believe to be "*true* worship;" and to allow the Presbyterians to *practice* their *belief* on this point, would be to allow them to invade the rights and tyrannize over the consciences of their fellow-citizens, to whom the same measure of religious rights is secured as to themselves. The same rule would apply to Catholics, or Methodists, or Episcopalians.

Finally: ECCLESIASTICAL RIGHTS are those privileges secured to individuals according to their stations, and resulting from the ecclesiastical constitution, or usages of the religious society to which he belongs. Thus, for instance, if the gentleman should be accused of heresy, like some of his brethren, he would have a *right* to a trial according to the usual forms among Presbyterians. He would be arraigned before his presbytery, and if the MAJORITY pronounced him innocent he would be acquitted. He might refuse the trial—tell his peers that he must "worship God according to the dictates of his *own* conscience, and not that of the presbytery:" "that if he submitted to their authority he would not be a *free* man, but a *voluntary slave*, and therefore a most base and ignoble slave." He might tell them that "aback of all conventions," &c. These are the rules, which in his pretended principles he has laid down for *Catholics;* and yet he knows that if he insisted on them, in such circumstances, he would soon feel the weight and the smart of the discipline—Calvinistic.

Thus, Mr. President, you perceive that there are RIGHTS of various and distinct orders. That the application of those *rights* must be in the *order of the subjects* to which they are applicable. That to confound them in one common mass, and then apply the principles of *one* order of rights to the circumstances of *another* order, as the gentleman has attempted to do, would be just as absurd (though perhaps not so striking in the minds of *this* audience) as if he undertook to prove the mysteries of the Christian religion by the axioms of mathematics, or to prove the problems of Euclid by texts of Scripture.

These principles are so clear, that they cannot be denied consistently with sense or reason. They are in the nature of things; and constitute the pulse of civil and religious organization. The individual who would exempt himself from the discharge of either social or ecclesiastical duties, as established in the state by lawful authority, or in the religious body of which he is a member, by an appeal to his *pretended natural rights*, would justly be regarded as unworthy to participate in the advantages of either. The culprit at the bar might, if this were not so, appeal for his *rights* to the tribunal of the "general assembly;" and the individual, deposed or condemned by that body for *heresy*, might carry his grievance before congress. All, to escape punishment, might reject the jurisdiction of society, and proclaim that there is no power on earth that has a right to rob them of their natural liberties, or make them "less free than God has made them free." Mankind could not exist under the shock of such doctrine. The frame of the social edifice would be broken to pieces by its application.

Now, the gentleman has himself argued that every man has a "right to worship Almighty God according to the dictates of his own conscience, without invading or injuring the rights of others." Therefore if my conscience dictates to me that the worship of the Catholic religion is that which is most pleasing to Almighty God, I have the absolute right to embrace and profess that religion. Having the right to profess that religion, it becomes my duty to comply with the terms of its communion *from the moment when I wish to be admitted a member.* How far this compliance abridges my natural rights is a question which is *personal* to ME, and on which I am not to be dictated to by others. It is a part of the judgment which all acknowledge the right in every man to form for himself.

The question, then, before this Society is, whether "that religion in any or all of its principles or doctrines is opposed to civil or religious liberty." By DOCTRINES you are to understand "those tenets of *faith* and *morals* which it teaches as having been revealed by Almighty God."

The gentleman has taken it for granted that he has proved the affirmative of this proposition; and when we know with what entire satisfaction of mind, men sometimes adopt the falsest conclusions, we may find charity to believe him sincere. What HE *conceives* to be Catholic doctrine may, and no doubt is, opposed to what HE *conceives* to be civil and religious liberty. But if his "conceptions" be erroneous; if his information be but partial and unsound; if his reasoning, even on the materials he has, be defective; and, in fine, if he be *unconscious* of all this, then his arriving at a false conclusion can be accounted for without the necessity of impeaching his sincerity. He has selected "Baptism," "Auricular Confession," and the "Liberty of the Press," as the triple foundation of his argument and inference. Here, then, it is manifest that the gentleman's information is *not* sound; otherwise, he would have known that Catholics do not teach that God made any revelation whatever on the subject of the "PRESS," and consequently that the "*liberty*, or the *restraint* of the *press*," forms no "principle or doctrine" of the Catholic religion. Common sense tells us that the press can be employed for the corruption of morals and the destruction of Christianity, and every virtuous mind would condemn such an abuse of it. But beyond this the Catholic Religion has no "DOCTRINE" on the subject.

The decision of the Council of Trent, on the subject of baptism, merely defines, as an article of *Catholic* doctrine, that persons baptized in infancy, are bound to discharge the duties of a Christian life, the same as if they had been baptized in adult age. And that the Church has a right to employ *other* means to enforce this obligation, besides "exclusion from the eucharist and the other sacraments." I presume that the gentleman does not deny the *right* of the Church to exclude heresy. He seems to have studied the Catholic religion just as Tom Paine studied the Bible. But let us, to show the nature of his argument, suppose *him* to carry his doctrine into some Presbyterian pulpit. Let him tell the young persons who were baptized in infancy, that they are free to remove the "indelible brand of slavery," and to become JEWS or MOHAMMEDANS, as they prefer. And suppose a number of them to adopt this doctrine, what would be the course of the Presbyterian Church in relation to the matter?—It would "*compel*" him and them to renounce the heresy. How?—By suspension from the Lord's Supper. But would this "punishment" be all the means of coercion within the power of the Church?—No: "Excommunication" might and would follow, in case of obstinacy. How then, I ask, can he advocate, in *this* place, a doctrine which he *dare not preach* in a Presbyterian pulpit? Shall the Catholic Church be *restricted* in the employment of censures, to suspension from the sacraments,—and the Presbyterian Church indulged with the right of employing the sword of excommunication? By virtue of Church censures, Presbyterians claim the power "*to* shut" and to "open" the kingdom; and shall it be "LIBERTY" to exercise this power *among them*, and "slavery," tyranny, to exercise it among Catholics? Let the gentleman consult his own "Confession of Faith." (1)

But he has told you that in the canon, the "doctrine of force is distinctly taught;—and not *moral* force, but *physical*." This assertion I pronounce to be emphatically FALSE. And I give it that designation, not out of any desire to offend, but to throw him on the necessity of furnishing the PROOF. The Council asserted the right of the Church to employ *other means* besides "exclusion from the eucharist and other sacraments;" and it does not follow, that those other means *must be* "physical."

His whole argument, then, may be stated in a few words; as follows :—

"The Council of Trent teaches, that "*physical force*" is to be employed to compel persons baptized in infancy, to lead a Christian life, as soon as they have grown up."

"Therefore this doctrine of the Church of Rome is directly and avowedly destructive of religious liberty."

The answer and the refutation are—that his *premises* are emphatically FALSE;—and the conclusion is like the premises, *false*.

I am surprised that the gentleman's mind did shrink back, affrighted at the absurdity of its own prejudice. At the period of the Council of Trent, when the standard of apostasy was raised on every side—when the pure light of the Gospel, as the apostates from the ancient faith were pleased to call *their* notions, was beaming in its morning brilliancy—when the echoes of Luther's coarse thunder were still reverberating throughout Europe—when Calvin was bringing up another reformation, and Socinus another still,—then it was, the gentleman tells you, that the Council of Trent decreed that the Church should employ "physical force," to *compel* men to be holy! If this be a doctrine of the Catholic Church, it has never been taught, and would have remained a secret to eternity, if HE had not discovered it in a canon of the Council—*where it is not to be found!* And he would denounce his Catholic fellow-citizens, because *he* ACCUSES *them falsely*, of holding a doctrine, which they abhor, and which exists only as a phantom in his own brain, if it exists even there!

From baptism he goes to confession. Here, again, if the gentleman had stated our doctrine as it is, and saved himself the

(1) Chapter xxx. p. 129, On CHURCH CENSURES.

trouble of *inventing* a creed for us, his apprehensions for the safety of "civil and religious liberty," from the dangers of "confession," would have dissolved into thin air. The question is not whether our doctrine on this subject is true;—it is enough that Catholics believe it to be so. It is then an article of our faith, that when Christ, speaking to his apostles, said, "*Receive ye the Holy Ghost: whose sins you shall forgive, they are forgiven; and whose sins ye shall retain, they are retained;*" they and their successors, the bishops and priests of the Catholic Church, received power to absolve any truly penitent sinner from his sins. God having thus given them the ministry of reconciliation, and made them Christ's legates,(2) Christ's ministers, and the dispensers of the mysteries of Christ,—and given them promise, that "*whatsoever they should loose on earth, would be loosed in heaven.*"—(3) It is an article of Catholic faith, that whoever comes to them, making a sincere and humble *confession* of his sins, with a *firm purpose of amendment*, and a sincere *resolution of turning from his evil ways*, may, and does, through their *ministry*, receive absolution and release from his sins. It is equally an article of faith, that whoever comes *without* the due preparation—without repentance from the bottom of his heart, and a sincere intention of forsaking his sins, receives no benefit from absolution, but adds sin to sin, by a high contempt of God's mercy, and abuse of the sacraments. Hence, the sacrament of penance, for the reception of which confession by the penitent is a condition, is the *opposite* of whatever is sin. The bishop or priest to whom the confession is made, is said to act in the capacity of *judge.*—1st. Because he has to judge from the *signs* of repentance, whether the sins are to be "forgiven" or "retained," *i. e.* not forgiven. 2dly. Because he judges of the penance which the sinner should undergo in this life, by acts of piety or self-denial. This confession is made to the minister of the sacrament *alone*, because, although in some instances in the early ages of the Church it was made in *public*, yet the danger of producing more scandal than edification by such public confession, has been considered as a sufficient reason for making the discipline uniform. The penitent must confess all his sins; for his concealing any of them *knowingly*, would indicate a want of sincerity, and render him unworthy of that mercy and forgiveness, which Jesus Christ exercises by the ministry of his priests. The Council of Trent observes, that without knowledge of the sins committed, the priest could not observe equity "in enjoining the penance." "Æquitatem servare in poenis injungendis,"—the gentleman's ignorance of our doctrine, has made him, on the misconception of these words, represent the priest as "INFLICTING equitable punishment." And though there may, in his case, be some excuse for a mis-translation, yet we know not how to account for his putting in the *English* quotation, a phrase which has *no original in the Latin* of the Council; as in the quotation from the 14th

(2) 2 Cor. v. 18, 19.   (3) Matt. xviii. 18.

session, the words "as a part of the sacrament of penance." The gentleman may, if he choose, take his learning at *second-hand*, but he himself must be accountable for the errors which it contains.

In the doctrine here stated, my opponent thinks he discovers "usurpation on the prerogatives of God," "blasphemy," "forcing the subject," &c. If God has appointed the sacrament of penance as the means of reconciliation; if he has imparted to the ministers of his church the power of absolving penitent sinners; if confession be a condition for the exercise of that power, as Catholics believe; then, according to his reasoning it is "blasphemy," "usurpation," tyranny, slavery, and what not, to do what *God has commanded!*—to comply with the conditions on which forgiveness and pardon depend! The children of fore-ordination and fatality may, as "American freemen," hold God obliged to pardon their sins, in the way most agreeable to themselves. Catholics are happy to receive that pardon in the way that God himself has appointed, although the means may be humiliating to the pride of the corrupt heart.

If, then, as the Catholics believe, and are able to prove, Christ appointed the sacrament of penance as the means of reconciliation between the repentant sinner and God, it is the duty of the "wife," the "sister," the "daughter," to have recourse to it as often as their conscience reproaches them with having violated the divine law. It is their *right* to do so—their inalienable right, and none but a *tyrant* would *interpose to prevent them.* Yet this is what the gentleman's argument goes to authorize, *forcing their conscience.* If this be a doctrine of revelation, as Catholics believe, then it is as compatible with freedom as any other doctrine of revelation. The gentleman is utterly mistaken when he says that priests know all the "*secrets of all the villians connected with their church.*" These persons, for the reason that they *are villains*, never go to confession. They unite Catholic theory with Presbyterian practice, and their restoring ill-gotten property to Protestants, is a sign of their conversion—that they have been at confession and mean to be "*villains*" no longer.

As for the "state of every priests' mind," in consequence of their having to listen to the confessions of the penitent, the gentleman need not be at all uneasy. There have been, and there still may be bad priests. But as a class, they will not shrink from a comparison with the Presbyterian clergy, for purity, zeal, learning, charity, and disinterestedness. And in confirmation of this remark, it is sufficient to observe, that the *corrupt* and *fallen* priest, who is cast forth from the sanctuary he has profaned, is nevertheless hailed as a trophy, if he can descend to turn Presbyterian.

The argument, then, on this subject may be stated as follows:
"The doctrine of penance is a system of '*usurpation*,' '*espionage*,' '*blasphemy*,'" and "'*tyranny*.'"

"Therefore, it is opposed to civil and religious liberty."

Answer and refutation. The doctrine of penance is a revelation of Christ. In administering or receiving that sacrament Catholics are "worshipping God according to the dictates of their conscience"

—doing what Christ commanded. And since in doing what Christ has commanded there is neither "*usurpation*," nor "*espionage*," nor "*blasphemy*," nor "*tyranny*," therefore, in the doctrine of penance there is *nothing* opposed to either civil or religious liberty. The gentleman would not have hazarded such an argument, had he not been ignorant of our doctrine; his conclusion is not sustained by arguments drawn from Catholic theology, but must have rested, in his mind, on those absurd Presbyterian prejudices which he imbibed in the nursery, and from whose thraldom his subsequent education was not calculated to emancipate him.

It is true, that the doctrine of penance may be *abused*, but in this, it is like every best gift of heaven to men. But the stern discipline of the church *degrades for life* the faithless minister, who would sacrilegously pervert it to any other end, save that for which it was instituted.

The third argument on which the gentleman would make it appear that the doctrines of the Catholic church are opposed to "civil and religious liberty," is the *freedom of the press*. Now the freedom of the press is as much a DOCTRINE of the church as Symmes' Theory of the Poles. Hence, the objection on this ground has no force. There is not in the whole creed, a doctrine which forbids me, as a Catholic priest, to advocate the most unbounded freedom of the press.

If the gentleman knew a little more of the history of printing, as an *art*, it would not be necessary to inform him, that the popes, and cardinals, and bishops, were its patrons, and the first use to which it was applied was the publication of the Scriptures. If he will consult the writings on bibliography, of Le Long, or of Clement, a Protestant, he will discover that there had been published *in the Italian language* alone, forty different editions of the Scriptures, before the first Protestant version of Geneva, which was in 1562. There had been ten editions of the Italian Bible of Malhermi, printed between the years 1471 and 1484. These facts ought to shame the *ignorance*, and silence the *hereditary slanders*, of those who, like the gentleman, pretend that printing, and the publication of the Holy Scriptures are against the doctrine of the church. One single Italian city, within thirty years after the invention of the press, and *before Protestantism was born*, publishes the Bible in the Italian language, at the rate of an edition every year, of eight out of ten years, and yet it is said that this was against the doctrine of the Catholic church, and credulity swallows the falsehood!

The object of all the regulations made in regard to the printing, publishing, and reading of books, was to preserve the faith of Christ from the admixture of errors, introduced at the apostasy of the 16th century. It was to check the *licentiousness*, not to destroy the *liberty* of printing, publishing, and reading. The church, as the depository of the true doctrines, has a right to condemn and exclude, by the exercise of *spiritual authority*, all heretical and impious

4

books, those of Calvin as well as those of Voltaire. Wherever this right has been maintained by *temporal* penalties, the penalties are for the violation of the laws of the state. The rules of the Index from which the gentleman has multiplied quotations, never took effect, except where the civil power had adopted them. There were many Catholic nations in which they were never published or heard of,—a sufficient proof that they constitute no portion of Catholic doctrine.

The gentleman says that, in page 80, the Index "actually FORBIDS the reading of the Bible, and not the Protestant Bible, (as my reverend friend tried in the late controversy to make appear,) but the very Roman Bible with all its parts, sanctioned by the church, in every *possible translation* is prohibited, as follows : Biblia vulgari quocunque idiomate conscripta," that is, "THE BIBLE IN WHATEVER IDIOM WRITTEN, (is prohibited.)" I have not seen his copy of this Index, but I have no hesitation to pronounce the statement here made to be *false*, and unwarranted by the original. I challenge the proof. He must furnish it, or stand accountable to public opinion for having falsified the text, and adduced *forged* documents to prop his cause.

Finally, he adduces the Encyclical letter of the present Pope. Well, what does he find in it, except a praiseworthy solicitude to preserve the truth of God pure, *in books* of doctrine as well as preaching; complaints that the world is inundated with *bad books*, to the corruption of faith and morals, and the destruction of souls. The Pope asserts that those who recognise the spiritual authority of the church, are wicked in denying her right to exercise censorship over books. He denounces the conduct of those men who labour to seduce the faithful into the mazes of error and doubt, by circulating among them *mutilated and spurious copies of the Scripture*, and telling them to reject the church of Christ, and to become their own guides. He warns the flock over which Christ has placed him, against those who come among them in sheep's clothing, or when they cannot do this, send their errors of doctrine most innocently bound up in calf-skin. He has a right to do all this—he is bound to do it, as he will have to appear before God, to answer for the discharge of his duty.

But it does not follow that he has any right, or temporal authority, to punish by civil disabilities, those who are not subject to the civil laws of his own state, for the violation of those principles. He does not pretend to have any. And hence the gentleman may discover that the "Pope and the Priest" do not "differ." That both recognise the right to denounce counterfeit copies of the Scripture, the writings of Calvin, those of Voltaire, Thomas Paine, and all works contrary to pure morals and sound doctrine. Neither does it follow that they are enemies of the "liberty of the press," unless by liberty, the gentleman means licentiousness.

"*Is the Roman Catholic Religion, in any or in all its principles or doctrines, opposed to civil or religious liberty?*"

AFFIRMATIVE II.—MR. BRECKINRIDGE.

THE gentleman began his reply by charging me with attacking *the liberty of the press*, because, forsooth, I demanded the name of a scurrilous writer, who has anonymously assailed me in the "*Catholic Diary*," and who refers to the Rev. gentleman as the person from whom he got a *part* of his information. Of course Mr. Hughes *knows* who he is, and whether he did not get the *whole* from the same quarter. Now, if calling for the name of a *libeller* be an invasion of the liberty of the press, (as the gentleman says it is,) can any one believe him in *earnest* when he attempts to *excuse* and even *defend* the present reigning Pope, for his open attacks on the *freedom of the press*, read by me when I last addressed this audience?

The object in calling for the name was not "personal chastisement," as the gentleman intimates; but such associations of mind are, I allow, very natural to his system; and especially from the *nearness* of the author to the *gentleman*, I can excuse him for desiring to shelter him. But I repeat the charges already uttered, and pledge myself to make them out to the full, whenever the name of the author is announced. In the mean time, and especially since the gentleman has become the *advocate* of the *writer*, I here publicly lay the *article* on the table, and hold the gentleman responsible for its contents.

The distinction which the gentleman has striven to make between this *piece* and that which appeared in the Presbyterian, is not a little remarkable, especially when we remember that he *opposed* the society's *acting* on it *this evening, as out of place*,—and now makes their *not acting on it* a ground of fault! Is this consistent, or candid? But in due time they *will* act on it, as we are assured, and give to the author good reason to continue in a darkness which wisely shuns exposure. I dismiss this subject, with the remark, that the *fulsome compliments* paid to Mr. Hughes in that piece, is another reason why the name is withheld; and really, Mr. President, they are in such strong contrast with the *history of the evening*, which was so mortifying to his friends, that I should have mistaken the praises for *irony*, but for other parts of the production.

And here allow me, thus early in the debate, to say, that nothing but the love of liberty as an American, and of truth as a Protestant

Christian, could induce me to subject my feelings to the coarse and ill-bred impertinence of a priesthood whose temper and treatment toward other men alternate between servility to their spiritual sovereigns and oppression of their unhappy subjects. I can and will bear, for the sake of the *great cause*, whatever may be made necessary—though I am, thank God, not forced to do it either as a minion of the Pope, or the subject of an arrogant and vulgar *Jesuitism*.

The first thing I notice is, the *gentleman's* quibble on my statement of the *rights of minorities*. On the first evening of our meeting, (which, happily for him, was not a part of the series of regular debates,) he had said *that a man did not drop down from the clouds, —but grew up under an existing state of society: and finding a certain government established by the majority of the people, who had a right to rule, that he had no right to interfere with the order of society already established.* Now my principle, as stated this evening, is, *that the majority have no right to rule in violation of certain rights of the minority.* He pertly replies, "of course the Presbyterian doctrine must be, that the right of ruling belongs to the minority." I answer, *no.* That is as *wrong* as the other—that is aristocracy, that is despotism.—*Both* are wrong. There are certain rights aback of all *minorities* and *majorities*, which are not lawfully in the *power of man*, such as the *rights of conscience*. For example: the Pope of Rome *has established by law the Roman Catholic religion, and no subject is allowed to exercise any other worship.* Allowing that a *majority* of the *people* wish it to be so, I contend, that, in this case, the majority have no *right to enforce such a regulation.*—The *minority* (and we have good evidence, from year to year, that even in Rome there exists a minority) have a right to worship God as *Protestants*, if they so please. But it will be replied, this cannot be done without violating the laws of the land. The gentleman has said, "*The individual who would exempt himself from the discharge of either social or ecclesiastical duties,* AS ESTABLISHED IN THE STATE BY LAWFUL AUTHORITY, *or in the religious body of which he is a member, by an appeal to his pretended natural rights, would justly be regarded as unworthy to participate in the advantages of either.*" This is truly a candid admission. Then, "*by lawful authority, civil and ecclesiastical duties may be established* in a state !" Yes, and so it is established at Rome at this day, that every child born there, and every subject, *must be a Catholic!* Now I say, this law, if passed by a *majority*, (which, however, is only a *majority of Austrian bayonets*,) makes the *majority* voluntary slaves, and *oppresses the minority.* The minority have no right to *enforce*, but to *enjoy their religion ;* so with *majorities.* If this be not so, we ask the gentleman, does he approve or condemn the Pope's enforcing his religion at Rome? Is it consistent with freedom of conscience ? Is not the temporal power by which he enforces it an usurped and tyrannic exercise of power? If he were in this land, and a constitutional majority of the states were to *alter the constitution*, so as to make *the Pope* temporal and spiritual head of the nation for life, and his successor *eligible* for life by a few Cardinals, would it not be an *evasion of our rights?* Of the rights of the minority? And would not the majority be voluntary slaves? But this is the way the Pope rules; and this is the way he is elected. We beg, then, a candid, direct answer to these questions. If they be evaded, we shall readily know why it is; and you, gentlemen, will please to remark it well.

Now my principle is this: there are certain *rights* which no majority or minority can give or take away, or interfere with, except to prevent men, in their exercise, from invading the rights of other men. Of these, as most important, I selected, as a specimen of the rest, *the right of worship*, which God confers on every man as a natural, indefeasible right. This right is sometimes called a *religious right;* but our admirable constitution justly regards it as a *civil right:* that is, though it refers to *religion*, it is a right belonging to man in civil society. The constitution does *not confer*, and no constitution can *take away* this right. It does not except it; but on the contrary adopts it, declares it, and secures it, as a civil right to all American citizens in the following noble language:—

"*All men have a natural and indefeasible right to worship Almighty God, according to the dictates of their own consciences. No man can of right be compelled to attend, erect, or support any place of worship, or to maintain any ministry against his consent; no human authority can in any case whatever control or interfere with the rights of conscience, and no preference shall ever be given by law, to any religious establishment or any modes of worship.*" But at Rome, in Spain, and in every Roman Catholic country upon earth, this is denied; and even in the Spanish American States, *the rights of conscience* are trampled in the dust. The gentleman himself also on the first evening took the same ground in substance, when he vested all *rights, civil and religious*, in the *majority*. Frightened by the consequences of his own principles, he has half receded and half retains this ground, in the last speech. It is indeed a curious offspring of a *Roman* conscience, trying to speak *American* principles. He denies, for example, that the majority-principle, as he calls it, has any thing "*to do with those natural and imprescriptible rights* which lie aback of all conventions." But if the *right of worship* be secured to us by the constitution as a *civil right*, then the *majority principle has much* to do with it. It has to *protect* it. It would at Rome put down the tyrant called the Pope. It would in South America put down Popery as the established religion. It *would not erect another* in its stead. It would *protect* it, while it did not burn heretics. It would close the inquisition. It would say to Jew, Protestant, Papist, we protect you all, while you *mind your own business*. In England, and Scotland, and Ireland, it would break down the Episcopal and Presbyterian establishments; and expelling the word *toleration* from the earth, would put in its place *protection to all,—equal rights to all.* So far, therefore, the majority-principle "*does* belong to this category," and so far do these *rights* which "lie aback of all conventions," enter directly into the question of *civil* liberty.

But again: the gentleman says that "*the right of the majority to rule*, is circumscribed in a *free government* by the boundaries of civil jurisdiction. True: but in a government *not free*, how is it? What is the gentleman's view of the *rights* of a people having a sovereign like the Pope? What is the *governing power* there? And what are the rights of the *minority?* Have they any on the gentleman's principle but *submission?* And he seems quite to forget his usual discretion in avoiding the disclosure of his true principles, when he says,—"In short, the gentleman might have been more concise, and told us at once, that ALL jurisdiction, both in church and state, is a usurpation on the natural rights of man, save and except that which is exercised by CONGRESS, and the General Assembly of the Presbyterian Church." It is surely no small *throw* at our American principles to speak just so of the national congress! Yet let the gentleman tell us *where* entire freedom, civil or religious, *is* enjoyed, "*save* and *except*" in that land which receives its laws from "*Congress.*"

The gentleman seems strangely at a loss to understand the meaning of "*voluntary slave;*" and infers from my principle, that *all subjection to law* (e. g. to the laws of Pennsylvania) is *voluntary slavery*. Not so. But this is the principle:—The papacy, by *restraining liberty* of *conscience*, is a system of oppression. *Its* doctrines are *forced on man*, (in Rome for example,) on every subject; and they who reject them are punished *civilly*, and *temporally*, and once were *mortally; for heresy was death* by the *law*. Now all *good Catholics choose* to submit. As the church excludes from salvation all who reject her doctrines, so her true followers *abandon their rights of conscience*, rather than expose themselves to her wrath and damnation. *This is voluntary slavery*. This too will explain "*the* article" (which the gentleman cannot discover, though it stares the world in the face) in the American constitution, *in which Protestants and Roman Catholics cannot concur*. The article is "*that no human authority can in any case whatever control or* INTERFERE *with the rights of conscience.*" This is an American, Protestant, Bible principle. Now conscientious papists do not, and *cannot believe* this; for they ascribe to the *Pope* the *right and the power* to *dictate their creed, and to enforce obedience to it;* and they are *voluntary slaves* by giving up their rights of conscience; and in all Catholic countries, they concur by civil and if necessary by military force, to compel submission in others. Hence no good Catholic can be a consistent American.

Now whereas the gentleman thinks, on my view, the human mind were like the ass—between two bundles of hay—I must own that between the gentleman and his *incognito* friend, (at whom we now and then get a glimpse,) the poor American constitution is like a bundle of hay *between two such animals*. And then as to all that he has said in abuse of Presbyterians in this and *other lands* and *ages*, though but about one hundredth part of it is true, we have never hesitated to own that our fathers very imperfectly understood the rights of conscience. Our principles strike at the *root* of *all* establishments, everywhere, *Protestant* as well as *Papal*. Our *fathers learned* to persecute from the Church of Rome; but *happily* we are not professedly *infallible*, and therefore not *unchangeable*. Popery, on her own principles, cannot *change;* but is the same persecuting power now, and everywhere she can be, that she ever was. The question (whose terms however the gentleman very little respects) limits his investigation "*to the Presbyterian Church in the United States, in connexion with the General Assembly.*" This church has never persecuted— no, *never;* and so little candour is there in stating her principles, that in quoting from her standards only *four words* the gentleman has transposed even a part of them; has put a *false* phrase *in*, and left the *true* one *out;* as he once extracted a *paragraph* from another *confession* and published it as *ours*. When we pass however to that form of the question which concerns the Presbyterian Church, it will be time enough to begin her defence. In the mean time, why does he leave his own unhappy communion so unsheltered; and while weaving subtle distinctions to entangle the unwary, pass untouched all the difficulties of his system? And even allowing, for the sake of argument, that *Presbyterians do persecute*, does that *prove* that *Catholics* do not?

It is needless to pursue the gentleman through his learned and pointless definition of "rights natural," "rights political," "rights divine," "rights ecclesiastical."

We may take an example of his confusion of ideas, and see even through his *effort* to conceal his *principles*, their anti-American, and (as we hold) anti-Christian character. Speaking of "divine right," (a favourite term with *kings and Romish priests*,) he says, "this is the authority with which God has invested certain men, and conditions of life, for some purpose of good.", He then refers to Moses, to the apostles, and their *putative* successors, viz.: the *priesthood of Rome*. "*These rights are peculiar to those* only to whom God has given them"—" now rights and duties are correlative"—of course we are all bound to obey the *priesthood* of Rome. But the American constitution allows *diversity of religions;* and the gentleman has said " *the individual who would exempt himself from the discharge of either social or ecclesiastical duties* as ESTABLISHED IN THE STATE BY LAWFUL AUTHORITY, or in the *religious body of which* he is a member, by an appeal to his *pretended natural rights*, would justly be regarded as unworthy to participate in the *advantages of either.*"

These things united give a stronger squinting at the *rights of Romanism* than might have been expected from so wary a disputant in North America. This is the *germ* of the canon law—that vilest, shrewdest of all human tricks,—to *mingle things temporal* with things *spiritual;* to enthrone *kings* on the necks of the people, by *divine right;* and, by *still diviner rights, the priesthood* on the necks of *the kings.* He says *divine rights* "are not *natural.*" Nor, says he, "*can they be derived from civil authority.*" What are they? Our constitution makes *rights of conscience* a part of the *civil rights* of every man, and guards Jew, and Christian, and Gentile, and Mohammedan *equally*, in their proper exercise. But it owns no peculiar divine rights claimed exclusively by the Pope, and "*to which duties are correlative.*" We reject the canon law. Whatever God in his blessed revelation has made known to man, enters under the broad banner of the rights of conscience; and it is no contradiction of natural right, or departure from it, to receive it, and exercise it as divided between a *ministry* of *persuasion*, and a laity voluntarily associated to be instructed and directed in certain duties, without the surrender of any original right. But how different from papal domination, and papal doctrine about the Pope, and priesthood, and confession, and the rule of faith, &c. &c. &c.

But we will meet the gentleman's wish for a more specific examination of *civil liberty.* The definition adopted by us is this, viz.:

"*The absolute rights of an individual restrained only for the preservation of order in society.*"

"*Absolute*"—not in respect to the Creator. As it respects him, all human rights are precarious and dependant. He may take away life, liberty, and happiness. "In him we live, and move, and have our being," is the language of a heathen, but adopted and commended by an inspired apostle. In respect, therefore, to God, the absolute rights of an individual can mean no more than his natural rights. But these may be called absolute in respect of the laws of men. They are absolute in essence so far as they are indefeasible. And they are absolute in fact so far as they are not divested by the just powers of government.

"*Restrained.*" The Declaration of the American Independence will show us in what sense *restraint* is lawful.

The second paragraph of that instrument reads thus:—We hold these truths to be self-evident—that all men are created equal; that they are endowed by their Creator with certain inalienable rights; that among these are life, liberty, and the pursuit of happiness; that to secure these rights, governments are instituted among men, deriving their just powers from the *consent* of the governed."

From this it appears, that the end of government is to secure to individuals the enjoyment of their inalienable rights, and that the foundation of all just government rests upon the *consent* of the governed; and, therefore, if our definition is just, the restraint intended must be *self-imposed*, or such as rests upon *consent* freely given.

"*Order in society.*" This phrase cannot be intended to apply to the *actual forms* of government, if the preceding remarks are just; for if we should so understand it, civil liberty would be a variable quantity, ranging between the extremes of a pure democracy and an absolute despotism. In the United States it would be one thing—in England another—in France another; in Austria another—in Russia another—in Italy another—*alia Romæ—alia Athenis:* yet this is the very ground that the gentleman has already taken. It would be any thing or nothing. Civil liberty, therefore, is not the *residuum* of freedom, after making such deductions or subtractions from the absolute or natural rights of man as are necessary to preserve the *particular* order established in the country where he happens to be, or to be born; but it is the residuum of freedom, after making *such deductions only* from his natural rights, as the social condition, *in its best form*, requires. These deductions are few, and consequently the *residuum* is large—such at least were the views of the signers of the Declaration of Independence; such cannot be the gentleman's. They declared that the object of the institution of government is to preserve the *inalienable* rights of individuals, comprising in this class life, liberty, and the pursuit of happiness. But we are not left to inferences—they declared in express terms, that when any form of government becomes destructive of these ends, *it is the right of the people to alter and abolish* it. If this sentiment be just, it puts an end to the doctrine of legitimacy and the divine right of kings; and it shows that civil liberty is much more than that miserable pittance of freedom, which the established order of society throughout the whole, or almost the whole, of Europe allows. It proves the right of *expatriation*, notwithstanding the claims and pretended rights of monarchs to the persons of their subjects; it proves the right of *revolution*—the instrument itself is professedly a revolutionary paper, and *justifies that as a right, which legitimacy denominates rebellion and treason;* and we should like to know whether the gentleman thinks our revolution was rebellion, our resistance, treason? The instrument asserts that the people are the source of all just government—that the rightful continuance of it in any form depends upon their will—that they have the right "to alter or abolish it, and institute a new government, laying its foundation on such principles, and organizing its powers in such form, as to them shall seem most likely to effect their safety and happiness." It is evident therefore that by *order in society*, cannot be intended the *established order*, unless civil liberty may consist with acts of despotism; for such acts are *consistent* with the order of society in despotic states; and they may be *necessary* to maintain the established order of society in such states. The tenants of the Bastile and of the Inquisition may have suffered according to *law*—the law of the state to which it was their misfortune to belong. Indulgence to the full measure of the rights of man, only *duly* restrained, might often result in a dethronement and a revolution. The laws of England would have condemned Washington and Hancock and their associates to the gallows, and the Prince of Orange would doubtless have suffered a similar fate from the hands of Philip II. And if such a fatality had befallen the cause of liberty, it would have contributed no doubt to preserve the *established order* of society. But the right to punish such men for disturbing the established order of society, is no better or greater than the right of the robber to murder or imprison his victims for the preservation of his plunder. No: in arbitrary governments (by which I mean all governments not founded and dependant for their continuance on the consent of the governed) the original wrong is the usurpation, and that cannot be rightfully defended. Despots, like Zaccheus the publican, ought to make restitution of their extortions. If they refuse to do it, their suffering subjects have a right to compel it. If they attempt it without success, the event proves nothing as to the *right*, but only the comparative *force;* it only shows that fetters may be forged which are too strong for the victim. These are the principles of the American governments. They are too repugnant to the ideas of *order in society*, as defined by legitimacy, to be popular at St. Petersburg, Vienna, Madrid, and Rome. They indicate also a reason for the preference entertained by the Holy Alliance for Louis XVIII. over Napoleon; although, in truth, the claims of Napoleon were at least as well founded as those of the head of the Bourbon race. They also show a reason for the concern which the advocates of legitimacy manifest for the diffusion of European notions of *order in society;* and their deadly opposition at Rome, at Vienna, at St. Petersburg and Madrid to the diffusion of American principles.

Now if the gentleman will apply these principles to that strange mixture of vulgarisms, affected American principles, and Popish enmity to human freedom, which, in verbose confusion, undulate through his reply, he will find it possibly no easy matter to escape from their application.

But it is time for us to pass to a brief review of the gentleman's reply to my specifications against "the principles or doctrines" of Romanism.

I. AS TO BAPTISM—beginning, as it does, with the beginning of life—I asserted and brought proof that the doctrine of Popery on this point was destructive of liberty. The gentleman denies it. The passage to which I especially referred, was the fourteenth canon of the Council of Trent on this sacrament. As the gentleman has not answered the argument already presented, we need not dwell here. The word in the original is *cogendos*. Now we assert, that the plain, obvious, and common meaning of this word, is the *application of force*; not implying choice, or leaving an alternative. Ainsworth gives for the meaning of the word *"to be forced,"* and in the common use of the term among classical authors, this is the idea where it is applied to this or kindred subjects: *e. g.* Cicero, *cogendus est armis*—*"to be forced by arms."* And then the connection of this word as used by the council. It anathematizes those who say *"that when these baptized children grow up they are to be asked whether they* will confirm the promises, &c. &c.; *"*and that if they say they *will not*, are to be left *to their own choice,"* &c. Here the freedom of will is forced—it is slavery downright. Now the Presbyterian Church does not at all proceed as the gentleman supposes, with baptized children. It is wholly a false and gratuitous statement. But when we do discipline adult members, they are visited only with spiritual punishments, such as suspension, excommunication. There we stop. Not so in the Catholic Church. Where they *can* and *dare*, as at Rome, " they are *not left to their own choice,"*—no, but "are to be *compelled to lead a Christian life by other punishment than exclusion from the sacraments!"* This is very plain to a candid mind. And why is the gentleman so cautiously silent about *the practice of the church;* go *to those who* have *left* this church ! go to the history of this system, and this, better than a criticism on words, by the comment of facts, will confirm my construction, and seal my proof.

II. On the head of *auricular confession*, the gentleman is so feeble, though so verbose, that I think really he has shown *what he cannot do*, and left little need of reply. The question now is not on the truth of the doctrine, but its *tyranny*. He adduces Christ's commission to his apostles, and *assuming* that Romish priests are their successors, and owning that *auricular confession* was the invention of his church, yet infers the *propriety* of it, from the *failure* of proving it. Now who made any man, and above all a Roman priest, "judge" of sins, and lord of conscience ! Is it not anti-Christian tyranny to say as the catechism of this council does, *"that the priests hold the place,* and POWER, and AUTHORITY OF GOD ON EARTH?" Is it not *blasphemy,* and unbounded oppression? *Is it not saying, through me you pass to heaven, or without me to hell?* In vain does the gentleman quibble and explain. *"Judges,"* and of men's sins and consciences, and in Christ's stead, and in the exercise of his *power!* He charges me with misunderstanding his doctrine. Is it not written near at hand—*"Pœnam quam opportet pro illis pœnitentibus imponere?"* i. e. *"the punishment which ought to be inflicted on the penitent;"* which a Jesuit would soften into *"penance enjoined."* As to the translation of which he last complained, I followed the faithful Cramp, and the gentleman well knows it: he also knows that the more literal translation is even worse for his suffering cause ; and that the sense is not varied by the expletive term which the translator has employed, as will be seen by reference to the original.

The syllogisms of the gentleman are so profoundly absurd, I see not their bottom or intent; but, like circumvallations of mud, they must be left as proof against all logic, and a terror to all "*clean and goodly arms.*"

When he argues so profoundly, "IF *God* has appointed the sacrament of penance;"—"*If* he has imparted to his *ministers the power,*" &c.; "*If* confession be a *condition*," &c.; "*If,*" &c. &c. And what *if!*

"Said Paddy with a hop,
If I had a horse, how'd ye swap!"

Pardon my poetic impulse, gentlemen. I feel inspired by this battalion of *ifs*; by argument without reasoning; and triumphs without the toils of ratiocination.

The practical effect of the doctrine of confession has been to make the priesthood the most corrupt of all men, and to put all men, all kings, all power, of all who confessed to them, at their disposal. Can such effects flow from *divine* doctrine? Are such demands compatible with *human rights?*

III. In reply to my argument so largely dwelt on, concerning *the freedom of the press, of reading,* &c., the gentleman says: "*Now the freedom of the press is as much a doctrine of the church as Symmes's Theory of the Poles. Hence the objection on this ground has no force.*" This is surely an ominous confession! Do her doctrines assert no liberty of thought? Do her Scriptures enjoin no inquiry after the will, and into the word of God? Has she not forbidden, in the manifold citations just given by me from councils and popes, the free printing and reading of books in general, and especially of God's holy *word?* Does her system hold *no doctrine* which would forbid such tyranny on the soul, and such daring restraint on the Bible? Then does not that *omission* ruin her system? Or will the gentleman tell me it is only *discipline?* Then can that church regard the rights of God or man, which will tolerate, nay, which will enact and enforce, such *discipline?* and with such temporal and spiritual pains and penalties?—*Impossible!* The gentleman says that "*forty editions of the Scriptures were published in the Italian language, before the year* 1562!" Admitting it true, (which however is *not*,) and what then? Does this disprove what the Lateran and Trent Councils did, and what a host of popes did against the printing, and reading, and circulating the Bible, and of other books? Bibles were printed—therefore the popes and councils did not oppose reading them! But, sir, here are *decrees* of councils, and bulls of popes! No matter! forty editions of Bibles were printed in Italy before 1562! But, sir, the decrees *forbade* any to print or read *without the Pope's license!* Had the church a right to make such decrees? Oh they were only *discipline!* Then you own that the discipline was wrong, and repressed freedom; and that no *doctrine* of your church forbids such discipline? No! doctrine has nothing to do with it. But what is doctrine? will you please give me an infallible *definition of doctrine?* I find, when you speak of the Presbyterians of Scotland as punishing those who read the prayer-book, you consider it *doctrine*. How are similar things in your church only *discipline?* How is it so wrong for Scotch Presbyterians (as it was, I think, very wrong) to hold such a principle as to restrain free inquiry, and yet is *no error* in the Church of Rome to do infinitely more, and greatly worse things, *under the same principle?*

The gentleman says the "*object of all such regulations, made in regard to printing, publishing, and reading of books, was to preserve the Church of Christ from the admixture of errors,*" &c. I know it; so Christ told his disciples the object some men would have in view in putting them to death, would be "*to do God service.*" But was it right? The gentleman then owns "*that the end justifies the means?*" Was it compatible with the civil and religious rights of Roman Catholics to pass such regulations? Were they not "*voluntary slaves*" to *submit* to it? Did they submit *willingly?* Were they *not forced?*

Again. He says, "The church, as the depository of the true doctrines, has a right to condemn and exclude, by the exercise of *spiritual authority,* all heretical and impious books—those of Calvin as well as those of Voltaire." Ah! "*a right to exclude!*" This is a full admission of the whole thing in debate. Here we might end the question, for we know what "SPIRITUAL AUTHORITY" means in the Church of Rome.

The gentlemen still further says, "Whenever this right has been maintained by *temporal* penalties, the penalties have been for the violation of the laws of the state."

That is, the Church of Rome can so unite with despotic states, as to permit and encourage such states to enforce her spiritual laws with temporal pains and penalties. The church makes laws for her subjects: and then, "whenever" she can, she influences the state to enforce them. Now at Rome the temporal and spiritual power are united in the same sovereign head—the *Pope.*

Query. When he, as prince, by *civil penalties,* and military power, if need be, enforces the laws, or, as the gentleman is pleased to call them, "regulations," against the freedom of the press, does not the church, in him, exercise *temporal power to enforce* "*the spiritual?*" I beg for a direct answer. Is it not tyranny? and do not the general councils sanction it? Has the church ever forbidden it? Has she not legislated on it, with *command* to enforce the oppression? Will the gentleman deny it? If the Pope were here, with like *power,* would he respect *our rights,* when he does as we have seen in *Italy?* Are our rights of one sort, and those of Rome of-*another?* What makes the *differ-*

ence? If no difference, is it not clear that the church, by her *acts,* and this her *head,* "*whenever she can,*" *opposes* the civil and religious rights of man. But, says the gentleman, *printing* is like "*the use of gunpowder,* or of steam-navigation—*an acquired right.*" Then, of course, according to his own principles, "the majority-principle" may alienate it! He says, "it is as natural and unalienable a right, *not* to circulate the Bible, as to circulate it." True, I have a *right* to do it, or to *omit* it. But have the Pope and general councils a right to "*forbid me to do it,*" if I please to do it? Or, have they a right to forbid me "steam-navigation," as they once did forbid all Europe to furnish the Saracens with ships, arms, &c. &c. The gentleman *more than hints* that *they have!* And, worst of all, the gentleman calls the tyrannic acts of the present Pope *against the press,* "*a praiseworthy solicitude.*" He says, "*The Pope asserts that those who recognise the spiritual authority of the church,* ARE WICKED IN DENYING HIS RIGHT *to exercise censorship over the press.*" * * * "*He has a* RIGHT *to do all this*—he is BOUND to do it," &c. Here he admits then, that the *Pope* has a *right* and *is bound to restrain the liberty of all Catholics;* and *all* men ought to be Catholics. Is not *this slavery?* Is not this conceding fully the point in debate? Is not this surrendering a *part* of their liberty? And then *can* a *good* Catholic be a *consistent* American citizen? But the gentleman goes still further: "But it does not follow that he (the Pope) has any right, or temporal authority, to punish, by civil disabilities, those who are *not subject to the civil laws of his own state, for the violation of those principles!*" *His* own state! Who made him a ruler! A few cardinals! *Not* the people! Who passed "*the civil laws of his state*" against the freedom of the press? General councils of the church! and popes elected by *cardinals,* who were created *by* popes! Yet the gentleman owns that the *Pope,* the head of the church, "*does enforce* by *civil disabilities,*" the laws *against* a free press "in *his own state.*" What if a papal majority should make France or America a part of "his state," will he not "*have a right,*" and "be bound" to enforce the same laws? And the gentleman ventures so far as to say, speaking of himself, "THE 'POPE' AND THE 'PRIEST' DO NOT DIFFER!" In this confession he yields up the question; finally exposes his indefensible principles, and insults the feelings of his injured country. As to the index, whose testimony he questions, here is the book, and here the very words. It was printed at Rome, too! and forbids the *reading in the vulgar tongue of the Catholic Bible, no matter in what idiom!* How much, pray, were the *forty editions* of Italian Bibles worth to an oppressed and benighted people?

IV. I next proceed to show from *various decrees of professedly infallible councils embodying principles on all the leading relations of man,* "*as to life, liberty, and the pursuit of happiness,*" that the Church of Rome is opposed in many of her doctrines to civil and religious liberty.

And first, from the Fourth General Council of Lateran held at Rome, A. D. 1215, under Pope Innocent III.—Present 2 patriarchs; 70 metropolitans; 400 bishops; 812 abbots, priors, &c. with imperial ambassadors, strumpets, &c. &c.

We give entire the whole of the third chapter. *Concerning Heretics.*—We have the *original* on the table, and it may be referred to by the gentleman, if he has any doubt of the justness of the translation—which we endeavour to make very accurate.

"We excommunicate and anathematize every heresy extolling itself against this holy, orthodox, catholic faith, which we before expounded, condemning all heretics, by whatsoever names called, having indeed different faces, but having their tails bound together by a common agreement in falsehood, one with another. And being condemned, let them be left to the secular powers present, or to their bailiffs, to be punished with due animadversion; if clergymen, let them be first degraded from their orders, so that the goods of persons thus condemned, if of the laity, may be confiscated; if of the clergy, they may be devoted to the churches from which they have received their stipends. But if any shall be found, who are notable by suspicion alone, let them be stricken with the sword of anathema, and shunned by all, until they have rendered full satisfaction; unless they shall have proved their innocence by a clearing of themselves, suitable to the degree of suspicion and the quality of the person; but if they continue under excommunication for a year, they shall after that be condemned as heretics. And let the secular powers be warned and induced, and if need be, condemned by ecclesiastical censure, what offices soever they are in; that as they desire to be reputed and taken for believers, so they publicly take an oath for the defence of the faith, that they will study in good earnest to exterminate to their utmost power, from the lands subject to their jurisdiction, all heretics devoted by the church; so that every one that is henceforth taken into any power, either spiritual or temporal, shall be bound to confirm this chapter by his oath. But if the temporal lord, required and warned by the church, shall neglect to purge his territory of this heretical filth, let him by the metropolitan and com-provincial bishops be tied by the bond of excommunication; and if he scorn to satisfy within a year, let that be signified to the Pope, that he may denounce his vassals thenceforth absolved from his fidelity, [allegiance to him,] and may expose his country to be seized by Catholics, who, exterminating the heretics, may possess it without any contradiction, and may keep it in the purity of the faith; saving the right of the principal lord, so be it he himself put no obstacle thereto, nor oppose any impediment; the same law not withstanding being kept about them that have no principal lords.

"And the Catholics that taking the badge of the cross, shall gird themselves for the extermination of heretics, shall enjoy that indulgence and be fortified with that holy privilege, which is granted to them that go to the help of the Holy Land.

"And we decree to subject to excommunication the believers and receivers, defenders and favourers of heretics, firmly ordaining that whenever such person is noted by excommunication, if he disdain to satisfy within a year, let him be *ipso jure* made infamous; nor let him be admitted to public offices or councils, nor to aid in electing such, nor to bear testimony. Let him also be intestate, so that he shall neither have power to bequeath or inherit. Besides—no one shall be required to answer him about any business—but he shall answer all others. If he be a judge, his sentence shall be null; nor shall any causes be brought for a hearing before him. If an advocate, he shall not be permitted to plead. If a public register, his instruments shall have no force, but be condemned with their condemned author. And we command the like to be observed in like cases. But if he be a clergyman, he shall be deposed from all office and benefice; because the greater the offence the heavier should be the punishment, (vindicta.) But if any persons shall contemptuously refuse to shun those whom the church has devoted, (as heretics,) let them be smitten with the sentence of excommunication, until they have made full satisfaction. Moreover, let not clergymen administer to such pestilent persons the sacraments of the church; nor let them presume to bestow on them Christian burial; nor to accept their alms or offerings; but on the contrary, let them be deprived of their office, and not restored without a special grant from the Holy See. In like manner all regulars, on whom the same shall be inflicted, shall lose their privileges in that diocese in which they have committed said excesses.

"And because some, under '*the form of godliness,* but *denying its power,*' as the apostle saith, have assumed the authority to preach, although the same apostle saith, '*How shall they preach except they be sent.*' Therefore, let all who presume to preach without the authority of the Holy See, or of a Catholic bishop, either publicly or privately, be bound with the chain of excommunication; and unless they quickly repent, let them be visited with other condign punishment.

"We enjoin, in addition, that every archbishop and bishop, either in person, by his archdeacon, or by fit and honest persons, shall twice, or at least once a year, make the circuit of any parish in which heresy is reported to exist, and there compel three or more men of good report, or if it is thought expedient the whole neighbourhood, to swear that if any one shall thereafter know of any heretics therein, or any holding secret conventicles, or any differing in life and morals from the conversation of the faithful, that he shall studiously point them out to the bishop. And the bishop shall call the accused to his presence, and the accused shall be canonically punished, unless they do clear themselves from the suspected guilt; if after a show of being cleared, they relapse into their former perfidy, or if any such despising the sacredness of an oath, shall with damnable heresy refuse to swear, let them for that thing be reputed heretics."

Such is the "Magna Charta" of *Papal rights*—the great infallible *Black Letter Commentary* on the power of the priesthood—the *germ* of the inquisition—the tender mercies of the only true church, *out* of which there is no salvation, *in* which there is no *liberty*. In vain did Draco write his laws in blood—or *heathen* Rome legislate against Christians. This is the masterpiece of spiritual and temporal despotism. But, as I need some respite, I reserve my analysis and comments for the last hour of the evening. We shall now be entertained by the gentleman's skill in showing that there is not a *word of doctrine in it;* and if men were destroyed in millions by the disciples of the church, why, that was not to be charged upon her principles; for she never *touched* a heretic—she only handed them over to the *civil power* —that did the business.

Her doctrines are those of perfect freedom! And as for the heretics, they deserved to die; and if *discipline* put them out of the way, the world was well rid, while *doctrine* is still full of *love* and full of liberty to man.

"Jesuitism," says De Pratt, "*embarrasses itself very little with the means*—scruples are trifles. This is what Mirabeau called *la grande morale;* leaving what he disdainfully termed *la petite morale* to the commonalty." The church killed millions by *discipline*, leaving *doctrine* reposing in the higher parts of the *system.* See now how skilfully her chosen son will exemplify the tactics of his school and the ethics of Rome in explaining away this tremendous decree.

"Is the Roman Catholic Religion, in any or in all its principles or doctrines, opposed to civil or religious liberty?"

NEGATIVE II.—MR. HUGHES.

Mr. President,—I am glad that, in demanding the name of the writer in the Diary, the gentleman's object is *not* to inflict "personal chastisement." If the name could be of any use to him, for any *other* purpose, I should have no hesitation in making him acquainted with it. His memory seems to be sore in relation to the subject, and I really cannot imagine why. He considers himself as having triumphed over me on that occasion, and why does he repine? The writer in the Diary spoke of him in terms of great respect, called him a gentleman, &c., but he has just discovered that the writer was "ironical" throughout. The gentleman's manner of referring to this, will have the effect to make persons doubt the solidity of his own convictions on the subject. For if he *can* prove it to be a libel, (which it is not,) an assault on him, (which it is not,) then people will say, "why does he not do so?" "Why does he *pretend* that the name of the author is necessary, when every one of common sense sees that it has no more to do with the statements, than the size of the town clock?"

As to the society's acting on it, it was for them to do so, not in the hour of discussion, but afterward, when they are on business. Let them treat its statements as they did those of the Presbyterian,—point out and specify the *falsehoods;* if they do not this, the legitimate inference is that there are none. The gentleman might be consoled for the "fulsome compliments" that are paid to me by the discovery, of which he is the author, that the writer spoke "ironically." But all will not do—*lateri hæret arundo.*

The sweet contemplation of the laurels which the article would wickedly dispute his right to wear, must have inspired him with the following *polished* specimen of Christian meekness, and literary refinement : " *Nothing but the love of liberty, as an American, and of truth as a Protestant Christian, could induce him to subject his feelings to the coarse and ill-bred impertinence of a priesthood, whose temper and treatment toward other men, alternate between servility to their spiritual sovereigns, and oppression of their unhappy subjects. He can and will bear, for the sake of the great cause, whatever may be made necessary;*

though, thank God, he is not forced to do it, either as the minion of the Pope, or the subject of ever-arrogant and vulgar Jesuitism."

Do you not, sir, pity the gentleman? The Chesterfield of the Presbyterian church—the *magister elegantiarum*—to be exposed to the retorts of a Catholic priest! But, for sake of " the great cause" he is willing to be a martyr.—Still it is hard to have his fine, delicate feelings exposed to such rude treatment! He ought, however, to remember, that aiming at the immortality of an author, he must be prepared to encounter the trials to which his ambition has exposed him. When he uses language in reference to his present position, which is a violation of the most common politeness, he must not expect that it can be allowed to pass unnoticed. Is not every *term*, in the foregoing extract, chosen—is not every sentence arranged, for the express purpose of gross insult? He would now claim sympathy as the reward of a position which he has sought with assiduity. HE it was who kept up a standing advertisement, challenging me to an " oral discussion." HE it was who rudely, as I conceive, thrust himself between me and my relation to this society. HE it was who addressed to me the most unwarrantable letter I ever received in my life, praying that I would give him the opportunity to meet me in this discussion. And now, forsooth, his truly delicate feelings are exposed, not by his own seeking, of course:—Oh no! but for " the great cause." Give him sympathy, then, all ye that love " the great cause."

The gentleman knew that I disliked to have any thing more to do with him, after the close of our late controversy; and I leave it to the connoisseurs in good breeding to determine how far his *forcing* himself on my notice can be reconciled with those pretensions to refined feelings which he has set forth. He promised himself immense glory from an oral discussion. He drew inferences from my reluctance to meet him, which the case did not warrant. It was not that I dreaded his arguments, nor distrusted my own. But I had been obliged to expose the gentleman during the controversy, in a way so disagreeable to myself, and necessarily discreditable to him, that I regarded him as having suffered literary shipwreck.

When a writer affects to be learned, and quotes from an author something as evidence, he ought to know for certain the truth of his quotation. When the sense of the author is perverted, either by *additions*, or *omissions*, or *garblings*, then the proceeding is entitled literary forgery. And when this is exposed in a controversy, either political, literary, or religious, the individual who is convicted is regarded, by men of high honour, as *hors de combat*. He is done.—Neither is it enough to say that the forgery was *copied*, and not original. The man who is necessarily at the mercy of *second-hand authority*, ought not to rush into a discussion where the *fountains* are to be consulted. In the course of that controversy, and in the duty of defending my religion against reckless and unfounded assertion, I was compelled to offer a premium of five hundred dollars to any professor who should find a certain quotation, by Mr. Breckinridge, in the place in which *he* professed to find it, *but where it did not exist*. The advertisement is still on record—and the premium unclaimed. (1) While the gentleman stands in this position before the public, he will see a reason why I desired to have nothing more to do with him, in the way of controversy. Others, too, will discover that the gentleman's claim to fine, sensitive feelings (refuted, however, by the very gross language in which he asserts it) comes too late. His position, as one who trifled with authors, and made them speak falsehoods to support his argument, was a much harder trial for his honour, than to encounter the *vivâ voce* refutation of his arguments. I recommend patience under contradiction. Whenever he errs in history, philosophy, logic, theology, it will be my duty, *if I can*, to advise him of it; and this, I am aware, will be hardly borne by one who has been accustomed to have his *ipse dixit* received as the gospel.

As to the points of his speech which relate to the argument, and not to himself, I am happy to perceive that his views on principles of civil government are much improved since he last spoke. He had censured my argument for maintaining the right of the majority to rule. In reply I retorted that, since he *denied* this right to the majority, he must, of course, ascribe it to the minority; and, in *that case*, there is no reason why the Presbyterians might not now begin to rule for the nation at large. Startled at the evidence of this consequence, he turns back in his last address, and states that *his* principle is "that the majority have no right to rule *in violation of certain rights of the minority.*" Now this is common sense; and if the gentleman had stated his proposition *thus qualified*, in his first speech, there would have been no disagreement on the matter. He is mistaken, therefore, when he represents me as replying *"pertly,"* or otherwise, to what did not exist. This is a new proposition. I agree with him, that in relation to certain *rights* of the minority, no majority has a right to rule. And this doctrine I have stated at large in my answer to his first speech.

I had laid down as a principle, that the man who, as a citizen, refuses to discharge the duties lawfully imposed on him by that relation; or, as a member of a church, refuses to comply with the regulations of the *religious society to which he belongs*, " by an appeal to his pretended natural right, would be justly regarded as unworthy to participate in the privileges of either:" viz. of the government, or of the church to which he belonged.

(1) See Controversy, p. 411, Johnson's edition.

There is not in the community, a man of common sense, to whom this proposition is not self-evident; and yet my opponent, struck apparently with its novelty or extravagance, calls it a "candid admission." It was not candid in him, however, to suppress a portion of my statement, in order to misrepresent me by the other portion. He makes me say, that "by lawful authority, civil and ecclesiastical duties may be established *in a state;*" as if I recognised in the state the right to appoint ecclesiastical duties. I spoke distinctly of *civil* duties as established in the state; and of *ecclesiastical duties* (as established) "*in the religious body of which one is a member.*" The gentleman's artifice, therefore, in suppressing a portion of the statement, and perverting the rest, must redound to the glory of Presbyterianism. On this perversion he builds a series of inductions, which, inasmuch as they are built on a *false imputation*, deserve no reply. He winds up, however, with the following question, which contains the cream of his logic: "*If he* (the Pope) *were in this land, and a constitutional majority of the States were to alter the constitution, so as to make the Pope a temporal and spiritual head of the nation for life, and his successor eligible for life by Cardinals, would it not be an invasion of our rights?*" ANSWER—IT WOULD. AND WE SHOULD BE GREAT DUNCES IF WE SUBMITTED TO IT. "*Would it not be an invasion of the rights of the minority?*" YES, MOST DECIDEDLY. "*And would not the majority be voluntary slaves?*" I think not; since the case supposes them to act "constitutionally," and by the impulse of their own FREE and SOVEREIGN CHOICE. The principle of the hypothesis is the same, no matter on whom the choice should fall. However, IF they were to "alter the constitution," and appoint "the Pope and all his successors," they would, in my humble opinion, do a very foolish thing. It would exceed, in absurdity, even the hypothesis itself.

The gentleman has undertaken to prove that the doctrines of the Catholic religion are opposed to civil and religious liberty. In order to refute his position, it is sufficient to show, that Catholics can be the most strenuous promoters of both civil and religious liberty, without violating any doctrine of their creed. To assert a proposition, and *maintain* it against the doctrine of the Church, is regarded as heresy; and such Catholics as do so, are permitted to become Presbyterians as soon as they wish. Therefore, if there were any doctrine, in the Catholic Church, opposed to civil and religious liberty, it would be *heresy* to advocate the principles of civil and religious liberty. Now, this principle has been advocated by Catholic individuals and Catholic nations, and in this they have never been accused of violating any doctrine of their religion. France is certainly a Catholic nation; and yet all religions are equal. Poland is a Catholic country; and yet Catholic Poland has always been conspicuous among the nations for its advocacy of civil and religious liberty If, therefore, Catholic nations and individuals can be, and have been, the advocates of civil and religious liberty, it follows that the most unbounded freedom, both political and religious, is perfectly compatible with the principles and doctrines of the Catholic religion.

Now, the gentleman's reference to the political and religious condition of the Papal dominions, must be intended only for the ignorant portion of his hearers. His argument betrays itself the moment you bring it to the test of reason. Supposing that I were to grant him all he requires, and agree that the subjects of the Papal dominion are oppressed by an arbitrary and absolute government, his inference that, therefore, the doctrines of the Catholic religion are opposed to civil and religious liberty, is a *non sequitur* in reasoning, and a contradiction of history in point of fact. The opposition which the *political views* of popes have had to encounter from *Catholic* governments in past ages, is a sufficient evidence that the political creed of the Roman States constitutes no part of the Catholic religion. If the gentleman would condescend to read history on the subject, he would learn, that the only connection between Catholics and the Pope, is the connection between the *visible* head and the *visible* members of the Church—Christ, its founder, being the supreme invisible head. He would learn that the object of this connection is the unity of belief in one Lord, one faith, and one baptism. He would learn that in *the Bishop of Rome*, Catholics have always distinguished between the legitimate authority of the Pontiff, appertaining to a kingdom, *which is not of this world*, and the pretensions of the temporal prince. And while the doctrine of the Catholic religion taught them to be submissive to the one, it left them the right not only to resist, but even to chastise, the temerity of the other. In short, any man who is acquainted with history, and honest in the use he makes of it, will discover in the *religious unity* between Catholic nations and the see of Rome, and in the *political resistance* to the pretensions of various popes, when they undertook to meddle in the civil concerns of other states, the broad historical evidence, that, as regards civil and religious liberty, Catholics are as unshackled in their doctrines as any other denomination. This the British nation have acknowledged, by restoring the Catholics to their political rights. And it is worthy of the Presbyterian parsonhood, to take up the cud of bigotry and persecution—which even England had thrown away, after having chewed it for three centuries—and present it to the palate of AMERICANS.

But the gentleman tells us, that *he* recognises, "as a natural and indefeasible right, the right of worship which God confers on every man." This he calls *his* principle: to which I reply, that it is as much my principle as *his*. Yet it does not follow, that I have "a natural and indefessible right" to SAY MASS in the halls of the Princeton Theological Seminary, under the *plea of wor-*

ship. Neither does it follow, that he has a right to preach Calvinism under the Pope's window, denouncing the civil head of the Roman States, as a "USURPER," and the supreme Bishop of the Catholic Church, as "ANTI-CHRIST." This would be not merely an act of worship—it would be preaching sedition: and if the doctrine took effect, bloodshed must be the consequence. To say mass, however, *is* an act of mere worship, having no other *effects* or relations, than those which relate to God, and the consciences of the worshippers. And yet, the Presbyterian laws of Scotland held it enacted, that the individual who should be convicted of performing or assisting at this act of mere worship, "THREE TIMES," *even in the caves of the mountain*, SHOULD BE PUT TO DEATH.

Now the gentleman himself disclaims this article of Scotch Presbyterianism, and contends for the unbounded freedom of conscience and right of worship. Let me, then, ask him a question, (and I beg you, gentlemen, to mark his answer well:) Supposing that the wife or daughter of a PRESBYTERIAN MINISTER should *claim* the right of worshipping God according to the doctrines of the Catholic Church—I ask the gentleman, whether *that* Presbyterian minister is *bound* to grant her the right which she demands, in the name of conscience and of God? Let him answer that. Is he bound to allow her to go to confession, when her conscience prompts her to do so? If he answers in the negative, then, you will understand how hollow are his professions of zeal for the "rights of worship and of conscience," which he calls "*his* principle." This will test all he has said on this subject.

The gentleman misrepresents me, when he charges me with having "vested all rights *civil and religious*, in the majority." Whenever I spoke of the majority, I spoke of them in connection with those things in which the principles of a free government acknowledge their right to rule; and already it becomes manifest, that the success of his cause will depend on the success with which the arguments of his opponent can be misrepresented. The rights of conscience, and of worship, are *older* than all civil government. They are coeval with the human mind; their existence is independent of civil laws—which have only the power to *recognise* or *not recognise* them. Catholic constitutions have *sometimes* recognised them—Presbyterian constitutions, NEVER.

In the oracular mood of his last speech, the gentleman had gone into a very minute detail of the "usurpations" in church and state, with which the world is afflicted. The Congress of the United States, and the GENERAL ASSEMBLY of the Presbyterian Church, were the only two sources of authority that did not enter into his catalogue. I took the liberty of observing, that he might have saved a tedious enumeration, if he had said *at once*, that "ALL *jurisdiction is an usurpation, except what is exercised by Congress and the General Assembly*." He intimates that I have spoken disrespectfully of Congress, by associating it with the General Assembly. This was not my meaning; and he would again mistake me, if he were to suppose that I ascribe to the said General Assembly any of those blessings of "civil and religious freedom," which he very properly ascribes to another source. Yet, though it is my privilege to regard the authority exercised by the General Assembly, as "usurpation," still I must say, with every man acquainted with the mode in which it is organized, that for the purposes of popular and political government, its structure is little inferior to that of the Congress itself. In any emergency that may arise, the General Assembly can produce a uniformity of action among its adherents to the farthest boundaries of the land. It acts on the principle of a radiating centre, and is without an equal or a rival among the other denominations of the country.

Catholics, in the adoption and profession of *their* religion, are actuated by the power of the evidences that establish, in their mind, the truth of their creed. Whenever men profess a creed *from other motives*, they become hypocrites, and are incapable of rendering worship to God, who is a Spirit, and who desires to be adored in spirit and in truth. Hence it is as absurd, as it is tyrannical, to attempt to *force* the *consciences* of men.

The faculty of the human mind, which *decides* on the question of creeds, is the JUDGMENT, which cannot be coerced by civil laws. Civil governments would be as well employed in passing laws to regulate the WILL and MEMORY of the subject or citizen, as in attempting to regulate the UNDERSTANDING. I submit to all the duties of religion prescribed by the Catholic Church, *because*, in the unfettered exercise of MY UNDERSTANDING, I have come to the conviction that the doctrines of that church are the doctrines promulgated by Jesus Christ and his apostles. The *motive*, therefore, which induces me to be a Catholic, is as much superior to all HUMAN authority, as God is superior to man, or as mind is superior to matter. Why then, if the gentleman holds these principles, does he associate himself with those, who, in contempt of the American constitution, are, as far as they can with safety, persecuting Catholics for conscience sake? Are not the misguided fanatics, who are covering the Catholic name with the slime of vulgar calumny, low invective, and mere Billingsgate argument—who are passing from town to town, and from city to city, appealing to the worst passions of ignorance and prejudice—and stooping from their pretensions as ministers of Christ, to the office of mere political haranguers, are not these trying to induce "human authority to interfere with the rights of conscience?" As a specimen of their style, I have only to quote from the gentleman himself. He says that Catholics must believe in the right of human authority to interfere with the rights of conscience. This is a gross calumny. I am a Catholic, and I have repeatedly asserted the contrary. He says that they "ascribe to the Pope the right and the power to *dictate their creed and to force obedience to it."* This is another gross calumny; the Pope has no such right, and the proposition *would be condemned by the Pope himself, and the whole Catholic Church, as* HERETICAL. He says that Catholics *"are voluntary slaves by giving up their rights of conscience."* This is equally a calumny. They worship Almighty God "according to the dictates of their conscience," and *this* is their crime in the estimation of the Presbyterian bigots, who persecute them now, as they have ever done, because they *refuse* to give up these rights. It was natural that, having made the foundation of his argument of "gross calumnies," his conclusion, that "*hence no good Catholic can be a consistent American,*" should be what it really is,—a gross libel. Let the gentleman inscribe it on the tomb of Charles Carroll of Carrollton, and the very marble will blush for him, if he cannot blush for himself.

The gentleman admits that persecution was a part of Presbyterianism in all other countries, but he says that the "question limits my investigation to the Presbyterian Church in the United States, and in connexion with the General Assembly." This is *not* the fact. The limits of the question are, the "PRESBYTERIAN RELIGION IN ANY OR ALL OF ITS DOCTRINES." Under the protection of the American Constitution it is no great merit to say that the Presbyterian Church has *not* persecuted other denominations; and this is about as far as the gentleman feels authorized to go. For the rest, he says that the Presbyterians learned persecution from the Church of Rome; and if so, it must be confessed that they remembered the *lesson* a long while, and practised it so uniformly, that it never would have been forgotten, had they not been obliged, in the development of national events, to submit to the influence of extrinsic liberality. He says, however, that the Presbyterian Church is not infallible, of which, indeed, there is sufficient evidence. Now when it shall be my privilege to investigate "the doctrines and principles of the Presbyterian religion," I pledge myself to prove that persecution, for conscience sake, *has been their doctrine.* And as they are fallible, they may discover in due time, that in disavowing this doctrine out of compliment to the AMERICAN CONSTITUTION, they were guilty of a departure from the "faith once delivered to the *saints."* Hence, their *fallibility* in doctrine is a very suspicious argument to prove that they will never relapse into their old habits. The gentleman says that the Catholic Church is, or claims to be infallible. This is true. She claims to have received the *doctrines of Christianity* from Christ and his apostles. She claims to have received divine commission to teach and transmit these doctrines, unchanged as she received them. Hence she claims to have been constituted a *witness* of what they are—with authority to expel from her communion those who would *add*, or *diminish*, or *pervert*. She makes no *doctrine;* she repudiates none that was *originally committed* to her testimony. In giving that testimony, she claims to be protected *from the attestation of falsehood*, by the promise of him who said, "I am with you all days till the consummation of the world." In this sense, therefore, *and in this sense* ALONE, she claims to be "infallible." If she teach as "A TENET OF FAITH OR MORALS REVEALED BY ALMIGHTY GOD" that "civil and religious liberty," or either of them, is sinful, then I am bound *as a Catholic* to believe accordingly, *and I should be guilty of heresy were I to deny it.*

Now it is known that all Catholics repudiate this charge; and consequently, that *either their* faith disclaims this imputed doctrine, or *else* they sin against their faith, and fall into heresy. But Catholics, it may be said, *have opposed* civil and religious liberty. Yes, and other, and perhaps *better* Catholics have *advocated* civil and religious liberty; their doctrines leaving them at perfect liberty to exercise their own discretion in the matter. The inhabitants of South America have vindicated their liberty by revolution—have they ceased to be Catholics on this account? And they might declare equal protection and privilege in the state, to the professors *of every other religion*, without violating one iota of the *doctrines* of the Catholic Church. They might follow the example of the Catholic colony of Maryland, who were the *first* to teach the Puritans of New England, and the bigots of the world, that no human authority has a right to interpose between the *conscience of man and his God;* and yet be even better Catholics than they are. All this proves that there is no doctrine in the Catholic creed opposed to "civil and religious liberty," and it proves that no such doctrine *can ever* become a portion of that creed, which would *forfeit* its claims to infallibility, the moment it should teach *as a* "tenet revealed by Almighty God," any article that had not been taught and believed from the beginning of Christianity.

The gentleman says, that in quoting from his standards, I *"put in a false phrase and left a true one out."* I deny the fact, and challenge him for the proof. Until he furnish the proof, I pronounce the charge unfounded in truth. It is a habit which I have had too much reason to despise in others, to be guilty of it myself.

My opponent finds himself unable to controvert any of my distinctions of "RIGHTS," or the definition given of them. Another, finding them just and logical, would have passed on. But not so the gentleman. He has discovered that I include the *legitimate ministers* of the Christian religion *as* persons exercising functions by "divine right." I gave Moses, and the apostles and their successors, as instances. He has not thought it too petty to insinuate that I was advocating the pretensions of "KINGS" to rule by "divine right." His motive for this little artifice cannot be mistaken. Now I shall show that every Presbyterian parson pretends to be a minister of Christ by "divine right." They are not *born* ministers. The *government* could not make them ministers. How then? By what right do they exercise the ministry? By divine right, as they say. They were called of God as they pretend, but *not* exactly "as Aaron was." This is their doctrine; and if I am mistaken I shall be glad to hear the correction, in the acknowledgment of the gentleman, that he is a Presbyterian minister, but *not* by divine right. If, therefore, this doctrine "squints," as he has elegantly expressed it, in favour of "kings," and against the Constitution, it follows that he is as much committed by it as I am. But the thing was almost too little to have deserved any notice.

We now pass to the gentleman's long commentary on the definition of "CIVIL LIBERTY." By this we agreed to understand "*the absolute rights of the individual, restrained only for the preservation of order in society.*" This definition, his own, must be very obscure, when four pages have been wasted in commentaries on it, which, however, only wrap it up in thicker folds of obscurity. It is much easier to understand the *text* than the *commentary*. The whole seems to be intended as a high-wrought panegyric of the principles set forth in the Constitution, of which I am as fond an admirer as the gentleman can be. Yet I must say, that this perpetual stooping to flatter the republican feelings of the audience, is but a lame way of maintaining an argument, while it is any thing but complimentary to their understandings. Now it is a singular fact, that while the gentleman affects to be almost an *idolater* of the American Constitution, other Reverend gentlemen, regarded by Presbyterians as sound in the faith, and as learned as my present opponent in Presbyterian theology, have denounced that Constitution as a GODLESS INSTRUMENT. The General Synod of the Reformed Presbyterian Church, held in Pittsburg, in the month of October, 1834, in two Overtures published as an appendix to its proceedings, contains the following propositions against the United States and State Constitutions. In the first Overture we find the following propositions explicitly laid down :—

"We proceed now to establish the charge of IMMORALITY against the Constitution of the United States." (1)

"1. It does not acknowledge or make any reference to the existence or providence of a Supreme Being."

"2. The United States Constitution does not recognise the revealed will of God."

"3. The Constitution of the United States acknowledges no subjection to the Lord Jesus Christ." (2)

Again, (3) "The Constitution of the United States contains the INFIDEL and ANTI-CHRISTIAN principle, that a nation, as such, *ought not to support nor even recognise* the religion of the Lord Jesus Christ. Congress shall make no law respecting the establishment of religion or prohibiting the free exercise thereof."

(1) Overture, p. 5.   (2) Page 6.   (3) Page 8.

The gentleman will tell you, that these are the doctrines *not* of the Presbyterians, but of the *Reformed* Presbyterians in the United States. But do not these kindred denominations exchange pulpits? Do they not exchange the right hand of Christian fellowship? And if they do, does it not follow that, in the judgment of the Presbyterian Church, there is no essential *heresy* in this doctrine of their reformed brethren? These are matters which it is difficult to reconcile with the "*blarney*" with which the gentleman treats the American Constitution, which his brethren denounce as containing "INFIDEL" and "ANTI-CHRISTIAN" principles.

Neither can I help believing that the gentleman has perverted the meaning and spirit of the American Constitution, when he tells us that "*it justifies as a right that which legitimacy denominates rebellion and treason.*" This is injudicious praise. I presume the advocates of "rebellion and treason" against this government, would find themselves mistaken in appealing to the Constitution for their *right to perpetrate rebellion and treason.* The gentleman wishes to know whether I think "*our revolution was rebellion, our resistance treason?*" I answer, that, *in my opinion*, our revolution was a successful experiment of popular resistance against unjust and tyrannical oppression, justified, not by the broad principles of anarchy laid down by him, but justified by the *particular grievances to which it owed its origin.* I believe it was so understood by the immortal men who wrought out the experiment and constructed the fabric of our national independence. *They* had no idea that the Constitution would ever come to be considered as the patent-right of what "legitimacy denominates rebellion and treason;" or that it should ever be denounced as containing "immorality," "infidel," and "anti-christian" principles. This is quite enough on the gentleman's four pages of political casuistry—for in the correction of his speech it extends to four pages.

His next matter is a return to, and repetition of, what he had said on baptism in his last speech, and what I had refuted in mine. He goes to Ainsworth's Dictionary for the meaning of what Catholics understand by the word "cogendus," in one of the canons of the Council of Trent. He does not adduce any *fact* to support his misapprehension of its meaning. I leave the explanation given in my last speech, as a sufficient reply to the vapid declamation, without either fact or argument, with which he has thought proper to return to it. It is a maxim of logic, that "what is *gratuitously* asserted may be *gratuitously* denied." When the gentleman adduces *facts* instead of *assertions*, to prove his construction, I shall be prepared to meet him.

There is one remark of his, however, which shows that his knowledge of the history of his own church is somewhat defective. I showed that Presbyterians themselves claim the right to "compel" members to lead Christian lives, by *other* penalties "besides exclusion from the sacraments"—such as suspension and excommunication. He informs me, however, that *these* are the only punishments by which Presbyterians "discipline their adult members." The Council of Trent prescribed no other. But I would beg leave to oppose to the gentleman's assertion, the authority of the historian Gilb. Stuart, who tells us that *one* of the ways in which they (Presbyterians) "disciplined their members," for breaking the fast of Lent, *was whipping in the church*.(1)

On the head of Auricular Confession, the gentleman still thinks and says it is "tyranny," "voluntary slavery," "blasphemy," "unbounded oppression," &c. &c., though he modestly abstains from producing any new argument against it, except what I shall notice presently. I refer the reader to my explanation of this doctrine in the last speech. Catholics believe that auricular confession, as *they* understand it, is a part of the religion of Christ. In practising this duty, therefore, they only *exercise the rights of conscience like other denominations*. They can pity the blindness, and pardon the bigotry, of those who *denounce them for the exercise of this right*, and who yet pretend to be advocates of freedom of conscience. I had, indeed, charged the gentleman, not only with "misunderstanding" our doctrine, but also with perverting the language in which it was expressed. By way of vindicating himself from this charge, he makes a show of appealing to the original Latin:—"*Is it not written*," says he, "*near at hand—pœnum quam opportet pro illis pœnitentibus imponere.*" And what will be the reader's disgust to learn that this beautiful specimen of Latinity, put forth as *a quotation* from the Council of Trent, is a FABRICATION—a FORGERY! The only sentence at all *like it*, (and the likeness is very remote,) is this . . . . *neque æquilatem quidem in pœnis injungendis servare potuisse* . . . . to which I referred in my last speech. The Rev. gentleman must have become quite *rusty* in his grammar, when he ventured on giving, as LATIN, a phrase which is a most palpable violation of all syntax. He says he follows the "faithful Cramp,"—author of the "Text Book of Popery"—and if so, I can only say that the master and the disciple are worthy of each other. The Scripture tells us, that "if the blind lead the blind, both will fall into the pit."

But if the gentleman, in making the fathers of the Council of Trent responsible for his own spurious and *ungrammatical Latin*, has given proof that he has forgotten his grammar, it does not follow that he has forgotten his *poetry*. His success in this department will surprise you the less; as, according to Horace, to be a poet does *not* depend on education—*poeta nascitur non fit*. The following beautiful lines, therefore, will gratify those who are sensible to the *delicate* and *sublime* :—

(1) Vol. ii. p. 94.

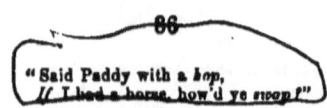

"Said Paddy with a *hop*,
If I had a horse, how'd ye stoop!"

After having *thus* proved that he had not perverted our doctrine of confession, (and such a proof!) he returns to the freedom of the press, in reference to which I beg again to direct the reader to my last speech. I am content with the judgment which people of common sense—united with common candour—will pronounce upon the objection and the reply. I stated a fact, in regard to the printing of the Bible, viz., that in Italy, where all are Catholics, under the notice, and with the approbation of popes, and cardinals, and bishops, no less than forty editions of the whole Bible, in the Italian language, had been published and in circulation before the *first* Protestant Italian copy was published. I stated this on the authority of a *Protestant minister*, the Rev. David Clements, in his Dissertation on Ancient Bibliography. The gentleman says, on his own *ipse dixit* authority, that the statement *is not true!* He despises the labours of literary research, as something beneath the dignity of an "American freeman." You state an historical fact, on the authority of an unimpeached historian, and the gentleman, because *he* never heard of it before, tells you *"it is not true,"* without giving a single reason for his assertion. Still I must say, that, under this head of the discussion, the gentleman makes up for the want of *knowledge* by a superabundance of *curiosity*. In three pages of his corrected speech, I have taken the pains to count no less than THIRTY different questions, followed by as many notes of interrogation—a proof that his mind is at length smitten with the *love*, or the *lack* of information.

On the discovery of printing as an art, all encouragement was given to it by the dignitaries of the church. It was employed to multiply copies of manuscripts in every department of knowledge. The Holy Scriptures were the first; the Greek and Latin classics, works of science, and elegant literature followed in order. This undeniable fact is a proof that printing in itself is by no means opposed to the doctrines of the church. But when the press became the *irresponsible agent of mischief* in the hands of wicked men, who employed it to *corrupt* the Scriptures, to *excite the people to sedition*, to *disseminate* FALSEHOOD instead of truth, the natural law of self-preservation, both in church and state, dictated the necessity of restricting the freedom of the press within such limits as would render it compatible with the safety of society. The object was to prevent the *abuse* of the press, and Protestant, Presbyterian governments were as prompt and as unrelenting in prosecuting this object as Catholic governments.

The Presbyterian parliament of England, on the 12th of June, 1643, (just two days before the calling of that Westminster Assembly which framed the gentleman's Confession of Faith,) published an act, commanding "*inquiry after private presses, and to search all suspected shops and warehouses for* UNLICENSED BOOKS *and pamphlets, and to commit offenders against this order to* PRISON, *to be* PUNISHED *as the parliament shall direct."* (1) Even at this day, Presbyterians hinder, as much as they can, the *reading,* and, if they could, would hinder the printing of Catholic books. The Pope, as the chief visible pastor of the Catholic Church, *has a right, and it is his duty,* to warn, exhort, entreat the whole flock, and every member of it, against the danger of printing, publishing, selling, circulating, or reading books, calculated to destroy their faith or corrupt their morals : this is a right exercised by every *Presbyterian minister in the country.* The civil restraints and penalties appointed by governments, whether Catholic or Protestant, are chargeable to those governments, and not to the *doctrines* which they profess. The Pope has no authority to inflict civil punishments out of his own dominions. I pass, then, from this head, by flinging back the consequences which the gentleman affects to draw from my arguments, but which are to be ascribed, not to *my language,* but to his garbling and misrepresentation of it. When he will condescend to dispense with abusive declamation, and substitute something like positive information, I shall be prepared to close with him. The gentleman can hardly expect to impose on his audience by these flourishes of stump oratory and grandiloquent assertion, when the question in debate is a matter of *historical evidence—a positive matter of fact.*

As to his assertion in his former speech, " that the Bible, in whatever idiom written, is prohibited"—I said, and I repeat, that it is *false.*—That it is not warranted by the original. The index has it, " Biblia *vulgari* quocunque idiomate conscripta." Therefore, it was not in " *whatever idiom,*" as the gentleman said, but in whatever " *vernacular* idiom." Again, in the fourth rule of the index, the reading of the Bible in the vulgar tongue is expressly *allowed,* under the prescribed qualifications set by the index. Therefore, the statement that it was " PROHIBITED," *even* in the vernacular idiom, is false. Again, still the authority of the index was never recognised beyond the limits of a few provinces. And, therefore, even if the gentleman's statement were true, *where the index prevailed,* which it was not, as we have seen, it would be, and is totally false, *in regard to all the other Catholics of the earth.*

The gentleman concludes with a republication of the third canon of the fourth Lateran Council, enacted specifically against the Albigenses. Having been obliged to convict him of garbling this canon in the written controversy, I shall not now take the trouble to examine his translation. It is probable that he follows the " faithful Cramp ;" and if so, we know what is to be expected. But there are a few questions involved in the subject. 1. Who

---

(1) Neal, Hist. of Purit., vol. iii. p. 72.

were these Albigenses? 2. What was their doctrine? 3. What were its effects on society? 4. What was the Lateran Council? and, 5. What was the *origin and authority* of the canon in question? The Albigenses were the religious descendants of the Manichæan heresy. Their principal establishment was in Bulgaria. Thence their horrible doctrines were translated into France, Italy, and Spain, in the tenth and eleventh centuries. They were called by different names—Poblicoli, Paterini, Cathari, Bogomili, Zurlupins, Beghardi, Brethren of the Free Spirit, &c.; but their general appellation was Albigenses. Their doctrines were, that there are TWO first principles or deities; one of them the creator of devils, of animal flesh, of wine, of the Old Testament, &c.; the other, the author of good spirits, the New Testament, &c.; *that unnatural lusts were lawful, but not the propagation of the human species.* (1)

These deluded and abandoned people, supported by the Counts of Thoulouse, Comminges, and Foix, had set their sovereigns at defiance, carrying fire and sword through their dominions, slaughtering their subjects without distinction of age or sex, and by their *conduct*, as well as their *doctrine*, waging open war against Christianity, morality, society, and human nature. As far back as the year 1022, Robert, King of France, had been obliged to take measures of safety against their doctrines and their crimes. The infamous name, which, even at this day, is given to unnatural lusts, is derived from their appellation—" Paterini et *Bugares* de quorum errore malo tacere quam loqui." (2) Knowing the errors and the infamy of the Albigenses, the man who is acquainted with ecclesiastical history must feel amused or shocked to behold them ranked, as they sometimes are, by ignorant advocates on the gentleman's side of the question, *among the religious progenitors of Protestantism.*

We must now turn to the Council of Lateran. The errors of the Albigenses were referred to, and condemned in the first and second canons. The object of the third canon, now in question, was to check the spread of those errors, and the progress of slaughter and desolation, which the Albigenses, on every opportunity, for two hundred years before, had not ceased to perpetrate. It was also to maintain the rights of sovereigns against the factious lords, who encouraged the excesses of the Albigenses, *for their own political purposes.* Besides the bishops and abbots, there were at the council ambassadors representing the temporal sovereigns of Germany, Constantinople, England, France, Hungary, Arragon, Sicily, Jerusalem and Cyprus; besides those of many other inferior states. Now the wording of the canon shows its

---

(1) See Bossuet's Variations, Book XI.—Acta Concil. iii. Lat.—Fleury, Histoire Eccles. L. 58, § 54.—Mosheim, Eccles. Hist. vol. i. p. 328, 329—et alibi passim.
(2) Matt. Paris, An. 1244.

limitation; first, to the Albigensian heretics alone; and, secondly, to the "*secular powers present*" at the council. The gentleman on a former occasion thought it advisable, in making the quotation, to suppress the word "*present*." Having been exposed for this, he now inserts it, and thereby *mars* his whole purpose, which was to extend the meaning of the text to ALL secular powers, whether *absent* or *present*. Now the fact is, that so far from its being the doctrine of the Catholic Church, and so far from its being an enactment of *universal* approbation, it never was put in force against any other heretics besides the Albigenses, nor even against them, except in the departments of the three counts mentioned above, who encouraged the outrages of these enemies of the human species. Its origin was owing to the crimes of those against whom it was specifically and *exclusively* enacted. And it is dishonest to charge on Catholics of the present day, a responsibility, which must rest, in time and in eternity, on those who were concerned in its enactment. But in all this I have admitted, *for sake of argument*, that it was enacted by the council, and this I have done, because, as respects the point at issue, it is of no importance by whom it was enacted.

The fact is, however, that the best critics, who have not been under the influence of the anti-Popery mania, have regarded this canon as SPURIOUS—an interpolation in the genuine acts of the council. In the Mazarine copy of the council, it is not found in either the Greek or Latin. In the earliest editions of the councils, it is not found. For two hundred and twenty years after the council, this canon was not known *as one of its enactments*. In the first edition of the councils, by Crabbe the Franciscan, published by John Merlin in 1530, it is not found. The first and *only* person who discovered it was John Cochleus, in 1537. By him it was sent to John Rincus of Cologne, and published in Crabbe's second edition of 1538. Some have ascribed it to Pope Innocent himself. Some have regarded it as a fragment of the imperial constitutions of Germany, probably the work of Frederick II., whose zeal against heretics and *rebellious barons* is well known. In support of these conjectures, it will be sufficient to mention such authorities as Platina, Rigordus, Gregory IX., Matthew Paris,(1) Nanclarus,(2) the monk Godfrey, &c., all of whom maintain that, whatever was its origin, it was not an act of the council. But as the gentleman is, probably, not acquainted with these authors, and probably never will be, I shall refer him to Dupin, vol. x. Bibliot. p. 104; or if he refuses the authority of this *half Protestant writer*, I refer him to Collier's Eccles. Hist. vol. i. p. 424. Collier was a Protestant, but a *learned* one; he pronounces this canon SPURIOUS. And the gentleman's authority, in opposi-

(1) Ad. An. 1215.
(2) Chron. Ad. An. 1215.

tion to that of Dr. Collier, would not weigh a feather, in regard to a matter of history. But at all events, Catholics of the present day, have no more to do with what is called the third canon of the Council of Lateran, than with the burning of Servetus.

In view of these historical facts, of which the gentleman seems to be most blessedly ignorant, I think he cuts a very ridiculous figure, when, in relation to this canon, he breaks out in the following strains of impassioned eloquence: *" Such is the Magna Charta of Papal rights—the great infallible Black Letter Commentary on the power of the priesthood—the germ of the inquisition—the tender mercies of the only true church, out of which there is no salvation; in which there is no liberty. In vain did Draco write his laws in blood—or Heathen Rome legislate against Christians. This is the masterpiece of spiritual and temporal despotism."* Here the gentleman gets out of breath, and, as he says, "needs a little respite." He is just able, before sitting down, to avow his ignorance of the difference between *"doctrine* and *discipline."* He should have reflected on *this state of his mind* before he rushed into the discussion. If he is serious in wishing to know what *doctrine* is, I refer him to his own definition. It is any *"tenet of faith or morals which a denomination teaches,* AS HAVING BEEN REVEALED BY ALMIGHTY GOD." Let him consult *larger* treaties of theology, when his leisure will permit. He had bound himself in relation to any disputed point, to show that it was taught by a General Council, or the bull of a Pope, as a "doctrine"—*i. e.* as a *tenet of faith and morals revealed by Almighty God,"* or else not to adduce it in argument. You all have seen how he redeems his pledge. You all have seen, that he insists on making Catholics admit as a *doctrine* of their religion, whatever nonsense or impiety *he* may think proper to ascribe to them. Now, it so happens, that neither Pope nor General Council possesses this right. They have the right to *attest* and *explain* what is the doctrine, but they have no right to *create* and *impose* new tenets. The gentleman, however, is determined to make us hold whatever doctrines he pleases. He first repeats the calumnies *that were invented for political purposes, in days of bigotry and rapine,* and then he denounces us for having been calumniated. It is with this view, that the slanders of every outcast from our communion, are put on file against us. It is with this view that De Pratt is quoted. I make the gentleman a present of him. Having the "faithful Cramp," and the infidel renegade, De Pratt, as his monitors, the gentleman is in a fair way of being correctly informed on the subject of the doctrines of the Catholic religion. Still, even under *their* guidance, I would advise him not to write any more *Latin* for the fathers of the Council of Trent.

"Is the Roman Catholic Religion, in any or in all its principles or doctrines, opposed to civil or religious liberty?"

AFFIRMATIVE III.—MR. BRECKINRIDGE.

MR. PRESIDENT:—The reason why I was so desirous to have the *name* of the anonymous writer in the "Catholic *Diary*," (better called *Noctuary*,) is the same which makes my Reverend friend so anxious to conceal it. Its loud, long praises of the *Rev. John Hughes*, (these praises it was that I said might *seem irony*, they were so *unapt*, had they not been meant for emphatic,) make it a curious document—since there is now so much reason to believe him the author of it. I am happy to say, that this society in a dignified letter to the editor of the Diary, has exposed the falsehoods of said piece—and demanded the publication of their reply to it. His refusal to do so is the proper, as it is the expressive, *finale* of this matter.

There is one very curious circumstance about this piece, which is worthy of notice before dismissal. The author says, "*I called on the Rev. Mr. Hughes the next evening, to obtain a copy of the conditions on which the debate is to be continued, which I send herewith.*" Having stated that the "Presbyterian Religion" was to be examined as the first question, he adds, on Mr. Hughes's information—"*The Westminster Confession of Faith of the Presbyterian Church in America, shall be a proof on the other side.*" Every member of the committee of arrangements knows this to be the case;—so does the whole society.—And yet the gentleman ventures to assert, "*that the question does not limit his investigation to the Presbyterian Church in the United States, and to that in connexion with the General Assembly.*" I appeal to the written rules, signed by the gentleman himself, in contradiction of his assertion. "*Oh, honour! thou hast fled to brutish beasts.*"

His reason for this course is very obvious. He says—"*The gentleman admits that persecution was a part of Presbyterianism, in all other countries.*" If so, then it is to be supposed that I would *defend it?* I *did* say that our forefathers in different ages, even Calvin himself, had some false views of religious liberty: and were to a certain extent intolerant; and that *so far* I condemned them—and that so far our church in the United States of America differed from them. The gentleman knows it to be so. He finds nothing in us to condemn,—and flies to other churches, and other lands, in quest of *matter*. This is, in fact, giving up the question, as to *Presbyterians*. He says truly, therefore, when quoting from the "*General Synod of the Reformed Presbyterian Church*"—a denunciation of the American Constitution—"the gentleman will tell you these doctrines are not of the Presbyterians." They are not our doctrines.—Far, far from them. When the gentleman, a little before, charges me with "*affecting to be an idolater of the American Constitution,*" HE answers the question. When he asks—"Do not these kindred denominations exchange pulpits?" I answer—*No.*

But we are now looking a little into *Popery, which is unchangeable, the same everywhere, and in every age. It cannot change.* And if, as he says, *we may relapse into the intolerance of our fathers, Rome can never (by her own confession) be reformed from her persecuting spirit.* When we come to the *Presbyterian* question, it will be the time to show that there are almost as many errors as paragraphs in the gentleman's attacks. But he cannot divert me, with all his *arts, from probing Popery.* I know it is a sore, and therefore sensitive, spot. But he must endure it;—for it is *not* I "*who have come and rudely thrust myself between him and his* relation with (to) this society." It is *he* who came, with unmanly officiousness, and thrust *himself* between the youthful disptutants;— it is *he* who quailed before the Rev. Mr. M'Calla, when he *unexpectedly* met *him,* on that occasion;—it is he who retreated from a half-finished debate of a former day—who, with the constancy of a martyr declined my reiterated call, for years—and whom I now meet by *invitation* of those very youths. *He* who has vitiated the stenographer's report after being beaten in oral debate;—*he* who yet refused to discuss it *orally* again—who was on the eve of a retreat to Mexico, had not the publication of the debate been pressed at the point of his honour, as well as the hazard of his cause; and who, (after six months of evasion and delay,) will now defeat the publication of this debate, without an almost superhuman patience, sagacity, and firmness, on the part of your publishing committee.

Sir, you have heard the audacity and coarseness of personal attacks. No Christian, no gentleman, can retaliate such language. *Here,* at least, I allow myself wholly his *inferior.* I yield the palm of *blackguardism* to him. He has entirely the advantage of me here. I make no pretensions to the title which he has conferred on me, "of the Chesterfield of the Presbyterian Church." But, sir, when we hear him wielding with such coarse and vulgar impertinence, the terms "*falsehood,*" "fabrication," "artifice," "forgery," *et id omne genus,* I cannot but be reminded of the origin, habits, breeding, and pretensions of the Jesuit priesthood, as the true explanation of the fact, that neither Chesterfield nor Elijah has *largely* cast his mantle over *them.* The fact is, they are used to so unquestioned a supremacy, that they cannot brook contradiction, or dissent. Their religion *deifies* each pope; and each priest is a *parish-pope,* a "household god," without the tiara and the temporal sword. The Catechism of the Council of Trent declares, "*that in the minister of God,* who sits in the tribunal of penance, as *his legitimate judge,* he (the penitent) *venerates the power and person* (awful profanity!) of our Lord Jesus Christ:" and "*were even the lives of her ministers debased by crime, they are still within* her pale, and therefore lose no part of the power with which her ministry invests them."(1)

The canon law makes it sacrilege to strike a priest; and *forbids* every one from bringing a bishop or priest before a secular judge for accusation of crime;—it exempts them from taxes, &c. &c. No wonder, then, a *Protestant heretic* is so illy borne with—and so much impatience discovered, under the freedom of American inquiry, and at the tribunal of public opinion. But, *still*, we must advance with the discussion, and we shall set down every ungentlemanly epithet, as so much conceded to *unanswerable argument.* These remarks will not appear too strong, when the gentlemen of the Society recall the following very insulting sentence of the reverend gentleman,—"I had, indeed, charged the gentleman not only with misunderstanding our doctrine, but also, with perverting the language in which it was expressed. By way of vindicating himself from this charge, he makes a *show* of appealing to the original Latin. 'Is it not written,' says he, 'Pœnam quam opportet pro illis pœni— tentibus imponere?' And what will be the reader's disgust, to learn that this beautiful specimen of Latinity, put forth as a quotation from the Council of Trent, is a FABRICATION, a FORGERY." If the *gentleman* were ignorant, we might account for, if not excuse, the reckless audacity of this charge. But he is *not* ignorant. I leave it for you, gentlemen, to *imagine* a reason for such a charge, especially when you hear that *every word* of my quotation *is* in the 5th chapter, 14th session, of the Council of Trent. I have been at the trouble to get another edition of the decrees of the Council, which exactly agrees with my former citation. The passage adduced by me, is part of a very long sentence, from which I extracted that for which the proof called. I own it is *barbarous* Latin. It appears in the following connexion, viz.:—"Ut de gravitate criminum recte censere possint, et *pœnam opportat pro illis pœnitentibus imponere.*"

We may better now explain a sentence in a former speech of the gentleman's, that not one in ten thousand of the people understood the language in which the decrees, &c. &c. of his church were written. Hence he ventures, trusting to this *ignorance*, to vitiate my quotations and assail my honesty. But happily, there are some men in the community beside the *Jesuits* who can read a *little* Latin, and who have in their hands the decrees of the councils. And now we ask, where does the charge of *"fabrication"* rest, and on whom must the *"reader's disgust"* fasten?

There is one part of this tirade which is truly diverting. He says of the passage quoted by me, it is *"a phrase which is a most palpable violation of all syntax:"* and at the close of his potential harangue adds, *"I would advise him not to write any more Latin for the Fathers of Trent."* It certainly is a curious fact that the *infallible fathers* of the Council of Trent should have written *bad Latin;* and "the Dutch have taken Holland," when the *son* thus laughs at the syntax of the inspired *fathers.* How he will settle

(1) Eng. Trans., pp. 242, 95.

this matter with his master at Rome I am at a loss to determine. But his corrections are two hundred years too late; and it is one of many proofs that the gentleman has arisen on the earth in the wrong age. But I think he will not venture again *"to make Latin for the fathers of the Council of Trent;"* and from this whole case we learn how far to trust the assertions of one who continues to illustrate the papal maxim, that *"the end justifies the means."* You may measure his charges of "artifice," "fabrication," &c. &c. by this specimen, and you will clearly see that he not only considers such things *"venial sins,"* but that any man who will practise these arts, shall still find himself a learner in the deeper counsels of my *more* practiced friend.

I have been thinking that it might be well to divide my answers to his speeches into two *parts*—one for the irrelative and indecent of the gentleman's remarks, viz.: the Billingsgate, the abusive, the "pathetic," the provocative, &c.; the other for the *argumentative* part: or perhaps if we could give him an entire evening to disgorge, he might feel better after it, and save us the trouble of so often exposing him.

There is another sample of *candour* and *logic* blended, which I must not omit to notice. He says, in reference to the III. canon of IV. Lateran, "Now *the wording of the* canon shows its *limitation* to the secular powers present at the council." Now, so far is this from being true, that there is not a schoolboy in America who has read the colloquies of Cordery that does not know better. The passage in the original reads thus:—Damnati vero, sæcularibus potestatibus præsentibus aut eorum balivis relinquantur animadversione debita puniendi. *But being condemned, let them* (the heretics) *be left to the secular powers* PRESENT, *or to their bailiffs to be punished by due animadversion.* He charges me with fraudulently omitting the word "present," and for this reason, that I thus make the persecuting canon apply *to all secular powers*, whereas, he says, it applies only to those "present" in the council. Can the gentleman be in earnest in this translation? (The *charge* I despise.) The decree is defining the *place* and the *powers* for punishing *"heretics"* at a future day; and orders that the *secular powers* in *whose territory they should be found, should punish them.* The terms *sæcularibus potestatibus præsentibus* are equivalent to " THE POWERS THAT BE." Just below, in the same canon, the *same "powers"* are named without *"præsentibus,"* and Caranza, the Popish author, in giving the contents of this canon, thus writes :—*Punitio hæreticorum sæcularibus potestatibus committenda.* "*The punishment of heretics* TO BE *committed to the secular power.*" "*Præsentibus*" is *omitted;* and in a just and pure translation not the least change in the sense is made by its presence or absence. Still the *omission* was an inadvertence, for I am accustomed to translate this barbarous Latin in almost a *babarously literal* way, knowing that I have to do with a Jesuit.

But *allowing* that "præsentibus" *does refer* to the powers present in *the council,* has not the gentleman told us that the council embraced "ambassadors representing the *temporal* sovereigns of Germany, Constantinople, England, France," &c., or as he says, in a former controversy, "*a general congress of Christendom in which the states and sovereigns were represented for the purpose of conferring together on such matters as concerned the general welfare.*"

Now, who was *not* represented here? Were not the "*secular powers present* from *all Christendom?*" Then wherever the decree went it would find the "*bailiffs*" of those very minions of the Pope who, in this "mingled theocracy and civil policy," "*this church and state*" in which the Pope was *head*, had allowed heresy to be denounced as a "civil offence" and as such to be devoted by the church of Rome, (the Pope presiding,) and through "all Christendom" doomed to extirpation by fire and sword.

These *dexterous* efforts of his are made to evade the powerful proof of Roman Catholic persecution found in the terrible canon of the IV Lateran, quoted by me at the close of my last speech. He first tries to distort its meaning, by telling us that its force is "limited," by the "wording of the canon," "to the *Albigensian heresy alone.*" It is truly incredible that he could believe so with the following words staring him in the face in the very first sentence:—"*We excommunicate and anathematize* EVERY HERESY (*omnem hæreism*) *extolling itself against this holy orthodox Catholic faith, which* (faith) *we before expounded, condemning* ALL HERETICS *by whatsoever name called.*" If these terms have any limitations save heresy and earth, I cannot see them. "*All heresy,*" "*by whatever name called.*" But I ask, what if it *were* limited to the *Albigenses?* Admit it to be so. What does the gentleman gain? Why this. The *infallible council, headed by the Pope, only persecuted one people*, not all. But what right had they to persecute *one* people? Or if *one*, why not all, when said church shall please? What right had Catholics to punish them with death for their *opinions?* Who put the sword into the Pope's hand? Who formed this "Congress of Christendom?" The Pope called it, headed it, drew up all the canons, and then confirmed them, published them, and ordered their execution in the name of the Holy Catholic Church, and by the authority of God! Yet the gentleman dares, in the light of this age and land, to defend this theocracy and fearful persecution!

But he says, "the Albigenses were *very, very wicked*, not only in their *doctrines* but *their lives*, by *lusts* and *bloodshed.* There are almost as many falsehoods as sentences in the account he gives of this persecuted people. You will remember, gentlemen, that he produced Mosheim's Testimony, and read, from his 3d vol., page 283, some sentences calling the Albigenses "*wretched enthusiasts*," charging them with "*abominable lusts,*" "*going naked,*" &c. &c. I was much shocked at the statement; declared it false, and a perversion of the historian; and promised to expose it as such. I had hoped to find it *a forgery of the Jesuits;* and thus the gentleman would escape. But as you will remember, on turning to the passage, it appeared that the gentleman had *omitted* the *real name* of the people denounced by Mosheim, (though but *one sentence above*,) and had *made* him say all those shocking things of the poor Albigenses. Now, how strange must it seem, when I tell you that the historian was there speaking of one of the sects classed with a people "*called Brethren of the Free Spirit.*" Of the Albigenses he gives a most opposite account, and in a different part of the work! This author says: (2) they were the *same with the Paulicans;* that "*even their worst enemies acknowledged the sincerity of their piety; but they were blackened by accusations which were evidently false; and that the opinions for which they were punished, differed widely from the Manichæan system.*" He adds, in the same page, a narrative of the character, vices, and errors of *those* whom my reverend friend made the slandered and perverted writer call *Albigenses.* I pronounce him a *falsifier* of Mosheim, and call on him to clear his character. If he will hear more of Mosheim, the historian goes on to say: (3) "*During the whole of this century* (the 13th) *the Roman pontiffs carried on the most barbarous and inhuman persecution against those* whom they branded with the *denomination of heretics; i. e., against all those who called their pretended authority and jurisdiction in question, or taught doctrines different from those which were adopted and propagated by the Church of Rome.*" Also, (4) he says of the *Inquisition,* "That nothing might be wanting to render this spiritual court formidable and tremendous, the ROMAN PONTIFFS PERSUADED the European princes, and more especially Frederic II," (the very prince on whom our priest would fasten the persecuting canon in question, and of whom he says, "*whose zeal against heretics and rebellious barons is well known,*") "and Lewis IX., king of France, to enact the most barbarous laws against heretics, and to commit to the flames, by the ministry of public justice, those who were pronounced *such by the inquisitors.*" When the proper time comes, I will show, by *Catholic historians,* that there is not one word of truth in what the gentleman has said of the Albigenses.

But allow it true. I ask again: What has the head of Christ's church, and the holy council, to do with burning heretics, with oaths of allegiance, with ruling, punishing, deposing princes? The gentleman's argument is: the Albigenses were *wicked and murderous;* therefore the church might lay hold on them. Princes were *represented* in the council, and these heretics had devastated their realms; therefore the church had a right to order a *crusade* against them, and promise a "*full remission of sins*" to all who fought against them, and to depose and punish all who refused. His argument admits that the Church of Rome *has been,* and of course, as she *cannot change,* is a *persecuting* church.

But the gentleman says this dreadful canon has *nothing to do with doctrine.* "*It is so far from having any thing to do with*

(2) Vol. II. p 580-2.   (3) Vol. iii. p. 266.   (4) P. 272.

doctrine," &c. Ah! it is only discipline. It is hard to see (as he tells us) how it is *doctrine* in Scotland to cut off men's *ears* for heresy, and only *discipline* in the *Catholic church* to cut off men's *heads* for the same thing? Poor *discipline!* she has a hard time of it. She is the *scapegoat* of all her infallible sister *doctrine's* sins. No wonder the gentleman refused so stoutly to discuss the *bearings of Catholic discipline.* But it will not all avail. That part of *discipline* which flows from doctrine, and for whose exercise the doctrine is pleaded, is doctrine in *amount.* For example: it is a part of *discipline* to take the *cup* from the people in the Lord's Supper. But it rests on the doctrine of the *real presence.* So here: It is a *doctrine* of the Church of Rome that heretics are in the power of the church, and to be punished by her. This decree announces the same doctrine, and directs its application. The gentleman, in a former controversy, (such writers need good memories,) said, "The *secular representatives had nothing to do with the definition of doctrines and morals.*" But the canon says: "This holy, orthodox, catholic faith which *we* have before *expounded.*" Of course, it was the pure doctrine—making council with no *secular admixture.* And then the decree proceeds to announce the sum of such *doctrines* as that those who "extol themselves against the Catholic church" are *heretics:* that God has empowered the church to *punish heretics* with spiritual pains and penalties, and to order the civil power to superadd *temporal ones;* that the civil power must be bound by oath to do it; that if it refuse it is to be excommunicated, and the subjects of said power absolved from their allegiance by the vicar of Christ; that indulgences, including great *spiritual* good, are purchased by going as crossbearers to exterminate the heretics, &c. &c. Not one of these but rests on a *doctrine, or is a doctrine.* Or else does the Church of Rome say, there is *no* revealed doctrine about the right of men to life and thought? Or did the holy council *err?* There is no escape.

This the gentleman finding, makes a last struggle (as if conscious that this terrible canon and his cause cannot both stand) to *vitiate the authenticity of the document itself.* This *new light* has unfortunately come too late. It is a pity the gentleman had not received it before the first controversy. It would have saved him the trials of his long and sad defence of this canon. But he had not even heard of it while the debate which we are now writing out was going on, else why *defend it then and discard it now?* He says: "The best critics have regarded this canon as *spurious;* an *interpolation* in the genuine acts of the council." Truly, if the authenticity of the *infallible decrees* be so uncertain, (as all this would seem to say,) that such a document could have been *interpolated* so as to deceive the infallible church, then her advocates may forever close their lofty speeches about *an unerring guide, and the faithful tradition of the Church of Rome!* But hear him: "In the Mazarine copy of the council it is not found in either Greek or Latin." This is false. It is only a *part,* not the *whole* of the canon that is wanting in that manuscript. Labbe, who follows it, gives the *whole* of the canon in *Latin;* and where he omits the *Greek,* he observes, in a marginal note: De est *hic folium* in codice Mazarino. *"Here a leaf is wanting in the Mazarine manuscript."* But this leaf contained only the *middle* portion of the canon, while both the *beginning* and *end* are *preserved.* This looks more like *excision* than *interpolation.* It is either too much or too *little* for the gentleman's purpose. And again; the *second* paragraph of this canon, as taken from the *same* manuscript, points out the *punishment to be inflicted on those who should be convicted of heresy.* Since, then, the *first part* and the *last* part, and the *punishment* to be *inflicted* are all retained by that MS., it is clear that only a *leaf* was wanting, not the *whole* as the gentleman ventures to say; and therefore we have the *exterminating* part at least. The rest I care not for. Again: the Rev. gentleman says, "Collier (a Protestant) pronounces this canon *spurious."* This *too,* I regret to say, is false. He barely states the above-named fact of its mutilation. Mr. Hughes says, again: "In the first edition of the Councils, by Crabbe the Franciscan, published by John Merlin, in 1530, it is not found." But why does the gentleman *not* tell us, that the said Crabbe *afterwards* published *three* editions of the Councils in which the said canon *is* found; and that the edition of 1530 contained *none of the fourth Lateran's canons?* Is this candid? to suppress the one *fact* and use the *other,* so as to make all who do not know better, think that the edition of 1530 *had all the* other canons of that council? But still farther. The gentleman claims Du Pin and Matthew Paris as rejecting it. But it is *still not true.* Du Pin says:(5) "Matthew Paris says that those canons seemed tolerable to some of the prelates and grievous to others. His words are these: *facto prius,* &c.; i. e. *an exhortatory discourse having first been delivered by the Pope, the seventy chapters* [capitula] *were then read in a full council, which seemed tolerable to some, grievous to others.* Let the case be how it will, it is certain that these canons were not made by the council, but by Innocent III., who presented them to the Council ready drawn up, and ordered them to be read; and that the prelates did not enter into any debate upon them, but that their silence was taken for an approbation." Here then is a falsification of the gentleman's statement by his *own authorities.*(6) And here, by the way, we see *what sort of a thing infallibility is.* The Pope draws up articles; the trembling prelates receive them in silence. Some think them tolerable, some intolerable; none satisfied, yet none speak!

Dr. Crotty, Catholic President of Maynooth College, thus testified before the British Commissioners of Education Inquiry,—(7) "I *acknowledge* that in the Councils of *Lateran* and *Constance,*

(5) Vol. xi. cent. xiii. p. 95.
(6) See on this whole subject the learned Grier's Epitome, p. 190-6.
(7) See 8th Report—note, p. 87, in Grier.

laws were enacted *inflicting severe temporal punishments* on persons who at those periods were labouring to subvert the *Catholic Faith* in Europe: that temporal lords who connived at, or favoured the heresy, should be excommunicated; and if within a year, they did not give a satisfactory account of their conduct, they should in addition, forfeit the *allegiance* and duty of their vassals." Will Mr. Hughes call this an opinion? Pray, is *his* better? Is not it as good as his?—yea, better. Yet what does it say?

Finally, (on this topic,) the Council of Trent has affirmed some of the Canons of the fourth Lateran; for example, its *Canon* on *Confession:* which it has adopted on its authority, and as its own. Yet it has not said one word of the *spuriousness* of any of the other canons. It has not *repealed* any of them. Yet it met since the other—and its decisions' *are law* with all true Catholics. Then, here is the broad seal of *the last, the great Council,* set to the *authenticity* of this third canon: and to the *authority* of all of them. And every Catholic on earth is under the following obligation : "I also profess and undoubtedly receive all other things, delivered, defined, and declared by the sacred *Canons,* and *general Councils,* and *particularly* by the holy Council of Trent."(8)

I regret to have spent so much time on a single document. But the discussion was important on many accounts. And now the terrific decree returns to us, as one of the "sacred canons" of the "Holy Catholic Church,"—to be received by all. Never was such a decree passed by any assembly secular or sacred, before or since. Consider for a moment its contents, as spread out at the close of my last speech.—1. Heretics are those who *differ* from Rome; and 2. SHE is to *denote* them. 3. The civil power is to *take oath* to inflict due punishment on them : 4. Which is to *exterminate them,* if they remain *contumacious;* and give their *lands* to *Catholics.* 5. If the civil power refuse, it is to be reported to the *Pope;* and 6. He *absolves the subjects* from the oath of allegiance, and excommunicates the prince, giving his lands to Catholics, and the throne to another. 7. All favourers of heretics were to lose all *civil* as well as all *religious rights:* as the right of inheritance, bequest, suffrage, &c. &c. 8. *Great indulgences* were, on the contrary, bestowed on their *persecutors.*

Is not this at war with all liberty—and with life, and the race itself, as well as with high heaven? But this decree is only as "*one of a thousand.*"

The 27th canon of the third Lateran, (which was also a general Council, held A. D. 1179,) is almost equally odious and persecuting. *This* the gentleman has not tried to vitiate ;—but stoutly charged me with garbling it, in a former controversy, because I followed Faber in citing its *substance.* The Acta Ecclesiæ give still less, I think, than Faber. This is the unlucky decree which the gentleman, during the debate, *made me say was in Caranza;* when, unfortunately, by turning to the page, I had just said the re

(8) Creed of the Church called Pius IV.

verse; viz.: that Caranza "with filial care had omitted the whole." Baronius himself does not give it continuously. I gave a full page; but because I omitted the nicknames and pretended sins of the heretics, he, as usual, charged me with "garbling;" for his great first resource is to taint the *documents*. Now, then, I refer you to his acknowledged edition of it in the late controversy.

This persecuting canon, in the name of God, "*curses the heretics and their favourers with an anathema.*" It "*enjoins on all the faithful for the remission of sins,*" "to take up arms." It enforces "*confiscation of their goods;*" and worse than all, adds, "LET IT BE FREELY PERMITTED TO PRINCES TO REDUCE MEN OF SUCH STAMP TO SLAVERY." It "*relaxes two years of enjoined penance, to those faithful Christians, who shall take up arms,*" and to "*longer time—longer indulgence;*" and those who refused, "*were inhibited from the body and blood of the Lord.*"

Surely this is *doctrinal*, ecclesiastical, and persecuting? Surely it relates to *morals*, to *faith*, to *duty?* We commend it to the gentleman's scissors! Let it but pass his alembick, and it will come out pure and ethereal, refined from "slavery," "persecution," and all that is opposed to civil or religious liberty!

Let us pass from these decrees of Councils to the *Catechism* of the Council of Trent—a source of proof recognised by the gentleman. In naming those who are excluded from the Church, it is said, "*Heretics and schismatics, because they have separated from the Church, and belong to her only as deserters belong to the army from which they have deserted. It is not, however, to be denied, that they are still subject to the jurisdiction of the Church, as those liable to have her judgment passed*" [the English translation recommended by the Reverend clergy in this country, here *forges* a word, which is not in the Latin—as if only *opinions* were to be judged—and puts in, "*on their opinions,*" whereas it is] "*on them, to be punished by her;*" [another forgery, for the translator interpolated 'spiritual,' but the Latin is simply '*puniantur*,'] "and denounced with anathema." Now, here is a claim full of despotism, which the translator's frauds could not conceal. It most fitly compares the Roman Church to an army, and us poor heretics to *deserters*, who are still *subject to her*. Yet does the gentleman talk about freedom of conscience, and of worship! But how is this? "Subject to her judgment still—like deserters." So they *act it* out in Italy and Spain; no thanks to them for *freedom* here! "TO BE PUNISHED *by her.*" Not "spiritual" alone, though that were destructive of liberty; but it is more than this, as any one will perceive who consults either the *force* of the *words*, or the *history and practices* of the Church of Rome.

We may learn what is meant above by referring to *other* testimony. For example, *Dens's Theology*, adopted by the Roman Catholic Bishops of Ireland, since 1808, as a standard book. What does it say?—"Although *Heretics* are without the church, nevertheless, they remain by reason of *baptism, subject* to the church, whence she justly seizes them as deserters from the camp of the church, and so they are under the obligation of returning."(9)

Under the question, "*Is it lawful to tolerate the rites of unbelievers?*" he replies, "The *rites* of other unbelievers, viz. of *Pagans* and *Heretics*, are not in themselves *to be tolerated;* because they are so bad, that no truth or utility can from thence be derived to the good of the church." (10)

"Unbelievers who have been *baptized*, as heretics, and apostates generally, and also *baptized schismatics*, can be *compelled by corporal punishments*, to return to the Catholic faith, and unity of the Church."

"The reason is, that they, by *baptism*, are made *subjects of the Church*, and therefore, the church has jurisdiction over them, and the power of *compelling* them by the *ordained means* to obedience, to fulfil the obligations contracted in *their baptism*."

"This also obtains in the case of those who have been baptized in their *infancy*" [I pray the gentleman to remember what I said of 'cogendos,' and of baptism as 'a brand of slavery;'] "as the Council of Trent teaches, sess. 7, can. 14," [the very proof adduced by me,] "and the fourth Council of Toledo, canon 55, vol. ii. pp. 79–81." The Toledo canon (11) is "*that even those who by force or necessity adopted the faith, should be forced to hold it.*" "Opportet ut fidem, etiam quam vi vel necessitate susceperunt, tenere cogantur."

"Heretics that are known to be such are infamous for this very cause itself, and are deprived of *Christian burial.*"

"Their *temporal goods* are, for this very cause itself, *confiscated;* but before the execution of the act, the sentence declaratory of their crime ought to proceed from the ecclesiastical judge, because the cognizance of heresy lies in the ecclesiastical tribunal." "Finally, they are also justly afflicted with other *corporal* punishments, as exile, imprisonment," &c.

"Heretics are justly punished with death, because God, in the Old Testament, ordered the false prophets to be slain; and in Deut. xvii. 12, it is decreed, that if any one will act proudly, and will not obey the commands of the priest, let him be put to death. See also 18th chapter."

"The same is proved from the *condemnation* of the 14th article of *John Huss*, in the Council of Constance." (12) That article denies the right of *handing one over* to the secular power for heresy.

Here is *proof* which he that runs may read. Will the gentleman tell me it, *too*, is *opinion?* Is *his* any more? Dens's is, to say the least, as good as *his*. But this is under the seal of the *Irish prelates*. Is it still *opinion?* When I adduced the *Pope*, it was *still opinion!* Either then you must *call a general council to repeal*, or rest in the fearful and full proof we have adduced. But again:

(9) Vol. ii. p. 114. (10) Vol. ii. pp. 82, 83. (11) See Caranza, page 55. (12) Dens's Theo. vol. ii. pp. 88, 89. See also Reports L and IL of Protestant Meeting at Exeter Hall, London, 1835.

We have the testimony of the *annotators of the Rhemish New Testament*, with full notes, prepared with much care, as an *exhibit of papal doctrines*. Note on Luke ix. 55, 56, "*The Church or Christian Princes, are not blamed for putting Heretics to death.*" Note on Revelations xviii. 6, "The blood of *Heretics* is not the blood of saints; no more than the blood of thieves, man-killers, and other malefactors:—for the shedding of which blood, by order of justice, no commonwealth shall answer." Rev. ii. 6, 20, 22, "He [Christ] warneth bishops to be zealous and stout against the false *prophets of what sort soever*, by alluding covertly to the example of holy Elias, that in zeal killed four hundred and fifty false prophets." John x. 1, " Arius, Calvin, Luther, and all that succeeded them in room and doctrine, are thieves and murderers." Acts xix. 19, [Please in each case refer to the Scripture-passage,] "A Christian man is *bound* to burn or deface all wicked books, of what sort soever, especially *heretical* books. Therefore *the Church has taken order against all such books*."

Here then is another collateral testimony full to my purpose. It is the declaration of a long accredited commentary that the doctrines of the Catholic Church not only justify but *command persecution*. But again. Besides this *testimony* from annotators, what says the GREAT BOSSUET? Of the power of the sword in matters of religion he says, "It cannot be called in question without weakening or maiming the public authority or power." "*No illusion can be more dangerous than making toleration a mark of the true church.*" No; *the church's holy severity*, and her holy delicacy forbade her such indulgence, or rather softness. (12)

We have also testimony to the intolerance of Romanism from Belgium as well as from France. As soon as the king of the Netherlands took possession of his dominions, the papal prelates made an effort to re-establish throughout Flanders the ancient despotism of the church over *conscience*. They addressed a letter to the king, to be found in the Annual Register, (London,) and portions of it in the History of the Jesuits, which is a reply to Dallas's Defence of them. They say, "Sire, the *existence* and *privileges* of the CATHOLIC CHURCH in this part of your kingdom *are inconsistent* with an article of the new constitution, by which equal favor and protection are promised to all religions." "*Since* the conversion of the Belgians to Christianity *such a dangerous innovation* has never been introduced into these provinces, unless by force."

"Sire, we do not hesitate to declare to your Majesty that the *canonical laws* which are sanctioned by the ancient constitutions of the country, are *incompatible* with the projected constitution which would give in Belgium *equal favour and protection to all religions.*" The "*canonical laws*, say the *Popes*, ought to be received *everywhere.*" But wherever they are received, *say these bishops* (and truly) *toleration is out of the question.* "The

(12) Œuvres de Boss, Tom. III. p. 411. Paris, 1747.

canonical laws have always rejected schism and hersey from the bosom of the church." Does Mr. Hughes deny this, or condemn the *effect*, if admitted by him to be true?

"The Council of Trent, *all* whose resolutions were published in these provinces, and have the force of ecclesiastical law, commanded the bishops carefully to *watch* not only over the *maintenance* of the *sacred pledge of the faith*, but also *that of the laws* which concern the essential discipline of the Catholic Church, and secure the consistency and inviolability of its government." One of these resolutions of the Council of Trent, and the object of the bull of Pope Paul the III. (observes the refuter of Dallas) which issued in consequence, was *the "extirpation of heresy."*

The bishops proceed to say *"Securing the same protection to all religions would be incompatible* with the free and entire exercise of our *official* duties." That is, wherever *Popery* really and fully exists there can be no *toleration*, for toleration *" is incompatible with the free and entire exercise of the official duties of its bishops."* In fine, they say, "We are *bound*, sire, incessantly to preserve the people intrusted to our care from the doctrines which are in opposition to the doctrines of the Catholic Church. We could not release ourselves from this obligation without violating our most sacred duties; and *if your majesty, by virtue of a fundamental law, protected in these provinces the public profession and spreading* of these doctrines, the progress of which *we are bound to oppose* with the care and energy which the *Catholic Church expects from our office, we should be in formal opposition to the laws of the state, to the measures which your majesty might adopt to maintain them among us, and in spite of all* our endeavours to secure union and peace, the *public tranquillity might still be disturbed."* Here is a bold, honest position taken; without disguise they declare that whenever the laws of the state shall *tolerate any other religion*, then the papal prelates and the Catholic system are necessarily opposed to those laws and to the government which should maintain them. Here observe, they do not say that *as* Popery was the religion of the state, therefore Protestantism was *against* the law. But they say *whenever* the law of the state shall so *change as* to tolerate *Protestants* (or heresy and schism) then Popery will be opposed to *the laws and government.* That is, Popery is in its own necessary nature *intolerant, opposed to liberty.*

It is a proper place here to introduce the Pope's letter to the cardinals universally, dated February 5th, 1808, declaring his dissent to Buonaparte's proposal to grant the free public exercise of religious worship to dissenters from Popery. He says, "*It is proposed that all religious persuasions should be free, and their worship publicly exercised; but we have rejected this article as contrary to the canons, and to the councils, to the* CATHOLIC RELIGION, *and to the welfare of the state*, on account of the deplorable consequences which ensue from it."(13) Here is the whole matter

(13) See Hist. Jesuits.

out. *Toleration* is *against* "CANONS," *against* "COUNCILS," *against* the "CATHOLIC RELIGION." Is not the Catholic religion, as a *system*, and in *many* of its doctrines, opposed to *liberty ?* Let the gentleman settle with popes, bishops, commentators and councils.

How well does the reigning Pope agree with his predecessor "of happy memory." He, as cited by me already, calls "*the liberty of the press*" an evil never sufficiently to be execrated and detested, and " liberty of conscience a pestilential error." It is a most striking fact, worthy of record, that even the *index to the decrees of councils* on the word "*heretic*" shows the persecuting and oppressive character of the church.

Hæretici, Judæi, ethnici, cum iis prepes habere communes vetatur.

Templorum hæreticorum ingressus prohibetur

Conjugium Catholici cum ethnicis, hæreticis, schismaticis, prohibitum.

Commercium cum iisdem omne vetitum.

Quomodo coercendi.

Hæretici pervicaces exterminentur. .

Damnati potestatibus sæcularibus relinquantur.

Multa circa eos qui favent hæriticis.

Pœnæ hæreticorum et illorum fautorum.

Incarcerentur usque ad mortem.

Relapsorum pœna.

Domus in qua inventus est hæreticus diraetur.(14)

TRANSLATION.

It is prohibited to pray with *heretics*, Jews, and heathens.

It is forbidden to enter houses of worship used by *heretics.*

Catholics are prohibited to marry with *heretics*, Jews, and schismatists.

All intercourse with them is forbidden.

By what methods they are to be coerced.

Pertinacious heretics are to be exterminated.

Being condemned they are to be left to the secular power.

Many things touching those who favour heretics.

The punishments of heretics and their favourers.

They are to be imprisoned even unto death.

Punishment of the relapsed.

The house in which a heretic is found is to be pulled down.

The great and good Baxter says: "*Smithfield* confuted the Protestants, *whom both the Universities* could *not* confute. *Their Inquisition* is a school where they dispute *more advantageously* than in academics. Though all the learned men in the world could not confute the poor Albigenses, Waldenses, and Bohemians, yet by these *iron* arguments they had men who presently stopped the mouths of many thousands, if not hundreds of thousands of them,

(14) Acta Ecclesiæ, tom. ii.

even as the Mohammedans confute the Christians. A strappado is a *knotty* argument. In how few days did they convert 30,000 Protestants in and about Paris, till they left them not (on earth) a word to say? In how few weeks' space did the ignorant Irish thus *stop* the mouths of many thousand Protestants? Even in Ulster, alone, as is strongly conjectured, by testimony on oath, about 150,000 men were *mortally silenced*. There is nothing like *stone-dead* with a papist. They love not to tire themselves with disputes, when the business may be *sooner* and *more* successfully despatched."(15)

Before closing, there are some multifarious matters which the gentleman has thrown in by way of "filling up," that I may be expected to notice.

As to the "premium of $500," I produced the book, and my friend, at the place appointed, *met with it*. But no *premium* has appeared, though I agreed to lay it out in Bibles for the worshippers of St. John's. Or, if the gentleman pleases, we will build with it *confessionals* for *priests* to confess *their* sins in.

As to "the majority principle," it is *he* who has *changed*, not I. On the first evening of this discussion, as also in the former Controversy, he avowed that *the majority* had the right (without making any qualifications) to rule the minority. Thus,(16) he says: "*I would ask, had not they the right, as the* MAJORITY *by a million to one, to take measures for the common welfare?* The doctrine of Christ teaches submission to 'the powers that be;'" and adds, "No *republican*, I should think, would deny it." Will the reader believe that this is in *defence* of the cruelties practised by the said Fourth Lateran Council, whose bloody canon we have so largely examined? Now apply the principle. In Italy, in Spain, the majority have established the *Catholic religion by law*. Now I ask him, again, "*had the majority a right to do so?*" Let him reply: yes, or no. He will not venture to do either. You will see that he will *evade* it. Yet the above *has* answered it. His shield was then on the other *side*, and he left his principles *exposed*.

That this is his principle, see Cardinal Bellarmine,(17) where he says distinctly, that when *Catholics* have the *majority* they have not only the right to *rule*, but to *extirpate heretics*. He who shall see a majority of our people *papists* shall stand at the tomb of liberty in this land. As to "voluntary slaves," he thinks the American people would not be such, though they *should* elect the Pope their head for life, and alter the Constitution to justify it? Could a Roman *monarchist* say more?

As to the charge of "artifice" in my statement of his "*candid admission*" "of the established order of civil and ecclesiastical duties in a state," I am willing to leave the matter to be judged

(15) Key for Catholics to open the juggling of the Jesuits.
(16) Page 72, IXth Letter of the late Controversy.
(17) Book III. chap. 23, of Laics.

of by every honest reader. The testimony of the *Belgian* bishops, given above, shows the gentleman's real system.

He denies that *the doctrines of his church* are opposed to liberty, because Catholics, as in France, Poland, &c., have sought and maintained liberty. The French conquered their liberty from the *priesthood*. And as to Poland, noble, bleeding Poland! if she had expelled the *Jesuits* a little sooner!!—Poland is but semi-papal—and she is the nursery of freedom and now its martyr, not in *consequence*, but in *spite* of popery.

"The cud of persecution will do for the *quid nuncs* of Jesuitism. But the doctrine, that "*Catholics can be submissive to the bishop of Rome*," and yet have nothing to do with him "as temporal prince," is hard of *digestion*, and especially in America. For example: He, as *bishop*, in the name of God, denounces "liberty of conscience," and, as "*temporal prince*," uses an *army to enforce uniformity of worship. As bishop, all* Catholics approve, and must approve of *the principle;* but yet the *practice* they condemn. Now can any man consistently hold to a *bishop* of such principles, and yet reject the principles; or, *consistently* uphold him as head of the church, when as *a prince* he is so foul a tyrant as to rest his throne on the hired bayonets of Austria. When (as the gentleman owns) the Pope, *as prince*, "*meddles* in the civil concerns of other states," and they resist him, as "*prince*," what becomes of the *bishop ?* can you separate them ? He asks, "*Is a Presbyterian minister bound to grant his daughter, if she demand it, the right to* be a Catholic?" Surely; or a Mohammedan, or an atheist, if she be "of age" to judge—and even in her *minority* he has no right to offer *force*. But what then ? If she should exercise the right of becoming a *papist*, and then the priest should *deny* her the Bible, make *his pardon the means of her salvation, require* her to confess her most secret sins to him, and she consent, that were "*voluntary slavery*."

I ask, in turn, if our "General Assembly" be, as he says, "*a radiating centre*," (which, by the way, he predicted some time ago, about to fall to pieces,) what is Rome? De Pratt says, "*Catholicism is not organized like other worships*. The latter have no *common centre*, no exclusive source from whence flows power in every religious society. They have no Rome, nor precedents of Rome, nor pretensions of Rome. The exaltation or depression of *these worships is of no importance in the political order of states*. Is it not so *with Rome;* every thing in *Catholicism tends to Rome*. The Pope is chief of 120,000,000 of followers." "Catholicism cannot have less than 400,000 ministers. This worship and its ministers are spread everywhere." "The Irish and the AMERICAN priests (my friend is both) *are more obsequious* to Rome than the German or French priests who are placed nearer to her. *Reverence is increased* with distance. Rome, viewed at a distance, is a Colossus." "*The Pope counts more subjects than a sovereign, more even than many sovereigns together. These have subjects only on* THEIR OWN TERRI-

TORY. The Pope *counts* SUBJECTS ON THE TERRITORY OF ALL SOVEREIGNS. *These command only the exterior.* The Pope penetrates deeper. *He commands the interior. The seat of his empire is placed in the conscience itself. If the whole world were Catholics the Pope* would command the world—what a power?—what would it leave to others? In a word, he would shake the world! *He did it for ages* in respect to Europe. *Not to know how to foresee is not to know how to govern or to judge the world."* This man was once an *Abbe* of the Pope. He knew what he was saying. Yet can Mr. Hughes talk honestly of the "radiating centre" of our General Assembly as *dangerous* to the land with Rome in his eye?

What the gentleman says of the forty *Italian* editions of the Scripture needs proving. I have searched extensively where such evidence should be found, and it is not to be had. Let us have the proof. Let us see the book.

But supposing it true, and also the gentleman's translation of "The Index" to be just, then what after all is the mighty benefit? Publish forty editions of the Bible, and then *forbid the people* to read them! Does he intend to insult our feelings by making a farce of this subject, or our reason by such logic? By the way, the gentleman denied that the Index contained what I asserted it did. He called for the book; I produced it. Pray has he had the justice to own that he was mistaken? I ask, did it or did it not contain the passage?

There is near the close of his speech this admission. *"The civil restraints appointed by governments, whether Catholic or Protestant, are chargeable to those governments, and not to the doctrines which they profess."* Then why does he just before charge *"the Presbyterian parliament of England"* with restraining the freedom of the press? "Was it not chargeable to the government, and not to the doctrines which they professed?" In the same page he defends popery and assails *Presbyterians* by a most palpable inconsistency for doing the *same thing.* In the former Controversy(18) he said, "Cæsar never was in the power of (Presbyterian) your church but once." Yet he has, during this controversy, again and again charged Presbyterians with abusing civil power for many ages and in many lands.

The gentleman *ridicules* my thirty questions; yet strange to tell he *answers none* of them.

I only notice in the last place this admission of the gentleman, "that *the doctrines of Catholics leaves them perfect liberty to exercise their own discretion about civil and religious liberty."* Is this not allowing that the civil and religious rights of man are not *sufficiently regarded by Romanism to be a part of their religion?* What, does not the *Bible* define the rights of conscience and of personal as well of civil liberty? *Presbyterians* hold that

(18) Letter 9, near close.

God has revealed a clear code of *rights in his word*, and that *"there is no discretion"* as to the matter of liberty. That we are *not at liberty* to destroy or repress the liberty of others, or alienate our own; in a word, that the Gospel is the *charter of freedom to man.* I have, in conclusion, only to beg the gentleman's pardon, that my poetical couplet, derived from his own native land, did not please him, and my only reparation possible is to furnish him a better.

> Well-spring of grief, and fierce wrath's hospital.
> The school of error, temple of Heresy,
> Once *Rome*, now BABYLON most wicked, all
> With sighs and tears bewail thy piteous fall;
> Thou mother of Deceit, *bulwark* of *Tyranny:*
> *Truth's persecutrix*, nurse of Iniquity,
> The *living's* HELL; a miracle it will be,
> If Christ in fury come not against thee
> Most shameless w****e.
>
> PETRARCH, Sonnet 149. tom. IV.

Or thus,

> The Inquisition, model most complete
> Of perfect wickedness, where deeds were done,—
> (Deeds! let them ne'er be nam'd,) and set and planned
> Deliberately and with most musing pains,
> How to extremest thrill of agony
> The flesh, the blood, and souls of holy men,
> Her victims might be wrought, and when she saw
> New tortures of her labouring fancy born,
> She leapt for joy, and made great haste to try
> Their force, well pleased to hear a deeper groan.
> The supplicating hand of innocence,
> That made the tiger mild, and in its wrath
> The lion pause—the groans of suffering most
> Severe were naught to her. She laugh'd at groans!
> No music pleased her more, and no repast
> So sweet to her, as *blood of men redeemed
> By blood of Christ.* Ambition's self, tho' mad,
> And nursed in human gore, with her compared was merciful.
>
> J. BRECKINRIDGE.

"Is the Roman Catholic Religion, in any or all its principles or doctrines, opposed to civil or religious liberty?"

NEGATIVE III.—MR. HUGHES.

MR. PRESIDENT:—You have been told by the gentleman who has just concluded, that "this Society, in a dignified letter to the editor of the Catholic Diary, has exposed the falsehoods of the piece" published in that paper. Now I have taken the pains to procure a copy of the letter referred to, and it turns out, that the Society have not exposed one single " falsehood." They merely complain (apparently to soothe the gentleman's feelings) that some of the remarks were *"in a great measure untrue."* This is supposing falsehoods. But to suppose them, and to "EXPOSE" them are two different things. On what authority, therefore, has the gentleman ventured to assert that any falsehoods were "exposed" by this Society, when the statement is discovered to be unsupported by facts? The editor gave his reasons at the time, for not publishing the letter of the Society—and the fact of their not having "exposed" the pretended misstatements, was one of those reasons. I know—for I was an eye and ear witness, as well as the Society—that the statements are substantially correct.

The gentleman pretends to discover a departure from the rules, when I go to other lands and other ages, to show the character of Presbyterianism. This inference is not just. I am at liberty to quote history, not indeed for the proof of Presbyterian doctrine, but for the illustration of Presbyterian intolerance. When I come to treat of the question of doctrine, I shall show, by the Westminster Confession of Faith, that the Presbyterians hold now, in the United States, some of the very doctrines which constituted their warrant for persecution in other countries. He ought to know, that I establish my point by showing that the creed of his church retains the doctrinal THEORY of persecution, in despite of the American Constitution, which has only taken away the right to put it in *practice.* Against the Catholics, he goes back a thousand years before Presbyterianism existed, and although his sect is only three hundred years old, I, forsooth, must not go back more than *fifty* years,—must not go beyond the boundaries of the United States, in which *the government had taken from them the power to persecute.* This is unjust and ungenerous. All that is required by the rules, is, that when he *denies* a doctrine, in the name of his church, I should *prove* by the Confession of Faith now adopted that it is a "DOCTRINE;" and he is at liberty to establish any point against me, by showing that such a point has been set forth as a "doctrine" of the Catholic Church, in some canon of a general council, or bull of a Pope.

If, therefore, I go to other lands "for matter," I only show what is, and has been, the *practical operation of the doctrines which are undeniably in the Confession of Faith*. To restrict the argument, then, to the United States, since the Revolution, is as absurd as it would be to restrict the inquiry respecting a man's moral character, to the period during which he was deprived of liberty by incarceration. His *principles* of dishonesty, his *perverse nature* are the same, as when he enjoyed liberty to indulge them; and it would be a poor vindication to say that he never *has* indulged them, since the *power* to do so was taken from him. And yet this is the defence which the gentleman sets up, by anticipation, for the Presbyterians.

The gentleman says, that there is no right-hand of fellowship between the Reformed Presbyterians and the General Assembly Presbyterians. This assertion is denied by members of both churches. Do the General Assembly look on their reformed brethren as *heretics?* The latter, it is known, reject the Constitution of the United States, as not being a moral ordinance of God; and yet the gentleman himself has pronounced them "as among the purest Presbyterians that ever lived!" How is all this to be accounted for?

Before entering on the main question, I must clear up a point in which my personal integrity is interested. It refers to my remarks on the gentleman's quotation from the Council of Trent. In order that the matter may be understood, it is necessary for me to remind you, that in a former speech he gave, *as a translation from the Council of Trent*, a passage setting forth that the priest, as the minister of the sacrament of penance, was to "inflict punishment." These are the words. Knowing the charge to be false, I replied, that the words in the original were "pœnam injungere;" which is, "to enjoin a penance." When a priest tells the penitent in confession to recite some of the Psalms of David, he "enjoins a penance." This is the true meaning of "pœnam injungere;" but the translation given by the gentleman, "to inflict punishment," might mean *personal castigation;* and there is little doubt but that he, or the "faithful Cramp," whom he followed, intended that it should be so understood by Protestants. On these evidences I charged him with having perverted our doctrine; and that charge still stands against him. For, in his reply, he flies from the original and translation, on which my charge was founded. He gives the *same translation*, and presents *another, different*, sentence of the Latin, which we shall presently examine. But in order to do perfect justice, I shall give the whole passage, as furnished in the corrected speech.

"Is it not written near at hand,—'pœnam quam opportet pro illis pœnitentibus imponere?' *i. e.*, 'the punishment which ought to be inflicted on the penitents.'" Now I pronounced this Latin a "fabrication, a forgery." According to the letter, I was mistaken; and according to the letter, I retract the expressions. And now I must explain, how far, and why, I was mistaken. 1st. The words "near at hand," did not signify the passage in dispute, *as I supposed*, but *another*, which had not been previously referred to. 2d. The English expresses the point in dispute. 3d. I supposed that the Latin was intended to express the same idea conveyed by the English. 4th. I saw that, *on this hypothesis*, it was such Latin as the fathers of Trent never would have used. It was a violation of all syntax: 1st, by putting the verb "imponere" in the infinitive mood, without any word to govern it; 2d, by writing the "oportet" with *two p's* instead of one, thereby putting it out of the Latin language; 3d, by putting the pronoun "illis" as an adjective; 4th, by putting the word "pœnitentibus," under the conflicting government of the verb "imponere," which requires the dative case, and the preposition "pro," which requires the ablative. Let any Latin scholar take the sentence, as *the gentleman quotes it*, and see whether it is not a flagrant violation of syntax, in all the particulars that I have pointed out. The Latin of the Council of Trent is not highly classical, it is true, but yet it is at least grammatical, as will be seen by the *connexion* in the original, on which the sense as well as the grammar depends.

"Colligitur præterea, etiam eas circumstantias in confessione explicandas esse, quæ speciem peccati mutant, quod sine illis peccata ista neque a pœnitentibus integre exponantur, nec judicibus innotescant, et fieri nequeat, ut de gravitate criminum recte censere possint, et *pœnam quam oportet pro illis pœnitentibus imponere.*" Here, there is nothing barbarous or ungrammatical; whereas the *garbled words*, marked in italics, when presented by themselves as they were by the gentleman, make complete nonsense. It is directed here, that those *circumstances* which alter the species of the sin should be confessed, as well as the sin itself; and among the reasons assigned, the last is, that otherwise the priests cannot "judge of the grievousness of the *crimes*, nor enjoin, on the penitents for them (pro illis) the penance that ought to be enjoined." This is very different from "the punishment which ought to be *inflicted* on the penitents." And this, too, as a translation of "pœnam quam opportet (oportet) pro illis pœnitentibus imponere."

I may as well here, as elsewhere, notice a few of the gentleman's scattering remarks. He says, for instance, that I "retreated from a half-finished controversy of a former day." I wrote the *last*, as well as the *first letter* of that controversy; and this is what the gentleman calls "retreating." He says, I was "beaten in the oral discussion." Still, for sake of appearances, he should let *others* celebrate his victory. I am perhaps less than his equal as to talents, but a good cause gives me advantages in every discussion involving the respective characters of Catholicity and Presbyterianism. If the gentleman wishes to triumph, there is but one way, in which he can succeed—let him carry on the *controversy* —alone.

In my last, I showed, by facts, that the sympathy which he claimed for his suffering in the "great cause," was unmerited. I detailed a *few facts*, which made it clear, that his *own pen* had furnished the hardest trials, to which his feelings could be subjected. Instead of meeting my facts with even an attempt at refutation, he very politely charges me with "*audacity and coarseness*," and then says that he is a mere novice in abuse, or, as he elegantly terms it, "blackguardism."

He says, I "refused stoutly to discuss the bearings of discipline." I say, that the offer was never made to me, and consequently I had not the chance to refuse it. But the charge proves that he was not quite so ignorant of the difference between doctrine and discipline, or what is termed canon law, as he pretended at the opening of the debate. The one is of Divine institution, and consequently unchangeable. The other is of ecclesiastical enactment—liable to be changed by the authority that ordained it, or like obsolete laws to pass into desuetude, when the object of it does not exist, or its application becomes injurious.

The gentleman, *after* denying that the Catholics had published forty editions of the Bible in Italian, before the Protestants had published one, *now* begins to hesitate, and wants to "see the book." Let him *deny* or *admit* the fact first, and then I shall consider of his request. For he goes on to say that, *even if true*, it was still nothing. "*Publish forty editions of the Bible, and then forbid the people to read them! Does he intend to insult our feelings by making a farce of this subject, or our own reason by such logic?*" Sure enough! If I had said that the translators had been allowed to translate the Bible into Italian, and the booksellers of the different cities to publish forty editions of it, with the express understanding, that none of them should ever be read, the gentleman would discover nothing "farcical" in the statement. The logic would be exactly like his own—reasonable, of course. As for the index, I have already disposed of it in a former speech. We shall now pass to the investigation of other matters.

The gentleman has returned to the canon of Lateran, against the Albigenses, although the remarks of my last speech, on that subject, should have been sufficient to satisfy any candid man. The growing light, and decaying bigotry of Great Britain, had wrung from king, lords, and commons, the public acknowledgment, that the gentleman's interpretation of this canon was a libel,—invented, as a pretext, for placing on the necks of the Catholics, that millstone of persecution which has been so recently removed. Still, as the creed of Calvin wraps its votaries in that mantle of "inamissible" intolerance, which is impervious to the rays of light and of liberality, the gentleman, as might have been expected, contends that *his* interpretation of the fourth canon of Lateran is the true one, and, of course, that the wisdom of the British senate was confounded, in blotting the infamous libel from the statute book. It remains for me, then, to show the true bearing of the case—not, indeed, in the hope that it will have any effect on the mind of those men, who, as a preliminary measure, conducive to the attainment of ulterior ends, have formed the unholy combination which is now in existence, for the destruction of the Catholics—but for the honest men of the country, in whose breasts justice, humanity, respect for *equal rights*, and liberty of conscience, prevail over blind attachment to the dictates of sectarianism.

I said in my last speech, that the canon in question related, *exclusively*, to the Albigenses, and those who should profess *their* heresy. Before I proceed to establish this proposition, it is proper to show, more at large, who were the Albigenses, and what was the nature of their heresy, from the testimony of contemporary writers.

The origin of the errors maintained by the Albigenses, is traced to the Manicheans. They were introduced into Bulgaria, shortly after the conversion of that province to Christianity.(1) The acts of the Council of Orleans (2) inform us, that under King Robert, their doctrines were discovered at Orleans, and were adopted by two canons of that church, named Heribert and Lisoius. At the same time their disciples appeared in Aquitania and at Toulouse.(3) They are expressly *called* "Manicheans," and "rejected baptism, the sign of the cross, the church, the Redeemer, (together with the incarnation and passion,) the veneration of the saints, the lawfulness of marriage, and the use of flesh meat."(4) Glaber, and the Chronicle of Saint Cibard, cited by Vignier, call them Manicheans. Renier, who had been one of their disciples for seventeen years, tells us that the errors of these sects, both in France and Italy, were derived from the *Manichean churches* of Bulgaria.(5) And Vignier says also, that the Albigenses were called Bulgarians.(6)

By these and other authorities, it is manifest, both in their descent and their doctrines, that the Albigenses were Manicheans.

(1) Petr. Sic. initio libr.   (2) Labbe, t. IX.: col. 830.
(3) Baron, t. XI.: an. 1017.
(4) Fragm. Hist. Aquit. edita a Petro Pithon, ibid.
(5) Rem. Cont. Vald. c. 6. t. IV. Bibl. P. P. part ii. p. 759.
(6) Bib. His. part ii. an. 1022. p. 672.

They were discovered at Goslar in Suabia, under Henry IV., by the determination with which they abhorred all animal flesh.(1) The Catbari, about Cologne, held the same abominable doctrines on the incarnation, and on marriage, as well as the other prominent characteristics of Manicheism.(2) Instead of water, they used *lighted torches*, and gave what they regarded as the "baptism of fire."(3) They held that all flesh was the creation of the devil, and consequently, that the propagation of the human species was aiding the devil in perpetuating his work.(4) St. Bernard went among them to recall them from their errors, by preaching and exhortation. He instructed himself thoroughly in their doctrines, in order to confute them; and besides their condemnation of the *baptism of infants, the invocation of the saints, prayer for the dead, he numbers also their condemnation of marriage, and of whatever resulted from the union of sexes.*(5) It is acknowledged by a Protestant historian, that the heretics whom Peter the Venerable labored to refute, were "Albigenses, under the name of Petrobrussians."(6) In their exposition of their doctrine at the Council of Lombez, near Albi, in 1176, they acknowledged that they rejected the "Old Testament," and *refused* to acknowledge the lawfulness of baptism or marriage.(7) Guy de Nogent says of them, in like manner, that they rejected all flesh meats, and all that resulted from the union of the two sexes.(8) Another historian of the eleventh century, gives the same account of them, and adds expressly their belief in "two creators."(9) William of Neudbridge, in England, and all other historians, give the same general account of their doctrine.

The authors of the time distinguish between the Albigenses and the Waldenses, who were entirely a distinct sect, and who were not even charged with having held the abominable doctrines which rendered the Albigenses so unspeakably infamous. Such were the origin, descent, and anti-human tenets of the Albigenses, as set forth by all the contemporary historians that ever wrote of them. They were, indeed, called by different names, as I mentioned in my last speech. And it is a mere quibble, to say, as the gentleman does, that they are to be considered as acquitted of these charges, on the ground that Mosheim does not *call them* Albigenses, when he is detailing their infamies. They are known by the generic term Albigenses, just as the descendants of the pretended Reformation are spoken of as Protestants. And to say that they

---

(1) Centuriat. in Cent. XI. c. 5.
(2) Eckbert, Serm. XIII. Adv. Cath. t. IV., Bibl. P. P. part ii.
(3) Serm. I. VIII. XI.
(4) Eckbert, Serm. IV.
(5) St. Bern. Serm. LXVI. in Cant. No. 9.
(6) Laroc: Hist. de l'Euch. 452, 453.
(7) Acta Con. Lumb. t. X. Labb. Con. col. 1471.
(8) De vita sua, lib. III. c. 16.
(9) Radulphus Ardens, Serm. in Dom. VIII. past. Trin. t. ii.

were not Albigenses, *because* Mosheim speaks of them as "Brethren of the Free Spirit," &c., is the same as to say that the members of the Church of Scotland are not Protestants, *because* they are *called* Presbyterians. Besides, Mosheim was their apologist. The Protestants wanted an appearance of ecclesiastical descent from the Apostles, and as the Albigenses had *protested* against the Church of Rome, they were considered a very important link in the chain of ecclesiastical ancestry. Mosheim, therefore, as was natural, was tender on the horrible vices of his religious forefathers; and when he speaks of their unnatural tenets, and the crimes which resulted from them, he calls them by some *specific* name, and sinks the general appellation by which they are known in contemporary history.

Let any man apply the doctrines of the Albigenses, simply on two points, viz. the tenet that the devil was the creator of the *visible* world; and that, in order to avoid co-operation with the devil in continuing his work, the faithful should take measures by which the human race should come to an end; and then say whether those errors were *merely* speculative. They were, on the contrary, pregnant with destruction to society. Was it persecution, or rather, was it not self-preservation, to arrest those errors? We shall see presently, however, that these men, like the Calvinists in France at a later period, took up the sword of sedition, and wielded it against the government under which they lived. We shall see, that *long before* the canon of Lateran was passed, their course was marked with plunder, rapine, bloodshed. And if so, it follows that their *crimes against society*, springing from their doctrines, constitute the true reason of the severity of the enactment against them.

Their existence was known from the year 1022. If, then, the extermination of heretics had been a *doctrine* of the Catholic Church, why were they not exterminated from the first? If it was not a doctrine of the church in 1022, it was not a doctrine in 1215; for the gentleman himself admits and proclaims that our doctrines never change. Why then did not the Catholics exterminate them at once? Is it that they were not able? No: for at first the heresy had but few supporters. But why were they *afterwards* persecuted? The reason is, that *in the interval* they had proceeded to sustain and propagate their infernal principles, by violence. They had placed themselves under the patronage of factious and rebellious barons, and had fought in pitched battles against their sovereigns. In the former controversy, the gentleman garbled the twenty-seventh canon of the third Council of Lateran, to show that these poor heretics were condemned to awful penalties, for nothing at all but protesting against the errors of the Church of Rome. This he did by quoting the *beginning* and *conclusion* of the canon, and, without indicating any omission, suppressing the crimes of these proto-martyrs of Calv'nism. It was proved, by the very document from which he quoted, that these lambs of the Albigensian fold were "EXERCISING SUCH CRUELTY ON THE CHRISTIANS, (*i. e.* CATHOLICS,) THAT THEY PAID NO RESPECT TO CHURCHES OR MONASTERIES, SPARED NEITHER VIRGINS NOR WIDOWS, NEITHER OLD NOR YOUNG, NEITHER SEX NOR AGE, BUT AFTER THE MANNER OF PAGANS DESTROYED AND DESOLATED EVERY THING."—When I discovered the fraud, and asked him to account for it, his defence is that he copied from the Rev. Stanly Faber!—or rather, in his own words, "Faber quotes just as I have done;" as if he and Faber were joint partners in the glory of the fraud! At all events the crimes of which they were convicted, show that the penalties enacted against them, a quarter of a century afterwards, at the fourth Council of Lateran, were founded on *other reasons* besides the mere fact of their heretical doctrine—blasphemous and shocking as this was.

Now, I leave it to the common sense and candour of any unbiassed man in this assembly to decide, even on the strongest case of supposed persecution recorded in ecclesiastical history—the case of the Albigenses—whether that case, adduced to prove that intolerance and persecution is a DOCTRINE of the Catholic Church, does not prove, in fair reasoning, the very reverse. Here is a sect, beginning, as all sects do, with a few individuals, appearing in the very heart of Catholic Europe, and, on the gentleman's hypothesis, creating a public, notorious sin—as extensive as the Church —viz. the sin of permitting these heretics to live and increase for *two hundred years* previous to the fourth Lateran Council, in open violation of their own supposed doctrine! If their extermination had been a doctrine; if, like the Presbyterians at this day, and in the United States, the Catholic Church had taught as the *commandment of God*, the obligation "to REMOVE all false worship," "according to each one's place and calling," binding the conscience of every man, from the Pope down to the acolythe, and from the king down to the peasant—I ask whether the Albigensian heresy would not have been extinguished in the blood of its first professors? Was it regarded as a sin, a violation of Catholic doctrine, to have let them live? Never. Was there any example in those ages, of what Presbyterians have since done, when, with hearts steeled by Calvinism, and faces bent upwards, they were appeasing offended Heaven for their "SIN;" and that of the English government, in "conniving at Popery?" Never. Were the Albigenses condemned to suffer death for an act of *private* worship, as the Catholics were by the Presbyterian laws of Scotland? Never. Did the Catholics destroy the Presbyterian "churches," "spare neither virgins nor widows, neither old nor young, neither age nor sex," "but after the manner of Pagans destroy every thing?" Never.—And yet, more than a quarter of a century *before* the fourth Council of Lateran, the Albigenses had committed all these excesses against the Catholics. Here then is a sect, in the midst of the dark ages, and in the midst of Catholic nations, and instead of being *extinguished* on its first appearance, it is allowed to grow, swelling its numbers, until it is able to set public authority at defiance, and to become the persecutor of those Catholics to whose *toleration* or *forbearance* it was indebted for its numbers, and even its existence! Will the gentleman say that the heretics were too numerous? But their very numbers is a refutation of his argument. To what were they indebted for their numbers, but to that forbearance which he says it was contrary to Catholic doctrine to exercise. Power for their extermination was not wanting at any time. And if that power *was* exercised finally, it was not until after their excesses, the result of their errors, had made it manifest that either *they*, or the *Catholics*, must yield to the superiority of *force*, instead of laws which they trampled on.

It was in this state of things, two hundred years after the first appearance of the Albigensian heresy, and twenty-five years after the third Council of Lateran in 1179, in which their crimes against public rights are specified, that the fourth General Council of Lateran was convened in 1215. Now the decree of that council, which the gentleman and his illiberal colleagues would manufacture into a Catholic *doctrine* binding on *all Catholics*, and applicable to *all* heretics, was directed, so far as it was penal in its enactments, against the Albigenses ALONE. Every other means had been resorted to, during the period of two hundred years, and the growing desperation of the disease seemed to require strong measures for the purpose of arresting its progress. Hence the ambassadors from almost all the governments of Europe concurred in, and probably instigated, the provisions of the canon, which were regarded as essential to their security.

In order not to be misunderstood, I deem it proper to state, that in detailing the facts and circumstances of the canon against the Albigenses, passed in the Council of Lateran, my object is not to vindicate the measure, but to submit the information that may enable this audience and our readers to form their own judgment and conclusion on the *whole* premises. The case will afford me an opportunity of establishing the distinction between the acts of a general council, which the doctrines of the Roman Catholic religion oblige every member of the communion to receive, as a "tenet of faith and morals revealed by Almighty God,"—and *other acts*, which have no such claim to our belief or obedience.

The Fourth General Council of Lateran was assembled especially for the purpose of condemning the errors of the Albigensian heresy. In this capacity, it was infallible—because, as the representative organ of the church, it was discharging the duty for which the church was divinely instituted—namely, "teaching all truth," and consequently, condemning all error. But when they pass from the definitions of doctrines to the enactments of *civil or bodily penalties*, their decisions are sustained by no promise of infallibility, and by no authority derived from God for that purpose. Whatever *right* they may have derived from other sources or circumstances to inflict *civil* punishment, it is certain that they have derived none from their vocation to the holy ministry or the imposition of hands. If Gregory XVI. were a wanderer on the Alps or Apennines, and like his divine Master, not having where to lay his head, he would be as much the supreme pastor of the Catholic Church, as he is, beneath the lofty dome of St. Peter's. It is not because he is the temporal ruler of a portion of Italy, that the eyes of the Catholic world are turned to him as the successor of St. Peter, and visible head of Christ's Church on earth. Hence the important distinction to which I have alluded. The power which God imparted to his church is *spiritual*. The exercise of temporal or civil power is of human origin, and constitutes no part or portion of the Catholic religion.

Here the gentleman ought to make a show of great surprise at the boldness of my assertion. He ought to pretend that I am guilty of heresy in making it. In fact, the assertions are not mine. They are the assertions of the *Universities* of Paris, Douay, Louvain, Alcala, Salamanca, and Valladolid, in reply to the questions put by Mr. Pitt in 1798. Does the gentleman wish a higher authority? Then I give him that of the Pope himself, Pius VI., in his rescript to the archbishops of Ireland in 1791.(1)

The principal question now is, whether the canon of the fourth Lateran was directed against *all* heretics and heresies, or whether it was, in its penal enactments, pointed against the Albigenses *alone*. Let us see. Here are the whole acts of the council on the table, and I challenge the gentleman to the investigation. Now the text of the council shows the nature of the heresy which it condemned. It defines the existence of *one* God or first principle, the *creator of all things*, and teaches that the devils were not from *all eternity evil*, but fell by sin; and it goes on to teach that persons are saved in the state of marriage, &c. Why define these DOCTRINES? Because the heretics, against whom the third canon was directed, held the errors *opposed* to these definitions. They believed that there were two first principles—*God* and the *devil*. They believed that *both* were eternal. They believed that God, the *good* principle, was the author of *souls* and of the *New* Testament; and that the devil, the *evil* principle, was the author of the *Old Testament*, creator of the *material world*, and of the *human body*; and hence, that *marriage*, with its consequences, was a co-operation with the principle of evil, and rendered salvation impossible.

Now I say that the provisions of the canon, of which there is now question, had reference to the believers in *these abominable*

---

(1) See the whole in the Appendix to "Catholic Question in America," by William Sampson, Esq., of New York.

impieties, and the evidence is found in the text itself, where the words "*hæc hæretica fœditas*," "*this* heretical *filth*," are expressly used. Again, where the words "universi hæretici, quibuscunque nominibus censeantur,"—"all heretics, under whatever name they may come," are employed; the same limitation is found in the context, in the words, "adversus *hanc* sanctam, orthodoxam, catholicam fidem, *quam superius exposuimus*." That is, "in opposition to *this* holy, orthodox, Catholic faith, *which we have exposed above*." What was that faith? The faith of one only eternal God—creator of all things, &c. Consequently, the extension of the third canon is restricted to those who held the opposite errors. Now, if the gentleman will only condescend to distrust his knowledge as a production of instinct or inspiration, and just take the trouble to examine the text, he will see all I have said. But, says he, they are not called Albigenses; and Mosheim speaks of them as connected with the brethren of the spirit. Now, if he will again condescend to examine the text, he will find that they are spoken of as having "different faces," but as yet being "joined together by the tails." That is, they had different appellations derived from their different "faces," but in the doctrines which constituted their *bond* of union, "hæc hæretica fœditas," one appellation was applied to them all—Albigenses. It was on this account, that in my last speech I remarked, that men of information must laugh or blush, as the matter may affect them, to hear ignorant advocates numbering the horrible Albigenses among the religious ancestors of Protestantism. I have now established the first fact, in opposition to the gentleman's hypothesis, according to which the canon of Lateran extends to all heretics that ever were, or ever will be. It is, in its very language, restricted to the Albigenses. The gentleman and all his anti-Catholic colleagues are sadly mortified to discover that the Catholic religion will not be as bad as they wish. If it would only accommodate them, by becoming all that malevolence has invented, and ignorance believed, it would suit their purpose exactly, and they could say what they do say of it, without the inconvenience of uttering calumnies.

We have seen secondly, by the highest Catholic authority, the Universities of France, Belgium and Spain, supported by the testimony of the Pope himself, that neither pope, nor cardinal, nor bishops, nor altogether have any right resulting from the doctrines of the Catholic religion, to dispense with oaths, release subjects from fidelity to their governments, depose rulers on account of difference of religion, or to exercise any civil authority over Catholics, by virtue of their ecclesiastical office. If, therefore, the canon in question confiscated the *goods*, and *punished the bodies* of the Albigensian heretics, my answer is, that the doctrines of the Catholic Church do not recognise or admit the *right* of a general council to either *confiscate goods* or *punish bodies*. If the gentleman can show me the "canon of a General Council, or the bull of a Pope, setting forth as *'an article of faith or morals revealed by Almighty God,'* " that such a right exists, or did exist in any age of the church, I give up the argument. But if he cannot, let him give up the attempt to prove it. Again, is it not surprising that the gentleman has not been struck with the absurdity of the conclusion to which his argument would lead? He makes us hold a doctrine, as he pretends, a canon which we never could comply with, until Protestants come to hold the abominations of the Albigenses, and till the world returns to that identical condition of civil governments, in which it was in the year 1215. Kings and feudal barons, vassals, and all gradations of the feudal system must return, before the provisions of this *canon could be* put in practice!

But when the gentleman is bent on carrying an argument, absurdities do not affright him, and impossibilities are but as straws in his way.

Having disposed of the substance of the gentleman's argument, I shall now proceed to take him on the small points with which it is surrounded.

He says, that in translating the words *"sæcularibus potestatibus præsentibus,"* the "secular powers *present*" at the council, I committed a mistake which "every schoolboy that has read Cordery could correct." Now, between "present" and "absent," there is no medium, and since he and the schoolboys have determined that *præsentibus* means "absent" or "*not* present," of course, I have only to bow submission to their authority. He says I charge him with having omitted the word "*præsentibus*" on a former occasion. I did; and he does not venture to say that the charge was unfounded. He says I qualified the charge by the word "fraudulently." I deny it, and call for his proof. Child of Antichrist although he supposes me, I have too much charity to suppose him under the influence of knowledge and malice at the same time. Another reason why our critic thinks "præsentibus" ought to be translated "not present," is that although expressed when the reference is *first* made to the "secular powers," it is not repeated at every subsequent reference—as if the original determination of the sense, did not render the repetition superfluous.

But admitting, as he does, *for argument sake*, that the word "præsentibus" means "present," he arrives at the conclusion, even by my own showing, that there was a "church and state"—as if this point of history were a new discovery.

The gentleman calls me a "falsifier of Mosheim." I fling the imputation back upon him, and call for his proof. I have already pointed out the reason of any apparent discrepancy, between my account of the Albigenses, and that given by Mosheim. I have access to the originals, and can see in every page of Mosheim the struggle between the Protestant and the historian. In his estimation, to have opposed the church, was, like the virtue of charity, enough to cover a "multitude of sins." But even Mosheim admits enough to sustain all I have said. He tells us that the term "Albigenses" was used in two senses. He states, on the authority of Petrus Sarmensis, that the *general appellation* of all the various kinds of heretics, who resided in the southern parts of France was *Albigenses*. He tells us that this term, "in its *more confined sense*, was used to denote those heretics who were inclined to the *Manichæan system*, and who were otherwise known by the denominations of Catharists, Publicans, or Paulicians and Bulgarians."(1) And pray have not I identified them by their "Manichæan doctrines"—their descent from the "Paulicians," who were Manichæans—and their having come from Bulgaria? Mosheim does not give any name to those "fanatics," as he calls them, whose "shocking violation of decency," he tells us, "was a *consequence of their* pernicious system." What was this but the Manichæan system? And since those who held or inclined to this system, were called, even in the stricter sense of the term, ALBIGENSES, as Mosheim tells us, was I a "falsifier" in calling them by that name? When Mosheim tells us, notwithstanding their "Manichæan system," that the Albigenses were very "sincere in their piety," he speaks as a partisan, giving his opinion; whereas the facts stated by himself, as an historian, are sufficient to prove their abandoned principles both in doctrine and morals. To talk about their "sincerity," is not to the purpose. He admits, and the gentleman quotes it as a vindication, that they were the same as the Paulicians; and this settles the question. The Paulicians being the name of the Manichæans in Armenia, from whence their doctrine passed into Bulgaria, and thence into Italy, France, and Germany, as we have seen above. Finally, Mosheim's testimony *against* the principles of these sects, is that of a friend; and it was on this account that I quoted him at all. For the rest, I have the *contemporary* witnesses of their abominable doctrines and practices; and who are the only sources of information on which modern writers, including Mosheim himself, have to draw.

When the gentleman tells us, on the authority of Mosheim, that the Pope "persuaded Frederic II. and Louis IX. to enact barbarous laws against heretics," he furnishes the refutation of his own argument, and I am surprised that he had not sagacity enough to see it. For since the Pope had *to persuade* them, it is evident that, to *this persuasion by the Pope*, and not to the *doctrine of the Catholic Church*, the persecution is to be ascribed. If it had been a *doctrine*, the Pope, instead of persuading them to *do it*, would have excommunicated them for having left it *undone*.

He charges me with having said that it was "doctrine in Scot-

(1) Mosh. Balt. ed. Vol. II. p. 375. Note.

land to cut men's ears off." He mistakes; it was New England, I said. In "SCOTLAND" something more than the "ears" was required as the penalty of worshipping God according to conscience. But he wonders why such things were "doctrine" among Presbyterians, and not doctrine among Catholics. I will inform him. The Presbyterians held that their right to do so, was a "TENET REVEALED BY ALMIGHTY GOD." Consequently with them it *was* a "doctrine." The Catholics never held, that their right to do so was a "tenet of revelation;" but invariably derived their right, so called, from either *the destructive nature of the heresy, the crimes of the heretics, the will of the government*, or *the dictates of self-preservation*, which the almost uniform seditious spirit of heresy often called into operation. Does the gentleman now understand the difference?

I said, in a former controversy, as he remarks, that "the secular representatives (at the Council of Lateran) had nothing to do with the definitions of doctrine and morals." I say so still, and the fact is as universal as the history of the church. Has he discovered any thing to the contrary? In consequence of my having said so, he remarks "such writers need good memories." What does he mean? Oh! I perceive. The "secular ambassadors" of Christendom were at the Council of Lateran—major. But the pronoun "WE" is found in the third canon against the Albigenses, in connection with the *faith* which had before been "expounded,"—minor. And therefore WE means the secular ambassadors, *helping* to "expound" the faith,—conclusion. This seems to be the gentleman's logic, and though it may pass in the anti-popery schools, it cannot pass wherever *common sense* is permitted to wield the ferrule. He uses also the term "doctrine-making council." Now you all recollect that the doctrine expounded was the existence of ONLY *one God*, and the sanctity of marriage, and you see how far the council deserves to be called a "doctrine-making" council—whether with or without the help of the "secular ambassadors." No; the time for these things was reserved for the minority of Presbyterianism, when orthodoxy was to be looked for in acts of parliament, and in oaths, leagues and covenants; and when the *civil magistrate*, good man, was to see that whatever should be done in ecclesiastical assemblies should be "according to the MIND OF GOD."(1)

I stated that the authenticity of this canon was disputed by Protestant as well as Catholic historians. The gentleman, as we shall presently see, has not been able to controvert the truth of the statement. But, he says, admitting it, what becomes of the "unerring guide, the faithful tradition of the Church of Rome?" I answer, that the "unerring guide" and "faithful tradition" would

(1) See [Genuine] Westminster Confession of Faith, Chap. 23,—"Of Civil Magistrates."

be no more affected by it, than the gentleman's identity would be, by his inability to tell whether a certain button on his coat, had been sewed on by his tailor, or by his laundress.

Now we come to the criticism on the authenticity of the canon in question. Before I notice what he has said on this subject, it is necessary to state, that what is commonly called the third canon of the fourth Lateran, is composed of five chapters or sections. Each of these has its own specific import, and in Caranza its own specific heading. The second, under the heading "Quod juramentum debeant præstare sæculares potestates," is the portion of whose authority there is a doubt among critics. And it was of this *section*, which is more properly a chapter than a "canon," that I said, it is regarded by critics as "spurious—an interpolation in the genuine acts of the council." This chapter is neither the beginning, "middle," or end of the canon; it is distinct and by itself—having no necessary connexion with what goes before or comes after. This is the section that is considered spurious. This is the section which is wanting in the Mazarine copy, "in Latin" as well as Greek. Here the gentleman has betrayed himself. He professes to quote the marginal note of Labbe, "De est hic folium in codice Græco *et Latino*," and leaves out the words "et Latino." He must have seen with his eyes, therefore, that the same leaf which was wanting in the Greek of the Mazarine copy was wanting also in the Latin copy. And yet he says that "*Labbe follows the Mazarine* copy," in giving that part of the canon which Labbe himself says does not exist in that copy, either in the Greek or Latin! If it does exist in Latin, why does Labbe say that it *does not; if* it does not exist, as the gentleman *saw by the marginal note*, why does he say that "Labbe followed it?" Let him answer that question.

He says, that independently of this omitted section, we have the "*exterminating* part at least." I deny the truth of the assertion. Here are the acts of the council, and I call on him for the proof. Collier, the gentleman has told you, *only* states that it is wanting in the Mazarine copy; and this was one of Collier's reasons for doubting its authority. Does not even this determine the *truth* of what my opponent has ventured to assert was "not true?" But why select Collier, and pass over the other authorities adduced in my last speech? I bring a host of witnesses, and instead of rebutting their evidence, he challenges the testimony of one, and he a Protestant, who sustains me nevertheless, whilst all the others remain unanswered, undisputed.

The gentleman represents me as "uncandid" for not stating that "Crabbe's edition of the councils published in 1530 *none of* the four Lateran's canons." There might be some foundation for the charge, if I had not assigned the reason why the portion of which I was speaking, could not have been published in 1530: namely, that it was not known as a part of what is called the third canon "until 1587." This seemed to me a sufficient reason why it should not be in the edition of 1580; and I was not speaking of the other canons.

He says that "the said Crabbe published afterwards *three editions* of the councils in which the *said* canon is found." If this be true, the fact cannot be explained except by taking it for granted that Crabbe published two editions *after his death*, just for the gentleman's accommodation.

We now come to Matthew Paris and Du Pin. I claimed these as rejecting the canon. He says this "is not true." And yet, he himself establishes the fact, by the very passages he brings to disprove it. Matthew Paris, even as quoted by the gentleman, says that the *whole* seventy chapters on being *read* in the council, "seemed tolerable to some, and grievous to others." Does this prove that the section of the third canon, now under consideration, was *then* incorporated in the seventy chapters? No. It leaves *that question* untouched. Does it prove that the seventy chapters themselves were the "genuine acts of the council?" No such thing. If it proves any thing, it proves the contrary. The document was read to the council—it "seemed grievous" to some, and only "tolerable" to others;—therefore it *was the genuine act* of the council, and Mr. Hughes says that which is "NOT TRUE" when he asserts the contrary! Du Pin says, "Let the case be as it will, IT IS CERTAIN that these canons were not made *by the council*, but by Innocent III." Therefore, says my logical friend, Mr. Hughes said what is "not true" when he quoted Du Pin as *not admitting* these to be the genuine acts of the council! But his commentary on Du Pin is worthy of his text. He tells us that on hearing them read "NONE WERE SATISFIED"—and yet he maintains that they were the genuine acts of the council! When he *contradicts himself*, it is not strange that he should contradict me.

But Dr. Crotty, the gentleman says, had admitted the substance of these canons to be the acts of the council—in his examination before the commissioners of parliament. Granted. So far as the doctrines of the Catholic Church are affected by them, I have no objection to make the admission myself. But it does not follow, that Dr. Crotty could not, or that I should not, give good reasons to prove that the documents, or at least a portion of them, which have been made a pretext for the persecution of Catholics in Great Britain for three hundred years, are of doubtful authenticity. My argument, however, does not require that I should avail myself of this circumstance. My allusion to it was merely *incidental*.

The gentleman betrays great want of information in what he says about the Council of Trent, as adopting the acts or reputed acts of the Council of Lateran. The Council of Trent adopts ALL the "tenets of faith and morals" that had been held as such by any, and by ALL the general councils that preceded it. To these "*tenets*" also, and to these *alone*, refer the words "*delivered, defined* and *declared*" in the creed of Pius IV. Thus the whole argument falls by knocking away the prop of ignorance by which it was supported.

As for Dens's Theology, which I have never seen, it is, I presume, like nearly all other treatises on the same subject, in which the prejudices of the author pervade the discussion of such questions as do not belong to the substance of faith. The gentleman has seen, or should have seen, that the Catholic Archbishop of Dublin, in the name of the Irish Prelates, had *disavowed* it. That it was published as a speculation by an ordinary bookseller, that it was not the standard or school book of theology in Ireland, that it was only referred to as a rule for the *order* or succession, in which the conferences of the clergy were to take up questions to be investigated. But the ebullitions of religious spleen, and the researches of reckless apostasy, furnished by Murtogh O'Sullivan, Mr. M'Ghee, dee, dee, and the rest of the "Fudge Family" at Exeter Hall, have come to the gentleman's aid, too late indeed for the discussion, but yet in time for the *correction* of his speeches. In quoting the real or pretended sentiments of Dens, my opponent deals in false premises, and absurd conclusions—by assuming, that the work called Dens's Theology contains nothing but Catholic doctrine, which is false; and by concluding from this false position, that therefore Catholics are bound to believe all that Dens has written; which is absurd, and consequently no argument.

As to the Rhemish Testament, I have no objection that he has referred to it. The notes put to it by the publisher are objectionable, and were condemned by the Catholics of England from its first appearance—a sufficient evidence that these notes are any thing but Catholic doctrine. The work was almost out of print when the clique to which the gentleman belongs, brought out an edition in New York, in order to make the Catholics of this country answer for the sins of the Rhemish note-makers. But iniquity lied to itself. For, in publishing the notes, they publish also the text; thereby refuting their own calumny about the Scriptures being forbidden.

Bossuet says, "there is no illusion more dangerous than to assign SUFFERING as a mark of a true church." His words are these—"Il n'y a point d'illusion plus dangereuse, que de donner 'LA SOUFFRANCE' pour un charactère de vraie eglise." As the gentleman does not know the French language, I can pardon him for supposing that "la souffrance" means "toleration." But Faber, no doubt, has "quoted it just as he has done."

The Belgian bishops quoted the ancient constitution of the country for their pretensions, and certainly neither English, French, Irish, Scotch or American Catholics, have any thing to do with the Belgic Constitution, ancient or modern.

The case of the Pope's letter to the cardinals, dated February 5, 1808, deserves a little explanation, which, for the gentleman's instruction in history, I will supply. The Pope was a prisoner in Rome, and Napoleon had proposed to alter the civil *constitution of the* PAPAL STATES, by which the Catholic religion had been exclusively recognised, from time immemorial. The Pope protested against this change, as being contrary to the "canons," "councils," and the "Catholic religion"—just as the Bishop of London would say, that it was against the "canons," "acts of parliament," and "the Church of England," as *by law established*, to admit the dissenters to take degrees in the Universities.

In a word, the gentleman may heap together scraps of books, five words from one place, and fifteen from another;—he may invoke the spouters at Exeter Hall, the apostate De Pradt, and one thousand other helps;—he may show what was done, but still he comes short of proving his proposition—which is, that the doctrines, that is, those "tenets of faith and morals which Catholics hold as having been revealed by Almighty God," are opposed to "civil and religious liberty." He knows well, that the Catholic Church cuts off from her communion those who reject her DOCTRINES. Thus it is a doctrine, that marriage lawfully and validly contracted, is indissoluble; and for the maintenance of this doctrine, she suffered Henry VIII. and his adherents to depart from the Church. In this respect she is perhaps inimical to *liberty*, as she would not allow his majesty the liberty of having two wives at the same time. But Catholic France and Catholic Poland made all religions equal, and there was no excommunication; because, in the exercise of civil sovereignty, they had the right to do so, and because, in so doing, they violated no doctrine of the Catholic Church. The gentleman, however, thinks that Poland did nothing, so long as she did not "expel;" in other words, persecute "the Jesuits." This shows *his* standard of religious liberty. His knowledge of the history of Poland seems to be as extensive as the article on that subject in the Encyclopædia Americana.

Let the gentleman now come on to "Huss," "the Council of Constance," "the massacre of St. Bartholomew," "the Inquisition," and the other stereotype topics of reproach ; and whilst I pledge myself to prove that the religion of Roman Catholics has no necessary connexion with them, I pledge myself also to show that the gentleman, like nine hundred and ninety-nine Protestants out of every thousand, is ignorant, or what is worse, *misinformed* on these subjects. I pledge myself to show that Presbyterianism has been more cruel in its laws than the inquisition itself. In the mean time, we are on the subject of the decrees, real or fictitious, as he may choose to consider them, of the Council of Lateran against the Albigenses. I have proved that they were confined to the Albigenses alone. 2. That it depended on the civil authority of the state, at whose instance they were probably enacted, to put them in force or not. 3. That they never were put in force except in one or two provinces in France. 4. That they were neither enacted nor enforced for two hundred years after the first appearance of the Albigenses. 5. That it was not for their *speculative errors*, but for their crimes against human nature—the "consequence of their pernicious system," as Mosheim expresses it, and not for these only, but for their ravages on the rights of society, in the destruction of life and property. 6. That the law for their suppression did not even pretend to rest for its authority on any *doctrine* of the Catholic Church, but upon the reward of confiscated lands and promised indulgences. And finally, that not only the political condition of society, which *then existed*, must be restored, but the Protestants must agree in "doctrine and practice" with the Albigenses, before the gentleman, with all his anxiety to do so, can bring himself and his brethren within the meaning of the obsolete politico-ecclesiastic enactments of the Council of Lateran. He may say that the council, as such, had nothing to do with the enactment of *civil penalties*. This is another question, on which I shall not enter further than by stating, in opposition to what the gentleman has undertaken to prove, that the doctrines of the Catholic Church gave them no authority to do so. He may say that the Albigenses have been calumniated, and get some Bancroft to give them a character, as he did the Calvinists. This will not do. I have stated the facts and *contemporary authorities*. Let the gentleman meet my position as a scholar and as a logician, by going to the original authorities. He mistakes the character of the public judgment, if he supposes that his declamation will pass for history, or his rhapsodies for reason.

The gentleman in quoting the index of what he calls the Acta Ecclesiæ, shows great fecundity of resources, if not depth of research. For, if he can make arguments from having perused merely the index, what would be able to resist him if he had made himself acquainted with the body of the work? He seems to think that every thing written by a Catholic is an article of faith; and that every action that was done by a Catholic, the more wicked the better for his purpose, was a defined tenet of Catholic morality. He is mistaken. The time allotted me, is too brief for me to refute his arguments, and point out to him the difference between canon law and Catholic doctrine.

But let him read some treatise, even Hooker's Ecclesiastical Polity, and he will find that there *is* a difference. Or to make the illustration more familiar, I would say, that "Acta Ecclesiæ," or the "Canon Law" of the Presbyterian Church, are the *sayings* and *doings* of the General Assembly; but the *doctrines* of the Presbyterian Church, are the Westminster Confession of Faith, as "revised" "corrected" and "amended," to suit the political condition of the country *for the time being*. But when I come to treat the Presbyterian question, I am prepared to show that what is *at most* only canon law with us, is *doctrine* with them. For instance, in the index of the Acta Ecclesiæ, as quoted by him, it is forbidden to *pray* or *marry* with heretics; a proof that, at least, it was *not* forbidden to let heretics *live*, as the gentleman has been labouring to persuade us. Now, in contrast with this, let us place the mild, liberal, charitable *doctrine* of the Presbyterian Church— "Such as profess the *true* reformed religion, should not marry with infidels, papists, or other idolaters: neither should the *godly* be unequally yoked."(1)

I had stated that Catholics *exercise their own discretion* on the subject of civil and religious liberty—that their religion leaves them free on the matter. I know that St. Paul was not a preacher of insurrection to the slave. In reply to this, the gentleman exclaims, "What! does not the *Bible define* the *rights* of conscience, and of personal as well as civil liberty? If we look at the black ruins of the convent near Boston, we should infer not; for the Boston people, and, indeed, the New England people generally, are great Bible readers. "*Presbyterians*," he says, "*hold that God has revealed a clear code of rights in his word*," and that there is "*no discretion as to the matter of liberty*." Now the magnanimous sacking of the convent was in strict accordance with this acknowledged "doctrine" of the Presbyterian Church. The midnight torch was applied, and, sure enough, there was "no discretion"—there was no alternative, but to perish in the flames, or go to enjoy "liberty" with the houseless beasts of the field. The consequences of this Presbyterian doctrine, which, I repeat, is not the doctrine of St. Paul, begin to be felt in the South, as well as in the North, making the master a criminal against God, for holding slaves, and the slaves criminals against God, for submitting to their condition. The Presbyterians hold, that according to the word of God, "there is *no discretion* on the matter of liberty."

(1) Confession, p. 108.

"Is the Roman Catholic Religion, in any or in all its principles or doctrines, opposed to civil or religious liberty?"

AFFIRMATIVE IV.—MR. BRECKINRIDGE.

MR. PRESIDENT,—

I HOPE the gentleman has recovered his composure after the discussions of the last night. If the *joints* of his *armour crack* under the power of the truth, it is not my fault; nor his: for he is the *"prince of dodgers."* If his cause *could* be defended, he could do it. It fails—not for want of an *able* advocate—but from its own *evil* nature. How affecting a spectacle it is, to see a mind possessed of powers fitted to bless his country and his age, stooping to every unworthy art, to defend a system on which God and man has written *"tekel,"* as with a sunbeam, and whose final and speedy overthrow is as certain as its dominion has been destructive of the best hopes of the race!

The gentleman denies that this Society has *"exposed"* the mendacious writer in "The Catholic Diary." Yet the Society (he owns) has said that *some* of the writer's remarks were *"in a great measure untrue."* This looks no little like saying that the author had told *"falsehoods;"* though I know the Jesuits draw a distinction between *lying* in whole, and lying in *"a great measure;"* and I am willing that the gentleman should *profit* by *his casuistry*. Yet *why* did the editor of the Diary refuse to publish the Society's letter? And why did he not call for the *proofs*, if he desired justice, or doubted the statements made in the letter?

It is really enough to excite the compassion of the audience, to see how the gentleman retreats from the charge which he made against me, of *"forging* a quotation" from the Council of Trent. He said, in so many words, *"And what will be the reader's disgust, to learn that this beautiful specimen of Latinity, put forth as a quotation from the Council of Trent, is a* FABRICATION, *a* FORGERY." In my reply, I produced *conviction*, even on *his* mind, that this *Latin*, at which he had *laughed*, and in regard to which he had so impertinently charged me, is indeed the very Latin, *verbum verbo*, word for word, of the holy council! Yet he called it "fabrication." You may see how much credit is due to his charges, by this example, for he is compelled to own "that his personal integrity is interested in this point," and with disingenuous, but forced acknowledgment, says, *"according to the letter, I was mistaken; and according to the letter, I retract."* But how could he be "mistaken," with the Latin before him, and in the very same chapter, a few sentences below! And *if mistaken* in his own decrees, what shall we say of his knowledge of his cause! *If not*, what shall we think of such outrageous charges against the *true citation* of the document?

Having failed "*in the letter*," he flies for refuge to the "*doctrine*," which I am still charged with "perverting.". In my first speech, I translated "injungere pœnas," to "inflict punishments." In his reply, he charged me, as usual, with *falsifying* the sense by this translation. To make it plain that this was the true sense, I referred, in my second speech, to a passage in the same connexion, just below, where the words *imponere pœnam* occur, and I quoted that *member* of the sentence which *contained them.* Then he denied that there was such a passage; but, corrected by my last speech, *owns* it was there; makes a ludicrous apology for ridiculing the *Latin of the holy infallible council,* and flies at me for a *mistranslation*. Now *pœna* means *punishment*, as my same little schoolboy will say: "*injungere*" means "*to join with,*" "to lay on," " to enjoin ;" and "*imponere*" "to impose," " to enjoin," " *to inflict,*" "*to lay upon one.*" *Pœnitentia* signifies "*penance ;*" but *pœna,* "*punishment.*" But the gentleman says, "*to inflict punishment, might mean personal castigation.*" So it might! and so it often does! Has this not been the fact in every age of the "Catholic Church," that she has enjoined and claimed the right to order, and even to inflict " personal castigation," by way of penance. Devoti, Vol. III., Book IV., § 21, tells us, "*that the church had prisons in former days, in which offending clergymen were cast,*" and he enumerates "CASTIGATION, *exile, fines, and other punishments inflicted by the church ;*" or, as the gentleman's Latinity is so pure, I will give him *the nut to crack*. " De verberibus, exilio, mulctis pecuniariis, cæteris que PŒNIS, quæ ab ecclesia dabantur, sequenti libro, suus erit agendi locus." Again, Book IV., §§ 9, 10, he discourses at large on the same subject, and tells us, among other things, that there are *prisons in monasteries,* for this very use. In the ninth section he *honestly avows that the church has power to coerce the laity as well as the clergy, with temporal punishments.* And this author has the *sanction of the Pope as* late as A. D. 1792—*saying that there is nothing in the book contrary to faith and good morals.* (But more of this hereafter.). Is any man a stranger to the fact, that all sorts of personal chastisements *have been enjoined,* some *self-inflicted,* as penance, and some inflicted by authority of the " holy mother," as *tender* mercies, to reduce the sinner to repentance?

In vain, therefore, does the gentleman struggle in his toils. His *bad Latin* is with him and his fathers of Trent. His *criticisms,* be on his guides; his "forgeries" on his own head! *As to Bossuet*—and French—I own "*I do not know as much about* the French" as I do of "*the Jesuits.*" But with my *little*, I proceed to expose his *wretched perversion* of *Bossuet*. The gentleman makes him say, "*there is no illusion more dangerous than to assign* SUFFERING *as a mark of the true church.*" "*La souffrance*" may mean either "*suffering*" or "*toleration*." The author is speaking of the *exercise of the power of the sword in* matters of religion and conscience; and he says that "IT CANNOT BE CALLED IN QUESTION WITHOUT *weakening, and, as it were, maiming, the public authority or power,*"(1) (then follows the passage before cited:) *so that there is no illusion more dangerous than to make* TOLERATION *a mark of the true church*." It would be pure nonsense to translate this word "*suffering;*" for he is *defending* the power to *enforce* religion; and is *opposing* "*la souffrance*" or "toleration." Now, if it be rendered "suffering," then you make him say that the power of the sword in matters of religion is *right*, therefore "*suffering*" is *not* a mark of the true church! But the same author elsewhere settles the question. "*It is this,*" the holy and inflexible incompatibility of the Catholic Church, "*indeed which renders her* SO UNCONCILIATORY, *and consequently so odious to all sects separated from her; most of which at the beginning desired only to be* TOLERATED *by her*, or at least not to be anathematized by her. *But her* HOLY SECURITY, and THE HOLY DELICACY OF HER SENTIMENTS, FORBADE HER SUCH INDULGENCE, OR RATHER SUCH SOFTNESS."(2) Will the gentleman then reapply his knowledge of the language "of the great nation," and tell us whether Bossuet really believed it right *to tolerate a false religion?* So far is he from this, that he admits that the Church of Rome *is the most intolerant of all Christian sects,* while quoting and affirming (on the previous page) the words of M. Jurieu.

The allusion of the gentleman to "*marriage*" is peculiarly unfortunate. For, on that subject alone, it were easy to show that the doctrines of his church are *directly at war with the civil law of the land,* as well as convey the *most horrible intimations on the legitimacy of all Protestant issue.*

"The Belgian bishops" are not to be put *aside* with a *word*. They quoted "*the canonical laws*" as opposed to the *new constitution*, and for the reason that the new constitution *tolerated all religions*, which the *canon laws forbade*. They say "*toleration* is incompatible with the free exercise of their official duties."

---

(1) Chose ausi qui ne peut être revoquèe en doute, sans énerver et comme, estropier la puissance publique.
(2) C'est en effect ce qui la rend *si severe si* insociable, et ensuite si odieuse à toutes les sectes séparées, qui la plûpart au commencement ne demondoient autre chose si non qu'elle voulût bien les tolérer ou du moins, ne le frapper par de ses anathemes. Mais sa sainte severite et la sainte delicatesse des ses sentimens ne lui permettoit pas cette indulgence, ou plûtot cette mollesse.— *Sixieme Acertiement*, sect. 115; Œuvres, tom. iv. p. 426.

They declare that their *duty to the church* will put them "*in formal opposition to the laws of the State*," viz.: to "*universal toleration.*" Now, if the bishops of a *whole nation* are right; if *they* understand the Council of Trent, the canonical law, and their duties to the Catholic religion, *toleration of any other religion is against all these!* Hence they call on the king to establish the Catholic religion again, by law, *as before*, or else threaten to oppose the "laws of the state." So would the bishops and priests do here if they had equal candour! Therefore, "*English, French, Irish, Scotch, and American Catholics* HAVE *much to do with*" this matter; and so have American *Protestants;* and they will understand it so!

We notice next the gentleman's confused and awkward account of the *Albigenses*. I see he would willingly *detain* me from the exposure of Popery, on the question of *their* heresies and immoralities. But this cannot be; though he is peculiarly open to exposure in their history. Now, allowing all he says of their character and doctrines to be true, what does it amount to? To this:—*that they were so wicked*, so *heretical*, and such enemies to the human race, that the *Pope and Council were compelled, after two hundred years of patience, to order their extermination!* We know that *laymen* never vote in popish councils. That is a *Presbyterian* heresy, to admit the *representatives of the people* to vote on the doctrines and discipline of the church. Of course it was by the *clergy* that this persecuting canon was passed. Therefore, the *clergy*, headed by the Pope, resolved that it was the duty of the *church* to take up arms against such offenders. This is confessing the whole point in debate. For, we repeat it, the *civil power alone* had a right to declare war against their *civil* transgressors. But the *holy* council did it. But the gentleman says, "the Fourth General Council of Lateran was assembled especially for the purpose of condemning the *errors* of the Albigensian heresy. In this capacity it was infallible." They *did* condemn the *errors*. But what next? They then proceeded to order the punishment of these heretics. Let it be remembered, the gentleman admits that they had been in *existence* for two centuries—and out of Rome's communion. Yet the holy council were determined, as they were like "*deserters from an army*, they were still subject to the jurisdiction of the church, and, *as such*, were *liable* to have *judgment* passed on them, and *to be punished* and *denounced with anathema.*"(1) Accordingly, the gentleman admits they had *the right* to inflict punishment, but denies that in doing IT they were *infallible*, or derived the right from their priestly office. "Whatever *right* they may have *derived* from *other* sources or circumstances to inflict *civil* punishment, it is certain they have derived none from their vocation to

(1) See Cat. Counc. Trent, p. 95.

the holy ministry or the imposition of hands." "When they pass from the definitions of doctrine to the enactments of *civil or bodily penalties,* their discussions are sustained by *no promise of infallibility."* How strange a picture! An *intermittent* infallibility! The same identical man, passing three decrees—*the first and second on doctrine*—the third ordering the punishment of those who held these doctrines, and who were enemies to society, &c. In the two former they were *infallible:* in the latter, *not.* They had right from God to do the two former, *i. e.* to *denounce* the *errors* and *sins:* in the latter, they had a *right* from "other sources and circumstances" to order their extermination! In a word, these holy butchers marked the *victims,* and then set their *bloodhounds* on them. When arraigned for it, they say, we condemned *doctrines,* as *infallible priests;* we ordered the extermination of the heretics, as *men.* Truly this is a terrific sort of defence? But this is the best that even Mr. Hughes himself can say. Now, to show the fraud as well as folly of such a distinction between the *definition* and *discipline* of the council, let me ask, is this *bloody discipline contrary to any doctrine,* or *to any bull ever uttered by the Church of Rome?* Of all the *general councils that have met since* A. D. 1215, (of which the gentleman admits no less than six,) and *of all the bulls of all the Popes* for so many hundred years, not one has in one line, or word, *denounced,* or in any way *recalled* or *altered,* this bloody canon! I call on the gentleman to produce one *sentence* which in the least goes to condemn it! If he cannot produce it, will it not follow that there is nothing in *persecution against the doctrines of his church?* The same remarks *apply with augmented force to the* twenty-seventh canon of the Third Lateran, against which he has no exception to make; only that I left out (in a former controversy) the *middle* of the canon, and gave the *first and last.* But I gave full proof of its *persecuting character.* I gave a *full page* of it; and gave all but the narrative of their pretended CRIMES. I did not know before that Mr. Hughes *conceded* that the council had jurisdiction over *them;* and, as the celebrated Faber set the example, I suppose that I shall be considered as at least in as good company, and under as hopeful direction, as if following a wily Jesuit. But now for the whole canon, crimes and all! Does he admit that to be *genuine?* He has already done so! It dooms its victims to *slavery!* It even hires men to slaughter the heretics for their errors and crimes, with heavenly gifts! and denounces all who refuse to take up arms against them! Has this canon of the third Lateran ever been repealed, or its *persecution* and bloodshed denounced, by pope or council? Yet it was passed as early as A. D. 1179—six hundred and fifty-six years ago!

But again, the gentleman, desperate in resource, and trusting to the *chance* of my not having the canons of the Fourth Lateran before me, says that the council was "assembled especially for the purpose of condemning the errors of the Albigensian heresy." Now Du Pin tells us, (on the 13th Cent., page 95,) "*the Pope, in his Letters of Indiction,* gives his reasons why he thought the council necessary, viz. '*the recovery of the Holy Land,* and *the reformation* of the Catholic Church.'" It passed no less than seventy canons—*one* of *these,* the bloody third, of which we are treating. They were *on the Greek Church,* on the drunkenness and bastards of the clergy—forbidding states to tax the clergy—regulating relics, excommunications, revenues, &c., and they *end* with a decree on the *crusade* for the *recovery of the Holy Land,* for which the *remission of sins was promised;* excommunication is threatened to those who *vowed* to go, and then *failed;* the holy army is ordered *when* to start, and *where* to convene, and such *like things, well becoming "Christ's vicar"* and Mr. Hughes's *infallible head!* Yet he says the *Albigenses* were *the chief* object; nay, "the exclusive" one! Again; he says, that the heretics *denoted* in the *third canon,* and the *heretics* denounced in the *first* and *second,* were *Albigensian,* and *restricted to them.* Strange! In the creed expressed in the first canon, the *doctrine of transubstantiation* is specially named, and *the impossibility of salvation* out of the Catholic *Church.* Now, I ask, were the Albigenses the *only sect* who opposed these, even in that age? But he owns that the *penal canon* was against all those who did not or *should* not hold *what is defined in the first canon.* But do not all modern, as well as ancient Protestants, reject and abhor the said defined doctrines of *transubstantiation,* and *no salvation out of the Catholic Church?* Then the canon applies to *them,* and to *all* of them, as well to the Albigenses. Besides, in the second canon, the council condemns the *errors* of Joachim, Abbot of Flora, and the *errors* of Amaury. After this broad and various definition, covering *every Protestant, then* or *now on earth,* the council proceed to say, (in the third canon,) "*we excommunicate and anathematize every heresy* extolling *itself against this holy orthodox faith,* which we have before (as above) expounded." And yet the gentleman tells us it only means these wicked Albigenses!

His motive in this is plain; but his weakness is plainer still. He cannot restrict the curses of that bloody act, and the *crimes* and murders which flowed after it, *to the poor Albigenses.* It has no limits less than *all ages of the world, and all Protestants against Rome;* or if there be a *limit,* it is in the *power* of Rome to carry it out. But once more: he says, if *persecution* were a doctrine of their church, why did they bear with the Albigenses *so long?* Answer. *They did not bear with them.* In 1179, as we have seen, the Third Lateran enacted its bloody twenty-seventh canon against heretics. The Council of Tours in 1163, that of Toulouse in 1119, &c., *passed persecuting canons.* As soon as they *dared,* the popes and councils began their persecution.

Du Pin says, (Thirteenth Century, p. 154,) "The Popes and prelates [perceiving that the notorious heretics contemned the spiritual power, and that excommunication and other *ecclesiastical* penalties were so far from reducing them, that they rendered them more insolent, and put them upon using violence] *were of opinion that it was lawful to make use of force, to see whether those who were not reclaimed out of a sense of their salvation, might be so by the fear of punishments, and even of temporal death. There* had been ALREADY several instances of heretics condemned to *fines*, to *banishments*, to punishments, and *even to death itself;* but there had never been any *war* proclaimed against them. Innocent III. was the first that PROCLAIMED SUCH A WAR AGAINST THE ALBIGENSES [a fine business for the *head* of the Church!] AND WALDENSES, [Mr. Hughes says, it was "restricted to the Albigenses," and that the Waldenses were a very different people,] and against Raymond, Count of Toulouse, their protector. War might subdue the *heads*, and *reduce whole bodies* of people, but it was not capable of altering the sentiments of particular persons, or of hindering them from teaching their doctrines secretly. Whereupon, the Pope thought it advisable to set up a *tribunal* of such persons, whose business should be to make *inquiry after heretics, and to draw up their processes*. . . . . . And from hence this tribunal was called the INQUISITION." My hearers know what IT IS. Du Pin was a Papist. We see, then, the gentleman is confuted, and exposed by his own historian. And when the gentleman asks, "*If their extermination had been a doctrine —I ask whether the Albigensian heresy would not have been extinguished in the blood of its first professors?*" I answer, it was finally *almost* literally *thus extinguished, in the blood* of an immense multitude, until at length they were nearly blotted out from under Heaven; though, as the gentleman says, they were at one time *exceedingly numerous.*

But lastly: The gentleman has *falsified the history* of this people, both as to their doctrine and lives. I cited *Mosheim*, because *he* first quoted him, and by *omitting* the name of one *sect*, which Mosheim *denounced*, and *inserting* falsely the name of *Albigenses*, whom Mosheim *defends*, made him *seem* to sustain Mr. Hughes's slanders, in utter variance with the author's whole history.

Mr. Hughes utters almost as many falsehoods as sentences, when he charges the Albigenses with being *Manichees;* and I pledge myself to prove on him an ignorance which has disgraced the Bishop of Meaux, (and which disgraces his *follower* now,) before I have done with this discussion. But allowing all he has said of their *errors* and their *vices*, does not this *plea for persecution, on that ground*, (for it is no less,) prove that Catholics think it a favour to let others exist who differ from them, and that they claimed and exercised the right to *denote*, as vicious heretics, those whose opinions and lives they disliked; that when society was in their judgment disturbed by such persons, especially if they became *numerous*, the Church claimed and exercised the right to declare *religious wars* against them, to *confiscate their property*, forbid the exercise of *all civil rights*, order *their extermination*, give their lands to others, and *depose* their rulers, if they refused to submit to it; and, finally, to *pay* the murderers with "*indulgences*," (of which the Church is exclusive depository,) by the act of the spiritual head, the Pope!!!

The defence which the gentleman makes of his vain attack on the authenticity of the canon, is both awkward and uncandid. In the former speech he had said, "the best critics have regarded this canon as spurious, and an interpolation in the genuine acts of the council." Now, driven from this ground by my convicting testimony, he says, the canon "is composed of *five* chapters or sections;" "the second section is the portion of whose authenticity there is a doubt among critics." But in the former speech he had said, "this *canon* is regarded as spurious." This is therefore a CHANGE from *five sections* to only *one section !* But he goes on —"*and it was of this section, which is more* properly a chapter than a 'canon,' that I said it is regarded by critics as spurious." This, I regret to say, is false. He said expressly, that "the *canon was considered spurious;*" not merely this *one section*. The *whole five sections* make one canon. He said the *whole* was spurious; now he *denies* it: and confounding *section* with *canon*, tries to confuse the subject. He has finally, however, owned, that only one of five sections is *supposed* spurious. Then my remark returns—allow it so. It is not the "beginning," nor the "end;" yet he denies it is the "middle." It may be the "*blind side*," for aught I care. *But take it out*, and what remains? The *first section*, as he calls it, *denounces all heretics*, ordering them to be delivered to the secular powers; their goods to be confiscated, &c.: the *third section* (as divided by Caranza, though it is all *one canon*, and *chiefly on one great subject*) offers *indulgences, such as were given to crusaders to the Holy Land*, (WHICH WERE IMMENSE BLESSINGS,) FOR EXTERMINATING HERETICS; and the *first* denounced canonical vengeance against the bishops who should neglect to purge their territories of this heretical filth. And this is only what Caranza's *abridgment* gives—I have the *whole* before me. He has left out nearly *half*, and some of the *worst parts too;* such as that the whole country was to be *put under oath to inform on heretics;* and those refusing to swear, were to be *treated as heretics; depriving lawyers, judges, clerks, voters, heirs, &c. of their civil rights*. Now I ask, even if the second section *were spurious*, is there not here persecution enough forever to expose the spirit of the council, and of the church? The third section expressly rewards those' who *exterminate heretics*— (ad hæreticorum exterminium.) Yet, gentlemen, can you believe it, he denies "*that independent of this omitted section, we have the exterminating clause.*" He says "*I deny the truth of the assertion.*" This is to me inexplicable. I do from my heart pity the position of the gentleman. The gentleman charges me with quoting Labbeus falsely, thus, "Deest hic folium in codice Græco."—*This is a falsification of my citation*. I quoted it thus "Deest hic folium in codice Mazarino."—"A leaf is here wanting in the Mazarine manuscript." As the *leaf* was wanting in the Mazarine manuscript, of course, *all* it *contained was wanting*; and yet the gentleman would make me say, though the *leaf* was *wanting*, yet *half* the *leaf* was *not wanting*. `I said Labbeus followed that manuscript; yet the fact that he *also* gives the *Latin* of the canon, shows that he believed it to be genuine, though the *leaf* was wanting. The gentleman ought to have more sense, or more candour, than thus to quibble. This then is my "answer" to his most *profound* "question."

Again: in the last speech the gentleman said, "Collier (a Protestant) pronounces this canon spurious." I replied, it is not true; he only says, it is *wanting* (as above) in the Mazarine manuscript. Does the gentleman, in answer to this, *prove* what he had before said? No. He *begs* the question, and shuns all proof, saying, "This was one of Collier's reasons for *doubting* its authenticity." "*Doubting!*" But before it was, "pronounced it *spurious.*" The *nerves* crack, and give way, from *certainty* to *doubt*. Now I again pronounce it *false;* and if not, give us the *proof*. These are *specimens* of his "*host of witnesses;*" you may measure the *rest* by *them*.

As to Crabbe, history tells us he published editions of the councils in 1538, 1551, 1558. Du Pin and Matthew Paris were claimed by the gentleman against the authenticity of the third canon. But lo! when I adduce their *real testimony*, it is directly *against* him. All he says, in reply, is, if Matthew Paris represented the council as of various opinions and feelings about the *seventy canons, does that prove that they passed,* and that the *third* is *genuine?* Answer. Matthew Paris was cited by the gentleman to *prove* the canon *spurious.* I proved, from Matthew Paris, that all he really said, was that the council *murmured over* the whole seventy; and Du Pin (though quoted by Mr. Hughes as on his side) expressly says the council did not debate the canons, but passed them in *silence*, which was received as *approbation*.

Mr. President, I regret this tedious discussion. But it was called for—and will be useful. I will here say, that never in my life did I know so many literary frauds in so short a compass as this gentleman has practised. I blush, sir, to have to expose them. There is one article in the Confession of Faith which the gentleman ought by this time to *believe*, even if he should not *like* it. He will find it in the 25th Chap. 6th Section, which *identifies* the *man of sin.*

The smart play upon the word *"præsentibus"* will not pervert my meaning; which was, that it referred to the secular powers present, when and where the decree should be *executed*; and hence, "secular powers," or secular powers present, or on the *spot* if you please, meant, in that instance, the same thing.

The gentleman quotes the *names* (*not a word* of *their testimony*) of the Universities of Paris, Douay, Louvaire, &c. &c., to disprove the authorities I brought. But pray did not the gentleman in the same speech discard the opinions of whole tribes of commentators and bishops, &c.? He also *refers* to Pope Pius Sixth's rescript to the archbishops of Ireland in 1791; and sends us to the appendix of the work of William Sampson, Esq., "on the Catholic Question in America." But why not give us "at least *five* or *fifteen words*" of this *rescript on liberty*. What is it? We cannot take his opinion, or *ipse dixit*. If his *word* will do, then (as is usual at Rome) we may save much trouble; and settle the question by *authority*.

The gentleman seems not at all pleased with *Dens's Theology*. Yet he is a *standard writer;* and *now* he is of special value, in evidence, because the "Catholic" prelates of Ireland have *publicly endorsed him*. It was proved by unanswerable testimony, at the said meeting of *Protestants* in Exeter Hall, London, June 20th, 1885, that as early as A. D. 1808, "*at a meeting of* the Roman Catholic prelates of Ireland, it was unanimously agreed *that Dens's Complete Body of Theology was the best book on the subject of the doctrines and discipline of the Roman Catholic Church, as a secure standard for the guidance of those clergymen who had not access to libraries." The work is therefore full authority*. Now from this book I made ample (and they were surely startling) quotations in my last address. Has the gentleman denied that they were the *author's belief* of Catholic doctrine? Who is right? Mr. Hughes, or the learned Dens and the *prelates* of *six millions* of Catholics? I ask you, gentlemen, to review my citations from Dens, in the light of the above facts; and I beg leave here, by way of refreshing the subject, to say that Dens declares "*all Protestants, as Lutherans, Calvinists,* &c., *worse heretics than Jews and pagans; that baptism brings them in the power of the church,* (*for they allow our baptism to be valid,*) *and that it is the right and duty of the church to compel heretics, by corporeal punishments, to return to the faith, or if they will not, that confiscation of property, exile, imprisonment, and death, are to be denounced against them.*" And now I invite the gentleman's attention to the *contents* of the book, and the *proofs* of the *sanction* of it by the *prelates of Ireland*. That the gentleman should complain of my introducing *new proof* is strange, when he it was who vitiated the *report* of the stenographer; and who insisted on rewriting the entire debate, after his own plan; and who has *not* ceased to desert his old ground on many points, and to introduce new topics and new matter.

But I will introduce an *old* acquaintance. Joannes Devoti, having the Pope's imprimatur to his *Canonical Institutes;* a late oracle from Rome; and pledged to contain nothing contrary to sound faith and good morals.(1) "*Actius first attempted to take from the church all ecclesiastical jurisdiction and legislative power; and the Waldenses,* John Huss, *Marsilius Patavinus, Jandunus, Luther, Calvin, Grotius, have followed his errors, having falsely thought* that the church had no *jurisdiction,* but that *all her authority consisted* in *government and* PERSUASION. After their example, *all Protestants who maintain the right of the prince, in sacred things,* deny JUDICIAL POWER *to the church.* These, with Puffendorf, *contend that the church is not* A DISTINCT *republic* or *state,* as they say, but only a *collegium;* and *with Mosheim, Bohemer, Budæus, and others, deny to the church all judicial power;* and *thinking it to pertain to the right of majesty in the secular prince, attribute only a collegiate right to the church.* . . . *In the same mire sticks* (in eodem lato hæsitat) P. Laborde, who, in his small work entitled 'Principles concerning the Nature, Distinction, and Limits of the *Two Powers, Temporal and Spiritual,*' endeavours to undermine and take away the *power given by Christ to the church,* not merely of *government by councils and persuasion,* but also *of decreeing by laws, and of compulsion, and of coercing* with punishment those who are worthy of it, [cogendique, et pœna coercendi eos, qui pœna sunt digni;] and who *subjects* the *ecclesiastical* ministry in such a way to the *secular power,* as to insist that to *it* belongs the cognizance and jurisdiction of all external and sensible government. *Benedict* XIV., (Pope,) *condemned this depraved and pernicious treatise* in Const. ad Assiduas, 44., t. 4, &c. &c.; and the *like error* of Patavinus and Jandunus was *long before condemned* by John XXII., Const. licet juxta doctrinam." Here we have an *honest Roman!* He has no prevarication; but freely tells the whole truth, and brings the authority *ex cathedra* of two Pontiffs to sustain his doctrine of the *judicial* and *coercive power* of the church with penal sanctions. The incidental testimony in *behalf of Protestant opinions* in the case of Luther, Calvin, the Waldenses, Huss, and "*the Protestants,*" is very striking; and as much contradicts Mr. Hughes on *that side,* as his papal claims do on *the other.* Huss was condemned to the stake by the Council of Constance, for holding such doctrines as "That the papal dignity savors of *Cæsar;* and the institution and headship of the Pope was derived from *his power;*" "that the doctrine of *handing over to the civil arm* those who, after ecclesiastical censure, refused to retract, was like the *high priests, scribes,* and *pharisees,*

---

(1) Book III., tit 1, sec. 3. " *On the Judicial Power of the Church.*"

who delivered Jesus to Pilate, saying, it is *not lawful for us to put any man to death;* and those who handed over such persons were worse homicides than Pilate:" "that *excommunications, interdicts, &c.* degraded the laity, exalted the clergy, and prepared the way for Antichrist;" and the like. To these the author quoted above refers. *The converse of these is popery;* so Huss's *sentence declares,* and its *execution seals* it.

It is worthy of remark also, that the *doctrines* attributed by Devoti *to Protestants* in the previous extracts, though retaining a *taint of church and state,* are so far *below* the *claims* of popery, that *they* were denounced as pulling down the *rights* and *judicial power* of the church! How lofty, then, must her pretensions be! But we are not left to *conjecture.* The same author tells us,(1) "*that the church has of right the power to punish clergymen,* and *of herself inflicts on offenders lashes, fines, imprisonment, exile, and other punishments.*" Now, when we collect the testimony of Bossuet, and Dens, and the Rhemish annotators, and Du Pin, and Devoti, (and to name no more,) *the reigning Pope,* it is clear they all concur in the *doctrine* that the Catholic Church has a right to *punish temporally;* that she is *intolerant* of *false religions* or *heresies;* and that *all modern Protestants are such heretics.* If Mr. Hughes says, these are their *opinions,* we ask, is he *infallible?* Are not his too *opinions?* Shall we believe *him against* so many, and so able witnesses, on the other side? And besides, they bring abundant *proofs!* What shall we say in reply to *them?* Were they all *mistaken* in their *proofs?* Is Mr. Hughes wiser than all these? The answer is very simple. He that runs may read. *They* lived in Rome, France, Belgium, Ireland. HE LIVES IN THE UNITED STATES!

We have now given several decrees of "infallible councils," which directly prove that the *doctrines of the Roman Catholic religion are opposed to civil and religious liberty;* and we have given *abundant testimony from commentators, a multitude of Belgian bishops, and divers authors of successive ages, and various nations,* showing that the meaning attributed to these decrees by us, was the common and received sense of Catholic Europe for ages. Surely it were a singular *accident,* that they should all concur to *slander their own church!* Yet if Mr. Hughes be *right,* they do. Now, if he may cite modern universities, I may adduce *all those authorities,* with some claim to be proof in the case. And if Mr. Hughes expects his *declarations* to have *weight,* why discard their overwhelming testimony—when so many are against him, (including the now reigning Pope,) and when *they* were in circumstances so much better fitted to give an unbiassed and true statement?

Reserving other councils for future use, I proceed to obey the

(1) Lib. IV., tit. 1, sec. 10.

gentleman's call for a *bull of a pope* in which *presecution* is *taught*,—I cite the bull in *Cœna Domini*. Of this memorable bull the PARLIAMENT OF PARIS, in its proceedings, (*as extracted from its Registers*,) A. D. 1688, upon the Pope's bull on the franchises in the city of Rome, &c. &c., thus speaks:—"And to give some colour to so scandalous an innovation, he (the Pope) refers to that famous bull styled *In Cœna Domini*, because it is read at *Rome every Thursday of the holy week*. True it is, that if this decree, whereby the popes declare themselves SOVEREIGN MONARCHS OF THE WORLD, be *legitimate*, the *majesty royal* will then *depend on their humour;* ALL OUR LIBERTIES WILL BE ABOLISHED, the *secular judges will no longer have* the power to try the possession of benefices, nor the CIVIL AND CRIMINAL CAUSES OF ECCLESIASTICAL PERSONS, AND WE SHALL QUICKLY SEE OURSELVES BROUGHT UNDER THE YOKE OF THE INQUISITION." Here is a great nation's parliament—I suppose the gentleman will again call it *infidel;* yet it may be presumed to *know evils* which it so grievously *felt*. The bull is taken from the Bullarium of Laertius Cherubinus, Rome, 1638, tom. iii., p. 183, the sixty-third constitution of Paul V. "*The excommunication and anathematizing of all heretics &c. &c., which is wont to be published on Maunday Thursday*. As for almost all the chapters of this bull [besides the third Extrav. of Paul II., and the first Extrav. of Sixtus IV. in the title of Penance and Remissions] you have *them before ordained* in the first constitution of Urban V., f. 215; in the twenty-fifth constitution of Julius II., f. 482; in the tenth constitution of Paul III., f. 522; and in the eighty-first constitution of Gregory XIII., f. 348, lib. 2. Other bulls of this nature, called bulls in Cœna Domini, I have purposely omitted, (says the compiler,) being content with these; from which it may appear that the popes have made some variation in them—according to the exigency of the times. Yet I would not omit those which follow, as being especially necessary, and particularly published upon the several chapters of this bull. There is extant, therefore, in this collection, a particular edict of Nicholas III., about the first section of this bull, in the Second Constitution, sup. fol. 143. Concerning section second there is extant Constitution fifth of Pius II., f. 290, lib. 1. Concerning section fourth there is extant Constitution seventh of Pius V., f. 137, l. 2. Concerning section seventh is extant Constitution third of Nicholas V., f. 283, l. 1. Concerning section ten is extant a canon of Callistus in CXXIII., Constitution twenty-fourth, q. 3." And thus the compiler proceeds to fortify, by *twice* as many authorities as we have here *recited*, all the great *principles* of this infamous bull. He adduced the acts of not less than EIGHTEEN popes, and some of them again and again, to prove that it rests on cumulative, undisputed, infallible authority; and I recite these otherwise disgusting details, to show that an *army* of popes will meet Mr. Hughes at every step of his denials and evasions. Truly this is a *cluster* from the vine of Sodom and the grapes of Gomorrah!

Here follows some material parts of the document itself:—

"*Paul, bishop, servant of the servants of God, in perpetual memory of the thing now decreed.*"

The introductory paragraph tells the *faithful* that *the unity of the whole church doth flow from the "Roman Pontiff, who is Christ's vicar and St. Peter's successor:*"—That "*the Popes of Rome, his predecessors, on the day dedicated to the anniversary commemoration of our Lord's Supper, have been accustomed annually to exercise the spiritual sword of ecclesiastical discipline, and the wholesome weapons of justice, by the ministry of the supreme apostolate, and to the glory of God, and the salvation of souls.*"

Here it is proved that this was an annual service.

Sect. 1. "We excommunicate and anathematize, in the name of God Almighty, Father, Son, and Holy Ghost, and by the authority of the blessed apostles, Peter and Paul, and by our own, all *Hussites, Wickliffites, Lutherans, Zuinglians, Calvinists, Anabaptists, Trinitarians,* and *apostates from the Christian faith,* and *all heretics by whatsoever name they are called, or of whatsoever sect they be.* Also their adherents, receivers, favourers, and *generally any defenders of them; together with all who,* WITHOUT OUR AUTHORITY, (sine nostra auctoritate,) *and that of the Apostolic See, knowingly* READ, KEEP, PRINT, *or any way, for any cause whatever, publicly, or privately, on any pretext or colour,* DEFEND THEIR BOOKS CONTAINING HERESY, OT TREATING OF RELIGION, *as also schismatics,* and those WHO WITHDRAW THEMSELVES and RECEDE OBSTINATELY FROM THE OBEDIENCE OF US, or the Popes of Rome for the TIME BEING." Here surely *more* than "*the* wicked Albigenses" are meant! *All, all out* of the Roman Church are *cut off,* and *doomed to* eternal woe! And the liberty of *printing, reading, and even of thought itself, is levelled to the dust.*

The second section CURSES, as above, and interdicts "all universities, colleges, and chapters, by whatsoever name they may be called, who appeal from the orders and decrees of Popes to a General Council;" and CURSES also, "*all who favour or aid the appeal.*" This usurps the *empire of letters,* and forbids all appeals.

The third section goes to SEA, not content with ruling all LANDS, and curses "all pirates"—that is, who trouble "*our seas.*"

The fourth legislates against "*wreckers*" in *all seas. These* laws are good: but, who ever set *Peter* and his *successors* over the sea? Ah, I forget! *Peter* was a FISHERMAN! therefore, *all seas* are subject to *the Pope.*

Fifth. "Also we excommunicate and anathematize all who impose or augment any new *tolls*, or *gables*, (excise taxes,) in their dominions, except in cases permitted to them by law, or by special leave of the apostolic see, or who *impose* or *exact such taxes forbidden to be imposed or augmented.*" Here he takes the *key of the treasury into his own hands;* as before, he had grasped the TRIDENT, the *spiritual sword* and the *"keys of St. Peter."*

Seventh, CURSES all who furnish to "*Saracens, Turks,* and *other enemies and foes of the Christian religion*, or to those who are expressly and by name declared heretics," (*as Hussites, Lutherans, Calvinists*, &c. &c.) "by the *sentence of us or this holy see— horses, arms, iron, wire of iron*, tin, *steel*, *and all kinds of metal and warlike instruments, timber, hemp, ropes made as well of any other matter*," &c. &c. Here he becomes *Head of Hosts, and commissary-general to the holy war against all foreign and domestic foes;* for there were *domestic* as well as *foreign* crusades; and he expressly includes *"all heretics named by us."*

There are no less than THIRTY of these SECTIONS, in which this "*great hunter of men*" raves through the world and *lays* his curse and his claim on all the civil and religious rights of man—leaving not even a *grave* for *a heretic!*

We must select some *specimens*.

Section thirteen CURSES those who carry *spiritual* causes before *secular tribunals*, by appealing from the *Pope's letters*, "to LAY-POWER," even though the civil power should require it.

Fourteen, CURSES those who "by their own authority and *de facto*," "*take away the cognizance of tithes*, benefices," &c. and "*from ecclesiastical judges*," even though the person doing it "should be presidents of councils, chanceries, parliaments, chancellors, &c. of any secular princes, whether emperors, kings, dukes, or any other dignitary."

Fifteen, CURSES those *who draw*, or *cause to be drawn*, "*directly or indirectly, upon any pretence whatsoever, ecclesiastical persons*, (as Mr. Hughes,) *chapters*, CONVENTS, &c. &c. *before them to their tribunal, audience, chancery*, council or *parliament*, AGAINST THE RULES OF THE CANON LAW. Here, on the *authority of the canon law*, all ecclesiastical causes and persons are declared by the Pope to be *exempted* from *civil courts*, and *he* excommunicates and anathematizes all who *oppose his will!* Did Presbyterians ever make such demands?

The sixteenth *curses* those who *hinder* these *ecclesiastical judges* in their jurisdiction, and rests *their claims* on "*the canons and sacred ecclesiastical constitutions and decrees of general councils, especially that of Trent.*" Here is "*infallible*" proof!

Eighteenth, *curses all who* impose, (without permission of the Pope,) *even with the consent of the clergy, any taxes of any kind on the clergy of Rome or on the rents of churches, monasteries*, &c., and he renews against them the canons of the last Lateran, as well as *other general councils*, with the *censures and pu-*

nishments contained in them. Here is complete exemption of the clergy.

Twentieth, *curses* all who dare to interfere, in any way with *St. Peter's patrimony*, and the *lands, cities*, &c. SUBJECT TO THE JURISDICTION OF THE CHURCH OF ROME." *This is the heart of Italy*, and a *temporal* DOMINION *over millions of subjects, whose emperor, the Pope, is elected for life by cardinals! Is this not opposed to liberty?*

Twenty-first. *These acts, not to be recalled,* except by the Pope; (*he has never done it,*) and to *continue in force and be put in execution.* (They are now binding upon Mr. Hughes and every Catholic on earth.)

Twenty-sixth announces *their publication*, "that those whom these processes concern may pretend no excuse or allege ignorance."

Twenty-seventh ORDERS THEIR PUBLICATION, by *Patriarchs, Archbishops, Ordinaries,* and *Prelates, directly or by others, once every year, or oftener,* (semel in anno—aut etiam pluries,) "*if they see fit, when the greater part of the people shall be met for divine service*—AND TO THE FAITHFUL, THEY are to be told, declared, and kept before *their minds*."

Thirtieth. The wrath of Almighty God, and of Peter and Paul, is denounced against all who dare to oppose these EXCOMMUNICATIONS, CURSES, INTERDICTS, &c. &c. Such is this terrific system, sustained by the authority of a *crowd of Popes*, and resting its claims on *divine right*, as *expressed by constitutions, general councils,* and the *canon law*.

Well did the French Parliament call the Popes "THE DECLARED MONARCHS OF THE WORLD." These Popes now head one hundred and twenty millions of people! We may now understand one of their mottoes: URBIS ET ORBIS. "THE CITY AND THE WORLD." The mistress of the world. If this bull be not published in Rome or in America at this day, it is still UNREPEALED, and *still* in force and lying in the Vatican,

> "*Hushed in grim repose,*
> *Expects its evening prey.*"

Let the day come which will make it prudent to republish it, and the nations will again hear this *Monarch's voice,*

> With "*Ate by his side come hot from hell,*
> *Cry havoc, and let slip the dogs of war.*"

Before I close, a few things in the gentleman's reply must be briefly noticed.

In my last speech I quoted from the *index* of the *Acta Ecclesiæ* to show *how rife persecution* is in the Church of Rome, when the *heads of chapters* were thus HEDGED WITH DAMNATION of all sorts, *temporal, social, spiritual,* against heretics such as we. He answers it with a sneer and a mild extract from our standards, stating the *duty of Christians to marry Christians*. He has furnished, without intending it, a most striking *contrast* between the two *religions*, as any one may see, who will refer to the *quotations* from that *index*, given by me in the last speech.

He also attempts to fasten the ABOLITION ODIUM on Presbyterians. In the former Controversy,(1) when he supposed the public mind felt a *little differently* on this subject, he insulted the nation after the coarse and ribaldrous manner of Daniel O'Connell, and actually retailed one of *Garrison's* anecdotes, as follows: "But when you wish to pay a *compliment* to '*our memorable Declaration of Independence*,' were you not rather unfortunate in coupling it with an allusion to *slavery?* It reminds me of the *negro slave*, who, on his way to GEORGIA through Washington, shook his manacled hands *at the capitol*, and began to sing, 'Hail Columbia, happy land.'" But NOW, he says, "the consequences of this Presbyterian doctrine, (which I repeat is not the doctrine of Paul,) begin to be felt in the SOUTH as well as in the *North;* making the master a criminal against God for holding slaves, and the slaves criminal against God for submitting to the condition." Now, SLAVERY, AFRICAN SLAVERY, ORIGINATED (in this hemisphere) with a CATHOLIC, the GOOD LAS CASSAS; and in the 27th canon of the Third Lateran, heretics are doomed to "*slavery,*" if not "*exterminated;*" and now the papal champion *squints* at its *defence*. The Presbyterian Church has often publicly avowed the *doctrine*, that slavery is a great evil, and as such, to be mourned over and removed *so soon* as the *highest interests* of the respective parties will allow. But we do not approve the ferocious spirit and false doctrines of *modern abolitionists*, any more than the *slavery doctrines* of the Council of Lateran, Las Cassas, or in Bohemia, and the conquest of South America. (It is strange that *Garrison* and *Priest Hughes* are the *most violent* in their attacks on *Presbyterians*.) The following very recent declaration of the Synod of Philadelphia may serve to show our views on this whole subject:

"In this day of public excitement and fanatical excess, the Synod feel called upon to warn the churches against the agitators of the public mind, who, reckless of consequences, and desperate in spirit, are endangering the integrity of the American Union, and the unity of the Presbyterian Church, by the unchristian methods which they adopt to advance the cause of *abolition*. The Presbyterian Church, through her supreme judicature, and other bodies, has often and freely expressed her views of the evils of slavery. But at the present crisis, it is earnestly recommended

(1) Letter 19.

to all our people, to discountenance the revolutionary agitations and unrighteous plans and doctrines of the *self-styled* abolitionists, who it is firmly believed are retarding, more than all other causes combined, the progress of universal emancipation. If they succeed, they must rend the Church and the Union in twain, deluge the land in blood, and destroy the best hopes of the unhappy slaves. The Synod would be very far from even appearing to excuse the spirit of misrule and lawless violence which has been exhibited of late in almost every part of our beloved country. But when such a spirit is known to be rife and abroad in the land, the friends of Christ are called on in a special manner to shun the occasions of such excitements; and to sustain, by every proper available influence, the dominion of law and public order. We cannot forbear to add, that those who take advantage of such a crisis to agitate the land, assume a terrible responsibility for all the consequences; and the guilt of such a system is aggravated by the consideration, that it seems to be a part of the design to *produce* public *excesses*, and then *profit by them.*"

The above reference to slavery grew out of the gentleman's perversion of an important principle *before* asserted and *now* maintained by me. He had said in a former speech, "THAT THE DOCTRINES OF CATHOLICS LEAVE THEM PERFECT LIBERTY TO EXERCISE THEIR OWN DISCRETION ABOUT CIVIL LIBERTY." I replied that it was not so with *Presbyterians*. THEIR PRINCIPLES PLEDGED THEM TO BE FREE, and to HOLD TO THE EQUAL, UNIVERSAL, CIVIL, AND RELIGIOUS RIGHTS OF ALL OTHER MEN, DENOMINATIONS, AND PEOPLE; *and that the gospel is the charter of freedom to man.* With these doctrines our standards are *erect and replete.* But a papist may be a *tyrant* or *submit* to be ruled by *spiritual and temporal* tyrants without violating his doctrines. So says Mr. Hughes: "May exercise his own discretion." Hence, when I call on him to show *one doctrine against* oppression, or one *oppressive* decree or bull that has been *rescinded*, he is *dumb*. He cannot show one article in all his creed, councils, catechism, or bulls, that *tolerate*, any religion but his own, much less that asserts "all are *equally to be protected.*" Now, this is really giving up the question in debate.

Again. He says the creed of Pius IV., (which binds all Catholics,) in avowing that it *"receives all other things"* delivered, defined, and declared by the sacred canons and general councils," means only *"tenets of faith and morals."* But how obviously false! It is written *"cætera item omnia"*—"ALL OTHER THINGS;" not "tenets" merely, but *all other things*, delivered, defined, and declared by the *sacred canons.* I ask, is not the third canon of Fourth Lateran, and the twenty-seventh canon of Third Lateran, *a sacred canon?* and were they not *"delivered by general councils?"* And all the other *persecuting canons* are included in this *"reception."* This is made clear by the next clause : " *and I like-*

wise also condemn, reject, and anathematize all things contrary thereto, and all heresies whatsoever," &c. Here two ideas are presented : 1, ALL THINGS CONTRARY to the sacred canons and general councils are condemned *in general;* 2, and particularly *"all heresies."* If the gentleman reply, then some things *besides heresies* are here *condemned!* True ; and *some things* besides what the gentleman calls *"doctrines delivered"* are *here received; viz., discipline,* which *persecutes* and *forbids to tolerate any other religion;* and, *by the authority of God, requires that heretics shall be exterminated.* This is "RECEIVED;" and call it "doctrine" or *"discipline,"* to this Mr. Hughes is bound this night by a solemn oath, and denies it at the *risk* of papal displeasure. Between his religion, his conscience, and his country's Constitution, I do most sincerely pity him.

THE RHEMISH TESTAMENT. THEN HE ABJURES IT. But it had great favour in Europe. What he says "of the text," exposing the *American* publishers, is laughable. The history of the book (my copy is *European*) is this: When it was found that it was impossible to keep the people from *having "the text"* in English, the papists at Rheims, in 1584, got up a translation attended by the *horrid notes* of which I gave *some specimens.* No wonder the gentleman *recoils.* But the notes speak the *opinions* of very learned papists about Roman Catholic *doctrines.* And pray, did the Pope ever *condemn the notes?*

The gentleman says, "the law for their (the Albigenses) suppression did not even pretend to rest for its authority on *any doctrine of the Catholic Church, but upon the reward of confiscated lands, and promised indulgences."* 1. Who passed the *law?* Answer. The "infallible council!" 2. Who *confiscated* the lands ? The *" infallible council." Laymen,* in both cases, were *silent.* The Pope and clergy did it. 3. Who promised *"the reward of indulgences?"* The infallible council. " The power of granting indulgences has been bestowed by Christ upon his church." (1) *Indulgences take away the punishment* (in this world and in purgatory) *due for sins; they are to be granted for reasonable causes, out of the superabundant merits of Christ and his saints.* Here then, for the REASONABLE CAUSE of *butchering multitudes* of men, women and *children,* THE CHURCH OF ROME, as Mr. Hughes tells us, *"promised indulgences;"* and " on this the *law* for the supression of the Albigenses rested for its authority." Then it seems the church does *persecute!* and *pays* out of "the merits of Christ" for it ? Only CALL IT NOT A DOCTRINE! Oh! tell it not in Gath ! publish it not in the streets of Askelon!!!

The gentleman *denies* he charged me with *"fraudulently"* abridging the twenty-seventh canon of Third Lateran ! It is well he can yet blush ! But in the very last speech he twice uses the

(1) See 25 Sess. Counc. Trent.

same *term* as to Faber and my *poor self;* so that *he* makes me Faber's *fellow,* though he condemns me for putting our names in *juxtaposition.*

Let me ask the gentleman if, as he allows, (in the case of the Pope and Napoleon,) "*it be contrary to the Catholic religion to alter the civil constitution of the papal states, by which the Catholics had been exclusively recognised,*" to what *part of the Catholic religion* it *was contrary?* And is not that *part* which is *violated* by breaking down a church-establishment, *contrary to civil and religious liberty?* Let the gentleman reply. Here the Pope, the principle, and the priest, are all involved; and the discussion is brought to a very point!

At the close of the last address, I asked the gentleman a question, which I then predicted he would not answer. Even so it is, But I repeat it once more. "HAD THE MAJORITY IN ITALY, or SPAIN, A RIGHT TO ESTABLISH THE CATHOLIC RELIGION BY LAW?" We *now* expect an answer!

I close with a word as to his "retreating from" the last Controversy. When our *second limits expired,* he insisted on writing the *last letter,* as he had the *first.* On my return to the city I proposed to *renew* and *finish* the discussion. He declined. I went on *alone* for many weeks. I invited him to oral *debate. He declined.* I finished the *discussion in public assembly, calling for him.* He declined. I left a *standing* invitation for him in the newspapers, as he has heretofore told you. He *declined.* And *you,* gentlemen, know *how* he came to meet me here! And you also know, how *hard* it was to hold him to the point. And the *public will* know how much he has striven to shun the publication of the debate; by refusing the stenographer's report, "going to Mexico," &c. I think all this looks like *retreating:* or if the gentleman calls this *courage,* we see his *standard:* But I really wish to *encourage* him. I am glad he feels *bravely.* We shall like him all the better, if his heart be the heart of a *man.* For my own part, I wonder that he can look his countrymen in the face, and advocate the *principles* of the papal hierarchy. I should run away from the first onset. It requires a *good cause* to inspire a *firm purpose.* The *militia* captain who told his heart to his general, was a *resolute, brave* confessor, after the gentleman's own school. "*Sir,*" said he, "*if you were frightened half as much as I am, you would run away from the enemy.*"

"*Is the Roman Catholic Religion, in any or in all its principles or doctrines, opposed to civil or religious liberty?*"

NEGATIVE IV.—MR. HUGHES.

MR. PRESIDENT,—

WHENEVER a disputant becomes the judge in his own cause—whenever the advocate assumes the office of umpire—you may take it for granted that he, himself, has but little confidence in the quality of his arguments, or in the character of the evidence by which he supports them. I refer you to the speech which you have just heard, as a striking illustration of this remark. The tribunal at which we stand is that of public reason; it expects us *to furnish evidence* in the case; and the gentleman, instead of being a pleader at the bar, becomes an oracle on the bench, and dictates the sentence. He will save the public from the trouble of forming a judgment, and leave it only the easy task of admiring the man who is at once his own hero,—his own judge,—and his own trumpeter. From all which, I am inclined to infer, that the experience which he has already acquired, has hinted to him the necessity of usurping the ermine, and *anticipating* the sentence.

He had said that this Society had exposed the falsehoods of a communication to the Catholic Diary. For this he had no authority in fact, and consequently has failed to produce any proof. But he makes no apology.

With regard to the Council of Trent, I am content with the explanation I have given in my last speech. Where I was mistaken, I had the candour to acknowledge it; and consequently, to vindicate my personal integrity in the opinion of honourable men. The manner in which I was led into the mistake does no credit to my opponent. A different sentence had given rise to the dispute, and instead of defending the passage which he had *first* perverted, he tears seven words out of their connexion in another sentence, (containing above forty,) repeats the translation "the punishment which ought to be inflicted on penitents," and gives for the Latin of *this* translation "pœnam quam opportet pro illis pœnitentibus imponere." Out of these seven words, one (opportet) is a barbarism; and the whole, *as a translation of the words* "the punishment which ought to be inflicted on the penitents," is ungrammatical—nonsense. Its sense and grammar depended on its connexion with the whole sentence, out of which the gentleman was pleased to garble it, and in which it escaped my notice, when I looked over the canon the first time. The matter being explained, then, according to the facts, I make him a present of all the glory, which the whole affair, including my mistake, is calculated to reflect on him in the minds of scholars.

The meaning of the word "imponere," as used by the Council of Trent, is to be determined by the sense in which Catholics understand it. Of that sense the practice of the church is the best interpreter. According to this, "injungere pœnam" means to "enjoin penance;" and "imponere pœnam" means the same thing. The gentleman thought it would help his argument with the ignorant, to translate the word, "injungere," by "inflict." But even the Dictionary refused to sustain him. The other verb, "imponere," has *among its meanings* "to inflict," therefore it does *not* mean "to enjoin." This is his logic. But the Dictionary itself refutes him.

His statement respecting the difference between "pœnitentia," "penance," and "pœna," "punishment," shows that he requires instruction. "Sacramentum pœnitentia" is the form of expression used by theologians to designate "the sacrament of penance." In the administration of this sacrament, the priest exercises that ministry which Christ instituted, when he said, "Receive ye the Holy Ghost, whose sins you shall forgive they are forgiven," &c. But it is not enough that the priest should be invested with this power, the *penitent* must have the *proper dispositions*, to receive the benefit of this ministry. He must be sincerely sorry for having offended God; and firmly resolved, by the assistance of Divine grace, never to offend him more. This is called CONTRITION—the first and most essential disposition to receive the sacrament of penance. The next is CONFESSION of the sins he has committed. The third is SATISFACTION, and consists in repairing, (as far as *he* can,) the injury which he has done to his neighbour, and the offences he has committed against God. If he has wronged his neighbour, he must retract the calumny, and restore the ill-gotten goods, before he can receive the benefit of the sacrament. Now all this *third part*, or *condition*, is prescribed, or "enjoined" by the priest, and is expressed by "pœna" in Latin, by "penance" or "satisfaction" in English. Hence, in the quotation from the Council of Trent, "injungere pœnam," "imponere pœnam," means simply to "enjoin penance"—to "prescribe the satisfaction." Hence it sometimes happens, that *restitution* is made through the priest. It is a part of the "penance," "satisfaction" —"PŒNAM"—that is enjoined, as an *essential condition* of the forgiveness of sin. *This* the gentleman may call "inflicting punishment," if he chooses. It is a condition, however, entirely foreign to the process of Presbyterian regeneration; although it would not be amiss, if the saints, in their ways of righteousness, would sometimes look a little to the *past*, as well as the present, and the future. To require them to do so, as a necessary condition of

Divine forgiveness, might, indeed, be considered as "inflicting punishment," but it would not be "corporeal castigation," notwithstanding the assertion of their minister.

The gentleman flies to Devoti for the proof, which, notwithstanding his talent at both garbling and perverting, cannot be made out from the Council of Trent. I meet him in Devoti. His first reference is to "Vol. III. Book IV. § 21." I have examined the reference, though there is no "Book IV." to be found. Devoti's work is on canon law, comprising *civil* and *ecclesiastical jurisprudence*, as it existed in countries where the church and state were united. It is chiefly historical. He speaks of laws and usages; he traces them to their origin; he shows what punishments the church inflicted *by her own divine constitution*, as distinguished from those *which the state authorized* her to inflict on ecclesiastics, or others. To the state belonged the power by which the church was authorized to punish ecclesiastics, by imprisonment or otherwise. He refers to the constitutions of the empire, and the code of Theodosius, for the proof. The gentleman *must have seen this* in the note; and a disposition to avoid deceiving his readers, should have induced him to say so.

Every one, who has read even a moderate course of history, must be familiar with the fact, that during the Middle Ages ecclesiastical offenders were tried *not by civil* but by *ecclesiastical judges*. This was by the concession of the state. And the same principles which authorized the church *to try* clerics for offences, authorized it also *to punish them*, when guilty, by civil penalties. It is in connexion with this state of things that Devoti speaks of "prisons, exile, pecuniary fines, &c." as having been used by the church. The gentleman's knowledge of history must have been very imperfect, if he remained ignorant of all this until he saw it in Devoti.

But this is not the question. The question is, does the Catholic Church claim, by virtue of any tenet of faith or morals revealed by Almighty God, the right to inflict *physical punishment* on any one? Devoti settles this question in the very paragraph to which the gentleman referred. He states distinctly, in that paragraph—
"*Sed ecclesiasticæ coercitionis summus est gradus* EJECTIO *eorum, qui in religionem, vel in societatem peccarunt. Si quis religionem violare ausus fuerit crimine, schismati, hæresi, neque monitus redierit in bonam mentem, eum sive clericus, sive laicus sit, ecclesia* EJICIT A SACRIS, ET SOCIETATE CHRISTIANORUM, *propter potestatim, et officium quod habet in omnes Christianos curandi, regendique cuncta, quæ ad religionem pertinent.*" (1) "But the *highest grade of ecclesiastical coercion*, is the *expulsion of those who have offended against religion or society. If any one has dared to violate religion by crimes, schism, heresy, and hav-*

(1) Vol. III. p. 20, 21.

ing been admonished, does not return to a good mind, him the church casts forth from her sacred things, and from the society of Christians, whether he be a cleric or a lay person, by the power and office which she has in reference to all Christians, of guarding and governing all things appertaining to religion." Here, therefore, is Devoti stating that excommunication is the "highest grade" of "ecclesiastical coercion" in the church. With this means of coercion Christ invested her; any other means of coercion, with which her laws have been enforced, at any time, were exercised or sanctioned by the civil power of the state, for the time and place being, and were revocable at the will of the civil government. When the civil constitution of states exempted the clergy from civil jurisdiction, it did not mean that *their offences against the laws should go unpunished.* It placed the authority to punish them, at the disposal of their ecclesiastical superiors. Otherwise they might claim impunity in defiance of *both* the civil, and ecclesiastical, governments. They might plead their privileges, as *ecclesiastics*, at the civil tribunal—and their rights as subjects of the civil state, at the bar of their ecclesiastical judges. They might say to the state, "I am not subject to your jurisdiction;" and to the church, "you have no right to punish me." But the fact was, that the state, in relinquishing its jurisdiction, authorized their ecclesiastical superiors, in certain cases, to exercise over them, its own powers of civil punishment. The dishonesty of the gentleman's attempt, therefore, consists in his representing this as a doctrine of the Catholic Church, *when he had before his eyes,* and in the *same paragraph, the author's statements to the contrary.* I shall have occasion to speak again of this in the case of John Huss, of which there is so much misapprehension.

I now turn to another quotation from Devoti which the gentleman has produced, and the purport of which he has most shamefully attempted to pervert. It is Vol. III. tit. 1, § 3. "On the Judicial Power of the Church." (1)

All Catholics hold, as a doctrine, that the church, inasmuch as it is a visible society, is invested by its Divine author with all powers necessary for its own government; that it has jurisdiction over all its own members; that it has authority to make laws, and require obedience to them; that it has authority to judge in controversies; condemn new doctrines; cast out heretics by excommunication, and do all other things necessary to the purity of doctrine and unity of faith, by the exercise of those spiritual weapons which Jesus Christ bequeathed for her defence, preservation, and government. Devoti lays this down as the Catholic principle of church government. He shows, or assumes, that the church has this power from Jesus Christ, and not from the authority of men. He then speaks of those who *denied* that the church has this

(1) See his last speech.

power—generally all those, who, from the beginning of Christianity until now, had been *cast out* of the church.

In opposition to this Catholic principle, he places "*in the same mud*,"—"*in eodum luto*"—Luther, Calvin, the Waldenses, Huss, and a few others, who maintained that the church had "no jurisdiction," but that *all* her authority consisted in "direction and persuasion." "*After their example*," he adds, "*all the Protestants who admit* THE RIGHT OF THE PRINCE IN SACRED THINGS, *take from the church all judicial power.*" Here are the two antagonistic principles. The one asserting that Jesus Christ invested the church with the right to judge, make laws, require obedience to them in all *ecclesiastical or spiritual matters*, and by penalties of the same spiritual order, to enforce their observance. The other denying all "judiciary power to the church," and *ascribing it to the civil "magistrates"*—"those nursing fathers to the church," as the gentleman's Confession of Faith has it. The one asserting that there is a *spiritual power* in the church, for the coercion of those who violate its laws. The other maintaining that the ministers have a right to make laws, and that the magistrates are bound, or at least authorized, to enforce them. This is the origin of the two great ordinances of Presbyterianism—MINISTRY and MAGISTRACY—of which I shall have occasion to speak in the next question. The reader can judge which of these two principles is the most dangerous to civil and religious liberty—the Catholic, which teaches that in the church itself, resides all necessary authority, jurisdiction, legislative, and judicial power *for its own government*—and the Presbyterian, which places the *execution of ecclesiastical laws in the hands of the civil rulers*. This is precisely the point of view in which Devoti discusses the question—as one of principle. Of those who would convert the magistrates of the commonwealth into mere *constables of the church*, for the execution of its laws, he says they all "*stick in the same mud together.*" Why? Because, acknowledging that in their church there is no authority that could produce a sense of obligation in the consciences of men, they require nevertheless that the civil magistrate should be the executive of their church, to regulate those *consciences in accordance with their will.* I again refer the reader to the quotation from Devoti, for evidence that the gentleman has made as gross a perversion of a writer's meaning, as ever disgraced the annals of polemical disputation.

On the perversion of Bossuet, by translating the word "souffrance" "toleration," I must make a few remarks, although the matter does not affect the main question.

Bossuet sets out(1) by showing that *by the doctrine of Luther, Calvin, Melancthon and the Genevan Church, the prince has a*

---

(1) Histoire des Var., liv. x. § lvi.

right to use the sword against the enemies of the church. On this question, he says, there was no dispute between him and them. Calvin had reduced their doctrine to bloody practice, by putting Servetus and Gentilis to death. He then goes on to say, that this right of the prince was admitted by the Calvinist author, who had most bitterly accused the Catholic Church of cruelty. He says, that to deny this right, would be to paralyze the public power—and concludes, " de sorte qu'il n'y a point d'illusion plus dangereuse que de donner LA SOUFFRANCE pour une caractère de vraie eglise;" by which it would seem that the Calvinists, whilst *suffering under the operation of their own principles,* acting in the French government, would represent their *sufferings* as a mark of their being the true church. Bossuet takes this plea from them, by showing that the descendants of the cruel Calvin, and the professors of his intolerant creed, *could not avail themselves of it;* that, if it were a true mark, it would be in favour only of the " Socinians and Baptists," *who denied the magistrate's right* to punish offences against religion. Hence, he says, in the words following: " et je ne connois parmi les Chretiens que les Sociniens et les Anabaptistes qui s'opposent à cette doctrine."

He had just proved that there was no dispute between him and the Calvinists on the question of toleration; that *their doctrine* was clear, from their own books, and Calvin's Commentary, written in the blood of his victims. *They* could not assign " toleration" as a mark of their church, but they *might* have assigned their *sufferings.* So that the gentleman shows his ignorance of the French language, when he says that " SOUFFRANCE" in this place, means " toleration," and produces the very nonsense which he affects to avoid. If Bossuet vindicates the magistrate's right to employ the sword, he does it by virtue of doctrines held by those against whom he was writing. It was the " argumentum ad hominem." He told them " you teach that right, and therefore *you* cannot complain of its exercise by the government."

The gentleman then quotes and perverts another passage of Bossuet, to support his perversion of the word " SOUFFRANCE" in this. The reference is Six. Avert. sec. 115, tom. iv. p. 426. In this passage Bossuet speaks of toleration, and uses the French word proper to express it. He does not speak of it, however, in the sense in which it is understood in our discussion. He speaks of it in the sense in which TRUTH must ever be *intolerant.* The author was assigning the reasons why the Catholic Church was so much hated by the Protestant denominations, who had separated from her. He says that at the beginning they only desired that the church would abstain from condemning their doctrines. But she was intolerant; she condemned their heresies, and would not allow their authors to propagate them within the pale of her communion. It was in this sense that she would not tolerate them, just as the Synod of York, *to which the gentleman has thought proper to refer*, would not tolerate the Rev. Albert Barnes. And with equal truth may it be said, in the words of Bossuet, that the "holy severity and the holy delicacy" of the old school party "forbade such indulgence, or rather such softness." The Catholic Church could not admit heresy to be orthodox doctrine. She was the original depository of the truths of revelation; and when men oppose them, she brands their opinions, and will not allow truth and falsehood to coalesce within the pale of her communion. *In this sense*, she is as intolerant as truth. In this sense, Protestant denominations *may be more tolerant*, because their doctrines being matter of opinion all round, they are in perpetual dispute as to *what is true*, and *what false*. But to pervert this into an evidence that, according to Bossuet, the Catholic religion would not allow "*toleration*" to persons *separated* from her communion, is one of those bold and desperate attempts to deceive the public which merit the reprobation of every honest man. But I ascribe it to the gentleman's imperfect knowledge of the French.

The Catholic "marriage," as a *civil contract*, is every thing that the laws of the land require. As a religious rite, it is in *harmony with the gospel*. So it has always been.

The Belgian bishops may *quote canon law in favour of intolerance*, yet they, with one exception out of four, voted the appropriation of money for the support of the Protestant ministers and churches; a very certain proof that their religion does not make intolerance *an article of faith*. Can the gentleman show a parallel?

In my last speech I exposed the case of the Albigenses;—the nature of their doctrine; their crimes against church and state, and human nature itself;—the measures that were then, *justly* or *otherwise*, deemed necessary to be taken against them. At this day there is no state, Catholic or Protestant, that would not suppress them. To that speech I refer the reader. They had set public authority at defiance, by their violence, and public authority put them down by the same means. The gentleman says I only wished to decoy him away "from the exposure of popery." I know he is abler at abusing popery than at discussing points of history, and therefore I give him credit for his ingenuity. He knows his forte. According to his view, it would appear, that the Albigenses had *only* to profess that all human bodies were the creation of the devil, and then, under the protection of their heresy, commit what crimes they would. He wonders that I should assert the infallibility of the council, in condemning the doctrine, and deny that infallibility in denouncing the persons, of the Albigenses. This puzzles him. "What a strange picture!" he exclaims. "An *intermittent* infallibility!" The quack, because he is a quack, is deceived in the symptoms. The educated physician knows that there is nothing "intermittent" in the case. The Council of Trent decreed that the ground on which a duel had been fought should be forfeited. None but a quack would look for "infallibility" in any such decision. So it was with that of Lateran, in appointing civil penalties against the Albigenses. It depended on the civil government in which they lived, to make war on them, or not, as their interests might direct. It is an abuse of language—a contempt of history—to represent the case of the Albigenses as a *persecution for worshipping God according to the dictates of their conscience.*

The gentleman, unable to find, anywhere, persecution recognised as a doctrine of the Catholic Church, except in the calumnies of her enemies, or in the perversion of what may have been said by her friends, as Bossuet, calls on me, as last, to show a condemnation of that principle. He set out to prove the charge; and now he calls on me to prove that he cannot do it. I am prepared to do this; but, in the mean time, let him look for the evidence, in the doctrines of the Catholic Church, to support the calumny which he and his associates in the anti-Catholic crusade have uttered. Let him find one tenet of faith and morals in the whole creed of the Catholic Church which is opposed to civil and religious liberty, as we have defined them. Let him show from any bull of a pope or decree of a general council that any such tenet has been proposed to the belief of Catholics, and then he will prove his proposition—not before. But if he cannot do this, let him retire with that portion of shame which ought to cling to those who bear "false witness against their neighbours."

He may prove that Catholics persecuted. This is not the question. *Did they persecute in obedience to any tenet of doctrine held by their Church?* If they did, let the gentleman point out *that doctrine* which required them to persecute. He refers to the 27th canon of the Third Lateran, in the quotation which I convicted him, and Mr. Faber by his testimony, of garbling to make out their cause. He makes a jest of the circumstance. *In his mind*, garbling and exposure for it, are not associated with dishonour. He has neither the courage to deny the fact, nor the humility to explain how it happened. He says, that canon "dooms its victims to slavery." The words of the council refute him. After enumerating their crimes, it simply states, "liberum sit principibus hujusmodi homines subjicere servituti,"—"*let it permitted, or free, for princes to reduce such men to slavery.*" Will he say that to "doom them to slavery," and to "*leave it free* for princes to reduce them to slavery," is the same thing. If not, the gentleman is convicted of another instance of false testimony. He asks, was the canon ever repealed? I answer, that it become extinct, when the Albigenses ceased from their warfare on "VIRGINS AND WIDOWS, OLD AND YOUNG, *sex and age, and their destruction and desolation of every thing after the manner of pagans,*" as the canon asserts; and as Mr. Faber and the gentleman thought proper *not to assert*, whilst they professed to give the canon. It became extinct *then*—or else when princes *had reduced* "such men" to slavery. And being extinct, it was not susceptible of repeal.

I stated, that the object for which the Lateran Council was "especially" convened, was the condemnation of the Albigensian heresy. And because they condemned *other* heresies, he affects to discover contradiction. They defined the doctrine of transubstantiation, and the gentleman hints, that in this, they had a *prophetic* reference to the Protestants, who were to come into being some three hundred years afterwards. They even excommunicated, and anathematized *every heresy*, extolling itself against this holy, orthodox faith which they had before expounded. And the gentleman thinks, after all this trouble, it is hard that the Protestants should not be included in the canon against the Albigenses. But he cannot be gratified. He is puzzled equally to account for the fact, that the Albigenses had been so long borne with in the midst of Catholic Europe. And he accounts for it, by saying, that "as soon as they *dared*, the popes and councils did begin their persecution." One would suppose that they might have "dared," *when the Albigenses were few*, instead of waiting till they perpetrated such outrages. Besides, there never was a period when popes did not "dare" to proclaim and practise *every article of Catholic faith*. Of the character and doctrines of the Albigenses, I said only what contemporary writers mention; and if the gentleman can refute my authorities, I beg him not to withhold his knowledge, until the *last night* of the discussion. It is possible, that my corrected speech has been *sent to college*, and if so, we all understand why the answer to it has been postponed for the present. The assertion, that Du Pin was a Catholic, is not to be depended on. His private correspondence with Archbishop Wake of Canterbury, proves that he was quite ready to be a Protestant.

As to the section of the canon, which I said was spurious, the gentleman cannot involve me in a contradiction, except at the sacrifice of truth, about which (to return his expression of "regret") I am sorry that he seems to entertain but little scruple. I did say, "this canon," when, in strict *hair-splitting accuracy*, I should have said "this section of the canon." This I did in my subsequent speech; and because I did so, he charges me as having intended to designate under the words, "this canon," the whole five sections, considered as different sections, as being spurious. It is in this that he sacrifices truth. I have a right, at least, to know my own *meaning*.

It is, however, of no importance in which section of the canon "THE exterminating clause" may be found. The gentleman would have found it equally in the second, if I had said it was in the third, and *not* in the second.

He does not yet answer my question about the Mazarine copy.

Neither did I do injustice to his citation of the marginal note. He now admits, that the section referred to, was wanting in *both* languages of that manuscript. Yet his former assertion was, that Labbe followed the Latin; and the insinuation, that the leaf *had been torn out*, proves his meaning. Now, he settles the matter, "of course." "As the leaf was wanting in the Mazarine manuscript, of course, all it contained was wanting." What next? "And yet the gentleman would make me say, that though the leaf was wanting, yet half the leaf was not wanting." No, I did not make him say any such thing. But since Labbe states, that *both languages* are wanting in the Mazarine copy, I wish to know how Labbe could follow the *Latin* of that copy, as the. gentleman asserted? If we believe the gentleman, Labbe followed the text, which Labbe himself says, did not exist. The difficulty remains; and the gentleman, instead of agitating the "leaf," will do well to meet it fairly.

Let me humour the gentleman in regard to Collier. That historian does not "*say*," that this section is spurious; he only rejects it for want of *evidence* to prove that it was the authentic act of the council. This is all I want. Now, if it was not the authentic act, was it not, *ipso confesso*, spurious?

As to Du Pin and Matthew Paris, I proved, in my last speech, that even by the use made of them by the gentleman, they sustain all I said on their authority. Du Pin gave the Pope himself credit for making the whole seventy canons; and M. Paris says, they were "READ," and, as the gentleman affirms, "THE COUNCIL MURMURED OVER THEM." This is the gentleman's own admission. But to make them "the genuine acts of the council," they should have been *submitted for deliberation*—they should have been *approved*—they should have been *adopted*. So far from this, on hearing them "read," "the council murmured over them;" and therefore, says Mr. Breckinridge, they are the genuine acts of the council; and, because they "murmured over them," they were "bloody butchers." The gentleman's intellects must be bewildered, or he would not refute himself so palpably. Having granted me all that I contended for, and more than was sufficient to sustain my position, he says he "blushes for having had to expose them." He exposed himself, and his "blushes" become him.

My reference to the decision of the universities on the question in debate, was for those who wish to know the truth, and gain correct information. As its *citation* was more than my argument required, I have postponed it for the present. But I may give it entire hereafter.

The document which I am bound to admit as evidence of Catholic doctrine, is the decree of a General Council, or the bull of a Pope—setting it forth as a "tenet of faith or morals. revealed by Almighty God." Unless it come under this definition, it is not a doctrine of the Roman Catholic religion; and unless it be a doctrine of the Roman Catholic religion, *I am not bound to defend it.* Catholics are to be judged by their doctrines—in which they all agree; and not by the opinions of individuals—which must be different and contradictory, according to the *age*, the *country*, the *government*, &c., in which they lived. The "learned Dens" is one of these writers. And when the gentleman asks "who is right? Mr. Hughes, or the learned Dens," I answer, that, as regards persecution, Mr. Hughes is right in condemning, and Mr. Dens was wrong in approving it. I answer, secondly, that, as regards the doctrines of the Catholic religion, there is no disagreement between Mr. Hughes and the "learned Dens." Both are agreed—and *both* are right. Has the gentleman ever seen Dens's Theology? I imagine not. But the tories in England, the men who will not allow Presbyterians to receive the honours of the UNIVERSITIES, founded and endowed by Catholics: these men, in order to check the progress of free principles and popular rights, have returned to the stale expedient of crying "NO POPERY." The chorus had died away for some years, and, in order to renew it, there was a congregation of the "Fudge Family" at Exeter Hall —headed by Murtagh O'Sullivan, and Patrick Maghee, dee, dee, —appropriate instruments to do the dirty work of political bigotry, by the excitation of religious hatred. These men made speeches on the subject of Dens's Theology, and to those speeches the gentleman appears to be indebted for all he knows of that work. He says it was approved of by the Irish bishops. It may have been, so, so far as it treats of those "tenets of faith and morals which the Catholic Church holds as having been revealed by Almighty God;" *i. e.* so far as Catholic doctrine is concerned. That the opinions of the author, in support of persecution, were approved of by them is *utterly false.* For three hundred years, the Irish Catholics have been the *victims* of Protestant persecution; and neither they, nor their bishops, would, or could, or did approve of the sophistry by which Dens would recommend the cursed principle. The whole matter was this:—a bookseller had published it as a matter of pecuniary speculation; he laboured to make money by it; and the bishops made it the rule, not for the *decision*, but for the *order* of such subjects as the clergy had to discuss in their conferences. The gentleman came here to show "those tenets of faith and morals held by Catholics" which are opposed to "civil and religious liberty;" and to prove the existence of such *tenets* by the "bull of a Pope, or the decree of a General Council." This he cannot do. But he quotes a canon of a General Council in which *no doctrine* is proposed, but in which permission is given, encouragement is held forth, to the governments in which the Albigenses existed, to drive them from their territories respectively; not as persons *simply exercising the rights of conscience*, but as *public enemies*, who, by their excesses against the rights of others, had forfeited every claim to have their own respected. He has quoted the supposed opinions of Dens; and the spouters at Exeter Hall are his witnesses even for *their* existence. And his reasoning is, that since Dens held those opinions —therefore they are doctrines of the Catholic Church, and are binding on all Catholics; for it is their boast that their DOCTRINES never change!! The premises are false, and the conclusion is absurd. The gentleman, in quoting Dens, Bossuet, the Rhemish annotators, admits that they only give their *opinions*. But, he says, "are not their opinions as good as that of Mr. Hughes? Is Mr. Hughes *wiser* than all these? The answer is very simple. He that runs may read. *They* lived in Rome, France, Belgium, and Ireland. HE LIVES IN THE UNITED STATES." I thank him for the admission. *Then* he acknowledges, that, in accusing the *Catholics of the United States* of holding the same opinions which have been put forth by writers in Rome, France, Belgium, and Ireland, he, and his colleagues, have been bearing "false witness against their neighbour." He acknowledges that Mr. Hughes can be a Catholic in the United States, without holding the *opinions* of Mr. Dens. In other words, he acknowledges that the anti-Catholic crusaders, with whom he is associated, *first calumniate* the Catholics, by charging on them tenets which they do not hold; and then denounce them for doctrines which they disclaim, at least in "the United States." I thank him for his candour, though I do not believe it was intentional.

Let the gentleman show me one of those writers teaching persecution as a Catholic *tenet of faith or morals*. Now, Mr. Hughes states, that it is NOT a doctrine. By what Catholic writer, then, has Mr. Hughes been contradicted? By Bossuet? No. By Dens? No. By the Pope? No. By the Rhemish annotators? No. Not one of them has ever said that *persecution* IS *a doctrine of the Catholic Church!* But they advocated the principle. If they did, it was in their *own name*, and on *their own authority;* not by any requisition of their religion, as Catholics. If it were a doctrine, Mr. Hughes *dare not* deny it in the name of his Church. Such a denial would be heresy, and would entitle him to a seat in the Synod of York. If it were a DOCTRINE, the Catholic wife would have to make an act of contrition every evening, for not having poisoned her heretical husband, during the day; and those Catholics in France and other countries, *where they are able to do it*, would be living in a perpetual state of *mortal sin*, so long as they abstained from *killing their Protestant neighbours*. In a word, the doctrine would lead to the same consequences among Catholics, which it produced among Presbyterians; and like them, we too should be asking God's pardon for *the sin* of tolerating a false religion.

The gentleman has taken *suspicious* pains to make it appear, that the bull IN CŒNA DOMINI rests on "accumulative and infallible authority." A few facts will suffice to prove the contrary. In 1510 the Provincial Council of Tours *rejected this bull* in the name of the French nation.(1) And in 1773, Pope Clement XIV. suspended the publication of it.(2) It is still read, however, in Rome every Thursday in holy week, as it *had been* long before the Reformation, so called. Out of one single church in Rome, it has not been read for more than sixty years. Since, therefore, it has *been rejected* by Catholics, it follows, that its *rejection* was *not inconsistent* with the *doctrines of the Catholic religion*. And since it has been suspended by the Pope himself, it follows that, if it ever had any authority, it has none now. It is another instance to show on what grounds the calumniators of the Catholics are obliged to build.

That Pope Paul should excommunicate the heretics and heresies, that were just springing into being, during his pontificate, 1536, is nothing wonderful. The Synod of York, for a mere difference of opinion, suspended the Rev. Mr. Barnes in 1835. And the gentleman himself instigated the General Assembly at Pittsburg to excommunicate the "whole Catholic Church," which they did accordingly. The "bishops," at his instance, constructed an artificial Vatican in the Western city, and with artificial thunder, that reverberated along the surrounding hills and valleys, for a considerable distance, cut off from the communion of the "Christian Church" nearly two hundred millions of as good Christians as themselves. Had not the Pope, in 1536, as good a right to excommunicate the Calvinists, as the General Assembly, in 1835, had to excommunicate the whole Catholic world of present and past generations?

After enumerating, with double emphasis on the word *curses*, of which I shall speak presently, all the clauses which he deems most suited to his purpose in the bull In Cœna Domini, he is forced to admit that "*some*" are good. But most of them had reference to times, and customs, and laws, with which we are altogether unacquainted. The world has changed, and it is probable that, *at the period of their promulgation*, these clauses were not at variance with the civil laws of any country that could be affected by them. But, at all events, the document is, in the Catholic Church, of no kind of authority; the state of things, in which it might be even tolerable, having passed away from every civilized nation, Catholic as well Protestant, in the world.

Making allowance for the age in which they were passed—let us see, after all, whether those clauses are so full of mischief. I shall just follow the gentleman, and we shall see.

The 1st section denounces heretics; and it is not for a member of the Synod of York to find fault with *this*.

(1) Bergier, vol. I. p. 475. (2) Ibid.

The 2d section denounces those who, *to gain time for the propagation of heresy*, or schism, or any thing else that might injure religion, appeal to a future general council. Does the gentleman, himself an enemy to heresy, find fault with this?

The 3d section denounces all "pirates." Was this wrong?

The 4th section denounces all "wreckers;" and pray was it wrong for the Pope to come with all the influence of his authority to the aid of the shipwrecked mariner, on whatever coast he might be cast?

The 5th section denounces the authors of oppression by the *illegal* imposition of taxes. Was this very inhuman?

The 7th section denounces those who assisted the Saracens in their wars against the Christians. Was there any thing so very bad in this? The gentleman makes it put the Hussites, Lutherans, Calvinists, &c. in the same predicament as the Saracens. This part of the bull, however, had existed a few hundred years before there were any Calvinists.

The 8th section denounces those who should appeal to *secular tribunals*, in spiritual matters. Was this a great crime? especially as the time had not yet come, when, as the Presbyterian Confession of Faith has it, the "*magistrate had to provide, that whatever is done in Synods, be according to the mind of God.*"

The 14th section denounces those who should take the cognizance of ecclesiastical affairs from ecclesiastical judges, to whom it belonged by the laws of the state, *as then existing*. Was this so very unnatural?

The 15th section denounces those who should invade the personal immunities of the clergy, as *then* recognised, both by canon and civil law. Is there any thing so shocking in this?

The 18th section denounces the invaders of their immunities *in property*, as equally secured by general laws.

The 20th section denounces those who should invade the papal states.

The 21st section directs, that these acts shall not be recalled, except by the Pope. And the Pope *has* recalled them; and with this item of *additional* information, I hope the gentleman will sleep sound, and not be disturbed by any apprehensions of the bull "In Cœna Domini."

In following him, I have used the word "denounced," while he uses the word "CURSES." This suits *his* purpose better, because it conveys the idea IMPRECATION. As a Greek scholar, he *must know*, that the intrinsic force of the word "anathema" is not "imprecation;" and, as an ecclesiastic scholar, he *ought* to know, that in ecclesiastical usage, it has not that meaning.

But it follows, on the gentleman's view of the case, that the Pope was not, even in the *Middle Ages*, that omnipotent monarch, who, by the frown of his brow, could lay nations prostrate in the dust, that he might trample on them. On the contrary, he had no means, it appears, to defend his own immunities and those of the Church, but anathemas, or, as the gentleman will have it, "curses." Which shall we believe? Again; since the Presbyterians hold, that the Pope is anti-Christ, *they* ought to rejoice, that he has excommunicated them; and be satisfied, that the "curses" of anti-Christ will only help them on their way to heaven.

The gentleman misrepresents me, when he says, I wish to fasten the "ABOLITION ODIUM" on Presbyterians. His own exposé of *Presbyterian doctrine*, setting forth that on the "subject of liberty, there is no discretion," is the only thing in this discussion, that can fix that odium. According to his own statement of the doctrine, it follows, as a consequence, that both slave and master are involved in guilt; since there is "no discretion on the subject of liberty." The uncalled-for disclaimer of the Synod of York will not remove the "odium," which I have no wish to fasten.

Of Garrison's writings on the subject of slavery, I have never read a line; and Daniel O'Connell goes out of his sphere, as I conceive, whenever he touches on the subject. From all I have seen of his writings, he seems to be, on this point, an orthodox Presbyterian, believing, in the gentleman's own words, that where *liberty* is concerned, God has left "no discretion."

The effort, the last struggle of the gentleman's argument, shows the desperate condition to which he is reduced. I explained, in my last speech, the meaning of the creed of Pope Pius IV. Still, he contends, that if not by "doctrine," at least by "discipline," all Catholics are bound to kill and exterminate heretics wherever they meet them. Poor man! To this (for it amounts to this by *his construction*) he says, "*Mr. Hughes is* BOUND *this night by a* SOLEMN OATH, *and* DENIES IT *at the risk of papal displeasure.*" The Catholics, throughout the world, the gentleman has told you, amount to 120,000,000; and the Pope would be quite angry, if they did not subscribe the creed of Pius IV., just for the pleasure of committing perjury by living *in the perpetual violation of its doctrine and discipline.* He will be equally displeased, if, *after having sworn to it,* they do not *commit apostasy,* as well as *perjury,* by denying it, as "Mr. Hughes does this night."

I say nothing of his charging me with *perjury.* Coming from *any other,* I should resent it as an insult—but from him, it is precisely what I expected—I know him to be capable of. When the gentleman has so far forgotten himself as to use such language to an opponent whom he himself selected, he authorizes that opponent to consider him as having forfeited that moral attribute which is essentially connected with even the *power* to insult. I, therefore, present him with carte blanche. But the fact of his having used such language, will explain, more clearly still, my motive for shrinking from any "oral discussion" with a gentleman, whom I judged so well to be capable of using it.

He admits that the notes on the Rhemish Testament are only the opinions of "very learned papists"—but he asks whether the "pope ever condemned them?" I really cannot answer the question, as I am uncertain whether the pope ever saw them. It would keep the pope too busy to read *all* the "opinions" that may be uttered and published by 120,000,000 of men. The book in which he would record the "opinions" that he approved; and the other book in which he would record the "opinions" that he condemned, would be too large and unwieldy. And *if* he were to do so, the gentleman would be among the first to accuse him of tyrannizing over, not only the "doctrines of the church," but the "opinions" of men. He must underrate the common sense of the audience and the public, when he asks such questions.

He has found out that "*indulgences take away the punishment (in this world and in purgatory) due for sins, they are to be granted for reasonable causes, out of the superabundant merits of Christ and his saints.*" This he has discovered in the Council of Trent. I am glad that he has lived long enough to prove, *with his own pen*, that when, in the recent controversy, *he* stated that "INDULGENCES WERE A BUNDLE OF LICENSES TO COMMIT SIN," he was deceiving the public by his testimony. He finds now that they are NOT licenses to commit sin, but simply the "taking away of *temporal punishment due* for sins" committed. He finds that they must be granted for "JUST CAUSES."

And now, for the use he makes of this discovery. Inasmuch as indulgences were offered to those who should aid in suppressing the Albigenses, he infers that the third canon of the Fourth Council of Lateran rested on the "doctrine of indulgences." This is his *last* resource for a doctrine to support it. Well, let us see how his argument will stand. "*Indulgences are the taking away of temporal punishment due for sins, and must be granted for reasonable causes.*" *Therefore*, Catholics hold the third canon of the Fourth Council of Lateran as a tenet revealed by Almighty God. This logic will not do. But then, the suppression of the Albigenses, provided for in the canon, *was deemed a sufficient*, "reasonable cause," for granting indulgences—*therefore* the canon, *going before*, was founded on the indulgences that were to come after. This will not do either. If, as historians write, the Albigenses were the destroyers of churches and monasteries—persons "WHO SPARED NEITHER SEX NOR AGE, NEITHER VIRGINS NOR WIDOWS;" those who risked their lives in *defence of these*, might be considered as furnishing "reasonable cause" for the application of indulgences. If, on the other hand, the Albigenses were those innocent lambs which the gentleman has promised to make them appear—then, it was an ABUSE of the doctrine to grant or promise an indulgence for their immolation. But in neither case can the doctrine be brought to sustain the canon.

The gentleman, copying after Faber, *suppressed* the middle of the twenty-seventh canon of the Third Lateran, and brought the other portions together, *as if nothing had been omitted*. This he calls "abridging." In speaking of it, I gave *him* the merit of a copyist, and on that ground excused him of "fraud,"—but not of culpable ignorance—considering his office. Rather than acknowledge that he had been deceived *by copying*, he stated that, "*Faber had quoted it as he had.*" On which I hinted to him that *he seemed to be ambitious of a partnership in the* "fraud" with which Faber is chargeable—for in *him* it could not have been ignorance.

The gentleman enumerates the efforts by which he endeavoured to engage me in controversy; to all of which the same monotonous result is ascribed. "He declined. He declined. He declined." I am not sorry that he should *boast*, except always where he goes beyond the facts. For, whilst it pleads my apology for the freedom with which I shall have to speak of Presbyterian doctrines; it will show, on the other hand, his want of title to that sympathy which he would otherwise claim for his suffering "in the great cause," if I should make a whip of his ecclesiastical ignorance, to chastise his anti-popery zeal withal. One thing I promise, however, that the gentleman himself, personally, shall but seldom engage my attention. As a gentleman he has entitled himself to impunity.

Finally, he asks me *my opinion* about the right of "THE MAJORITY IN SPAIN, OR ITALY, TO ESTABLISH THE CATHOLIC RELIGION BY LAW." I answer that, *in my opinion*, if the majority in Italy and Spain, by doing so, violated *no civil or religious right of the minority*, they had, *in that case*, the *right* to "establish the Catholic religion by law." But if, in order to establish it, they violated *any right, sacred* or *civil*, of the minority, then, in that case, they had *no* right to "establish the Catholic religion by law." They had no right to do evil, that good might come.

And now, having answered his question, I ask in turn, WHETHER HIS RELIGIOUS FOREFATHERS, IN SCOTLAND, WHILST YET A MINORITY, ARE TO BE BLAMED FOR PULLING ALTARS, IMAGES, AND OTHER MONUMENTS OF IDOLATRY, FROM PLACES OF PUBLIC WORSHIP AT THE REFORMATION? "We now expect an answer."

The gentleman has quoted some of the *doctrines* of John Huss, and especially on the subject of handing heretics over to the civil arm for corporal punishment. It is a little unfortunate for his argument, however, that Huss himself was an *advocate* for the corporal punishment of heretics; and this too, whilst he himself was under the imputation of heresy. Connected with the case of

Huss, is the supposed evidence on which Mr. Wesley constructed his famous syllogism, to prove that Catholics ought not to be tolerated among even "Turks or Pagans." The Rev. Mr. Nightingale, a Protestant clergyman, says, that Mr. Wesley wrote under "a mistaken impression;" and that if he were living "*at this time*," he would use his talents and influence in favour of "the cause of liberty and justice;" that "no man was ever more ready to acknowledge an error, of which he was once convinced, than was Mr. Wesley." I subscribe freely to these observations in favour of Mr. Wesley's sincerity and candour—at the same time I shall proceed to show that he was under a "mistaken impression."

His argument, in his letter of January 12, 1780, proclaims it as a "*Roman Catholic maxim, established not by private men, but by a public council, that 'no faith is to be kept with heretics.' This has been openly avowed by the Council of Constance, but it has never been openly disclaimed . . . . . . Therefore they (Catholics) ought not to be tolerated by any government, Protestant, Mohammedan, or Pagan.*" The whole of this argument depends on the *fact*, whether or not the Council of Constance "publicly avowed the maxim" ascribed to it by Mr. Wesley. If it did NOT, then it was impossible to "*recall*" what it had never published. If it did NOT—then, under a "mistaken impression," Wesley, too, has borne "false witness against his neighbour."

Mr. Wesley is dead—but Mr. Breckinridge has adopted his assertion; and I call on Mr. Breckinridge, here present, to show, in the acts of the Council of Constance, *now open before us on the table*, the "*maxim avowed* 'that no faith is to be kept with heretics.'" If *he cannot*, I call on him, as he professes to *hate a falsehood*, to aid me in denouncing the CALUMNY. There is no retreat. HE shall not have the plea, in his biography, that he wrote under "a mistaken impression." Here are the *original documents*.

A few words will be sufficient to explain the supposed foundation of this *cruel* slander. In the nineteenth session of the Council of Constance, it is laid down, that the spiritual authority of the church, being of Divine origin, cannot be *impeded*, or *hindered*, by *any safe-conduct* of any *prince, emperor, king*, or *secular power* whatever, from the just exercise of its function, in *condemning the errors of those who are subject to its jurisdiction*. It asserted the right of the church to judge of heresies or errors that might corrupt the purity of the faith, in despite of *all the safe-conducts that might be given by all the princes in the world*. It asserted this right and jurisdiction, even where the culprit depended on his safe-conduct in such a manner as that he would not have come to the place of judgment without it. It asserted that princes had no authority to give a safe-conduct which would *trench on the judiciary powers of the spiritual tribunal,* over which princes, as such, have no control. And finally, that supposing they did give such a safe-conduct, it could not bind them, only to the extent of *civil jurisdiction,* beyond which no-safe-conduct can be admitted as of any effect. Otherwise a heretic might appear before the council, argue his case, propagate his errors, and laugh at his spiritual judges, because he had a safe-conduct from the civil government. Let us make the illustration.

Supposing the Rev. Mr. Barnes, at the Synod of York, had pleaded, in bar of his suspension, that he had a *safe-conduct* from the governor of the state, promising that he should return to his congregation as he left them. What would Father Green and the "bishops" say? They would say, "*Sir, no safe-conduct can take from Synod the power to judge and punish you for heresy, in your notes on the Romans.* But suppose the governor were to appear, and say, "I have promised to see that Mr. Barnes shall return to his congregation *unsuspended,* and *uncondemned.*" They would tell him, that, as to civil rights, he might protect him as the laws directed, but if he promised to *prevent Synod from suspending* Mr. Barnes, the obligation was *unlawful,* and he was not obliged to fulfil it—inasmuch as it was out of his power. And supposing that, on this decision, we should build an argument to prove that "it is a Presbyterian maxim, established not by private men, but by the Synod of York, that 'no faith is to be kept with heretics,' and that, *therefore,* Presbyterians ought not to be tolerated by any government, Catholic, Mohammedan, or Pagan;" what would the gentleman say?

To prove that I have fairly stated the case, and fairly established the parallel, I shall quote the original in the words of the council.

"Præsens sancta synodus ex quovis salvo conductu per imperatorem, reges et alios seculi principes hæreticis, vel de hæresi diffamatis, putantes eosdem sic à suis erroribus revocare, quocunque vinculo se astrinxerint, concesso, nullum fidei Catholicæ vel jurisdictioni ecclesiasticæ præjudicium generari, vel impedimentum præstari posse, seu debere declarat, quo minus, dicto salvo conductu non obstante, liceat judici competenti ecclesiastico de hujusmodi personarum erroribus inquirere, et aliàs contra eos debite procedere, eosdemque punire, quantum justitia suadebit, si suos errores revocare pertinaciter recusaverint, etiam si de salvo conductu confisi, ad locum venerint judicii, aliàs non venturi; nec sic promittentem, cum aliàs fecerit quod in ipso est, ex hoc in aliquo remansisse obligatum."(1)

(1) Acta Cenc. Const., Sess. XIX.

TRANSLATION.

"*The present sacred synod declares, that, out of any safe-conduct whatever, granted to heretics or persons accused of heresy by the emperor, kings, or secular princes, by whatever tie they may have bound themselves, thinking thus to recall those persons from their errors, no prejudice to Catholic faith can or ought to arise, nor any obstacle be thrown in the way of ecclesiastical jurisdiction, by which it might be less lawful for the competent and ecclesiastical judge, notwithstanding said safe-conduct, to inquire into the errors of such persons, and otherwise proceed against them, and punish them, as justice shall direct, if they obstinately refuse to retract their errors—even though they come to the place of judgment, trusting to their safe-conduct, and otherwise would not have come: nor is he who makes the promise, when he has done what is in his power to do, bound by any further obligation.*"

I call upon the gentleman now, either to say that the "maxim" that "no faith is to be kept with heretics," is avowed in this passage, or that it is not. If it is, let him tell in which part of it. He has both languages before him. Let him quote from either. If it is not, (as is manifest to every Latin reader,) then let him, as an *honest man,* denounce the CALUMNY, as a false and wicked charge, and let him undeceive the American people so far as he has contributed to lead them astray by aiding in its propagation. But no retreat—no shuffling.

But did not, it will be asked by Protestants, the Council of Constance burn Huss, at the stake? *No.* Did it not *solicit* that he should be burned? *No.* But did it not condemn him as a heretic? *Yes;* and it had, at least, as much right to do so as the Synod of York had to condemn Mr. Barnes, as a heretic. But did it not "hand him over to the civil power?" It degraded him from his office as a priest, which it has a right to do, when he had rendered himself unworthy of that character by his anti-Catholic doctrines of heresy and sedition. How, then, came he to be burned? *The civil law of the country contained the barbarous enactment which authorized it.* By condemning Huss as a heretic, the church or council necessarily exposed him to the law of the state. But by *not* condemning him the council would have been under the necessity of APPROVING HERETICAL DOCTRINES. Now, the church could not allow Huss to preach heresy in *her name,* as a Catholic priest, for any consideration that might follow his suspension and excommunication, more than the Synod of York could allow Mr. Barnes to continue to preach heresy in the name of the Presbyterian Church, on the ground that the *loss of his salary* and *the suffering of his character,* might be the consequence of his suspension.

That Huss maintained heretical and seditious doctrines the gentleman himself will allow. One of his doctrines condemned in the council, was, that the "*authority* of the magistrate, prelate, or bishop is NULL, when he is in mortal sin."

Going to the council, Huss proclaimed his *willingness*, in case of conviction, to "*submit to all the pains of heretics.*" He knew by the laws of the land what they were. He had *appealed to the council*, and desired to be tried by it. He had obtained his safe-conduct from the emperor, *as going to the council*, only. And yet almost all Protestants, deceived by their writers and ministers, assert that the emperor had bound himself to bring him safe back. I call upon Mr. Breckinridge to meet me in this question; and *if he denies one single statement made by me in relation to it, I promise to furnish the evidence on the most indisputable authority.* But let him state his argument, and refer to something better than *popular prejudice* for his proof. The people will find out how their credulity has been imposed on, in relation to these matters.

It is not at all improbable that he will assert, or at least *insinuate*, that Mr. Hughes is an apologist for the Council of Constance, and of course approves of the burning of a heretic. The council will require no apologist; it did only what it had a right to do; and what is ascribed to it, *over and above*, is properly to be charged to the CALUMNIES *of political or religious enmity to Catholics.* As to the burning of Huss, as a Christian, a Catholic and a man, I reprobate the *barbarous and inhuman statute* of which it was the execution. But to make the church accountable, either for the *existence* of that law, or for *its execution*, is as false in history, and as absurd in reasoning, as to make it accountable for not having invented printing in the tenth century.

Another of the stereotype CALUMNIES which the gentleman and his associates, in the present crusade against the Catholics, labour to make as immortal as truth, is, that the Inquisition is a part of the Catholic religion. And whilst, with affected scrupulosity of conscience, they call our religion "POPERY," they become polite in their libellings of it, and say the "HOLY CATHOLIC INQUISITION."

I do not mean to enter into defence of the Inquisition; and none can have a deeper abhorrence of the cruelties, real or supposed, of which it was made the instrument. But I mean to show that Protestants are, for the most part, perfectly deceived in relation to it. They suppose that it is, or was, a part of the Catholic religion. In this they are DECEIVED. First, because it was unknown during the first twelve hundred years of the church. Secondly, because in very many *Catholic* countries it never existed. Of these, it will be sufficient to mention England, the kingdom of Naples, in Italy, and France, where an attempt was made to establish it, but without any lasting success. In Spain it was what the *civil government* made it. In no place did it exist except by the permission, often at the request, of the civil government. Those Catholic nations that rejected it, were as sound in their faith as the others that admitted it. Therefore, it was no part of the Catholic religion. The representative of the calumnies, that have been uttered against Catholics in relation to the Inquisition, is here present, and let him show from history that I have here made one single statement that is not true. If he does attempt it, I pledge myself to refute his argument. But if he does *not*, then let him aid me in denouncing the first great CALUMNY which he has helped to circulate, viz. that the Inquisition is a part of the Catholic religion.

The next great calumny which he has aided in circulating, is, that there are dungeons of, or for, the Inquisition under the Catholic Churches in this country; thereby exposing them to share the fate of the Convent at Boston. Now the fact is, and it argues great ignorance not to know it, that, at this day, out of the city of Rome the Inquisition does not exist either in fact or in name—either civilly or ecclesiastically—in any country under the sun. Does he deny this? Then let him point to the spot on the map of the world where it does exist.

And now I propose to show that, apart from the form given to it by the state, the substance of the Inquisition exists in every Protestant denomination. The word inquisition is derived from the duty of *inquiring* into the real or supposed errors which might corrupt the true faith. Thus when Mr. Barnes appended Notes to the Romans, Dr. Judkin became his accuser, and his Presbytery constituted the tribunal of INQUISITION—*to inquire* whether these things are so. This tribunal decided in the negative; but a higher tribunal of INQUISITION reversed the decision. The gentleman himself was one of the inquisitors. In this sense, all clergymen of all denominations, that hold tenets of doctrine, a denial of which *they* regard as *heresy*, are by office and profession inquisitors. The gentleman will not, *so far*, deny one word of this. Where, then, is the difference, *in principle*, between the Catholic and the Protestant Inquisition? So far as the *inquiry into errors*, and *condemnation of heresies* is concerned, it is common to both; and in principle, there is not a particle of difference.

The gentleman may tell me that, here there are no *civil penalties attaching* to the crime of heresy. True. But would this have been the case in Scotland, Holland, or Geneva? Thanks to the liberality of the age, and the freedom of our institutions, the inquisitors of *all denominations* are circumscribed within their proper sphere. *Here* men may be heretics, without kissing the stake that Calvin fixed for Servetus, or going through the ordeal of a Spanish auto de fe. There are heresy-hunters in every denomination that has a creed which *they call orthodox;* but it is to be hoped that the times have gone, forever, when there can be found *heretic-burners* in any.

The appointment of inquisitors, *as a special and distinct office*, was, if any thing, an encroachment on the inherent prerogatives of the episcopacy, whose special office it was and is to watch over the purity of the faith. As an ecclesiastical tribunal, their office was to inquire after heresy, and to judge whether those who were accused of it, were guilty, or not guilty. When they had done this, the power which their office gave them, *so far as it was derived from the Church*, was at an end. Now here is a statement that will startle the *victims of the delusion* which the gentleman has laboured to perpetuate, touching the "Holy Catholic Inquisition." But I make it, in order to bring him to the proof. He must not say that he *can prove* it, and yet withhold the testimony.

If, therefore, the ecclesiastical authority terminated at the same point, to which it extends in all denominations, even in this age, and in this country; if it neither *exacted*, nor *required*, nor *enjoined* any penalty in life or property, I ask him, is it CHRISTIAN, is it JUST, is it TRUE, or rather, is it not SHAMEFULLY *calumnious*, to charge on the *Catholic religion* the punishments which the CIVIL LAWS of Spain and Portugal had enacted against those who should be found guilty by the tribunal of the Inquisition. Let the gentleman not mistake the question. Let him not undertake to prove what I do not deny, but what I *do* deny.

Of all the blood that ever was, or was supposed to have been shed, let him show that the Catholic religion, or the authority of the Church, ever *expected*, or *required*, or *enjoined*, that so much as one drop should be shed for the *crime of heresy*. If he cannot, how will he stand before the American public, whom he has so much contributed to deceive? If he cannot, how will he answer to God, who is the source and *lover of truth;* and who rejects the aid which men think to render to *his* cause, by the employment of CALUMNY and "false witness against their neighbour."

"But the Church could have prevented it." Neither is that so clear. The Church had no jurisdiction to establish civil laws in France, and just as little to annul them in Spain. She judged of heresy as a crime before God; and so Presbyterians, as well as Catholics, regard it. When she had condemned it *as such*, her jurisdiction terminated. The civil laws of nations claimed the right to determine offences, and assign their punishment, and this, not as Catholics, but as *nations* exercising the rights of *national sovereignty*. Hence the Inquisition which was adopted in Catholic Spain, was rejected by Catholic France, on the ground that it would be consistent with the welfare of *neither* the church, *nor* the state. Neither was it established in the kingdom of Naples, because the Pope and King could not agree as to which should have the right to appoint the Inquisitor-General, and as neither would yield to the other, the Inquisition was never established in that kingdom. Will the gentleman contradict any of these facts? If he does, I shall cite the authorities to convince him and the public, how little he has read of the *true* history of the Inquisition.

"*Is the Roman Catholic Religion, in any or all its principles or doctrines, opposed to civil or religious liberty?*"

AFFIRMATIVE V.—MR. BRECKINRIDGE.

MR. PRESIDENT:—It ill becomes me to retort Mr. H.'s vulgar and unchristian assaults; for the sacred Scriptures forbid us to "*render railing for railing.*" The low abuse and indecent personalities of the *gentleman*, if I can consent to call him so any longer, reflect most unhappily on his spirit and his origin, and confirm, what I have long known, that he is *really ignorant* of what gentlemen owe to each other and to themselves.

I consider this a sufficient answer (and more than he deserves) to all his scurrility. Poor St. John's! It has set up for the fashionable and the refined world who wished to go to *heaven* without the trouble of being *holy*; and the priest at the altar was supposed by some to have sprung from a band-box. As for breeding, they would have found a real gentleman in the Rev. Charles Constantine Pise. As it is, (if any of that people venture on the *mala prohibita* of a controversy with heretics, or if, like the devouter papists, they read Mr. Hughes's argument alone,) I am sure they will find in his last speech that his breeding is *skin-deep*, and it is only *want of resolution* that keeps him from the frequent and free use of the ecclesiastical shillelagh. After all the gentleman's struggles about "the Latin of the Council of Trent," it ends in Mr. Hughes's *conviction* and uncandid confession of a flat misstatement! As to *my bad* Latin, I gave the *Latin* of the holy *fathers*, and gave in full the member of the sentence which the discussion called for; and he now makes the presence of a *superfluous word*, in that member, an apology for daring to charge me with "fabricating" and "forging" Latin for the Council of Trent, and then saying "what will be the reader's disgust," &c. &c. If I had left *out* that word, then he would have charged me with *criminal omissions affecting the sense.*

If this were a *solitary* misstatement of the gentleman, or if, being the repetition of the offence, he had with Christian candour acknowledged it, I should have said no more about it, for I do from my heart pity him. But you remember, gentlemen, that during the debate he produced Caranza, and represented me as having said that *a certain passage was in Caranza*, and told us that it was NOT in Caranza, and gloried in the apparent triumph over my character! When lo! on my turning to my letter in the former Controversy, (on which he charged the falsehood,) I *found* and *proved* before the *whole society*, that he had utterly falsified my letter, that I had distinctly declared that Caranza *omitted the passage!* And how did he excuse himself? By saying that when he *first asserted it, I had been silent*, and therefore he thought it true and admitted by me. But does the *silence* of a slandered man make the *slander true?* And pray, *why did he* say it the *first time?* Does one falsehood excuse *two?* I refer you also to his treatment of Mosheim, which made a shiver of involuntary horror run like a wave over this assembly when it was first exposed.

As to the "*infliction of punishment*" in the sacrament of penance if (as he says) "*satisfaction consists* in repairing (as far as he can) the injury which he (the penitent) has done to his neighbour," I would say that it is high time for him to seek a confessor himself, and recall his *slanders*, and confess his *false statements* in this debate. I do not wonder that he ridicules the doctrines of "*regeneration,*" which even the dark mind of Nicodemus, amidst his *marvel* at its mysterious character, durst not despise. When we come to show that "*immorality* is *necessary* to the *very nature of papal penance,*" we shall also prove that "*indulgences are a bundle of licenses to commit sin;*" as we have in the last speech showed, without *any reply* but a *denial* from the gentleman, that *punishment* is *supposed* in penance, and that *corporeal punishment* is *often* included. Sometimes, it is perhaps walking *barefoot*, at an *early hour before St. John's;* sometimes, it is to *pray* for a *long time*, each day, for many days, (for *prayer* is a great punishment to some people;) sometimes, self-castigation; sometimes, walking on the knees so many times around a *holy well*, or *idol*, or *altar;* or it may be *pecuniary fines*, (these are precious to priests,) or exile, or imprisonment in the dungeons of the monastery. It is from this very word, and this very use of it, that our term *penitentiary* is derived.

It is pleasant to me, though vain for the gentleman, that he has at length *attempted* to look at the testimony of *Devoti*. He tells us gravely, that Devoti in speaking "of *the power by which the state authorized the church to punish ecclesiastics by imprisonment or otherwise,*" (the OTHERWISE—*covers fines, exile, castigation*, &c.,) or in other words, that the author did not claim for the church any original power to inflict such punishments. But this is directly false; for in the very passage before his eyes, cited in my last speech, Devoti says, " P. La Borde *endeavours to undermine and take away* THE POWER GIVEN BY CHRIST TO THE CHURCH, *not merely of government, by counsels and persuasion, but also decreeing by laws and of* COMPULSION, *and of* COERCING WITH PUNISHMENT THOSE WHO ARE WORTHY OF IT." Here is a flat contradiction of Mr. Hughes, and the author cites *two popes*(1) who condemned this *very principle!*

The gentleman proceeds—"*During the Middle Ages, ecclesiastical offenders were tried, not by civil, but by ecclesiastical judges.*" Yes, this is by the *canon law*, (which is the *text-book of popish doctrine on the power of the church*,) not used as "*the concession of the state*," but *claimed as the right of the church*, and those are denounced who dare to do otherwise! Yet Mr. Hughes says it "*was by concession of the state.*" Query. If the *United States* were to *concede* this to Roman Catholics, does *their religion forbid it?* The Presbyterian Church *forbids* this as *contrary to the word of God.* "And the same *principles which authorized the church to* TRY CLERICS FOR OFFENCES, AUTHORIZED IT ALSO TO PUNISH THEM WHEN GUILTY OF CIVIL PENALTIES. It is in *connection with this state of things, that Devoti speaks of 'prisons,' exile, pecuniary fines, &c. as having been used by the church.*"

But Devoti expressly says, "*this power is given by Christ to the church*," and is, of course, inalienable and perpetual. If it fails to exercise it, then it is for want of *ability*, not want of *right*. And pray, *when* did the *church* cease to use them?—*never*, till forced by the *state*. *Where* did she ever cease to use them?—*nowhere*, till she was compelled to do it!

He next *cites and translates* a passage from the same author, to prove that "*the highest* grade of ecclesiastical coercion is expulsion" from the Church. But, unhappily for the gentleman, in the *next sentence* to the one so pompously quoted by him, the author goes on to say—"*But he who offends against society by any crime, if a clergyman, is subject to the judgment of the Church, not on account of the thing itself, which is proper to the civil commonwealth, but on account of the* PERSON, *because, forsooth, he is a citizen of the ecclesiastical commonwealth. Wherefore, the Church proceeds against him, by imprisonment, or other corporal punishment;* and if the *crime be still more weighty, for which the lenity and mildness of the church has no adequate punishment*, (pœnam,) *she degrades him—that is, permits him to be no longer a citizen of her commonwealth; but subjects him, like other laics, to the civil power.* It (the civil power) therefore exercises the jurisdiction *over this man who is now a citizen of its commonwealth, which it has over its other citizens;* and *visits him with death or other punishments, appointed by civil law.*"(2)

(1) See the whole extract in my last speech.
(2) Qui aliquo crimine societatem læsit si clericus sit ecclesiæ judicio subest, non propter rem ipsam, quæ propria est civilis reipublicæ, sed propter personam, quia silicet ecclesiasticæ reipublicæ civis est. Itaque in eum ecclesia animadvertit carcere, aut alia pœna corporali; et si gravius crimen sit cui non parem habeat pœnam ecclesiæ comitas et mansuetudo eum de gradu dejecit; hoc est non amplius suæ reipublicæ civem esse sinit, sed ad instar cæterorum laicorum subjecit civili potestati. Ipsa vero in hunc hominem, qui jam suæ reipublicæ civis est imperium exercet quod habet in reliquos cives suos, eum que coercet morte, cæteris ve pœnis quæ sunt a civilibus legibus constitutæ.

Here it clearly appears, that Devoti holds the doctrine, that the *clergy are punishable, temporally and corporally, by the Church,* (*which he says derived this power from Christ, as quoted by me above, and not from the State, as Mr. Hughes falsely says;*) *that the fact of being a clergyman gives the Church this power;* that he must be *degraded,* i. e. cease to be a clergyman in order to be reached by the civil power. How strangely must the gentleman feel to be thus caught in the same page, and in his own papal theology!

The gentleman "*mired*" "in the same mud," (to use the elegant figure of Devoti,) struggles to prove that I have perverted the author, and denies that he claims any thing for the Church, but spiritual jurisdiction. Yet, in the sixth page of the same book, § 5, he says—" For those who are placed over a commonwealth, in authority, have power over all the things which pertain to that commonwealth, viz. *over the persons* of which it consists; and the *things which* these persons use and enjoy in *prolonging life.* Wherefore, also the *magistracy* (magistratus) *of the Church ought to have judicial power over the things and persons of her commonwealth, which other magistrates have over theirs.*"

When we come to present the *proof* from the *Inquisition,* that the *institutions of popery* (*embodying* and expressing her doctrines and her morals) are opposed to *liberty* in all its lovely forms, then we will show how far the *gentleman's defence of,* or at least, *apology for,* "A GOOD THING ABUSED," has any claim to our regard by its *weight,* or any title to our *credence* by its *truth.*

In the mean time honest Devoti shall again speak. *He surely knows what the Inquisition is.* He wrote in sight of it. His work is *franked* from Rome itself. Let honest men compare the following statement with what Mr. Hughes says:—

Under the head "*Inquisitors of heretical pravity,*" he gives the following statements: "The cause of instituting the tribunal called the Inquisition, was this. At first every bishop in his own diocese, or a number of bishops assembled in a provincial council, made inquisition of those errors which arose in the diocese or province; but the more weighty matters were *always referred* to the apostolical see, (Rome,) and thus every bishop or provincial council took care to bring to its proper issue whatever was decreed by the apostolical see. But in process of time, when greater evils pressed, it became necessary for the pope to send legates into those regions in which heresy had long and widely spread, that they might assist the bishops in restraining the audacity of abandoned men, and in deterring Christians from foreign and depraved doctrines. But when new errors daily sprung up, and the number of heretics was greatly increased, seeing that the legates could not always be at hand nor apply the proper remedy, it was determined to INSTITUTE A STANDING TRIBUNAL that should always be present, *and at all times and in every country* should devote their minds to preserving the soundness of the faith, and to restraining and expelling heresies as they arose. Thus it was that the *inquisitors were first appointed to perform the office of vicars to the Holy See*. But as in a matter so weighty as the preservation of the purity of the faith, *the inquisitors* needed that close union of mind and sentiment which is proper to the apostolical see, as the centre of unity, *there was instituted at Rome, by the Popes, an assembly or congregation of cardinals in which the Pope presides. This congregation is the head of all inquisitors over the whole world, to it they all refer their more difficult matters, and its authority and judgment are final.*"

"It is rightly and wisely ordered that the pope's office and power should sustain this institution, for he is the centre of unity and head of the church; and to him Christ has committed plenary power to feed, teach, rule and govern all Christians."(1)

Surely one of these gentlemen has been guilty of no small departures from historical and doctrinal truth!

The same author (2) says expressly: "And since the power of the church is twofold, the one wholly spiritual given separately by Christ, which is exercised both in the inner and outer court, the other which she has in common with every perfect and distinct commonwealth, and which is *called* TEMPORAL, *it follows that there are two kinds of punishment ordained by her. That is, one kind is spiritual, which is to afflict the soul;* THE OTHER TEMPORAL, WHICH IS TO CASTIGATE THE BODY. *She exercises the right to* inflict spiritual punishments on all who by baptism 'are admitted among the children of the church, and who sin against religion. THE CHURCH ALSO HAS SET UP TEMPORAL PUNISHMENTS FOR ALL, BUT THE LAITY AND CLERGY IN AN UNEQUAL DEGREE." Now, if the gentleman ventures again to deny that this writer claims for the church the right to inflict *temporal and bodily punishments*, I will expose him in a way which he must deeply regret.

I am willing to leave the long contest about Bossuet to speak for itself; and so also that about the third canon of Fourth Lateran. The hearer and reader must have perceived that at every step the gentleman has given ground. First he tried to defend the canon, as being only *discipline against* murderers. Then, driven from that, he assailed the *authenticity of the canon*—the *whole canon;* and lo! in the last speech he is finally forced to own that it is only *one of five sections* of that canon which he can assail; and in a jesuitical way is constrained to confess, after being exposed, that he did misstate in condemning the whole canon.

I think, gentlemen, he will attempt to *spike* no more of these *canons*.

(1) Devoti, book iv., title 8, passim.   (2) Book iv., § 8, p. 12.

The gentleman scolds about Matthew Paris, but wisely forgets "DENS'S" Theology, and my challenge on that *book*, which has opened the eyes of millions on the other side of *the waters* to new evidences on the persecuting doctrines of the Church of Rome.*

The reason why all the *European authorities* quoted by me are more impartial than Mr. Hughes, is not "*that Mr. Hughes* (as the gentleman says) can be a Catholic in the United States," without holding doctrines opposed to liberty; but because Mr. Hughes has proved to us that he dares not honestly avow what the true doctrine of his church is, in the United States! The gentleman's defence of the Bulla In Cœna Domini, is a concession of the question in debate. I need not, therefore, dwell much more on it. For example, he says, was it wrong for the Pope to *condemn pirates?* Was it "*inhuman to condemn the illegal imposition of taxes?*" Why, Mr. Hughes! These taxes, says the Pope, were imposed in "*dominions*" of others, "*without the special leave of the apostolic see!*" Of course Mr. Hughes thinks it not against the liberty of states for the pope to interfere with their *taxation of their own subjects!* And so of all the invasions in this Bull, of the *rights* of *sovereign states;* he defends them, says they were according to the *canon law*, &c. &c. Yes! and for that very reason, *since* the Pope's bull, sustained by *the canon law*, thus claims jurisdiction over sea and land, armies, navies, battles, treasuries, coasts, &c. &c.; and since Mr. Hughes defends the acts and claims, he concedes being unable to defend the question in debate.

Of *Anathema* we shall speak, in its place, and too soon for the gentleman.

The gentleman in reply to my question—"*Had the majority in Spain or Italy the right to establish the Catholic religion by law?*" answers, "*in my opinion, if the majority in Italy or Spain, by doing so, violated no civil or religious right of the minority, they had in that case the right.*" This is *allowing* that the *Catholic religion may be in certain cases established by law, without violating the right of the minority.* This is *again conceding* the whole question. For *when can a majority do this*, without such a violation of the rights of the *minority?* I ask the gentleman *when*, or how can this be done? The *American* principle, the Bible doctrine, is, that it is violating the rights of a *minority* to *establish any religion by law!* That no *majority* can, in any possible case, *of right,* do such a thing! That if *all* were of the same religion, it were anti-Christian and anti-liberal to do it! Here we see leaking out the gentleman's *majority rights*—which he exposed the first night of our debate, then tried to retract; and now again, drawn by the debate and by his other principles, is compelled to admit!

As to our Scotch fathers, I say, unequivocally, that they *had no right,* however great a *majority* they may have composed, to "*pull down the monuments of papal idolatry by force.*" It was *wholly wrong!* Mr. Wesley "*being dead, yet speaketh.*" I am happy to honour the memory of that great and good man; and when Mr. Hughes answers, or even attempts to answer his arguments, as quoted by me, I will, on the ground stated when I cited his remarks, meet Mr. Hughes, and all the college of priests who help him, in and about St. *John's*, and the library of St. *Augustine.*

In the very terms of the gentleman's citation from the Council of Constance, the doctrine is avowed that the *faith*, the *pledged faith (of the emperor) that Huss should return in safety from the Council, was not binding.*

But we will hereafter, at large, put this matter in the light to make "*the defender of the Council of Constance's crimes*" blush once more, if that faculty has not been *lost* by him.

Having now disposed of the gentleman's despairing attacks on my *authorities*, I proceed to adduce others:—

We have seen from the disclosures of my former speeches how far the Rev. Mr. Hughes permits his zeal in defence of the papacy to carry him in denying the existence and obligation of documents, which make a part of the history of the world, and which are known to every well-informed man in Europe and America.

We have still stronger illustrations of the same reckless spirit for the present one.

In letter No. 15 of the Controversy, the Rev. Mr. Hughes said, "Show me then the decree of any Council, or the Bull of any Pope, proposing persecution as a part of our religion, and let that document be the proof of your charge." In answer to this call, I produced copious extracts from the Bull of Pope Innocent VIII. for the extirpation of the Vadois (or Waldenses) given to Albert de Capitaneis, A. D. 1477, stating at the same time, in proof of its authenticity, that the original was preserved in the University of Cambridge, England. And how did he meet its terrific contents? Why in this extraordinary way: "Pope Innocent VIII. was elected in the year 1484, and it is not usual with our Popes to issue Bulls *seven* years before their election: such Bulls come from another quarter." Here he implies that the Bull has been *forged;* that it was never issued from Rome; and the proof is drawn from an error of *ten years* in the date! But in my next letter, I corrected the date, which was 1487, instead of 1477, and which had been a misprint in the work from which I had extracted it. I then added: "do you deny that there *was* such a Bull? If you have any *doubts* on this subject, I refer you to Baronius's Annals, Vol. XIX., page 387, section 25th."

And now, guileless hearer, can you divine how any art could evade such testimony? He replies: "The Annals of Baronius come down only to the year 1198, and yet you quote his authority for a fact which should have taken place in 1487!!! How is this?" But Raynold, the accredited continuator of Baronius, brings down the history of the church to the year 1534! The reply then was, there is no such Bull, because Baronius *died* before it was issued? On such shallow evasions he ventures flatly to deny the existence of the Bull. In Letter 19, he says: "You ask me, do I deny it? and without waiting for my answer, you reply, that '*I dare not!*' Now, I reply that *I dare*, and do deny it *flatly*." And now see what Baronius's continuator, Mr. Hughes's authentic historian, says:

"By which indignity Innocent, much excited, ordered the Gauls, Savoyes, and Germans, within whose territories the impiety still remained firmly rooted, to take up arms for the destruction of the heretics; and he smote the *favourers* of the heretics with heavy punishments; at the same time he commissioned Albert de Capitaneis, Archdeacon of Cremona, with ample powers to publish a crusade for the extermination of the Waldenses, and to stir up Princes and Bishops against them. The date of this document is as follows: *Given at Rome at St. Peter's, in the year of our Lord's incarnation* 1487, 5*th of Kallends of May, and of our Pontificate the* 3*d.*"

Having then been' brought to such sad issues with his own historian and with notorious facts, his last vain struggle was this: "Does he say that such a Bull exists? No. The quotation merely testifies that Albertus Capitaneis was commissioned to preach a crusade against the Waldenses, &c. &c." Was there ever such evasion? was evasion ever more unavailing and palpable? "*Commissioned!*" But who commissioned him? Why the Pope! But *what* was the commission? A Brief? a Bull? Letters Patent? an Edict of Blood? The *name* matters not. It is the *thing* we look to? The historian tells us of this thing; and it was *a commission with ample powers from Innocent VIII., the Pope to preach a crusade against the Waldenses for their extermination, and to stir up Princes and Bishops against them.* And yet Mr. Hughes says the historian "MERELY testifies that Albertus was commissioned to preach a crusade against the Waldenses." "MERELY a CRUSADE!!!" Do we need any more proof of Mr. Hughes's secret feelings on this subject; or of the Papal system? *Merely a crusade!* in which, by authority of the Pope, a great army, headed by *prelates, and priests, and princes* invaded a territory over which the Pope had no civil control, and in the name of God, butchered thousands of men, women and children, *because they held doctrines in religion which the Pope called heresy?* In order to show the spirit of this Bull, as well as the recklessness of our American defender of the faith, I here spread it out in full for the use of Mr. Hughes, and of all our readers; and when we get a copy of the original Latin (as we expect soon to do) from the archives of Cambridge University, we will give it to the American people:

"Innocent the Bishop, *servant of the servants of God*, to our well-beloved son Albertus de Capitaneis, archdeacon of the Church of Cremona, our nuncio, and commissary of the Apostolical See, in the dominions of our dear son the noble Charles, duke of Savoy, both on this side and that side of the mountains, in the city of Vienne in Dauphiny, and in the city and diocese of Sedon, and the places adjacent; health and apostolic benediction.

"The chief wishes of our heart demand that we should endeavour, with the most studious vigilance, to withdraw those from the precipice of errors, for whose salvation the sovereign Creator of all things himself choosed to suffer the greatest of human miseries, and carefully to watch over their salvation; *we, to whom he hath been pleased to commit the charge and government of his flock*, and who most ardently desire, that the Catholic faith should prosper and triumph under our pontifical reign, and that heretical pravity should be extirpated from the territories of the faithful.

"We have heard, with great displeasure, that certain sons of iniquity, inhabitants of the province of Ambrun, &c., followers of that most pernicious and abominable sect of wicked men, called *poor men of Lyons,* or *Waldenses,* which long ago hath most unhappily (*damnabiliter*) risen up in Piedmont, and the other places adjacent, by the malice of the devil, endeavouring, with fatal industry, to ensnare and seduce the sheep dedicated to God through winding, devious paths, and dangerous precipices, and at last to lead them to the perdition of their souls; who, under a deceitful appearance of sanctity, and delivered up to a reprobate sense, have the utmost aversion to follow the way of truth, and who, observing certain superstitious and heretical ceremonies, say, do, and commit very many things contrary to the orthodox faith, offensive to the eyes of the Divine Majesty, and most dangerous in themselves to the salvation of souls.

"And whereas our well-beloved son Blasius de Mont Royal, of the order of preaching friars, professor in theology, *inquisitor-general* in these parts, transported himself into that province, in order to induce them to abjure the foresaid errors, and profess the true faith of Christ, having been formerly appointed for that service by the master-general of that order, and afterwards by our beloved son Cardinal Dominic, styled *Presbyter of St. Clement,* legate of the Holy See in these places, and at last by Pope Sixtus IV., of happy memory, our immediate predecessor; but so far from forsaking their wicked and perverse errors, like the deaf adder that shuts its ears, they proceed to commit yet greater evils than before, not being afraid to preach publicly, and, by their preachings, to draw others of the faithful in Christ into the same errors, to *contemn the excommunications, interdicts,* and *other censures of the said inquisitor,* to demolish his house, to carry off and spoil the goods that were in it, and those of other Catholics: to kill his servant, to wage open war, to resist their temporal lords: to destroy their property, to chase them, with their families, from their parishes, burning or demolishing their houses, hindering them to receive their rents, doing to them all the mischief in their power, as also to commit innumerable other crimes, the most detestable and abominable.

"We therefore, as obliged *by the duty of our pastoral charge, being desirous to pluck up and wholly root out from the Catholic Church that execrable sect*, and those impious errors formerly mentioned, lest they should spread farther, and lest the hearts of the faithful should be damnably corrupted by them, and to repress such rash and audacious attempts, we have resolved to exert every effort for this purpose, and to bestow hereupon all our care, and we putting our special trust in God as to your learning, the maturity of your wisdom, your zeal for the faith, and experience in affairs; and likewise hoping that you will execute, with honesty and prudence, all that we have judged proper to commit to you for extirpating such errors, we have thought good to appoint you, by these presents, our nuncio, and commissary of the Apostolic See, for the cause of God and of the faith, in the dominions of our dear son Charles, duke of Savoy, &c., to the intent that you may *cause the said inquisitor to be received and admitted to the free exercise of his office*, and that by your seasonable remedies, you may prevail with these most wicked followers of the Waldensian sect, and others defiled with the infection of any sort of heresy whatever, to abjure their errors, and *obey the orders of the said inquisitor;* and that you may be able to effect this with so much more ease, *in proportion to the greatness of the power and authority wherewith you are vested by us*, we, by these presents, grant to you a full and entire license and authority to call and instantly to require, by yourself or by any other person or persons, *all the archbishops and bishops* in the duchy, in Dauphiny, and in the parts adjacent, (whom the Most High hath appointed to be partners with us in our travail,) and to *command* them, in virtue of holy obedience, together with the venerable brethren our ordinaries or their vicars, or the officials general in the cities and dioceses wherein you may see meet to proceed to the premises, and to execute the office which we have enjoined you; and with the foresaid inquisitor, a man of great erudition, established in the faith, and of ardent zeal for the salvation of souls, that *they be assisting to you in the things mentioned, and with one consent proceed, along with you, to the execution of them; that they take arms against* the said Waldenses and other heretics, and, with common counsels and measures, *crush and tread them as venomous serpents;* and that they provide with care, that the people committed to their inspection persist and be confirmed in the confession of the true faith; and that, *in a work so holy and so very necessary as the extermination and dissipation of these heretics*, they apply all their endeavours, and willingly bestow all their pains as in duty bound; and, in fine, that they neglect nothing which may in any way contribute to that design.

"Moreover, to entreat our most dear son in Christ, *Charles the illustrious king of France,* and our beloved sons the *noblemen, Charles duke of Savoy, the dukes, princes, earls,* and *temporal lords of cities, lands,* and the universities of these and other places, the *confederates of higher Germany,* and *in general all others who are faithful in Christ in these countries, that they may take up the shield for defence of the orthodox faith,* of which they made profession in receiving holy baptism, and the cause of our Lord Jesus Christ, by whom kings reign, and princes rule; and that *they afford help* to the said archbishops, bishops, to you, to their vicars, or officials, and to the inquisitor, by suitable aids, and *by their secular arm,* according as they understand to be needful for executing such a necessary and *salutary perquisition;* and that they vehemently and *vigorously set themselves in opposition to these heretics,* for the defence of the faith, the safety of their country, the preservation of themselves and of all that belong to them, that so they *may make them to perish, and entirely blot them out from the face of the earth.*

"And if you should think it expedient, that all the faithful in those places should carry the salutary cross on their hearts and on their garments, to animate them to fight resolutely against these heretics, to cause, preach, and publish the *croisade by the proper preachers of the word of God,* and to grant unto those who take the cross, and fight against these heretics, or who contribute thereunto, the privilege of gaining a *plenary indulgence,* and the *remission of all their sins once* in their life, and likewise at the point of death, by virtue of the commission given you above; likewise to command, upon their holy obedience, and under *the pain of the greater excommunication,* all *fit preachers of the word of God, secular and regular, of whatever order they be, mendicants not excepted, exempt and non-exempt, that they excite and inflame* (exotiare et inflammare) *these faithful to exterminate, utterly by force and by arms, that plague, so that they may assemble with all their strength and powers for repelling the common danger;* further, to absolve those who take the cross, fight, or contribute to the war, from all ecclesiastical sentences and pains, whether general or particular, by which they may in any manner be bound, excepting those which shall be specially inflicted hereafter, from which the offenders are only to be loosed by previous satisfaction, or the consent of the party; as likewise to *dispense* with them as to *any irregularity* they may be *chargeable with in divine things, or by any apostasy, and to agree and compound with them as to goods which they may have clandestinely or by stealth acquired, or which they dishonestly or doubtfully possess, applying them only for the support of the expedition for extirpating the heretics;* in *like manner to commute all vows whatever,* though made with an oath, of pilgrimage, abstinence, and others, (excepting only those of chastity, of entering into a religious life, visiting the

Holy Land, the sepulchres of the apostles, and the church of St. James in Compostella,) to those who come forth to this warfare, or who contribute thereto, or who only give as much as the performance of their vows of pilgrimage might probably have cost them, having a respect to the distance of the places, and the condition of the persons, according as shall appear proper to you, or to the confessors deputed by you for that purpose; in the mean time to choose, appoint, and confirm, *in our name*, and in the name of the Romish Church, one or more captains or leaders of the war over the crossed soldiers, and the army to be convened, and to enjoin and command, that they undertake that charge, and faithfully acquit themselves in it for the honour and defence of the faith, and that all the rest be obedient to him or them; *to grant, further, to every one of them a permission to seize and freely possess the goods of the heretics whether movable or immovable*, and to give them, for a prey, whatever the heretics have brought to the lands of the Catholics, or, on the contrary, have taken or caused to be taken from them; to command likewise all those who are in the service of the said heretics, wherever they be, to depart from them within a limited time which you shall prescribe to them, under whatever pains you shall judge proper; to admonish and require them, and all persons, ecclesiastical or secular, of whatever dignity, age, sex, or order they be, under the pains of excommunication, suspension and interdict, reverently to obey and observe the apostolical mandates, and to abstain from all commerce with the aforesaid heretics; and, by the same authority, to declare, that they and all others, whoever they be, who may be bound and obliged by contract, or in any other manner whatever, to assign or pay any thing to them, shall not henceforth be obliged to do so, nor can they be compelled in any manner of way to it; moreover, to deprive all those who do not obey your admonitions and mandates, of whatever dignity, state, degree, order, or pre-eminence they be, ecclesiastics of their dignities, offices, and benefices, and secular persons of their honours, titles, fiefs, and privileges, if they persist in their disobedience and rebellion; and to confer their benefices on others whom you shall account worthy of them, and even on those who may be already possessed of, or expecting any other ecclesiastical benefices, in whatever number, or of whatever quality soever they may be; and to declare these deprived as aforesaid, forever infamous, and incapable, for the time to come, of obtaining the like or any others; and to fulminate all sorts of censures, according as justice, rebellion, or disobedience, shall appear to you to require; to inflict an *interdict*, and, when inflicted, either to remove it finally, or only to suspend it for a time, according as it may be found expedient, on good reasons and consideration, as you may know to be useful and necessary; but chiefly on those days on which perhaps indulgences are to be published, or the croisade to be preached; and to proceed directly and *simpliciter, without the noise and form of justice,* having only regard to truth, against those who carry to these heretics, or their accomplices, provisions, arms, or other things prohibited, and other aiders, abettors, advisers, or entertainers of them, whether open or secret, or who by any means hinder or disturb the execution of such a salutary enterprise; and to declare all and every one of the transgressors to have incurred the censures and pains, both spiritual and temporal, which are inflicted, of right, upon those who do such things; as also to restore and absolve those who are penitent, and willing to return again to the bosom of the church as formerly, even though they should have taken an oath to favour the heretics, or had received their pay to fight for them, or had supplied them with arms, succours, victuals, and other things forbidden; providing they promise by taking an oath of a different kind, or otherwise give sufficient security, that for the time to come they will obey our mandates, those of the church, and yours, whether they be communities, universities, or particular persons, of whatever state, order or pre-eminence they be, or in whatever dignity, ecclesiastical or civil, they may be elevated; and to reestablish and put them in possession of their honours, dignities, offices, benefices, fiefs, goods, and other rights, of which they were formerly possessed; *and, in fine, to concede, dispose, establish, ordain, command, and execute, all and every other matters necessary or in any respect conducive* to this salutary business, even though they should be such as require a particular order, and are not comprehended in your general commission; and to check and restrain all opposers thereof, by ecclesiastical censures, and other suitable and lawful remedies, without regard to any appeal whatever; and, *if need be,* to *call into your assistance the aid of the secular arm.* And our will is, that all privileges, exemptions, apostolical letters, and indulgences of any kind, granted by us, in general, or particular, or in manner aforesaid, under any form of words or expressions, shall be held void, and as letters not granted, so far as they are inconsistent with, and tend to hinder or retard these presents, we hereby deprive them of all force, together with all other things whatever that are contrary, though the Holy See should have granted to any, either generally or particularly, that they could not be interdicted, suspended or excommunicated and deprived of their dignities and benefices, or smitten with any other apostolical pain, if in the apostolical letters there be not full and express mention made, word for word, of such an indulgence.

"*Thou, therefore, my dearly beloved son, undertaking with a devout mind the charge of such a meritorious work, show yourself diligent, solicitous, and careful in word and deed to execute it, so that, from your labours, attended with the divine favour and grace, the expected success and fruits may follow, and that by your so-*

licitude you may not only merit for reward the glory which is bestowed on those who are employed in designs and affairs of piety, but also that you may obtain, and not undeservedly, the more abundant commendations from us, and from the Apostolic See, an account of your most exact diligence and faithful integrity. And, because it may be difficult to transmit these present letters to all places where they may be necessary, we will, and by apostolical authority appoint, that to a copy which may be taken and subscribed by the hand of any public notary, and attested by the subscription of any ecclesiastical prelate, entire faith may be given, and that it should be held as valid, and the same regard paid to it as to the original letters, if they had been produced and shown. Given at Rome, at St. Peter's, in the year of the incarnation of our Lord 1487, the 5th of the kal. of May, in the 3d year of our pontificate."

Such is the document! Has earth ever seen such outrages? Did heathen Rome herself ever issue and enforce such edicts of blood and terror, as "Holy Mother Church" belched forth upon the trembling tribes of men as they melted before her wrath! Well did the Fifth Council of Lateran, 1516, session 11th, forbid her priests "*on any account* to presume to fix, or in their sermons assert, any certain time of the evils to come, or of the *coming of Anti-Christ.*" (Tempus quoque præfixum futurorum malorum, vel Antechristi adventum..... prædicate, vel asserrere, nequaquam præsumant.) The denial of Mr. Hughes is its own best comment on the *character* of Papism, and the *means* of its defence.

We see in this decree from the head of the church, the claim of power over all things temporal and spiritual, as having *charge from God to govern his flock* by such means. The *Inquisition* is here *authoritatively set up in the dominions of a foreign prince; kings* invoked to sustain the work of *crushing the vipers, the heretics*—in the name of their *baptism, and of the faith, and of God; Archbishops, and other ministers of peace and love, ordered to take up arms* against them, and tread them down, and *exterminate* them; and all to unite in *blotting them from the earth.* We have also, as usual, the *"plenary indulgence" for murdering* by wholesale: and the good morals of *"compounding"* with thieves and robbers, so as to apply the goods fraudulently gotten, to the extirpation of heretics; also "*commuting vows, though made with an oath,*" for those who aid the crusade by hand or purse, and the like holy things, showing how *"Holy Mother"* loved *heaven and the rights of men!* This document alone is enough to settle the question at issue, with every candid man. The only possible apology which is attempted for this *diabolical* instrument is, that these heretics (WALDENSES TOO, so that it was not *only* the *Albigenses* whom the popes slaughtered) were public enemies of all *Catholics,* and of all *states.* This, if wholly true, (it is *wholly false,*) is in fact, giving up the question in debate; for it is saying, that *according to the Catholic religion,* whenever a people arise in a country, who are thought *at Rome* to be public enemies to all Catholics and all governments, then the Pope may order their extermination by a crusade—no matter whether in France, Portugal, or Italy,—whether in Europe or America! This is no less than claiming universal supremacy over church and state everywhere, for the support of the *Catholic faith.* It is claiming the right in the name of God, and as head of His church, to put men to death (or which is the same thing, *order* it to be done) for *crimes against the state,* and departure from the doctrines of the *Catholic* church.

While Mr. Hughes gives it as HIS OPINION, that the *Roman Catholic religion is not opposed to civil and religious liberty,* we may surely ask what other and abler men say, even allowing that they only give *their opinion* of Catholic doctrine on this subject. And if the Pope of Rome should endorse such *opinions,* (which he has never done for Mr. Hughes's opinion,) then the testimony would seem conclusive in favour of the truth of these opinions. Now, suppose Cardinal Bellarmine to be in Priest Hughes's place, and discussing this question, and should, under the Pope's sanction, argue for the fact and the right of persecution, in the following terms :—(1)

"THAT HERETICS CONDEMNED BY THE CHURCH MAY BE PUNISHED WITH TEMPORAL PENALTIES, AND EVEN WITH DEATH. We will briefly show that the *church has* THE POWER, AND IT IS HER DUTY, *to* cast off incorrigible heretics, especially those who have relapsed, and that the SECULAR POWER OUGHT TO INFLICT ON SUCH TEMPORAL PUNISHMENTS, AND EVEN DEATH ITSELF. 1st. THIS MAY BE PROVED FROM THE SCRIPTURES. 2d. It is proved from the opinions and laws of the emperors, *which the church has always approved.* 3d. IT IS PROVED BY THE LAWS OF THE CHURCH. 4th. It is proved by the *testimony of the fathers.* Lastly. It is proved from natural reason. For, *first;* it is owned by all, that heretics *may of right be excommunicated—of course they may be put to death.* This consequence is proved because *excommunication is a greater punishment than temporal death. Secondly; experience proves that* THERE IS NO OTHER REMEDY; *for the church has, step by step, tried* ALL REMEDIES ; 1st, *excommunication alone;* then PECUNIARY *penalties;* afterwards, BANISHMENT; *and lastly,* HAS BEEN FORCED TO PUT THEM TO DEATH, TO SEND THEM TO THEIR OWN PLACE. *Thirdly;* all allow that *forgery* deserves death, but heretics are guilty of *forgery* of the Word of God. *Fourthly;* a *breach* of faith *by man toward God* is a *greater sin* than of a *wife* with her *husband.* But a *woman's unfaithfulness is punished with death;* why not a heretic's? *Fifthly;* there are three grounds on which reason shows *that heretics should be put to death.* The first is, lest the

(1) Chap. XXI. Lib. iii. On Laity.

wicked should injure the *righteous;* second, that by the *punishment* of a FEW, MANY may be REFORMED. FOR MANY WHO WERE MADE TORPID BY IMPUNITY ARE ROUSED BY THE FEAR OF PUNISHMENT: AND THIS WE DAILY SEE IS THE RESULT WHERE THE INQUISITION FLOURISHES. *Finally;* it is a benefit to *obstinate heretics* to *remove* them *from this life, for the longer they live the more errors they invent, the more persons they mislead, and the greatest damnation do they treasure up to themselves.*

"Chapter XXII.—*Objections Answered.*

" It remains to answer the objections of Luther and other heretics. Argument 1st, *From* THE HISTORY OF THE CHURCH AT LARGE. THE CHURCH, says Luther, *from the beginning even to this time,* HAS NEVER BURNED A HERETIC. *Therefore it does not seem to be the mind of the Holy Spirit that they should be burned !* I reply. This argument admirably proves, not the sentiment, but the IGNORANCE or IMPUDENCE of Luther. FOR AS ALMOST AN INFINITE NUMBER WERE EITHER BURNED OR OTHERWISE PUT TO DEATH, Luther *either* did not know it, and was therefore *ignorant ;* or, if he knew it, he is convicted of *impudence and falsehood,* for *that heretics were often burned by the church, may be proved by adducing a few from many examples.* (*He instances, Donatists, Manicheans,* and *Albigenses.*)

"Argument 2d, *Experience shows that terror is not useful* (in such cases). I REPLY, EXPERIENCE PROVES THE CONTRARY—FOR THE DONATISTS, MANICHEANS, AND ALBIGENSES WERE ROUTED AND ANNIHILATED BY ARMS.

"Argument 13th. The Lord attributes (says the Protestant) to the church, *the sword of the Spirit, which is the Word of God,* but not *the material sword.* Nay, he said to Peter, who wished to defend him with a material sword, '*put up thy sword into the scabbard:*' John xviii. I answer: *As the* CHURCH HAS ECCLESIASTICAL AND SECULAR PRINCES, WHO ARE HER TWO ARMS, SO SHE HAS TWO SWORDS, THE SPIRITUAL AND MATERIAL; AND THEREFORE WHEN HER RIGHT HAND IS UNABLE TO CONVERT A HERETIC WITH THE SWORD OF THE SPIRIT, SHE INVOKES THE AID OF THE LEFT HAND, AND COERCES HERETICS WITH THE MATERIAL SWORD.

"Argument 18th. *The Apostles* (says the Protestant) *never invoked the secular arm against heretics.* Answer, (according to St. Augustine, in Letter 50, and elsewhere :) THE APOSTLES DID IT NOT, BECAUSE THERE WAS NO CHRISTIAN PRINCE WHOM THEY COULD CALL ON FOR AID. BUT AFTERWARDS, IN CONSTANTINE'S TIME, THE CHURCH CALLED IN THE AID OF THE SECULAR ARM."

Luther denied that the *true* church had ever burned a *heretic.* He often *convicts the Church of Rome of such acts.* Bellarmine here frankly avows *persecution,* yea, the RIGHT and THE DUTY of

THE CHURCH TO PUT HERETICS TO DEATH, and pleads the Scripture for the *authority;* and appeals to history for the fact that the church had put to death, before his day, "ALMOST AN INFINITE NUMBER."

It is this same writer who thus explains the stillness and peace of *Catholics* where they are not the *majority* of a community, in the very *next chapter:* "But when in reference to HERETICS, THIEVES, AND OTHER WICKED MEN, *there shall arise this question in particular,* 'SHALL THEY BE EXTERMINATED?' *it is to be considered according to the meaning of our Lord, whether that can be done without injury to the good, and if that be possible, they are without* DOUBT TO BE EXTIRPATED; *but if that be not possible, either because they be not sufficiently known, and then there would be danger of punishing the innocent, instead of the guilty;* OR BECAUSE THEY ARE STRONGER THAN OURSELVES, AND THERE BE DANGER, LEST IF WE MAKE A WAR UPON THEM, MORE OF OUR PEOPLE THAN OF THEIRS BE SLAIN, THEN WE MUST KEEP QUIET."

Hence, in the *United States,* we may expect life while we have *numbers.* You see, gentlemen, what our friends at Rome (not *priests,* but CARDINALS, whose works are *sanctioned by the Pope,* and in this case a nephew of the Pope) think of the *rights of minorities!* they are summed up in this—*they may die by the hands of papists!*

Now, with these *declarations* of a great cardinal, we may compare the bulls of popes, and decrees of councils, already adduced —and see how forcibly they illustrate and confirm each other.

One of the most striking proofs of the opposition of *popery, as a system,* to civil and religious liberty, is found in the *interference of the popes as the avowed head of the church, with sovereign states of Europe.* There was scarcely a form of oppression which they did not practise, or a *right,* civil or religious, on which they did not encroach. A system is often best known by its *practical operation;* and when the effect is not only such as the system might be expected to produce, but such as the system fearlessly avows, no one can refuse to it a character which it openly assumes. What follows will explain itself.

We present to our readers a chapter from Du Pin, *a Roman Catholic historian,* which gives a most striking picture of the spirit of papism in the 17th century. It is a detailed history of an outrageous assault made by the Pope on the Republic of Venice. For the fidelity of the narrative we have not merely the character of Du Pin, (who as a papist would hardly do the Pope injustice,) but the confirmation of contemporary writers. The events are too notorius to be denied, at least in their essential parts. It may be proper here to say a word of the Inderdict which the Pope fulminated against the State of Venice, for daring to assert rights which are inseparable from every government, and which no ruler but the Pope ever had the audacity to question.

The papal Inderdict was designed to shut Heaven against the offending people; and to expose them as heathen to the wrath of God until they submitted to the Pope. I have before me a large folio, JUS ECCLESIASTICUM UNIVERSUM; or The Universal Ecclesiastical Law of the Church of Rome, in which a whole chapter is taken up on the nature, form, force, &c. &c. of an Interdict. The following is a part of the form there given, which has been often used in other days and other lands:

"Bind the whole land of ———— with the bond of public excommunication, so that no one, except a clergyman, or poor mendicant, or stranger, or infant of two years or under, be allowed burial in the whole territory ————. No one shall be permitted to marry a wife, or to salute another; nor clergy, nor laity, nor inhabitants, nor strangers in all the land shall be permitted to eat flesh or any other food, except what is allowed in Lent, while the Interdict continues. Let no layman or clergyman be shorn of his hair or shaven, until the rulers are subdued, and the leaders of the people are made obedient. But if any one shall be detected in the violation of this bond, in any way, he shall not be restored without condign punishment."

This is a part of the terrific sentence passed by the Pope only two centuries ago, against a sovereign state, and that a republic, over which he had no more right to lord it, than over our own.

Now, I ask, why should the minions of the Pope in the United States be believed when they talk of LIBERTY? Can any man believe the Rev. Mr. Hughes, when he *professes* to be *subject* to the Pope, and yet love liberty? One or other of these must be given up. Let Mr. Hughes tell us why in the 17th century the Pope oppressed Venice, and yet in the 19th century *spares us?*

THE HISTORY OF THE INDERDICT OF VENICE, FULMINATED BY POPE PAUL V. (1)

"The difference of the Republic of Venice with Paul V. is one of the most important points of the ecclesiastical history of the seventeenth century; not only by reason on the subject of the dispute, but also much more on account of the great number of questions which were agitated on occasion of that difference, by the most able divines and lawyers of that time. The Senate of Venice made two decrees in the beginning of that century; by the first of which it was forbidden under severe penalties, to build hospitals or monasteries, or to establish new convents or societies in the State of Venice, without the permission of the senate. By the other, which was made the 26th March, 1605, a law made in 1536 was renewed, confirmed and extended over all parts of the State, forbidding all the subjects of the republic to sell, alienate,

(1) From Du Pin's Ecclesiastical History, Vol. viii. Book ii. Chap. 1, Century 17th.

or dispose in any manner whatsoever, of immovable goods in perpetuity, in favour of ecclesiastical persons, without the consent of the senate: upon condition nevertheless, that if any legacies of immovable goods were bequeathed, those goods should be sold within two years after, and the purchase given to discharge those legacies. There happened at the same time two criminal affairs, which concerned the ecclesiastics. *Scipion Sarrasin*, canon of Vicenza, who had taken off the seal of the magistrates, affixed to the Episcopal chancery, at the request of the chancellor, the see being vacant, was seized by the senate, and put into prison for having insulted one of his kinswomen, whom he intended to debauch; and some time after, Count Baldolin Valde-marino, Abbot Feveza, being accused of many enormous crimes,(1) was imprisoned by order of the senate. The Pope Paul V. being persuaded that the decrees and enterprises against the clergy, encroached upon ecclesiastical jurisdiction, complained of them to the ambassador of Venice, and demanded of the senate by his nuncio, that the decrees should be revoked immediately, and the ecclesiastics, imprisoned by the authority of the senate, delivered into the hands of his nuncio, to be tried by ecclesiastical judges; threatening to interdict the republic, if he was not obeyed immediately. The senate answered, the 1st of December, 1605, that they could not release prisoners accused of crime which belong to the recognisance of the secular judges, nor revoke the laws which they had a right to make, and which they believed necessary for the good of the state. The Pope having received this answer by letters from his nuncio, and by word of mouth from the ambassador of Venice, despatched on the 10th of December two Briefs; the one addressed to Marin Grimani, Doge of Venice, and the other to the republic by way of monitory, exhorting the state to revoke their decrees, which he thought contrary to the canons, and prejudicial to the liberties of the church; declaring that they who made these laws, or caused them to be executed, had incurred ecclesiastical censures, from which they could not be freed but by revoking those statutes, and re-establishing affairs in their former state. He commanded them under the penalty of excommunication, *latæ sententiæ*, to revoke them, which, if they refused, he protested that he should be obliged to put in execution the penalties annexed to such offences, without any other citation; being not willing that God should call him to account one day for having thus failed in his duty; and not being able to dissemble, when he saw the authority of the holy Apostolic See infringed, the ecclesiastical immunities trampled under foot, the canons and holy decrees neglected, and the rights and privileges of the church subverted."

The Pope sent these briefs to his nuncio at Venice, with orders

---

(1) Oppression, incest with his sister, and murder.

"to present and publish them," and acquainted the cardinals in a consistory held the 12th of that month, with the subject of complaint he had against the republic of Venice, and with what he had done thereupon. Nevertheless the republic appointed Leonardo Donato, procurator of St. Mark, to go express, and treat of this affair in the quality of ambassador at Rome. The nuncio not having received those briefs till the day after Donato had been chosen ambassador, thought he ought to put off the publication of them, and wrote to the Pope, who ordered him to present them. The nuncio received this order on Christmas-eve, and presented, the day following, the briefs to the counsellors assembled to assist at a solemn mass, in the absence of the Doge Grimani, who was extremely ill, and died the day following. His death was the reason why the briefs were not opened, the senate having ordered that no affair should be transacted, but that of the election of a doge. The Pope on his side wrote to the nuncio, to protest to the senate that they ought not to proceed to a new election, because it would be null, as made by excommunicated persons. The nuncio pressingly demanded audience to make this declaration; but the senate would not give it him, it being not customary to receive any memorials from the ministers of foreign princes during the interregnum, but compliments of condolence. The electors were not a long time in choosing a new doge. The 10th of January, 1706, Leonardo Donato was advanced to that high dignity. All the ambassadors went immediately, according to custom, to visit the new doge, and pay him their compliments. But the nuncio would not visit him. The doge did not omit in writing to the Pope according to custom, to notify his election to him; and the Pope received his letter. The first affair which was transacted at Venice after the election of the doge, was the difference of the republic with the Pope. It began with nominating the Chevalier Duodo in the place of Leonardo Donato (who was elected doge) ambassador at Rome. After this the briefs were opened; and when the senate saw what they contained, before they returned an answer to the Pope, they determined to have the advice of some divines and lawyers. The lawyers whom they principally consulted were Erasmus Gratian of Udina, and Mark Antonio Pellegrin of Padua; and the famous Fra-Paolo Sarpi of the order of the Servites, was appointed the divine of the republic. It was also resolved not only to consult the doctors of the university of Padua and of Venice, but also the most able lawyers of Italy and Europe, who sent them their opinions, with the laws of the other kingdoms and churches of Christendom, which had any relation to the affair in question. Then the senate, after having understood the opinion of the doctors, returned this answer to the Pope the 28th of January: " That they heard with a great deal of grief and astonishment, by letters from his holiness, that he had condemned the laws of the republic, (observed with success for many ages, and with which his predecessors had found no fault,) as contrary to the authority of the holy apostolic see; and that he regarded those who had made them (who were men of piety, and had well deserved of the see of Rome) as persons who broke the ecclesiastical immunities; that according to the admonition of his holiness, they had caused to be examined their ancient and modern laws, and that they had found nothing in them which could not be ordained by the authority of a sovereign prince, or which infringed on the power of the Pope; because it is certain that it belongs to a secular prince, to take cognizance of all societies which are founded within his own jurisdiction, and to take care that no edifices may be raised which may prejudice the public safety, when there are in a state as great a number of churches and places of devotion as is sufficient. That they never refused giving leave to build them; the republic even contributing thereto very liberally on her part. That the law prohibiting the alienation of the goods of the laity forever in favour of the ecclesiastics, regarding nothing but temporal affairs, it cannot be pretended that they have done any thing by that against the canons. That if the Popes had power to forbid the ecclesiastics to alienate in favour of secular persons the goods of the church without her consent, it might be lawful for princes to prohibit seculars also to alienate theirs in favour of the ecclesiastics without their permission. That the ecclesiastics lose nothing by their decrees, because they receive the value of the immovable goods which are given or bequeathed to them. That this alienation weakening the state, is not less prejudicial in spiritual than temporal concernments. That the senate cannot believe they have incurred any censure by making these laws, since princes have by a divine law, from which no human authority can derogate, the power of making laws in temporal affairs. That the admonitions of his holiness have no effect but in matters that are purely spiritual, and not in a temporal affair, which is in all things separate, and wholly exempt from the pontifical authority. That the senate does not believe his holiness, who is full of piety and religion, will persevere without knowledge of the cause, in his menaces. That these were an abridgment of the senate's reasons, which their extraordinary ambassador would give him to understand more largely.

"The Pope having received this answer of the senate, declared to the ambassador that he could not relax his severity if they did not revoke their laws, and deliver into the hands of his nuncio the prisoners. He complained still more of another decree they had made upon the emphytheoses,(1) and caused his complaints to be delivered by his nuncio to the senate. As he knew they would give him no satisfaction thereupon, he gave orders for another brief to be presented, the 10th of December, to the senate,

(1) A term of law for a long lease, from ten to a hundred years.

whereby he required that the two prisoners should be delivered to his nuncio, under the penalty of excommunication. The senate answered, that they would not divest themselves of the right which they had to punish the crimes of their subjects, which they had always enjoyed from the establishment of their state, with the consent of the sovereign pontiffs. The extraordinary ambassador of the republic came to Rome, and represented to the Pope the reasons of their proceedings; but nothing was able to move his holiness. He caused a monitory to be drawn up against the Republic of Venice, and having communicated it to the cardinals in consistory the 15th of April, he ordered it to be published and fixed up in the public places at Rome. This monitory imported that the Senate of Venice being not willing to revoke the laws which they had made in prejudice of the ecclesiastical authority, nor to deliver their prisoners, he declared these laws to be null, and pronounced the doge and Republic of Venice excommunicated, if within the space of twenty-four days, to begin from the day of the publication, they did not revoke, break, and annul the aforesaid laws, and actually deliver the canon and the abbot into the hands of his nuncio. That till such time as they should pay obedience to this order, he forbade them to bury in consecrated ground those who happened to die; and that if, within three days after the twenty-four were expired, they did not comply, he laid the whole state under an interdict; and forbade all masses and divine offices to be celebrated, except in such cases and places as were privileged by common law. And that he deprived the doge and senate of all the goods which they possessed in the Roman Church, or in other churches, and of all the privileges or indultos which they had obtained from the holy see, and especially from those which they had to proceed against clerks in certain cases. The monitory was addressed to the patriarchs, archbishops, bishops, their vicar-generals, and to all the clergy, secular and regular, having ecclesiastical dignity in the State of the Republic of Venice.

"The senate being informed that the monitory bull was published, recalled their extraordinary ambassador; forbade all ecclesiastical prelates to publish or set up the bull of the Pope, and commanded that all they who had copies of it should carry them to the magistrates of Venice. The Pope on his side recalled the nuncio who was at Venice, and dismissed the ordinary ambassador of the republic. At the same time the chiefs of the Council of Ten sent for the superiors of monasteries, and of the other churches of Venice, and declared the intention of their sovereign to be that they should continue to perform the divine offices, and that no one should leave the ecclesiastical state without leave, assuring those who stayed of protection; and declaring, that they who departed should not carry with them any of the goods and ornaments of the churches. They commanded them, in case any brief was sent to them from Rome, or order from their superiors, to send it to the magistrates before they read it. And the governors of all the cities of the state were enjoined to give the same orders in the places of their jurisdiction. The superiors immediately all promised to obey the orders that had been given them, and to perform divine service as before. A council was held upon what was proper to be done concerning the monitory of the Pope. Some gave their advice to appeal from it, as many princes, and the republic itself had done on the like occasion. But others believed there was no occasion for having recourse to this remedy, pretending that the briefs were notoriously null of themselves. This opinion was followed, and, nothing was done, but a mandate made in the name of the doge, addressed to all the ecclesiastics of the republic, wherein he declared, that, having received advice of the publication, April 17th, at Rome, of a certain brief fulminated against him, and the senate, and sovereignty of Venice, he thought himself obliged to employ his cares in maintaining the public tranquillity, and supporting the authority of the prince. That he protested before God he had not omitted any means of informing, and laying before the Pope, the strong and convincing reasons of the republic. But that having found his ears closed, and seen the brief he had published against all kind of reason and justice, in opposition to the doctrine of the Holy Scripture, the fathers and canons, and to the prejudice of the secular authority which God has bestowed upon sovereign princes, the *liberty of the state* and the public repose, and to the great scandal and offence of the whole Christian world; he held that brief to be not only unjust, but also null, unlawfully fulminated in fact, and contrary to the rules of law, and that he would use the same remedies which his predecessors and other princes have used against the popes who abused the authority which God had given them to edification, and passed the bounds of their power. And this he was the more inclined to do, forasmuch as he was certain that this brief would be looked upon in the same light, not only by all the subjects of the republic, but also by the whole Christian world. That he was persuaded they would continue, as before, to take care of the souls of the faithful, and to perform the divine offices, being fully resolved to persevere in the Catholic and apostolic faith, and the respect which is due to the holy Roman church. This mandate, dated the 6th of May, 1606, was immediately published and set up at Venice, and in all the cities of the state.

"As the term of twenty-four days allowed by the briefs approached, and the *Jesuits*, who had received particular orders from the Pope, showed plainly, that they were inclined to observe the interdict, and would at least abstain from saying of mass, they were commanded on the 10th of May, to give an express declaration of the measures they designed to take. They acknowledged then, that they could not celebrate mass during the interdict, and that if the senate obliged them to do it, they chose rather to retire from Venice. Upon this answer, the senate resolved to send them away, and appointed the grand Vicar of the Patriarch to receive the ornaments of their churches, and gave them order to depart immediately. They went out that evening, carrying each of them a consecrated host about their necks; and being put into two barks, retired to Ferrara. The Jesuits in the convents which were in the other cities of the republic departed also. As it was manifest that the Capuchins, Theatins, and other regulars, after the example of the Jesuits, were resolved to observe the interdict, the senate published a decree the last day of the term, by which all those who refused to celebrate the divine offices, in the accustomed manner, were enjoined to retire out of the jurisdiction of the republic; upon which the Capuchins and Theatins departed also, and the other Religious were placed in the government of their churches. The Capuchins of the Territories of Brescia and Bergamo stayed, and continued to perform divine offices, like the other ecclesiastics, secular and regular, of the republic.

"The nuncios of the Pope who were in the courts of Catholic princes of Europe, endeavoured to exclude from divine service, the ambassadors and envoys of Venice; but their attempts were fruitless. They continued to be treated as they used to be, and were admitted to prayers, assemblies, and the ecclesiastic ceremonies, as heretofore, in France, Spain, Italy, and Poland. The ambassador of the republic assisted in person at Vienna, in the first solemn procession of the Holy Sacrament, which was made by the Jesuits. But the nuncio, who was not present for fear of meeting the ambassador, gave out such menaces, that the ambassador did not think fit to be present at the two following ones. Though the interdict was not observed in the States of Venice, it occasioned *tumults* and *seditions* in several places, which the senate, having attributed to the suggestions of the Jesuits, made a decree the 14th of June, whereby they declared, that the Jesuits should nevermore be received for the future in any place of the State of Venice, and that this decree should never be revoked, before there had been first read the whole process in presence of all the senate, which should be composed at least of a hundred and four score senators, and unless there were five for one who voted for the revocation.

"Nevertheless the Christian princes interposed to accomodate the difference between the Pope and the Venetians. But these would not hear any proposition of accommodation, before the Pope had taken away the interdict, and the Pope demanded before all things the revocation of the decrees. The ambassador of the most Christian king exerted himself more strongly and efficaciously than any one else in bringing matters to an accommodation, and at length effected it. The *king of Spain* assured the Pope that he *would assist him* with all his forces, and that he had given orders for that purpose to his ministers in Italy. But these promises had no other effect, than to retard the accommodation, and had like to have kindled a war in Italy. Some unknown persons having set up in the state of Venice a placard by which the republic was exhorted to separate herself from the Roman Church, the senate commanded, that search should be made after the author of it, and protested that their intention was, never to depart from the Catholic religion, nor the obedience due to the Holy See. They published afterward several orders to maintain a war in case they should be attacked. The Pope on his side solicited the princes of Italy to put *himself* into a condition to *attack* the Venetians, or to defend himself, if he should be attacked by them. On each side preparations of war were made, but the dispute never came to an open rupture. It was not so in the war which was carried on by the pen, for a very great number of writings were published on both sides, with heat, vivacity, and learning. Though the affair had a lowering aspect, and all things threatened a rupture, the ambassadors of France did not cease, nevertheless, to negotiate an accommodation."

The above passage from a Roman Catholic historian, is the narrative of a transaction which is full of interest to the American people. From it we learn that the Pope only two centuries ago, when his claims were asserted without disguise, excommunicated a whole people, for daring to extend the jurisdiction of the state to the *punishment* of *ecclesiastics*, to the *erection* of *convents*, monasteries, &c. &c. The clergymen were arrested by order of the Republic of Venice, the one for debauch, and the other for incest and murder. These are offences against the *state;* they are cognizable in civil courts, and in them alone. The courts of the church cannot inflict *temporal* punishment, or try civil cases, without infringing the liberty of the state, and violating the order which God has established. No Papist will venture to deny this in this country, though in Spain and Italy it is far otherwise. But the Pope demanded these criminals of the republic, to be tried by *him* in his ecclesiastical court; and threatened an interdict of the republic, if instant obedience was not shown to his mandate! What would the American people say if a certain priest who not many years since, in a neighbouring town, attempted a similar offence to the one mentioned above, (instead of flying the country,) had been arrested by the civil magistrate, and had been demanded by the Pope, with the threat of an interdict, if we refused to give him up?

In the other case, the republic forbade convents, monasteries, &c. &c. to be erected without the permission of the senate, and passed salutary laws regulating the bestowing of property on ecclesiastics. Monasteries were filling, and ruling the land; and the clergy (as in South America, and once in Great Britain) were getting possession of the wealth and even the soil of the commonwealth. These salutary laws were intended to restrict their encroachments. But the Pope had no idea of permitting a free state to govern *his subjects*, though they lived in that state! Let the reader refer to the first part of this chapter from Du Pin, and then read these remarks—and he will see how the Pope claims temporal, as well as spiritual power, over all his followers, everywhere.

The next note we make on the above narrative is that the historian tells how faithful the JESUITS (whom the Rev. Mr. Hughes so much admires and lauds) were to the Pope. *They* left the republic, and publicly espoused the cause of the Pope, as a military foe, against their native and free state!! And the oath of allegiance of every Jesuit, bishop and priest, if faithfully observed, will lead to the same results, in the same circumstances.

Again: *"The Pope,"* (says our Catholic historian,) *"solicited the Princes of Italy to put himself into a condition to attack the Venetians, or defend himself, if he should be attacked by them."* A very Christian attitude truly for the *Head* of the Church! Heading an army to crush a republic! And that for daring to punish priests who had been guilty of incest and murder! How would it sound to say—The Apostle Peter raised an army in Jerusalem to rescue James from prison? Peter once *did* try the sword, and in how just a cause! But his master *rebuked* him! "Put up thy sword; they that use the sword shall perish by the sword." Yet this is the vicar of Jesus and the successor of Peter! The Pope is indeed the *successor* of Peter in his follies and sins—in using the sword, and in denying his Lord; but not in repentance, obedience, and the ministerial office.

"Is the Roman Catholic Religion, in any or all its principles or doctrines, opposed to civil or religious liberty?"

NEGATIVE V.—MR. HUGHES.

MR. PRESIDENT:—Nothing is more disagreeable than to be obliged to argue with a man who trifles with those rules of reasoning, on the observance of which, the soundness of an argument depends. Logic is to reasoning what grammar is to language, with this difference, that the principles of logic are founded in common sense, and derive but little authority from usage: whereas, those of language are frequently sustained by usage alone. All men reason, and yet there are few who pay attention to the rules of reasoning. Now I will take up the *prominent* points of the gentleman's last speech, in order to show that they are what logicians term "FALLACIES."

FIRST. What had he undertaken to prove? He had undertaken to prove, that there are doctrines in the Catholic religion which are hostile or opposed to civil and religious liberty. This is his proposition. As long as he does not *prove this proposition*, he beats the air! But what are we to understand by "DOCTRINE?" Any "*tenet of faith or morals which Catholics hold as having been revealed by Almighty God.*" Consequently, the first step to be taken, is to select the "DOCTRINE." If it is admitted as such, then he has only to proceed with the argument. If, what he imputes as a "DOCTRINE," be denied by his opponent, then he must either abandon it, or show that it was taught in the acts of a general council, or the Bull of a Pope, "AS A TENET OF FAITH OR MORALS THAT HAD BEEN REVEALED BY ALMIGHTY GOD." When he has proven this, then he may again proceed to build his argument on it, notwithstanding the denial of his opponent.

SECOND. His next duty, as a logician, is to show in what manner, the "DOCTRINE" is opposed to civil and religious liberty, according to the admitted definition of these words. If, instead of this, he trusts to popular prejudices in the minds of his audience, and substitutes declamation instead of logic, then he appeals to the tribunal of passion, and REASON will assuredly disclaim the verdict.

THIRDLY. I shall now proceed to show wherein the "FAL-

LACIES" of the gentleman's argument consist. The foundations on which he builds are the sayings and doings of popes, cardinals, canonists, and Catholic writers. Now, this is fundamentally illogical; for, there are many things *said*, and *written*, and *done*, by these, which are *not* Catholic doctrines. Thus the interdict of Venice does not pretend to be either a "tenet of faith or morals."

In making this the *foundation* of an argument, therefore, he assumes FALSE PREMISES, by assuming as a "doctrine," what is not doctrine, and he arrives at a FALSE CONCLUSION. Herein is the fallacy.

If it were *true*, that Catholics hold the Interdict as "a tenet of faith or morals," then, the argument would be logical. But, as this is false, so the reasoning which is founded on it, is false, so far as regards the question in debate. If I had asserted that the Pope had *never issued an interdict*, the case of Venice would have been in point, to refute me. But the question is not about INTERDICTS, but about DOCTRINES. The same remarks are applicable to the other facts, real or pretended, adduced in his speech. They may be true in themselves, but it does not *follow* that, *therefore*, they are doctrines of the Catholic religion. The Synod of York, or the Assembly at Pittsburg, may have said very foolish, and done very naughty things; but it does not *follow* that, *therefore*, the Confession of Faith is a book of heresy. This must be proved by other arguments. Now, when I shall come to show what doctrines of the Presbyterian religion are inimical to civil and religious liberty, I shall begin by proving, that they are held by that denomination, as "having been revealed by Almighty God." Whenever the gentleman disclaims the doctrine, I shall point it out to him, put his hand upon it, and "compel" him, as a Presbyterian, to acknowledge it. His introduction of the acts and opinions of *individuals*, instead of stating the acknowledged "DOCTRINES" of the Catholic religion, as *evidence* in the case, is a FALLACY in argument, which proves, either that he knows not the laws of sound reasoning, or, that he believes his *hearers* and *readers* to be ignorant of them.

FOURTHLY. The case of Venice furnishes a few facts which go to *refute* the gentleman. Venice was a REPUBLIC. And Venice was CATHOLIC. Therefore, the Catholic doctrines have nothing in them *inconsistent with republicanism*. Here then, is a fact which refutes the slanders of the whole tribe of anti-Catholic crusaders, who are going about disturbing the harmonies of society by their malevolent zeal. Again, the CATHOLICS of THAT REPUBLIC, when the POPE attempted, as they conceived, to govern the TEMPORAL, which belonged to the state, by means of the SPIRITUAL, which belonged to the church, they resisted him, and were prepared to resist him at the POINT OF THE BAYONET. Were they heretics for this? No: they were never accused of it, and this proves that they violated no "doctrine" or principle of the Catholic religion. The gentleman in his comments on this, confounds the "interdict" with the "excommunication," but this I ascribe to the defectiveness of his historical and theological information.

FIFTHLY. The pretended Bull of Innocent VIII. I have long since pronounced spurious. It is not in the BULLARIUM MAGNUM, which contains others quite as objectionable. It is not to be found in ROME. But Mr. Breckenridge promised, more than eighteen months since, to procure its authentication from "Cambridge, England." He has not redeemed his promise. Why? HE knows, and let him tell why. He wants the "original Latin." This will be no proof; for a document may be spurious *in Latin*, as well as in English. Yet he gives the document, under all these circumstances, as if it were genuine. But even *if it were* genuine, it would be no proof; because it does not constitute any doctrine of the Catholic religion. This is the point which the gentleman overlooks, and on which the FALLACY of his induction rests. It purports to be a letter of "INNOCENT, THE BISHOP," to his "WELL-BELOVED SON ALBERTUS," "Commissary, &c. both on THIS SIDE and on THAT SIDE of the mountains," &c. Now, what I have to defend, are the DOCTRINES of the Catholic religion; and as this is no such thing, even if it were genuine, and as besides it is spurious, I have nothing to do with it. The gentleman has first to prove, that it is authentic in history; secondly, that it is regarded as containing doctrines, and then I shall recognise it as an argument.

He first said it was issued in 1477. This was before Innocent was elected. I sent him back to his authorities. Then he found he had ante dated the document ten years, and charged me with "evasion" FOR HAVING DETECTED THE ERROR. Then, he quoted Baronius. I told him, that Baronius wrote only as far down as 1198. He then says, it was "Raynold" (Raynaldus) who continued the work of Baronius, and instead of thanking me, for compelling him to be *more exact in his information*, he again charges me with *evasion*. Finally he finds in Raynaldus, reference to a document on the subject, Rome, 1487, and concludes that, THEREFORE, THIS IS THAT DOCUMENT!! Now, I deny its authenticity, and I call for the proof. I know that it is worthless, for his argument, even if it were authentic. But as a matter of *historical criticism*, I demand his proof. Oh! says he, the "Latin original" is in "Cambridge, England?" What proof have we for that either? I deny the fact, and pronounce the document spurious, and worthy of the cause which employs it. There is no difficulty in admitting that the Waldenses, as well as the Albigenses, were *persecuted* by the Catholics. This is not the question. But the question is, did ever Catholics persecute by virtue of any "TENET OF FAITH OR MORALS HELD BY THEM AS HAVING BEEN REVEALED BY ALMIGHTY GOD?" I answer boldly, NEVER.

And I call upon their accuser to point out the TENET or DOCTRINE in their religion that requires of them to persecute. He is bound to do this, at the risk of being looked upon as a public CALUMNIATOR of their civil and religious character.

SIXTHLY. Bellarmine was an advocate for the punishment of heretics by the state, and it is a remarkable fact, that he was so far from pretending that any doctrine of the Catholic Church required this, that his principal authorities for his views, were the writings of the infallible Calvin himself. Now, my obligation in this controversy is not to defend all that was ever done, or said, or written by Catholics. I am here to defend the *doctrines of the Catholic religion*, and not the opinions of its members. The DOCTRINES ARE BINDING ON ALL CATHOLICS; the opinions of individuals are BINDING ON NOBODY. Here, then, is the FALLACY again, which pervades the whole of the chapter. Let Bellarmine answer for himself; I do not hold his sentiments on the subject of heretics. I prefer the more humane views of the OTHER individuals, and if Bellarmine had attempted to put forth these views as the DOCTRINES of the church, and not as his own opinions, he would have been unquestionably called to account for them. Does he lay them down, as tenets of Catholic faith? Not he; and yet the gentleman would have his readers believe, that the speculations of an author and the DOCTRINES which Catholics " hold as having been revealed by Almighty God," are the same thing! Silly artifice! He knows that the doctrines of the Catholic Church are no more affected by the writings of individuals, giving their opinion as individuals, than the Constitution of the United States is affected by the bubblings of a pettifogger. His system of logic would make the ravings of Garrison a part of the American Constitution, and those of Doctor Ely, or Mr. M'Calla, a part of the Presbyterian creed. Catholics, as such, are accountable for doctrines held by the church as having been revealed by Almighty God.

SEVENTHLY. He asked me, whether the majority in Italy and Spain had a right to establish the Catholic religion by law. To this, I replied that, if in doing so, they violated no right of the minority, they had, in that case, but not otherwise, the right to establish it. He says, the case can *never occur*, and I reply that, if it can never occur, it can never be right for any majority to establish any religion by law. I asked him in turn, whether his Scotch forefathers had a right, being a minority, to pull down by force the altars and religious emblems of the Catholics, who were the majority. To this he replies, " IT WAS WHOLLY WRONG." This flat denial of Presbyterian DOCTRINE is what I expected. Any book, which is used as a CATECHISM, with the approbation of the church, is to be regarded as a STANDARD; and such a book is Fisher's Catechism, which answers the question very differently. In explaining the gentleman's Confession of Faith, it has this " Question. Are our forefathers *to be blamed* for pulling down altars, images, and other monuments of idolatry, from places of public worship, at the Reformation? Answer. No. THEY HAD SCRIPTURE PRECEPT AND WARRANT FOR WHAT THEY DID. (1) 'YE SHALL DESTROY THEIR ALTARS, AND BREAK DOWN THEIR IMAGES, AND CUT DOWN THEIR GROVES, AND BURN THEIR GRAVEN IMAGES WITH FIRE.' "(2) Here we see the HERESY of the gentleman's reply when he says it was "WHOLLY WRONG." This identical Scripture is quoted or referred to in his Confession of Faith, and shows the "SCRIPTURE WARRANT" for burning the Convent at Boston.

EIGHTHLY. The gentleman admits, that Devoti proclaims expulsion from church communion, to be the "highest grade of ecclesiastical coercion." Now, this settles the question, so far as the present discussion is concerned. The same means of "ecclesiastical COERCION," is used by *every petty sect*, in existence. This belongs to DOCTRINE, and all the rest is touching what is called canon law, or rules that were observed in states where the ecclesiastical law was so *mixed* up with the civil, as to be part and portion of the law of the land. Is it honest then, I would ask, to take advantage of the ignorance of those who are unacquainted with the political conditions of other times, and by a perversion of truth, represent as portions of Catholic DOCTRINE, those things which Devoti himself, shows to have been the result of positive state and church laws? If the author in question says, that Catholics are *bound* by the obligation of their religion, to do what he tells us has been done, then I want to know, in what part of his work the assertion is found. The whole speech, being a laboured effort to compel Catholics to believe, what they would in fact BE HERETICS in believing as TENETS OF REVELATION,— shows how the ACCUSER is straitened for evidence. He must first swear, that Catholics believe it as a principle or tenet of their religion—and when *they* swear, that they do not,—he must then swear in reply, that they are not to be believed on oath. He bound himself in the agreement, to confine the question to their DOCTRINES, and yet he never touches a DOCTRINE, but selects out the history of eighteen hundred years, and of the Christian world, such portions as would prove his point, IF it were not CALUMNY of the GROSSEST KIND, to call them doctrines, or hold Catholics of the present day accountable for them.

NINTHLY. I have explained the circumstances, connected with these times, as much as the limits at my disposal would admit. I have shown, that in no case, has the gentleman met the question at issue. I defy any man to fix on any single DOCTRINE, PROVED TO BE SUCH, which is opposed to civil and religious liberty. I have, in former speeches, pointed out what

---

(1) Numbers xxxiii. and Deut. vii. 5.   (2) Page 66, 67.

are the principles of Catholic doctrine. They are TENETS, held by the church, as having been revealed by DIVINE AUTHORITY—are believed by ALL CATHOLICS—in ALL TIMES—in ALL PLACES—and which it would be HERESY TO DENY. These, and these only, are Catholic "DOCTRINES." And these are what the gentleman shuns, although it was in these that he bound himself to discover hostility to civil and religious liberty. I shall argue the case for him, by taking up some of those grounds, which the calumnies of Protestant writers have assigned, as evidence in the case. But, before I do this, I have to call upon the gentleman, to explain a few points, in which he has had the *infirmity* to sin against *truth*, without having the grace or humility to acknowledge it. I have been under the necessity of admonishing the audience, that his statements were not to be depended on, and as this implies a very serious charge, it becomes necessary for me, to establish, and to prove it. And here I must protest against *unfounded* accusation of "abuse and personality." If I were to go out of the record, to examine his *private* affairs, that would be "PERSONALITY." If I were to imitate his example, by retorting on him epithets of contempt and odium, such as he has applied to me, "Jesuit," "papist," "foreigner," "minion of the pope," &c. &c., that would be "ABUSE"—too vulgar, I trust, for my imitation. But I have done nothing of this kind. I have been invited expressly to controvert *his statements*, to examine *his authority*, and *expose him*, whenever he uses bad logic or false assertion. I hope he did not expect me to come here, at his invitation, to *sanction by my silence, the calumnies by which the public,* (to an almost incredible extent,) have been so long deluded, on the subject of the Catholic religion, and its doctrines. If he did, he is mistaken. He stands forth as a PUBLIC ACCUSER, and he must expect that his claim to veracity will be scrutinized. He who tries to take away the character of a large body of his fellow-citizens, must not *complain*, when his unamiable zeal pushes him to the daring experiment of risking his own. If he makes a false statement—and I prove that it *is* a false statement, has he any right to complain, that I am "*abusive or personal?*" I should think not. If he were scrupulous, he would never leave such an advantage in my power. I have already given some instances, in my former speeches, in proof of the fact, that his statements are not to be depended on. I shall now give a few more.

In page 89, (Johnson's edition,) of our written Controversy, he gives a quotation from the "Third chapter" of the Fourth Council of Lateran, as divided by Caranza. He says, at the head of it, "*I have the original before me, but for want of space, I give the translation.*" In regard to this translation, the following questions were put by me. "*First, do you give it as a* LITERAL *and* CONTINUOUS *translation? Second, do you affirm, that in the origi-*

nal, it has the same GENERAL MEANING *that it seems to have in the translation?*" (p. 100.) His answer to the first question is—"*I answer unhesitatingly*, I DO." And yet, the *fact is*, that it WAS NOT CONTINUOUS! The *truth is*, that no two sentences of this "continuous" *translation*, follow each other *in the original*, without words or sentences intervening, which he omitted. He had "the original before him." And *if he had*—he must have known that it was NOT *continuous*. How then, and I ask him for a reply, how could he *say*, that it was continuous?—First instance. Again, having the original before him, how could he say in reply to the second question, "*I consider the second question an indignity offered to the feelings of any honest man.*" (p. 106.) This second question was, "*Whether, in the original, it had the same* GENERAL MEANING, *that it seems to have in the quotation.*" His reply is an indignant mode of asserting, that *it had*. And yet the TRUTH IS, that it HAD NOT. The original had it, "the secular powers PRESENT;" which limits the meaning, by the word "present,"—qualifying the "secular powers," to whom the execution of the decree was entrusted. To make the "meaning *general*," Mr. Breckinridge OMITS the word "present," in the translation, "having the original before him,"—and yet *affects* to be indignant, that I should have *suspected him* of having done so! He *denies it*, and regards the question as an insult. And yet, what HE DENIED, WAS TRUE. SECOND "INSTANCE."

Again still, he says, (same page,) "I answer, that it is from your own 'Caranza's Summa Conciliorum,' that I quote." Now, the *proof* that this is NOT to be depended on, is, that the last sentence of the quotation is NOT in CARANZA—at least not in the part from which the rest was taken. THIRD "INSTANCE."

He says, (same page,) "I omitted the original *for want of space alone.*" This could not be the fact, if, as we have seen, he had "space" left *for what was not in the original at all*. FOURTH "INSTANCE." Now, I challenge the gentleman to deny one single statement here made. If he does *deny one*, I shall quote the omitted passages, and show that the denial is to be regarded as *another* "instance." If he does not deny one, then he admits the facts, and I call upon him for the explanation. I might add many more, but I shall reserve them for future occasion, not wishing to press too much, *at once*.

This may be as convenient a place as any other, to notice the gratuitous, and unmixed "abuse and personality," with which Mr. Breckinridge introduced his last speech. If he can *show*, that my statements are unfounded in truth, I shall not complain But when, *unable to do this*, he travels out of the discussion, to treat of matters that have nothing to do with the question in debate, then I maintain, that the "LOW ABUSE, and INDECENT *personalities*," are *his own*. His reference to what he calls, my

"SPIRIT and ORIGIN,"—to "ST. JOHN'S," "THE FASHIONABLE CONGREGATION," the "*band-box*," the "PRIEST AT THE ALTAR," the "BREEDING SKIN-DEEP," the "ECCLESIASTICAL SHILLELAGH," &c., all on the same page, are specimens (I will not say, of mere *personality*, but) of GROSSNESS, for which no parallel can be found in my writings. I ask, what have these things to do with the question? If I were disposed to *retort*, I should say, that there are *some* men, in whom VULGARITY and PRIDE are inseparably blended,—alternately betraying each other;—in whom, this complex quality is so *innate* and *constitutional*, as to bid defiance to the influence of education, good manners, and even religion itself. I might quote the GROSS and ABUSIVE EPITHETS, which the Rev. John Breckinridge has applied to his opponent, during this discussion, to prove, that the gentleman himself (if to use his own words, "I must call him by that name any longer") is *one* of those men. But, such retorts do not edify. However, lest the gentleman should mistake my motive for abstaining, I wish him to know, that, as to FAMILY, ORIGIN, GOOD-BREEDING, EDUCATION, PRIVATE HISTORY, PUBLIC CHARACTER, I have no reason to shrink from a comparison with HIM, the said Rev. John Breckinridge. *If he brings on the discussion*, he will find me as competent to *rebuke arrogant pretensions*, as he has found me to refute bad logic. I shall hold myself ready to *balance the account*, as soon as he may think proper to present it. But, let the responsibility be on him. The first, and most essential ingredient in the *moral composition* of a WELL-BRED MAN, is a strict and scrupulous regard *for truth*. There are violations, however, of truth, which have no evil consequence, except to the speaker himself. But when truth is violated, *for the purpose of* DEFAMATION, then it admits of no palliation. I shall here give one additional "instance," in which the gentleman has violated truth, precisely in this way. It is found in the written Controversy, p. 325, (Johnson's edition,) where he gives, or professes to give, a note from the Rhemish Testament, and bad as those notes are, he *falsifies the citation*, in order to make it appear even worse than they are. The note is on Hebrew v. 7.

The note is this:	AS FALSIFIED by Mr. Breckinridge:
"But IF the good reader knew *for what point of doctrine they (the Protestant translators) have thus* FRAMED THEIR TRANSLATION, *they would abhor them to the depth of hell.*"	"*The translators of the English (Protestant) Bible* OUGHT TO BE *abhorred to the depths of hell.*"

Here the gentleman makes that a positive and universal proposition, which is in the text, only conditional—"if the good reader knew." &c. 2. He makes that a *duty*, which the authors say, would be a conseq .nce. 3. He FALSIFIES *the text absolutely*, by inserting the words, "OUGHT TO BE," which are not in the original. 4. By his omis-ion of the *true*, and inserting of the *untrue*, the citation would make it appear, that the crime of translating the Bible into English, was *that*, for which the translators "ought to be abhorred," &c. Now the truth is, that the annotators were censuring them for preverting the Bible, after the example of Calvin. They are censuring that preversion, by which these translators, would have Christ to have "SUFFERED THE PAINS OF THE DAMNED IN HELL." And the Rhemish annotators say, that "*if the good reader*" knew this, he would abhor *them* to the depth of hell. Now, Mr. President, the public must determine, how far this gentleman is sustained by HO-NOUR, in thus CORRUPTING the INTEGRITY, and ALTERING the *language of his witnesses*, for the PATRIOTIC purpose of *blackening* the reputation of Catholics, and helping a desperate cause.

During that controversy, it became necessary for me to point out so many instances of a sinfilar kind, that, as it would seem, his friends became a little alarmed. Accordingly, shortly after its close, there appeared a volume of the usual slander and calumny against Catholics, under the insulting and *lying title* of "A HISTORY OF POPERY." The author appears to have been ashamed to put his name to it. But he got Doctor Miller to endorse the ribaldry.

The venerable Professor in an "Introductory Essay," to that compilation of falsehoods and buffoonery, took occasion to allude to the controversy, in language that shows how necessary *he* must have considered it to repeat the charges, and support them on his *own* authority, when they had been found to rest on no other. I do not pretend to judge of his heart or motives, but speaking of his language in as much as it can be considered apart from its author, I venture to assert that it is impossible to find in so small a compass, a larger quantity of condensed malignity, slander, and sanctimoniousness. Of the sanctimonious portion, I shall quote at present two sentences, which I recommend to the *serious consideration* of the Rev. Mr. Breckinridge. Speaking of the controversy, the venerable Professor says, "*Misrepresentations the most gross were not only made, but after their* FALSEHOOD *was* DEMONSTRATED, *was persevered in with a recklessness truly astonishing.*" Yes, we have just "demonstrated" the "falsehood" of some of them. "With such adversaries," he continues, "it is difficult for men of TRUTH and of DELICACY, to carry on a contest."(5) Yes, it is extremely "difficult" when their own statements, and even their citations, as we have seen, are not to be depended on; and when their language becomes surcharged with scurrilous

(5) Ibid. p. 16.

epithets and indelicate figures, such as graced the introduction of Mr. Breckinridge's last speech. This smooth moral of the Doctor's was intended as a charge against the Catholic side of the controversy; but facts prove that its application properly belonged, and belongs to the other.

It is in this "Essay," that this meek Professor denounces the Catholics—those who in the *exercise of the rights of conscience*, prefer the religion of Carroll, of La Fayette, of Kosciusko, and of Gaston—as the "foes of God and man." Think you, sir, that the spirit of Calvinism, which inspired *him* with this language, would not impel his followers to *actions* corresponding, if the Constitution did not interpose?

But enough of Doctor Miller for the present. As to the slanders with which his Essay is crowded, I shall take another occasion of placing them in company with those which I am now engaged in refuting, so far as they belong to this question.

I shall now take up such of the small points of the gentleman's speech, as deserve notice. As to the seven words torn out of a sentence in the Council of Trent, and applied as a translation of an English pretended quotation, I have already established the fact, that, *as the gentlemen used them*, they comprised bad grammar, barbarism, and nonsense; although in the context from which they had been taken, they are exactly correct. The gentleman never attempted to *meet me* on that head. I said they were a forgery; but as soon as I discovered my mistake, I retracted the expression. Notwithstanding this, contrary to all parliamentary usage, he avails himself of my candour to accuse me of injustice. Now, the fact is, that the analogies of the case are, as if A had charged B with forging the name of C: And as if B should affect to triumph, *on the ground that he had not forged*, but had only *cut out* and *transferred the signature*. This would not be *exactly* FORGERY, but it would be almost as disreputable; at all events, it would be nothing to be *boasted* of. He says that this is not a "solitary misstatement." I assure him and the audience, that I will retract every "misstatement" that he can prove to be such, if he will have the goodness to point it out. I challenge him to convict me of any "misstatement," which I am not ready to correct. The side of the discussion which rests *on truth*, requires no other support; and though it is possible that I may commit mistakes, I only wish to have them pointed out. It is by this purpose of honesty, that I have escaped, and always shall escape, those straits into which the gentleman has betrayed himself by his *rashness*, or *readiness*, to assert what is *not true:* and his obstinate reluctance in correcting it, when pointed out and proven to a demonstration, as in the foregoing "instances."

As to Caranza, I have already furnished evidence which ought to make Mr. Breckinridge wish to forget his name. He states, that in reference to this author, I "gloried in the apparent triumph over his (Mr. B's) character." Now, from what I have already established in this speech, the audience will judge whether the "triumph" was not *real* and *complete*. But to me it is no "triumph,"—truth alone claims the victory. I understood distinctly the gentleman to account for the iniquitous suppression in the Twenty-seventh Canon of the Third Council of Lateran, by stating, when charged with it, in the debate, that he followed Caranza; and the PROOF that I understood him correctly, was the silence with which he *admitted* the charge. It appears that afterwards he discovered his mistake, by a reference to the written text of the Controversy, and then attempts to hold me *alone* accountable for a position, which *he created by his assertion*, and *confirmed by his silence, when called upon for an explanation*. And to show how strong his propensity is to use abusive language, and how weak the pretexts on which he indulges his taste, he asks: "*But does the silence of the slandered man make the slander true? And pray, why did he* (Mr. H.) *say it the first time? Does one falsehood excuse two?*" No: but if Mr. Breckinridge, in the debate, gave Caranza as his guide, and I took the excuse which he gave, and whilst I used it in argument, *he was silent as he admits*, thereby showing that I had *not misunderstood* him, then he himself was *positively, by his assertion,* and *negatively, by his silence,* the WITNESS against himself. It was on his authority and admission that I argued; and the gentleman overreaches himself a little, when he applies the words "slander" and "falsehood," to what was said on *his own testimony*. He may keep these precious phrases where they belong.

But the gentleman is mistaken if he thinks that he can escape the charge of *faithless* citation, in regard to the Twenty-seventh Canon of the Third Lateran, by any such silly flourish, as that which I have just exposed. And since he did *not* follow Caranza, in citing the canon, I CALL UPON HIM to say from whom he copied. I DEMAND HIS AUTHORITY. He cites the beginning and end of the canon, *conceals the middle by suppression*, which contained a narrative of the crimes and cruelties of the Albigenses, and makes it appear that the punishment which was awarded *for their crimes,* was simply *for their speculative heresies.* The object of all this malignant artifice, and dishonest citation, was to blacken the Catholic name, and excite hatred founded, in so much at least, on deception, in the minds of Protestants. If he says HE translated from the original, then I charge him directly with the fraud. If he says HE DID NOT COPY from the original, then I demand the name of the author, from whom he *did* copy—that Protestants who love truth, may know in what geometrical progression are propagated from generation to generation, those calumnies which are invoked to prove that Catholics *ought to be hated*. The name MUST BE GIVEN, otherwise the FALSIFICATION must rest at the gentleman's own door. Supposing I were to quote a document to show that

Presbyterians put heretics to death, and *suppress* the part of the document which attested that these heretics were guilty of murder and violence of every description, what would honest and honourable men say? I may be told, that this does not justify the canon ;—that is not the question. I want to know *who it was*, that cited it dishonestly, *for the first time :* whether it was Mr. Breckinridge himself, or another from whom he copied.

The gentleman had stated that there were only four words of the second commandment, in the catechism of the Council of Trent, followed by an *expressive* "et cætera." I showed by no less than five different editions of that work, that it *contains every word of the whole decalogue*, and you may recollect, gentlemen, how he blanched under the testimony—how, on standing up, he spoke of his character, and promised that, if "God would spare his life," he would go to New York, and procure the copy of that work, on which he depended for his vindication. He brought it from New York; and after a long dissertation on the injury that had been offered to his feelings, he exhibited the work. He was courteous enough to trust it into my hands, that I might examine it, when lo! the *entire of the second commandment* was found in it, the same as in all the rest! He spoke no more about his "feelings;" but with great coolness said, that it was not all on the same *page*, which contained the first sentence! The commandments are all divided in that work, and explained clause by clause. Now, I call upon the gentleman to do homage to the truth, under *this head*, and to undeceive the public by acknowledging that the catechism in question, contains not only "four words," but the WHOLE OF THE SECOND COMMANDMENT. Will he have the moral courage to do it? I fear not. He represents me as ridiculing the "doctrine of regeneration." I protest against the charge. I am not conscious of having employed "ridicule," but if I did, it was in reference to that *mockery* of regeneration, which allows men to consider themselves holy from the moment when they become conspicuous in contributions to present or future *schemes* of benevolence towards others, without first going back to make straight the crooked ways of past, private, and personal transactions.

I have had occasion already to observe that Devoti's work is not a work on the doctrines of Catholicity, but a Treatise on the External Policy of the Ecclesiastical Laws and Usages, *as existing in Catholic countries*. He speaks of the church as a VISIBLE SOCIETY, having within itself, and from the very nature of its constitution, all the powers of self-government, implying authority to make laws, and the right to punish those who violate them. Now these punishments, so far as they result from the constitutional powers of the church, were necessarily given by Christ. They consist of ecclesiastical censures, suspensions, and finally excommunication, which the author calls "THE HIGHEST GRADE OF COERCION."

These are the punishments, (pœnæ,) or penalties, by which men are to be "compelled (cogendos) to the observance of the laws and obligations of church membership." These are the powers which Devoti says were given by Christ—as I proved in the arguments of my last speech. I then stated, that Devoti did not claim by virtue of any power given by Christ to the church, the right to punish *by fines, imprisonment, or otherwise*, in a civil sense. The proof was, that Devoti, to support that right, referred *expressly* to the "constitutions" of the empire, and the code of Theodosius. The gentleman says this is "false, directly false." And what proof does he give that it is so? He says that Devoti claimed for the church, as a power *given by Christ*, the right, not merely of governing by counsel, and persuasion, but also of decreeing by laws, and of compulsion, and of coercing with punishment, those who are worthy of it. Mr. Hughes says the same, provided that the "decreeing laws," the "compulsion," "coercing," and "punishment," be in the *spiritual order* such as the Synod of York has exercised in "punishment," of Mr. Barnes, when they could not "coerce" him, to fall down and worship *their* infallibility. Devoti nowhere says, that the use of corporeal punishment, by prisons, fines, exile, or otherwise, was by virtue of a "power given by Christ." This is the proposition which the gentleman says is "directly false;" and I repeat his words to show another "*instance*" in which his statements are not to be depended on. There was no dispute between Devoti and La Borde, on the subject of *bodily* or *civil punishments*. The former wrote in opposition to the principles laid down by the Reformers, so called, which La Borde's treatise favoured. What were those principles? That the "judiciary power" in the church belongs to the civil magistrates, under the pretty title of "NURSING FATHERS TO THE CHURCH." And thus was formed that coalition between ecclesiastical apostasy and political ambition, of which the thousand and one religions, called the Reformation, were the amphibious offspring.

I refer the audience to my remarks, in my last speech, for the circumstances in which Devoti speaks of "prisons, fines, banishment, &c.," as having been used by the church. The gentleman, after quoting my words, tells us in his corrected speech, that Devoti expressly says "this power is given by Christ to the church." It is not true. And to show that it is not true, I pledge myself to make a public apology, if he can produce the words of the author, stating "expressly that the power of 'imprisoning,' 'banishing,' or 'imposing pecuniary fines,' WAS GIVEN BY CHRIST TO THE CHURCH." If he cannot, his *inability* will *convict him* of another "instance" in which his statements are not only not to be depended on, but are absolutely false and unfounded. From these, his false statements, he may draw what inferences against Catholics he pleases, the public will understand the *true* consequence.

His quotation from Devoti, beginning *"But he who offends against society, &c.,"* (which he gives in Latin too,) is another attempt at establishing a false conclusion, on the belief of false premises. Devoti is speaking of the rights of the "ECCLESIASTICAL TRIBUNAL," to judge those who were subject to ITS JURISDICTION, being clergymen, and in those cases not subject to the *civil judge*. But does he say that the right to judge and punish them had been conferred on the church BY CHRIST? Not at all. On the contrary he refers expressly, in the note, to the LAWS OF THE EMPIRE, for the *source* of that jurisdiction which the church, he says, exercises over the "persons" of the clergy, who had been guilty of crimes. Whenever these crimes, he says, were so great that the lenity of the church had no adequate punishment for them, then the clergy were degraded, and the state punished them directly as *lay persons*. Did the gentleman see this? If he did, how could he honestly suppress it? If he did not, it only proves that he reads Devoti as the deist reads the Bible. But whether he saw it or not, it furnishes another "instance" still, to prove that his statements are not to be depended on. I may now address him in the language which he applies to me. He says that Devoti speaks of the power by which the church inflicted *bodily punishment on the clergymen who had committed any civil crime against society*, as "given BY CHRIST *to the church:*" whereas Devoti, *first*, does *not* say this—but, secondly, he states that it was derived from the civil laws of the empire, to which he expressly refers. The gentleman asserts what is *not* true, and suppresses what is *true*. "How strangely then must he feel, to be thus *caught,*" *making* Devoti speak falsehood to support a Calvinistic argument. His reasoning, when founded on false premises, falls of itself.

Now, for his last quotation from Devoti, it is what every body acknowledges in every sect. The Church, as a spiritual commonwealth, has governors, or magistrates, and has power, in the *order of its constitution*, over all persons who are its members, and all things that belong to it, for its use. This is all true, not only in the Catholic Church, which received it from Christ, the *original* proprietor, but also in the Presbyterian Church, which claims it without a title, and exercises it most graciously, as Mr. Barnes knows.

With regard to the INQUISITION, I proved, in my last speech, that it is, and ever was, as much unconnected with the Catholic religion, and the doctrines of the Catholic Church, as the TRIAL BY JURY. I have said and proved, that the *essence of the inquisition* is in every church that has a creed which it calls *orthodox;* and that the gentleman himself, and his "orthodox" brethren, have been but recently discharging the genuine functions of inquisitors. As long as he does not assert that *such* or *such* a *doctrine* of the Catholic religion *requires* the existence of the Inquisition, he shrinks from his proposition. He may abuse it as much as he pleases, and he will accomplish nothing. "The question" is about the DOCTRINES of the Catholic Church, and unless he can make it appear that the Inquisition is one of them—to which I challenge him, as the representative of all the calumniators that have ever said it was—he proves nothing to the point in debate. Devoti gives an account of its institution, and the gentleman concludes that either *"Devoti or myself has been guilty of no small departures from historical and doctrinal truth."* He will again have to excuse me, for saying that his statement is *not to be depended on,* until he will have the goodness to point out *in what* these " DEPARTURES" consist.

After this unfounded statement, he goes back from the Inquisition to the commencement of the volume, as if he had forgotten something very important. Devoti speaks there, as he speaks throughout, of the church, *as she existed in conjunction with the ancient imperial laws.* He speaks of her " twofold power" of punishment. The ONE " WHOLLY SPIRITUAL, given separately by Christ." Now if the gentleman were not bent on making his attempt at argument infinitely ridiculous, he would have stopped here. He had accused Devoti of saying that the "power" to punish " by fines," " imprisonment," " castigation," "exile," &c., had been given *by Christ* to the Church. Now, however, the truth has leaked out, and he is convicted by his own showing. The Church has a " twofold power." After telling us what was the nature of the power *given by Christ—that it is* " WHOLLY SPIRITUAL," exercised in " foro intimo"—the conscience, and in " foro externo," laws and censures; he, Devoti, tells us that she has "ANOTHER POWER" which she has in common with every perfect republic, and which " is called temporal." " *It follows, says he, that there should be a twofold kind* of punishment:" What is this "other" power that was *not* given by Christ;—and " is called temporal?" Precisely that which he had traced to the imperial statutes, with a fidelity of reference which the gentleman *would not* notice, and with a depth of erudition which the gentleman *could not* fathom.

I thank him, however, for having at length done justice to Devoti, at the expense of his own statements. When the imperial laws allowed " ECCLESIASTICAL" OFFENDERS to be judged and punished by the " ECCLESIASTICAL TRIBUNAL," then the church, or the authorities of the church " inflicted bodily punishment." But by what power? By power given by Christ? No; *that* was "WHOLLY SPIRITUAL." By what "power" then? By the power of those imperial laws which Devoti has most abundantly cited. Here again the gentleman has convicted himself; when, *contrary to the truth,* he asserted, and repeatedly asserted, that Devoti had claimed for the church, " AS A POWER GIVEN HER BY CHRIST," the right to *inflict bodily or civil punishment.* He says, that for denying his assertion he will " expose me in a way which

I must deeply regret." His assertions and arguments have inspired me with every feeling but respect for the cause that could employ them; and I can assure him that his *threats* shall not deter me from my duty to truth, and its opposite: I shall continue to defend the one, and expose the other. I have no doubt, however, but he will verify the words of the poet, "furor arma ministrat."

He is willing to "leave the long contest about Bossuet to speak for itself. It *has spoken*, and the gentleman is wise in his silence. And also, he says, "that about the Third Canon of the Fourth Council of Lateran." Not exactly, sir. The gentleman must *first* tell us why he said he quoted from "our own Caranza," literally and continuously, when *the fact was not so*. He says that, in relation to this canon, "*at every step I have given ground. First I tried to defend the canon, as being only discipline against murderers*." This is not the fact; I never said it was "discipline," and never "*defended*" it at all. I showed that it was no "doctrine;" and then the gentleman represented me as wishing to make it "discipline." I showed that the Albigenses, through whom Calvinism is claimed to have *descended from the apostles*, were a sect whose doctrine and practices could not be tolerated in any country or age; and *then, he* said, that I " defended" the canon. As to its authenticity, I assailed it, but not after having been "driven" from what he incorrectly calls my " defence" of it. I showed that he had nothing to reply, except that he *should reply* in time; from which I inferred that my speech had been sent to college for an answer. I showed that, *admitting* its authenticity, it proved nothing *for* the affirmative of the question. I proved that I MIGHT HAVE AVAILED MYSELF of its spuriousness, as established by numerous evidences. I drove the gentleman off on *this* point; and by a kind of delusion which appears to be natural to him, he has mistaken his *own* flight for mine. It is true that, taking the division of Caranza, I used the word "canon," when I should have said "chapter" of the canon; I corrected myself, and then the gentleman "exposed" me. The only difference, therefore, between the gentleman and myself is, that, whilst I have "*spiked*" the canon effectually, after its mischief against the Albigenses, *he* has been *sponging* it with the *leaves of Caranza*, to make it shoot Presbyterians. And unfortunately his hands have not been as yet *purified* from the operation.

The gentleman's authorities return periodically, like the arms of a windmill. He tells us that "Dens," an author which neither of us have ever seen, "*has opened the eyes of* MILLIONS, *on the other side of the waters, to the new evidences of the persecuting doctrines of the Church of Rome.*" He does not give any authority for the statement, however, not even "our own Caranza." A book that has been for sale, for *thirty years* on the shelves of the Protestant booksellers in Dublin, has at length been *miraculously discovered*, and "has opened the eyes of millions," yes; *not*, however, to see what the gentlemen supposes, but to see by what low, base, and contemptible tricks Protestantism in England tries to sustain itself on the crutches of MAMMON, conscious that it cannot walk, nor even stand without them. "Opened the eyes of millions;" yes, to see that the "no popery" tricks will avail no more. "Othello's occupation's gone," and Murtagh O'Sullivan, and Dr. Magbee, dec, dee, cannot recall it. The ghost of Peter Dens will frighten nobody. The people of England are looking for freedom, not because they *love* Catholic doctrines, but because they are disgusted with *Protestant oppression*.

The gentleman says, I HAVE PROVED THAT I DARE NOT HONESTLY AVOW WHAT THE TRUE DOCTRINE OF MY CHURCH IS, BEING IN THE UNITED STATES." How he found his way into the *cabinet of my thoughts*, is more than I can conjecture. Or WHY I SHOULD BE AFRAID to avow the doctrines of my church "in the United States," is a question which would hardly have occurred to any citizen, except a Presbyterian, *familiar with the secrets and designs of the anti-Catholic conspiracy, which has begun to show itself in bigotry and* DARKNESS, *except at Boston, where its darkness was turned into light.*

He says, I "*defend the Bull In Cœna Domini.*" This is not true. I stated that it had been SUPPRESSED; and that was surely not defending it. Can he show where I "defended" it? Does he not perceive that he injures not only his cause, but himself, by such assertions. And, on this unfounded assertion, he builds almost a page of very confused and vapid declamation.

The gentleman promises to speak of "Anathema," in its place, and "*too soon for me.*" He cannot take it up too soon for himself, however; for he has said that it means "CURSE," and I have proved that it does not. And, consequently, that he has "borne false witness against his neighbour."

The gentleman tells us, that the "Bible doctrine" forbids the establishment of any religion by law. I shall prove from his own "CONFESSION OF FAITH," that his assertion is not the doctrine of his church. Was not the Jewish religion established by law? And is not this the Bible? Ay, and that very portion of the Bible which Presbyterians, as the "people of God," in "New Testament times," have ever been ready to imitate.

I had refuted Mr. Wesley's false charge against the Council of Constance, in a way that *bids defiance to my respondent.* I proved that Mr. Wesley, supposing him to have been sincere when he asserted the calumny, had been deceived; and the arguments adduced by me for that purpose, have left the gentleman without any future pretext for the wilful malignity that would *repeat* the charge of Wesley; knowing, as he *now* does, that the charge was, and is, and shall ever be, an atrocious calumny. He has no reply to my facts; no answer for my proofs. The *original documents* have confounded him. As for "help from priests," *I do not re-*

ceive it; and the gentleman knows that *I do not stand in need of it.* If, instead of meeting the " College of Priests," he will only meet my arguments, it will be much more to his credit. By those arguments I have proved that the man who asserts *"that it is a Roman Catholic maxim,"* or *"doctrine,"* *"that no faith is to be kept with heretics,"* is a slanderer of the Catholic body. Now this has been asserted by Mr. Wesley, Dr. Miller, and the Rev. Mr. Breckinridge; I call upon the last-mentioned individual, therefore, to prove the charge, or, like a man who loves truth, to ACKNOWLEDGE THE SLANDER, and undeceive his countrymen.

He says, that " *in the very terms of my citation from the Council of Constance, the doctrine is avowed, that the* FAITH, *the* PLEDGED FAITH (of the Emperor) THAT HUSS SHOULD RETURN IN SAFETY FROM THE COUNCIL, WAS NOT BINDING." Now this is not true. And the proof is, that *no such faith had been pledged by the Emperor.* The Passport was a common passport, to protect Huss, travelling through Germany, where he had many private and personal enemies. The Emperor told him, that if he did not retract, " he, with his own hands, would kindle the fire to burn him."(1ˢ) He says, again, *the Emperor's conduct was not so much violated by the execution of Huss, as by his imprisonment. For if, after an examination, according to the due course of law, the Council had found John Huss a heretic,* THEY WERE IN THE RIGHT, ACCORDING TO THE USAGE OF THOSE TIMES, *to sentence him to the flames, and deliver him over to the secular arm."*(2)

I shall now proceed to a more *critical* examination of the *Presbyterian calf,* which the gentleman sets forth as the *Bull of Innocent* VIII. I have already stated, that there is no external evidence of history to prove that it is authentic. Now, I purpose to show, that it bears in its bosom the *intrinsic* evidences of spuriousness and falsehood. 1st. It enjoins on " *archbishops and bishops to take up arms.*" Whereas, by a law of the church, the shedding of blood, even *accidentally,* or in a just war, *disqualifies a man from becoming a clergyman*—unless by a special dispensation. There never was a case, in which it was allowed for clergymen, by either pope or council, to shed human blood, *in war or otherwise.* This command for " *archbishops and bishops to take up arms,*" is *alone* sufficient to stamp the character of the document. 2d. After having ordered all the ecclesiastical and *civil powers,* to " *make the heretics perish, and entirely blot them out from the face of the earth,"*—as we read in the middle of the document,— this " beloved son, Albertus," is " PERMITTED," towards the close, " if *need be, to call into his assistance, the aid of the secular arm."* This is the second evidence, that it is spurious—and that the imposture is a bungling concern. 3d. But what seals the

(1) L'Enfant, B. III. No. 6. (2) Ib. B. IV. No. 32.

evidence, is, the *suspicion* which the Pope is made to have had about its being regarded as spurious, and for which he takes *prophetic* measures. "*And because,*" he is made to say, "*it may be difficult to transmit these present letters, to all places where they may be necessary, we will, and by apostolical authority appoint, that to a copy which may be taken and subscribed by the hand of any public notary, and attested by the subscription of any ecclesiastical prelate, entire faith may be given, and that it should be held as valid, and the same regard paid to it, as to the original letters,* IF THEY HAD BEEN PRODUCED AND SHOWN."

This was rather overdoing the business. But with all due respect for Innocent VIII., and his calumniators, I would prefer to see the "original letters," or an ATTESTED copy of them. Mr. Breckinridge is not a "notary public,"—and he has not procured the "subscription of any ecclesiastical prelate;" therefore, I cannot "pay the same regard to it," as if it were authentic, notwithstanding the orders of his holiness.

Now, Mr. President, I call on the gentleman to give me the SOURCE *from which he derived this document.* From whom did he copy it? I demand his answer to that question. Was it from the Rev. Dr. Brownlee? Or Mr. M'Calla? What proof has he, that it was ever treated as genuine, by any respectable writer? What then, will the audience and public think of the cause that requires, and the man who could produce such a document in evidence? Must he not have a delicate sense of literary pride,— a high respect for the understandings of his audience,—a sincere disposition to confer honour on the Presbyterian Church, the American name, and human nature? A document surrounded with *external*, and surcharged with *internal*, evidences, of spuriousness—produced by a man who tells us, that there is a "Latin translation" of it in "Cambridge, England." I have a right to demand his authority, and to consider it, what it is, a vile attempt at imposture, UNTIL he shall have furnished us with its history, and the proofs of its authenticity. The inference and commentary are worthy of the document; founded on falsehood, they perish with its exposure.

When the gentleman introduced Bellarmine discussing, as an individual in the exercise of his private opinion, the proposition— "*That heretics condemned by the Church,* MAY BE *punished with temporal punishment, and even with death,*" he should have stated one fact, which the Cardinal sets out with, viz. that HE and CALVIN were agreed on that point,—a pretty strong evidence that he was not arguing an article of *Catholic doctrine.* He proves his opinion by various arguments, which were no doubt satisfactory to his own mind—but though he quotes imperial statutes, and facts to show that heretics had been put to death, and though he quotes Calvin to prove, that they *ought to be* put to death,—he never attempts to prove it, by any reference to the DOCTRINE OF HIS OWN CHURCH, that such a principle of "BELIEF or of MORALS," is a part of the *Catholic religion*. The gentleman affects to say, that he (Bellarmine) was giving on this head, his *opinion* "OF CATHOLIC DOCTRINE." This is not true. He was giving his *own* opinion, and the *reasons why* he entertains it. His opinion is of no authority;—no man's opinion, not even the Pope's, is of any authority in the Catholic Church, farther than as an opinion. But the gentleman knows, that where "doctrines," "tenets of faith or morals revealed by God,"—are in question, there are NO OPINIONS among Catholics. Christ made a revelation of FACTS, TRUTHS,—Catholics believe them as FACTS and TRUTHS,—whilst Protestants make OPINIONS of them.

When Bellarmine lays down the rule to be observed with "heretics, thieves, and other wicked men," when they are not known *distinctly enough*, or when they are too powerful and numerous, he remarks, that he gives the answer *given to the same question by St. Augustine*, who is in high veneration among the Calvinists. Why did the gentleman suppress this?—Since the blame which he would throw on Bellarmine, belongs equally to St. Augustine. Another deception in this passage is, the meaning attached to the word "extirpate." He is speaking of the text, in the gospel of St. Matthew, in which the Saviour was explaining the parable of the "good seed," and "the cockle,"—the one representing the good, the other the wicked;—and Bellarmine following out the figure, contended, that the "cockle" in the field of the Lord, were the *heretics, thieves*, and *other wicked men*, who were to be rooted or plucked out, (EXTIRPANDI,) unless in the cases which he excepted, after St. Augustine, and St. Chrysostom. This is the *fact*, and the gentleman must have known it, if he ever saw the work. He takes up this case, suppresses the circumstances that explain it, metamorphoses Bellarmine's private sentiment, into a doctrine of the Catholic Church, carries it from Rome to America,—makes the Catholic citizens of the republic adopt it, *against their creed and conviction*, and with a *logic worthy of the school he belongs to*, infers on this evidence, that Catholics are bound to cut the throats of all heretics, as soon as they find themselves in the majority! Are they not the majority in France, Austria, Belgium, Ireland, Italy, and in short, in the whole Christian world? If this had been their doctrine, could they not have destroyed the Reformers, in any stage of their increase, from Martin Luther, up to millions? Does the gentleman not see how ridiculous, in presence of THESE UNIVERSAL FACTS,—public, notorious, and obvious to common sense, —he renders himself, when supported by his perversion of Bellarmine, he draws the following sweeping conclusion, discreditable to his feelings, and to the understandings of the audience: "HENCE," says he, "*in the United States we may expect* LIFE, *while we have numbers. You see, gentlemen, what our friends at Rome* (not priests, but cardinals, *whose works are sanctioned by the Pope, and in this case nephew of the Pope*) *think of the rights of the minorities; they are summed up in this,—*THEY MAY DIE BY THE HANDS OF PAPISTS." This is silly slander, founded on yet more silly reasoning.

The gentleman says, that Luther, in maintaining "that the church had never put a heretic to death," meant, *not the Catholic Church,* but some other. That he, after, even *" convicts the Church of Rome of such acts."* I thought he entertained more respect for the character of Luther, than to charge him thus, with a palpable *equivocation.* I call upon him, therefore, for the reference in Luther's works, for the authority on which he makes these two statements. 1st. In which he states, that "THE CHURCH NEVER BURNED A HERETIC,"—and 2d, in which he "CONVICTS THE CHURCH OF ROME OF THESE ACTS." I suspect that something *is wrong here,* as usual. My reason is, that history is entirely silent, touching the existence of TWO CHURCHES, previous to Luther. And I do not like to hear the gentleman, imputing to Luther, a contemptible equivocation on that subject. At all events, I wish to see his *authorities* for the statement.

He says, that Bellarmine *"here frankly avows persecution, yea, the right and the duty of the church to put heretics to death,—and pleads to Scripture for the authority,—and appeals to history for the fact, that the church before his day, had put an almost infinite number to death."* Now, although Bellarmine's opinion, on the matter has nothing to do with the question in debate, yet I cannot hear such atrocious imputations falsely made against Bellarmine, more than against Luther. The question was, whether "heretics, condemned by the church, MIGHT be punished *by temporal punishments,* and even death." Bellarmine contended, that they might, and should,—in opposition to Huss and Luther, who having been liable to this consequence in their own persons, contended, very naturally, that they *should not.* Hence, Bellarmine begins his chapter in these words. *"Joannes Huss, art.* 14, *in Concilio Constantiensi, sess.* 15, *recitato, asseruit, non licere hæreticum incorrigibilem* TRADERE SÆCULARI POTESTATI, *et* PERMITTERE *comburendum.* `Idem Lutherus in art.* 33, *et in assertione ejusdem." "John Huss, in article* 14, *in the* 15 *session of the aforesaid Council of Constance, asserted, that it is not lawful to* DELIVER *an incorrigible heretic* TO THE CIVIL POWER, *and* PERMIT HIM *to be burned. Luther asserted the same, in article* 33, *and in his defence of that article."* The first witness adduced by Bellarmine, to refute both Huss and Luther, was JOHN CALVIN. But what does he undertake to prove? He undertakes to prove, that it is lawful for the church, to leave incorrigible heretics, *to the civil laws of the state, even where the pu-*

nishment of heresy is burning. This was *the only point* in dispute, between him and Huss or Luther.

He lays down the proposition which he is about to prove, in these words :—

"*Nos igitur breviter ostendemus, hæreticos incorrigibiles, ac præsertim relapsos, posse ac debere ab ecclesia rejici, et a sæcularibus potestatibus, temporalibus pœnis atque ipsa etiam morte mulctari.*"

"*We, therefore, shall briefly show, that incorrigible heretics, and especially those who have relapsed,* MAY AND OUGHT TO BE CAST OUT FROM THE CHURCH, AND BE PUNISHED BY THE SECULAR POWERS, *with temporal punishment, and with death itself.*"

Here, then, are the two points of his thesis:—

1st. That heretics MAY AND OUGHT TO BE CAST OUT OF THE CHURCH; and

2d. That (being cast out) they MAY AND OUGHT TO BE PUNISHED WITH CIVIL PENALTIES, *and even death,* (not *by the church,* as Mr. Breckinridge states in opposition to Bellarmine's own words, but, BY THE CIVIL POWER. That first part of the proposition is held by the gentleman himself, viz. "That heretics *may and ought to be cast* out of the church." Bellarmine, then, turning to the CIVIL POWER, says, that the state (sæcularibus potestatibus) "may and ought" to put them to death even, or lesser punishments. The arguments by which he attempts to prove *this part* of the proposition, are those from which Mr. B. presents the garbled quotations, which he shamefully perverts. Bellarmine says, that it is the RIGHT AND THE DUTY OF THE STATE to punish heretics, with civil penalties and even death. Mr. Breckinridge, contrary to this, charges him with "avowing the right and the duty of THE CHURCH to put them to death." In which he only furnishes another "instance" to prove that his statements are not to be depended on. Every instance adduced by Bellarmine of this, is an instance by the authority of the state or by some Emperor; but, inasmuch as the civil rulers, who *made* and *executed these laws* against heretics, *were Catholics,* and the church had "cast those heretics out," he speaks of it as if the church itself had executed the laws. DOES HE say that there is any *doctrine* of the church, any *law of the church,* requiring heretics to be put to death ? No ! DOES HE say the church ever put them to death except by *not shielding them under* the ecclesiastical laws ? No ! DOES HE say that she ever claimed the *right* to put them to death, that she exercised it, that she ever put any one to death for *heresy,* except by leaving them exposed to the law of the state, the secular power ? No ! Has not the gentleman accused Bellarmine falsely ? He will probably say, that I "defend" Bellarmine—yes, from *unfounded accusations,* but as to his *opinion* on the right and duty of the magistrate, or temporal powers to punish heretics, I hold it *indefensible;* and the only way I can account for his having attempted to maintain such an opinion, is, by supposing that his judgment had been twisted into obliquity of vision by the sophistries of Calvin and Beza, on the same subject—for he places *their works and example* at the head of the chapter.

Such, Mr. President, are the amount and detail of the gentleman's speech; a compound of false premises, supporting false logic, and giving occasion to that kind of wholesale assertion and bloated declamation which constitute the very acme of eloquence and evangelism, in the anti-popery meetings which have been organised by the propaganda of bigotry in New York. Any thing, sir, that is said to blacken popery, being, of course, Protestant doctrine, *must be true.* This delusion has lived too long, and spread too far. It may be convenient for the gentleman, whenever he shall think proper to make good his promise of "carrying on the controversy *by himself.*" But it will not suit *here.* He has invited me to come and examine the quality of his information and the character of his reasoning. It is in obedience to this invitation that I make so free in my analysis of both. The child of his anti-popery zeal would be, perhaps, admired elsewhere; but when he sends it forth *here,* as a young giant, that is to slay the man of sin in the United States, I have only to bring it near the light, and hold it up. The first ray that falls upon it from the lamp of truth in history, and of logic in debate, proves it to be a little monster of moral deformity, which, instead of killing the pope, will only disgrace its parentage.

By the way, there is one thing that has struck me as somewhat extraordinary. It is, that the gentleman, after having been in the field publicly against the Catholic religion these several years, is evidently unprepared for the facts of the question. He was unprepared for the case of the Albigenses, and the *facts* connected with it. He was unprepared for the *facts* regarding Huss and the Council of Constance. He was unprepared for the meaning of "anathema," according to the facts. He was unprepared for the character of the Inquisition, according to the *facts* of history. He was *familiar with the calumnies* which are founded on all these subjects, and made abundant use of them. But the *facts,* which he had never condescended to examine at the *original source,* took him by surprise; and he adjourned the topics with a—*promise.* A gentleman who has kept himself so long advertised as *the champion,* should have been better prepared: one who had so long and so often *instructed the public,* should not have been obliged to wait for information on subjects with which he had professed himself so well acquainted. The unexpectedness of the position should have been an excuse for *me,* if I were found unable to meet the gentleman at every point. It was impossible for me to have made any special preparation; and yet, to my surprise, my arguments on the very topics on which the gentleman has been so clever, *when there was no one to oppose him, are obliged to wait unanswered* till the advent of *"new light."* And as I never wish to make an assertion without supporting it by proof, I give an additional instance of a topic for which I venture to predict that not only he, but the authorities at Princeton are unprepared. Has he ever asserted in public, or proclaimed in print, that in the Catholic Church the *Scriptures in the vernacular language are withheld from the laity?* If he has, he has aided in perpetuating the calumny, without taking pains to know, or make known the *facts.* Doctor Miller has this very calumny in his Introductory Essay, coupled with others "whose name is legion." " Does she not," says he, "after all her multiplied denial of the fact, continue to LOCK UP *the Scripture from common people?"* No, Doctor, not at all; *you are misleading the public (unintentionally, I hope)* when you say so. Do you ask for proof? Then I give it. It consists of the following FACTS, which you *should* have known.

The Catholics in this country have published *more editions* of the Scriptures in the English language than any other denomination, during the same time. They have one in folio, four in quarto, one in octavo,—making SIX DIFFERENT EDITIONS OF THE WHOLE BIBLE. Of the New Testament, there have been published separately, one in 4to, two in 8vo, two in 12mo, and two in 32mo, making SEVEN EDITIONS OF THE TESTAMENT SEPARATELY—THIRTEEN EDITIONS in all, and *one in French, for the French Catholics, published under the auspices, and by the direction of Bishop Cheverus.* Protestants do not buy them,—the clergy do not require them in English, having them in other languages, especially the Latin. Who bought them, and paid the publisher for printing, and even stereotyping them? The "COMMON PEOPLE," from whom, Doctor Miller says, falsely, that "THEY ARE KEPT LOCKED UP." Is the gentleman prepared to meet me on this topic, in regard to which he has so often asserted the calumny? Shame on the men who can thus bear " false witness against their neighbour."

Mr. Breckinridge may say that in *this country* the Scriptures could not be kept out of the hands of the people; and that though the charge is false, *as regards American and English Catholics,* yet it is true where the power of the church prevails, as in Italy. This is equally false, and the proof is the letter of Pope Pius VI. addressed to Martini, in *approbation of his labours as translator of the Bible into Italian,* for the use of the *"common people."* For *this,* and other service to religion, said Martini was made archbishop. This reference to the Italian Bible reminds me of a pledge given by me in presence of the society, which it is fitting that I should redeem.

You remember, Mr. President, the evening on which DOCTOR BROWNLEE honoured the meeting with his presence, I had to answer the young gentleman who opened the debate with so many beautiful figures of speech. I had to answer the Rev. Doctor Brantley, who thought that it was possible and incumbent on me to "*prove* the NEGATIVE." I had to answer the gentleman himself, who had come *prepared.* In his speech, he brandished the usual calumnies around the head of "popery." Among others, this very one of Doctor Miller's, about keeping the Scriptures "*locked up from the common people.*" In my answer to his speech, I mentioned as a refutation of *this particular calumny*, that the Catholics had published FORTY EDITIONS of the Scriptures in Italian, before the first Protestant edition came out, which was that of Geneva in 1562. This was something *new* to the bench and to the meeting. Dr. Brownlee, as you recollect, stood up to interrupt me, and on being informed that he must address himself to the chair, he stated that he wished to ask a question "*for information,*" and on leave being granted, he inquired, "WHETHER THOSE EDITIONS OF THE SCRIPTURES WERE IN THE VERNACULAR LANGUAGE?" I replied that THEY WERE; to which his rejoinder was, "I DENY IT." Then, sir, I promised to *prove it,* and show that the Doctor ought not to deny the existence of FACTS, after having avowed his ignorance of them, and his *desire* to be "informed." Now for the PROOFS.

1st. In the year 1471, SIXTEEN years after the *first book was printed with type,* and FIFTY years before that fusion of DOCTRINE into PRIVATE OPINION, which is called the "Reformation," and TWELVE years before the BIRTH of Martin Luther, the Bible was printed and published in the Italian language, in VENICE. This edition was published in August, as appears by the title-page; "*impresso fu questo volume nel l'alma patria di Venitia negl' anni de la salutefera incarnatione del Figliolo de l'eterno et omnipotente Deo,* 1471, *in Kalende di Augusto; per Vindelino Spira.*" It was the translation of NICHOLAS MALHEMI, a MONK. Another edition was published in October of the same year, in the same city, and a third in Rome, making three editions in large folio in the year 1471. In 1475, a fourth was published "*in Pignerolo, per Gio de Rossi.*" Fifth, sixth, and seventh editions in VENICE, *all three in* 1477, *of different type,* and the last being an "improvement" on the translation of Malhemi, by Squarzaticco, as stated in the preface. Eighth, VENICE, in 1481. Ninth and tenth, VENICE, in 1484, when Martin Luther was a *baby of about one year old.* Eleventh, VENICE, in 1487, a curious and elegant edition, a copy of which David Clement saw in the biblical collection of the Duchess of Luneburg, "*nitide et accurate excussa.*" The twelfth and thirteenth have disappeared entirely. The fourteenth and fifteenth editions are of the years 1502 and 1507. The latter is the first edition of the celebrated GIUNTI. The editions of 1517, '25, '32, '35, '46, '53, '58, all of Malhemi, in folio, bring the number to twenty-one. The editions from twenty-two to thirty-five, both inclusive, were the translation from the Hebrew, of Bruccioli, published by Giunti, VENICE, with the *privilege of the senate;* the first appeared in 1532. A version by another translator, Marmochini, a Dominican, which he professed to have made from the Hebrew, and Greek, was published by GIUNTI, first in 1538, and again in 1546, making editions thirty-sixth and thirty-seventh. Edition thirty-eighth, was by another translator, with a *poetical version of Job and of the Psalms,* in 1547.

The 39th and 40th editions were published in 1541 and 1551, being the translation of Bruccioli *with some alterations.* ELEVEN years after the date of the *last,* and NINETY-ONE years after that of the *first* edition of the Bible in Italian, the Calvinists ALTERED the version of Bruccioli to suit their purpose, as the editor declares in the preface, and published in Geneva, the FIRST PROTESTANT edition of the Scriptures in the Italian language. But on what authority does all this rest? Must I send for "*Latin to Cambridge, England,*" to prove it? No, sir. The proof is the testimony of DAVID CLEMENT, A CALVINISTIC MINISTER, *and librarian to the king of Prussia, in his "Bibliotheque curieuse, ov catalogue raisonne de livres difficiles a trouver,*" in ix vols. 4to, published at Gottingen, 1750–60. (See letter B.) What will the gentleman say for his fanatical associate, Doctor Brownlee, who DENIED this fact? What will he say for his own calumnies, and those of Doctor Miller, in maintaining that the Catholic religion is hostile to the Scriptures, and "*locks them up from the common people?*" Sir, these gentlemen ought to instruct themselves before they teach others, and if they really are ignorant of these facts, it is a disgrace to the age that they should labour as they do in regard to this matter, to engraft their own ignorance of the fact, on the American mind, *as a part of knowledge and education.*

What was true of Italy, was equally true of Germany, France, Spain and Belgium. Does the gentleman *deny* it, like Doctor Brownlee? If he does, I pledge myself to prove it. But I took Italy, *the heart of the Catholic Church.* Will the gentleman, therefore, as he loves truth, aid, with the pen that has contributed to lead the uneducated astray on this subject, to undeceive them? Will not GOD approve of such a course, proceeding from such a motive?

But why was a partial restriction put to the reading and circulation of the Scripture afterwards? The reason is obvious. The religious wars in Germany, France and Switzerland—the crimes and fanaticism that had been witnessed, and for all which was quoted, some *text of Scripture,* as authority, had presented a *new* and *alarming view* of the case. When the demagogues of the reformation, in order to seduce the people from allegiance to all powers *but themselves,* taught them that they could understand the Scriptures without difficulty, and engaging them in wars and sedition against their governments, applied the principle of Mohammed with more subtlety, but with equal effect, to persuade them, that in doing so, they were contending "FOR THE GOSPEL," then it was deemed prudent to regulate the circulation of the Scripture in the vernacular language, until the delirium of the social and religious condition, which the abuse of the Scripture and the degradation of its character had produced, should have subsided or passed away.

The regulation was restrictive, local, temporary. And never was PROHIBITORY, UNIVERSAL, or PERPETUAL, as Protestant misrepresentation has asserted. The facts of the immense circulation of the Scriptures in the various languages of Europe, before the Reformation, (*considering how recently printing had been invented,*) are such as should make these false accusers ashamed of their vocation. The circulation of the Scriptures in the United States, where the Catholics, few as they are, have had them in every size and form, is a direct refutation of the calumny, by facts, against which it is ridiculous for them to reason. Even the Spaniards, in whose country the Inquisition was most jealous and oppressive, have their Spanish Bible, by the Bishop of Segovia, a copy of which, *mutilated* by the Bible Society of New York, I now hold in my hand. It is regarded as the word of God, and yet it is sent by the Bible Society to the ignorant Spaniards of South America, with a FALSEHOOD printed on the title-page. It purports to be from the Vulgate, as translated by the Bishop of Segovia, in order not to startle the prejudices or suspicions of the Spaniards. And yet the books, which Protestants call "Apocryphal," but which Catholics believe to be inspired, ARE ALL OMITTED. With this omission, of which nothing is said, it is no longer the Bible of the Bishop of Segovia; and, consequently, it 'carries on its title-page a FALSEHOOD. Now, let not the gentlemen say that in this, I *calumniate the Bible Society*, or the gentlemen who compose it. I state the FACT. It is a FRAUD, known as such to its authors, whoever they may be, and ought to be denounced by every honourable member of that society. They ought not to associate, nor allow their agents to associate, with the circulation of the "WORD OF GOD," so legitimate an evidence of their holding, or at least *practising* the maxim, that the "*end* justifies the *means.*"

"*Is the Roman Catholic Religion, in any or in all its principles or doctrines, opposed to civil or religious liberty?*"

AFFIRMATIVE VI.—MR. BRECKINRIDGE.

MR. PRESIDENT,—After holding the copy of my speech about *thirty days*, the gentleman has returned me his *windy* response. During half of that time, he also had in his possession my reply on the alternate question also, though, by agreement, his reply was due on the delivery of my speech on the affirmative. I do not *wonder* at his delay. I *shall* wonder, if he ever permits this debate to see the light. But I here notice these facts to show the public in what a position the man stands who complains that I am *never prepared to meet him*. Was I not prepared to meet him in the discussion? Did I not meet him on *all* the *points* as they arose? And after the debate was brought to a close, is not the whole Society witness to the fact, that he *refused* to publish the *reports* of the *stenographer;* and insisted on delaying even the *writing out anew* of the debate, as we are now doing, until he should go to Mexico?

No, sir, the fact is this. The gentleman finding his cause pressed sorely, tried *first* to divert me from its exposure, by shifting the grounds of the discussion. But I chose to pursue my own course, as it is my right and duty to do, while in the *affirmative*. I did not choose to discuss the character of the *Inquisition*, till I had finished the *direct proof of the enmity of his Church* to *liberty*. He then tried the virtue of attacking my reputation through the contents of a former controversy. I then turned aside, for the greater part of one evening, to meet and expose his malignity and falsehoods, to the satisfaction, I am sure, of every candid mind; and afterward resumed the line of my discussion. In the *writing out* of this debate, he has bespangled every part of it with these personal attacks, and these vain efforts at diversion from the main question. Besides having met these *personalities* in my *late* controversy with him, and besides, having exposed them in the oral debate, I have met them as they have been brought up by him in the manuscript. Some of them reappear, in meagre and dejected forms, in his last speech, evidently showing that the author, having little to say *for* his cause, wishes to do all he can *against his* adversary. Pascal, a *Catholic*, but a *Jansenist*, has explained all this in his fifteenth Letter, (Provincial Letters,) of which the heading is this: "*the Jesuits omit calumny in their catalogue of crimes, and make no scruple of using it against their enemies.*" Pascal, whom Mr. Hughes has *denounced*, exposes the Jesuits, whom Mr. Hughes has *praised*, for wickedly justifying *horrible calumnies* known to be so, in self-defence. "It is certain," says Caramuel,(1) "it is a probable opinion that it is no mortal sin *to bring a false accusation for the sake of preserving one's honour, for it is maintained by twenty grave doctors*, Gaspar, Hurtado, Decastillus, &c. Hence, if this doctrine be not probable, there is scarcely any one that is so in the whole system of divinity." Well might Pascal exclaim, "*Oh, what an execrable system is this!*" This is the morality of the school which the gentleman sustains; which is head of popery in this country; and which adequately explains all Mr. Hughes's calumnies.

By these attacks the gentleman compelled me to hold up *three cases* of *fraud committed by him before the whole society*, viz.: 1. The case of Mosheim, where he omitted the *first sentence*, and read what the historian had said of a set of *fanatics*, and told us it was a *description of the Albigenses, who were* not *named* there; and of whom the same writer *gives a totally different account*. 2. The case in which he *took one sentence of mine* from a *certain page*, and another, some fifty pages *off;* and by putting them together, made me say the very reverse of what I had really said, and then charged it on me as falsehood. 3. The case in which he *omitted whole pages* of a manuscript which he was reading as part of his speech, and yet handed it in to be reported, thus robbing me of my time, (for we spoke by portions of time alternately,) and thus dishonourably charging Presbyterians with horrible principles and crimes, which I *did not know* were in the paper, and which would have gone before the public unknown, and, of course, unanswered by me, if I had not demanded a copy from the stenographer. These were openly exposed, and charged upon him publicly. They *have not* been, they *cannot* be explained. When they occurred, I should have left the discussion, but for the sake of the cause: for since that moment he can have no claim to my respect; nor can I own him as an equal, or a gentleman. I once tried to explain Mr. Hughes's conduct by the apology of his bad breeding and ignorance of the decent proprieties of life. Now, we must refer all to the *morality of Jesuitism*. And now let the *gentleman explain*, if he can; *deny*, he dare not; and even should he be unable to do it, if he will repent, and reform, I will *forgive*.

As to Caranza; I have already, and fully explained, as he well knows, the *omission* of a single word, "*præsentibus*," by *mistake*, which he *knows* did not in the *least* affect the *sense*. And I call on him to tell me publicly, whether *the extract*, from the third

(1) N. 1151.

chapter of Fourth Lateran, contains *one word* that is not in the *original*. He says, the *translation overruns Caranza, from whom I quote*. If, then, what I give in English, is not in the *original Latin*, here will be the way to detect me. If he will say that translation is not *faithful;* if, what overruns Caranza, is *forged*, let him say so. If he will, then *I will* tell him what translation I followed. By his declaration, that *Caranza's* Latin is overrun by my English, he either asserts that I *fabricate matter*, or else that Caranza has *not given all*. The former he dare not say. The latter is the fact. Caranza suppresses much of the decree. I gave a *page* of his abridgment, and gave the *continued sense* of the decree; following him as far as he *went*, and then continuing it from other sources. This Mr. H. knows. Let him venture to deny it. Yet he charges me with garbling the decree; and justifies Caranza for doing the very same thing. And now I challenge Mr. H. to show that, in my long extracts from Caranza, I have *at all* affected the *continued sense*, or *mistranslated, in the smallest measure, a single word*. My citations were taken largely from consecutive portions of the infamous decree, to prove the *persecution* of the Church of Rome. I have given the whole chapter in my second speech, first night. Let any reader refer to the former Controversy. I challenge Mr. Hughes to cite the passage in his next speech, and show that my said extracts *altered the sense of the* canon. If not, his charges are base. If I did, let him show it.

Mr. H.'s *evasion* about the false charge of "forging Latin for the Council of Trent," which he so ludicrously urged against me, is too palpable to call for any thing but my pity at his embarrassment. When, by accident, I omitted *one word* in a *page of Latin*, he says I "*suppressed;*" when I cite a passage, and give a *word too much*, he says it is "a *forgery*." I then refer to the passage with new *proofs* of its *genuineness;* he says I am *right* in the *letter*, but wrong in the *spirit*. When, of a decree covering several pages, I give the *substance* in one page, he says, I *suppress* a *part*. Yet, at the end, I *overrun* a *papal abridgment*, and give an additional sentence from another and fuller work, he charges me with doing wrong again. Because I say I follow the abridgment, (as far as it goes,) I *sin* if I go any farther, though *every word I add is a part of the decree* which the popish abridger *had left out!!* For such attacks, there is no explanation but the desperation of the man.

His explanation of his fraud on my quotation, I cannot receive. It will not do, Mr. H. Your character calls you to try it once *more!*

He rings *new changes* on the *old* charge, and the *true one* made by me, *that* the *Catechism* of the *Council of Trent gives* only *four words* of the second commandment. The *copy* to which I referred is in the *public library* of New York. When he called up the subject, on the rostrum, *two years after* I had *asserted the fact*, (in the first Controversy with him,) I promised to get the book, and exhibit it. In due time I did so. It was just as I had said. The *four words* were given; the *rest*, instead of being *announced*, were *suppressed*, and brought up *many pages after*, in the *tail* of the *exposition*, and kept out of view as much as possible! That the gentleman produced *some copies* of one or more *editions*, in which the whole was honestly announced *on one page*, is only a proof, that *Rome* is *wise*. She gives out the word of God as she *must;* and has different *degrees* for different *regions* of the earth. Sir, every scholar knows that the Church of Rome is guilty in this thing. She even mistranslates the words of the Bible, which forbid us "to *bow down*" to graven *images*; *falsely* rendering them "*adore*," &c.; for you know her people do *bow down* to *graven images*. But in most cases the Church has *suppressed the true second commandment*, after merging it in another, and splitting the *unique* tenth, so as to make *two of it;* and thus covers the fraud. That Church has different editions of her standards for different countries; and whenever she dare, she suppresses the commandment which forbids *idolatry*. I will prove what I say. The most Rev. James Butler's Catechism, revised, enlarged, improved, and recommended by the four Roman Catholic Archbishops of Ireland, printed at New York in 1826, at page 21, has the following question and answer:—

"Lesson XIV. On the Commandments.

"Ques. Say the ten commandments of God.

"Ans. I. I am the Lord, thy God; thou shalt not have strange Gods before me, &c.

"II. Thou shalt not take the name of the Lord, thy God, in vain.

"III. Remember that thou keep holy the Sabbath day." Is there any thing here about *images?* Not a word! Surely, they who keep the Bible from the people, ought, at least, to give them the ten commandments in full! The *next* proof is from a Philadelphia edition, published by authority, by Eugene Cummiskey in 1827. *Not one word is here about graven images.* *Next*—Mr. Cummiskey, four years after, gives another edition. There was time for *repentance*. But still the *same thing*. *Fourth proof.* "The Christian Doctrine," composed by Father Lederma, Priest of the Society of Jesus, and printed "*by permission of the superiors*," A. D. 1609 and 1624,(1) gives the following version of the commandments:

"I. I am the Lord, thy God; thou shalt have no other Gods but me.

"II. Thou shalt not take the name of God in vain.

"III. Remember to sanctify the holy days." Is there any thing here about *graven images?* Yet, while suppressing the

(1) See Preface to Vis. Tuta.

law of God against *idolatry*, he *adds*, (*wickedly*,) a charge to keep *Roman holy days!*

Again; the version used in Ireland has not one word of the second commandment.

And again; the version used in the Highlands of Scotland (1) wholly suppresses the second commandment. And now, no one need be at a loss to understand the *reason*, to estimate the *guilt*, or know *the fact* of this *suppression*. I ask now, who is the *calumniator?* And as *I* have no Jesuit-morality to shelter *me*, I wish the calumny to attach where it belongs. I know, however, that it is hard for Mr. Hughes to *explain*, or *disprove* this terrible iniquity.

As the gentleman's ideas fluctuate in elegant confusion, through his pages, it matters little in what order the reply to them be arranged. We make the *order of importance* our guide; and next return to Cardinal Bellarmine. He says, that I "introduce Bellarmine discussing as *an individual, in the exercise of his private opinion*, the proposition, '*that heretics may be punished with temporal punishments, (penalties,) and even with death.*'" But, sir, the gentleman well knows that Bellarmine speaks, like DEVOTI, under the Pope's *expressed sanction*, and utters the true Catholic doctrine! The Pope did hang him up in the Index for *one error*, viz.: for saying, that the Pope had only INDIRECT TEMPORAL POWER, whereas he ought to have said, he has DIRECT temporal power. The rest is *approved*, and declared to contain no doctrine contrary to the Catholic faith. It is no *private opinion, then;* but the publicly approved, avowed doctrine of the Church of Rome! If Calvin agreed with Bellarmine, then Calvin was so far *wrong*. But Calvin spoke *his* tenet; Bellarmine spoke for the Pope, his master, and *his Church.* Mr. Hughes says, that infamous passage which directs to *kill heretics*, if Catholics have the *majority*, was derived from Augustine, by the author. Yes, and that is another *proof*, that it is *Catholic doctrine;* "the *consent of the fathers.*" Chrysostom, also, says the same. Mr. Hughes says, again, that I "suppress the circumstances which explain it." What are they? The above is one of them! Another is "that Bellarmine is speaking of the text (passage) in the Gospel of St. Matthew, in which the Saviour was explaining the parable of the good seed and the cockle; the one representing the good, the other the wicked; and Bellarmine following out the figure, contended that the *cockles* in the field of the Lord, were the *heretics, thieves, and other wicked men*, who were to be rooted or plucked out, (extirpandi,) unless in the cases which he excepted, after St. Augustine and St. Chrysostom." Now, if this be not *enough* to prove, that Bellarmine *thought* it a papal doctrine to *extirpate heretics*, unless, to use his own words, "THEY

(1) See M'Gavin on this subject.

ARE STRONGER THAN OURSELVES," I know not the force of words. But see how Mr. Hughes and Bellarmine reason. The Lord said, "*let the wheat and the cockle grow together till the harvest;*" i. e. "*the end of the world.*" Bellarmine says no! Pluck them up now, *if you can!* Mr. Hughes says, that I "suppress circumstances." What circumstances? Does Bellarmine say, it is his opinion! No. He says, in the same chapter, (in answer to the objection, that it *was contrary to the mercy of the Church, to wish the death of heretics,*) " THE CHURCH HAS TRIED ALL *other methods, before* she could be induced to inflict this extreme punishment, (death;) for, at first, as we have said before, SHE only excommunicated; but afterwards, seeing this would not suffice, SHE added pecuniary penalties; then confiscation of goods; afterwards exile; at length she reached this, (death;) as is sufficiently apparent from the various laws of the ancient emperors, in the chapter entitled *De Heretics.*" Here is no *opinion;* but a fact; viz., that as soon as the emperors allowed her, THE CHURCH DID *fine, rob, banish, and kill heretics!*

But Mr. Hughes asks, "Are not Catholics in the majority in France?" No. Protestants and infidels are now! . Once they were. And what then? Has Mr. Hughes forgotten the edict of Nantz, and St. Bartholomew's day? " In Austria?" But are Protestants tolerated in *Austria?* So as to have room to increase? "In Belgium?" But she goes with France. Have you forgotten the Belgian bishops, who said, that it was anti-Catholic to tolerate any other religion? " In Ireland?" It has been tried there! Force alone has hindered it! " In Italy?" Are Protestants tolerated in Italy, Mr. Hughes? "And the Reformers?" Why, yes? The Reformers lived only because the wars of near half a century could not extinguish them. No, Mr. Hughes; it is not from the Carrolls, and Gastons, and Careys, and other patriots, that we look for these things, as you try to make me say, concerning the wicked and polluted bands of the *Jesuit priesthood*, under their names. No. The Catholic laity, such as these, are not Roman Catholics! on the question of *liberty.* The *priesthood* is the *Church;* the hierarchy of Rome is the despotic power; and they must change, or fall from the confidence of American citizens. But if the priesthood can but rally from the dark papal states of Europe, a full band of their unlettered and deeply subjected militia, then may we see this land ruled by a *papal mob;* and then these slumbering doctrines will awake for new carnage in this confiding nation. But we proceed. Mr. Hughes, in the face of Bellarmine's own words, says, that "they" (heretics) "may, and ought to be punished with civil penalties, and even death, *not by the Church*, as Mr. Breckinridge states, in opposition to Bellarmine's own words, but by the civil power." Now, see the truth. In this very chapter, Bellarmine says, "It is proved; [the proposition, that the civil power OUGHT to punish, even with DEATH, the IN-

CORRIGIBLE HERETICS CAST OFF BY THE CHURCH.] I. BY THE SCRIPTURES. II. It is proved, from the opinions and laws of the emperors, WHICH THE CHURCH HAS ALWAYS APPROVED." Is this an OPINION of Bellarmine? He appeals to history. III. "IT IS PROVED BY THE LAWS OF THE CHURCH!" Is this an *opinion?* Do the *laws* of the Church EVER VIOLATE HER DOCTRINES? If these *laws* were anti-Catholic, would "*the Church always approve them,*" and *pass them,* and *never* to this day repeal them? IV. "*It is proved by the testimony of the fathers.*" Were these fathers *heretics?* Their *opinions* make part of the *rule of faith* in the Roman Church! He afterwards says, "THAT HERETICS WERE OFTEN BURNED BY THE CHURCH, MAY BE PROVED BY ADDUCING A FEW FROM MANY EXAMPLES;" and he names "DONATISTS, MANICHEANS, AND ALBIGENSES, who were routed, and *annihilated by arms:*" nay, he says, "AN ALMOST INFINITE NUMBER (OF HERETICS) WERE EITHER BURNED, OR OTHERWISE PUT TO DEATH," (by the Church.) But Mr. Hughes ventures to say, "*every instance,* adduced by Bellarmine, of this, is an instance by the authority of the state," (but, he says, the Church *approved* this! Is it not then her *doctrine?*) or by some emperor; but inasmuch as the civil rulers, who made and executed these laws against heretics," (but, Mr. Hughes! Bellarmine says, "THE LAWS OF THE CHURCH called for it!") "were Catholics, and the Church had cast these heretics out; he speaks of it as if the Church herself had executed the laws." But Bellarmine says, "The apostles did not invoke the secular arm against heretics, because there was no Christian prince whom they could call on for aid. But afterwards, in Constantine's time......... the Church called in the aid of the secular arm." And he here quotes Augustine again. And more; he says, (all in Mr. Hughes's face, in the self-same chapter,) "As the *Church has ecclesiastical and secular princes, who are her two arms,* so she has *two swords,* the *spiritual and material;* and, therefore, when her *right hand* is unable to convert a heretic, with the *sword of the Spirit, she invokes the aid of the left hand,* and coerces the heretics with the material (*ferreo— iron*) *sword.*" Here he makes the Church the HEAD; and the state, "the left arm, with the iron sword" moving at her will; and as soon as ever the emperors would, she set them to work to burn heretics! Yet, Mr. Hughes has the *rashness,* I use no stronger term, to say, "EVERY INSTANCE, adduced by Bellarmine, is AN INSTANCE OF THE AUTHORITY OF THE STATE!" Oh! shame, where is thy blush! As well say, that the *man who kindled the fire that burned them, did it, and not the emperor; for the emperor did not touch the match!* The Church *cut off the heretic;* she then ordered, or *begged, according to her power, the state to burn him; the state ordered the executioner to do it! Pray who did it?* And yet Mr. Hughes gravely asks, "Does he say there is any *law* of the Church requiring heretics to be put to death?"

Yes. He says, "IT IS PROVED BY THE LAWS OF THE CHURCH!" What is proved? Why, that when the Church casts off incorrigible heretics, the civil power should inflict on such temporal punishments, even death itself. He quotes, in proof, no less than *four chapters* from the *canon law*, which I will spread out in my next speech, if Mr. Hughes dares deny these proofs again. How futile, how childish, then, his quibbles on *the assertion of doctrine in form?* How reckless, and how impotent his foul, vulgar charges against me, as the perverter and corruptor of this author! But I think we shall next hear him say, *Bellarmine is not a standard author!* "The grapes are sour," said the wily fox, when he reached for them in vain. I know not where the gentleman gets the phrase, which he charges on me, "*that I carry on the controversy by myself.*" This "*lingo*" is familiar at home with him, I suppose. But truly, if his defence of his Church falters hereafter, as it has done of late, after *thirty days delay*, and then such replies, I shall almost cease to believe what others say, that he has *helps at hand*.

The gentleman cannot forget "the barbed" arguments of Dr. Miller! Adapting my figure to my present associate, I have only to say "*the galled jade winces.*"

Next he assails the able Dr. Brownlee, and calls him a *fanatic!* Strange that a *fanatic* routed the banded triumvirate of the New York priesthood. You remember, Mr. President, that on the preliminary evening of the debate, Dr. Brownlee, Dr. Brantley and his son, as well as Mr. Hughes and myself, took some very small part in the debate. The *terms* had not finally been agreed on. Young Brantley, with great modesty, dignity, and effect, according to the rules of your society, opened the debate. Dr. *Brantley stated a single point,* and "proved" Mr. Hughes a "negative" for the evening; Dr. Brownlee denied the assertion made by Mr. Hughes, as to *forty editions of the Italian Bible* being printed *before one Protestant edition*. Now Mr. Hughes drags *him* and the other gentleman in, and very rudely insults them. The truth was, we had much difficulty in getting Mr. Hughes *to* the meeting; in keeping him *at* it, (for his *canonical* hours came on early that night;) or in drawing him out *in* it.— Hence it was an irregular meeting; though the gentleman gave *himself* a good share of glory, and us a terrible awful defeat, in his communication to the "*Catholic Diary.*" I am thus minute, that those who may read this Discussion (having not witnessed the debate) may know the history of that scene.

And now, as to the *forty Italian editions of the Bible*. I say first, I demand better proof than Mr. Hughes's word. Let us have it in *full*. Second, I ask Mr. Hughes if he will assert that there was no restriction on the reading of the Bible *before* the Council of Trent? Third, Will he say that *these editions* of Italian Bibles circulated *freely*, and were by their *cost*, &c., in the reach of the mass of the people? Fourth, how *large* were the editions? But allowing his *forty editions*, let us see his *reasoning. Forty editions of Italian Bibles were printed by Catholics, before the first Bible was printed by Protestants: therefore the Scriptures were not, and are not forbidden to the laity!* Surely there is great *profundity* here. It seems to be thought by Mr. Hughes of no consequence to the argument to know, whether there was not a *restriction* on the *use* of these books. But the FACTS shall speak by the side of his *logic*. FIRST FACT. In 1515, about half a century after the first use of *types*, when printing began to *frighten* the Church of Rome, the Council of Lateran under Leo X. *muzzled the press*, when, by Mr. Hughes's own showing, *only fifteen* of his *forty* editions had appeared; and when knowledge had begun to spread, and Luther was on the *point* of appearing as a *Reformer*, the Council forbid *any book to be printed anywhere under heavy penalties*, unless *examined and approved*, by the *Pope's vicar, or some inquisitor*. SECOND FACT. The first rule of the *Index* of prohibited books prepared by order of the Council of Trent, informs us *that books were condemned before* the *year* 1515, *by Popes and Councils*. THIRD FACT. The Index prepared by authority of the Council of Trent, which I exhibited to *the society* during the debate, and which Mr. Hughes has examined at his own house, in so many words *forbids the use* (not of the *Protestant* but) of the *Roman Catholic Bible, in every vulgar tongue.*(1) *Biblia vulgari quocunque Idiomate conscripta!* Pray, of what use then, were, the *forty* editions in the *Italian language, except to* THE *priesthood?* FOURTH FACT. The fourth rule of the Index *forbids the Bible,* (the CATHOLIC Bible) *translated into the vulgar tongue to be indiscriminately used, because it was manifest from experience* [these forty *editions* had begun to do *mischief* it seems!] *that such use would cause more evil than good; and therefore no man without a written permission from a bishop or inquisitor, should read or possess a copy of the Bible, and offenders were punished—the possessors and readers—by refusing absolution to them, till they gave up the book; and the venders by fines and forfeitures, and other penalties.* These rules I produced at large on the first night of the debate. *Now* I ask of what *use* were these Bibles, these "forty editions," under such *restrictions?* And is it honest, with these *four* facts in his house, in his hand, in his eye, to make so great a flourish with his *forty Italian* editions? It were just as fair, and as fitting, to give us the history of "*the forty thieves!*" FIFTH FACT. *Even this license has since been recalled.* I have before me, and will give, from the Index, the order of Pope Clement VIII. RECALLING THE LICENSE-GIVING POWER MENTIONED ABOVE; and EXTENDING the PROHIBITION to

(1) In page 30.

the READING or KEEPING OF THE BIBLE, OR ANY PART, EVEN A COMPEND OR SUMMARY OF IT, IN ANY IDIOM. If Mr. Hughes questions it, I will give the passage in the original.

Now where are your *forty Italian editions?* They are buried in your convents—used as *pillows under* the heads of lazy monks, hid from the sight of men—forbidden to God's creatures, as hurtful to the hierarchy of that "man of sin" who would take God's place, and full well knows that *darkness* is his *fit* dwelling-place, and his only *defence!*

In truth—the gentleman owns that there *was a "partial restriction"* afterwards! I ask why? Who dare do it? Is not this against human liberty? He says it was "local," "temporary." I pronounce it utterly, deliberately false; and defy the author of so outrageous a perversion of facts to show me, in all the above citations, one proof that these restrictions were not *"prohibitory," "* universal," and " perpetual." Let him but give me *one* rebutting fact or word. His knowledge is too large to acquit his character. It is the height of reckless audacity and folly.

And now a word of the bull of Innocent VIII. Not for his impertinence, will I give my authority—but for the information of the country—for the confusion of the man, who knows, while he denies it, that there is such a bull. He will find it spread out at large in "Free Thoughts on Popery," by Bruce, of Great Britain. He will find an abstract of it in Jones's History of the Christian Church, Vol. II. Chap. 6. He will find it in Morland's Churches of Piedmont, pp. 188–198; and in *Alix's History* of that persecuted people against whom the "infernal machine", was levelled. The original, Mr. H. once called for. I promised to send for it to the Cambridge library, England. I have done so. It may yet make him *blush.* He evidently fears it; for *now,* he says, if it comes, *it* may be a *forgery.* He thus makes a *bull*, in *denying one.* In the *continuation* of Baronius's Annals, as proved in the late Controversy, the fact, that such a bull was given, is distinctly stated. I now ask, does Mr. H. deny that Albert de Capetaines was commissioned by the Pope to carry on the crusade, as stated in the bull? By what authority did he execute his commission? Let us have *honest* answers to these two inquiries. Let the reader also observe, that the bull is so *horrible* that the gentleman finds his only safety in *denying its authenticity.* To its *contents* he will never venture a reply.

And you see *all* he says, or can say, of the Pope's treatment of the *Republic* of *Venice!* Venice was a *Republic;* therefore *Catholics* are not opposed to liberty! profound ratiocination! But what did the *Jesuits*—the Pope's soldiery, do? Why, impelled by the *doctrine,* that the Pope is head of the church, and the church over the state, they left their *country to join the Pope,* who was in arms against it! And so would it be with Jesuits in America, in the same circumstances. Venice, like Poland, and

Switzerland and France, had some noble spirits—some deep-laid principles of liberty, not in *consequence*—but in *spite* of popery. Popery has well nigh ruined them all. But, *in so far* as they were *free*, did they find the Pope trying to oppress them. Spain had *good Catholics*—hence Spain was enslaved: so Portugal. In each, as liberty rises, popery sinks. The liberal party in both countries has the priesthood *against them*. The thousand monasteries and nunneries, lately annihilated in Spain and Portugal, show what the lovers of the *rights* of the *people*, and of a more *free constitution*, think of Popery, and its anti-liberal fruits. The Pope's bull against the government of Portugal, and his sympathy with his dear son, Don Carlos, show how he feels towards liberal institutions, and the destruction of church-power and priestly domination. So it was, in Venice; ask Father Paul—ask Du Pin —ask De Thou, (Thuanus;) you have denounced them as *Protestants*. They were *Catholics*, but in Venice and France stood up for liberty. I say not, that *all Catholics* are in *doctrine* or in *spirit, enemies to liberty*. Far from it. All men love it. But the *priesthood* ride on the necks of men. They keep them debased, ignorant, oppressed, by *doctrines* and *discipline* opposed to all *liberty*. The most enlightened rise up to resist; and at last the hierarchy will fall; and all people will be free. Then there will remain the *catholicism* of *truth*, which now lies neutralised under the weight of despotism, as the Alps under *eternal snows*. But the *system* is constructed to darken, enslave, corrupt, and govern the world. Not *all* the *doctrines;* not *all* the *discipline;* but the *system* is tyrannic. It refuses to reform—it must then expire. God speed the day!

In the case of Devoti, the gentleman feels himself to be on perilous ground. I have *forced* him to admit that Devoti, (a writer approved at Rome late in the eighteenth century,) says, that the Church of *Rome did directly inflict bodily punishments, and fine and banish men*. This is enough. Does Mr. Hughes deny this to have been the fact? Did the Church of Rome do it or not? Let him reply. I defy him to *deny it*. You will see he *dare not*. She did. Then there was a time when the Church of Rome held no *doctrine which forbid* this tyranny. But, she *says, she changes not*. Then she is still the same; and can, without any violation of her doctrines, do it still. If, then, she gets the power in America, is she to be trusted? Are not her doctrines as *ready* for it as *ever?* Now, the American Protestant churches say, that it is anti-Christian, anti-liberal for *them to do it*. If the gentleman can show any such declaration of his church, let him do it. If not, that settles the question. But, he says, Devoti only *claimed the church's right to do these things from the constitutions of emperors*. Suppose it to be so. If the American Constitution should give to the Catholic Church the power to fine, imprison, banish, castigate men, *is there any thing* in her doctrines which forbids it? No. If there be, let it be stated, chapter and verse. But the American Protestant Churches—the Presbyterian Church, for example, in *her standards*, declares, that it is not right, not Christian, not competent to her, or any church of Christ, to have, or to hold, or to exercise, such power. Here is the grand difference. But the author Devoti goes farther, and distinctly says, (in a passage quoted at large by me in my first speech, second night,(1) to which I refer the reader,) "Labarde...... ENDEAVOURS TO UNDERMINE AND TAKE AWAY THE POWER GIVEN BY CHRIST TO THE CHURCH, *not only of government by councils, and persuasion, but also of decreeing by laws, and of compulsion, and of coercing with punishment, those who are worthy of it, and who* SUBJECTS THE ECCLESIASTICAL MINISTRY IN SUCH A WAY TO THE SECULAR POWER, AS TO INSIST THAT TO IT BELONGS THE COGNIZANCE AND JURISDICTION OF ALL EXTERNAL AND SENSIBLE GOVERNMENT."

Again, § VIII. "And since the power of the church is twofold, the one *wholly spiritual*, given *separately* (i. e., to her alone) by Christ, which is exercised both in the inner and outer court; the other, which she has in common with every perfect and distinct commonwealth, and which is called *temporal*, it follows that there are two kinds of punishments ordained by her: the one kind is spiritual, which is to afflict the soul; the other *temporal, which is to castigate the body: she exercises the right to inflict* spiritual punishment on all who, by baptism, are admitted among the children of the church, and who sin against religion. THE CHURCH HAS ALSO SET UP TEMPORAL PUNISHMENTS FOR ALL; BUT THE LAITY AND CLERGY, IN AN UNEQUAL DEGREE." In § X. he says, "So long as she (*the church*) has punishments equal to their (*the clergy's*) *offence, she inflicts them by that right which every republic has over its citizens,* and *punishes a guilty clergyman with lashes, fines, imprisonment, and other inflictions, with this end, that the* offenders may be reformed, and others may, by the example of their punishment, be induced to abstain from crime." It is in illustrating this section, (as well as in Book III. tit. 1, sec. 21,) that he gives the account of the prisons of the church, in monasteries, for example. [Are our nunneries thus furnished?] Now, we ask, is not here a *right claimed to exercise temporal power?* Whence is it derived? Not from the *state?* No. For he says each power, civil and religious, has its distinct prerogative! It is "*eo jure,*" *by that right which every republic exercises over its citizens.*" This DENS contends for, over all baptized persons, as I have already showed—the gentleman not *disputing his* testimony. Bellarmine, also, as I have just shown, claims this power, not as the gift of the *state*, but *possessed before* the state permitted the church to exercise it; and says, it was exercised as soon as it was in the power of the church to do so. When I

(1) Page 139.

said, then, in my last speech, "*this writer claims for the church the right to inflict temporal and bodily punishments,*" I said just the truth; and my promise to expose Mr. H. is so far fulfilled, that I am well assured his friends will feel it, if he does not.

But to end the dispute. Devoti says, § V., "Peace having been given to Christians, [in Constantine's reign, and afterwards,] *the church passed judgment on crimes, not only by* HER OWN RIGHT, (suo jure,) *but by the laws of the emperors.*" Here, plainly, *she claimed the right before* the emperors conceded and confirmed it. But what were these *crimes* and *judgments?* "*And truly these judgments* were not only about *crimes against religion, but they also comprehended all causes in which the clergy were convicted, of any crime against the republic,*" (or state.) He proceeds through the whole *title*, or chapter, to distinguish, or more properly to *confound*, the two republics, as he calls them, namely, the *church* and the *state;* and comes to the result, that the essential nature of the church's constitution as a republic, gives her temporal power over *all*, in certain respects, but especially *over the clergy;* whom she fines, whips, imprisons, banishes; and, if all will not do, then hands them over to the last vengeance of the *civil arm*, by *excommunication;* which is higher punishment than all others; and which infers all the rest, if the *state* does its duty to *heretics.*

As to the Rhemish Testament, I really think that all honest men will say Mr. H. has made a *distinction* without a *difference* in his comments on one of my citations from it. I gave a page of *extracts.* It seems in *one* of them I make them say, "the translators of the English (Protestant) Bible, OUGHT *to be abhorred to the depths of hell.*" They say, "but if the good reader knew for what point of doctrine they (the Protestant translators) have thus framed their translation, they WOULD abhor them to the depths of hell." In both cases, they are to *be abhorred to the depths of hell*—only, gentle reader, it is the *great difference*, that a right judgment *would* so ABHOR *them;* and not that they *ought* to be so *abhorred!* How hard pressed is a man, a cause, that thus *sinks*, *catching at straws.* But I stand corrected. Yet pray, Mr. Hughes, why pass over *all* the other *citations* in *silence?* One of them says, "*the zeal of Catholic men ought to be so great toward all heretics, and their doctrines, that they should give them the anathema, though they* are never so dear to them; so as not even to *spare their own parents.*" Am *I* right in this *citation?* If so, are *they* in *doctrine?* "The *blood of heretics, is not the blood of saints, no more than the blood of thieves, mankillers, and other malefactors; for the shedding of which blood, by order of justice, no commonwealth shall answer.*" Is it faithful? Is it true Catholic doctrine? They *seem* to say so. These are their comments, as *good* Catholics, on *Gal.* i. 8, and Rev. xvii. 6; and are specimens of those *not noticed* by Mr. Hughes.

The charge against the *American Bible Society* bears malice and falsehood on its front. But the Pope has *begun* to denounce these noble institutions; well may the vassal follow his "*most holy lord.*"

Under what he calls "*7thly,*" he tries to cover a former admission, which was, "that the *majority* had a right, as in Italy, or Spain, to establish the Catholic religion by law, if, in doing so, they violate *no right* of the minority." Now, I ask, if this does not *imply that* such a thing *may be done without violating such rights?* But to test his principle, I still farther ask, *Is it possible ever to establish any religion by law, and yet not violate the rights of the minority?* Or to the cases in hand. Was not that done in Spain and in Italy, by establishing the Catholic religion by law?

On the third page, he admits that *Catholics* have *persecuted.* I ask, has one *bull* or *decree* of *council*, by which they justified their persecution, ever been repealed? Please show me *one.* Whereas, American Protestants have renounced and changed those articles which their fathers derived from Rome, and once plead in justification of persecution. For example, the citation from "Fisher's Catechism" is not held by Presbyterians in America.

He says, "*Was not the Jewish religion established by law?* And is not that in the Bible?" This is a strong squinting at defending establishments. But, Mr. Hughes, that was a theocracy, and not an *example;* or to be a *plea* for the Roman hierarchy, though I know your church so thinks, and your government is so modelled.

His pertness about Luther answers itself: it is too puerile to be worthy of notice.

Having met the statements, and exposed the fallacious and evasive reasonings of the gentleman, I now return to the *line of my argument.* In my last address, I showed conclusively, both by the declarations and the acts of the Pope, that he claimed, by divine right, POWER OVER BOTH SWORDS, that is, to be the head of the state, as well as of the church. The honest and high-toned papal writers make no qualifications on this subject. Of these there is a great crowd. Let us take an example. SUAREZ:—

"*A king legitimately deposed is no longer legally a king;* and, *if after such deposition,* he continues obstinate, and retains the kingdom by force, he then deserves the title of tyrant. After the sentence is pronounced, (by the Pope,) he is entirely deprived of his dominions, so that he can no longer justly retain possession of them. Hence he may be treated in all respects as a tyrant; and, consequently, it is lawful for every individual to kill him. James, king of England, in order to turn Bellarmine into ridicule, observes, *this is a new and admirable rendering of the words of Jesus,* 'FEED MY SHEEP, *which makes them signify destroy, proscribe, and depose, Christian princes and kings.*' But Bellarmine and ALL OF US (FOR IN THIS CAUSE WE ARE ALL AS ONE) do not allege these words to prove the *direct* primacy of the Pope in temporal affairs. The king of England should not, therefore, assert that we explain these words as signifying *destroy*, &c., which no Catholic ever did; but, if he will attend to our sincere testimony, we maintain, that among other things contained in these words, and in the extent of power which they ascribe, this is comprised—DESTROY, PROSCRIBE, DEPOSE HERETICAL KINGS WHO WILL NOT AMEND THEIR WAYS, AND WHO ARE DANGEROUS TO THEIR SUBJECTS IN MATTERS PERTAINING TO THE CATHOLIC FAITH."(1)

This is comparatively a *modern* author; and he tells us what ALL hold in the CATHOLIC Church, *Mr. Hughes excepted.*

Cornelius, a Lapide, is still more *bold*. He says: " The sacerdotal kingdom of the church appears first in the bishops and the episcopate; but it is above all to be found in the *Pontiff*, and the *pontificate, whose power, great and most ample, extends to all parts of the universe—a power by which he commands kings, (who, therefore, prostrate themselves before him as suppliants, casting their crowns and sceptres at his feet,) by which, when rebels to the church, he deprives them, as he* HAS OFTEN DONE, OF THEIR KINGDOMS."(2)

Let it be observed too that these are men of what they would call *moderate views*, only contending for an *indirect temporal power.* The sixth chapter of Bellarmine, fifth book, on the Pope, has this for its heading:—" Papam habere summam temporalem potestatem indirecte"—*the Pope possesses supreme temporal power indirectly.* By *indirectly*, we see what he means, in the following passages from the seventh chapter. *" It is not lawful for Christians to tolerate an infidel or heretical king, provided he endeavours to seduce his subjects to his heresy or infidelity. But to judge whether or not he does seduce them to heresy, pertains to the Pope, to whom is committed the care of religion: therefore, the Pope is to judge whether or not a king is to be deposed.*"

The same writer, in the eighth chapter, adduces examples in proof of the fact that popes have exercised this *right of deposition*; and from the *fact*, he proves the *right.* He gives no less than *twelve examples!* His first examples are from the Old Testament: such as Uzzia, 2 Chron. chap. 26, and Athaliah, 2 Chron. chap. 23; where he distinctly implies a *theocracy*, as transmitted to the Catholic Church, with authority to do *by the Pope* what the ancient high priests did. He then enumerates the cases of Gregory I.; Gregory II.; Zachariah; Leo. III., &c. &c., who respectively exercised the deposing power; and one of whom,

(1) *Defensio* Fidel, Cath., &c., lib. 6.
(2) Com. in Acta. Apos., cap. 2.

LEO III., "*translated the empire from the Greeks to the Germans, because the Greeks were not able to help the western church in her trials.*" He also quotes divers parts of the canon-law in support of his reasoning; and to every *Catholic* his arguments are *unanswerable*: for he brings authorities which they dare not refuse or discredit. This is an *honest Roman!* Oh that they were all *honest;* if they will be *Romans!* And this is the *Catholic doctrine.* Baronius, Binius, Carnoza, Driedo, Suarez, Perron, Pighius, Cajetan, Sylvester, Hortiensis, Panormitan, yea, a crowd of such writers of the first authority; many quoted by Bellarmine sustain him in the assertion that this is the *principle of popery.* The French parliament cite no less than SIXTY-EIGHT papal writers, who were advocates of this terrific doctrine.

But we have the SPECIFIC CLAIMS OF POPES ON THE SAME SUBJECT.

In the Decretals (1) it is thus written, (by Pope Gelasius to the Emperor Anastasius) "O, august emperor, there are two by whom the world is chiefly ruled—the sacred authority of the Popes and the kingly power. In the which that of the *priests* preponderates, inasmuch as in the divine examination, they will have to answer for the kings of men."

"Be well aware, therefore, that in these matters you depend upon their judgment; and they cannot be subservient to your will." And at the close, he quotes a passage from Ambrose, in proof of the subjection of *kings* to the *priesthood:* "*for as much as you see that the necks of kings and princes are put under the knees of priests;* und that when they have kissed their right hands, they believe themselves to be partakers of their prayers."

Again: (2) the heading of the title or chapter is "Omnes Christi fideles de necessitate salutis, subsunt Romano Pontifici, qui utrumque gladium habet, et omnes judicat, a nemine judicatur"— "*It is necessary to the salvation of all the faithful in Christ, that they be subject to the Pope of Rome; who has the power of both swords, and who judges all, but is judged by none.*" Here is, 1. Damnation to all out of the visible communion of Rome; 2. A claim to all temporal and spiritual power; 3. A superiority to all human tribunals. This is stated at large in the extracts which are cited by the canonist, in proof of the *text* quoted above. Thus we are told that "*of the two swords, one must be subject to the other; and that the temporal power must be subject to the spiritual;*" and to leave no doubt of the infamous bigotry and uncharitableness of the system of popery, closes with this awful declaration, as *a defined tenet* of the Church of Rome, viz. "Porro subesse Romano Pontifici omni humanæ creaturæ, decla-

(1) First Part, Dist. 96, chap. 10.
(2) Extravag. Comm., book L, tit. 8.

rimus, dicimus, definimus et pronuntiamus, omnino esse de necessitate salutis ?"—"*Moreover, we declare, affirm,* DEFINE *and pronounce* (is not this a doctrine delivered ex cathedra ?) *that it is altogether necessary to salvation for every human creature to be subject to the Pope of Rome.*"

The Pope of Rome professes to be the vicegerent of God on earth—to dispose of the church and the state at his will. Hence the Pope gave a grant of America to Spain, (which has never yet been revoked,) even before America was discovered. The Pope, Pius V., in his bull against Queen Elizabeth, recites his prerogative in no measured terms. In that bull he deprives her of her kingdom, and releases her subjects from their allegiance to her. "He who reigns on high, to whom is given all power in heaven and on earth, hath committed the one Holy Catholic and Apostolic Church, *out of which there is no salvation*, to one alone, on earth, namely, to Peter, Prince of the Apostles, and to the Roman Pontiff, successor of Peter, to be governed with the fulness of power. *This one man hath he appointed prince over all* NATIONS, AND ALL KINGDOMS, *that he may pluck up, destroy, scatter, ruin, plant, build.*" To this latter trust he has been eminently faithful! Here is *godship on earth in church and state.* Where any *liberty* can lurk, in these pretensions, or under this universal theocracy, I am at a loss to conceive.

Again: the bull of Sixtus V. against Henry, king of Navarre, and the prince of Conde, thus runs:—"The authority given to St. Peter and his successors, by the immense power of the eternal King, excels all the powers of earthly kings and princes. It passes uncontrollable sentence upon all, and if it find any of them resisting God's ordinance, it takes a more severe vengeance of them, and, casting down the most powerful of them from their thrones, tumbles them down into the lowest parts of the earth, as the ministers of the proud Lucifer."

Among the twenty-seven celebrated Sentences, or Dictates, of Pope Gregory VII. are such as these, viz.

8th. That the Pope alone can use imperial ensigns.

9th. That all princes must kiss the feet of the Pope only.

12th. That it is lawful for him to depose emperors.

17th. That no chapter or book may be accounted canonical without his authority.

18th. That his sentence may be retracted by none; and he alone may retract all men's.

19th. That he himself ought to be judged by no man.

27th. That he may absolve the subjects of unjust men from fidelity, (to their princes.)

These Dictates are papal *definitions* of *papal power.* They have been preserved by the papal writers; believed and observed by the priesthood; and never revoked, rescinded, or condemned by any council, or any pope. Of this Cardinal Baronius is a good witness who asserts, concerning these *Dictates*—Sententias eas hactenus in Ecclesia Catholica, usu receptas fuisse, quibus reprimetur audacia schismaticorum principum hoc tempore in Romanam Ecclesiam insurgentium. *That these sentences had heretofore* (to the eleventh century) *been received into use in the Catholic Church; by them the audacity of schismatic princes, who had during that time arisen in the Roman Church, had been restrained.*

It were a curious and instructive piece of history to compile into one table, after the example of Bellarmine, not the *dozen*, but the *two hundred* examples, in which *popes* have actually carried their principles into effect in the excommunication, or deposition, or both, as the case might be, of offensive kings and emperors.

We give below an imperfect tabular view, promising to add, alter, or diminish, at the suggestion of Mr. Hughes, on good evidence of error. We have no doubt his *superior knowledge of this topic in history* will enable him greatly to enlarge the table.

Popes.	Princes *excommunicated*, or *deposed*, or *both*.
Gregory II............	Leo. III., ⎫
Gregory III..........	Leo. III., ⎬ Emperors.
Pascal I.	Leo. V., ⎭
John VIII...........	Lewis, King of Germany.
Gregory V...........	Robert, King of France.
Adrian II.	Lothario, } Emperors.
Gregory VII......	{ Henry IV., Balislaus, King of Poland.
Urban II...........	{ Henry IV., Emperor. Philip I., King of France.
Pascal II...........	{ Henry IV., Henry V., ⎫
Calixtus II...........	Henry V., ⎬ Emperors.
Gelasius II...........	Henry V., ⎭
Adrian IV	William, King of Sicily.
Alexander III....	{ Frederic I., Emperor. Henry II., King of England.
Celestine III......	{ Henry VI., Emperor. Alphonso, King of Galicia.
Innocent III......	{ Philip and Otho, Emperors. John, King of England. Philip II., of France. Ladislaus, King of Poland. Louis VII. and Louis VIII., of France.

This was the monster who said—"It has pleased God so to order the affairs of the world, that those provinces which had anciently *been subject to the Roman Church in spirituals*, were now become *subject to it in temporals."* And again : " Jesus Christ, the King of kings, and Lord of lords, and Priest according to the order of Melchizedeck, hath so united the royal and priestly power, in his church, that the kingdom is but a royal priesthood, and the priesthood the royal power."

He said, "the church, my spouse, is not married to me without bringing me something. She hath given me a dowry of price beyond all price, *the plentitude of spiritual things, and the full extent* (latitudinem temporalium) *of temporal things.* She hath given me the *mitre,* in *token of things spiritual; the crown,* in *token of things temporal:* the mitre, for the priesthood; the crown for the kingdom—making me the *lieutenant* of Him who hath written upon his thigh and upon his vesture, King of kings, and Lord of lords : I ENJOY ALONE THE PLENTITUDE OF POWER, THAT OTHERS MAY SAY OF ME, NEXT TO GOD, *'and out of his fulness we have received!!!'"* Such were his blasphemous claims, which the Church of Rome has not *denounced, but sustained.*

But to continue our list :—

POPES.	PRINCES.	
Honorius	Frederic II.,	} Emperors.
Gregory IX.	{ Frederic II., Wincessaus.	
Innocent IV.	Frederic II., Emperor.	
Urban IV.	Manfred and	} Kings of Sicily.
Clement IV.	Conradin,	
Gregory X.	{ Alphonso, King of Portugal. Alphonso X., King of Castile.	
Nicholas III.	Charles, King of Anjou.	
Martin IV.	{ Peter of Arragon. Michael Paleologus, Emperor.	
Honorius IV.	{ James, Alphonso,	} Kings of Arragon.
Nicholas IV.	Alphonso,	
Boniface VIII.	{ Philip IV., King of France. Eric VIII., King of Denmark.	
John XXII.	Lewis, of Bavaria,	⎫
Benedict XII.	Lewis,	} Emperors.
Clement VI.	Lewis,	⎭
Urban VI.	{ Jane, Queen Charles, King	} of Naples.
Boniface IX.	{ Lewis of Anjou. Richard, Edward, Wenchelaus, Emperor.	} Kings of England.
Innocent VII.	Ladislaus,	} Kings of Naples.
Alexander V.	Ladislaus,	
Sixtus IV.	Ladislaus, King of Bohemia.	

POPES.	PRINCES.
Julius II............	{ Albert, King of Naples. { Lewis XII., King of France.
Leo X.................	Stenon, King of Sweden.
Clement VII.	Henry VIII., } King of England.
Paul III...............	Henry VIII.,
Pius V.................	Elizabeth, Queen of England.
Sixtus V............	{ Henry III., King of France. { Henry, King of Navarre.
Gregory XIV........	Henry IV., King of France and Navarre.
Innocent VI.........	Ambassador of Louis XIV. of France.

This terrific list needs no comment! It speaks the *doctrine* of the Church in its superabundant *practice*. It is no longer merely an ABSTRACT *point to be proved*. It is a part of the *history* of the Church and of its creed, for ages. It is *quod erat faciendum*. It is in vain to cry out now, this was only *discipline*. Does *any doctrine* of the Church *forbid* it? Have all these Popes done all these things with the *connivance* of the Church? Then is such a Church to be trusted, *doctrine*, or no *doctrine?* Do so many Popes *assert* their divine right to depose kings; dissolve the tie that bound their people to them; transfer kingdoms, from Asia to Europe, from country to country, and from man to man; and yet all their *infallibilities* mistaken, and a self-styled insulated interpreter of catholicity contradict this great cloud of witnessing Popes? And shall we take *his* word against *all these?* Impossible. HISTORY is on one side; *John Hughes* on the other! The history of Popes, with few exceptions, is a history of usurpation of human rights; enmity to human liberty; lording it over human conscience; and oppression, when possible, of the *temporal*, by the *spiritual power*.

"It is well known," says an admirable author, "that the papacy is a species of universal monarchy of a mixed nature, partly *ecclesiastical*, partly *civil*, founded upon the pretence of *divine right*, and promoted under colour of religion; that it ever aspires to unlimited extent, universal dominion, and worldly wealth and grandeur; that it claims a *divine authority to govern the world*, and subject princes not only in *spirituals*, but in *temporals* also, directly or indirectly; that the Roman pontiffs consider themselves as *kings*, as well as *priests*, uniting the *imperial diadem* with the *mitre*, and grasping the *sword*, together with the *keys of St. Peter*; yea, as possessed of the *power and prerogatives of divinity*, boasting that all power is committed to them in heaven and in earth; *in consequence of which they claim a right to dispose of crowns and kingdoms*, to set up or depose princes, and to pluck up and destroy, at their pleasure. In consequence of that absurd and monstrous system, Rome gradually began to show herself with glory and eclat among the nations, till that *great city actu-*

ally became once more *the mistress of the world*, 'RULING OVER THE KINGS OF THE EARTH;' her fallen empire was again set up under a new form, and her *pretended vicars of Christ*, in the end, outdid, if possible, her *Pagan Cæsars* in pride, magnificence, despotism, and cruel tyranny, as well as in idolatry, luxury, and every abominable vice. Having obtained repeated donations of cities, lands, and provinces, they rose to the rank of *temporal princes*. But these being entirely unequal to their insatiable avarice and ambition, they enlarged their claims without end. Not satisfied with taxing and giving laws to the patrimony of St. Peter, they began to *consider all Christendom as his patrimony;* and accordingly claimed HIS PENCE.(1.) By methods unheard of before, they found the secret of raising immense revenues, and of drawing the wealth of the world to their coffers. They used the style of the most haughty and arbitrary sovereigns. They affected more than royal titles, powers and honours; were crowned in state; carried about on men's shoulders in procession; received homage and adoration; imposed oaths of fidelity and allegiance on the clergy; kept a numerous train of servants and attendants; had their guards, fleets and armies; they inflicted capital punishments; wore the imperial ensigns, and in military armour have gone in person to battle; they had their courts and tribunals, with long lists of dependent officers and ministers of state; they received ambassadors; despatched their *nuncios* and legates *a latere*, (a sort of sub-Popes, to go abroad from Rome, and represent his majesty,) into all nations; they have meddled in all the affairs of princes; managed perpetual intrigues; fomented endless discords; mingled in all broils; sustained themselves judges in all causes, umpires in all controversies, and supreme arbiters of peace and war. False and absurd as the principles are, on which the papal empire is built, ... yet they have, in innumerable instances, been reduced to practice, and too often with admirable success. There is no state where the papal supremacy was at all owned, but the temporal authority has also been *tried*, and exercised, even in some of its highest branches. So that, whether gained by subtlety, extorted by force and terror, or yielded up by voluntary abject concessions, one way or other, these *usurping Nimrods* found themselves actually possessed of that sovereignty which they so much wished for, and so falsely pretended to be their right. Appeals of all kinds were made to them, and all differences submitted to their decision. *They crowned and constituted the emperors;* in competitions and controverted elections they preferred whom they pleased; they not only *demanded* the surrender of every kingdom in Europe, as tributary fiefs of the Roman See, but *made the greater part of them really to be so;* imposed oaths of fidelity and vassalage on princes, enlisting them

---

(1) A tax levied by the Popes on every family in England, paid annually.

under their banners, and sending them on their frantic expeditions against infidels, to break them more tamely to the yoke. Royal titles and dignities have been created, or annihilated at their word; and kingdoms, like toys, given away, or sold to their sycophants and slaves. Against all who have offended them, or dared to resist their will, they have armed themselves with thunders, denouncing *anathemas upon anathemas;* sacrilegiously profaning sacred institutions, to which they have added others of their own invention, to gratify their lust of dominion, their diabolical pride, resentment, and revenge; times without number, have they excommunicated princes, deposing them from their governments, interdicting their dominions, or transferring them to others; absolving subjects from allegiance, exciting them to revolt, and authorizing them to depose or murder their excommunicated sovereigns; and their iniquitous sentences and barbarous mandates have often been but too well obeyed. If the objects of their resentment have escaped falling an instant sacrifice to it, and overcome by a series of insults and dangers, they have at any time applied for favour, the terms of reconciliation have proved more intolerable, than all they had before either suffered or feared, by the most humiliating ceremonies, the basest and most abject submissions and concessions, and sometimes by the most mortifying penances, they have been constrained to sacrifice at once the majesty of kings, and the dignity of men. Intoxicated with their success, the Popes disdaining to acknowledge any limits to their dominion, have attempted to grasp and wield the sceptre of the universe........ They have extended their sovereignty to every quarter of the globe; to islands and continents; to the east and to the west; to countries civilized and barbarous, Christian and Indian, known and unknown; to land and sea; and what is more, to heaven and hell: no wonder to find this lower world trembling at their voice, and poor mortals paying abject homage to their triple crown, when they can summon all the celestial thrones and principalities above, and command the whole *infernal* hierarchy, without exception, to obey them." Now, there is not one of this vast catalogue of *crimes* and usurpations, which we do not stand prepared to *prove.* If the Reverend gentleman will select from them *one,* or one *dozen,* we will, at once, make out the proof, as in the example given of the *excommunication and deposition* of princes, from almost every throne in Europe.

But can an American audience, or *any* honest man, look at this sketch of the *claims and practices* of *the head* of *the church,* and not own that *liberty* lingers not in a communion or a country which she controls?

There is still extant in Europe a book, of which the celebrated George Finch, Esq., a living British writer, thus speaks:—
"Through the kindness of Dr. Sadler, who favoured me with a sight of the original work from Trinity College Library, Dublin,

I was enabled to verify the quotations. (Some of which we give below.) The title of the work is as follows: *Three Books of the Sacred Ceremonies of the Holy Roman Church; printed at Cologne,* 1571." The quotations which follow, illustrate how *popes* treated, and felt towards, kings and emperors in the days of their power and glory. When the Pope had a procession, it was ordered,

"1. The emperor shall hold the Pope's stirrup.
"2. The emperor shall lead the Pope's horse.
"3. The emperor must bear the Pope's chair on his shoulder.
"4. The emperor shall bear up the Pope's train.
"5. Let the emperor bear the basin and ewer to the Pope.
"6. Let the emperor give the Pope water.
"7. The emperor shall carry the *Pope's first dish.*
"8. The emperor shall carry the Pope's first cup."

Think, gentle auditor, that this is the man who calls himself *servant of servants,* "*servus servorum;*" think, *in contrast,* of our blessed Lord, whose VICAR the Pope calls himself, *washing his disciples' feet,* and Peter, the *"first Pope,"* saying, *"silver and gold have I none."* Is not this he of whom the Apostle Paul speaks, when he tells us of *"that man of sin, and son of perdition; who opposeth and exalteth himself above all that is called God, or that is worshipped; so that he, as God, sitteth in the temple of God, showing himself that he is God."*(1)

Take, for illustration, the following facts: "But now we proceed to relate the things which were then transacted from the annals of Roger, which were compiled at that time. On the morrow after his consecration, the lord Pope went from the Lateran to the church of the blessed Peter, and Henry, king of the Germans, met him there, with Constance, his wife, and a large body of armed men....... Our lord, the Pope, after this, led them into the church, and anointed him as emperor, and his wife as empress. But our lord, the Pope, sat in the pontifical chair, holding the imperial crown between his feet, the emperor, bending his head, received the crown; and the empress, in the same manner, from the feet of our lord, the Pope. But our lord, the Pope, instantly *struck with his foot the emperor's crown,* and *cast it upon the ground, signifying that he had the power of deposing him from the empire if he was undeserving of it. The cardinals, however, lifting up the crown, placed it upon the head of the emperor.*"(2) This was Pope Celestine III., crowning Henry of Germany! "The Pope was conducted to the church of St. Peter, and after being elevated on the great altar, at the foot of which are the tombs of the Holy Apostles, he sat upon the throne that was prepared for him, and *was there adored by the cardinals,* (et y fut adore des cardinaux,) afterwards by the bishops,

(1) See 2 Thes. chap. ii.
(2) From Cardinal Baronius's Annals, A. D. 1191.

and lastly, by the whole people, who crowded to kiss his feet."(1) The former shows, that he claims divine power over *temporal princes and kingdoms;* the latter, *that he claims divine worship audaciously, venturing to ascend the altar of God, and there to receive the adoration of men!* Finally, the Pope has permitted himself to be *called* God; and has *called himself God.*

In the Council of Lateran, A. D. 1512, 1513, 1514, 1515, the Pope was expressly called God. And in Roscoe's account of the inauguration of Pope Alexander VI. we are told, that "while the new pontiff passed through the triumphal arches, erected to his honour, he might have read the inscriptions, which augured the return of the golden age—and HAILED HIM A GOD." Of these, the following one may serve as a sufficient specimen. "*Rome was great under Cæsar, but now she is greatest;* Alexander VI. reigns; the former was a man, the LATTER IS A GOD." Cæsare majora fuit, nunc Roma est maxima; sixtus regnat Alexander; ille VIR, iste DEUS.(2)

Pope Nicholas, in his letter to the Emperor Michael,(3) says, "*it may very evidently be shown, that the Pope,* who, [as we have already related,] was CALLED GOD, by Prince Constantine the Pius, can neither be bound nor released by the secular power, FOR IT IS MANIFEST THAT GOD CANNOT BE JUDGED OF MEN." (Satis evidenter ostenditur, a seculari potestate, nec ligari prorsus nec solvi posse pontificem, quem constat a pio principe Constantino, (quod longe superius memoravimus,) DEUM APPELLATUM; neo posse Deum, ab hominibus judicari manifestum est.)

Here, after all quibbles have been tried, in vain, the Pope claims exemption from human authority, on the ground of GOD-SHIP. It is true, the Rev. gentleman had tried, by much evasion, to weaken the force of this terrible testimony. In the progress of the debate Mr. Hughes called on Mr. Kearney, (a gentleman of the Roman Catholic Church, who was present, and who was commended by Mr. H. as a scholar,) to translate the passage just quoted. Mr. Breckinridge called for Dr. Wiley, but he was not present. Mr. Kearney then rendered the passage as follows: "*It is shown sufficiently evident, that the Pontiff cannot be bound altogether, nor dissolved, by the secular power, who, it is evident, from the pious Prince Constantine, was called a God— and that God cannot be indicated by men is manifest.*" Being again asked, as to the last member of the sentence, Mr. Kearney looked more closely at the Latin, and said, he had been misled by the old spelling, and had mistaken *judicari* for *indicari.* He then rendered the last clause thus: "*that God cannot be* JUDGED *by men is manifest.*" Mr. Hughes asked him to say whether it was the

---

(1) Fleury, Ecc. His. tom. 15, lib. 5.
(2) Corio-Storia di Milano, par. 7, p. 188, as cited by *Finch.*
(3) See Decretals, First Part, Dist. 96, chap. 7.

Pope who said this, or *Constantine?* Mr. Kearney replied, it was *Constantine.* Mr. Breckinridge resumed. The gentleman laid stress on the fact, that these were the words, *not* of Pope Nicholas, or Pope Leo, but *of the Emperor Constantine.* But the *Pope* Nicholas had cited them to the *Emperor* Michael, to prove that a *previous* emperor had called a *previous Pope, God!* For what did the Pope quote the words? To show that *the Pope was above human tribunals, because he was a god on earth.* It is evident that this is the very use for which the Pope cited the words. If not for this, for what purpose? But Mr. Hughes would have it, that *"pontificem"* meant not the *Pope,* but *every priest!* that is, that NO PRIEST *could be bound by the secular power;* and why? Because *he was a god* on earth; and *God* could *not* be *judged* of *men!* It came then to this, *that all priests were gods!* We had thought before, that there was but *one god among* them, and that was *the Pope.* But he stood corrected; for it seemed, by Mr. Hughes's own interpretation, *every parish priest is a god!*

The above narrative is taken, in substance, from the *stenographer's report of the debate.* This specimen may help to show *why* it is that the gentleman did not wish that report published; and why this debate is now nearly *one year behind its time.*

"Is the Roman Catholic Religion, in any or in all its principles or doctrines, opposed to civil or religious liberty."

NEGATIVE VI.—MR. HUGHES.

MR. PRESIDENT :—

THE gentleman intimates that I have refused to publish the report of the stenographer, and that I have caused the delay of the publication. I shall state the facts of the case, and leave the public to decide. 1st. As to the stenographer, *we had* NONE *during the first three evenings of the discussion.* Was that my fault? 2d. Of the remainder, he did not return some of the speeches for about *four months* after the close of the debate. Was that my fault? 3d. Both he and Mr. Breckinridge, almost immediately after its close, had to attend the General Assembly at Pittsburg; the latter to help to *excommunicate the whole Catholic Church* present, past and future; and the former, to make a report of the proceedings. Was that my fault? 4th. The stenographer had to go, then, to Cincinnati, where Doctor Beecher was to be tried for *heresy.* Was I the cause of this delay? Finally, when it suited the convenience of the stenographer to return the remainder of the speeches, he did so; and when I was making arrangements to go to Mexico, the gentleman became quite impatient to have the debate published. Now the only difficulty was to know how, by what rule, the report of the stenographer should be corrected? That it required the correction of the speakers is undenied, as the stenographer himself frequently put in the margin, "This, I do not understand," "here I could not make out the notes," "this is spoiled," &c. &c. In order, therefore, that the mode of correction might not be an occasion of new and interminable disputes, I proposed that each speaker should correct, as he thought proper. The gentleman, unable to discover any better rule, adopted it, and led the way, in the correction of his first speech, which has been followed up to the present time. These are the *facts of the case.* The blame, therefore, must rest on those to whom it belongs, and not on me.

When the gentleman says, that I have kept his speech a great many days, he ought to recollect, even if the fact were as he states, that I have duties to attend to, which I deem much more important; and that it is only the intervals of leisure, which are few and far between, that I can devote to him and his speeches. As to his charges of "personality," "attacks on his reputation," "MALIG-

NITY AND FALSEHOOD," and other scurrilous matter in which his speech abounds, I look upon them as ebullitions of temper, which plead for pity, at the same time that they destroy all claim or title to it. His charges are silly, vague and unfounded. Let him SPECIFY, and then let him PROVE. But as long as he withholds the proof, his crimination is ridiculous. When *I* make a charge, I prove it. I begin with a fact, which he cannot deny. I reason from that fact, with a strict and just induction of consequences, which he does not venture to dispute. I have never gone out of the question, to find matter of censure; but confined myself strictly to his labours, as the gratuitous defamer of his Catholic fellow-citizens. When I wish to prove that in carrying on this work of defamation, he sinned against both truth and knowledge, I found abundant testimony *in his own writings and assertions*, to establish the fact; and the fact, once established, remains. His own pen, his own words have been the true, *real enemy* of his reputation. Before he takes pains to account for my pretended calumnies by citing " Pascal, a Catholic, but a Jansenist," (he might as well have said a " Catholic but an *atheist*,") let him first *specify*, and *prove* one single charge of calumny against me. He does not, he cannot. Neither need he be at a loss for an immoral principle, to authorize the dishonourable means by which he attempts to sustain himself in this discussion. The same doctrine of his creed, which teaches him that good works have no merit, and that evil works, cannot hinder his salvation, if he is one of the " foreordained," *makes all means equal*. Calumny itself never imputed to the Jesuits so broad a shield for the covering of iniquity, as this, under which his creed protects its members. By this, Calvin was a saint, although guilty of the blood of his victims. And if such crimes could not hinder the master from being a saint, smaller transgressions cannot defeat the destiny of the disciples, who expect to be saved by the "decree" of God, and by faith *alone*. Nay, they are never so much in danger of hell, as when they believe that good works could avail any thing, in aiding them to escape it.

He says " he has held up three cases of fraud committed by me." There is not a word of truth in the statement, as I have shown before. I proved that Mosheim himself applies the name of Albigenses to the "fanatics," whom he describes, and of whom I spoke. Is there any fraud in this? I refer the reader to my former speech, in which I settle the question in a way which left the gentleman not a word to say in reply. So much for the *first* fraud. The second was a mistake, in which the gentleman participated with me, but which I promptly corrected, as soon as I discovered it. Was there any fraud in this? The third is that in which he charges me with having suppressed the reading of a portion of a document which I handed in to the stenographer, which, he says, " charged Presbyterians with horrible principles and crimes." The principles here referred to, are those of absolute "predestination," and the gentleman characterizes them properly, when he calls them "horrible." But they are in the "CONFESSION OF FAITH," and he defends them. So far, therefore, there could be no motive to suppress the reading. But when he says I charged Presbyterians at the same time, with "horrible crimes," he only bears false witness against his neighbour. This I have also cleared up in a former speech. I showed that, *according to this doctrine*, Presbyterians *might* commit any crime, without risking their hopes of happiness, or fear of punishment in the next world, where every thing is fixed by eternal, immutable, absolute election and reprobation, irrespective of good works or bad works done in the flesh. But I did not charge Presbyterians with being guilty of the "horrible crimes," to which this doctrine *invited them*. That I may have omitted, on any occasion of reading manuscript, a sentence by mistake, *is possible*, and those who recollect the many interruptions to which both parties were subject on such occasions, will not be surprised that such a thing should have occurred, although I have no reason to believe that it did occur even in this instance. But the charge of "fraud," implies that it did occur, and was *intentional*. I deny the first as unfounded in fact, and the latter as equally FOOLISH and FALSE.

How could the gentleman charge me with an *intention* fabricated in his own mind, and imputed to me on the strength of a fact, which he has asserted, which I have denied, and which he has not proved? What motive was there? What evidence is there, that in one place I suppressed the reading of an argument which I have developed again and again, throughout the discussion? There is not in the assembly, another mind, perhaps, that would harbour such a suspicion, on such absurd grounds; and it is no evidence of "conscious rectitude," in the gentleman himself, that he should have harboured, and even ventured to express it, without the shadow of proof. I fling it back upon him with the indignation which it is calculated to excite, and with only this rebuke, that *his example*, even if I had not known it before, has taught me and this audience that "*honesty*, in literary, as well as social intercourse, is the best policy." If he had paid strict attention to this moral adage, he would not have been what he now is. This is the second time that I have had to refute these charges; and, like bubbles floating on the sea of temper, to blow them into thin air. But let us turn to something substantial.

You must have been amused, gentlemen, to observe the variety of expedients employed by Mr. Breckinridge to evade the question about Caranza. Poor human nature! How much better would it have been for him to have acknowledged the facts, and do honour to injured truth, of which he calls himself a minister? How much more honourable for him to have acknowledged, that when he said that "HE COPIED FROM CARANZA," he was betrayed by his pen! That when he said he copied "CONTINUOUSLY," he was deceived by his *spectacles*. That, when he said he "HAD THE ORIGINAL BEFORE HIM," he was only copying from Faber, or some other blind guide. That, when he said he "omitted" part of Caranza, "FOR WANT OF ROOM," he deceived his readers *unintentionally.* That the part which he has quoted, as being *in Caranza*, and which is *not* in Caranza, was found *just so*, in the book from which he copied, *and that he does not know to what author it belongs*. Yes, yes; any other course would have been mercy to his own reputation, compared with that which the gentleman has thought proper to pursue. Addison has remarked somewhere in his SPECTATOR, that falsehood is like a house without a foundation, "it requires to be supported by props." And, although I cannot praise the gentleman as an architect, yet he has displayed considerable talents in finding and applying props. He shuns the real question, and agitates points that are not in dispute. He talks about "substance," and "sense," &c. &c. This is not the question. He shifts it from what is in dispute, to what is not in dispute. The question is, DID HE STATE TRUTH, when he said "unhesitatingly, that he copied from Caranza—literally and continuously?" I say, he did not; and I say more, that if I were in his situation, I should never stand in a Christian pulpit, until I had proved the truth of that assertion, or acknowledged its falsity. I bring him to the point; it is the only advantage that oral disputation can have over written controversy, that you can call your opponent to account, point out his words, and, face to face, hold him responsible for them, when they are, as Addison expresses it, a house that requires to be *supported by props*, for want of a foundation. Sir, I cautioned the gentleman to beware of his authorities; he slighted my advice, and compels me to defend truth, at the expense of what may seem, but is not, charity. I take no pleasure in exposing facts, which must necessarily have their influence in public judgment, against the gentleman's pretensions.

As to the charge about the second commandment of the Council of Trent, the gentleman bears me out in regard to all I said in my last speech. It was found in the *very edition* which he brought from New York to sustain his calumny!! This he acknowledges, and this settles the question;—convicting him, by his own testimony, of having uttered what was "untrue," when he said it contained *"only four words of the second commandment."* His display about its being "suppressed," and then "brought up," and "kept out of view as much as possible," is to be charged to the chapter on "PROPPING."

The exhibition of his false statements, with regard to the other catechisms, must be reserved to another time. If he understood the history of the Protestant Scriptures, he would know that the word *"image"* is one which their translators *supplied*, but which is not in the original. But it is useless to waste time in giving him what he vastly stands in need of—information.

In attempting to cover his misrepresentation of Bellarmine, he says that his writings, except one portion, ascribing only indirect power to the Pope over temporal matters, are approved of, and "declared to contain NO DOCTRINE CONTRARY TO THE CATHOLIC FAITH." Yes; but does this make it appear that when he gives, not the "doctrine of Catholic faith," but the opinion of the writer on political questions, Catholics are to receive *his opinions* as doctrines of their Church? I believe not. I wish the gentleman would review his logic, if he ever studied any.

He says that "Calvin agreed with Bellarmine." Indeed! Calvin, who died in 1564, *agreed* with Bellarmine, who wrote and lived more than half a century afterwards!! Bellarmine copied Calvin's doctrine on persecution, just as the gentleman *copied* from Faber, stating that Faber "had quoted as he had done." But if persecution had been a Catholic tenet of faith, Calvin's authority would never have been adduced. Bellarmine gave citations also from Augustine and Chrysostom, and hence the gentleman quotes *this as the criterion* of Catholic *doctrine*—"the consent of the fathers." Even here *he garbles*, by leaving out the word which determines the rule. The words are, the "UNANIMOUS CONSENT OF THE FATHERS." He knows the word too well to have omitted it by accident. Now, many of the fathers, Tertullian, St. Ambrose, Leo the Great, and others, condemned persecution; and since their "UNANIMOUS consent" is the sign of doctrine, we see the reason why the word "unanimous" was suppressed. I explained, in my last, the meaning of Bellarmine, and the gentleman has nothing to say in reply, except by notes of interrogation. "Does Bellarmine," he asks, "say it is opinion?" No;—for he did not conceive that any one should be so ignorant as to suppose it to be any thing else but opinion. Mr. B. tells us, (stupite gentes!) that "Protestants are now the majority in France!" Such ignorance is too gross not to be feigned. He asks, are Protestants "tolerated in Austria, *so as to have room to increase?*" Yes; except that they are not yet allowed to increase by pulling down the "monuments of idolatry." So in Belgium—so in Italy itself; we never hear of their putting Protestants to death by virtue of a Catholic majority. Now, if it were a Catholic doctrine, to be practised wherever Catholics have the power, as he interprets Bellarmine, here is the power in all these countries; and yet the doctrine, so falsely imputed, is never heard of.

The gentleman's account of the Reformers is truly amusing. As an argument and evidence that the Catholic religion is not so exterminating as his Commentary on Bellarmine would make it appear, I referred to the case of the Reformers. Surely the Catholics were a majority then. All they *wanted* to extirpate the Reformers, was a doctrine of their religion requiring them to do so. The reason why they did not do so, was, it appears by the gentleman's philosophical account, that the "*wars of near half a century could not extinguish them.*" Then they carried on wars!! Against whom? Against *their countries.* Against their *lawful governments.* A beautiful "Reformation," truly! Admirable apostles of the new religion, who spread their gospel by *civil wars!* What simpletons the first Christians were, who knew how to *suffer;* whereas, if they had possessed a spark of the Geneva Revelation, they would have been trained to *fight.* The gentleman has told the *secret of the Reformation.*

The compliment paid to the patriotism of "the Gastons, the Carrolls, and the Careys," will, no doubt be duly appreciated, coupled as it is with the charge that they are *faithless to the principles of the religion which they profess.* I will give one single passage from the speech of the eloquent Judge Gaston, before the convention of his State, which is enough to refute all the gentleman has said in the whole of his effort to support his cause against the Catholic religion:

"But it has been objected that the Catholic religion is unfavourable to freedom, nay, even incompatible with republican institutions. Ingenious speculations on such matters are worth little, and prove still less. Let me ask who obtained the great charter of English freedom but the Catholic prelate, and barons at Runnemede? The oldest—the purest democracy on earth, is the little Catholic republic of St. Marino, not a day's journey from Rome. It has existed now for fourteen hundred years, and is so jealous of arbitrary power, that the executive authority is divided between two governors, who are elected every three months. Was William Tell, the founder of Swiss liberty, a royalist? Are the Catholics of the Swiss Cantons in love with tyranny? Are the Irish Catholics friends to passive obedience and non-resistance? Was La Fayette, Pulaski, or Kosciusko, a foe to civil freedom? Was Charles Carroll, of Carrollton, unwilling to jeopard fortune in the cause of liberty? Let me give you, however, the testimony of George Washington. On his accession to the presidency, he was addressed by the American Catholics, who, adverting to the restrictions on their worship then existing in some of the states, expressed themselves thus:—'The prospect of national prosperity is peculiarly pleasing to us on another account; because, while our country preserves her freedom and independence we shall have well-founded title to claim from her justice the equal rights of citizenship, as the price of our blood spilt under your eye, and of our common exertions for her defence, under your auspicious conduct.' This great man, who was utterly incapable of flattery and deceit, utters in answer the following sentiments, which I give in his own words: 'As mankind becomes more liberal, they will be more apt to allow that all those who conduct themselves as worthy members of the community, are equally entitled to the protection of civil government. I hope ever to see America among the foremost nations in examples of justice and liberality, and I presume that your fellow-citizens will not forget the patriotic part which you took in the accomplishment of their revolution, and the establishment of their government, or the important assistance which they received from a nation in which the Roman Catholic faith is professed.' By-the-by, sir, I would pause for a moment to call the attention of this committee to some of the names subscribed to this address. Among them are those of John Carroll, the first Roman Catholic bishop in the United States, Charles Carroll of Carrollton, and Thomas Fitsimmons; for the character of these distinguished men, if they needed vouchers, I would confidently call on the venerable president of this Convention. Bishop Carroll was one of the best of men and most humble and devout of Christians. I shall never forget a tribute to his memory paid by the good and venerable Protestant Bishop White, when contrasting the piety with which the Christian Carroll met death, with the cold trifling that characterized the last moments of the skeptical David Hume. I know not whether the tribute was more honourable to the piety of the dead, or the charity of the living prelate. Charles Carroll of Carrollton, the last survivor of the signers of American independence—at whose death both houses of the legislature of North Carolina unanimously testified their sorrow as at a national bereavement! Thomas Fitsimmons, one of the illustrious convention that framed the Constitution of the United States, and for several years the representative in Congress of the city of Philadelphia. Were these, and such as these, foes to freedom and unfit for republicanism? Would it be dangerous to permit such men to be sheriffs or constables in the land? Read the funeral eulogium of Charles Carroll, delivered at Rome by Bishop England—one of the greatest ornaments of the American Catholic church—a foreigner indeed by birth, but an American by adoption, and who, becoming an American, solemnly abjured all allegiance to every foreign king, prince, and potentate whatever—that eulogium which was so much carped at by English royalists, and English tories—and I think you will find it democratic enough to suit the taste, and find an echo in the heart of the sternest republican amongst us. Catholics are of all countries, of all governments, of all political creeds. In all they are taught that the kingdom of Christ is not of this world—and that it is their duty to render unto Cæsar the things that are Cæsar's, and unto God the things that are God's."

There, sir, is enough to put to shame the ignorant revilers of Catholic principles. There is the *true* state of the case. "Catholics are of all countries, of all governments, of all political creeds." And who was that "Archbishop Carroll" to whose virtue the "venerable Bishop White" bore such honourable testimony? He was a Jesuit; belonged to that body which the gentleman, with a grossness familiar to his pen, has designated as the "WICKED AND POLLUTED JESUIT PRIESTHOOD." Now I will only say in answer, that from this priesthood, the Presbyterian parsons, (at least the class of them to which the gentleman belongs,) might learn much of PIETY, HISTORY, PHILOSOPHY, SCIENCE, GENERAL INFORMATION;—but, above all, much of what is much needed,—HUMILITY and *good manners*. Whether this land is to be ruled by a "papal mob," or a "Presbyterian mob," time only can determine. I hope it will never be ruled by either. At present the aspirants to rule are the gentleman himself and his "gallant colleagues" in the propagation of the anti-Catholic conspiracy.

The gentleman repeats himself in such detail, that I must leave him to his "ingenious speculations." He is determined to make out the evidence in some shape, and what Bellarmine does *not* say for the church, *he says* for Bellarmine. He does not argue, he *asserts*. He seems to think that to employ *reasoning* for his readers, would be throwing pearls to swine. I think he is mistaken. I think there is a portion of them, even Presbyterians, who will expect to see the DOCTRINE of the Catholic Church, which is opposed to civil and religious liberty, and who will be disappointed, if not disgusted, to find that he can only torture the *assertions* of Bellarmine by *assertions* of his own.

He boasts of the "barbed arguments" of Dr. Miller, and it is but fair that the meeting should have a specimen of them. I shall take it from his ribaldrous compilation, entitled the "HISTORY OF POPERY." In order to give his readers a correct idea of the Catholic religion, this venerable calumniator is not ashamed to copy into his work the burlesque *excommunication of* TRISTAM SHANDY, part of which is as follows—"*May he be cursed in living and dying, in eating and drinking, in being hungry, in being thirsty, in fasting, in sleeping, in slumbering, in waking, in walking, in standing, in sitting, in lying, in working, in resting. May he be cursed in all the powers of his body. May he be cursed within and without. May he be cursed in the hair of his head; may he be cursed in his brain. May he be cursed in the crown of his head, in his temples, in his forehead, in his ears, in his eyebrows, in his cheeks, in his jawbones, in his nostrils, in his fore-teeth, in his grinders, &c. &c.*" Is not this a "barbed argument" of which the friends of Dr. Miller may be proud? Is it not evidence of extensive erudition, and a delicate conscience? Is it not worthy of the man who lifts his face to heaven, and tells God that the "Catholics are his enemies."

But let us give another of these "*barbed arguments.*" It is a story about a Scotch lady who happened to be on a visit in Dublin on a very interesting occasion, when a number of souls were to be translated out of purgatory. The operation was to take place in one of the Catholic chapels, and it appears that *purgatory was under the floor.* The priest having received his wages, and all things being ready, the doctor goes on to tell us that, "*Immediately a movable part of the floor, unoccupied of course, opened, and there issued forth from it living creatures as black as jet. When the little creatures began to move about, in order to prevent the deception from being detected, the lights were all extinguished, as if by magic.* The lady had eyed the souls' representatives very narrowly, and had observed that there was one of them within her reach; and with a degree of courage that would not be exercised by every one in her circumstances, she seized and secured it. She took it home, and showed it to the gentleman who had introduced her to the chapel, when it turned out to be a CRAB DRESSED IN BLACK VELVET."

Such is Dr. Miller's "History of Popery." Such his "BARBED ARGUMENTS." The author was ashamed to put his name to it; but Dr. Miller became father to the offspring, which its own parent would not own. He is satisfied, he tells us, in his Introductory Essay, that the work "MAY BE READ WITH ENTIRE CONFIDENCE, AND THAT IT IS ADAPTED TO DO MUCH GOOD." . . . "*That it is well worthy of the careful perusal of all who wish to be able to give* 'A REASON OF THE HOPE THAT IS IN THEM,' *and to warn their children and others around them, against those delusions which destroy the soul.*"

Do you wonder, sir, that the common lights of Presbyterianism are destined to cut a sorry figure in discussing this question, when the great luminary of their church is found in such works of ignorance and absurdity; bestowing *such* recommendations on *such* nonsense, and blessing God that he is to be saved by absolute predestination?

I have long since answered the objection which the gentleman brings forward again on the subject of the Scripture. In my last I proved by facts unanswerable, that in the interval between the invention of printing and the invention of Protestantism, the Scriptures were extensively circulated in the common language of the people. The clergy used them in the *Latin language*, as they still do. The gentleman explains the forty Catholic editions of the Scriptures in Italian, preceding the first Protestant version, by supposing that they were for "monks." This is a mistake. The monks, unlike many of the parsons of the present day, did not require that books should be in their "mother tongue" in order to understand them. It is to *their* labour and learning that we are indebted for the preservation of the Scriptures, and the fragments of literary or scientific works that have come down from antiquity. It was by the labours of the monks that they were all saved from the deluge of ignorance and barbarism that swept in upon Europe after the fall of the Roman Empire.

As to the spurious bull ascribed to Innocent VIII., he might as well quote Dr. Miller's History of the "crabs in black velvet," or his own authority, to prove its authenticity, as the writers whom he has quoted. They do not touch the point. They quote it, but it does not become the less spurious on that account.

In his allusion to my remarks on Venice, the gentleman gives us a new view of liberty. According to him, it consists in the *destruction of monasteries and nunneries*, and the triumph of anarchy and Voltaire over the rights of order and the authority of the pope. He admits, in fine, that he cannot prove his proposition. His words are, "*I say not that all Catholics are* IN DOCTRINE *or in spirit enemies to liberty.*" He knows that "*in doctrine*" all Catholics are the same. And, consequently, since he allows that *some* can be friends to liberty without violating their doctrine, it follows that *all can be*, if they will; and, consequently, it follows that the Catholic religion is not opposed to liberty in any of its doctrines. Its *doctrines* are the same for all—for the pope and the peasant, the rich and the poor, the learned and the illiterate, the priesthood and the people. The gentleman is disposed to acquit the people, and fix the charge on the "priesthood." Hinc illæ lachrymæ. But he is confused; and it would be wasting time to follow him through all his contradictions, not only of others, but of himself also.

But I must not be so fast. The gentleman, to "END THE DISPUTE," as he tells us, comes out with an argument from Devoti, § V. He does not say what volume, nor is it at all important. Devoti, it appears, says, "*Peace having been given to Christians*, (in Constantine's reign and afterwards,) *the church* PASSED JUDGMENT *on crimes, not only by her own right (suo jure) but by the laws of the Emperors.*" "Here," says Mr. Breckinridge, plainly, "she claimed the right before the Emperors conceded it." Certainly, Mr. B., and she claims it still; and so does your own church. But what then? Why she claims to "*pass judgment*" on crimes against the state, as well as against religion." Certainly, and so she does still. If a priest or lay person were to be involved in treason against his country, has she not a right to *judge him*, and even punish him by expulsion from her communion? This she has (*suo jure*) by her own right. But the rights which were *conferred* on ecclesiastical tribunals by the emperors, were those of *penal chastisement*, whose origin Devoti points out, as derived from the state, and not inherent in the church (*suo jure*) by her own right. This, therefore, does "end the dispute."

In my last speech I convicted the gentleman of altering and thereby corrupting a citation from the notes of the Rhemish Testament; and, instead of apologizing for such dishonourable proceeding, he says I am "catching at straws," and wonders why I did not stop to expose ALL the rest of his citations in the same way. I had not time.

Those notes are censurable enough in themselves; and as such were condemned from their first appearance, by the Catholics of England and Ireland. But it seems they were not bad enough for his purpose, and hence he *counterfeits them* by inserting words which they do not contain, and omitting others that are contained in them. This he admits: but he is not ashamed of it.

He volunteers to defend the "AMERICAN BIBLE SOCIETY." I did not attack it. I did not say one word against it. I stated that it had printed and sent to South America, a pretended Spanish Bible, with a falsehood stamped on its title-page. The gentlemen does not, dare not, deny the fact. He knows it is true. And what is his reply?—that my "charge bears malice and falsehood on its front." But so long as *the fact is undenied and undeniable*, his abuse, and the epithets in which he expresses it, must recoil on their source. The proceeding is a scandal to public morals. They circulate what they profess to believe a CORRUPTED version of the word of God. They call it on the title-page, the BIBLE OF THE BISHOP OF SEGOVIA, and they know that they have *omitted intentionally*, several books which *that* Bible contains. Why is the title preserved? To deceive the Spaniards, to whom it is sent. Why are portions of the original *suppressed*, whilst the title is retained? To *protestantize* the sacred word, and by a clandestine process, unworthy the Bible Society, to debauch the faith of the Catholics, whom they have selected as the victims of this contemptible artifice. Why have they circulated it at all, if they believe it to be a *corrupted version?* There is only one possible answer,—the assumed lawfulness of "doing evil that good may come." The proceeding, I say, claiming for its support the name and respectability of the American Bible Society, IS A SCANDAL TO PUBLIC MORALS. I state facts. I have no doubt but hundreds of individuals, of high and honourable feelings, will learn of this proceeding, with disgust and indignation at the iniquity which perpetrated it in their name.

The gentleman takes up my admission that Catholics have persecuted, as something highly serviceable to his cause. But has he been able to show, by any doctrine of their religion, *that they were required to persecute?* Has he been able to show that they *violated* any doctrine of their religion, when they not only did *not* persecute, but granted equal civil and religious freedom to Protestants, flying from the persecutions of their fellow-Protestants, as in Catholic Poland, and in Catholic Maryland? He has not, and he cannot. Will he be able to show that Presbyterians in power *ever granted such freedom?* Never, as we shall see under the next question.

I asked him to explain the equivocation which he ascribed to Luther, in making him distinguish between the Catholic Church and some other church, when he said, in opposition to Bellarmine, that "the church never put a heretic to death." To this, he replies, that my "perjness is too puerile to be worthy of notice." The gentleman has frequently alluded to the temporal power claimed by and attributed to popes, during the Middle Ages.

On this subject he has only "a little learning." It may be proper for me to make a few observations on it.

The Pope, according to the DOCTRINE of the Catholic religion, is the supreme visible head of that kingdom, which is not of this world—the chief visible pastor of Christ's universal world. The doctrines of that religion gave him no title, by virtue of his high spiritual trust, to any civil power or temporal right for the management of purely secular things. Therefore, what has been called the temporal authority of the Pope, must be traced to some other source, than that by which he is appointed to feed the sheep as well as the lambs of the Christian fold.

THE POPES—during the first three hundred years, were distinguished, amidst the brightness even of those ages of primitive Christianity, for the innocence, holiness, humility, and heroic fortitude of their lives. The greater proportion of them sealed their faith by martyrdom. Those of the fifth and sixth century were equally distinguished for their zeal, talents, science, and laborious ministry. Contemporary writers bear witness to the correctness with which those of the seventh and eighth centuries laboured to stem the torrent of barbarism, that was threatening to inundate the church, as well as the empire. In the ninth and tenth centuries, the regions of northern barbarism were invaded by the apostolic missionaries, sent by the popes to preach Christ, and establish the gospel on the ruins of paganism. So far, enmity itself has been unable either to obscure the virtues of the men who succeeded in the chair of St. Peter, or to deny the salutary effects of their zeal, in promoting all that was most beneficial for the temporal and eternal interests of man. It is a remarkable fact, that ALL the nations that have ever been CONVERTED *from* PAGANISM, have been converted *to* the Catholic religion, and by missionaries appointed by, or in connection with, the successive popes, who have governed the church. Fifteen hundred years of Christianity had passed away, before the Protestant religion was invented—breaking communion with the pope and the church—and three hundred years since; and it is equally remarkable that Protestants have failed in their attempts to convert pagans. They *seduced Catholics*, but they have failed *among the heathens*. From the tenth to the fifteenth century, the state of society and civil government in Europe was such, as it is impossible for us, at this day, to conceive or realize, even in imagination. The military spirit that prevailed—the feebleness of law—the unsettled order of claims to political power—the strifes and rivalships,—all presented an ocean in which were rocks and whirlpools, shoals and tempests, and through which the popes as pilots of divine appointment had to steer the vessel of the church.

It was during this period that occurred those events which furnish half-educated Protestant writers with the everlasting theme of crimination against the popes. Those events, to be judged *with justice*, ought to be judged in connection with the character of the age, customs of the nations, and the other specific circumstances in which they occurred. For their own temporal power, the popes enjoy it by as ancient and as just a title as any government in Europe or America. When the emperors were busied in the East, and unable to protect the states of Italy, the pope became, by the choice of the people, sovereign of the Exarchate of Ravenna; and their title is confirmed by a prescription of eleven hundred years. It matters not whether that authority was the gift of Pepin, after the expulsion of the Lombards, or not. The pope became the temporal ruler de facto, and his successors, with scarcely any *addition* or *diminution of their territory*, have remained so to this day.

But they are charged with claiming a right to dispose of the crowns of other nations, and releasing their subjects from their oaths of fidelity. Some few have, indeed, cherished and proclaimed this pretension. But who is the prince that was ACTUALLY DEPOSED by any pope? You will look for his name in history, and you will not find it. The Presbyterians deposed FOUR GOVERNMENTS, and brought two crowned heads to THE BLOCK, in less than a century. The popes never so much as one. Who is the prince on whom the popes conferred a crown and dominions, *which he did not possess before?* NOT ONE. These are the *facts of the case*, and show the value of the gentleman's learning and industry, as exhibited on this subject in his last speech.

The pope did not give America to Spain, and much less did he give it before it was discovered. The countries discovered in these seas by Spanish and Portuguese navigators, were taken possession of in the name of the two governments respectively; and when a dispute arose about the boundaries, the Pope Alexander VI. was appealed to as arbiter; it was in this capacity that he gave those governments what they possessed already.

The popes in some cases, as that of Queen Elizabeth, did affect to release subjects from their allegiance. This was exercising an *assumed power* for an *unlawful end*. It was an abuse, consequently. And the Catholics of England and Ireland condemned it, and proved that *whilst they were ready to suffer persecution for conscience' sake at the hands of Elizabeth*, they were also ready to fight in defence of her rights, notwithstanding the pretended release from their fealty, and her excommunication. Even Hume, the habitual reviler of the Catholic religion, shows how distinguished was the loyalty of the Catholics of England against the pretensions of Philip. But facts that are palpable, are the best test to decide. Presbyterians overthrew four governments, and brought two sovereigns to the block in less than a century : and the Popes have never overturned so much as *one*. The gentleman has copied an *index* in his catalogue of popes and kings, and he very modestly requires of me to write out the history. Nearly the whole of his speech is made of assertions, which he calls history. From whom he copied the long extract of borrowed assertion, with which he fills up, it is not worth while to inquire. It is *assertion*, mere *assertion*, and nothing else. Its violence betrays its origin. Copied, no doubt, from some writer as fanatical and as ill-informed as the gentleman himself. It is from beginning to end, a fiery, foolish rhapsody, which a man who pretends to give *proof* and *reason*, instead of *declamation* and *abuse*, would not offer to an assembly whose intellect he did not despise. It was not worthy of the gentleman to undergo the humiliation of borrowing such gratuitous ABUSE from another; whereas in that department, which requires no proof, he is known to be equal to the sublimest originality.

About the pope calling himself God, and some other points in which the gentleman has borne false witness against his neighbour, I shall sum up the evidences presently. In written controversy, it is easy for one who is not restrained by the " belief in good works," to give such a partial colouring to isolated facts, as to pervert them from the truth of history. But here, he cannot escape detection. I have collected a number of the gentleman's calumnies from the written controversy, with the very books to which he referred for their proof. These books, the original works, are now *marked at the place of each reference*, AND ON THE TABLE BEFORE US. The gentleman has an opportunity to sustain his assertions, in presence of this meeting, and if he does not, the audience will not be slow to understand the reason.

It is a painful process, sir, to have to contend with a man against whom the interests of truth, the rights of reputation, the protection of innocence, accused and villified, oblige you to prove, face to face, the charge of CALUMNY. I charge the gentleman with calumny: not in his absence, but in his presence; and I have brought to this meeting the ORIGINAL WORKS, said to contain the statements which he has ascribed to them, *but which they do not contain*. Yes, sir, it is painful to be obliged to undertake such a work. But it is the glory of the Catholic religion, that in order to prove it guilty of the charges that sectarian zeal has preferred against it, recourse must be had to artifice, perversion of authorities, imputation of doctrines which Catholics disclaim, and in many instances abhor. Recourse must be had to every species of refined speculation, misrepresentation, and, with a sense of humiliation for human nature, I must add, falsehood. I shall now give a list of those particular calumnies, which I have selected, and if the gentleman will venture to deny the truth of *my statements*, HERE ARE ALL THE BOOKS, THE PAGES, AND PASSAGES MARKED.

which will decide in presence of this meeting who speaks the truth, and who has spoken or written the *untruth* in the matter. I request the gentleman to pay attention, and not flinch from the ordeal.

Be it known then, to all posterity, that, in the year of our Lord 1835, in the month of February, in an Oral Discussion between the Rev. John Breckinridge and the Rev. John Hughes, in the city of Philadelphia, the following CALUMNIES against the holy Catholic religion have been refuted by a reference to original documents:

FIRST CALUMNY. "*That according to the Council of Constance, Catholics are not bound to keep faith with heretics.*" Whereas, this has been stated by nearly all Protestant controversial writers, and believed by their unsuspecting followers, and lastly has been referred to, *as a settled point*, by the Rev. John Breckinridge in his first letter of the written Controversy with said Rev. John Hughes; (1) and whereas, the TRUTH is, that no such doctrine is contained in the acts of said Council, now open before us, therefore, the charge is a CALUMNY; FALSE in itself, and injurious to the rights of Catholics.

SECOND CALUMNY. "That according to the Sixteenth canon of the Third Council of Lateran, an oath contrary to ecclesiastical utility is perjury, not on oath."(2) And whereas, the said canon, NOW PRODUCED IN THE ORIGINAL, contains no such doctrine, therefore, the charge is FALSE and INJURIOUS, as above.

THIRD CALUMNY. "That the Fourth Council of Lateran, A. D. 1215, Third canon, freed the subjects of such SOVEREIGNS as embraced heresy, from their fealty;"(3) whereas, the ORIGINAL CANON NOW PRODUCED, contains no such doctrine, therefore, the charge is again FALSE and INJURIOUS, as before.

FOURTH CALUMNY. That "if the Pope should err in commanding vices, and prohibiting virtues, the church would be bound to believe vices to be virtues, and virtues to be vices." And whereas, Bellarmine has been referred to, as maintaining this doctrine, (4) and whereas, Bellarmine teaches no such doctrine, but the reverse, therefore, the charge is FALSE and INJURIOUS to Catholics. Bellarmine's work, with the passage marked, is now on the table before us.

FIFTH CALUMNY. "That the Catholics have suppressed in the catechism of the Council of Trent, that part of the first commandment which forbids idolatry."(5) And whereas he (Mr Breckinridge) persisted in this CALUMNY, and attempted to prove it

---

(1) Johnson's edition, p. 20. (2) Mr. Breckinridge, same page.
(3) Mr. Breckinridge, same page. (4) Mr. Breckinridge, ibid., p. 19.
(5) Mr. Breckinridge, ibid., passim.

(*even after six different editions had been shown to him*) by referring to a copy which was in New York, and whereas, he has exhibited *that copy* to this assembly as proof in his favour, and whereas, THAT COPY CONTAINS IT, like all the others, therefore, the charge is cruelly FALSE and INJURIOUS.

SIXTH CALUMNY. "That there is a *dishonest* difference in the sense of two translations of the Catechism of the Council of Trent, in certain particular passages." And whereas, the pretended difference *does not exist* in the works referred to, but was predicated on *what turns out to be a falsification of the text*, by making a *full stop* in the middle of a sentence, and otherwise mutilating; therefore, the charge is FALSE and INJURIOUS as above. And since Mr. Breckinridge disclaims having copied from the "Text-book of Popery," it remains for him to explain, 1st. *How he came to* MUTILATE *it at all?* And 2d, *How he came to mutilate word for word, as was done in the above "text-book" of falsehoods.*

SEVENTH CALUMNY. "That Catholics call the Pope God." As proof of this, Mr. Breckinridge (6) quoted the epistle of Pope Nicholas to the Emperor Michael, in the Corpus juris Canonici; and whereas, said epistle now produced in the original, contains no such proposition; therefore the charge is FALSE and INJURIOUS to Catholics, and shows great STUPIDITY in the minds of those who make or believe it.

EIGHTH CALUMNY. "That the DOCTRINES of the Catholic Church are hostile to civil and religious liberty." In proof of this calumny, the Rev. Mr. Breckinridge cited the Twenty-seventh canon of the Third Council of Lateran, A. D. 1179, against the Albigenses.(7) And whereas, said canon is *no part of the Catholic religion*, but a special regulation for a particular case, made in concurrence with the civil power of the states from which alone it could derive any authority; and whereas, the said Mr. Breckinridge in quoting the said canon, SUPPRESSED the section which enumerates the *crimes* of the sects referred to, and thereby DECEIVES his readers, making it appear that the punishment was for *their speculative errors in doctrine*, and not for their crimes against society and the state; therefore, the charge is FALSE and INJURIOUS to Catholics. And whereas, the said Mr. Breckinridge alleges that *he copied this suppression of the truth*, without being aware of it, FROM FABER; and whereas, we do not know from whom FABER copied; and whereas, the *greater the multiplication of copyists and copies*, the greater the *extent of injury done to Catholics;* and whereas, it is a divine trait of the religion of Christ, that it OBLIGES US to repair an injury even to a pagan, when it is in our power; therefore, it would *refresh the face of Christianity*, if Mr. Breckinridge would undeceive the public with the same pen

(6) Controversy, p. 86.   (7) Ibid., p. 175.

which contributed to lead that public astray. FABER will have to see to it in the *next world*, if not in this.

NINTH CALUMNY. "That the Pope claims the right of exterminating heretics." In proof of this, the said Rev. Mr. Breckinridge quoted (8) a supposed Bull of Innocent VIII. against the Waldenses; and whereas, said bull, even if genuine, *is no part of Catholic doctrine;* and whereas, the gentleman who quoted it, had no certainty of its existence, and whereas, it is not to be found in the collection of bulls, in which the worst, as well as the best, are preserved, nor among the archives in Rome, which have been particularly examined; therefore, the charge, so far as it depends on this spurious document, is equally FALSE and INJURIOUS to the rights of Catholics.

TENTH CALUMNY. "That according to the Third Canon of the Fourth Council of Lateran, *sovereigns may be deposed*, and their subjects released from their allegiance, when *they become heretics;* and that they are to be excommunicated when they *neglect to exterminate heretics* from their lands." In proof of this, the said Rev. John Breckinridge quoted a mangled extract of said Canon.(9) And whereas, *said Canon is no part of Catholic doctrine,* except in so far as it condemns all heresies in the abstract; and whereas, it expressly refers to those *particular heretics whose crimes, growing out of their errors,* had threatened the welfare of the state and of society, as appears by the ORIGINAL DOCUMENTS NOW BEFORE US; and whereas, it refers to *inferior lords* who held their territory and power by the conditions of feudal tenure, and expressly excepts the rights of the sovereign or principal lord, who held by what was termed divine right; and whereas, it was enacted with the concurrence, probably at the request, of all the sovereigns of Europe, and depended on them for its authority; and whereas, it is denied by learned Protestant authors, that said Canon was passed in the Council;(10) and whereas, admitting it to be genuine, *it does not prove the accusation;* therefore the charge is equally FALSE and INJURIOUS.

And whereas, the said Mr. Breckinridge in reply to the question, whether the quotation was literal and continuous, answered unhesitatingly, "that it was;" that "he had the original before him; that "he copied from Caranza;" that his opponent might "compare his translation with the original;" that he considered the question an indignity offered to his character, &c. And whereas, his opponent *has compared;* and has the ORIGINAL and TRANSLATION HERE PRESENT, and finds that the said translation is *neither "continuous"* nor *"literal:"* because, 1. Whole sentences are left out, without the usual marks to indicate the omission. 2. Other sentences are *begun* or *broke off in the middle.* 3. The

(8) Controversy, p. 174. (9) Ibid, p. 89.
(10) Collier's Eccl. Hist., vol. L p. 424.

word "præsentibus" is omitted, as an important qualification. 4. The last paragraph is *not in the original*, and we must be informed where the gentleman found it. Hence, the following questions are to be answered. 1. Did he quote from Caranza? *If he did*, why did he mangle his authority in order to make out his proof? *If he did not*, why did he say that he did? 2. Had he room for the *whole Canon* as it is abridged in Caranza? *If he had*, why did he *not* give all? *If he had not*, as he says, why did he introduce a passage which is *not in Caranza at all?* 3. Did he *know* how much his translation differed from Caranza? *If he did*, why did he say that it was "continuous?" *If he did not*, why did he say that *he had the original before him?* Challenge a comparison of his translation with the original, and *affect* to be offended at the intimation of a doubt, which facts have proven to be but too well founded?

Here are the charges, and here are the witnesses, the original works, to prove them. Will the gentleman vindicate himself now, or will he wait till the witnesses are *removed?* If I were in his situation, I know what I should do. I should appeal to the witnesses to prove my innocence, and if *their* testimony condemned me, I should apologize to my Catholic fellow-citizens for the injury I had done them.

But the fact is, that the gentleman, hoping to be saved by the patent-right of predestination, which God was pleased to bestow on Calvin and his followers, seems to make a jest of truth and literary honesty. After having acknowledged the error of his citation of one of the notes appended to the text of the Rhemish Testament, he adds, "*Yet pray, Mr. Hughes, why pass over* ALL *the other citations in silence?* One of them says: 'The zeal of Catholic men ought to be so great towards all heretics and their doctrines, that they should give them the anathema, though they are never so dear to them; so as not even to spare their own parents.' Am I right in this citation?" Why, Mr. Breckinridge, you are *wrong. If you ever saw the text*, YOU MUST KNOW *that you are wrong.* The annotators were writing on the 8th verse of the 1st chapter to the Galatians, where the apostle gives the "anathema" to even an angel who should preach another Gospel, besides that which he had preached. On this, after giving the explanation St. Vincent Lerius and St. Augustine, they conclude in *these words:* "*Lastly, Hierome useth this place, wherein the apostle giveth the curse or anathema to all false teachers, not once but twice, to prove that the zeal of Catholic men ought to be so great towards all heretics and their doctrines, that they should give them the anathema, though never so dear to them. In which case, saith this holy doctor, I would not spare mine own parents.*" This is the *true* citation. Proving the gentleman guilty of 1st. Garbling, by beginning in the *middle of the sentence, and* ALTERING THE PUNCTUATION. 2d. Of suppressing the words "*in which case saith that holy doctor, &c."* 3d. Of foisting into the text words which are not in it, viz. *"so as not even to spare, &c."* And yet with a boldness which indicates nerves of iron, he asks in reference to this citation—"PRAY, MR. HUGHES, AM I RIGHT, OR AM I WRONG?" Let the public judge. I have been obliged to expose him in this way from the beginning. During the written controversy he gave a quotation from Baronius, composed of only a few lines; but what is its history? *He gave it as one unbroken passage,* and on examining Baronius, it was found to be made up of "scraps" taken from *four different paragraphs* of a page, in two columns, folio. The first SCRAP was from the 5th paragraph, the second from the 6th, the third scrap from the 5th again, the fourth scrap from the 4th paragraph, the fifth scrap from the 5th again, and the 6th scrap from the 7th paragraph. Of what use is it, therefore, to contend with a man, who, to supply the absence of truth in the support of a bad cause, is obliged to have recourse to these means?

I have now examined the evidence which he has brought forward, to show that the Catholic religion contains doctrines opposed to civil and religious liberty, and I believe that no man who understands what it is TO PROVE A PROPOSITION will risk his reputation so far as to say that the gentleman has not signally and triumphantly FAILED. He has trifled with truth. He has perverted authors, and authorities. He has corrupted citations. He has exposed himself, and done no credit to the cause which he had thrust himself forward to maintain. He has told us what Bellarmine and Devoti said, and yet admitting, for argument sake that he has told us correctly, still he has signally and triumphantly FAILED, whenever he attempted to show that the sayings of these individuals, and *the doctrines of the Catholic religion are the same thing.* He has stated facts of history, and by reasoning backwards, he has inferred that they MUST be sanctioned by DOCTRINE; as if the transgressions of our citizens were a *proof* that the American Constitution sanctions immorality. He has quoted Canon law, and whilst he shows in every instance that he does not understand what it means, he seems to expect that I should supply the instruction of which he is deficient. Canon signifies a rule or regulation. Now every subject, to which a rule can be applied, may be said to fall under the operation of a canon. Hence there are CANONS OF DOCTRINE in the Catholic religion, which are THE SAME IN ALL AGES and COUNTRIES, OF THE CHURCH AND OF THE WORLD. These canons of doctrine are *defined* sometimes by General Councils, sometimes in the Bulls of Popes. It was in *these doctrinal canons* that the gentleman had bound himself to find those "tenets of faith or morals" in the Catholic religion, which were supposed to be hostile to civil and religious liberty. Did he find them? Not one. They do not exist. But there have been other canons, of which doctrine was not the object. They were temporary laws made for particular exigencies, and as these were subject to the *vicissitudes* of time and place, so the rules or canons to which they gave rise were necessarily various, different, and often contradictory. They are like a COLLECTION OF CIVIL STATUTES under the *Constitution of England;* and it would be just as absurd to say that the inhabitants of Great Britain are obliged to observe ALL THE STATUTES THAT EVER WERE PASSED from the foundation of the empire, as to say that Catholics are bound by what was, at *one period*, or in *other countries*, Canon law, but is so no more, or is so, but in other countries. Most of those canons have become, like other laws, obsolete. They *were*, but are not now. They are not even universal laws of the church; much less, DOCTRINES; which are confined to those tenets of faith and morals that Catholics believe to have been revealed by Almighty God. Where they existed, they were incorporated into the civil code, and formed part of the law of the land. Neither was this regulation, in those times, deemed an invasion of either civil or religious liberty, in as much as the Catholic religion was the religion of the people and rulers as well as of the popes and bishops.

From these, the gentleman would prove DOCTRINE. They *never were* doctrine; and wherever they affected the external relations of men, they have become obsolete, except in those countries in which they still remain incorporated in the civil code as laws of the land. Consequently in adducing these as evidence of doctrine, he signally and triumphantly FAILED.

He spoke of the INQUISITION. I have proved that every denomination has all of the Inquisition, for which the Catholic religion is responsible; viz. *the right* to hunt out heresy, and expel the obstinate heretics; and that no denomination exercises this right, with more rigour and less mercy than the Presbyterian would-be orthodox, as Mr. Barnes can testify. But as for the *penal portion* of that tribunal, it belonged to the civil governments, and was used by them as a *political engine*. To the facts by which this distinction is established, the gentleman has been utterly unable to reply.

He spoke of the CRUSADES. Mr. James, who has studied the question, and written upon it, and who being a Protestant, cannot be suspected of partiality, has decided that they "were as *just* as any wars that ever were undertaken." Whether his opinion, or that of Mr. Breckinridge carries more weight, I shall not pretend to decide. At all events, they have no more to do with the *doctrines* of the Catholic religion, than the English wars have to do with the thirty-nine articles.

He spoke of the MASSACRE OF ST. BARTHOLOMEW. He did not, however, relate the facts connected with it, or rather antecedent to it. The followers of Calvin's religion had attempted to dethrone their king, and put a successor of their own creed on the throne. For this they had invited *foreigners to aid them in their war against their country.* They had assassinated the Duke de Guise; sacked and pillaged hundreds of towns; massacred thousands of their countrymen; and spread desolation and bloodshed wherever they went. On the occasion of the St. Bartholomew, it was maintained by the French court, afterwards, that they had formed a plot, to get possession of the young king, and thus accomplish their object by stratagem. Whether they had or not, is now not clear; they were known to be capable of it. But THIS was the PLEA on which the court attempted to justify the horrid crime, by which it escaped the real or pretended conspiracy of the Calvinists. This is notorious matter of history; and those who understand it otherwise, are like the gentleman, under the dangerous influence of "a little learning."

On the civil wars in Ireland, I advise the gentleman to read Mr. Carey's erudite and unanswerable work, the VINDICIÆ HIBERNICÆ. But all these matters are unavailing for the purpose in hand, which is to show that there are DOCTRINES, TENETS OF FAITH, AND MORALS, in the CATHOLIC RELIGION, opposed to civil and religious liberty. He has signally and triumphantly—FAILED, in this; whatever else he may have done.

And now having seen that every attempt to prove *the affirmative of this question* has been a FAILURE, I shall try whether, difficult as is the proof of *a negative*, I cannot establish FACTS from which it will appear clearly and conclusively, that there is no doctrine of the Catholic religion opposed to civil or religious liberty.

FIRST FACT. That the Catholic Church teaches, and has always taught, that the kingdom of Christ is not of this world. For proof of this, we have the testimony of popes and fathers, all agreeing that religion cannot be enforced by violence, nor defended, unless by patience. See St. Irenæus,[10] St. Justin,[11] Theophilus Alexandrinus,[12] Eusebius,[13] Tertullian in his Apology.[14] He says in his book ad Scapulam,[15] speaking of the Christians—" *We worship the emperor as it befits him, and as it is lawful for us, to wit, as a man next to God, dependent for what he possesses on God,* AND INFERIOR ONLY TO HIM." St. Optatus maintains the same doctrine.[16] Also Osius of Cordova, cited by Athanasius.[17] St. Augustine[18] says, "We do *not assign* THE RIGHT OF GIVING *kingdoms or empires except to the true God.*" The doctrine of Origen,[19] and in short, of all the fathers that have ever written on the subject is the " UNANI-

[10] Lib. 5, chap. xxiv.
[11] Apol. 2.
[12] Lib. 1, ad Antilogium.
[13] Lib. 7, chap. x.
[14] Chap. xxx.
[15] Chap ii.
[16] Lib. 3, Cont. Parm.
[17] Tom. I. p. 371.
[18] Lib. 4, de Civit. Dei, c. xxxiii.
[19] Tom. II. p. 118.

MOUS CONSENT," that the *civil powers* of the world, and the *spiritual powers of the Church*, are both *original* in their source, and mutually independent of each other. If individual popes, or individual writers have claimed, for popes, the right to dispose of kingdoms, it was on some *other ground of right*, besides any doctrine of the church:—some human title, or some text of Scripture, employed on the hazard of " private interpretation," which is contrary to the rule of determining *doctrine* in the church.

SECOND FACT. That Catholic nations invariably RESISTED, and that without even the charge of having violated any DOCTRINE of their religion, the attempts of popes to dispose of their civil sovereignty. And it does not appear that the popes have *actually* ever succeeded in deposing a sovereign, or bestowing a crown.

THIRD FACT. That before Luther and Protestantism were heard of, crowds of Republics had flourished under the auspices of the Catholic religion, and public liberty. VENICE rose up from the ocean, with all her republican glory round about her, and for *five hundred years* remained a lofty democratic government. Genoa, Florence, and other free states, are proof that liberty and Catholicity are perfectly congenial, notwithstanding the infinite ignorance that asserts the contrary. Even Spain had its Catholic Cortes, a free assembly, which imposed upon the monarch an oath, in which they told him, that they were individually as good, and, taken altogether, far better than himself, and that *his power was derived from the people*. This was before what is called the Protestant Reformation, and it was the *excesses of that era*, that frightened Spain into a despotism—in self-defence.

FOURTH FACT. That the Catholics of Great Britain and Ireland have disclaimed all right of the Pope or cardinals to civil or temporal jurisdiction in the British dominions. This they have not ceased to do since the pretended Reformation; and disclaimed it ON OATH, as a calumny imputed by their oppressors, and *not* contained in the doctrines of the Catholic religion. During most of the last 300 years since the importation of Protestantism, the Catholics, who have continued to disclaim this calumny under the solemnity of an oath, have constituted one-fourth, and at present constitute one-*third*, of the entire population of Great Britain and Ireland. In this, no portion of their fellow-Catholics throughout the world, ever accused them of denying a DOCTRINE OR PRINCIPLE OF FAITH.

FIFTH FACT. That in 1791, the following questions, at the instance of Mr. Pitt, then Minister of State, were sent to the foreign universities in France and Spain, and were answered unanimously, as follows :—(1)

(1) See Butler's Book of the Church.

"1. *Has the Pope or cardinals, or any body of men, or any individual of the Church of Rome,* ANY CIVIL AUTHORITY, POWER, JURISDICTION, OF PRE-EMINENCE *whatsoever, within the realm of England?*

"2. CAN THE POPE OR CARDINALS, *or any body of men, or any individual of the Church of Rome,* ABSOLVE or DISPENSE *with his majesty's subjects,* FROM THEIR OATH OF ALLEGIANCE, UPON ANY PRETEXT WHATSOEVER?

"3. *Is there any* TENETS OF THE CATHOLIC FAITH, BY WHICH CATHOLICS ARE JUSTIFIED *in* NOT *keeping faith with heretics, or other persons differing from them in religious opinions, in any transaction, either of a public or a private nature?*"

THE UNIVERSITIES ANSWERED UNANIMOUSLY:—

"1. *That the Pope or cardinals, or any body of men, or any individual of the Church of Rome,* HAS NOT *any civil authority, power, jurisdiction, or pre-eminence* WHATSOEVER, *within the realm of England.*

"2. *That the Pope or cardinals, or any body of men, or any individual of the Church of Rome,* CANNOT ABSOLVE or DISPENSE *with his majesty's subjects, from their oath of allegiance,* UPON ANY PRETEXT WHATSOEVER.

"3. *That there* IS NO PRINCIPLE IN THE TENETS OF THE CATHOLIC FAITH, BY WHICH CATHOLICS ARE JUSTIFIED IN NOT KEEPING *faith with heretics, or other persons differing from them in religious opinions, in any transactions, either of a public or a private nature.*"

SIXTH FACT. That the Catholics of Great Britain and Ireland have suffered themselves to be robbed of their TITLES, their CIVIL RIGHTS, their PROPERTY, their REPUTATION, &c., rather than *swear a false oath.* They were required to swear, that they believed in the religious OPINIONS set forth in various acts of parliament, and that they did *not* believe in the DOCTRINES of their own Church. This, they knew, would be *perjury.* And because they would not commit this *perjury,* they were doomed to submit to the grinding and degradation of the PENAL CODE, which brands Protestantism with such indelible crimes of *persecution* for conscience' sake, as ought to make its votaries *blush,* whenever the words "religious freedom," "rights of conscience," are *accidentally* pronounced in their presence. A Protestant has thus described the barbarous operation of that infernal code:

"In ENGLAND, this code, (the penal code,) I. Stripped the peers of their hereditary right to sit in parliament. II. It stripped the gentlemen of their right to be chosen members of the Commons House. III. It took from *all* the right to vote at elections; and though Magna Charta says, that *no man shall be taxed without his own consent, it double-taxed every man who refused to* ABJURE HIS RELIGION, and thus become *an apostate.* IV. It shut them out from all offices of power and trust, even the most insig nificant. V. It took from them the right of presenting to livings in the Church, though that right was given to *Quakers* and JEWS. VI. It fined them at the rate of TWENTY POUNDS A MONTH, for keeping away from that Church, *to go to which they deemed apostasy.* VII. It disabled them from keping arms in their houses *for their defence;* from *maintaining suits at law;* from *being guardians or executors;* from *practising in law or physic;* from *travelling five miles from their houses,* and all these, under heavy penalties, in case of disobedience. VIII. *If a married woman kept away from Church, she forfeited* TWO-THIRDS OF HER DOWER; *she could not be executrix to her husband,* and *might,* during her husband's lifetime, *be imprisoned,* unless ransomed by him at ten pounds a month. IX. It enabled *any four justices* of the peace, in case a man had been convicted of *not going to Church,* to call him before them, to COMPEL *him to* ABJURE HIS RELIGION, or, if he refused, to sentence him TO BANISHMENT FOR LIFE, (without judge or jury,) and, if he returned, HE WAS TO SUFFER DEATH. X. It enabled *any* two justices of the peace to call before them, without any information, any man that they chose, above sixteen years of age, and if such man *refused to abjure the Catholic religion,* and continue in his refusal for six months, he was rendered incapable of possessing land; and *any land, the possession of which might belong to him,* CAME INTO THE POSSESSION OF THE NEXT PROTESTANT HEIR, who was not obliged to account for any profits. XI. It made such man incapable of purchasing lands, and *all contracts made by him, or for him,* WERE NULL AND VOID. XII. It imposed a fine of about TEN POUNDS A MONTH, *for employing a Catholic schoolmaster in a private family,* and two pounds a day on the schoolmaster so employed. XIII. It imposed a fine of one hundred pounds for sending a child to a Catholic foreign school, and the child so sent was disabled from ever inheriting, purchasing, or enjoying lands, or profits, goods, debts, legacies, or sums of money. XIV. *It punished the* SAYING OF MASS, *by a fine of one hundred and twenty pounds, and the hearing of mass, by a fine of sixty pounds.* XV. Any Catholic priest, who *returned from beyond the seas,* and WHO DID NOT ABJURE HIS RELIGION IN THREE DAYS AFTERWARDS, and also any person *who* RETURNED TO THE CATHOLIC FAITH, or procured *another to return to it,* this merciless, this sanguinary code, punished with HANGING, RIPPING OUT OF BOWELS, and QUARTERING.

"In IRELAND, the code was still more ferocious, more hideously bloody; for, in the first place, ALL *the cruelties* of the *English code had,* as the work of a few hours, a few strokes of the pen, in one single act, *been inflicted upon unhappy Ireland:* and *then,* IN ADDITION, the Irish code contained, amongst *many other* violations of all the laws of justice and humanity, the following *twenty most savage punishments.* I. A Catholic schoolmaster, private or public, or even usher to a Protestant, was punished with IMPRISONMENT, BANISHMENT, and FINALLY, AS A FELON. II. The Catholic clergy were not allowed *to be* in the country, without being registered, and kept as a sort of prisoners at large; and *rewards* were given (*out of the revenue raised in part on the Catholics*) for discovering them; fifty pounds for an archbishop or bishop; twenty pounds for a priest, and ten pounds for a schoolmaster or usher. III. *Any two justices* of the peace might call before them any Catholic, order him to declare *an oath*, where and when he heard mass, who were present, and the name and residence of any priest or schoolmaster he might know of; and if he refused to obey *this* INHUMAN INQUISITION, they had power to condemn him, (without judge or jury,) *to a year's imprisonment in a felon's gaol*, or to pay twenty pounds. IV. No Catholic could purchase any manors, nor even hold under a lease for more than thirty-one years. V. Any Protestant, if he suspected any one of holding property *in trust* for a Catholic, or of being concerned in any sale, lease, mortgage, or other contracts for a Catholic; any Protestant, thus suspecting, might *file a bill* against the suspected trustee, and TAKE THE ESTATE OR PROPERTY FROM HIM. VI. Any Protestant seeing a Catholic tenant of a farm, the produce of which farm exceeded the amount of the rent by more than one-third, might DISPOSSESS THE CATHOLIC, *and* ENTER ON THE LEASE IN HIS STEAD. VII. Any Protestant seeing a Catholic with a horse, *worth more than five pounds*, might *take the horse away from him upon tendering him five pounds*. VIII. In order to prevent the smallest chance of justice in these and similar cases, none but *known Protestants*, were to be *jurymen* in the trial of any such cases. IX. Horses of Catholics might be seized for the use of the militia; and, besides this, Catholics were compelled to PAY DOUBLE towards the militia. X. Merchants, whose ships and goods might be taken by privateers, during a war with a *Catholic Prince*, were to be compensated for their losses *by a levy on the goods and lands of Catholics only*, though, mind, Catholics were, at the same time, impressed and compelled to shed their blood in the war against that same Catholic Prince. XI. Property of a Protestant, whose heirs at law were Catholics, was to go to the nearest *Protestant* relation, just the same as if the Catholic heirs had been *dead*, though the property might be entailed on them. XII. If there were *no Protestant heir*, then, in *order to break up all Catholic families*, the entail and all heirship were set aside, and the property was divided, *share and share alike*, amongst all the Catholic heirs. XIII. If a Protestant had an estate in Ireland, he was forbidden to marry a Catholic in or out of Ireland. XIV. All marriages between Protestants and Catholics were ANNULLED, *though many children might have proceeded from them.* XV. Every priest, who celebrated a marriage between a Catholic and a Protestant, or between two Protestants, was CONDEMNED TO BE HANGED. XVI. A Catholic father could not be guardian to, or have the custody of, *his own child, if the child,* HOWEVER YOUNG, PRETENDED *to be a Protestant;* but the child *was taken* FROM ITS OWN FATHER, and put into the custody of a Protestant relation. XVII. If any child of a Catholic became a Protestant, the parent was to be instantly summoned, and to be made to declare, *upon oath,* the full value of his or her property, *of all* sorts; and then the chancery was to make *such distribution of the property as it thought fit.* XVIII. ' Wives, be *obedient* unto your own husband,' says the great apostle. 'Wives, be *disobedient* to them,' said this horrid code; for if the wife of a Catholic chose to *turn Protestant,* it set aside the will of the husband, and made her a participator in all his possessions, in spite of him, *however immoral, however bad a wife or bad a mother she might have been.* XIX. ' Honour thy father and thy mother, that thy days may be long in the land, which the Lord, thy God, giveth thee.' 'Dishonour them,' said this savage code; for if any one of the *sons of a Catholic father* became a Protestant, this son was to possess all the father had, and the father could not sell, could not mortgage, could not leave legacies or portions, out of his estate, by whatever title he might hold it, even though it might have been the fruit of his own toil. XX. Lastly, (of this *score,* but this is only *a part,*) 'the Church, as by *law* established,' was, in her great indulgence, pleased not only to open her doors, *but to award,* (out of the taxes,) thirty pounds A YEAR FOR LIFE, to any Catholic priest, who would *abjure his religion, and declare his belief in hers."*

Such is but *a part* of the punishment which Catholics *might have escaped,* if the doctrines of their Church had only permitted them to swear a lie, by which Protestants would have hailed them as *converts to pure Christianity.* And yet, after an ordeal of three centuries of persecution, the Catholic religion is found to have been gaining ground for the last one hundred and fifty years, in spite of human efforts to crush and extinguish it. But although the Presbyterians were themselves sometimes sufferers by penal laws, yet it is a fact, that in all their grievances against the government, *the neglect to put these sanguinary and inhuman laws into rigorous and merciless execution against the Catholics* was always at the head of the list. And yet they talk about being friends of religious freedom!!

SEVENTH FACT. That the FIRST *declaration* of religious and civil freedom and equality, that was ever published by a legislative body, was by the Catholic Colony of Maryland. They had fled from persecution; they offered an example which *none had given,* and which few other denominations were prompt to imitate. Did they, in this, violate any doctrine of the Catholic religion? As the Protestants of Germany, persecuted by their fellow-Pro testants, found protection and liberty of conscience in Poland, with its Catholic population of 20,000,000, so did the victims of Protestant persecution in this country find an asylum in Catholic Maryland, where conscience was declared free.

EIGHTH FACT. That the last *Catholic* king that sat on the throne of Great Britain, was expelled from his dominions for being a Catholic, *and for not being a persecutor*. It is acknowledged, that the profession of the Catholic religion, and the attempt to establish *universal toleration*, lost the crown and kingdom to James II. and his son.

NINTH FACT. That some of the *most democratic and free cantons* of Switzerland are the Catholic cantons.

TENTH FACT. That the independence of this country was won by the efforts and blood of Catholics, as well as Protestants. That Archbishop Carroll, then a Jesuit priest, was among the most zealous in co-operating with the other Catholic and Protestant patriots by whom it was secured.

Will any man, therefore, who is endowed with common understanding, and is not bent on gratuitous falsehood and misrepresentation, say, that a religion, whose members MAY and CAN *individually and collectively furnish* SUCH EVIDENCES, both of principle and of practice, on the question of civil and religious liberty without violating any doctrine of their creed, is opposed to civil and religious liberty? And whilst the gentleman on the other side has *signally* and *triumphantly* FAILED;—in every attempt to prove the affirmative, I submit to the cool, sober, and just judgment of reflecting men, whether I have not established the negative of the question. I am willing to abide by their judgment.

And now we have to pass to the Presbyterian religion. There I shall show, first, that its doctrines, not falsely imputed, *but avowed in the Confession of Faith*, are truly hostile to civil and religious liberty. I shall show, that they have led to persecution, and, if reduced to practice, that they would lead to persecution again in the nineteenth century, and in this very country. If I do not prove my proposition, so as to make the gentleman shrink from an attempt to answer my arguments, I shall ask no man to believe me. FACTS and LOGIC shall be my auxiliaries, leaving to the gentleman all the advantages of popular prejudice, and of his peculiarly ingenious mode of spreading *it*, as a mantle, over the weakness of his arguments.

PART II.

"Is the Presbyterian Religion, in any or in all its Principles or Doctrines, opposed to Civil or Religious Liberty?"

DISCUSSION.

"Is the Presbyterian Religion, in any or all of its principles or doctrines, opposed to civil or religious liberty?"

AFFIRMATIVE I.—MR. HUGHES.

MR. PRESIDENT:—

BEFORE I enter on the arguments in proof of the affirmative of the question, I beg to be indulged in a few remarks, by way of introduction. Some time before the commencement of the present discussion, my attention was drawn to the subject by a notice, in the public papers, that the religion of a large body of American citizens was to be made the subject of crimination and defence, in a Debating Society. Having attended on the occasion, I took the liberty to suggest, in the most respectful manner, the inexpediency of treating such a question in such a place. Prejudice and popular calumnies might make many members eloquent in attacking;—whilst incompetency to detect sophistry, and want of specific information on that subject, might render others unequal to the task of defending. The consequence would be so far injurious to the Catholic body, in their civil and religious rights. I did not imagine, nor do I believe now, that the members of this Society could be induced to be employed, *knowingly*, as tools, in the hands of a combination of bigotry and malice, whose centre is New York, and whose contemplated circumference is the boundary of the land. The man must be blind to clear evidence, who does not see the existence of a dark conspiracy, having for its ultimate object, to make the Presbyterian Church the dominant religion of this country,—the workings of the same spirit, which, having been foiled in its attempt to stop the Sunday mail, has now hit upon a more popular, more cunning, and, therefore, a more dangerous expedient for the accomplishment of its unhallowed purpose. This expedient is, to combine all Protestants in a general effort to put down, *first*, the denomination that is most unpopular, and then, by the same rule, to graduate the scale in reference to other sects, until Presbyterians shall be predominant. The watchword is well selected. Under the pretence of solicitude for the preservation of CIVIL AND RELIGIOUS LIBERTY, the Catholics are to be robbed of both. They are to be denounced as "foreigners;"—and foreigners are at the bottom of the plot for their destruction. These intriguing adventurers, who come inflated with the spirit of John Knox, care not what dissensions may ensue, what charities may be broken up, what blood may flow, provided that, under the plea of guarding against "foreigners," they may be allowed to sting the Republic, and distil into its veins the poison of bigotry and intolerance, which will soon reach its heart. But they would have the work of their own creation to appear as the spontaneous manifestation of *American* feeling. And hence, we find, by a coincidence, too striking to be natural, that the same question, which was selected for debate in this Society, was, at the *same time*, undergoing discussion in New York, Ohio, Kentucky, and the Eastern States. They knew very well, that throughout the country, for every man that has read the Council of Trent, there are ten thousand who have read the popular treatises, written expressly to misrepresent the tenets of Catholicity, and to villify the professors of that creed.

Presbyterian clergymen had left their own pulpits, where their ministry might have been salutary, in teaching their congregations the meek doctrines of the Saviour, in preaching good will and charity among men,—and were passing from city to city, and from district to district, rousing the worst passions of the human breast into hatred and enmity against Catholics. Their object was to agitate the elements of strife, and the pulpit, from whence men should learn to forget and forgive, was selected as the *laboratory*.

It was in this state of the case that the discussion of the question, respecting the Catholic religion, was announced on the part of the Union Literary and Debating Society; and, although I believe that the gentlemen composing it were too high-minded, too American, to become tools in the hands even of parsons, *knowingly*, yet it was manifest, that the purposes of those fanatics would be equally subserved by a discussion, when all could attack, and none, perhaps, were qualified by education to defend. It was on these accounts that I attended, with a view to see how such a question would be disposed of, in such an assembly. My anticipations, in this regard, were not disappointed. Hence, I made some remarks, showing the injustice done to Catholics, under these circumstances. At the request of the respected President, I consented to deliver an address on the principles involved in the discussion, and on the distinction between the doctrines of the Catholic religion, and the sayings or doings of its nominal members. This, after my arrival on the evening appointed, was refused by the Society. I should either depart, or else speak for a certain time, when I might be answered by any respondent. I chose the latter, because I knew that, if I did not, the trump of triumphant falsehood would proclaim my retreat, and ascribe to a wrong motive. In fact, as it was, the veracious Presbyterian, and another paper, published in New York, called the Protestant Vindicator, proclaimed that I was pulverized, annihilated, and that, after having been reduced to nothing, I fled. You all know how that was. But if they could publish such a statement, unsupported by one tittle of truth, how much more, in case I had, in fact, declined the discussion? On that evening I had to encounter the Rev. Wm. L. M'Calla, a gentleman whom, for various reasons, I was by no means ambitious of meeting. He was in keeping, however, for the occasion, and made his debut, by the significant declaration, that *he* was no "green horn," and, "as Sam Patch said, there was no mistake in *that*." He was only a substitute, however, appointed by my present Rev. opponent. This appointment was made, according to his own explanation, *in Philadelphia* on *Friday* evening. And yet he writes *from New York* on the *Wednesday* following, that he had "*just learnt*," that I was to address the society on the following evening. He complains that by this I impeach his veracity. I answer that for the statement of both facts, he is himself my author, and of course, it is for him to explain in the best way he can, how he should have learnt *in New York, on Wednesday,* what he acknowledges he knew *in Philadelphia* on the *Friday previous*.

He returned from New York in due season. The first evening the debate was opened by a young gentleman of the Society, followed by several others. The anti-Catholic battery was manned by a goodly number, including the venerable gentleman, on the left of my opponent. I, sir, had to stand the fire of them all, and I hope they will be prepared to defend Presbyterians, when the time shall come, and to receive a shot in return. The venerable gentleman's mind, as I remember, laboured strangely under the conflicting claims of friendship and duty. "Out of this place, no man had greater respect for Mr. Hughes than he had, but *here* he knew no man." Presbyterian charity is always *geographical,* mine is catholic. I respect age everywhere, and, therefore, I dismiss the subject. Yet the gentleman's remarks came in the richness of Scotch-Irish accents, that brought back the years of my childhood, when Presbyterian lads were my school-companions, and would have flogged the urchin who should have attempted to impose on me.

Subsequently, the definitions of liberty, civil and religious, as well of doctrines, and the rules of the discussion, were agreed upon, and signed by the gentleman and myself, in a private interview. I thought then, that he would have complied with his own deliberate agreement, and have "kept faith with a heretic." But no. He agreed that nothing should be adduced against the Catholic religion, as argument, except what should be admitted, or *proved by a General Council, or the bull of a pope*, to be a DOCTRINE of that religion. And yet, on the first evening of the debate, he assumed, that every document emanating from either of these sources, *must be* a doctrine. Discipline, history of events, legislation, enactment, every thing was *doctrine*. He was as innocent of the knowledge of what constitutes *doctrine*, as the child unborn. Two or three days before, he had defined "*doctrines as those tenets of faith and morals, which a denomination teaches*, AS HAVING BEEN REVEALED BY ALMIGHTY GOD." But on the entrance into this Hall, his memory was overtaken with a most unaccountable "backsliding and shortcoming." Then every thing that a Council *said*, or a Pope *did*, was a doctrine. When I reminded him of his contract, that, unless it had been taught by the council or the Pope, as "having been revealed by Almighty God," he should not assume it as a doctrine of the Catholic religion, his answer was, that I meant to "cramp the discussion." But even with this latitude, the councils and Popes were soon relinquished for the authority of the renegade, the *apostate* De Pradt; and this apostate, and outcast from the Church, the gentleman would pass off for a Catholic. Was this ignorance? was it disingenuousness?

When De Pradt failed, Tristam Shandy was adduced to prove Catholic doctrine—and the records of the Parliament of Paris, from which the gentleman drew mighty inferences, although he never got farther than the *Index*. Still he proceeded uncontrolled, turning every thing into doctrines, and obstinately determined to make Catholics hold, as tenets revealed by Almighty God, Whatever he or Tristam Shandy charged them with believing.

It was not for me to instruct the gentleman as to how he should conduct his argument. Still, I must observe, that so palpable a violation of an agreement I have never witnessed. In the whole six evenings, the gentleman never touched on a "doctrine," except one or two. He took liberties with the few bulls of popes in the way of additions and suppressions, and the exposure which followed show that the animals wheeled upon him and horned him. There he remains, and the only consolation he has, is, that, in his falsification of documents, he only copied after the Rev. G. Stanley Faber—clarum et venerabile nomen.

His tirade against the Catholic religion passed through the three stages of the facetious, the furious and the flat. He opened with the story of "Paddy and his horse"—this was funny; he continued by "oceans of blood"—"millions of butchered Protestants"—these were *furious* figures; he terminated with the anecdote of the "butcher and his ham"—and the "hen laying eggs"—this was flat. In a word—

<blockquote>
He commenced with a "wen,"
And he closed with a "hen."
</blockquote>

I recognise the fitness, as well as humility, of the emblem.

Still, if I were ambitious of immortality as an author, I should have selected a nobler bird; I should have endeavoured to mount on the eagle's pinions, and gone down to posterity in a style of which posterity need not be ashamed. But all this is past, and the "Presbyterian Religion" is now on its trial, *mine* being the right to prosecute, and *his* the duty to defend.

Now, Mr. President, I charge that religion with holding "doctrines"—"tenets of faith and morals, as having been revealed by Almighty God," which are opposed to the "civil and religious liberty" of all men who are not Presbyterians. That religion, under the head of "God's Eternal Decree,"(1) teaches that God from all eternity did "freely and unchangeably ordain whatsoever comes to pass." The same doctrine is taught, in Larger and Smaller Catechism,(2) where the word "foreordained" is applied to "whatsoever comes to pass." I am aware that the text goes on to disclaim the consequences of this doctrine, by stating that God is not on this account "the author of sin," which I do not assert him to be. And further, that "neither is *violence* offered to the will of the creatures," of which I also say, let that pass. But when it goes on to assert, that the "liberty or contingency of second causes is not taken away, but rather established," by this doctrine,—I must beg leave to demur. How an act can be "*unchangeably foreordained*," and yet the agent, who was "foreordained" to do that act, be at liberty to leave it *undone*, is what I leave to the gentleman or the General Assembly to explain.

Let us illustrate this doctrine by a particular case. In the year 1553, Michael Servetus was burned alive for heresy, in Geneva, by John Calvin, or through his influence. Now, according to this doctrine, the *time*, the *place*, the *agent*, had all been determined and "foreordained unchangeably;" and, if so, Calvin *could not* avoid the part assigned to him in this tragedy of blood. If he *could not* avoid it, where was his "liberty" as "a second cause?" If he had no "liberty" to avoid it, where could be his guilt? And here is the reason, that, whilst all other denominations regard him, in connexion with this matter, as one whose hands were purpled with blood of a man, who was not amenable to his tribunal, the Presbyterians regard him as a saint, who is not to be held accountable for having done what God from all eternity had "unchangeably foreordained" that he should do! Apply this principle to John Knox and his associates, in the assassination of Cardinal Beaton; and to the others, in the assassination of Archbishop Sharp—the execution of Laud, Strafford, Charles I., &c.—and, last of all, to the burning of the Convent at Boston. The doctrine that God has "unchangeably foreordained what-

(1) Confession of Faith, Chap. III. p. 15.
(2) Page 146 and 321.

soever comes to pass," is applicable to all these cases, and to all the crimes that ever were, or ever will be committed. The agents were but the irresponsible tools of *omnipotent power*—"foreordained" to execute "whatsoever comes to pass"—the *evil* as well as the *good;* for the word "*whatsoever*" comprises both. Now there can be neither merit nor crime in executing the decrees of God; and where there is neither, there can be no *punishment*—no *reward*. Hence, it follows, that this doctrine is subversive of that fundamental principle, on the admission of which, the safety of states, the authority of human laws, the welfare of society depend—viz. the principle of future "*rewards* and *punishments.*" The doctrine of the decree "unchangeably foreordaining" whatsoever comes to pass, destroys the doctrine of free will and moral responsibility. I do not say that Presbyterians *act out* this doctrine of their Confession of Faith; but that its tendencies are such as I have described, no man who has a mind capable of tracing the connexion between principles and their consequences, can, for a moment, deny. The gentleman will not venture to deny the doctrine; and I challenge him to refute the argument, which it confirms, as here laid down, and proven. Reduced to the form of a syllogism, it may be stated thus:—

Any religion that holds, as a "tenet of faith revealed by Almighty God," that "whatsoever comes to pass" was "unchangeably foreordained," is opposed and dangerous to civil and religious liberty, by reducing *its votaries* from the position of moral, free, responsible agents, to that of the mere instruments of God's eternal decree, for the execution of "whatsoever comes to pass."

But the Presbyterian Religion holds this doctrine:

Therefore the Presbyterian Religion is, in this respect, opposed and dangerous to civil and religious liberty. FIRST ARGUMENT.

Intimately connected with this, is the Presbyterian doctrine of "election and reprobation." The belief that God would render to every man according to his works, in the judgment of another life, has been the conservative principle of all social rights since the beginning of the world. It furnishes the check by which the conscience of a good man curbs and restrains the passions of cupidity and self-interest. It furnishes the motive, reaching to the inmost soul, for which we should avoid evil and do good. It supposes, that, with the help of divine grace, we are not only free, but able to fulfil the requisitions of justice towards God and our neighbour. Wherever this salutary belief is rejected, there the corner-stone of social safety is removed, and the edifice, unless sustained by other support, will totter and fall. Now this principle is rejected by the Presbyterian Religion, which teaches that our *good* or *evil works*, in this life, do not in any wise contribute as a help or a hinderance, to our eternal happiness or misery in the life to come: consequently, there is no motive of reward or punishment, among the believers of that creed, springing from the considerations of eternity, to counteract and subdue the workings of temporal self-interest.

Their doctrine is, that, "by the *decree* of God, for the manifestation of his glory, *some men* and angels are *predestinated* unto everlasting life, and others foreordained to everlasting death." And this (for the elect) out of his mere free grace and love, without any foresight of faith and good works, or perseverance in either of them, or any other thing in the creature, *as conditions*, or causes moving him thereunto; and all for the praise of his glorious grace." "The *'rest* of mankind, God was pleased.. . . . to pass by, and to *ordain* them to dishonour and wrath, for their sin, to the praise of his glorious justice."(1) Since this consequence was "for their. sin," it *would follow* that God had foreordained their sin. But as Presbyterians *disclaim* this blasphemous consequence, I will not urge it, although I cannot see how they can escape it, consistently with the doctrine that God has "unchangeably *foreordained* whatsoever comes to pass."

But it is manifest from the doctrines here stated, that "good works" cannot contribute to secure the salvation, nor to hinder damnation of Presbyterians. Whence it follows, that with them, all is fixed as fate; that those who are to be saved, will be saved, whatever may be the extent of their wickedness; and that those who are to be damned, will be damned, in spite of all their efforts to avoid it, by a virtuous, upright, honest life. The gentleman cannot deny these consequences consistently with the Confession of Faith. Whence I conclude—

That any religion which makes *eternal happiness* and *eternal misery* depend on an *absolute decree*, "excluding the foresight of faith and *good works*, or perseverance in either of them, or any other thing in the creature, *as conditions*," is dangerous, and *opposed to* civil and religious liberty; by inculcating implicitly that the invasion of the civil and religious rights of others, in this life, cannot affect the destinies of the soul, in the life to come.

But the Presbyterian Religion holds the doctrine of which this is the logical and undeniable consequence:

Therefore, in this doctrine, that religion is opposed to civil and religious liberty. SECOND ARGUMENT.

I am not ignorant that Presbyterians disclaim this consequence, but I dispute their right to disclaim it. It is deduced from their doctrine as fairly as ever consequence flowed from premises, and those who deny it, must either have minds incapable of making inductions, or else be persuaded that all reasoning is a farce. According to their doctrine, I am foreordained to everlasting *life* or everlasting *death*, by the eternal decree of God; and no actions of mine can disappoint my eternal destiny. Now this principle pervades the whole Presbyterian denomination, and takes from

(1) Confession of Faith, pp. 17, 18, 19.

them the MOTIVE which would render the civil and religious rights of other denominations *sacred* in their estimation. How is that motive taken away? By their belief that God will judge them, *not by their actions, but by his own eternal decree.* To the influence of this doctrine, I ascribe that dark, morose, restless, aspiring, turbulent, intolerant, and persecuting spirit, which has characterized the ardent disciples of this sect, from the hour of its birth;—distinguishing it from all other sects and denominations. Assuming that God had elected *them* as special favourites, they naturally grow proud by the distinction in comparison with other men, who, in the language of their creed, have been "passed by." Hence, as the Christian heirs of these prerogatives, which God bestowed on his chosen people under the Jewish law, they would exercise over every country, that right of exclusive domination which the children of Jacob, by divine permission, exercised in reference to the inhabitants and territory of Canaan. You can find no period in their history, in which they were not oppressed—or oppressing—and sometimes both. Whilst the laws and government of Protestant England were severe, and severely executed against them, their cry was that the oppression of the Catholics was not sufficiently grinding. They emerged from every persecution with the fierce spirit of intolerance, unquenched and unquenchable. Even in this country, without a single legitimate motive to stimulate them, they are now attempting to rob their Catholic fellow-citizens of the civil and religious rights secured by the Constitution. Other denominations of Protestants are used by them as "cats'-paws;" and will, no doubt, in due season, receive their *merited*, but unwelcome recompense, at the hand of predominant Presbyterianism. They are the *favoured class;* with the decree of election and reprobation as a patent of impunity in the other world for actions done in this, they have *conscientious facilities,* for the accomplishment of projects dictated by private or sectarian ambition, which are denied to the consciences of those who hold, as a doctrine, that their conduct in this life will have a serious influence on the judgment of their souls in the life to come.

This difference accounts also for the fact, that the Presbyterians in every instance, where their numbers gave hope of success, aimed, and often successfully, at the supreme civil power of the state; perfectly indifferent as to the means by which it might be acquired. Hence their libels on governments, which they wished to overturn, and then civil war to be followed by defeat or victory. It was thus, trampling on the civil and religious rights of the Catholics, that they established their religion in Scotland, England and on the Continent of Europe. The excitement of popular commotion, the circulation of libels, the inflaming of the passions of the multitude, were the usual precursors of some political stroke which should place Presbyterians uppermost. The attack on

Catholics which they are now exciting the people to make, is not their first attempt in this country, to obtain the control and direction of the civil government. We all remember the effort made by them, as a trial of strength, to have the Sunday mail stopped, and by *an act of Congress*, save the country from the national sin of transporting letters on the Sabbath-day. The experiment failed. We all remember the efforts to have the "Sunday-school Union" incorporated; and the anticipation that was indulged in of the political influence which would be placed at the disposal of the Presbyterians, through its instrumentality, in ten or at most twenty years. We all remember the boast of Dr. Ely, that Presbyterians alone could bring half a million voters to the poll, and his effort to establish "a Christian party in politics." All these efforts failed. But the untiring, indomitable spirit of Presbyterian ambition returns to the onset, and, out of pure, disinterested zeal "for civil and religious liberty" undertakes to deprive Catholics of both. It will be again defeated;—as soon as it will be discovered that there is an ulterior object towards which the putting down of the Catholics is but the first stepping-stone.

Another point of danger in the creed of this denomination is the right claimed by them to *alter* their doctrine, according to the interests of their position on the scale of political ascendency. Thus, the principles of the "Solemn League and Covenant" constituted their doctrines so long as they were able, *by means of the civil power*, to force their adoption on others. But after the restoration of the Episcopalian interest to supreme power under Charles II., it was found that a more relaxed creed would suit their interest better. And the small band of Presbyterians, called "Covenanters," preserved alone the profession of their principles. The Westminster Confession of Faith became the nominal standard of doctrine, among the degenerate sons of defection. This document taught, as a *doctrine*, that for publishing or maintaining certain erroneous opinions, persons might be called to account, and proceeded against, by the censures of the church, "and by the power of the civil magistrate." That the "civil magistrate" may suppress blasphemies and *heresies*.' That it is a sin to tolerate a *false religion*, &c. After the Revolution in this country, these "tenets," hitherto held as "having been revealed by Almighty God," were also discarded from the books, as being unsuited to the soil of new-born liberty and of equal rights. The Constitution declared that opinions were free, and should *not* be proceeded against "by the civil magistrate," that he should suppress *no heresy*, that it was *no sin* to tolerate a "false religion"—and lo! the Confession of Faith is forthwith *amended* so as to suit the Constitution, and the new order of things. When reminded of these several rejections of what God had revealed, the answer is, that they do not pretend to be infallible; and consequently have a right to change and modify their creed when they find it wrong. But the question is which of their creeds is right? May they not discover that they are now in error, and recall the doctrines of the magistrate's power, and of the sin of tolerating a false religion? They may. And there is reason to believe that they will, when it can be done with safety. Whence I argue,—

That any religion which maintains as a doctrine the right to resume its intolerance, whenever the civil power is prepared for it, is, in this respect, dangerous to the civil and religious liberty of other denominations.

But the Presbyterian religion teaches this right as a doctrine. Therefore this religion is opposed to the civil and religious liberty of other denominations. THIRD ARGUMENT.

As it exists at this time, and in this country, Presbyterianism is in a false position. It embodies in its composition all the essence of persecution, and yet, awed by the genius of the country, it is compelled to do violence to its nature, and *profess* that liberality which it does not feel and cannot *practise*. But let such a change of political circumstances arise as will authorize another revision and *correction* of its doctrines, and the scenes of other days will be renewed, supported by a new Confession of Faith, and texts of Scripture. Richard will be himself again. The "ordinance of magistracy" may be revived, and days of humiliation and prayer appointed for the sin of having ever abandoned it. Under the sanction of this "ordinance," whipping, cutting off the ears, hanging, may again be introduced, as they were practised in New England, which was always remarkable for its *love* of civil and religious liberty.(1)

Before going farther, it may be proper to expose a sophism, of which the gentleman has more than once attempted to avail himself. It consists in denying that the colonies of New England were Presbyterians, and this for no other reason except that he must be ashamed of professing a religion which sanctions their deeds of blood and persecution. "*They* were PURITANS," he has said, "whereas *we* are *Presbyterians*." They differed only, however, in the form of church government, and not in the doctrines of intolerance. Both agreed in holding as a {"tenet revealed by Almighty God," that the civil magistrate had a right to enforce the observance of the "first," as well as the "second table" of the decalogue. Now the first table has reference to the worship of God, the sanctification of his name, and of the Sabbath-day. So that the right of every man to worship Almighty God, according to the dictates of his own conscience, is contrary to *all* that *was* doctrine among Puritans and Presbyterians, previous to the declaration of American independence. Their doctrine was that he had a right to worship Almighty God, according to the dictates of the civil magistrate. This I shall have abundant occasion to

(1) See Backus's History of the Baptists, *passim.*

show in the sequel of this argument. Consequently, then, since both hold the same doctrine on all the points that are essential to this question;—it follows that the pretended difference or distinction on which the gentleman claims to disown the Puritans, is nugatory. We shall find that in both denominations it produced the same blood-stained fruits.

The plan of civil and religious government contemplated by the doctrine of the Presbyterian, and indeed, all the Calvinistic sects, is a coalition and consolidation of church and state. Geneva was the model. The clergy were to constitute the legislative body and the judiciary, in all matters appertaining to doctrine, worship, and "the power of godliness." The civil magistrate was to be the executive, the mere constable of the church. Neither let it be supposed that Presbyterians have yet relinquished this dangerous doctrine. The present Confession of Faith tells us, that although the civil magistrates may not "interfere in matters of faith, yet, AS NURSING FATHERS, it is the duty of the civil magistrates to protect the church of our common Lord, without giving the preference to any denomination of Christians, above the rest," &c. This last clause is put in as a salvo ad captandum;—for the gentleman has made amends for his want of charity, by his abundant candour in admitting that, according to Presbyterian doctrine, Catholics, Quakers, Unitarians, and I know not how many other sects, are excluded from the meaning of the words, "church of our common Lord," and consequently, excluded from the protection which the "nursing fathers" are bound to afford. But I fear the Confession of Faith, which is better authority, cuts off a few other denominations. In page 3, it tells us that the "visible church . . . consists of all those throughout the world, that PROFESS the true religion; together with their children; and is the kingdom of the Lord Jesus Christ, the house and family of God, out of which *there is no ordinary possibility of salvation.*" Whence it follows that those who do not "profess the *true* religion," do not belong to the "church of our common Lord," and are not of the happy few whom it is the duty of the civil magistrates, as "nursing fathers," to protect. Now the "true religion," according to Presbyterian belief, consists in the doctrines of the Old and New Testament;—and the book called the Confession of Faith, "contains the system of doctrine taught in the Holy Scriptures."(1) Here then the profession of the *true* religion is made to consist in the profession of the *Presbyterian* religion. And since the profession of the *true* religion, alias the Westminster Confession of Faith, with all its doctrine of fatalism, under the caption of "GOD'S ETERNAL DECREE," constitutes the "church of our common Lord," "out of which there is no ordinary possibility of salvation," it follows that those who do not hold the

(1) Page 378.

system of doctrine taught in the Confession of Faith, have no title to the protection of the civil magistrates, as not being included in the "church of our common Lord," which turns out to be nothing more than the *Presbyterian* church. To reduce the matter into a more condensed form, it may be stated in the following propositions:

Any religion which teaches, as a doctrine, that the CIVIL MAGISTRATES, in these United States, are bound, "as nursing fathers," to protect the church of one sect, or of a specific number of sects, under pretext that it, or they alone, constitute the "church of our common Lord," to the exclusion of other denominations, is adverse to the constitution of the country, and dangerous to civil and religious liberty. This proposition is self-evident.

But the Presbyterians, as has been shown, by the foregoing facts and reasoning, holds this doctrine:

Therefore, the Presbyterian religion is opposed, in this respect, and dangerous to the civil and religious rights of other denominations. FOURTH ARGUMENT.

Let this doctrine be carried out, and you will see the magistrates of your republic converted into dry nurses of Presbyterianism, the President dandling the baby on his knee, and the Secretary of the Treasury gathering pap for it. The vision is enchanting enough, as it recalls the palmy days of the church, when, at her bidding, the magistrates of Geneva, Holland, Scotland, England, maintained the "power of (Presbyterian) godliness," by the power of the sword. Still it is but a *vision*.

All other denominations, with whose doctrines I am acquainted, hold, that it is the duty of the civil magistrates to administer the constitutional laws of the country, in justice and mercy, leaving "the church of our common Lord" to protect itself. "The church of our common Lord" is a thing unknown to the Constitution; that instrument guarantees the protection of citizens, leaving them at full liberty to choose their religion unbiassed by political preferences, extended to one sect more than another. The orthodoxy of the Dutch Reformed Church is fully admitted by the denomination to which the gentleman belongs. And the anti-constitutional doctrine, of the duty of magistrates, which is cunningly enough disguised in the Westminster Confession, is openly and honestly stated in the creed of the Dutch Reformed brethren, where it is taught, that the "office" of the civil magistrates is . . . "that they protect the sacred ministry; and thus may remove and prevent all idolatry and FALSE WORSHIP . . . . . . wherefore, we detest the Anabaptists and *other* seditious people, and in general all those who reject the higher powers, and magistrates . . . . ."(1) This coincidence of intolerant doctrine accounts for the fact, that

(1) Confession of Faith of the Reformed Dutch Church in North America, New York, 1819.

the politico-religious excitement which is now raging against the Catholics, has been mainly stimulated by the fiery harangues and writings of certain fanatical or malevolent preachers, of those two denominations. They endeavour to enlist the passions of other sects of Protestants, in the nefarious attempt to put down the adherents of that religion, which they impudently term of anti-Christ. But let their credulous allies not be deceived; the same warrant of Revelation which authorizes them to do this, makes it equally incumbent on them to put down "ALL FALSE WORSHIP," and to "*detest* the Anabaptists."

The gentleman takes credit to his cause, on the ground, that, in this country, Presbyterians have not persecuted since the Declaration of Independence. If he means that they have not put men to death or in prison, for the crime of worshipping God according to the dictates of their conscience, I admit the truth of his observation. But I ascribe the happy circumstances to the constitution and laws of the United States, and to the buoyant energies of young American liberty and liberality. The American eagle, which has hovered over the equal rights of all denominations, both civil and religious, would have picked the eyes out of the sect that should have dared to execute the work of religious persecution. But let the hand of Presbyterian intolerance only *succeed* to pluck only one feather out of the noble bird's wing; and its pinions will soon be broken, and a *cage* found for it by the General Assembly. The church will become the guardian of "civil and religious liberty," and the civil magistrates will become the "nursing fathers" of the Church.

It might be supposed by those who are unacquainted with the subject, that these observations are made without regard to facts that warrant them. This would be a great mistake. It was said by a great statesman, Patrick Henry, that the light which should guide our course, in regard to the future, must blaze from the lamp of *experience*. And on this subject, what does experience teach? Open the history of Presbyterianism and see. If the gentleman can show me an instance, in the history of the world, in which Presbyterians did not invade by civil penalties, extending in most cases to life and death, (when they had the political power to do so,) the "right of every man to worship God, according to the dictates of his own conscience," I bind myself to give up the argument. *Other* general rules have *exceptions*,—this has *none*. Let him name one instance. I challenge him to the test.

"Is the Presbyterian Religion, in any or in all its principles or doctrines, opposed to civil or religious liberty."

NEGATIVE I.—MR. BRECKINRIDGE.

Mr. President:—

It would seem as if the gentleman had determined to make a deep impression on your *pity*, if not on your *reason*, in the introduction of his address. It is surely a strong indication of the progress of truth, and human freedom, as well as of the spirit of the age, when a priest of Rome is heard appealing to public sympathy, under *any* circumstances. We may truly bless God, and take courage, when we compare Rome, in the fifteenth century, making the earth to tremble at her rebuke, with Rome, in the nineteenth century, calling for *pity*. *Rome complaining of persecution!* Sir, Romanism cannot endure free inquiry. It is always, therefore, either *"heresy"* or *"persecution,"* to question this infallible mother of churches, and mistress of nations. It is *heresy*, if *in power; persecution*, if *not*. But, sir, Roman Catholics *are not persecuted*.

It is a custom of the American people to examine every thing. It is an attribute of the American system, to reject every thing which cannot stand the test of an examination by the standard of truth and right. Rome is not used to this. She cannot stand it. She cries out against it. *Hinc illæ lachrymæ.* Hence, those lugubrious cries with which the gentleman moved your pity at the sorrows of that poor weak people, only 120,000,000 strong, whom a few Presbyterian *"parsons"* are persecuting to death! No, Mr. President, the *"origin"* of this question is not truly stated by the gentleman. It is no new thing, that popery and liberty have no affinity, or love for each other; and it is natural for the American people to watch narrowly what is so well known to be hostile to the rights of man.

Well; it had been observed, with some solicitude for many years, that a large number of Jesuits (you remember how sternly and fondly the gentleman has defended them) were coming into the United States; some *in*, some *out of* the priesthood. Talleyrand (a Jesuit) was once a *teacher* in this country! Crowds of such were seen passing with other *goods* through our customhouses into the bosom of the nation—from France, Spain, Germany, Portugal, Italy, and Ireland. The Jesuits were known to be the most subtle, strongly united, and numerous body of Romish emissaries; the militia of the Pope, the enemies of all freedom; who had ruled, corrupted, and been expelled from almost every government of Europe; and having recently been restored to power and rank by the Pope, were rapidly extending their missions to the New World, and to this garden of it.

Again: The emigration to this from Roman Catholic countries, was observed to be immense; and, with many honourable exceptions, this population was confessedly the most ignorant, unruly, and vicious in the country; and, also, very much devoted to popery.

Again: It was seen that *European despots* were deeply interested, and published, in the annual reports of organized societies, as patrons of plans to send priests and Catholic emigrants to the United States: (witness the Leopold foundation of which I have largely spoken already, headed by Prince Metternich, sending vast sums of money to America to spread Catholicity:) and this was done in connexion with the periodical visits to Europe of American Roman Catholic prelates; as, for example, Bishop England's late tour.

Roman Catholic politicians also in Europe, had avowed alike their enmity to our institutions, and the fear of their influence on the European system of despotism.

A high officer in the Austrian government, Schlegel, had said, in his *Lectures on the Philosophy of History*,(1) "THAT THE REAL NURSERY OF ALL THESE DESTRUCTIVE PRINCIPLES, THE REVOLUTIONARY SCHOOL OF FRANCE, AND THE REST OF EUROPE, [Poland, Belgium, Holland, he names,] HAD BEEN NORTH AMERICA!!"

And still more. We had been warned by *writers*, especially *Frenchmen*, who have most freedom of all the Catholic states, that the priesthood of Rome would destroy our liberties, if they prevailed in America. De Pradt, who had certainly *once been* a Catholic, and an *Abbe*, one of the first writers and politicians in Europe, has thus warned us: "In IRELAND, Holland, and THE UNITED STATES, (Rome) does every thing by apostolic vicars, as in the countries of missions. This *regime* pleases Rome; for it gives her the *means* of being *mistress* everywhere. The CLERGY OF THE UNITED STATES, like that of Ireland, is very *devoted* to the Pope. It is very rigorous. IN TIME IT WILL GIVE EMBARRASSMENT TO THE UNITED STATES, AS THAT OF IRELAND DOES TO THE BRITISH GOVERNMENT."(2)

All these, connected with an unparalleled zeal for proselytism, and a daily augmenting arrogance, and self-consequence among the priests, awakened the simultaneous attention of American citizens, politicians, and Christians; and, at the same time, American Epis-

(1) Lecture XVII., Vol. II. p. 236.
(2) Modern Jesuitism, p. 305.

copalians, Baptists, Methodists, and Congregationalists, as well as Presbyterians, without collusion, by the call of these concurrent events and disclosures, began to inquire *"what can this mean?"* It is wholly false, however, that this coincidence was *by concert,* as the Rev. gentleman has said. For, even supposing that these various and powerful Christian denominations could be thought capable of a *concerted, simultaneous* attack of the sort, " in New York, Ohio, Kentucky, and the Eastern States," it is hardly likely that they would have joined in *"a dark conspiracy—to make the Presbyterian Church the dominant religion of the country;"....* and *"under the pretence of a regard for civil and religious liberty, rob the Catholics of both."*

And then, as to the respectable Society before which we appear, I hardly suppose the young gentlemen will feel much flattered by the charge of "being employed," "though not knowingly," "as tools in the hands of a combination of bigotry and malice." For myself, sir, the first intimation that I ever had of the *existence* of this Society, was AFTER the question *" On Civil and Religious Liberty"* had been brought up, and debated for at least *one night;* and after the Rev. gentleman had *participated* in the discussion. It was in consequence of that very appearance of his, at this Hall, that I was asked to attend and meet him, (a week after,) *in case* he should finally consent to debate again. This was on Friday, when I was on the eve of a journey to New York. On the next Wednesday I received *official* notice that Mr. Hughes *had* committed himself to appear again. *Then* it was, that I addressed to him the letter which he has so ungenerously tried (though in vain) to distort into a contradiction. All I intended to say, in a hurried letter, written in a sick chamber, was this: that having just been *officially assured* of his pledged appearance in the discussion, (what he had *promised* before, what the Society *hoped he would,* and I *feared* he *would not* do,) I then, and thus agreed to meet him on the pending question. What motive had I to affect ignorance of his intention? I had, for more than a year, publicly, by a standing call, invited him to an oral discussion. He had all this time declined, after having abruptly and pertinaciously closed a former *written* discussion with me; and left me to carry it on *alone.* You lately had a specimen of the gentleman's resolution in debate—when this Society earnestly and unanimously requested us to add two evenings to *each of the questions,* that the important subjects involved might be fully examined; yet against our united entreaties, he did most *heroically* and zealously *refuse.* The gentleman is a great admirer of that prudent adage —*" The better part of valour is discretion;"* and if ever he redeem his pledge to finish and publish this debate;—if he do not make reasons to decline it, to delay it, to vitiate it, I shall be both surprised and gratified.

His unhappy grudge against my gallant and able friend, the

Rev. Mr. M'Calla, who sometimes attends this debate, is easily divined by those who witnessed their late meeting in this place. The Rev. gentleman is so much disturbed by his presence, that I shall be constrained to beg him to leave the house—or at least to require him to turn his eyes away from my friend; and especially to drop not an arrow into my quiver.

Let me add, on these preliminary matters on which the gentleman has so largely dwelt, that it was natural, manly, seasonable, and *American*, for these young gentlemen to bring up this question; and the promptitude with which all the parties interested have agreed to examine (at Mr. Hughes's request) the relation of *Presbyterian* principles to civil and religious liberty, proves alike the liberality and justice of the Society, and the fearless candour and confidence of Presbyterians in the goodness of their cause. It puts to shame also the gentleman's *cry of persecution;* for if discussions of charges *against* Romanism constitute persecution, and intend the destruction of Roman Catholic rights, then, when the name shall be changed to *Presbyterian*, will it not be equally true of *Presbyterians* and their *rights?* Do the gentleman's attacks on Presbyterians, *intend* the destruction of their rights? Does he *intend* to persecute them? *He first* appeared in the debate! He proposed, nay, *urged*, as *a condition*, the discussion of Presbyterianism! Will he say it is retaliation? or self-defence? But the Society is not *Presbyterian;* it is of *no* sect; and numbers many *Catholics* who consented to the original question; nay, aided to adopt it. No, sir; we understand this cant; and it comes with an ill grace from a priest of the Vatican, holding allegiance to the author of the crusades, and the mistress of the inquisition, "drunk with the blood of saints."

The gentleman has attempted to excite the public mind against "Presbyterians"—on the ground, that they were indiscriminately attacking "*foreigners.*" Sir, no men feel more, or do more for deserving "foreigners" than Presbyterians. Does the gentleman forget their sympathies and co-operation in the memorable case of the exiled Poles—those injured, noble men? Have we not hailed them, and loved them, and helped them, as the peculiar objects of the public care, as the *orphans* of *the nation?* It is only the corrupt, degraded, intractable, that we fear. Beside what has been said before, let me subjoin that this is a topic on which the wise and good of all names, sects, and parties, both secular and religious, even now tremble; and our various state sovereignties are wisely beginning to make provision against the immense evils which threaten from that quarter. Mr. Jefferson, whom the gentleman loves to quote in garbled extracts against Presbyterians, long ago lifted up his warning voice, saying, in his Notes on Virginia—" To these [the principles of our government] nothing can be more opposed than the maxims of absolute monarchies. Yet from such we are to expect the *greatest* number of *emigrants*.

They will bring with them the principles of the governments they have imbibed in their early youth; or if able to throw them off, it will be in exchange for an unbounded licentiousness, passing, as is usual, from one extreme to another. . . . . In proportion to their numbers, they will share with us the legislation. They will infuse into it their spirit, warp and bias its directions, and render it a heterogeneous, incoherent, distracted mass." When we add to this almost prophetic language (whose fulfilment is now daily transpiring before our eyes, in all our large cities) the fact, that so many of the emigrants come from *papal* countries, and bring with them, or meet here, Jesuit priests, who are ex officio *monarchists*, and stifle, as it rises in the bosom of the people, the love of liberty, we may well be excused for a wise fear of impending danger to our free institutions.

I fear, sir, you are already impatient at these prefatory matters; yet, as the gentleman has introduced them, I must meet them. As to the charge of following " Faber" in falsifying the *decrees*, &c. of the church, I refer this body to my *full exposure* of these slanders on a previous evening; and to the several *reversed cases*, in which I convicted him of falsifying me, and of garbling divers authorities to suit his own purposes.

And then as to the rules: I agreed to use the decree of a General Council, the brief or bull of a Pope, the Catechism of the Council of Trent, and the admitted doctrines of a pope, in proof; it being understood that each party was to prove that what was used was a doctrine. I appeal to the train of my arguments, and to the decision of the chair, already given, whether I have violated these rules. The Rev. gentleman agreed that the Westminster Confession of Faith of the Presbyterian Church, under the care of the General Assembly in the United States, should be his *source of proof.* Yet you will perceive, from every allusion almost which he makes, that he is perfectly reckless as to this rule. The gentleman has an *intermittent sensibility* of conscience about the rules, which fluctuates, with amusing alternacy, from one side to the other. When we were probing the Roman hierarchy, he was often crying aloud for "*rules*"—"*rules.*" Now, while he charges me with deviation, what does *he* do? I offered him the broad question of Protestantism, as exhibited in the *twelve creeds* issued at the Reformation. He refused; and chose the *Presbyterian Church, and its Confession of Faith, as held by us.* I agreed joyfully to that selection; and so the rules fixed it. Yet now we find him running for proof to the *Congregational churches* of New England, and then to the Reformed Dutch Church; and then to the Covenanters; and then to the churches of Scotland, Holland, England, Geneva, &c. ! Now, it is true, that all these churches *are*, or *were*, Calvinistic—as we shall presently see; and most of them are *Presbyterian.* But it is to the *doctrines of the Presbyterian Church, under the government of the*

General Assembly in the United States, that he agreed to confine himself. Here he finds scarcely a *point* on which to *alight:* therefore he goes to other communions and other continents. For example, he charges Presbyterians with burning "*the Convent.*" Now the charge is too base to be replied too—in the name of our Protestant brethren of Massachusetts. But there is not a Presbyterian Church, nor, as far as I know, member, within ten miles square of *Boston*. It is, therefore, not "*a sophism,*" as the gentleman says, but "*a truism,*" that "the New England colonies were not Presbyterian," and their descendants are not—though nearly allied to them in their general principles, and in the noble love of liberty and divine truth.

It may be as proper here, as anywhere, to say that the *American churches* (we mean of course *Protestant*) stand in a very peculiar relation to their *European progenitors*. The European Protestant Churches are *Protestant* in regard to *Rome*. The American Protestant Churches are so in respect of *established religions*, as well as in regard to *Rome*. This peculiarity exists in North America alone. For example: in England, the Episcopal church is established by law; in *Scotland*, the *Presbyterian*. But in this country, no American Presbyterian or Episcopalian can approve of those establishments; nor are these churches *branches* of the parent stock in this respect; nor can they tolerate or have any fellowship with an establishment as such. The American system disclaims all *force* as a means of preserving unity, and as a means of maintaining and extending the visible church. We deny and reject the *right* of the civil magistrate *to legislate* for the *conscience*. That is the prerogative of God alone. Nor has the *majority* the right to do it for the *minority*. American Protestant Christians, as citizens, have declared this to be their system in their American constitutions; and, with equal explicitness, in their creeds and public formularies. In this the Presbyterian Church has ever held a most conspicuous position, and taken a decided part. The pages of our standards stare the gentleman full in the face, and bespeak him a slanderer, in a hundred paragraphs, which he declares the reverse.

Thus,(1) it is thus written:—"They (that is, Presbyterians) are unanimously of opinion, that God alone is Lord of the conscience, and hath left it free from the doctrine and commandments of men, which are in any thing contrary to his word, or beside it in matters of faith and worship: *therefore, they consider the rights of private judgment*, in all matters that respect religion, as *universal and unalienable;* they do not even wish to see any religious constitution, aided by the civil power, *further than may be necessary for protection and security, and at the same time,* BE EQUAL AND COMMON TO ALL OTHERS."

(1) On page 343, Form of Government, Chap. I., Sect. I.

Again;(1) *civil magistrates may not assume to themselves the administration of the word and sacraments; or the power of the keys of the kingdom of heaven; or, in the least, interfere in matters of faith.* Yet, " as nursing fathers,"(2) it is the duty of civil magistrates to PROTECT the church of our common Lord, without giving the *preference to any denomination* of Christians above the rest, in such a manner, that *all ecclesiastical persons whatever shall enjoy the full, free, and unquestioned liberty of discharging every part* of their sacred functions, without violence or danger. And, as Jesus Christ *hath appointed a regular government and discipline in his church, no law of any commonwealth should interfere with, let, or hinder, the due exercise thereof, among the voluntary members of any denomination of Christians,* according to their own profession and belief. It is the duty of civil magistrates to protect the person and good name of all their people, in such an effectual manner as that no person be suffered, either upon pretence of religion or infidelity, to offer any indignity, violence, *abuse or injury* to *any other person whatsoever;* and to take order, that all religious and ecclesiastical assemblies be held without molestation or disturbance." This covers all; no *less* Catholics, *than* Protestants; and, it is PROTECTION, not MERELY TOLERATION.

Here are surely some pretty explicit declarations—of the full and equal rights of all denominations—and the utter rejection of all establishments. And this is the general position of the American Protestant Churches. This is the American system—American Protestantism; or, more properly speaking, a return to that position in which Christ and his apostles left the church, and which she maintained while she continued in the purity of the faith, and until corrupted by union with the state.

Now, if the gentleman will show me *one such principle* in all his creeds, decrees, missals, bulls, briefs and canons, I will own that he is right, and I am wrong. Let us for a moment inquire how all this is with respect to Rome. The gentleman says his church is *infallible* and *unchangeable:* the same, therefore, in Rome, Spain, and North America. Protestant American churches have *denounced* and *divorced* the alliance of church and state. They have adopted American principles. But *American Papists change not.* They cannot change. Therefore, the genius of the church, and the institutions of the church, here, and in Europe, are the same. The Pope, their *spiritual* head, is *the temporal* head of a state; *a monarch; elected by cardinals,* that *popes* appoint. *It is church and state united;* and all priests, and all papists, owe allegiance to this monarch *of spiritual and temporal*

---

(1) Pages 105, 106, Of the Civil Magistrate, Chap. XXIII., Sect. 3.
(2) And kings shall be thy nursing fathers, and their queens thy nursing mothers.—*Isaiah,* chap. xlix., ver. 23.

things mixed; and are under this universal head. And that said head, the Pope, in his last *universal circular,* thus writes:—
"Nor can we augur more consoling consequences to religion and to government, from the zeal of some TO SEPARATE THE CHURCH FROM THE STATE; AND TO BURST THE BOND WHICH UNITES THE PRIESTHOOD TO THE EMPIRE. For it is clear that this *union* "*is dreaded by the* PROFANE LOVERS OF LIBERTY, *only because it has never failed to confer prosperity on both.*" Here it is plain that the Pope declares *it profane* to sunder this tie. *He honestly* announces a *papal doctrine;* and no consistent Catholic can *decline* the *authority* announcing, or the *principle promulgated.*

Again, he says, "*May this our zeal for the welfare of religion and public order,* (we see what he considers '*established order in a state,*') *acquire aid and authority from the princes,* our *dearest sons in Christ, who, let them reflect, have received their power, not merely for their temporal rule,* BUT CHIEFLY FOR THE PROTECTION OF THE CHURCH." If, because Dr. Ely, the clerk (*not the secretary of state*) of the General Assembly, in his private capacity, being a busy, loquacious man, talked about "*a Christian party in politics,*" the Presbyterian Church is accused by Mr. Hughes of aiming at an establishment; then what will he say to this *official* and direct *avowal* of the propriety and necessity of an establishment, by the reigning Pope! And, if we are to be charged with *holding to a theocracy,* because, as Isaiah said, so say we, *rulers should be* "*nursing fathers*" to the church, what will the gentleman do with the Pope's avowal, that the protection of the Catholic Church is the *chief end* of rulers, and that the Pope is the *father of "princes,* his dearest sons?"

The result is clearly this, that the *Church of Rome everywhere, is one, and unchangeable;* that, at Rome, it not only courts, but enjoins the union of church and state; and that, therefore, what the head and centre holds, the *branch* holds also *in this land;* and, hence, the Roman Catholic Church in America is anti-American, anti-liberal; and, in order to take the right, or the safe ground, and to secure the confidence of the American people, American Catholics must declare themselves independent of Rome; and *change their doctrines* on the subject of civil and religious liberty.

Again; it follows, from the above exposition, that whatever principles or practices the gentleman may have found in European Presbyterians opposed to civil and religious liberty, yet they attach not to *American Presbyterians.* That *some* such things existed, we own; we regret them; we denounce them. They were learned from Rome; they were only as a "drop in the bucket" compared to Rome. But they are not ours; and the American Presbyterian Church is stainless on this *subject*—both in principle and practice.

But, the gentleman says, we were *forced to change:* as follows, viz.—"After the revolution in this country, *these tenets* (of the Westminster Confession, making heresy punishable by law) hitherto held as having been revealed by Almighty God, were also discarded, as being unsuited to the soil of new-born liberty and of equal rights."....... "The Confession of Faith is forthwith *amended* to suit the constitution and the new order of things." "Presbyterianism, awed by the genius of the country, is compelled to do violence to its nature, and profess that liberality which it does not feel, and cannot practise." These truly are fine specimens of the "charity" about which the *meek* and loving man preached, with so much pathos, at the opening of his harangue. But observe; he *owns*, in the very basis of the argument, that our Confession is *now right:* that it has *"discarded"* its objectionable *"tenets;"* and stands *"amended to suit the constitution,* and *the new order of things."* Very well. So far it is good; and, by his own confession, *right.* For this unconscious admission, which settles the question in dispute, we devoutly thank him. And now, if Rome will only change too, and "adapt herself to the new order of things," we will not ask her *why,* or abuse her for the blessed *"amendment."*

But again; he has repeatedly said that the clause in our Larger Catechism,(1) which *"requires every one, according to his place and calling, to remove* all the *monuments of idolatry,"* is a persecuting clause, and distinctly points to *force* against the papacy. He also charges the Reformed Dutch Church, and the Covenanters, with *retaining* persecuting articles, even until now. If so, how does it happen that the "constitution" did not *force* a change? Did the constitution "compel us to do violence to our nature," and "amend the Confession to suit the new order of things?" The gentleman says so. Then there can be no persecution in it! But he says there is. Then we did not do what we did, in the way of change, "by force," and "against our nature;" for here, he says, is persecution *"still."* Here is a flat contradiction. But still further. The changes in the Confession of Faith were made *before* the adoption of the American "Constitution." The men that legislated and fought for American freedom— for the whole term of the American war—they were the men who altered one or two clauses in the *Confession* of their Faith *before* the adoption of the American Constitution. "Father Green," as the gentleman calls him, and well does he deserve it of his country and his church, carried his musket; and, as a chaplain, in the *rebel* army, preached freedom, civil and religious. And the father of the said Dr. Miller, whose *heavy blows* on "the beast and the bull that has turned to gore us," make him so hateful to my Reverend friend; I say, his father *preached* freedom, and *rebellion,* as Rome would call it, at the origin of the revolution.

(1) Page 217, Ans. to 108 Ques.

Ask the country, and ask the American army; ask the British leaders, where the Presbyterians were? How they felt? How they fought? Ask Tarleton! Ask the American Congress how Washington felt, and thought. No, sir. There was no *force* about it. The American Constitution was the *effect* of Puritan and Presbyterian love of civil and religious liberty, as much perhaps, as of any other cause; and, I repeat it, our present Confession was adopted before the American Constitution. And, until we change back, by the gentleman's own logic, we are "suited to the new order of things," which we helped, with all our power, under God, to produce.

We pass, as it is here in place, to consider the gentleman's argument from the *fact* of the *change*. We own that a change was necessary, in all or nearly all the European Protestant Confessions on the point of *establishments*, and of *religious freedom*. We own that Presbyterians of Scotland, Holland, and Geneva, as well as Episcopalians of England, and *Catholics* everywhere, needed to change their principles on the right of the civil magistrate to legislate for conscience. We Presbyterians did change *before* the American Constitution was adopted. Episcopalians changed. Have Catholics? No. The gentleman says they cannot. Nay, he argues against our change. He says, "*may they not discover that they are now in* error, *and recall the doctrines of the magistrate's power, and the sin of tolerating a false religion?*" . . . . "*They do not pretend to be infallible.*" . . . . "There is reason to believe they will [change back] when it can *be done with safety.*"

Now when I charged Romanism with persecuting what it calls "*false religions*," not merely to the "cropping of ears" but by the *crusades* and *inquisitions* founded on decrees of councils and bulls of popes, destroying many millions of lives, he said "OH, IT WAS ONLY DISCIPLINE," "not doctrine." How does it come that "*not to tolerate a false religion*" *with us* "IS DOCTRINE?" You see his *consistency!* But to the argument. If we, being *fallible*, may change to wrong, when right, can Catholics, believing themselves *infallible*, if *wrong*, ever become *right?* I have proved for six long nights of unanswered arguments, that in doctrine and discipline they do persecute, and *ever have done it.* Hence they must be so *forever;* for he says they *cannot change.* Therefore they are now what they were on St. Bartholomew's night, at the Council of Constance, in the crusades, in the inquisition; and they are in *America*, what they are in Spain, in Portugal, in Goa, and at Rome. Fatal logic to the gentleman's cause! Yet it is his own reasoning. Now we *own* that we are fallible, and therefore may change. But we claim no *right* to do *wrong*. We claim no right to change to a *renounced error. Till* we change we are owned by him to be *right. When* we change back to Rome's principles, then the gentleman will love us more. Till then the slanderous charges and false logic of the gentleman will be estimated on the same standard which can claim *infallibility to the worst men that ever cursed the earth;* and which glories to give eternity to error, by refusing to change even from *bad to good,* from *wrong to right,* from *slavery to freedom.*

One of the most remarkable instances of *audacity in assertion,* is his charging a "*theocracy*" on Presbyterians, and "indeed on all the Calvinistic sects." I know no motive for this, but the advantage of "*calling hard names*" *first.* Why, sir, the whole system of popery is one grand consolidated theocracy, corrupting and then extending the *Jewish system* to the *whole world.* Does not the pope claim to be "father of princes," "*vicar of Christ,*" "*head of the Universal Church,*" above all *civil power,* and as we have showed abundantly on the previous question, "a god on earth?" Even the famous writer Robinson,(1) adduced by the gentleman *against Presbyterians,* says, "*The canon law is a body of high treason against the rights and consciences of mankind.*"(2) The canon law is Rome's *magna charta.* He says too,(3) "*The pope's public political end was to be the absolute ruler of all the priesthood; and through them of all mankind.*" And, again,(4) "It is a *Jewish Christianity, having in it the seeds of a hierarchy;* "they *sunk* the *people* to elevate the *order:*" "the order created a *master like Aaron,*" &c.; and again, "If this dispute had been only about the right of wearing bells and pomegranates, as Aaron had done, and a breastplate that nobody but a Jew could read, it might have created *mirth;* but it took a very serious turn when it was *perceived that Aaron had under all his fine things, a* KNIFE *and a* BLOOD-*basin.*" De Pradt says "Jesuitism is EMPIRE BY RELIGION." .... "The general of the Jesuits is a *veritable king.*" The Pope is *master* of the *general.* He says, "It is organized intolerance." .... "Who is chief of this immense family, this militia present everywhere? THE POPE. *He counts more subjects than any sovereign;* more than even *many* sovereigns together." .... "IF THE WHOLE WORLD WERE CATHOLIC, THE POPE WOULD COMMAND THE WORLD." ... When we add to these shocking truths that the Catholics number 120 millions, and have *one* and *only* one common centre, and boast of their *unity* and *indivisibility,* and *common principles,* it becomes truly terrific. De Pradt says "Catholicism is not organized like other worships. *The latter have no common centre—no exclusive source from whence flows power in every religious society.* THEY HAVE NO ROME."(5) Protestants are incapable, if they *would,* of *consolidation. Catholics* cannot *exist without* it. When *it* ceases, the system ceases. When, therefore the gentleman talks of a *theocracy,* and says it endangers civil and

(1) Eccles. Researches. (2) Page 142.
(3) Page 163. (4) Page 121.
(5) See Modern Jesuitism, *passim.*

religious liberty, we wonder at his temerity; we rejoice in his admissions; and turn his principles back upon his own "*eternal city.*" Where the *great tyrant* reigns in the name of God, "calling himself God" on the ruins of religion, liberty and law.

The gentleman has said so much about the spirit of *European Presbyterians*, that it may not be amiss to examine this matter a little, and see what others thought of our venerable ancestors. While, as we have said, we own they brought out of Rome a *remnant* of her spirit, yet they have ever been foremost, in each age, in the love and defence of human liberty. Dryden, who has done so much with his sarcastic pen for popery, in his political poem, called "*The Hind and Panther,*" thus traces the origin of *republicanism*. Observe, the HIND was the *Romish Church;* the *English Church* was the *Panther;* the *Presbyterian* the *Wolf;* the *kennel,* Geneva; the *puddle,* its beautiful *lake,* and the *wall,* its noble *mountains.*

> "Last of all, the *litter* 'scaped by chance,
> And from Geneva first infested France.
> Some authors thus his pedigree will trace,
> But others write him of an upstart race;
> Because of Wickliff's brood no mark he brings,
> *But his innate* ANTIPATHY TO KINGS.
> What tho' your native kennel still be small,
> Bounded between a puddle and a wall?
> Yet your victorious colonies are sent,
> Where the North-ocean girds the continent.
> Quickened with fire below your monster's breed
> In *fenny* Holland, and in fruitful Tweed;
> And like the *first,* the last effects to be
> *Drawn to the dregs of a democracy.*
> But as the poisons of the deadliest kind
> Are to their unhappy coast confined,
> So PRESBYTERY and its pestilential zeal,
> CAN FLOURISH ONLY IN A COMMONWEAL."

This is the good, honest testimony of a Papist. It needs no comment. Surely Dryden did not think Presbyterianism and republics at war with each other!

Again; listen to Dean Swift. In a sermon, preached on "the Martyrdom of Charles II.," he said, "Upon the cruel persecutions raised against the Protestants under Queen Mary, among the great number who fled the kingdom to seek for shelter, *several went and resided at Geneva, which is a commonwealth, governed without a king, where the religion contrived by Calvin is without the order of bishops.* When the Protestant faith was restored by Queen Elisabeth, those who fled to Geneva returned among the rest home to England, and *were grown so fond of the government and religion of the place they had left,* that they used all possible endeavours to *introduce both into* their own country......

"From hence they proceeded by degrees to quarrel with the KINGLY GOVERNMENT, *because, as I have already said, the city of Geneva, to which their fathers had flown for refuge, was a commonwealth, or government of the people!!*" Here is the testimony of a Tory and high-churchman! Surely the Dean differed with our Papist priest about *Presbyterianism and liberty!*

And then, as to "*Mr.*" Luther and "Mr." Calvin, especially the latter! why, Mr. President, these upstart Jesuits, who have never learned as much, "with all their philosophy" and monarchy, as Calvin *forgot*—I do not wonder that they hate his memory. He was not infallible. He is not our "Pope." We condemned him for his conduct to Servetus. It has been much exaggerated, and they only did at Geneva, what the Papists tried to do, but failed, *at Vienne.* Yet it was very wrong. But, if *one victim* makes Geneva so *vile*, what shall we say of the millions of the victims of papal crusades and inquisitions? Has the gentleman forgot? or does he adopt the famous principle—"*one murder makes a villain*"——"*millions a hero!*"

Hooker, the immortal defender of Episcopacy, says, of Calvin, in his Preface to his "Ecclesiastical Polity," on the origin of popular Church government, "that he was incomparably the wisest man that ever the French Church did enjoy"—that in Exposition of the Scriptures, "the perfectest divines in the Reformed Churches were judged to be they who were skilfulest in Calvin's writings, his books being almost the very canon to judge both doctrine and discipline by."

And our own eminent and admirable historian, Bancroft, though himself a *Unitarian*, thus writes—not only of Calvin, but *Calvinists*, and of *American Calvinists!*

"They who have no admiration but for wealth and rank, can never admire the Genevan Reformer, for though he possessed the richest mind of his age, he never emerged from the limits of frugal poverty. The rest of us may be allowed to reverence his virtues, and regret his errors. He lived in a day when nations were shaken to their centre by the excitement of the Reformation, when the fields of Holland and France were wet with the carnage of persecution; when vindictive monarchs on one side threatened all Protestants with outlawry and death, and the Vatican on the other sent forth its anathemas and its cry for blood. In that day, it is too true, the influence of an ancient, long-established, hardly disputed error, the constant danger of his position, the intensest desire to secure union among the antagonists of popery, the engrossing consciousness that his struggle was for the emancipation of the Christian world, induced the great Reformer to defend the use of the sword for the extirpation of error. Reprobating and lamenting his adhesion to the cruel doctrine, which all Christendom had for centuries implicitly received, we may, as republicans, remember that Calvin was not only the founder of a sect, but foremost among the most efficient of modern republican legislators. More truly benevolent to the human race than Solon, more self-denying than Lycurgus, the genius of Calvin infused enduring elements into the institutions of Geneva, and made it for the modern world the impregnable fortress of popular liberty, the fertile seed-plot of democracy.

"Again; we boast of our common schools; Calvin was the father of popular education, the inventor of the system of free schools.

"Again; we are proud of the free states that fringe the Atlantic. The pilgrims of Plymouth were Calvinists; the best influence in South Carolina came from the Calvinists of France; Wm. Penn was the disciple of the Huguenots. The ships from Holland, that first brought colonists to Manhattan, were filled with Calvinists. He that will not honour the memory and respect the influence of Calvin, knows but little of the origin of American liberty.

"Or do personal considerations chiefly win applause? Then no one merits our sympathy and our admiration more than Calvin; the young exile from France, who achieved an immortality of fame before he was twenty-eight years of age; now boldly reasoning with the King of France for religious liberty; now venturing as the apostle of truth to carry the new doctrines into the heart of Italy; and now hardly escaping from the fury of papal persecution; the purest writer, the keenest dialectician of his age; pushing free inquiry to its utmost verge, and yet valuing inquiry only as the means of arriving at fixed principles. The light of his genius scattered the mask of darkness which superstition had held for centuries before the brow of religion. His probity was unquestioned; his morals spotless. His only happiness consisted in 'tasks of glory and of good;' for sorrow found its way into all his private relations. He was an exile from his country; he became, for a season, an exile from his place of exile. As a husband, he was doomed to mourn the premature loss of his wife; as a father, he felt the bitter pang of burying his only child. Alone in the world, alone in a strange land, he went forward in his career with serene resignation and inflexible firmness; no love of ease turned him aside from his vigils; no fear of danger relaxed the nerve of his eloquence; no bodily infirmities checked the incredible activity of his mind; and so he continued, year after year, solitary and feeble, yet toiling for humanity, till, after a life of glory, he bequeathed to his personal heirs a fortune in books and furniture, stocks and money, not exceeding two hundred dollars, and to the world a purer reformation, a republican spirit in religion, with the kindred principles of republican liberty."

How impartial, how true, how noble. How such light dazzles as it discloses the "bats" of the gloomy Vatican!!!

We come, at length, to the gentleman's famous "*argumentum ad captandum,*" on "*decrees*" and "*election.*" He has truly given a sad caricature of our system, and then denied to us even the right of "disclaimer," and to *our doctrine* the *benefit of clergy*, and decent burial in holy ground. He raises two arguments—but they are one. The first is—"*that the doctrine, that whatever comes to pass, is foreordained unchangeably,*" is destructive of *free* agency, and therefore of moral freedom, and therefore of civil and religious liberty. The other is its necessary corollary: viz., that "the making of eternal happiness or misery to depend upon the decrees of God, without conditions of faith and good works," destroys motives to duty, and therefore all regard for the *rights* of others. The very statement of the argument shows, that the gentleman was *hard run* for *matter*. We are not now on the *truth*, but the *tendency* of these doctrines; yet, if they *be* true, (not as distorted by a Jesuit, but as spread out in our standards,) this must disprove the tendency charged on them by him, as well as exhibit him in a light of shocking profanity and presumption. I will not argue the *truth* of these doctrines, as that is *not* the *question;* but since the gentleman has an infallible interpreter always present on earth, I beg, in reply, that he will tell us what he makes of the following passages: "Him being delivered by the *determinate counsel and foreknowledge* of God, ye have taken, and by *wicked hands* have crucified and slain."—*Acts* ii. 23. "Thou couldst have no *power* at all against me, *except* it *were given* thee from *above;* therefore, he that delivered me unto thee, hath the greater sin."—*John* xix. 11. Here the *sin* is made the greater, by the certainty and divinity of the decree. Also, Ephes. i. 11; Roms. ix. 10-24; Ephes. i. 2-4. A candid Hicksite once said to me in debate, "*Paul certainly agreed with thee.*" Paul's is surely good company. Where *this* gentleman will put him, I am at a loss to determine.

Now, as to the *tendency* of these doctrines, we hold, and so our standards abundantly *declare*, that so far from making men unholy, the moment a man freely adopts them, he is humbled, purified, and made a Christian. We also *hold*, that it is only by the power of God a man can be *made* or *kept* holy; and we also hold, that God's decrees *establish*, instead of *destroying* moral freedom. That good works flow from God's decrees; and that, "without holiness, no man shall see the Lord;" and it is *because* "*the Lord worketh in us,*" "*that we work out our salvation with fear and trembling.*" We think the *means* are predestinated, as well as the end. As Paul told the *crew of the ship that not one of them should be lost;* and yet, *after that*, he said, if the men *left the ship, all would be lost;* so we hold, as to the *means* and the *end*. *Good works*, therefore, are a *part* of *the system;* not as *causes*, but as *effects;* not as *merit*, but as *fruit;* not as *conditions,* but as *means.* The doctrine, on the contrary, of *papal merits,* we hold, not only dishonours Christ, but tempts men to licentiousness and self-dependence; and the whole system of penance, indulgences, confession, unction, remission by priests, purgatory, prayers for the dead, supererogation, and the mass, is vile *human patchwork*—to fill the pockets of the priests, and cheat the souls of the people. Well have these hocus-pocus arts and heathen exorcisms been described—

> "Supplied with spiritual provision
> And magazines of ammunition,
> With crosses, relics, crucifixes,
> Beads, pictures, rosaries, and pixes,
> The tools of working out salvation
> By mere mechanic operation."

How finely contrasted with this system of self-salvation, is the description given by Sir James Macintosh:(1) "It was fortunate also, that the enormities of Tetzel" [*the Pope's retailer of indulgences*] "found *Luther* busied in the contemplation of the principle, which is the basis of all ethical judgment, and by the power of which he struck a mortal blow at superstition:" namely, "men are not made truly righteous by performing certain actions which are *externally good,* but men must have righteous *principles* in the first place; and then they will not fail to perform virtuous actions." He calls it "a PROPOSITION EQUALLY CERTAIN AND SUBLIME;" and adds, that *Luther, in a more special application of his principle, used it to convey his doctrine of justification by faith.*"....... And again says, "in justice to him, the *civil historian should never omit the benefits which accrued to the moral interests of society from this principle.*"..... This principle is the merit of Christ made ours by the power of God working faith in us; and by union to Christ, making us free from guilt and pollution. To this Christians are by God's decree predestinated. This secures moral liberty, and moral rectitude; makes a man "a law unto himself"—and, therefore, a good citizen; the freest, noblest, and most just of men.

But let us pass from *principles* to *facts.* Who held these doctrines? Why Augustin, and the *flower* of the papacy. And at the Reformation, the whole of Protestant Europe! The *twelve* creeds of the Reformers, uttered by many millions in the same illustrious age, from Germany, Switzerland, Holland, France, England, and Scotland, were *all, all* what you term "CALVINISTIC." And they were the most free, and most virtuous millions of all Europe.

Who are Calvinists now-a-days? Why, not only the *Presbyterians* of Europe and America, but the great mass of the *Congre*

---

(1) History of England, Vol. II. pp. 120–1.

gationalists of New and of Old England; the Baptists, as a body, of both continents; and the *articles* of the Episcopal churches, on both sides of the Atlantic, if not *all* their clergy. And our Methodist brethren, the potent and dreaded enemies of popery everywhere, disclaim and abhor the "merit-system," and "salvation by words"—of priest-craft, though they reject the peculiar doctrines of Calvinism. Now, the appeal is *to facts*. Are not these Calvinistic masses of men among the purest and freest upon earth? Nay, is there a nation on earth that is not grossly corrupt, and deeply enslaved, in which there is not a strong leaven of *Calvinism?* There, then, is your false logic; and here are my triumphant facts: for whose truth, I appeal to the history of virtue, liberty, and man.

Finally, it is curious that the Council of Trent has contradicted itself flatly in its decree on this subject; and, as Father Paul, a Catholic, has told us (1) that on predestination and freewill it did not agree; and could not agree. Two large parties, the Dominicans and Franciscans, quarrelled over the *meaning* of the decree; and to this day, it is a contradictory system, evidently shaped with *unity of words*, and *contrariety* of *doctrine*. In fact, they *would* not admit, and they *could* not wholly stifle, the *truth*.

As to being the "exclusive favourites" of heaven, our principles, as already quoted, falsify the charge. It is true, we hold Rome to be apostate from God. But our creed avows that "all men are to be protected in the exercise of their religion," true or false; and we embrace Rome in our *pity*, and "all who hold the head" in our Christian *fellowship*. Complaints of bigotry from a Roman priest, if they were sincere, were cheering truly; for heretofore papists have excluded even *unbaptized infants* from heaven; and the Catholic creed expressly says "OUT OF THE TRUE CATHOLIC FAITH [not out of the pale of the Church] NONE CAN BE SAVED." But *all* Protestants are *out of* both *pale* and *faith*.

I regret the gentleman is not pleased with my illustration of the "hen." I adapted my *figures* to my *friend*. The American eagle spreads too free a pinion to descend to a papal quarry. Besides, the Pope has been legislating lately about the use of *eggs* on days of abstinence; which brought the good dame to my mind. But I truly hope there is no offence, at least with the poor fowl—for I should fear that the next orders from Rome will not only forbid *us* to *eat*, but *her* to lay *her eggs*. If, however, my Rev. friend would like a graver fowl, and a fitter exemplar, I would respectfully remind him that Rome was *once before saved by the cackling of a goose*.

We shall, in our next, reply to his last question, about Presbyterians abusing power when they had it.

(1) Hist. Counc. Trent, Book II.

We now close, as we have not room to go on with that question, by asking that gentleman to tell me of one people under heaven, for the ages on ages in which papacy prevailed over the world, of one country where Roman Catholics ever had the power to persecute, and did not do it; or one country in those ages that was, or in this age, that now is really free, where Roman Catholics have the majority.

"*Is the Presbyterian Religion, in any or all its principles or doctrines, opposed to civil or religious liberty ?*"

AFFIRMATIVE II.—MR. HUGHES.

I AM far from supposing, Mr. President, that the good sense of this meeting, will be satisfied with the gentleman's mere declamation, instead of the *facts* and *reasoning*, which it had a right to expect, and with which he had promised to astound the nation. I may characterize his speech justly, by saying of it, that what is *new* is not *true*, and what *true* is not *new*. I do not complain that Catholics are persecuted by Presbyterians in the sense in which he would represent. But I complain of their *disposition* and *efforts to bring about a persecution*. Thanks to the better genius of the age and country, they have not yet succeeded.

The cause to which the gentleman ascribes the present excitement against Catholics, for exercising the rights of conscience, is not the true cause. He says that, in as much as poor foreigners, escaping from the oppressions of their various countries, seek an asylum on these shores, "American Episcopalians, Baptists, Methodists, and congregationalists *as well as Presbyterians*," are guarding the coast against the landing of the emigrant who comes to better his condition, and to breathe, *as he supposed*, the air of religious and civil freedom. He is a foreigner, as all of us have been, either in ourselves or in our ancestors, but his son will be an American, and his grandson will wear gold spectacles. He may be poor, but is this a reason why "*ministers* of the *gospel*," should denounce him? He may be ignorant, but does not this strengthen his claim to our pity and humanity? Should we not rejoice that he and his posterity are transplanted into a region, where human rights are recognised; and that a race of victims have been rescued from the present, and prospective, grasp of iron-handed despotism, both civil and religious. But he is a Catholic; that is, he *worships God, according to the dictates of his conscience*,—and has he not a right to do so? And shall we be told that all the other Protestant denominations join the Presbyterians in denouncing him for this? I do not believe the assertion. He comes to earn his bread by the sweat of his brow, to tame the forests, and to make the highways of commerce through the very cornfields, by canals and railways; and is *this* an injury to your country? But he is a Catholic, ignorant and vicious; then teach him virtue *by example*, and if this will not do, teach him by the *laws*. But the accusation is a calumny: the great body of Catholic emigrants, exposed as they are, are industrious, hard-working people, who live, not by *knavery*, but by their daily toil. And the vicious among them, are themselves the victims of their own folly and wickedness. This plea, therefore, for the pretended combination of all Protestant denominations is equally unfounded and absurd.

But there are "foreign associations in aid of Catholic missionaries." And so there are here,—for the aid and support of foreign Protestant missions. Of which then, on the score of political economy, has the country more reason to complain—of those who send the money *out* of the country, or of those who bring it in? The receipts of the American Bible Society, since its commencement to the year 1830, have been $909,291.15, almost a million of dollars. The receipts of the Board of FOREIGN MISSIONS, in 1834, was $152,386.10.(1) This society has been in operation for twenty-five years, and the whole sum expended by it, in FOREIGN missions, is probably not less than two millions. All that was ever received by Catholics from foreign sources *together*, would not equal in amount the *annual* income of the American Board of *Foreign* Missions. It is an injury, therefore, that for all the money which *they* send out of the country, the Catholics should bring a little in? But they build colleges with it. Well, that only proves that they are the friends of education; and are the friends of education, the enemies of freedom? Education ought not to be a *Presbyterian* monopoly—we do not burn down *their* houses of education. But "European despots" . . . . . . The Catholic religion has flourished *in despite* of them; it can flourish without them./ They are its enemies at home, and we cannot expect them to be its friends abroad. But the "LEOPOLDINE FOUNDATION"—What of it? Its members, very limited in number, choose to tax themselves about one cent a week, in aid of foreign missions in America. And supposing all the people of Europe were to do the same, it would only . . . bring more money into the country. Yes, but it is to aid in spreading *Catholicity*. And is Protestantism afraid of being *bought out?* The *Presbyterians* seem to think so. But "PRINCE METTERNICH," the gentleman tells you, "SENDS VAST SUMS FOR THE SPREAD OF CATHOLICITY." I am aware that the gentleman is not *original* in making this assertion, and I have the less difficulty, on this account, in pronouncing it to be, what it is, *a positive falsehood*. I challenge his proof. But "Bishop England" has made a "late tour" in Europe, and of course *he* was about no good. And pray, is the POLICY OF CHINA to be adopted, by the American people, that a citizen may not go *when* and *where* he pleases? According to the gentleman's

---

(1) See Report, page 44.

apprehension of things, Rome is the "beau ideal" of civil and religious despotism, and yet in Rome, as elsewhere, the institutions of America, found in Bishop England not only a willing, but a willing and *able* advocate. It is true that the BURNING of the CONVENT gave the advocates of absolutism a momentary advantage over him, but it was only until he had time to discriminate between the genius of our institutions, and that dark, cold, remnant of Calvinistic bigotry, which the sun of our government has not been able to thaw into humanity, or enlighten into virtue.

But "Schlegel, in his Lectures on the Philosophy of History," says that the "nursery of all the revolutions that occurred in Europe, has been North America." To be sure,—and he says the fact. And a fact of which "North America" is not ashamed. Nay, it is her boast. On the fourth day of July, every year, this very fact makes every tongue, east and west of the Alleghany, eloquent with liberty and patriotism.

As for the "JESUITS," there are a few facts in their history, which make me appreciate the united compliment the gentleman pays me, when he represents me as their "defender." One is, that they have done more for EDUCATION and SCIENCE, than all the Presbyterians that ever did, or ever will, exist. Another is, that they have suffered persecution, and rejoiced that they were found *worthy* to suffer, for the name of JESUS. Another still, is, that *their* enemies, the infidels of the last century, were the enemies of Christianity. Frederick the Great, who was in the secrets of the *infidel conspiracy*, said of the Jesuits, that they were the "*foxes*," between the sheep of the Christian fold and the "wolves," that wished to devour them. I have no objection, therefore, to see the gentleman putting on the panoply of Voltaire and Rousseau, against the Jesuits, though I do not think it becomes him. The *reasonable* motive of hatred against them in this country, is, that they can give a BETTER and a CHEAPER education than *Presbyterians*.

I have taken, Mr. President, almost too much notice of the gentleman's loose and vague, and I may add, unfounded, assertions. You have observed that, like all declaimers who wish to reach an *end*, and have not the *means*, he deals exclusively in *general* statements, without proof. The only authority in fact that he could adduce is that of an anonymous libeller in New York, who, under the signature of "BRUTUS," and in a tract of silly slander against Catholics, entitled "Foreign Conspiracy," insulted the understanding of the country, by pretending, that the governments of Europe were preparing to invade our liberties—as if such a thing were possible. They have enough to do at home. But, sir, these Presbyterian gentlemen are haunted by strange visions. Some time since, there was a division in the synod of Cincinnati, (no unusual thing by-the-by,) and a reverend peacemaker addresses them, as I remember, in this wise—"Ah! brethren, how the Pope of Rome will chuckle, *when he hears of your divisions!"*

The gentleman, however, I must do him the justice to say, has ventured on *one* specific statement. In order to make you believe that crowds of "Jesuits" are smuggled through our custom-houses, he tells you that " TALLEYRAND (A JESUIT) WAS ONCE A TEACHER IN THIS COUNTRY." Here is something tangible. Here is a sentence of only ten words, and yet it contains *two positively false* statements. Talleyrand never was either a " Jesuit," or a " teacher."

Such is the analysis of the pretended events which have roused, as the gentleman asserts, the "American Episcopalians, Baptists, Methodists, Congregationalists, *as well as Presbyterians,*" to "inquire what can this mean?" That some of each of these denominations may have been *used* to stir up the fanatical excitement, is highly probable:—but that the genius which presides and directs, is the genius of Presbyterianism, no man at all acquainted with the character of the machinery will for a moment deny. The only denominations, so far as I am aware, that have brought the politics of the country into their pulpits—are the Presbyterians, and possibly their step-brethren, the Congregationalists of New England. The only denomination that have itinerant haranguers *on pay*, who go about like roaring lions, for the express purpose of stirring up the people against Catholics, are the Presbyterians. The only denomination that seem to have despaired of being able to pluck arguments *from heaven,* for the refutation of Catholic doctrine, and who have, therefore, *stooped* to dig them out of the earth, are the Presbyterians. Yet I know some Presbyterians, and I hope there are many whom I do not know, who blush for and condemn these proceedings. The gentleman, however, I regret to say, is not of the number. Dr. Beecher of Cincinnati, whose visit to Boston last year was as if he came to "bring fire on earth, and only wished that it might be kindled"— who had scarcely finished his third sermon against Catholics, when the Convent was in flames—he is not of the number. The conductors of the Cincinnati Presbyterian Journal, who gave the first circulation to what the CHRONICLE of that city calls "AN IMPUDENT LIE," viz., the story about knocking a senator down, and, "HATS OFF, GENTLEMEN, THE BISHOP'S COMING," are not of the number. They knew, and most of their colleagues knew, that this was "AN IMPUDENT LIE." They published the falsehood, and they have refused to publish the correction. Nay, a Presbyterian minister in New York, Mr. Mason, has made this falsehood *immortal,* by treating it as a matter of historical record, in his Preface to History of the Inquisition.

But, if there be a man in the country whose sentiments are a fair index of the genius and temper of Presbyterians, that man is Dr. Miller, of the Princeton Theological Seminary. In his Introductory Essay to the History of Romanism, a compilation of calumny and buffoonery, this venerable professor, in the nineteenth century, and in the United States of America, denounces his Catholic fellow-citizens "AS FOES OF GOD AND MAN!" and compares them to "HIGHWAYMEN AND ASSASSINS IN THE DARK." Out of the Presbyterian communion, I question whether there is a man on the American continent capable of giving utterance to a sentiment, so unchristian and so inhuman; for, let it be recollected, that the crime of the Catholics is their worshipping God according to the dictates of their *own* conscience, rather than of that of the General Assembly, or of Dr. Miller.

No, sir, the glory of stirring up, or causing to be stirred up, the smouldering embers of *religious hatred*, (what a contradiction!) belongs to the Presbyterians. The other denominations of whom the gentleman has made an artificial parade, are, no doubt, persuaded that we are wrong in our belief: our conviction is precisely the same in regard to *their* creed. But they are, in the main, content to allow us to conduct our affairs in our own way, and we certainly do not disturb them in the management of theirs. Not so the zealots among the Presbyterians. Believers in their own "election," and in the "inadmissibility of grace," they *seem* to think that God has commanded them to take charge of all the rest of mankind. I can admire their zeal, but I would admire it much more, were it tempered with a little more charity, and a little less overbearance.

But the gentleman tells you that the American people "EXAMINE EVERY THING;" that popery, as he insultingly calls my religion, cannot stand the test of inquiry; and that its votaries have no other way to hide its deformities, than by endeavouring to check free inquiry and discussion.

I suppose we may take the scene that was exhibited in Mr. M'Calla's church last winter, as a fair specimen of what the gentleman means by "free inquiry." A platform—a crowd of curious and uneducated people of both sexes—a circle of ministers, amusing the audience with burlesque and ribaldry, at the expense, not of the Catholic religion, but of what the speakers might think proper to represent as such: this is what we are to understand by "FREE INQUIRY." A scene unworthy of the temple and its ministers; at which, though the profane might laugh, piety, of whatever sect, might find enough to weep. This is "FREE INQUIRY." That is, your enemies attack your character, by *clubbing* their calumnies or prejudices against you: one says that you knocked down an American senator, because he would not take off his hat when "the bishop was coming;" another, that you have cells for the inquisition, and infants' skulls in your cellar; a third avers that you are as bad as "a highwayman, and an assassin in the dark;" a fourth proves that you are "THE FOE OF BOTH GOD AND MAN;" and, then, the assembly closes, as it commenced, with a *prayer* You remonstrate against the injustice of thus attacking your character; and you are gravely told that you are an enemy to "free investigation;" and that the "American people investigate *every thing.*"

The Catholic religion courts investigation, but not *this kind* of investigation; and Presbyterians do not allow it the benefit of any other. If they wished the American people to be informed correctly on the subject, they would direct them to our catechisms and books of instruction, and not to our enemies. The Catholic clergy throughout the country, though not obtrusive, are, nevertheless, always ready to explain our doctrine to those who are sincere in their inquiries. But the object is to distort the public judgment, by the exhibition of caricatures, and the concoction of old slanders with modern seasoning. The object is to vitiate the public taste; so that, like the Chinese, who never relish eggs till they are *stale*, nothing may go down but what, in a healthier tone of the literary and religious palate, would have created nausea and disgust. Witness Miss Reed's book. Witness the "DOWNFALL OF BABYLON," by a Miss Reed of the other gender, the unhappy Mr. Smith, a little two-penny concern of abuse against the Catholics, of which Dr. Ely said, with a good deal of malicious wit, "every *little* helps." It is by such means as these that the Catholic religion and its professors are enveloped in the slime of calumny, and so presented for the judgment of the "American people:" just as the anaconda wraps up its victim in saliva, in order to facilitate the process of swallowing.

I have already said, that, with regard to the young gentlemen who introduced the question in this society, I could not for a moment suppose that they would knowingly introduce any question for the purpose of injuring any sect or denomination. So far as I know them, I have too high an opinion of their honour and sense of justice, to harbour the thought for one moment.

It is true that the gentleman was the advocate of the unfortunate Poles, who were not only foreigners, but Catholics, and I give him credit for it. When he portrayed the agonies of their separation from their country, and their friends, whom they should see no more, until they meet "around the throne of God," the picture was touching, and did honour to his feelings; but, alas! the vision of the orator, and the man, was soon dissipated by the dogmas of the Presbyterian. In this capacity, the gentleman, against the better feelings of his nature, is obliged to regard them, and all Catholics, as—idolaters! so that their meeting "around the throne of God," was, after all, only a figure of oratory.

The Society remember that I exposed the gentleman's falsification of the Council of Lateran, in the place in which, *suppressing the crimes* of the Albigenses, in the middle of the quotation, and bringing the beginning and end together, without indicating any *omission*, he made it appear that the penalties enacted against them, were for their *speculative errors*, and *not* for their crimes against society; his excuse was, that "he had quoted as Faber had done." If, therefore, this is "slander," as he now says, you are all witnesses that he himself is my authority! Quo ipse ducit, sequor. When I falsify, let him expose; that he has done, or *can do so*, I emphatically deny.

The speech which you have just heard is sufficiently accommodating. It admits the fact that persecution was a part of Presbyterianism, from the origin of the sect, down to the last amendment of the Confession of Faith. Then, it follows, that down to this period, the Presbyterians were themselves heretics; by holding "as having been revealed by Almighty God," a tenet, which, just after the Declaration of Independence, it was discovered that God had *not* revealed! Here, then, is a Presbyterian minister, acknowledging that, down to that period, all Presbyterians were *heretics by doctrine*, and *persecutors by heresy!* This is candid, though perhaps some of his brethren may regard it as somewhat humiliating.

By this candid acknowledgment, the gentleman has saved me, *for the present*, the necessity of entering on the horrible facts of persecution by the Presbyterians. It only remains to show that persecution is at this day, and in the UNITED STATES, an avowed doctrine of the Presbyterian Church. When I say "avowed," I do not mean that they avow it *under that name;* but that they avow it, in other words, no man acquainted with the Confession of Faith will for a moment deny. Since the revolution they have cut down the tree, whose fruit was death to other Protestants, as well as Catholics, in the various countries of the earth in which Calvinism prevailed. But its *root* remains. The Presbyterians hold not only as a *doctrine*, but as a positive commandment of Almighty God, that THEY are bound "TO REMOVE ALL FALSE WORSHIP, AND ALL THE MONUMENTS OF IDOLATRY." If, therefore, they are *bound* to do this, by the commandment of God, what other religion will remain, after they have begun to "keep the commandments?" Every other religion but their own, is a "FALSE WORSHIP;" and, as they are bound to "remove all false worship," it follows that they are bound to remove all other religions. In the Confession of Faith, under the head of the Second Commandment,(1) among the obligations which the commandment imposes, we find "*the disapproving, detesting, opposing all false worship, and, according to each one's place and calling, removing it and all the monuments of idolatry.*" Not only is this obligation imposed on the Presbyterians by the Decalogue, it is confirmed to them as the true heirs of the Jews in their complex rights regarding the land of Canaan. The Confession of Faith takes the confirming warrant from the seventh chapter of Deuteronomy—of which the text is clear.

(1) Pages 218, 219, Quest. 108.

The gentleman has had the candour to admit, that by "monuments of idolatry," are meant whatever is appropriated to, or in connexion with the Catholic religion. Hence, according to the Presbyterian mode of interpreting the seventh chapter of Deuteronomy, we, as IDOLATERS, are to be treated by them, the PEOPLE OF GOD, as the Canaanites were treated by the Jews. It is not for me to say who the "seven nations" are. But if the *true* worship be the Presbyterian, the "*false* worships" are pretty numerous, and it will be difficult to "REMOVE" them. However, as the Presbyterians are bound to aim at this object, "ACCORDING TO EACH ONE'S PLACE AND CALLING"—*i. e.* the minister in the pulpit—the author at the press—the teacher of schools as teacher,—the session of the church, the Synod, and the General Assembly, in their accumulating, and concentrated influence—the Sunday-school Union, as the Sunday-school Union—the various religious societies holding this abominable doctrine, in their respective capacities—the merchant in his commerce,—the judge on the bench,—the jurymen in the box—the legislator as legislator—the ordinary citizen at the ballot-box—the pious ladies who have hearts to pity the objects of persecution, except they are steeled with Calvinism, in their domestic influence: in a word, ALL PRESBYTERIANS, being bound by the Confession of Faith, and the *supposed* commandment of the holy and just God, to "REMOVE ALL FALSE WORSHIP," *may* succeed, by the mode which they are bound to follow, "each according to his *place* and *calling*."

This, therefore, being the DOCTRINE of the Presbyterian church, throws considerable light on some of their recent efforts to disturb the equilibrium of the constitution and laws of the country. Their petitions to Congress to have the Sabbath sanctified by legislative enactments; their attempt to drive out of circulation every elementary book of education not favourable to their doctrine of arrogance, as well as despotism; their attempt, frustrated by the timely but unintentional disclosures of that "busy and loquacious man," as the gentleman calls him, Dr. Ely, to "form a Christian party in politics;" these were the beginnings of that intolerant policy which in the name of *God Almighty* calls upon all Presbyterians to labour "according to each one's place and calling," to "*remove* all false worship, and all the monuments of idolatry." Since the failure of these, it has been thought more expedient not to attempt the fulfilment of the *whole* commandment at once; and it is thought wiser to begin by putting down the "monuments of idolatry" first, and the "false worships" will be more easily "removed" afterwards.

I would now appeal to any twelve conscientious men in the United States, and ask them, under the moral responsibilities of a jury, bound to decide according to truth, whether this doctrine of the Presbyterian Church in the United States is not in deadly conflict with the constitution under which we live. Here is a constitution securing to every man the right to worship God according to the dictates of his conscience; and here is a Confession of Faith obliging, by a commandment of God, the Presbyterians to "remove all *false* worship, and all the monuments of idolatry." The Presbyterians, therefore, must be either faithless to God, by bearing with those "false worships and monuments of idolatry," which, according to their narrow and intolerant creed, he has commanded them to "*remove;*" or they must be traitors to the constitution which protects those "false worships," and will not allow them to keep the commandments of God, by removing the monuments of idolatry. I did not say, as the gentleman affects to understand me, that the Convent at Boston was burned down by Presbyterians; but what is certain is, that the Presbyterians have, what they call a commandment of God, and according to that commandment, the incendiaries who fired it were doing God's service, though against the American constitution. The chivalrous men who made war on the dwellings of defenceless ladies and female children, in mask, and at the dead hour of midnight—the men who, by this act of barbarism and ferocity, violated the American constitution and fixed a *blot* on the national escutcheon, and on the nineteenth century, did nothing more than what the commandment of God binds all Presbyterians to do—"according to each one's *place and calling*"—they "removed a false worship, a monument of idolatry." With this doctrine, therefore, in their Confession of Faith, is it not an evidence of singular contempt for the attestations of history and the understandings of men, that the *Presbyterians*, above all other denominations, should put themselves forward as the *advocates* of civil and religious liberty; whilst—under the *divine obligation* of removing "ALL FALSE WORSHIP," and all the "*monuments of idolatry*"—they would allow it to none but themselves?

I shall now proceed to show that the purposes avowed by Dr. Ely are in strict accordance with the doctrine and history of the Presbyterian Church. The gentleman would account for the avowal, by telling you that the doctor is a "busy and loquacious man;" but it has a deeper origin. The doctor may have been "imprudent," and it is well for the country that he was so. But for the rest, I ask, whether he was not discharging the duties of a sincere Presbyterian minister? He was commanded, with all his brethren, by the Confession of Faith, and on the pretended authority of God, to "REMOVE ALL FALSE WORSHIP, AND ALL THE MONUMENTS OF IDOLATRY." And this he was commanded to do according to his "PLACE AND CALLING." Now, his "place and calling" are the ministry and the pulpit; and hence, he was only discharging honestly the duties imposed on him by the Confession of Faith, when, on the 4th of July, 1827, he preached the doctrine of his Church in the following passages:—

"*Our rulers, like any other members of the community, who*

are under the law to God, as rational beings, and under law to Christ, since they have the light of Revelation, ought to search the Scriptures, assent to the truth; profess faith in Christ; keep the Sabbath holy to God; pray in private, and in the domestic circle; attend to the public ministry of the word; BE BAPTIZED, AND CELEBRATE THE LORD'S SUPPER." This is specious and general; still, it is a *religious test* of qualifications for office. But the doctor, being a "busy and loquacious man," unfolds a little more of the doctrine in the following passage, given as explanatory of the above:—

"*In other words, our presidents, secretaries of the government, senators, and other representatives in Congress, governors of states, judges, state legislators, justices of the peace, and city magistrates, are just as much bound, as any other persons in the United States, to be* ORTHODOX IN THEIR FAITH."

Now, if Presbyterians could see all these *offices* filled by men who are "ORTHODOX IN THEIR FAITH," then they might begin to keep the commandment of God, as set forth in the Confession of Faith, by which "they are bound," according to each one's *place* and *calling*, to "remove all false worship, and all the monuments of idolatry." However, the doctor's "place and calling" was to labour for this remote end. Accordingly he goes on:—

"*I propose, fellow-citizens, a new sort of union; or, if you please, a* CHRISTIAN PARTY *in politics, which I am exceedingly anxious all good men in our country should join, not by subscribing a new constitution, and the formation of a new society, but by adopting, avowing, and* DETERMINING *to act upon truly religious principles in all* CIVIL MATTERS."

"*The Presbyterians* ALONE *could bring half a million of electors into the field.*"

"*It will be objected, that my plan*," (of making orthodoxy a test for office,) "*of a truly Christian party in politics, will make* HYPOCRITES. WE *are not answerable for their hypocrisy, if it does.*"

"*I am free to avow, that other things being equal, I would prefer for my chief magistrate, and judge, and ruler,* A SOUND PRESBYTERIAN."

Now, the end of the second commandment, as laid down in the Confession of Faith, is the removal of "all false worship, and all the monuments of idolatry." And when all public rulers shall be "ORTHODOX IN THEIR FAITH," "SOUND PRESBYTERIANS," and *each* obliged to labour for the end, according to his "*place and calling*," it is easy to foresee the consequences. Let the gentleman not think, therefore, that he can get over this avowed doctrine of the Presbyterian creed, by charging Dr. Ely with being a "busy and loquacious man." The truth is, that the doctor only preached what all Presbyterian ministers should preach, if they were as *imprudently honest* in proclaiming their tenets, as the Reverend clerk of the General Assembly. Their doctrines, under the second commandment, oblige them to it. The doctor allowed the "simplicity of the dove" to prevail over the "cunning of the serpent:" it was his misfortune, by proclaiming openly the doctrines of his Church, to give the alarm to the friends of civil and religious liberty; and hence, he is called a "busy and loquacious man."

The Sunday-school Union, in perfect harmony with these sentiments—in various reports made about the same time—had the candour to avow their desire and intention "*to force out of circulation*," such elementary books as did not coincide with their views—to "revise and alter"—to become, in their own language, "the DICTATORS TO THE CONSCIENCES OF THOUSANDS OF IMMORTAL BEINGS." And what were their anticipations of reward for this labour of love? They themselves explain it. "IN TEN YEARS, OR CERTAINLY IN TWENTY, THE POLITICAL POWER OF OUR COUNTRY WOULD BE IN THE HANDS OF MEN, WHOSE CHARACTERS HAVE BEEN FORMED UNDER THE INFLUENCE OF SABBATH-SCHOOLS."(1)

It is generally known, that Presbyterians soon became the prominent and efficient managers of all the concerns of the Sunday-school Union. It was under their supervision and authority, that these bold and daring purposes were thus publicly avowed.

They proclaim themselves "DICTATORS to the consciences of thousands," by "*altering*" the sources of early information, and they look forward to the time, when the " political power of our country shall be in the hands of men, whose *characters* have been formed under this dictation."

The gentleman will tell you, that some of our most respectable citizens are, or have been, managers in this institution. I would not detract one iota from their respectability. But the more respectable they are, the more reason there is to dread a religion, the influence of which could so far pervert their judgment. "If these things be done in the *green* wood, says the Scripture, what shall it be in the *dry?*" If respectable men can so far forget what is due to the CIVIL and RELIGIOUS RIGHTS of the American people, as to become "DICTATORS," to the "consciences" of *confiding childhood*, merely because the second commandment of the Presbyterian creed requires of them, "according to each one's *place* and *calling*, to remove *all* false worship, and all the monuments of idolatry;" then, sir, you may imagine what it will be when these same principles are brought to operate on men of bad or of no character. That is the aim of their effort now. Their object is to stir up—the mob.

No Christian can entertain much respect for the character of Thomas Jefferson, who is known to have had little or no respect for the Christian's religion. But, viewed as a *statesman*, his

(1) Appendix to Second An. Rep. S. S. U. 1826, p. 93.

character appears in a very different light. In political sagacity, in the direct or indirect bearings of religious or political principles, he was a deep reader of the human heart, and thoroughly instructed. He warned his country against the possible danger which *might* arise from the monarchical or other predilections, that might be introduced by emigrants. But he warned it also against a danger more immediate, for his knowledge of which he depended not on speculation, *but on facts*. This was the danger growing out of the superior intolerance, for which Presbyterianism had been, and would be, distinguished in all ages. He wrote *history*, and yet those who are acquainted with the violent proceedings of Presbyterians within the last twelve months, may see that he wrote *prophecy* at the same time. In vol. iv., p. 358, Letter clxvii., he says:—

"*The atmosphere of our country is unquestionably charged with a threatening cloud of fanaticism, lighter in some parts, denser in others, but too heavy in all. I had no idea, however, that in Pennsylvania, the* CRADLE OF TOLERATION AND FREEDOM OF RELIGION, *it could have risen to the height you describe. This must be owing to the* GROWTH *of Presbyterianism. Here, Episcopalian and Presbyterian, Methodist and Baptist, join together in hymning to their Maker, listen with attention and devotion to each other's preachers, and all mix in society with perfect harmony. It is not so in the districts where Presbyterianism prevails undividedly.* THEIR AMBITION AND TYRANNY WOULD TOLERATE NO RIVAL, IF THEY HAD POWER. SYSTEMATICAL *at grasping at an ascendency over* ALL *other sects, they aim at* ENGROSSING THE EDUCATION OF THE COUNTRY; *are hostile to every institution that* THEY *do not direct; are jealous at seeing others begin to attend at all to that object.*"

On the same subject, he says, in his letter to William Short, p. 322:—

"*The Presbyterian clergy are the* LOUDEST, *the most* INTOLERANT *of all sects; the most* TYRANNICAL *and* AMBITIOUS; *ready at the word of the lawgiver, if such a word could now be obtained, to put the* TORCH TO THE PILE, *and to rekindle in this virgin hemisphere the flames in which their oracle, Calvin, consumed the poor Servetus, because he could not subscribe the proposition of Calvin,* THAT MAGISTRATES HAVE A RIGHT TO EXTERMINATE ALL HERETICS TO CALVINISTIC CREED. THEY PANT TO RE-ESTABLISH BY LAW, *that holy inquisition, which they can now only infuse into public opinion.*" Be assured, sir, Thomas Jefferson understood the genius of Presbyterianism, not in its theological deformity, but as a *statesman*, in its bearings upon the principles we are now discussing; viz., "civil and religious liberty."

But we have other testimony besides that of Thomas Jefferson. We have those who are good Presbyterian theologians, explaining the intolerant doctrines which the gentleman would disguise, by pretending that nobody ever thought of them, except Dr. Ely, who is "a busy, loquacious man." We have, in our own city, the testimony of the Rev. Dr. Wylie, a gentleman of learning and humanity, from whose breast not even the intolerance of the creed he defends has been able to drain the milk of kindness to his brother—man. The testimony of this writer is unanswerable proof of the arguments which I have already deduced from the Westminster Confession of Faith. The gentleman will tell you that Dr. Wylie is a *Reformed* Presbyterian. But I can tell you, and my opponent will not venture to gainsay the statement, that the principles now maintained by Dr. Wylie are the true principles of honest primitive Presbyterianism. They are the principles of the Westminster Confession. The work from which I am about to quote, is a short doctrinal treatise on the "Duty of Magistrates and Ministers," entitled the "TWO SONS OF OIL," and published by Dr. Wylie, in 1803. The audience and the public will judge of the principles;—in regard to which the author says, in his short Preface, "*The time has been when the whole body of Presbyterians, in Scotland, England, and Ireland, unanimously subscribed them.*"

The first object of the argument is to show that the doctrine of what is called "UNION OF CHURCH AND STATE," is conformable to the law of God, in the institution of the two great ordinances of MAGISTRACY AND MINISTRY." The second is to show that the government of the United States and the State governments are NOT MORAL ORDINANCES OF GOD, precisely because they *reject* these notions of a scriptural magistracy, and allow UNIVERSAL LIBERTY OF CONSCIENCE. What is definitive in support of my argument, and in showing that the doctrines of the Presbyterian religion are opposed to civil and religious liberty, is, that to establish the above points, the author of the "Two Sons of Oil" quotes repeatedly the text of the Westminster Confession—*the present creed of the General Assembly.*

On the Presbyterian doctrine about the magistrates being "nursing fathers" to the church, Dr. Wylie speaks out with a degree of manly candour and fearlessness, which does him credit. "*He* (the magistrate) *ought, by his* CIVIL POWER, *to* REMOVE *all external impediments to the true religion and worship of God, whether they be persons, or things; such as persecution, profaneness,* HERESY, IDOLATRY, *and* THEIR ABETTORS, *as did Asa, Hezekiah, Josiah, and other pious kings.*"(1) Now this is plain dealing. This is the *end*, and Dr. Ely's "CHRISTIAN PARTY IN POLITICS" is the means by which to accomplish it. If the gentleman denies this doctrine—he denies his *faith*. It is neither more nor less, than what his *creed* requires of all Presbyterians, under

---

(1) Two Sons of Oil, p. 19.

the second commandment, viz., to "REMOVE, ACCORDING TO EACH ONE'S PLACE AND CALLING, ALL *false worship, and all the monuments of idolatry.*" Of the want of qualifications for the ministry, the candid Presbyterian writer whom I have already quoted, says,—"*Such are the clouds of illiterate, Methodist locusts, which darken the horizon of these states ...... the infuriate zeal with which they propagate their* POISONOUS DOCTRINES, *resembles much the character of the Scribes and Pharisees, mentioned* in Matthew xxiii. 15."(1) In this assembly, it has suited the gentleman to be loud and long in the praise of the American General and State Constitutions, inasmuch as this audience respects the Constitutions, and do not know its creed.

Now, the *fact* is, that the Constitution and the doctrines of the Presbyterian religion are directly opposed, one to the other. Hence, the stricter sort of that denomination condemn the whole political system. Their reasons are, that first, the federal Constitution does not even recognise the existence of God.(2) Second, That the State Constitutions contain "positive immorality," And what is this immorality? "*Their recognition of such rights of conscience*" as are contrary to sound Presbyterianism.(3) "*The government gives a legal security and establishment to gross heresy, blasphemy, and idolatry,* UNDER THE NOTION OF LIBERTY OF CONSCIENCE."(4)

The Confession of Faith teaches, as a doctrine, that the "*civil magistrates are* NURSING FATHERS *to the Church.*" And the gentleman pretends not to understand this perversion of the Constitution, as containing any thing at which the friends of civil and religious liberty need feel alarmed. Let him see its explanation in Dr. Ely's "Christian party in politics." Let him read its meaning in the "Two Sons of Oil." "*Kings shall be thy nursing fathers. Would he not be a hard-hearted father, who would put his* CHILD *upon the same footing with the* WOLVES, TIGERS, *and* OTHER VORACIOUS BEASTS *of prey? The* POLITICAL FATHER, *who leaves the child* TRUTH *in the jaws of enemies, still more deadly, cannot be allowed to possess much more tender feelings. Will the Church of Christ enjoy no* OTHER PRIVILEGE *than this,* '*by sucking the breast of kings?*'"(5)

In short, I put it to every honest member of the Presbyterian Church, whether there is not a palpable contradiction, between his implied oath as a citizen, and his implied oath as a Presbyterian. As a Presbyterian he binds himself to "REMOVE, according to his *place* and *calling,* all false worship, and all the monuments of idolatry." As a citizen, he binds himself to support the Constitution, and consequently, to *protect* "all false worship, and all the monuments of idolatry." Consequently, he binds himself to "re-

(1) Two Sons of Oil, p. 31.   (2) Ibid. p. 34.
(3) Ibid. p. 35.   (4) Ibid.   (5) Ibid. p. 38.

move" the very things which he binds himself to protect, and not "*remove!*" If he tells us that he *can* keep both, he must either be a fool, or else believe those to whom he makes the assertion to be fools. He swears, either actually or implicitly, of the same thing, that he *will* "REMOVE," and that he will NOT "*remove*" it. Which of these contradictory oaths will he keep? If he keeps his *Presbyterian* oath, he is a traitor to the Constitution, a foe to the rights of conscience, to civil and religious liberty, and a dangerous citizen. If, on the other, he keeps his *civil* oath, he is a hypocrite, and a traitor towards God. For, as a Presbyterian, he is obliged to believe that God has commanded him to remove *all false worship;* and, instead of obeying God, he turns round, and swears to support a Constitution which protects all false worship! To be an honest man, therefore, he must renounce one or other of these incompatible obligations. If his creed is correct, the Constitution is a document of iniquity—opposed to the commandment of God. If the Constitution is correct, he ought to renounce his creed. But, at all events, it is manifest, that, under this government, the Presbyterians have not liberty of conscience. It will not allow them to keep the commandments of Jehovah, by REMOVING "all false worship," as the Almighty has appointed in the Westminster Confession of Faith. This is the reason why the *honest* Presbyterians—the Covenanters, whose orthodoxy in the faith, the gentleman will not dare to deny, reject the American Constitutions as *not being a moral ordinance of God.* This is the reason why Dr. Ely would prefer, for his "chief magistrate, a sound Presbyterian." This is the reason why the Sunday-mail experiment was tried. This, in fine, is the reason why the Presbyterian parsons have, in such numbers, entered into a political conspiracy against their Catholic fellow-citizens. If they can only enlist the other Protestant denominations *in aiding them* to remove the "monuments of idolatry," they will know how to dispose of *their allies afterwards*, and the removal of "all false worships" will follow, as a matter of course.

The doctrine of the Reformed Presbyterian Church is notoriously opposed to the civil and religious liberty guaranteed by the American Constitutions. Yet they are held to be *sound in the faith*, by their brethren of the General Assembly. What does this prove? The Dutch Reformed Church, another head of the original hydra of intolerance, the representative of which is the gentleman's colleague, holds the same anti-American doctrine that I have pointed out in the Confession of Faith. All of them hold, as a tenet revealed by Almighty God, that magistrates of this Republic are, (or rather *ought* to be,) "nursing fathers to the Church." The Dutch Confession says :—"*And their office is not only to have regard unto, and to watch for the welfare of the civil state; but also, that they protect the sacred ministry; and* THUS *may* REMOVE *all idolatry and* FALSE WORSHIP, *that the kingdom of anti-Christ may be* THUS *destroyed, and the kingdom of Christ be thus promoted."*(1) "THUS"—*i. e.*, by the "nursing fathers," the MAGISTRATES!!.... "Wherefore," says this *liberal* and charitable document, "*we detest all* ANABAPTISTS *and other seditious people,* &c."(2) And why detest the "*Anabaptists?*" Because *they* denied that the magistrates had any right to meddle with the rights of conscience. For this, they are "detested," and ranked with "seditious people."

Now, I would leave it to any man of sound mind, and impartial judgment, in the United States, to say, whether these several tenets of the Presbyterian creed are not pregnant with all that is destructive of religious liberty, and the rights of conscience. Their creed is not, indeed, as arrogantly intolerant in the *letter*, as it *was* before the rights of men, proclaimed at the period of American Independence, obliged them to curtail its tyrannical prétensions. But the gentleman reckons without his host, when he represents me admitting, that it "is *now* right." He asks why the Dutch Reformed Church, and the Covenanters, were not obliged to change *their* persecuting principles, as well as their brethren of the General Assembly. I know no reason, except that they appear to have been more consistent, and less *time-serving*. They seem to have felt that it was too late in the day, to persuade the world, that Presbyterianism *could be other* than a persecuting creed. They judged rightly; for at this day *they* would be trusted with the guardianship of civil and religious liberty, just as fast, and as far, as those who thought it more advisable to hide the more ugly features of their religion, in hypocritical conformity with the shiftings of the political gale.

The gentleman wishes me to *repeat* my refutation of assertions against the Catholic faith. I refer the reader to my vindication during the first six evenings. He says that "Father Green" carried his musket during the Revolution. To which I reply, that for this he deserves well of his country. But Catholics did the same. The Catholic armies and officers of France and Poland helped "Father Green" to *survive the day of battle.* The gentleman says, what is unfounded in fact, when he represents the said "Father Green" as being "hateful" to me. He is to me an object of great indifference; and, I trust, that I can live without *hating* any one.

It will be time enough for the gentleman to call on the Catholics to change their *creed*, when he shall have proven that they ever held, as "a tenet of faith or morals," any of the avowed doctrines of the Westminster Confession of Faith on the subject of domineering over the religious rights of other denominations. The doctrines of the Catholic Church are as immutable as the truths of God. Men *professing* those doctrines have, sometimes,

(1) Page 486.   (2) Ibid.

persecuted, but their faith did not require them to do so; they would have been better Catholics if they had left it alone. But the Presbyterians cannot comply with the *revealed tenets* of HIS FAITH, without being a persecutor. Here is the difference.

The gentleman characterizes my charging " theocracy on Presbyterians," and indeed, " on all the Calvinistic sects," as an instance of "*audacity in assertion.*" By this, it is plain, that he is ignorant of the history of his own Church. Is it not known to every man of information, that Calvin and Knox justified their shedding of blood, by claiming for *their magistrates* the rights and duties exercised by the magistrates under the old law ? Nay, is not the present Confession of Faith crammed with texts and references to the same effect ? Is it not on this principle that they claim a divine right to " burn our graven images with fire," and to " remove all false worship ?" I should not wonder any more to find the gentleman ignorant, as he is, of Catholic doctrine, when he is so palpably unacquainted with his own.

The opinions of Robinson and De Pradt, two enemies of the Catholic religion, are of as much weight in the argument as his own opinion. He tells us, on the contrary, that European Presbyterians were great democrats. The attestations of history are, that they were invariably *seditious* under the civil governments of *other denominations*, and as invariably *tyrants* when *other denominations were under them.* The dethronement and violent death of Charles I., and the penalty of imprisonment, for reading the Episcopal Common Prayer Book, are proofs of their character under this double aspect.

The gentleman, unable to find facts for the vindication of his cause, calls in Hooker and Bancroft, two zealous Protestants, to say a good word for Calvin and for Calvinists. This proves, that the evidence of facts is felt to be strong against the culprit. But the audience will judge of them by their *deeds* and avowed *principles*, and not by the flourishes of rhetoric employed by their friends. The gentleman could have made *almost* as good a panegyric himself.

I showed, in my last speech, that the doctrine of " PREDESTINATION, as held by Presbyterians, has an adverse bearing on the civil and religious rights of all other denominations of Christians. And the gentleman answers my argument by asking me to explain a text of Scripture for him ! This shows that he understands the force of the argument, and cannot meet it. Then let it remain unanswered, to teach others, that when Presbyterians talk about " civil and religious liberty," they ought to be acquainted with their own doctrine, and not rush into a position in which they cannot help appearing a little ridiculous.

But though he cannot meet the argument, he can quote doggerel ribaldry, abusive of the Catholic religion and practices. This, however, is no argument—and the audience know it. The infidels can write and utter many stupid witticisms against Christ and his religion, without being able to affect the solidity of Christianity. So with the gentleman; he has studied Catholic Theology, as far as the "inquisition," "hocus-pocus," "Tetzel, and the sale of indulgences—" and few of the clique to which he belongs, have gone farther. Macintosh's testimony is like that of Hooker and Bancroft—*opinions* —mere *Protestant* opinions.

The gentleman states, as *facts*, that St. Augustine, and the flower of the Catholic Church, held the Presbyterian doctrine on what are called in that system of fatalism, "the decrees of God." Now the Presbyterian doctrine is that God "*foreordained* WHATSOEVER *comes to pass*."(1) Hence, since evil—murder, adultery, calumny, crime of every description, "come to pass," it follows according to this doctrine, that God has "*foreordained*" them. And he tells us that Augustine and the flower of the Catholic Church held this *blasphemous* and dangerous principle! That many of the Reformers held it, I admit, but their doctrines have been *reformed* in their turn, by their successors. And the only denomination, that I know, who have not become ashamed of the avowal of this article, are the high-toned Presbyterians. I defy the proof, that it is held by the other denominations of Protestants, whom he has mentioned.

He says that that the "Presbyterian creed" avows that all men are to be protected in the exercise of their religion, "whether true or *false*." Yes, but what comes of the second commandment in the mean time? The State had determined that all religions should be protected. But when, as Dr. Ely says, we shall have a "Christian party in politics," and a "sound Presbyterian for our chief magistrate—" then we shall learn the meaning of that divine precept of the decalogue, that obliges the Presbyterians, "according to each one's place and calling, to REMOVE *all false worship and all the monuments of idolatry*." *This is the kind* of "protection" which Presbyterianism never failed to afford when it had the power—as I shall prove in the sequel of this argument. The concluding portion of the gentleman's speech does not deserve a reply.

(1) Confession of Faith, page 321.

"Is the Presbyterian Religion, in any or all of its principles or doctrines, opposed to civil or religious liberty?"

AFFIRMATIVE II.—MR. BRECKINRIDGE.

MR. PRESIDENT:—

NOTHING is farther from my intention than "to insult" the Rev. gentleman by calling him a *Papist.* It is only calling things by their *proper names.* On this side of the Atlantic, the temper of the times and the spirit of the people, make it advisable to keep the Roman monarchy out of view. But in Papal (I beg pardon) "*Catholic*" Europe, they glory in the very title which Mr. H. rejects with scorn. Baronius, the great historian of Rome, says (in his Martyrology,) glorying in the name " *The modern heretics, call Catholics* PAPISTS.: *certainly they could not give them a more glorious title. Let it therefore be our praise while living, and our epitaph when dead, ever to be called papists.*"—And Gother perpetuates the sanction of this name, by calling his book "THE PAPIST MISREPRESENTED." What shall we call him? *A Catholic?* But that were to give up the whole question in debate between him and Protestants; for the name imports that his is the *universal*, and therefore *the only true church; and that, without its faith, none can be saved!* shall we admit this? The canon-law which is binding on every priest and member upon earth goes still farther, and expressly excludes from salvation all who are not *subject to the Pope. Omnes Christi fideles de necessitate salutis subsunt Romano Pontifici, qui utrumque gladium habet a nemine autem judicatur.* (1) (The book is now in my hands, and is the property of a Roman Catholic Priest.) "*It is necessary to the salvation of all the faithful in Christ, that they be subject to the Pope of Rome, who holds both swords; but is himself judged of no man.*" Here in *one* sentence it is declared, 1, That *all who are not papists perish:* 2, That the Pope has control of *civil* as well as of *religious* affairs: 3, Yet that he is *above all human jurisdiction.* Shall we not then call his *servant* and *priest* by his name? Truly, Mr. President, I think the gentleman ought to carry his *shame* to the thing *signified*, and not stop at the *name.* He has much more reason to be ashamed of the title of "*Jesuit*," in which he *glories*, calling it "*a compliment*," and this too in the face of all the disclosures made by me on that subject!

(1) Extrav. tit. viii. chap. i.

It is but too evident, from the tone of the gentleman's remarks, on my account of the *origin* of this Controversy, that he feels their force not a little. His attacks on the Presbyterian Church at large, are most virulent and bitter. It is hard to say, whether there be a greater *dearth* of *argument*, or profusion of ferocious scandal. "*He draws upon his imagination,* and *his passions, for his facts —and on his memory for his wit.*" "Fools"—"Hypocritical conformity to the shiftings of the political gale," &c. &c., flow with elegant ease from the refined and lordly priest, "*in* WHOSE PERSON" (according to his Catechism,) WE VENERATE THE POWER AND PERSON OF OUR LORD JESUS CHRIST." What a contrast!

From the fact, that it was at his own instance that the "Presbyterian Religion" was brought under review at this time, we may learn how sincere he is in charging us with wishing to deprive *Papists* of their rights, by freely examining their principles. On this whole subject, Dr. Beecher, whom the gentleman seems most cordially to hate and fear, has well expressed the feelings of Presbyterians, when he says, in a recent publication:

"But have not the Catholics just as good a right to their religion as other denominations have to theirs?" I have said so. I not only admit their equal rights, but insist upon them; and am prepared to defend their rights as I am those of my own and other Protestant denominations. The Catholics have a perfect right to proselyte the nation to their faith if they are able to do it. But I too have the right of preventing it if I am able. They have a right freely to propagate their opinions and arguments; and I too have a right to apprise the nation of their political bearings on our republican institutions. They have a right to test the tendencies of Protestanism by an appeal to history: and I, by an appeal to history, have a right to illustrate the coincidence between the political doctrines and the practice of the Catholic Church, and to show that always they have been hostile to civil and religious liberty. The Catholics claim and exercise the liberty of animadverting on the doctrines and doings of Protestants, and we do not complain of it;—and why should they or their friends complain that we in turn should animadvert on the political maxims and doings of the Catholic Church? Must Catholics have all the liberty—their own and ours too? Can they not endure the reaction of free inquiry? Must we lay our hand on our mouth in their presence, and stop the press?—Let them count the cost, and such as cannot bear the scrutiny of free inquiry, return where there is none; for though we would kindly accommodate them in all practicable ways, we cannot surrender our rights for their accommodation."

But the gentleman denies that other Protestant denominations in the United States participate with Presbyterians in their views and feelings about popery, except as *dupes*. He owns that "*these denominations may have been used by Presbyterians to stir up this* fanatical excitement." He is certainly very complimentary to them! He admits that the Reformed Dutch Church, which he styles " another head of the original hydra of intolerance, the representative of which is the gentleman's colleague," (Dr. Brownlee, whom popery has reason to mourn was ever born,) is in harmony with us. This is surely no mean ally. He admits also, that " our step-brethren, the Congregationalists of New England," are with us. They are of themselves a *nation ;* and the *cradle of liberty* is in their midst. But the naughty Yankees will not let the Pope *rock* it, or put the spirit of liberty (nursed in it,) to sleep, and *Mr. Hughes* is very *angry* at it—What a pity!! But does the gentleman doubt the feelings of American Episcopalians? Let him ask Bishop McIlvaine, or the Gambier Observer, or the Episcopal (Philadelphia) Recorder. Does he doubt the feelings of the Baptist Church: or the Methodist Episcopal Church? surely the " Catholic Herald" does not exchange with the " Christian Advocate," or the " Christian Watchman." If the gentleman will bring me the certificate of one *Baptist* or one *Methodist minister of Christ, in the United States,* who believes that *the Roman Catholic doctrines, as a system, are favourable to civil or religious liberty,* I will then own that, out of many thousands, I have mistaken *one.* The gentleman will remember Wesley! His views are *strong,* but they have never been answered. In letter No. 15, of our late Controversy, the gentleman charged that celebrated man with *intolerance,* and tried to prove it, by a garbled extract, *plucked out* of its connexions. In a subsequent letter, I cited the whole paragraph, it is as follows:

" With persecution I have nothing to do; I persecute no man for his religious principles. Let there be as boundless a freedom in religion as any man can conceive. But this does not touch the point; I will set religion, true or false, out of the question. Yet I insist upon it that no government, not Roman Catholic, ought to tolerate men of the Roman Catholic persuasion. I prove this by a plain argument, let him answer it that can : that no Roman Catholic does, or can give security for his allegiance or peaceable behaviour, I prove thus: It is a Roman Catholic maxim established not by *private* men, but by a *public council,* that ' *no faith is to be kept with heretics.'* This has been *openly avowed* by the Council of Constance; but it never was *openly disclaimed.* Whether private persons avow or disavow it, it is a fixed maxim of the Church of Rome. But as long as it is so, nothing can be more plain than that the members of that church, can give no reasonable security to any government, for their allegiance or peaceable behaviour. (Here follow the words quoted by Mr. Hughes.) *Therefore they ought not to be tolerated by any government, Protestant, Mahometan, or Pagan.* (The author proceeds.) You may say, ' nay, but they will take an oath of allegiance.' True, five hundred oaths; but the maxim, ' no faith is to be kept with heretics' sweeps them all away as a spider's web. So that still, no governors, that are not Roman Catholics, can have any security of their allegiance. The power of granting pardons for all sins, past, present, and to come, is, and has been for many centuries, one branch of his (the Pope's) spiritual power. But those who acknowledged him to have this spiritual power, can give no security for their allegiance, since they believe the Pope can pardon rebellions, high treasons, and all other sins whatever. The power of dispensing with any promise, oath, or vow, is another branch of the spiritual power of the Pope. All who acknowledge his spiritual power must acknowledge this. But whoever acknowledges the dispensing power of the Pope, can give no security for his allegiance to any government. Nay, not only the Pope, but even a priest has the power to pardon sins. This is an essential doctrine of the Church of Rome, but they that acknowledge this cannot possibly give any security for their allegiance to any government. Oaths are no security at all, for the priest can pardon both perjury and high treason. Setting, then, religion aside, it is plain that, upon principles of reason, no government ought to tolerate men who cannot give any security to that government for their allegiance and peaceable behaviour.... Would I wish, then, the Roman Catholics to be persecuted? I never said or hinted any such thing. I abhor the thought; it is foreign from all I have preached and wrote these fifty years. But I would wish the Romanists in England, (I had no others in view,) to be treated with the same lenity that they have been these sixty years; to be allowed both civil and religious liberty; but not permitted to undermine ours." (2)

While Wesley disclaims persecution, he insists that popery "undermines civil and religious liberty" if allowed its genuine influences.

Now the American system is one of unqualified and universal *protection*, and is more than *toleration;* and we glory in it, just as it is. But we hold that no consistent Roman Catholic can be ex animo, an admirer of the American system. The people, happily false to popery, present many noble examples of devoted freemen. The *priests*, they are the *monarchists;* they are the *hierarchy of Rome;* they are the church, the foes of *divine truth*, and *human liberty.* In these views, we repeat it, American Protestants as a body agree.

The gentleman's rejoinder to my argument "on the decrees of God"—as he calls the *doctrine*, halts to the last degree. His previous position was that the doctrine of *election* led to *immorality*—and to the destruction of a due regard for the rights of other men; and therefore was opposed to civil and religious liberty. In reply, I forbore to discuss the *truth* of these doctrines, as out of place; but yet presented a *few passages* of God's word, by way of *nuts* for his *infallible interpreter*, begging, in passing, an explanation of their sense. These passages (see my last

(2) See Wesley's Works, vol. v. p. 817, 818, 826.)

speech) assert that *moral liberty* is *secured by the decrees of God;* and are therefore direct rebutters to his false logic. And what does he say ? " I showed in my last speech that the doctrine of predestination, as held by Presbyterians, has an adverse bearing on the civil and religious rights of all other denominations of Christians. And the gentleman answers my argument by asking me to explain a text of Scripture for him ! This shows that he understands the force of the argument, and cannot meet it." But with all this bravado, what has he done? I appealed to *history* in proof of the *fact that* "Calvinistic denominations" and "Calvinistic nations," were foremost in the ranks of the *free* and *prosperous* and *virtuous.* Did he deny it? Did he disprove it? I have already shown abundantly that popery is the parent of *vice,* and vice in its vilest forms; so that if the argument to immorality is of any weight, as I think it is of much, his logic rebounds on his cause; and *history* is witness that his principles have ruined it. Tacitly admitting that the denominations and nations enumerated by me, were signalized by their liberty and virtue, he makes the only effort possible to disengage himself, by denying that they held the doctrines of "the decrees," and "predestination." "The only denomination that I know, who have not become ashamed of the avowal of this article, are the high-toned Presbyterians. I defy the proof that it is held by the other denominations of Protestants whom he has mentioned." To the proof then we go. The XVIIth Article of the Episcopal Church, while it wisely guards against the torture and perversion of this doctrine, is *fully* Calvinistic. " Of *Predestination and election.*" "*Predestination to life is the everlasting purpose of God, whereby (before the foundations of the world were laid,) he hath constantly decreed by his counsel, secret to us,* to deliver from curse and damnation those whom he *hath chosen* in Christ out of mankind, and to bring them by Christ to everlasting salvation, as *vessels made* to honour. Wherefore, they which he endued with so excellent a benefit of God, *be called according to God's purpose,* by his spirit working in due season; they, through grace obey the calling; they be justified freely; they be made sons of God by adoption; they be made like the image of his only begotten son Jesus Christ; they walk religiously in good works; and at length, by God's mercy, they attain to everlasting felicity." Pray is this no " proof?" It is ample proof that the *doctrine is Episcopal;* and it closes with a charming refutation of the gentleman's reasoning, when he says the doctrine leads to immorality. Here, as in our Confession, it is declared, and facts prove it, that the doctrine *calls for,* and its belief produces, *good works.*

When he denies that the Baptists hold this doctrine, he only exposes his ignorance. Let him ask Gill, Fuller, Robert Hall, Carey, Ward, and their standards of faith, for the conviction which he desires. He *cautiously* denies that Augustine held this doctrine. Proof (1)—"*We are therefore to understand calling, as pertaining to the elect; not that they were elected because they believed;* but that they were elected in order that they might believe. God himself makes this sufficiently plain, when he says, *ye have not chosen me but I have chosen you.* For if they were elected because they believed, they would *themselves elect* by *believing* in him; so that they would *merit election.* But he takes all this away, when he says, 'ye have not chosen me, but I have chosen you.' They have not chosen (non elegerunt) Him, in order that he might choose them; but he chose, (elegit eos) them that they might choose him; because his *mercy* prevented them, by grace, and not by debt. Therefore, He chose them *out of the world,* when they lived in the flesh, but He *chose them in himself before the foundation of the world.* For what does the Apostle say, "as he hath chosen us in Him before the foundation of the world."

Again; (2) "*No one cometh to Christ unless it be given to him; and it is given to those who were chosen in Him before the foundation of the world.*" (3)

We need not enter into the proof as to the *twelve creeds* of the Reformers; for the gentleman *admits* that "*some*—" of them held it. He *knows* that nearly "all" *did.* It is true, *some* of their descendants have abandoned these views. But look at Scotland, England, Ireland, Holland, and the United States of North America, for the liberty, science, and piety of those lands. Are they not the most free, enlightened and virtuous of nations? and are they not the most *Calvinistic:*—and are not the *Calvinists* among them abreast of any other population, and far, far ahead of the "Catholic," population, in intelligence, and piety, and good order? Again, I say LET HISTORY REPLY.

But the gentleman, in calling this "*a blasphemous and dangerous principle,*" treads on delicate ground; for, strange as it may appear, the *best part* of the Council of Trent (if such a term be not a contradiction) held to this very doctrine; and the divided conventicle actually trimmed their *creed* to heal the breach that was threatened to their *infallibilities.* The Twelfth Chapter, sixth Session, in a scared way, admits the truth of this doctrine, in the following terms: "*That the rash confidence of predestination is to be avoided. Let no man, while he continues in this mortal state, so far presume respecting the hidden mystery of divine predestination, as to conclude that he is certainly one of the predestinate; as if it were true that a justified man cannot*

---

(1) Book I. Chap. 17. tom. 7. *Of The Predestination of Saints.*
(2) Tom. 7. chap. 10. "*Of Perseverance,*" &c.
(3) Neminem venire ad Christum nisi fuerit ei datum; et eis dari qui in eo electi sunt ante constitutionem mundi.—See at large Corpus et Syntagma Confessionum, &c. on Augustine.

sin any more, or that if he sin he can assure himself of repentance ; for no one can know whom God hath chosen for himself, unless by special revelation." Here the *truth* of the doctrine is acknowledged.

Father Paul (referred to in my last speech, but cautiously *shunned* by his papal brother Hughes) on the same subject, viz. predestination and election, that man doeth nothing, but all is in the will of God ; thus writes :—" In examining the first of these questions, the opinions were divers : the most *esteemed divines among them* thought IT to be Catholic, and the *contrary, heresy,* because the good school-writers, St. Thomas, Scotus, and *the rest, do so think ; that is, that God, before the creation, out of the mass of mankind, hath elected by his only and mere mercy, some for glory, for whom he hath prepared effectually the means to obtain it,* which is *called* to PREDESTINATE. That their number is certain, and determined." The writer goes on to say, that they quoted in proof, the ninth chapter of Romans, in the case of Esau and Jacob, and the example of *the potter and clay,* and that the apostle calls "divine *predestination* and *reprobation* the *height and depth of wisdom unsearchable and incomprehensible . . .*" " They added divers passages of the Gospel of John, and *infinite authorities from* St. AUGUSTINE, *because that saint wrote nothing in his old age,* but in *favour of this doctrine."* (1) On page 202 he adds, that after the decree was adopted the Dominicans and Franciscans wrote laborious controversies, showing directly opposite senses to it ; and, that when it was sent to the Pope, and he gave it to his friars and learned men for consultation, *" it was approved by them because every one might understand it in his own sense."*

From this circle of proofs then, it appears, that the doctrine "of divine decrees," as held by the Presbyterians, is held now, by the great body of the professed Protestant Churches, in all those countries most remarkable for the freedom of their institutions, and the diffusive intelligence of the people ; that Augustine *did* teach most *clearly* the same doctrine, and that the Council of Trent itself gave it a *scanty* existence, in its decrees, and enacted an evasive canon on the subject, in order to have unity without candour or sense.

As to this doctrine, I am well aware, that many excellent men, and some Christian denominations, differ with us. But they have the candour to own, that it makes us not the *less* respectful of the rights of *man,* and of *the obligations* of religion. Indeed, they have, many of them, paid a generous homage to the virtues of "Calvinists," as we are sometimes called. It was to this *purpose* we cited the testimony of the great Hooker, who was NO *Presbyterian,* of the elegant and impartial Bancroft, *a Unitarian,* and of Sir James Macintosh, a great statesman, and *not* a

---

(1) Hist. Counc. Trent, Book II, p. 196. Lond. edit. 1576.

Presbyterian. Such testimony to *facts*, are not "*mere opinions;*" and from learned, impartial, and virtuous men of other denominations, have great weight. Besides, this was called for by the dishonourable course pursued by Mr. Hughes. He agreed in " the *rules*" to confine himself to "*The Presbyterian Church under the General Assembly in the United States.*" But he soon found *nothing* in our standards *against liberty;* and he flew to European Presbyterians. I followed him, admitting that *our ancestry had erred* as to the *rights of conscience*, (he falsely says, I owned that *persecution* was a *part* of Presbyterianism in all time till now.) I owned, that formerly Presbyterians had *persecuted*, but *his Church exceedingly more*. Presbyterians had, from the first, been the leading advocates for liberty, and distinguished for good morals. In *proof*, I brought the testimony of *other* denominations, and of statesmen of *no* denomination, and even of *Roman Catholics*. For this reason I called in *Swift*, and *Dryden*, a " Catholic," as well as Hooker, Bancroft, and Sir James Macintosh. And now, he says, they were but "*opinions.*" And pray, is his *doctrine* any more? I brought *our standards*. He says, *they* were *altered* to suit the country. Very well. I ask him to do the same with *his* system. But he cannot, will not; it *is infallible*. And so it stands. The papal system *cannot become liberal*, and they will not renounce it; and here we join issue—here we fix our final opposition to it, as anti-American, as well as anti-Christian.

The abuse which the gentleman pours upon Dr. Miller, speaks *well* for the doctor's *labours*, for truth and liberty. Mr. Hughes seems to covet the honour of being in such *good* company. But it is not for *porcupines* to fight with *lions;* nor *rats* to demolish the *stately pillars* of the Church.

I confess, it is more appropriate *game* to go after Dr. Ely. And yet, how has our Jesuit friend garbled even Dr. Ely! He has left out, as usual, the explanatory parts, and *uprooting* from their connexions *other* parts, has falsified *his* sense, and then charged the *perversion* on the Presbyterian Church. For example, Dr. Ely says, " *We do not say that true, or even pretended Christianity, shall be made a constitutional test of admission to office, but we do affirm, that Christians may, in their elections, lawfully prefer the avowed friends of the Christian religion, to Turks, Jews, and Infidels.*" But Robert Bellarmine says, (1) "But when, in reference to heretics, thieves, and other wicked men, there arises this question in particular, '*shall they be exterminated?*' it is to be considered, according to the meaning of our Lord, whether that can be done without injury to the good; and if that be possible, they are, without doubt, to be EXTIRPATED,

---

(1) Book III. Chap. 23, of Laics—his works being *approved and published by authority* of the Pope, except that he condemned him for *not being strong enough* on the temporal power of the Pope.

(exterpandi sunt proculdubio.) Dr. Ely says, (speaking of a Christian President,) "Let him be a man of a good moral character, and let him profess to believe in, and advocate the Christian religion, and *we can all support him.* At one time he will be a *Baptist;* at another an *Episcopalian;* at another a *Methodist;* at another a *Presbyterian* of the American, Scotch, Irish, Dutch, or German stamp, and always a friend to our common Christianity." I suppose, his being a *Christian,* would not be a *radical* objection in the mind of Mr. Hughes! The sermon was surely a silly production. But while Mr. Hughes cries "wolf," "wolf," over *it*, the present Pope says, (and I beg him to notice it as it has been before presented, and *not* noticed,) "NOR CAN WE AUGUR MORE CONSOLING CONSEQUENCES TO RELIGION AND THE GOVERNMENT, FROM THE ZEAL OF SOME TO SEPARATE THE CHURCH FROM THE STATE, AND TO BURST THE BOND WHICH UNITES THE PRIESTHOOD TO THE EMPIRE. FOR, IT IS CLEAR, THAT THIS UNION IS DREADED BY THE PROFANE LOVERS OF LIBERTY, ONLY BECAUSE IT HAS NEVER FAILED TO CONFER PROSPERITY ON BOTH."

Here the head of the universal and only true Church announces, in a public letter, addressed to "Catholics," over the whole world, that it is a *profane love of liberty to oppose the union of Church and state,* and that *said union* is necessary to the *prosperity of religion and government!* Will Mr. Hughes meet this? Will he explain it, by the side of his inference from Dr. Ely's proposal to form "*a Christian party* in politics."

Dr. Wilie is next introduced. He is first assailed for his opinions; then devolved on us; then praised for his candour. Dr. Wilie is an able and a good man. I wish that "a drop of oil" from "the good olive trees," that I believe feed his soul, might fall on the husky conscience of his *wily* eulogist. Dr. Wilie belongs not to our communion. His views, as uttered in the sermon adduced, on the question now before us, are very much at issue with our *standards. We are* not responsible for them. We deeply regret them. They greatly surprise us. Mr. Hughes, however, as usual, has distorted them. But Dr. Wilie, with whom, I presume, on all *other* leading points I should essentially agree, "*is of age,*" and will, if he think it worth while, "*speak* for himself."

And then for "*The Dutch Reformed Church.*" I refer Mr. Hughes to my gallant "colleague," whose heavy blows yet ring on the broken bosses of the *three priests,* who united against him in New York; but who treated him anon as my *discreet* friend did Mr. M'Calla, profiting by the venerable maxim:—

"He that fights, and runs away,
May live to fight another day."

Of the *caricature* which he has given us of the meeting at Mr. M'Calla's church, I will only say, that though the gentleman *seems* to have been *present*, he did not *accept* the *invitation* publicly given, to any *priest*, to defend his cause; and that the efforts made to disturb that meeting, plainly prove what "Catholics" *would* do, if they *could*.

Mr. Smith is *now* despised. When he was a *Popish priest*, as his testimonials fully show, he was *much esteemed*. Now he is *blackened*. The truth is, his "two-penny" sheets are making, week by week, such disclosures of what he saw among *nuns* and *priests*, that I do not wonder Mr. Hughes "*despises even the day of small things.*" The gentleman excuses us from the charge of *actually putting the torch to the Convent;* but he still insists that we are labouring to excite "*a disposition and efforts to persecute Catholics.*" I need not, I will not stoop to repel such malignant but powerless thrusts. But I will say this: that there is a *certain kind of houses*, which the Pope used to license at Rome, which the "boys and mobs" in America, taking Judge Lynch's laws, sometimes *pull down*, not as *Protestants* against *popery*, but as enemies to *gross immoralities*, which we cannot name.

When he comes to Mr. Jefferson, the gentleman says, "He (Mr. Jefferson) depended for his knowledge (of the Presbyterians) *not on speculation, but on facts.*" But did not De Pradt, and Robinson, and Hooker, and Bellarmine, have "facts" also? yet their's were only "opinions;" and De Pradt, and the Parliament of Paris, were "*Infidels,*" and in both cases, he told us they had *no weight;* you see his *consistency*. The gentleman ought to have a *better memory*, or not so *bad spirit*. But we proceed: Mr. Jefferson has shared the fate of *all authors* that pass through Mr. Hughes's *household expurgatory Index*. He gives the *part* that suits his case, "*for* the rest," as he says, let it go to the winds. Just *above* Mr. Hughes's second quotation, Mr. Jefferson says of Paul, "OF *this band of dupes and imposters, Paul was the great Coryphæus, and first corrupter of the doctrines of Jesus.*" You see we are in good *company:* and you can judge how impartial he is towards us in other matters. Mr. Hughes *omits* a passage about the *Trinity*, and begins his citation in the midst of a paragraph, of which the following is an integral part: "The history of our University you know so far. An opposition in the mean time, has been gotten up. The *serious enemies are the priests of the different religious sects*, to whose spells on the human mind, its improvement is ominous. Their pulpits are now resounding with denunciations against the appointment of Dr. Cooper, whom they charge as a *monotheist*, in opposition to their *tritheism*. *Hostile* as these sects are in every point to *one another*, they *unite* in maintaining their mystical theology, against those who believe there is one God only." Then comes in the quotation by Mr. Hughes, the *reason* for the omission is obvious. Mr. Jefferson includes "*priests of the different religious sects;*" Mr. Hughes wished to *confine* it to *Presbyterians*. Query? Did Mr. Jefferson mean to exclude *Popish priests* from any claim to be " *Christians?*" Again. When he speaks of the "*holy inquisition*," does he intend to say that Presbyterians ever had one, or that they *originated* it, and *kept it alive* in Rome, and Spain, &c.? The tyranny of Rome is *incorporated* into the *elements* of language. If we would express *cruelty*, we go to the *abstraction* of Rome's *inquisition*. If *fraud*, we borrow *Jesuit* from Rome's magazine; so that Mr. Jefferson, in abusing Presbyterians, and Mr. Hughes in quoting him, unconsciously publishes the *shame* and *oppression* of the papal system !

The quotation from Mr. Jefferson, (see my last speech) on *emigration* from Europe, has been *put by*, but not *answered*. We do not object to worthy emigrants. We welcome the patriot, the persecuted Poles. They come loving liberty, and we trust long to enjoy it. The Poles, by the way, as a *nation*, think very differently of *the Jesuits*, from Mr. Hughes. The Jesuits began their ruin: they know it, and judge accordingly. But to return. The emigrants we dread, are such as "dig our canals," and "rail-roads," and make mobs by way of chorus, and keep the land in commotion, wherever they are: such as are now figuring in Baltimore, living at the *public charge*, and enjoying trial by jury, for riot and bloodshed on the Baltimore rail-road. The *poor*, the well-principled, intelligent, industrious *poor*, we welcome and confide in.

Let such freemen multiply in our midst. But let them not be priest-ridden, degraded men, who think it a crime to read the Bible: a merit to hate a Protestant: and that liberty is freedom from law and order.

Washington said to the American people, in his Farewell Address, "*Against the insidious wiles of foreign influence, (I conjure you to believe me, my fellow-citizens,) the jealousy of a free people, ought to be* CONSTANTLY AWAKE, *since history and experience prove that foreign influence is one of the most baneful foes of a republican government.*" May we profit by his oracular and paternal warning !

There is a very interesting and important document connected with our *colonial history*, which speaks volumes on this subject, especially in reference to *papal emigrants and influence*. I quote from the *Address of the Continental Congress to the People of Great Britian, Oct.* 21, 1774. (1)

" And by another act, the dominion of Canada is to be so extended, modelled, and governed, as that by being disunited from us, detached from our interests, by civil, as well as religious pre-

---

(1) See *Journal of Cont. Cong., in* 4 *vols.* 1774 to 1788 vol. i. p. 30. See Life and Writings of John Jay, 2 vols. octavo, New York—J. & J. Harper—1833. Vol. i. p. 473. See also p. 382-3, Oct. 19—" Dated by paragraphs." See p. 382.

judices, *by their numbers daily swelling with Catholic emigrants from Europe,* and by their devotion to an administration so friendly to their religion, that they might become formidable to us, and, on occasion, be fit instruments, in the hands of power, to reduce these ancient, free, PROTESTANT colonies, to the same state of slavery with themselves.   *   *   *   *   *

"Nor can we suppress our astonishment, that a British Parliament should ever consent to establish in that country A RELIGION THAT HAS DELUGED YOUR ISLAND IN BLOOD, and dispersed IMPIETY, BIGOTRY, PERSECUTION, MURDER, AND REBELLION, *through every part of the world.*"

We see then, what our fathers felt and feared, *long before Presbyterians began to excite the nation* (as Mr. Hughes has said) to *persecute Catholics.* Who were *they* that uttered these strong opinions? Not a General Assembly of the Presbyterian Church! Not a convention of Protestant preachers! But *a Congress of the Colonies, on the eve of the American Revolution.* Let us see were the gentleman will place these patriots! Let us hear to "*what category*" this document belongs! Surely, if Presbyterians are mistaken in this matter, they are not *alone.* These fears are strangely sustained by our patriot fathers.

In reply to the challenge for proof of immense sums being expended in this country for propagating popery by foreign despots, I need only refer you to my extended disclosures already made on that topic in the history of the *Leopold Foundation,* and the acknowledgment of *Catholic* documents, both in America and Germany, as already exhibited. Our *foreign missions,*" he complains, drain the country of money; also, "*the American Bible Society:*" and this he professes, as a *political economist,* and boasts that Catholics send money *into* the country. But political economists tell us that such monies, say on Bibles, made at home, and circulated chiefly at home, directly quicken trade; and even foreign expenditures do the same. But we would not complain of "Catholic despots" sending us *good* money, if it were not that they send *with it bad* men, and for *bad* uses. But, surely, the gentleman forgets, when he ventures on the ground of "*political economy.*" It is estimated that in the states of Eroupe there are a million of different sorts of ecclesiastics; who are usually not *taxable,* though, as a body, they command vast wealth (as in South America), and who are, as to public service in the state, *idle,* and, if *fathers,* not *husbands;* and "most of this *million* subsist on the plunder of the people." Again; the number of monasteries and nunneries in popish countries is incredible. They are *seats* of idleness, if not *sinks* of corruption. It was at one time boasted that there were forty-four thousand in the empire of the Pope. Again; nearly *one-third* part of the year is wasted, in papal countries, in feasts, and fasts, and worshipping saints, &c. &c.; all which is sunk to the state, in *money,* while it also corrupts the *morals* of the people. The *treasure* sunk in *kind*, in adorning images, chapels, cathedrals, and in sacred vessels, &c. is immense. This is lost to the state. The result is, that Rome, (for example) the centre of the finest country on earth, once the *greatest* city, is surrounded by boundless desolations. Italy, and Spain, and Portugal! Why are they now, degraded, enslaved, and a century behind their *sister nations?* It is popery—popery, alone, makes them decay; and, until it is destroyed, they can never rise. Popery closes on them the Bible. Popery is the *malaria* of the nations. Popery makes the very *land to decay*, while it *enslaves and destroys the soul.* I challenge a reply to these astounding facts. No. Never mention political economy again, while you love popery! And now let the gentleman visit Scotland, England, Holland—*Protestant states.* Does he see such desolations? Does he see such in North America? They abound in *papal* South America. Why? Let the gentleman inform us.

His attack on "the American Sunday School Union" is eminently fitted to disclose the aversion of popery to *universal and Bible education;* and is a lasting disgrace to its author. It is not a Presbyterian but a Protestant association. Episcopalians, Baptists, &c. share with Presbyterians equally in its control; and no book is edited by it which has not been *revised* by a committee composed of all these, as well as of Presbyterians. If, as he says, Presbyterians *give most* to it, and *labour* most for it, why I hardly know how to apologise for so atrocious a crime. But, while a *foreign priest* denounces this noble charity, what do impartial *Americans* say? At a public meeting held in our capital, during the session of Congress, in 1830, the Hon. Senator Grundy presided. William Wirt addressed to the meeting a *letter*, being sick in his chamber. William Wirt—a name dear to letters, liberty, and religion—said : " *I regret that it is not in my power to be with you this evening, that I might have united my humble efforts with those of my fellow-citizens* who will be present in advancing this great, and, as I believe, heaven-directed cause." " It has been the ignorance of the people which has so long enabled tyrants to hold the world in chains." "Viewed in a temporal and political light, merely, it deserves the strongest support of all who wish the continuance of our free and happy institutions at home." Does he who opposes such influences, sincerely love them, or really desire their "continuance ?"

The Hon. *Theodore Frelinghuysen*, the pure politician, the eloquent statesman, *himself a Sunday School teacher*, ably advocated this holy cause, saying, " *It is the most benignant enterprise of modern benevolence.*" " *He is unfaithful to his country who would seek to impair its influence.*" The President of the United States sent an apology for his absence, (having promised to be present) enclosing a donation. And, to name no more, DANIEL WEBSTER addressed the meeting, saying: "*The usefulness of Sunday Schools is universally acknowledged. Most great conceptions are simple. The present age has struck out two or three ideas, on the important subjects of education, and the diffusion of religious knowledge, partaking in a very high degree of this character. They were simple; but their application was extensive, direct, and efficacious. Of these, the leading one, perhaps, was the distribution of the Holy Scriptures without note or comment, an idea not only full of piety and duty, and of candour also, but strictly just and philosophical also. . . . . . . The object of Sunday Schools, and of the resolution now before the meeting, was, as he understood it, of similar large and liberal character. It was to diffuse the elements of knowledge, and to teach the great truths of revelation. It was to improve, to the highest of all purposes, the leisure of the Sabbath; to render its rest sacred, by thoughts turned towards the Deity, and aspiring to a knowledge of his word and will. There were other plans of benevolence about which men might differ. But it seemed to him there could be no danger of error here. If we were sure of anything, we were sure of this, that the knowledge of their Creator, their duty, and their destiny, is good for men; and that whatever, therefore, draws the attention of the young to the consideration of these objects, and enables them to feel their importance, must be advantageous to human happiness, in the highest degree, and in all worlds.*" Such is the noble testimony of this great man, this disinterested patriot—called by emphasis the champion of the American Constitution! He *was* not, *is* not, a Presbyterian. Oh! how small, and how ashamed, must a *priest of Rome* feel before the sublime conceptions, the manly rebuke, the just defence of an American layman pleading for an open Bible and universal education, against the chosen representative of the "only true Church,"—"the *exclusive* depository of God's word and ministry!!" I have looked at the gentleman's reference in vain, for the declaration charged by him on the institution—that they desire to become "*the dictators of the consciences of thousands of immortal beings.*" I believe it utterly false; or, if found in it, whenever identified, it will be seen to mean wholly another thing from what the gentleman says. I call for the reference. And as to the passage about "the political power of the country," it is a private letter from Connecticut, and only asserts, that *in ten* years, minds formed, not by *Presbyterians*, but by the *Bible*, and in *Sunday Schools*, would predominate in the country.

Will not our "Catholic" laymen, such as Mathew Carey, blush for *their priest*, who so recklessly assails such institutions? By way of a very striking *contrast*, I remind the audience of the "Inquisition," and the "Jesuits." Is it not passing strange that this gentleman can be the *apologist* of the former, and the advocate of the latter, and yet assail "*Sunday Schools?*"

But it is time for me to notice his argument, drawn from the *Larger Catechism*, on the duties required in the second commandment, which, among other things, is said to require "*the disapproving, detesting, opposing all false worship; and, according to each one's place and calling, removing it, and all monuments of idolatry.*" If I understand the reasoning, he means to charge us with holding, that *force* of some kind is a duty; or that some *method* of "*removing the monuments of idolatry,*" at war with the rights of others, is expressed. For, I suppose, he will not say, that if we *oppose false worship,* and remove these *monuments* of *idolatry,* in a constitutional way, and *without* disturbing the rights of others, this would be *wrong;* or *against* liberty, civil or religious? I am aware, however, that he has a *warm side towards these things,* which, indeed, is not to be wondered at. But he will not say that it is *persecution,* to oppose idolatry by discussion, moral influence, and prayer. The question then is, as to the *manner* of *doing it.* Does our doctrine utter, or imply tyranny? or force? or a hindrance to the free exercise of religious worship? If so, we should like to know it. So far is this from being the fact, that he has himself owned, "*that the Confession of Faith was amended,* (at the adoption of the American Constitution,) *to suit the Constitution, and the new order of things.*" What he thus admits (as "*an amendment,*") to be true, may be easily shown, by reference to all those parts of our standards, which relate to the freedom of worship, and the use of force by the civil magistrate in matters of conscience. For example: (1) "*It is the duty of civil magistrates to protect the person, and good name, of all these people; so that no person be suffered, either upon pretence of religion, or infidelity, to offer any indignity, violence, abuse, or injury, to any other person whatsoever; and to take order that all religious and ecclesiastical assemblies be held without molestation or disturbance.*" "It is the duty of civil magistrates, *as 'nursing fathers,' to protect the Church of our common Lord without giving the preference to any denomination* of Christians, above the rest." Here is surely a disclaimer of *all force.* "But the nursing fathers!"—Why, yes. Isaiah said so before us. But he ought to have known, that he would give offence to Mr. Hughes, native of Ireland, emigrant to the United States, priest of Rome, pastor of St. John's in the nineteenth century, by such a passage? Yet it is not said *our* particular church, but all Christian denominations, that the civil magistrate should protect. Religion is one of our *common* rights—and a *civil right* to be protected in it. But Mr. Hughes replies, this "*excludes us idolaters.*" No. We say "all *religious* and

---

(1) Chap. XXIII. Confession of Faith.

ecclesiastical assemblies" are to be "*protected*," though it be an anti-Christian system. But shall we, for this reason, be *silent* about their errors? May we not use the liberty of speech? It is a part of the daily worship of St. John's, and of every "Catholic" altar upon earth, whenever full service is performed, to denounce us heretics; and every time the creed of Pius IV. is said, we are excluded from salvation. But they have a right to do it; and it does not hurt us—nor do we try to *hinder* them. But shall we not use our liberty in turn, and freely inquire into these things? This is all we ask, and all we do. This is what the gentleman *dreads*—this is what his system cannot *endure*.

But he insists we are not *sincere*. That we have a secret sense, and a private purpose, which Dr. Ely has let out for lack of Jesuit cunning. If our *profession* of faith be discredited, the appeal, of course, must be *to facts*. The only one he has adduced, is, that at Boston, the riotous rable taking the *Convent* for a ********, wickedly burned it down. But these were not Presbyterians. No. But they well *deserved* to be! We appeal then to our *standards*, and, passing from them, we *appeal* to our history, in refutation of these uncandid and shallow attacks.

One thing must have struck every hearer. I mean the *dearth of matter;* when "election," and "removing all the monuments of idolatry," constitute the burden of his argument, (if such it may be called,) on which he has so long rung the changes of hopeless declamation, and ingenious sophistry.

On the other hand, have not my hours been *crowded with testimonies* against the oppressive system which he attempts to defend?

Before I close, let me notice some of the gentleman's evasions, devices, &c.

He says the Jesuits were opposed by Voltaire, and other infidels; and were therefore good; yet he cites Mr. *Jefferson* to testify to Presbyterian character.

Under the second commandment, our standards refer to Deuteronomy vii. 7., to prove that idolatry was to be abhorred, and, by all proper means, prevented. He argues, from the reference, that we hold to a *theocracy*, and to *force* as a duty. Is he sincere? Then let us turn to his own Catechism, (1) where it says, "*heretics are to be punished.*" (The translator has interpolated the word "*spiritual*," and *struck out* all *the references*.) But on turning to the honest Latin, I find, it quotes Deuteronomy xvii. 12. "*And the man that will do presumptuosly, and will not hearken unto the priest that standeth to minister there before the Lord thy God, or unto the judge, even that man shall die—and thou shall put away evil from Israel.*" If the gentleman is honest,

(1) Counc. of Trent, page 96, English edition.

then, he is forced to own, by his own reasoning on our Confession, that *his* is a *persecuting theocracy*. But, still more. It also refers, for further proof, to Romans xiii. 4. "*He beareth not the sword in vain,*" &c.; and, in the margin, it says, *Unde leges in hæreticos latæ*. *Hence laws are passed against heretics*. This, also, the *pious* translator left out. Now, this *confirms* and *interprets* the persecuting clause. Now, in our Confession there are abounding passages, which *disclaim* all purpose, or right, to enforce religious opinions; or to persecute heretics, or to require the civil power to do it; and all pretensions to be exclusively the true Church. Whereas, in the Roman Catholic standards, directly the reverse is true. It *professes* to be the *only true* Church; it *professes* that the civil power is *bound* to punish all persons "*denoted by the Church*" as heretics; it *professes* to be a theocracy, a mixed power, *commanding both swords*. And I defy the gentleman, I hereby challenge him, to bring me one passage, in all his *standards*, condemning the union of church and state; or *permitting* the *toleration* of a false religion; or the *protection* of any religion; or announcing that all religions ought to be placed by the state on an equal footing! I call on him to do it. Here, then, he adduces a passage of our standards, and construes it, (in a way which contradicts all the *other parts* of it, as he has allowed,) to mean *persecution*. Whereas I produce a passage sustained by his own use of our standards, and by many kindred parts of his, *avowing* the doctrine and the *duty* of *persecution*.

And that there may be no doubt of this, let me close with an extract from his own Cardinal Bellarmine. (1) "The spiritual power does not mingle in temporal affairs, but *permits* them to proceed in their ordinary course, *provided* they *present no obstacle* to the spiritual purpose, or are not necessary to *forward* them. But if any such thing should happen, the spiritual *power may* and *ought* to *repress* the temporal, by *every means and expedient* which she *may deem* requisite;—may change kingdoms, taking them from one and giving them to another, as the sovereign, spiritual prince may deem necessary to the *safety* of *souls*. It is not *permitted* to Christians to *tolerate* an infidel, or heretical king, if *he endeavours* to draw his subjects into *heresy;* but it belongs to the *sovereign pontiff*, who has the *care* of *religion*, to JUDGE, *whether the king does or not;* to the sovereign pontiff it consequently remains, to *decide, whether the king shall* be deposed or not."—ILLUSTRATION. King John, of England; the Pope's *interdict*, and *deposition* of the king; his doing homage to the Pope for his crown; and agreeing to pay an annual tribute to the Pope, called, from this, "Peter's Pence!" In different periods of papal despotism, not less than *sixty* emperors, kings, and princes, have

(1) Lib 5. chap. 6. De Rom. Pon.

been excommunicated, deposed, &c. by the Popes of Rome! Yet, we are told, Rome regards the rights of man!

P.S. When a Jesuit denies a Jesuit, what shall we say? There is proof positive, in the *history* of Talleyrand, that he *taught mathematics* in the state of New York. There is proof in his *character*, that he is a Jesuit.

"Is the Presbyterian Religion, in any or in all its principles or doctrines, opposed to civil or religious liberty ?"

AFFIRMATIVE III.—MR. HUGHES.

Mr. President :—

I HAVE had but little intercourse with the gentleman, except as a controversial opponent, and yet, notwithstanding the violation of all the rules that usually govern the intercourse of gentlemen, which you have witnessed in his last speech, I have reason to know that he *can be* courteous, when he is in good humour. "Papist," "Jesuit," "native of Ireland," "foreigner," and every epithet that can awaken a dormant prejudice, or excite a feeling of hatred, is employed to designate the individual whom HE HIMSELF SELECTED, as his equal in every moral quality. Still, sir, I can trace his violation of propriety to his bad humour; and I can trace his bad humour, to his bankruptancy in argument. His conduct reminds me of those disputants, who would overthrow the influence of the Saviour's preaching, *not* by *argument or reasoning*, but by saying that he "*intended* to destroy the temple," that he was a "Samaritan, and had a devil."

He represents me as attacking the reputation of individuals,—slandering the character of institutions,—"hating" this one, "fearing" that other—and above all, publishing "ferocious scandals" of the Presbyterians. But all will not do. HE has assigned my position in this Discussion, and the history of his creed and its professors furnish me with arguments to maintain it. Catholics are not in the habit of meddling with the religious concerns of other denominations; but when circumstances of the gentleman's own choice and creation, have made it my *duty* to examine the bearings of Presbyterianism on "civil and religious liberty," then the fault, if there is any, must rest on his own head. The examination of Presbyterianism is an operation to which he is evidently unaccustomed, and for which his temper is constitutionally unfitted. I am not surprised, therefore, that it should betray him into a forgetfulness of what is due to himself as a "minister of the gospel" and a refined gentleman. That he should experience pain, is natural enough. But the man who is so *ready to inflict* it on Catholics, should be prepared to endure in return. Neither should he mistake the *source* of his suffering—by making the instrument responsible for what belongs, rather, to the depth and inveteracy of the disease. I give chapter and verse for every fact stated in argument. Does he dispute my citation of authorities? It would be useless. Does he grapple with my reasoning, in deducing consequences from those facts? No, but he calls me a "Jesuit," a "papist"—and for those who will not be convinced by *this kind* of argument, there is no remedy. Least, however, that even this should go unrefuted, I shall cite a counter argument from the Rev. Mr. Nightingale, a Protestant clergyman, who says "*The reproachful epithets of 'Papists,' 'Romanist,' 'Popish,' 'Romanish,'* &c. *are no longer applied to them (Catholics)* by ANY GENTLEMAN OR SCHOLAR." (1) The gentleman says, that to call us "Catholics" "would be to give up the whole question of debate between us and Protestants." I am sorry that Protestantism has to depend *for its existence* on a *breach of politeness*—and the hope of appropriating to itself a title which *had been ours* for 1500 years previous to its existence.

He seems to think that the other Protestant denominations join the Presbyterians in the crusade against Catholics. That they believe Catholics to be in error, is easily admitted. But this does not constitute evidence in the case. The Presbyterians *alone*, so far as I know, are the only denomination who have seen their "ministers of the gospel" resigning their congregations to be saved by "God's eternal decree," in order to devote themselves to the preaching of *religious and political hatred* among citizens in a country where the *rights of all are equal*. I believe that the great body of the sober-minded Presbyterians themselves, have beheld with regret and mortification, the proceedings by which certain Rev. agitators of their sect, were fixing the attention of the country, as to what might be their ulterior object. The stories about "gunpowder plots," and "foreign conspiracies," were a little too absurd for the belief of rational and reflecting minds, such as are found in all denominations. Their very authors, I am persuaded in my heart, do not believe one word of them.

Passing over the gentleman's charges against the Catholic religion, which I have answered under the former question—passing over for the present his irrelevant matter about "Dr. Beecher," "Dr. Miller," "Dr. Ely,"—"lions," "porcupines," and "rats," —I shall proceed to the question, and the argument at once. My first argument to show, that Presbyterians hold doctrines "opposed to civil and religious liberty," was founded on their doctrine of predestination; which Calvin called the "horrible decree." I showed that any doctrine which destroyed *free-will, and transferred the responsibility of moral transgression from the* CREATURE *to the* CREATOR, whether true or false in itself, is opposed *in its*

(1) Pourtr. p. 14.

consequences, not only to morality, but to the foundation of all moral laws. But does the Presbyterian doctrine warrant such a conclusion? It certainly does. It teaches that God "FORE-ORDAINED WHATSOEVER COMES TO PASS." (1) Pass in review, then, all the crimes that have been committed since the world began, including the first and the last; and, since it is undeniable that they "HAVE come to pass," it follows, according to the Confession of Faith, that God had "fore-ordained them." And since God had "fore-ordained" them, it follows that their perpetrators *could not* avoid committing them. And since they could not avoid committing them, it follows that they had *no reason* to be sorry for them. And since they had no reason to be sorry for them, it follows that there is no motive *for exertion* to avoid them. Since, if God has "fore-ordained" them, they will happen in despite of effort. Here, therefore, is a doctrine which makes all human actions—virtuous as well as vicious—and vicious as well as virtuous, the result of God's "fore-ordination," in the carrying out of which, man is no longer a *free, moral agent*, but the mere automaton of the eternal decree. According to this it was "FORE-ORDAINED" that John Huss should be burned at Constance; and yet the gentleman charges the Council for it. But I ask him whether it was not "fore-ordained" that it should be so? *If he says it was*, then he blames the Council for *not* DEFEATING *one of God's "decrees."* *If he says it was not*, then he abandons his doctrine. But he must admit that it was. And I ask any one, whether a doctrine which tells the *offender* against the *rights of his fellow-men*, that God had "fore-ordained" the *offence*, is not a dangerous doctrine?

In answer to this, he says, that St. Augustine, the Episcopalians, and Baptists hold, and that the Council of Trent *almost* held this doctrine. I say that, with the exception of what are called *Calvinistic* Baptists, the fact is not so. St. Augustine, in the passage quoted, is speaking of election to the *grace and knowledge of Christianity*, as the original clearly shows. The Episcopalians, even in England, are known to have had, especially since the time of Archbishop Laud, "Calvinistic articles, and Arminian clergy." The doctrine was in the book, but they neither professed nor believed in it, as their *Presbyterian opponents* have been eloquent in showing. As to the Council of Trent, it taught no such impious tenet. But it is of no importance. The difficulty remains the same. A second attempt at answering, which has been made, is the citation of the *good opinion* which Hooker, and Bancroft, and Sir James Macintosh entertained of Presbyterians. This is not the question. But the question, what is the plea which this doctrine gives to wicked men *who* CHOOSE *to act upon it?* A man trained in this belief, for instance, has committed a crime. Before

(1) Page 321.

detection, he soothes his conscience by the reflection that the "eternal decree of God, foreordained" him to commit it. But he is detected, and condemned by the laws of his country. Before receiving his sentence, he pleads, in bar of judgment, that God had "foreordained" him, by an "UNCHANGEABLE DECREE," to commit the act for which *man* is about to punish him. The human law required him *not* to do it—the DECREE of God put it out of his power to abstain from doing it; the consequence is, that he is to be *punished for not having resisted the decree of God!* Now let the gentleman show where there is an error in this reasoning. Let him reconcile the doctrine of "the foreordination of *whatever* comes to pass," with the JUSTICE of those primitive laws, by which the equal rights of men, social, civil, and religious are protected; and I shall admit that there is nothing in this doctrine of the Presbyterian Church, "opposed to civil and religious liberty." Nay, I shall never bring it forward again, if he does. But let us have no more certificates of good behaviour from "Hooker and Bancroft." For they do not remove the difficulty. Neither does Swift or Dryden remove the difficulty.

Another argument was founded on the Presbyterian doctrine, by which the "magistrates" are constituted "nursing fathers of the Church of our common Lord." This was the language of the Westminster Assembly, *and their own understanding of its meaning is the best interpretation.* Dr. Wilie gave the true interpretation in the passage I read from his sermon in my last speech. *Before,* Dr. Wilie was ranked among the *"purest Presbyterians that ever lived;"* now, the gentleman says, *"he (Dr. W.) does not belong to our communion.* But how comes it, that the identical texts of Scripture, by which Dr. Wilie supports those arguments, which the gentleman sees with so much "regret and surprise," are for the most part the same that are referred to or expressed in the Confession of Faith? Did the gentleman not study in his theological course the meaning which *the Westminster divines gave to them?* Were they not Jehovah's warrant, authorising those laws of persecution and intolerance, by which the brief ascendancy of Presbyterianism in England was so distinguished? What are they now? Have *they,* too, altered their meaning? If they have, why did not the republican edition of the Confession say so? If they have *not,* why does he disclaim the persecuting principles, which they were originally employed to support? Thus, the text, to prove that magistrates are to be "nursing fathers to the church," is Isa. xlix. 23. *"And kings shall be thy nursing fathers, and their queens thy nursing mothers."* Is this the manner in which the Presbyterian Church has *repudiated* the state? The fact is that the state, happily for the country, would not marry the church; but if the visions of Dr. Ely should be realised, it will be found that the "banns" have been long on record, in the Confession of Faith.

But I am told, that this article, making the magistrates of the republic "nursing fathers to the Church of our common Lord," means something else. It means, that they should protect all denominations of Christians. Well, this duty the magistrates can learn from the Constitution. But let us see what is meant by the "Church of our common Lord." Let the confession speak.

"*The visible Church, which is also Catholic or Universal under the Gospel, (not confined to one nation as before under the law,) consists of all those throughout the world that* PROFESS THE TRUE RELIGION, *together with their children; and is the kingdom of the Lord Jesus Christ, the house and family of* GOD, OUT OF WHICH THERE IS NO ORDINARY POSSIBILITY OF SALVATION." (1) Hence, to belong to the "Church of common Lord," to which the magistrates are to be "nursing fathers," it is necessary to "profess the true religion;" in other words, to be a Presbyterian. If the magistrate is bound to "REMOVE ALL FALSE WORSHIP, ACCORDING TO HIS PLACE AND CALLING," as the creed elsewhere teaches, is it not contradictory and absurd to say, under this head, that he is bound to "*protect all?*"

There is one circumstance connected with the gentleman's vindication of Presbyterian doctrine, from the charge of persecution, to which I beg to direct your attention. It is this—that he confines himself within that portion of *history* and *geography*, in which it was impossible to *practice* the doctrine of his Church, and unpopular even to profess it. But the honest Presbyterians, who have adhered to their principles in *adversity, as well as prosperity*, determined the question of doctrine by a thousand attestations. I have given already abundant evidence to establish this, both from their synodical expositions and individual testimonies, in our own times and country. We shall now hear their doctrines expounded by themselves, and we shall discover in them the broad avowal of civil hostility to all freedom of conscience opposed to Presbyterianism. Let it be understood, that I do not hold the gentleman responsible for the *intolerance of individuals*, but I quote those individuals as faithful interpreters of the standards of the Presbyterian Church; and we have his own candid acknowledgment of their character, when he tells us, that "they are among the *purest Presbyterians* that ever lived." I quote from the work of the Rev. Mr. Houston, of the Reformed Presbyterian Church in Ireland, published in 1833, entitled "THE REVIEWER REVIEWED."

In order to understand the merits of the argument, it is necessary to premise that, the reviewer, a Mr. Paul, had undertaken the difficult task of vindicating the Presbyterian standards from the persecuting doctrines, which all the world knows them to contain; and which Mr. Houston being, like Dr. Ely,

---

(1) Chap. xxv. Art. 2.

perhaps, "a busy, loquacious man," had imprudently set forth. Here the question was identically the same that is now under discussion, and the disputants being *both* of that class, which the gentleman designates as among the "*purest Presbyterians that ever lived,*" every justice will be done to the standards.

Mr. Houston, with that intellectual refinement of intolerance, for which the disciples of John Calvin have always been characterized by a singular aptitude, maintains, that Presbyterian magistrates have a right, and it is their duty, to punish "HERETICS and IDOLATERS," with the civil sword, and yet *that this is not persecution!* It is true, if magistrates of any *other* denomination, were to wield the civil sword against Presbyterians, *then* it would be persecution; because, says he, persecution " is the endurance of trouble for the TRUE *Christian religion,* in doctrine and worship."(1) From this position, he deduces, as consequences, that the Protestants, or at least the Presbyterians, were martyrs when they suffered for conscience sake; but that this was *their exclusive* privilege, as professors of the " TRUE Christian religion."

As the Presbyterian was a *martyr,* whenever *he* suffered by civil law, so, whenever he made the *professors of other religions* suffer by the civil sword, he was not a persecutor, but a zealous minister of God. Hear the Presbyterian, who had no motive to disguise the principles of their creed. "*Actuated by* HOLY ZEAL *for the honour of God, and feeling a deep interest in the safety of the* TRUE RELIGION, *the magistrate may restrain its daring enemies; and if free from malignity in so doing, he incurs not the guilt of a persecutor, according to the* TRUE IMPORT *of the word.*" (2) Let the Presbyterian magistrate only say, with the associate of John Knox, and the murderer of Cardinal Beaton, that he is not moved to the shedding of heretical blood, by any "private malignity," and he is, from that moment, not a persecutor, but a zealous minister of God. Having established this Presbyterian distinction, the author goes on to say—" *The most enlightened of our Reformers, too, whether churchmen or statesmen, and the most devoted and faithful martyrs to the Reformation cause, drunk deeply into the same spirit,* BEING AVOWED ABETTORS OF MAGISTRATICAL INTERFERENCE IN FAVOUR OF THE REFORMED RELIGION."(3) The author is here candid and honest, and we shall have abundant occasion to show that the ministers of the Reformed religion, made use of the magistrates' power, and that without it, Protestantism never would have succeeded. But Mr. Houston supports his assertions by the authorities of the Westminster divines, and their cotemporaries, and from the gentleman's Confession of Faith. The London ministers had laid it down, that " *The magistrate is, in a civil notion, the supreme governor in all causes ecclesiastical,* THE KEEPER OF BOTH TABLES, THE

(1) P. 20.   (2) P. 16.   (3) P. 21.

NURSING FATHER OF THE CHURCH, &c." (1) The gentleman pretended, that the magistrate's being denominated a "nursing father of the church," had no kind of connexion with civil and religious liberty; although he must be truly unacquainted with Presbyterian theology, if he did not know that in the mind of *those who made his creed in Westminster*, it meant to authorize the tyranny over conscience, which Presbyterians invariably exercised, when they had the power. Mr. Houston proceeds to show the meaning of the doctrines on this subject, embodied in the Westminster Confession of Faith, and other Presbyterian standards, from "such venerated men as Rutherford, Guthrie, and Gillespie," and from those very texts of Scripture, by which the Westminster divines proved the right of the civil magistrates to regulate the consciences of men, and which texts are still in the gentleman's Confession. "*Now*, says he, *it is plain that all those false teachers of old, who aimed to withdraw the Israelites from the worship of the true God, and to cause them to go after other gods, were regarded by the law as heretics. Such is the interpretation given to the laws recorded in Deut. XIII. by Calvin, and the most eminent expositors of former times, and Scott, of more modern days. 'It deserves to be remarked, that,* OUR WESTMINSTER DIVINES REFER TO THESE VERY PASSAGES, (2) *in proof of the positions which they advance, that it is the magistrate's duty to take order that all heresies should be suppressed.*" (3)

After the independence of this country was secured, it was found that the doctrine of using the civil magistrate as a *tool in the hands of Presbytery,* for "suppressing heresy," would not take. These odious words were omittted, accordingly, in the Confession of Faith; but the original Scripture on which their persecuting import was founded, remains to the present day. And it is probable that this is one of the reasons why that "busy, loquacious man," Doctor Ely, desired to form his "Christian party in politics," and preferred, ("other things being equal,") to have a "good sound Presbyterian for his chief magistrate." Mr. Houston, in developing the standards, says—"*It is so notorious that at the period of the Reformation, the Reformers and* REFORMED CHURCHES *held the principle of magistratical care about religion, and that the* PROTESTANT POWERS, *such as the* SENATE OF GENEVA, *the Elector of Saxony, and others who favoured the Reformation,* CARRIED THIS PRINCIPLE INTO EXECUTION, *that the advocates of the* NEW-LIGHT DOCTRINE *generally represent them as but partially enlightened on this article; and if they go not the length of condemning them as bigots, they represent them as not fully emancipated from the shackles of Antichrist.*" (4) We shall see more of this by-and-by.

(1) P. 38.   (2) Deut xiii. 5, 6, 12.
(3) P. 54.   (4) P. 58.

Again. "*The penal statutes enacted in various Reforming parliaments, against idolaters and heretics, prove incontestibly, that, at that time at least, and by those men,* WHOM WE ARE ACCUSTOMED TO VENERATE, *as valiant witnesses for the truth, the suppression of idolatry and heresy, by the authority of the civil magistrate, was regarded as* AN INDISPENSABLE DUTY." (1)

"*The article of the Westminster Confession,* (2) *which asserts, that all blasphemies and heresies should be suppressed, by the magistrate's authority; and the solemn league and covenant, a deed which was sanctified by the highest legislative council in the nation, and cheerfully taken by persons of all ranks and conditions at that day, in which the* SWEARERS *bind themselves, each* 'ACCORDING TO HIS STATION, AND MEANS COMPETENT THERETO, *to extirpate* SUPERSTITION, HERESY, SCHISM, PROFANENESS, &c.,' *exhibit with a* CLEARNESS NOT TO BE MISUNDERSTOOD, *the doctrine which they maintained on this subject.*" (3.)

After having noticed the "gratuitous assertions," as he calls them, of "infidel writers" and "pretended liberals," Mr. Houston states a fact, which shows how little Mr. Breckinridge's statement, as to Presbyterians having been the friends of liberty of conscience, is to be depended on. "*Besides, the* SECTARIES *who abetted the cause of liberty of conscience and toleration, both in the Westminster Assembly, and the councils of the nation, were men of learning and address, and possessed of extensive influence. Notwithstanding these powerful obstacles,* THE GOOD HAND OF THE LORD WAS VISIBLY UPON HIS SERVANTS." (4) Here is the acknowledgment, that the *pleaders* for toleration, were the *Sectaries*, and that the Presbyterians *defeated their purpose*. Yet you have heard their liberality spoken of. The gentleman will say this is Houston, a Reformed Presbyterian. Yes; but he is unfolding the principles of the Confession of Faith. For instance, "*When the abettors of error are restrained by the civil magistrate, and when he acts in every respect as a true* 'NURSING FATHER TO THE CHURCH,' *faithful ministers will be encouraged in their labours, and the difficulties that now oppose their success in the ministry, will be in a great measure removed.*" (5) He goes on to say, that "In no country, *without the aid of the civil magistrate, can Christianity* (Presbyterianism) *universally prevail.*" And as a proof of this, he cites an example which ought to make the gentleman and his colleagues blush. "*Popish delusions received no effectual check in Scotland, till the rulers and nobles of the land put their hand to the work, and called into exercise* THEIR OFFICIAL AUTHORITY, TO RESTRAIN AND PUNISH THE ENEMIES OF THE TRUTH." (6) What is this, but to acknowledge that the

(1) P. 59. (2) Chap. xxiii. (3) P. 62.
(4) Ibid. p. 63. (5) Ibid. p. 65. (6) Ibid. p. 66.

Presbyterian religion was established by *the magistrate*, and the Catholic, refuted by the argument of the sword?

After showing the advantages of the magistrates being, as the church requires, and as they *used* to be, "nursing fathers," he shows the evils of the opposite, which he calls the "new-light," system. "*Consequences of the new-light scheme exemplified in France, and in the United States of America.*" (1) For the evils of the system in this country, he quotes from Doctor Dwight and Doctor Beecher. (2) "*The United States afford another specimen of the working of the new-light scheme, though even there, the principle is by no means carried into full extent. The government of this land of freedom, as it is boastingly called, not only contains no direct recognition of the moral Governor of the Universe, offers no homage to Messiah, but makes it essential, that no favour should be extended to the Church of Christ, more than to any merely civil institution, while her avowed enemies are eligible to all places of power and trust, and the fullest toleration is extended to every species of error and irreligion.*" (3) Let any one compare this with the doctrine of the "nursing fathers," and the "Christian party in politics," and the late political campaign of the Rev. junto of Presbyterian ministers, and see whether every expression, and every movement, is not in accordance with the doctrines which I have already quoted from the Confession of Faith.

Among the evils deplored by this writer, as the consequence of our free American government, is the very one with which my Rev. opponent and his colleagues are endeavouring to stir up the people to intolerance. "*With all the vigour and zeal of the churches in the United States,* IN CONSEQUENCE OF THE NEGLECT OF THE CIVIL RULER ON THE SCORE OF RELIGION, *the idolatry of popery is spreading with rapidity.*" (4) . . . . . . What is all this but the acknowledgment that, without the help of the civil magistrate, Presbyterianism cannot flourish? The whole, and only defence that the gentleman can make, is, that *he* does not hold these doctrines. *He!* Of what importance is he in the question? I bring expounders of his doctrines, who wrote in the absence of the motives which seem to operate on the gentleman *just now*, and he flings them all overboard! He is not "answerable for Dr. Miller;" Dr. Ely is a "busy, loquacious man;" Dr. Wilie "belongs not to our communion;" and he "regrets," and is "surprised." The only one whom he has not disowned is Dr. Brownlee, of the Dutch Reformed or Presbyterian Church. And this man's Confession of Faith makes it a duty, imposed on the *civil magistrates* of this free country, to "*protect the sacred ministry;*" and "REMOVE AND PREVENT ALL IDOLATRY AND FALSE WORSHIP.". . . "Wherefore," the doctor and his associates

(1) Ibid. p. 67. (2) P. 69. (3) P. 69. (4) P. 70.

"*detest the Anabaptists and other seditious people*," who do not agree with his creed in holding these anti-American doctrines. The representative of this creed, a Scotch foreigner, the gentleman calls his "gallant colleague;" by which it is manifest that the doctrine obtains his approval, as being orthodox, and in strict conformity with his own creed, which obliges all Presbyterians to "REMOVE ALL FALSE WORSHIP, AND ALL THE MONUMENTS OF IDOLATRY."

Sir, the gentleman's disclaimer of intolerance, in the name of the Presbyterian doctrine, is a sufficient evidence that he is better acquainted with "Cramp's Text Book of Popery," than with the standards and theology of his own communion. I will now quote but one single doctrine, which he is bound by his ordination vows to preach and maintain as a "tenet of faith or morals revealed by Almighty God." It is, that all Presbyterians are commanded by Jehovah, not only to DETEST and OPPOSE, but also "ACCORDING TO EACH ONE'S PLACE AND CALLING, TO REMOVE ALL FALSE WORSHIP, AND ALL THE MONUMENTS OF IDOLATRY. As a *commentary* on this avowed doctrine, I shall quote the standards of Presbyterians of other countries, to show that this single article contains the *essence* of all the intolerance which was honestly expressed by this sect, previous to the national establishment of liberty of conscience in this republic—to which its spirit is so emphatically adverse.

STANDARDS OF THE PRESBYTERIAN RELIGION.

"That papistry and superstition may be UTTERLY SUP-
"PRESSED, according to the intention of the Acts of Parlia-
"ment, repeated in the 5th Act, Parl. 20, King James VI.
"And to that end they ordain all papists and priests to BE
"PUNISHED WITH MANIFOLD CIVIL AND ECCLESI-
"ASTICAL PAINS, as adversaries to God's true religion,
"preached, and BY LAW ESTABLISHED, within this realm,
"Act 24, Parl. 11, King James VI.; as common enemies to all
"Christian government, Act 18, Parl. 16, King James VI.; as
"rebellers and gainstanders of our sovereign lord's authority,
"Act 47, Parl. 3, King James VI. (Acts of Parliament
"embodied in the National Covenant, and afterwards approved
"by the compilers of the Act and Testimony)."

This shows the character of that Gospel *by which* Presbyterianism was established in Scotland; and sufficiently indicates the duty of the magistrates, as nursing fathers." But again—

"That all kings and princes, at their coronation, and reception
"of their princely authority, shall make their faithful promise,
"by their solemn oath, in the presence of their eternal God, that
"during the whole time of their lives, they shall serve the same
"eternal God, to the utmost of their power, according as he hath

"required in his most holy word, contained in the Old and New
"Testament; and, according to the same word, shall maintain
"the true religion of Christ Jesus, the preaching of his holy
"word, the due and right ministration of the sacraments now
"received and preached within this realm, (according to the
"CONFESSION OF FAITH IMMEDIATELY PRECED-
"ING) and shall ABOLISH and gainstand ALL FALSE RE-
"LIGION CONTRARY TO THE SAME; and shall rule the
"people committed to their charge, according to the will and
"command of God, REVEALED IN HIS FORESAID WORD,
"and according to the laudable laws and constitutions received in
"this realm, no wise repugnant to the said will of the eternal God;
"and shall procure to the utmost of their power, to the kirk of
"God, and whole Christian people, true and perfect peace in all
"time coming; and that they shall be careful to ROOT OUT
"OF THEIR EMPIRE ALL HERETICS and enemies to the
"TRUE WORSHIP of God, who shall be convicted by the
"TRUE KIRK of God of the foresaid crimes." (1)

Here is the origin of that commandment which requires Presbyterians to ..... "oppose and REMOVE, *according to each one's place and calling*, all *false worship*, and all the monuments of idolatry. Again, still—

"That we shall, in like manner, without respect of per-
"sons, endeavour the extirpation of popery, prelacy (that is
"church-government by archbishops, bishops, their chancellors,
"and commissaries, deans, deans and chapters, archdeacons, and
"all other ecclesiastical officers depending on that hierarchy),
"SUPERSTITION, HERESY, SCHISM, PROFANENESS,
"and whatsoever shall be found to be contrary to sound doctrine
"and the power of godliness; lest we partake in other men's
"sins, and thereby be in danger to receive of their plagues; and
"that the Lord may be one, and his name one, in the three king-
"doms." (2)

This was in England, in 1643—more than a hundred years after the so-called Reformation. But let the standards proceed.

"When any thing is amiss, we will endeavour a reformation
"in a fair and orderly way, and where reformation is settled, we
"resolve, with that authority wherewith God hath vested us, to
"maintain and defend it in peace and liberty against all trouble
"that can come from without, and against all HERESIES,
"SECTS, AND SCHISMS, which may arise from within." (3)

"We shall be bold to warn your majesty really, that the guilt
"which cleaveth fast to your majesty and to your throne, is such
"as (whatsoever flattering preachers or unfaithful counsellors may

---

(1) Coronation Oath in the National Covenant.
(2) Solemn League and Covenant, Art. 2.
(3) Acts of Assembly, 1638.

"say to the contrary) if not timely repented, cannot but involve
"yourself and your posterity under the wrath of the ever-living
"God, for your being guilty of the shedding of the blood of many
"thousands of your majesty's best subjects; for your PERMIT-
"TING THE MASS and other idolatry, both in your own
"family and in your dominions." (1)

This was the Assembly which framed the gentleman's CONFESSION OF FAITH. The king was so far friendly to liberty of conscience, as to "permit" the saying of mass, and this was to draw upon him the "wrath of God." Again—

"So, it cannot be denied, that upon these passages and pro-
"ceedings, hath followed the interrupting of the so much longed
"for reformation of religion, of the settling by Presbyterian
"government, and of THE SUPPRESSING OF HERESIES
"AND DANGEROUS ERRORS, which works the PARLIA-
"MENT HAD TAKEN IN HAND." (2)

"We are also very sensible of the great and imminent dangers
"into which this common cause of religion is now brought by
"the growing and spreading of most dangerous errors in England,
"to the obstructing and hindering of the begun reformation; as,
"namely, besides many others, Socinianism, Arminianism, Ana-
"baptism, Erastianism, Brownism, Antinomianism, Independency,
"and that which is called (by abuse of the word) LIBERTY
"OF CONSCIENCE, being indeed liberty of error, scandal,
"schism, heresy, dishonouring God, opposing the truth, hinder-
"ing reformation, and seducing others. (3)

Will the gentleman say that this is not evidence to show the bearing of Presbyterian doctrines on civil and religious liberty? These were the men who *understood* the Confession of Faith—and explained it.

"The General Assembly, considering how the errors of INDE-
"PENDENCY and SEPARATION have, in our neighbour
"kingdom of England, spread as a gangrene, and do daily eat as
"a canker; insomuch that exceeding many errors, heresies,
"schisms, and blasphemies have issued therefrom, and are shelt-
"ered thereby; and how possible it is for the SAME EVILS TO
"INVADE AND OVERSPREAD THIS KIRK AND KING-
"DOM, (lying within the same island,) BY THE SPREADING
"OF THEIR ERRONEOUS BOOKS, PAMPHLETS, LI-
"BELS, AND LETTERS .... that some course may be
"taken to hinder the dispersing thereof; *and hereby all Presby-
"terians and synods are ordained to try and process such as shall
"transgress against the premises, or any part of the same:* And

---

(1) Remonstrance to the King—*Acts of Assembly, February*, 1645.
(2) Declaration and Brotherly Exhortation, in the *Acts of Assembly August*, 1647.
(3) Declaration and Brotherly Exhortation.

"*the Assembly also doth seriously recommend to civil magis-
"trates that they may be pleased to be assisting to ministers
"and presbyteries in execution of this act, and to concur with
"their authority in everything to that effect." (1)

* * * * * * *

* * "That notwithstanding hereof, the civil magistrate ought
"to suppress, by corporal or civil punishments, such as, by
"spreading error or heresy, or by fomenting schism, greatly dis-
"honour God, dangerously hurt religion, and disturb the PEACE
"OF THE KIRK. WHICH HEADS OF DOCTRINE, (how-
"soever OPPOSED by the AUTHORS and fomentors of the
"foresaid errors respectively,) the General Assembly doth FIRM-
"LY BELIEVE, OWN, MAINTAIN, AND COMMEND
"UNTO OTHERS AS SOLID, TRUE, ORTHODOX,
"GROUNDED UPON THE WORD OF GOD, consonant
"to the judgment both of the ancient and THE BEST RE-
"FORMED KIRKS. (CXI. Proposition, 8th Head.")

The profession of faith, in divinity of Christ, by the Council of Nice, is not more emphatic than the doctrine of magistrates here laid down—as TRUE, ORTHODOX, grounded on the word of God," &c.

"As also, that, as the ambassadors of Jesus Christ and his
"watchmen, you will give seasonable warning to the honourable
"Houses of Parliament, that now, (after the loss of the oppor-
"tunity of so many years,) they would, IN THEIR PLACES,
"repair the House of the Lord, that lieth so long desolate, and
"promote the work of reformation and UNIFORMITY accord-
"ing to the Covenant. For, if the honourable Houses of Parlia-
"ment had timely made use of that power, which God hath put
"in their hands for suppressing of sectaries, and had taken a
"speedy course for settling of Presbyterial government, (a spe-
"cial and effectual means appointed by God to purge his Church
"from all scandals in doctrine and practice,) then, had not THE
"INSOLENCY OF THAT PARTY ARISEN to such a
"height, as to give occasion to the MALIGNANTS of both king-
"doms to justify and bless themselves in their old opposition to
"the work of reformation, and to encourage one another to new
"and more dangerous attempts. (2)

Some of the audience may not be aware that "*malignants*" was the term employed to designate the EPISCOPALIANS—the old argument of nicknames, instead of reason.

"And because the POWERS which God hath ordained, and
"the liberty which Christ hath purchased, are not intended
"by God to destroy, but mutually to uphold and preserve one

---

(1) *Acts of Assembly, August*, 1647. This was the Assembly that received and approved of the Westminster Confession of Faith.
(2) Acts of Assembly, August 2, 1648.

"another; they who, UPON PRETENCE OF CHRISTIAN
"LIBERTY, SHALL OPPOSE ANY LAWFUL POWER,
"or the lawful exercise of it, whether it be CIVIL OR ECCLE-
"SIASTICAL, resist the ORDINANCE OF GOD. And for
"their publishing of such opinions, or maintaining of such prac-
"tices, as are contrary to the light of nature, or to the known
"principles of Christianity, whether CONCERNING FAITH,
"WORSHIP, or conversation; or to the power of godliness; or
"such erroneous opinions or practices, as, either, in their own
"nature, or in the manner of publishing or maintaining them, are
"destructive to the external peace and order which Christ hath
"established in the Church: they may lawfully be called to ac-
"count, and proceeded against by the censures of the Church,
"(and by the power of the civil magistrate.") (1)

The words in parenthesis are omitted in the present *republican
edition*, as something offensive to the eye. But the rest of the
article makes the sense complete; and besides, omission is no
contradiction.

("The following Scriptures, amongst others, are referred to by
"the compilers, in proof of the doctrine which they have here
"advanced:—Ezra, vii. 23. 'Whatsoever is commanded by the
"God of heaven, let it be diligently done for the house of the God
"of heaven: for why should there be wrath against the realm of
"the king and his sons?' Ver. 25. 'And thou, Ezra, after the
"wisdom of thy God that is in thy hand, sit magistrate and judges
"which may judge all the people that are beyond the river, all
"such as know the laws of thy God; and teach ye them that
"know them not.' Ver. 26. 'And whosoever will not do the
"law of thy God, and the LAW OF the king, let judgment be
"executed speedily upon him, whether it be unto death, or to
"banishment, or to confiscation of goods, or to imprisonment.'—
"Zech. xiii. 2. 'And it shall come to pass in that day, saith the
"Lord of hosts, that I will cut off the names of the idols out of
"the land, and they shall no more be remembered: and also I
"will cause the prophets and the unclean spirits to pass out of the
"land.' Ver. 3. 'And it shall come to pass, that when any shall
"yet prophecy, then his father and his mother that begat him
"shall say unto him, thou shalt not live; for thou speakest lies
"in the name of the Lord; and his father and his mother that
"begat him shall thrust him through when he prophesieth.'")

"The civil magistrate may not assume to himself the adminis-
"tration of the word and sacraments, or the power of the keys of
"the kingdom of heaven; (yet he has authority, and it is his duty,
"to take order, that unity and peace be preserved in the Church,
"that the truth of God be kept pure and entire, that all blasphe-
"mies and heresies be suppressed, all corruptions and abuses in

(1) Westminster Confession, Chap. XX. Art. 4.

"worship and discipline prevented or reformed, and all the ordinances of God duly settled, administered, and observed. For the better effecting whereof, he hath power to call synods, to be present at them, and to provide that whatsoever is transacted in them be according to the mind of God.") (1)

The words in parenthesis are omitted since the Revolution; and the very ambiguous phrase, appointing the magistrates of this country to be "nursing fathers to the church," substituted. But the magistrates not being always *orthodox*, the "baby" has been much neglected, and Dr. Ely, naturally enough, wished to see all offices filled by Presbyterians.

"Lev. xxiv. 16. And he that blasphemeth the name of the Lord, he shall surely be put to death; and all the congregation shall certainly stone him; as well the stranger, as he that is born in the land, when he blasphemeth the name of the Lord shall be put to death." 2 Chron. xxxiv. 33. "And Josiah took away all the abominations out of the countries that pertained to the children of Israel, and made all that were present in Israel to serve, even to serve the Lord their God, and all his days they departed not from following the Lord, the God of their fathers."

In perfect keeping with all the foregoing, is the following article, which requires only to be understood. It appears smooth; but every clause is pregnant with hostility to the rights of conscience, and to "civil, as well as religious liberty."

"*And also the disapproving, detesting, opposing all false worship; and according to each one's place and calling, removing it and all monuments of idolatry.*" (2)

Let us now see whether this was not the doctrine of the Presbyterian Churches on the continent of Europe, as well as where the Westminster Confession prevails.

The celebrated Francis Turretin, PROFESSOR OF THEOLOGY IN GENEVA, expresses himself fully on this topic, and by various arguments, shows the right of the magistrate to punish with civil pains, gross heretics, idolaters and blasphemers. In endeavouring to establish this point, he lays down this position, that "MAGISTRATES have the right to restrain contumacious and OBSTINATE HERETICS, who cannot be CURED of their errors, and who disturb the peace of the Church, and even to inflict upon them due punishment." "Since magistrates," he adds for confirmation, "are keeper of BOTH TABLES, and the care of religion pertains to them, they ought to provide that it should suffer no injury, and should in wisdom oppose those who assert it, lest the poison insinuate itself more widely, and be diffused through the whole body. But magistrates cannot protect religion, unless they restrain the obstinate and factious contemners

(1) Westminster Confession, Chap. XXIII. Art. 3.
(2) Larger Catechism, Quest. 108.

'thereof. Such interference, both the glory of God, of which
"they are the defenders, and the safety of the commonwealth,
"of which they are the guardians, demand. If less evils are
"restrained by heavy penalties, this, which is the greatest, which
"injures the trust of God, which blasphemes his name, which
"rends the Church, which corrupts the faith, and brings into
"danger the safety of the faithful, should not be permitted to
"go unpunished. Rather is there frequently required, that a
"speedy and powerful remedy be applied; inasmuch, as from
"this quarter, the destruction of the whole body is threatened,
"unless the application be quickly made."

"For this purpose, the laws of Moses against apostates, blas-
"phemers, false prophets, &c. were given, as in Deut. xiii. 5, and
"xvii. 12; Levit. xxiv. 16, with the same design, there are set
"before us the examples of Moses, and of pious kings in the Old
"Testament, who reformed religion, and restrained FALSE PRO-
"PHETS, HERETICS, and IDOLATERS, and never hesitated
"moreover, to inflict upon them various civil punishments; and
"also the examples of Christian princes, in New Testament times,
"who passed several laws against heretics, and visited them not
"only with imprisonment and exile, but coerced them likewise
"with severer punishment." Again he asserts, that "the magis-
"trates can restrain heretics, and punish them, and according to
"the nature of their crime; if, for instance they are blasphemers,
"and factious and seditious, he may inflict on them capital pun-
"ishment." And afterwards he advocates the application of capital punishments in such extreme cases, from, 1. The atrocity of
the crime; and 2. The authority of God declared in the law. (1)

The confessions of the Reformed Churches, expressly assign to
the Christian civil magistrate this coersive and punitive power,
in matters of religion. The first confession of Helvetia, declares,
"Seeing that every magistrate is of God, his CHIEF DUTY, ex-
"cept it please him to exercise tyranny, consisteth in this: to de-
"fend religion from all blasphemy, to promote it, as the prophet
"teacheth, out of the word of the Lord, to see it put in practice,
"as far as lies in him." The *latter* confession of Helvetia, which
was expressly approved by the Church of Scotland, and other reformed Churches, teaches, that " magistracy, of whatever sort it
"be, is ordained of God himself, for the peace and tranquill ty of
"mankind; so that the magistracy ought to have the chief place
"in the world. If he be an adversary to the Church, he may
"greatly hinder and disturb it; but if he be a FRIEND and MEM-
"BER of the Church, he is a most profitable member, and may
"excellently aid and advance it. His principal duty is to procure
"and maintain peace and public tranquillity; which doubtless he
"will never do more happily than when he is seasoned with the

(1) See Turret, De Polit. Ecc. gubern. quæsti xxxiv.

"fear of God, and true religion, particularly when he shall, after
"the examples of the most holy kings and princes of the people
"of the Lord, advance the preaching of the truth, and the pure
"unadulterated faith, shall EXTIRPATE FALSEHOOD, and
"ALL SUPERSTITION, IMPIETY, and IDOLATRY, and
"shall defend the Church of God; for indeed we teach that the
"care of religion doth chiefly appertain to the holy magistrate."
The confession of Saxony declares, that "the word of God doth
"in general, teach this, concerning the power of the magistrate;
"first, that God wills that the magistrates, without all doubt,
"should sound forth the voice of the moral law among men, ac-
"cording to the ten commandments, or law natural, by-laws for-
"bidding idolatry and blasphemies, as well as murders, theft, &c."
for well has it been said of old: "THE MAGISTRATE IS A
"KEEPER OF THE LAW, *i. e.* OF THE FIRST AND SE-
"COND TABLE, as concerning discipline and good order. This
"ought to be their special care, (of kingdoms and their rulers,) to
"hear and embrace the true doctrine of the Son of God, and to
"cherish the Churches, according to Psalm ii. and xxiv. and
"Isaiah xlix., and KINGS AND QUEENS SHALL BE THY
"NURSES, *i. e.* let commonwealths be NURSES OF THE
"CHURCH, and to godly studies." The Dutch Confession
teaches, that God "hath armed the magistrate with a sword, to
"punish the bad, and defend the good. Furthermore, it is their
"duty to be careful not only to preserve the civil polity, but also
"to endeavour that the ministry be preserved: that all idolatry
"and COUNTERFEIT WORSHIP be abolished, the kingdom
"of Antichrist be brought down, and the kingdom of Christ be
"enlarged; in fine, that it is their duty to bring it to pass, that
"the holy word of the Gospel be preached everywhere, that all
"men may serve God, purely and freely, according to the pre-
"scribed will of his word." And the French Confession declares, "that God hath delivered the sword into the magistrate's
"hand, that so sins committed against BOTH TABLES OF
"GOD'S law, not only against the second, BUT THE FIRST
"ALSO, MAY BE SUPPRESSED."

Here, sir, are not the *opinions* of individuals. Here, the speculations of Doctor Ely, and Mr. Dens, of Bellarmine, and of Doctor Wilie, are all out of the question. Here are the *doctrinal foundations* of the Presbyterian Church. Here we have, on the subject of "magistracy," "nursing fathers to the church," "heresy," "false worship," "monuments of idolatry," "both tables of the law," &c. &c., "the TENETS *of* FAITH and MORALS, *which that denomination held, and holds, as having been revealed by Almighty God.*" Compare them one with another, beginning at Geneva, you will find that royalists or republicans, Swiss, Saxon, Dutch, French, Scotch, English and American, they all agree in the same DOCTRINE, more or less developed: expressed boldly in Geneva, Holland, Scotland, and England, (during Presbyterian ascendancy in the State,) expressed cautiously in the United States, since the revolution, but expressed sufficiently everywhere.

But, says the gentleman, where have Presbyterians persecuted in the United States? I answer, wherever they *obeyed* their own doctrine, rather than the American Constitution. They had to *break the second commandment,* in order to abstain from violating the rights of their fellow-citizens, by "REMOVING FALSE WORSHIP, AND MONUMENTS OF IDOLATRY." But, at all events, they did not "REMOVE THEM." Thanks to the Constitution, and their own good sense, but none to their doctrine, or some of their parsons.

There is one thing to which I beg leave to direct the attention of this meeting, and of the public. It is, that the gentleman's quotation of my language is not to be depended on. I will give one or two instances, as a sample of the rest, too numerous to notice. He represents me glorying the title of "JESUIT," and, as ashamed of that of "PAPIST." There is no truth in either of his statements. I said, that the title JESUIT did not belong to me, although I might be proud to be the defender of that calumniated body. I said, that he "insultingly" used the term popery; but not that I was ashamed of being insulted, nor of the term by which the insult was conveyed. In purporting to repeat my remarks about the other denominations of Protestants, he makes me say, that "these denominations may have been used by the Presbyterians to stir up this fanatical excitement"—and then adds, that I am "certainly very complimentary to them." He falsifies my language, and then charges me with the result of his own oversight or dishonesty. My words were, *"that some of each* of these denominations may have been used, &c." He charges me with applying the word "fools" *to my opponents*; and yet, though I used the word, there is no truth in the charge. By what name, then, is it customary to designate those who assert what is false? He says, that I "hate" and "fear" Dr. Beecher. The fact is not so. That gentleman has entitled himself to the "love" which every "enemy" has a right to claim from the Christian disciple. The defenceless females and children of Mount Benedict, have had reason to "fear" him. And yet, I do not say, that the burning of the convent was the direct motive of his fiery sermons in Boston and Charlestown. The fact is, the doctor *wanted money,* and, like some of his brethren, knew that he could extract more by denouncing popery than by preaching the gospel.

He says, of Dr. Miller, that "I seem to covet the honour of being in such good company." Now, the fact is, that I do not. I know and speak of Dr. Miller only as an AUTHOR. In this capacity, the portion of honour that remains to him, is *too small* to be divided. He has been equally various and unfortunate in his controversies. His literary career has been one series of polemical drubbings, which few writers have so richly earned, or so regularly received. His bad logic has been immortalized by the Rev. Mr. Duncan, of Baltimore; and his abuse of authors, by faithless citation, in the *Episcopal Controversy*, has been placed on the pinnacle of notoriety, by Dr. Cooke, of Kentucky. Still he *may* be, as the gentleman will have it, a "lion;" although the only trait of the noble animal that I can discover in the doctor's polemical career, is the *majestic silence* with which he retires to his *den*, as often as he is foiled in the open field. There the gentleman may have had an opportunity of admiring him, but, as "porcupines" are not permitted to enter, I cannot tell how he looks. If it be "*abuse*," to state a fact from his own book, and make the proper commentary on it, then I have "abused" Dr. Miller, but not otherwise. I know nothing of him, except as an author, and, as such, his fame excites no envy.

The gentleman has altered his tone about foreigners. The poor men on the "railroads" and "canals" are the foreigners he dreads. "The *poor*, the well-principled, intelligent, industrious *poor*, WE welcome and confide in." I thank him, in their name. The feeling does honour to him. But then, there was "riot and bloodshed" on the Baltimore Railroad; and, therefore, he says, "The emigrants we dread, are such as dig our canals and railroads, and make mobs by way of chorus," &c. If, instead of making "mobs by way of chorus," they had made mobs by way of removing a false religion, or a monument of idolatry, his sensibilities would not be shocked in the least, as appears from the almost inhuman manner in which he seems to triumph over the destruction of the convent. His language is this:—"*But I will say this, that there is a certain kind of houses, which the Pope used to license at Rome, which the boys and mobs in America, taking Judge Lynch's law, sometimes pull down, not as Protestants against popery, but as enemies to gross immoralities, which we cannot name.*" And again, "..... *the riotous rabble, at Boston, taking the convent for a * * * * * * WICKEDLY burned it down.*" The malignity of malice itself, was foiled, in every attempt to fix a stigma on the *moral character* of the inmates of the convent, and no one will envy the feelings of that man, who, in addition to the *injuries already inflicted on them*, can give utterance to so foul and false an insinuation. He, the advocate of "civil and religious liberty!!"

The gentleman speaks of my "attack on the Sunday School Union," and quotes William Wirt and Mr. Frelinghuysen, to prove that it is a good institution. He says, I "denounce this noble charity." And again; "Will not our Catholic laymen, such as Mathew Carey, blush for their priest, who so recklessly assails such institutions." Now, if he will quote from my speech the passage in which I made an "attack on the Sunday School Union," in which I "denounced this noble charity," in which I "assailed this institution," in which I spoke of the *merits of the institution, as such,* I promise to make a public apology. But, since he has accused me of all these, then, if *he cannot furnish the proof from my speech,* I charge him as A CALUMNIATOR of my character. I now put him to the test; and honest men will see, whether Presbyterians have not more occasion to blush for their "Minister of the Gospel," than Catholics have to blush for me. I have made the penalty emphatic, in order to bring him to the *test.* I have stated facts. I have quoted from the RECORDS *of the Sunday School Union,* and if the quotations reflect on its character, the fault is *theirs*—not mine. He says, "*Oh! how small and how ashamed must a priest of Rome feel before the sublime conceptions, the manly rebuke, the just defence of an American layman pleading for an open Bible and universal education...*" This is a hundred miles from the argument. Does the American laymen plead for their becoming "DICTATORS TO THE CONSCIENCES OF THOUSANDS OF IMMORTAL BEINGS?" Is THIS the "open Bible?" for "CHANGING EVEN THE IDEAS" of authors? Is this "universal education?" The legitimate object of the Sunday School Union is *one* thing—the abuses into which faithless agents, or *sectarian* ambition may betray it, are another. I did not attack the institution itself; and, therefore, its defence was supererogatory, except to keep time with the calumny on which it was based. The gentleman says, he could not find my quotations, by which he insinuates, that he will defend them, *if discovered.* He will find them in the Appendix to Dr. Ely's Sermon, published with remarks, by the doctor himself, at the office of William F. Geddes, in 1828. We shall see, whether he will be able to prove, that they are nothing but "an open Bible, and universal education." He says, "he believes it" (dictators to the consciences of thousands of immortal beings) "to be utterly false;" but he will find, that he is "utterly" mistaken.

I stated, in my last, that for all the money which the Presbyterians *send out* of the country, for *foreign missions,* it can be no great harm if Catholics should bring a *little into* it. In reply, he assumes, that in Catholic countries, one-third part of the year is wasted in "worshipping," &c.; "immense treasures are sunk in adorning images," &c.; that they are "poor" and "desolate;" whereas, Protestant countries are rich and prosperous, &c. All this is the gentleman's assumption, and, if it were true, would only prove, that Catholic countries are poorer than Protestant countries. But what becomes of the other part of his story, setting forth, that these "rich," "enlightened," "prosperous Protestants," were to be bought up by the vast sums of money, which the poor, ignorant, debased Catholics were sending for that purpose? How is that? Since one part of his argument refutes the other, he ought to have told us which we are to believe.

Having calumniated me as an "assailant of the Sunday School

Union," it is *not* "passing strange," that he should represent me as the "apologist" of the inquisition, and the "advocate" of the Jesuits. On the subject of the inquisition, I proved, that it had no necessary connexion with the Catholic religion; that it was employed as an engine of state policy, for political purposes; that the Catholic religion existed more than one thousand years before the inquisition was thought of; that even in parts of *Italy itself*, it never did exist: in a word, I enlightened the ignorance of the gentleman in relation to it. If he states, that I was the "apologist" of the inquisition, he states what is *false*. I did not say one single word in its justification.

He had stated, that Talleyrand was a "JESUIT, and had been a TEACHER" in this country. I denied the assertion, knowing it to be unfounded. In a postscript to his corrected speech, he says, "*There is proof positive, in the history of Talleyrand, that he taught mathematics in the state of New York. There is proof in his character that he is a Jesuit.*" Now, I CALL FOR THE PAGE OF THE HISTORY WHICH ATTESTS THE FORMER FACT. AND I CAUTION THE GENTLEMAN NOT TO TRIFLE WITH HIS REPUTATION FOR VERACITY.

The JESUITS are known to every man of education, in both hemispheres, to be a society of men in the Catholic Church, the object of whose institute is the promotion of religion, piety, and learning. That there may have been *bad members* in that society, is readily admitted. But, as a body, they have deserved well of religion, of science, and of humanity. This I have proved under the former head. It was of *this society*,—and in *this sense*, that I was the "DEFENDER," although I am not a member. The gentleman stated, that Talleyrand was a "JESUIT"—that is, as *honest men* would understand, *a member of this society*. He is caught in the assertion; and, instead of feeling ashamed at its *want of truth*, he seems to smile at his own smartness, in effecting a dishonourable retreat. "There is proof in his (Talleyrand's) *character*, that he was a Jesuit." That is, "all SCOUNDRELS are JESUITS; and Mr. Hughes, (who attacked the Sunday School Union, and apologized for the Inquisition,) is the ADVOCATE of the Jesuits." *In this sense*, there are JESUITS of all denominations. And the man who is willing to be their "ADVOCATE," need never be at a loss for a *brief* and a *client* among the *Presbyterian Jesuits* of the country. I hope the gentleman will tell us in future *which kind* of Jesuits he means.

He has said, that Dr. Brownlee has given the Catholics occasion to regret that "ever he was born." Now, the only definite result that I have been able to trace to the doctor's labours, was the public statement made by two respectable gentlemen in New York, that *his writings* had induced them to *renounce the Protestant*, *and embrace the Catholic faith*. If the doctor "had not been born," it is probable that these persons would never have come to the knowledge of the truth.

The gentleman says that Mr. Smith is "now despised." It may be, but Catholics entertain more of *pity* than contempt for him. As to his being "esteemed" when he was a "priest," it may be true, so long as he was regarded as a *good* priest. But when they came to know him better, he discovered, 1st, that he *would not be employed* in the ministry; and then he discovered, 2dly, the errors of popery. On the 15th of August, 1833, he addressed to me a letter, in which he states:—"*If I am not considered altogether too unworthy, I wish, like the prodigal child, to return to the house of my father.*" "*That I am still worthy of nothing but stripes I am fully aware, although my soul is bleeding under the bitter lacerations of a wounded conscience.*" ....."*I congratulate you on the success of your controversy with Mr. Breckinridge.*"......"*Here I drop a tear; and, involuntarily grasping the sword of the Spirit, long to be by your side, fighting in the cause of* TRUTH."......"*May I be so happy as to be one of your number.*" When Mr. Smith wrote this letter, he knew of "priests" and "nuns" ALL that he knows now. His experience had all been *before.*

At all events he was "*considered* ALTOGETHER *too unworthy*" to exercise the priesthood; and the consequence was that he renounced his religion. It appears he was bent on "fighting;" and, since he would not be permitted to fight by "my side in the cause of truth," he determined, unhappy man, to fight in the cause of error. He is now, I believe, a saint—having broken his vows, abjured his faith, and published the Downfall of Babylon.

As to the gentleman's "challenges" about Catholic principles in relation to "civil and religious liberty," I have met them all under their head, during the first six nights. *Then*, it was *his right* to "challenge" and affirm—and my duty to meet his "challenges" and refute his assertions. If I have failed—let the public judge—let the FACTS decide. But now, *by the gentleman's own regulation*, I have a right to enter the sanctuary of the Presbyterian religion. I have a right to take it down from its pedestal, on which people of *moderate information* have been accustomed to venerate it, as the "beau ideal" of all that is friendly to religious and civil liberty, and to lay it open by dissection. All this, the gentleman has given me a *right* to do. Consequently, my business during these six nights, is to lay before the public, the anatomy of Presbyterianism, and to show that, notwithstanding its long and sanctimonious *visage*, to which its advocates point with such confidence, there is the deadly seed of intolerance and persecution in every joint and muscle of its whole frame and structure. Now, the gentleman having given me the *right* to do all this, as an equivalent for *his* privilege to examine the Catholic religion, during the first six nights, must not expect that I can suspend the operation to refute *again*, what I *have already refuted.*

You would suppose, from the tone of the gentleman, that his religion is entitled to the credit of all that is liberal in the genius of the civil government of the country. "WE *protect* all religions." No, sir, the Constitution of the country does this. ALL *denominations protect all denominations, and are protected by them.* The protection of all denominations which the creed of Presbyterians furnishes, is the commandment of Almighty God to. . . . . . . "to oppose all false worship, *and, according to each one's place and calling, to* REMOVE IT, *and all the monuments of idolatry."* The protection of the Constitution is to FORBID what Presbyterians say God COMMANDS; and to prevent *their* "REMOVING *of any false worship, or any monument of idolatry," except their* OWN.

The gentleman finds fault with me for not giving more of Mr. Jefferson, Dr. Ely, &c. Where should I fix the limits? Must I publish their whole works, in order to make a quotation? I shall show, in the sequel of the argument, the gentleman need not go out of the annals of his own church to find language to express *cruelty,* not in the "*abstraction*" but in the practice. The name of its founder, Calvin, conveys the idea in a much more concrete form than the word inquisition.

The extract from the continental Congress is just such a broad, sweeping, but unfounded assertion, as the gentleman himself would make, during a violent paroxysm of devotion to "civil and religious liberty." Protestants who have not taken the pains to examine the FACTS, have been much accustomed to deal in such figures of rhetoric. *I* do not repeat what Catholics *said* of Presbyterians, to show their doctrines and practice, but I give their actions, *when* and *where;* and this, too, on Protestant authority. I deem it no disrespect to the memory of that Congress, to say, that, with all their patriotism, and magnanimity of character, they were unacquainted with the principles of the Catholic religion, and misinformed as to the matter of which they assert. When they assert that the Catholic religion had "deluged England with blood," they assert what history does not sustain. If they had spoken *thus* of the civil wars by which Presbyterianism fought its way to WESTMINSTER, when the island *was* deluged with the blood of the prince and the peasant—then, indeed, HISTORY would have borne them out.

"Is the Presbyterian Religion, in any or in all its principles or doctrines, opposed to civil or religious liberty ?"

NEGATIVE III.—MR. BRECKINRIDGE.

MR. PRESIDENT :—

WHETHER, if the question of a mere choice of "an equal and a companion" were before me, I should select the Rev. priest of St. John's, is a matter which I do not feel now called on to decide. I am glad, however, to see that he has not forgotten *the name* which defines a well-bred man. His *presumption*, in *comparing himself to Jesus Christ*, and his *compliment*, in resembling me to *the murderers of our Master*, may be left among the *memorabilia* which need no comment.

My arguments already given, are enough, without repetition or enlargement, to set the question of "the decrees" in its proper light.

He unwittingly answers all his own cavils, on the subject, when he says, "ACCORDING TO THIS IT WAS 'FOREORDAINED THAT JOHN HUSS SHOULD BE BURNED AT CONSTANCE. AND YET THE GENTLEMAN CHARGES THE COUNCIL FOR IT." *Even so.* This shows, in a word, "*that the gentleman* (Mr. B.) *denies*, as *every* Presbyterian does, that *foreordination* takes away accountability. This is the very distinction that we make. So the Lord Jesus said to Pilate : ' *Thou couldst have no power at all against me, except it were given thee from above; therefore he that delivered me unto thee hath the greater sin.*' " (1) It was this text I asked the gentleman to explain ; you have seen his reply !

In *Acts* ii. 23. Peter (" *the first Pope*,") said : " *Him* (Jesus) *being delivered by the determinate counsel*, and *foreknowledge of God, ye have taken*, and by wicked hands have *crucified and slain.*" Here God is directly called the decreeing cause ; yet the agents are called the "wicked" agents, who DID the murderous deed. And again, Acts iv. 26-28. " *The kings of the earth stood up, and the rulers were gathered together, against* the Lord, and *against his Christ;......for to do whatsoever thy hand and thy counsel determined before to be done.*" Here is *foreordination by God*, and yet *guilt* charged on *men* for doing what God had determined *before was to be done.*" Now, this is our doc-

---

(1) John xix. ii.

trine. Moral agency is not disturbed by *divine foreordination;* or will the gentleman tell us *what* the passages mean? if not, what I attribute to them? If he be *silent after this*, then it will be owning that God's word teaches a doctrine which *makes* God to authorize sin, and which takes away the guilt of all actions; and all motives to good actions. So he says of this doctrine! *Now let him speak!*

My answer, "that Augustine—the Baptists, and Episcopalians," &c. held this doctrine, was in reply to this statement in his previous speech, viz.: " *The only denomination that I know who have not became ashamed of the avowal* of this article, (predestination,) are the high-toned Presbyterians. I defy the proof that it is held by the other denominations whom he has mentioned." I had, in my first speech, mentioned " the Congregationalists of old and New England" *as a body,* "*the great mass;* " and the *twelve creeds* of the original Reformers—in Germany, Switzerland, Holland, France, England, and Scotland, as " *Calvinistic,*" as well as "Augustine, the Episcopalian *articles,* and the Baptist." As he denied it, so I brought *proof.* Now, he " *lets go*" about half of the whole number, and denies that "Augustine, Episcopalians," and *all* the Baptists, hold it. He is in the face of a mass of *Catholic evidence,* if he deny that Augustine held this doctrine; and now, if he will only *venture to deny it like a man,* and *in plain words,* I will expose him before all the world. He *admits* that the Episcopal ARTICLES are *Calvinistic.* I have to do with no more. But surely, when he says the " *clergy are Arminian,*" he pays them no enviable compliment. He says profoundly, "*with the exception of those called Calvinistic Baptists,*" *the Baptists are not Calvinists !* But who are Calvinistic Baptists. I refer to history in England and America, in proof that the great body are *Calvinistic;* though I must own that those *who are not Calvinistic, are not !* In reply to all I said (including a passage from the decrees) of the Council of Trent, he remarks, "as to the Council of Trent, it taught no such impious tenet." This is *summary,* though it *may* not be very *conclusive* reasoning. The point of my argument was to show, that the freest, wisest, most virtuous, and most flourishing nations on earth, have been distinguished by "Calvinistic" doctrines; and that the Council of Trent *contradicted* itself, being *divided* on the doctrine, in trying to reconcile parties.

Foiled on this topic, the gentleman returns, for the *twelfth time,* (I think,) to " the *monuments of idolatry.*" He says, as the magistrate is by our Confession bound to remove " *all* the monuments of idolatry ; " and as, by the same Confession, " those only belong to the true Church, who profess the true religion "—therefore, it is absurd to say, that they ought to "*protect all religions.*" I grant it is so, " on Catholic principles ; " which are, that "*heretics are to be exterminated.*" But while we hold, that " out of the universal Church there is no ordinary possibility of salvation," we also hold, that "*civil government*" is not to protect *only the true Church*, but all churches—even congregations of infidels in Tammany Hall, if they commit no civil offence. But the Catholic "church and state doctrine" interwoven in his argument, as now stated, makes protection *stop* where *heresy begins*. Again: we hold, that not only Presbyterians, but "all, everywhere, who love the Lord," are of Christ's Church; and so wide is this principle, that we believe a part of the true Church lay hid, in the Church of Rome, at the occurrence of the Reformation.

He next remarks, as if it were a new and extraordinary thing, that "he (Mr. B.) *confines himself within* that *portion* of *history* and *geography* in *which* it was *impossible to practice* the *doctrine* of *his Church, and unpopular to profess it.*" Here the gentleman admits impliedly, the *terms* of our *discussion*. It was "*the Presbyterian Church, in connexion with the General Assembly in the United States,*" and *the Confession of Faith of that Church,* which were by the rulers, (for which, to help the short memory of the gentleman, I appeal to the records of the Society,) defined, for his *attack*, and my *defence*. Early in this debate I distinctly declared, that I considered *our fathers* in Europe mistaken in some of their views of "religious liberty;" and that, at this day, the Presbyterian Church in Scotland, like the Episcopal Church in England, was most seriously wrong, in *permitting*, and, still more, in *cherishing* an *union* with the state: that American Presbyterians, like American Episcopalians, had renounced this system, as *contrary* to *liberty* and the *word* of God. The gentleman said it was *forced* on us by the American Revolution. I showed that *the alteration in our* Church *preceded* the Revolution of the *United States*. But *force*, or no *force*, here is the *change*. In this respect, the *American system* differs wholly from the *European system*. Now, we call on the American Catholics, to make the same *change*. They *pre-eminently*, and *originally*, held to the *duty* and *necessity* of an *union* of church and state; and at Rome this union is such, that the Pope refused to tolerate any other religion, (when even Napoleon proposed it,) saying, IT WAS CONTRARY TO THE CATHOLIC RELIGION TO ALTER THE CIVIL CONSTITUTION, BY WHICH THE CATHOLIC RELIGION WAS EXCLUSIVELY RECOGNIZED (in the papal states).

Now, in those very states, above all others, the Pope had the power to *alter this clause!* But he says "it is CONTRARY to the CATHOLIC RELIGION *to do it*;" and refused. It is clear, then, that in Rome "*religious liberty is contrary to the Catholic religion.*" Now, the *Catholic* religion is *unchangeable*, (says Mr. Hughes) and *is one and the same every where*. In *America*, then, "religious liberty," or, what is the same, the protection equally of all religions, is *contrary* to the Catholic religion. Here, then, is the difference. The American Presbyterian religion ha$ rejected this vile, and barbarous, and anti-apostolical principle. So has the American Episcopal Church. The gentleman goes to Europe to find *proof* that *we* in *America*, as Presbyterians, oppose *liberty*. We point him to the *change*. But his Church, he says, cannot *change*. Then, till it *can*, and *will*, and *does*, the American people will and must believe that it is a *persecuting church;* and, it is as fair to go for *proof* of *this* to Europe, and especially to *Rome*, and the *Pope*, as it is for Mr. Hughes to go there for his *creed* and *ordination*, and *right* to administer the *"sacraments."* To settle this question, I will record this inquiry:—" DOES MR. HUGHES THINK IT CONSISTENT WITH THE CATHOLIC RELIGION TO ESTABLISH IT BY LAW, AS THE EXCLUSIVE RELIGION OF THE PAPAL STATES!" *Now*, I will nail this inquiry up at the *portal* of the debate, till he gives a direct reply. Whenever he shall do so, I promise you, gentlemen, to settle this question—by his own showing. Till he does, you will know the *reason of his silence.*

The above statement disposes entirely of all his citations from *" Mr. Houston,"* of the Reformed Presbyterian Church, Ireland. And so far as these citations are honestly made, we cordially join with the gentleman in saying that every *Presbyterian act,* as *well as every papal* which went to apply *force* and use the *civil power* in *aid* of *religion*, was contrary to the rights of men and the word of God. *Popery began persecution in Scotland.* Cardinal Beaton, of bloody memory, burned men at the stake *before Presbyterians* had the *power to resist*. *Episcopalians*, afterwards, in a way full of horror and fierce crime, persecuted *Presbyterians;* and Presbyterians *persecuted* also, in their turn, and often with a high hand. For these things American Episcopalians and Presbyterians condemn their ancestors. But *popery* is the same. It cannot change. The butcher, Beaton, is a *saint and martyr.*

The gentleman, with *poetical* license, makes me to say, " *I am not answerable for Dr. Miller.* This is *only* directly *false!* He says the " only one whom he has not *disowned is Dr. Brownlee.*" This also is false. I commended Dr. Brownlee. The discomfited priests of New York praise him still more. " His works praise him." Hence the gall of the gentleman's attack. But I still reverence Dr. Wilie—as a learned divine, who, in *all other* respects, so far as I know, is a *sound Presbyterian,* as well as an able and good man. The views of his communion on the subject of the American Constitution differ much from ours. But if his assailant would read *" the Original Draft of a Pastoral Address from the Eastern Subordinate Synod of the Reformed Presbyterian Synod,"* he might learn a little of the doctor's real doctrine ; and spare the ignoble exhibitions of his own dishonourable attacks, under the guise of professed respect.

The gentleman says of me, " *The whole and only defence that the gentleman can make, is,* that *he* does not hold these *doctrines."* I defy him to produce such a defence, from all that I have said. He adds, *"Of what importance is he in the question?"* True— or *Mr. Hughes?* Let us remember this—when with a word he *dismisses* a pope, a canon, or a decree. *I go to our standards for defence;* he to his—NEVER; save to vitiate, deny, or becloud them.

In his long citations from acts of English and Scotch Assemblies, he has found it necessary to save his own character, by throwing in here and there a saving clause, wherever any *persecution* is found; as, for example, in presenting you the *Scotch Article* of the Confession corresponding to our Art. 4, Chap. XX. he says, *"The words in parenthesis are* OMITTED *in the present republican edition.* These words are, (AND BY THE POWER OF THE CIVIL MAGISTRATE); and this is the only *persecuting part.* In a word, he shows what *is not* in our standards; and *chafes* himself, not a little, that it is *wanting.* In another place he has the audacity to insert a long passage from the same foreign standards, and affix it to *our Confession,* (1) and then to add, *"The words in parenthesis are* OMITTED *since the revolution; and the very ambiguous phrase, appointing the magistrates of the country to be 'nursing fathers to the church,'* SUBSTITUTED.*"* That is, the *persecuting part* Mr. Hughes regrets to find is *not* in the *Confession of Faith of the Presbyterian Church in the United States."* Here again he *clears us,* by his own impertinent exposition. This is only *not forgery.* He then says :— *"Let us see whether this was not the doctrine of the Presbyterian Churches on the continent of Europe;"* and, *travelling out of the record at the first step,* quotes from Turretine and the Helvetic Confession.

Still there is no proof of *the opposition* of our doctrines to civil and religious *liberty;* for he has, at the close of these *long extracts,* still to own that they are *not ours;* and, therefore, though they help him to wend his weary way through the appointed half hour, they only show what *our doctrines* ARE NOT. They do serve one other purpose. They show that, from the days when popery fastened its yoke on the necks of the race, until the *asylum of liberty* was opened by Heaven, in a new world, that all Christendom had been *more* or *less* astray on *"the rights of conscience;"* and the relations of *the church to the state.* In *these errors Roman Catholics* led the *way* with supreme dominion. *The reformers,* rejecting the chief part of their *persecuting* principles, *retained some of them,* in a *milder form,* but still, retained a *portion.* Episcopalians in England, and Presbyterians in Scotland, retain establishments to this day. Popery remains the same *every where, unchangeable and unchanged—*

(1) Art. 3, Chap. XXIII.

till God shall destroy it with the brightness of his coming. In America, Presbyterians and Episcopalians, &c., have wholly renounced all appearance of the old leaven. Mr. Hughes says we are *dishonest*. We condemn the *errors* of our *fathers*, while we *own them errors*. Mr. Hughes says we are *dishonest* still. Very well. We know he regrets that we are not in the *same condemnation* with him and his system. If he will honestly abjure *papal persecutions*, we will then cease to charge him with the system of tyranny, *which* riots through his standards, and reigns *wherever it dare*, and where it *can*. Till then, American citizens must watch these emissaries of the Pope; and expose their anti-American, anti-social, anti-Christian discipline, doctrine, and morals.

The gentleman, in a late speech, made a most flourishing exhibition of Bishop England, as the representative of our country in the eternal city, and as puzzled to *defend* our *national* character, after the news reached Rome, of the *burning* of the *convent*. This is surely a most unfortunate allusion. It is not a long time since that man wrote to his Irish friends, one of the most barefaced letters, *against the American system of religious liberty*, that was ever penned. I give below an extract from his *patriotic opinions*. It was *published* in a *Charleston* (S. C.) *paper;* and the Bishop was at hand to *deny* or to *explain*, had that been possible. It is as follows :

" How often did I wish my voice could be heard across the deep, proclaiming to your meetings what I have seen and heard since I left you! *A people valuing freedom—and in the plenitude of its enjoyment—destroying religion—nay, having nearly effected its destruction by reducing to practice here, the principle which the Vetoists and Conciliators contend for amongst you.*

"*The Americans are loud in their reprobation of your servile aristocracy, who would degrade religion by placing its concerns under the control of a King's minister;* and could your aristocrats and place-hunters view the state of Catholicity here, *they would inveigh against the democrats, who would degrade religion by placing its concerns under the control of a mob, and I am perfectly convinced both are right. In both cases the principle is exactly the same—the mode of carrying it into operation is different.*

" I am convinced that if those gentlemen of the Irish hierarchy who are suspected, and I fear with good reason, of being favourable to vetoistical arrangements, had each one month's experience *of the operation of the principle here, their good sense, and piety, and zeal for religion, would compel them to suffer inconvenience, rather than commit the fate of the religion of millions under their charge, and myriads yet unborn, to the influence of a most destructive principle*, to release themselves and their flocks from the mitigated persecution under which they still suffer.

"*The people here, claim, and endeavour to assume, the same power which the clauses and conditions would give to the Crown amongst you*—though not to the same extent. *The consequence is, that religion is neglected, degraded, despised, and insulted with impunity.*"

Now if the Bishop is an American in heart, he has become so very *lately*. The above, is the boldest and basest attack I have ever seen, on our free institutions, from any pen, save those of George Thompson and Daniel O'Connell. The American people will be not a little disgusted to hear, in contrast with the above extracts, Bishop England's adulation of the *religious statesmen at Rome*. While in Rome, in his late visit, he actually wrote *a book* on the "*furniture, &c. of a church, vestments of the clergy,*" &c. &c., which he dedicated to "His eminence Cardinal Weld," &c. &c., "*my Lord Cardinal,*" &c. He tells him "*that the grain of mustard seed,* (the papal church in America,) *cultivated with success, under the auspices of Pius VI., has rapidly grown to a mighty tree, and protected by Gregory XVI. is now extending its branches above an enlightened community, reposing in peace under its shadow.*" He adds (in the dedication to a second work bound in the same volume, "*On the Ceremonies of the Holy Week.*") "In the venerable successor of St. Peter, I *behold the* former, active, zealous, and enlightened prefect *of the Propaganda,* whose DEEP INTEREST, and LABORIOUS EXERTIONS in THE CONCERNS OF THE CHURCH OF THE UNITED STATES, have *been so* BENEFICIAL." He calls the company of the Cardinals "THE VENERABLE AND EMINENT SENATE OF THE CHRISTIAN WORLD;" praises the Pope for that very effort against "liberty," which breathes through the detestable "*Encyclical Letter*" so repeatedly alluded to in the Controversy, (that letter was published Aug. 15th 1832, and the Bishop's book appeared at Rome, March 26, 1833,) and he says, "*that stripping the Holy See of its temporal independence, would inflict a deep wound on religion.*" Yet Mr. Hughes says, the *temporal prince* has no *relation to the Ecclesiastical Head of the Church.* In a word, this prelate by his public defence of ministerial dissipations, by his unworthy and antirepublican sycophancy at Rome; and by his direct attacks on the institutions of his country, not to name his *open defence* of the Inquisition, has disgraced his prelacy, and sundered every tie that could constitute or continue him *an American.*

But this spirit is not peculiar to him. A papal journal in our country, holds the following language. (It is from the "Catholic Telegraph," Cincinnati, and was called out by the trials of Boston in relation to the burning of the Convent.)

"*A system of government,* which admits a feeling of alarm in the execution of the laws, from the vengeance of the mob, which Mr. Austin (the prosecuting attorney,) distinctly allowed to be the case, a vengeance exhibited by letters to the public officers and threats to the public authorities, may be very fine in theory, very fit for imitation on the part of those who seek the power of the mob, in contradistinction to justice, and the public interest. But it is not of a nature to invite the reflecting part of the world, and shows at least that it has evils. A public officer in England, who would *publicly avow such a fear of executing his duty*, and carrying into effect the law of the realm, ought and would be thrust out of the office, by public opinion. THIS ONE FACT IS CONDEMNATION OF THE SYSTEM OF AMERICAN INSTITUTIONS, CONFIRMED LATELY BY NUMEROUS OTHER PROOFS." That is, our institutions are a *failure*, because a *mob burned a Convent;* and the Court did not find a bill for the Catholics, as strong as was expected. "*Therefore our institutions are to be denounced as worthy of imitation only, by those who seek power of the mob.*" Such is the audacity of *foreign emissaries; renegado-Jesuits*, the bondsmen of the Pope, who come here to *corrupt* and to *traduce* the country. In *substance*, Mr. Hughes has told us, that our nation is disgraced by that conflagration. These haughty bondsmen of a foreign despot, the Pope, seem to think indeed, that *this world was made for them*, and their master; and that we are honoured by holding their *sacred persons* in the land; or even by being noticed by their lordly anathemas.

But Bishop England is not *alone* in denouncing our "democracy," and RESPONSIBILITY TO THE PEOPLE, AS THE GREAT PRINCIPLE OF THE AMERICAN SYSTEM. "My Lord Bishop Flaget, of Bardstown, Kentucky, (says the admirable Brutus,) in a letter to his patrons abroad, has this plain hint at ULTERIOR POLITICAL DESIGN; *and that no less than the entire subversion of our republican government.*" Speaking of the difficulties, and discouragements, the Catholic missionaries have to contend with, in converting the Indians, the last difficulty in their way, he says, is "*their continual traffic among the whites*, WHICH CANNOT BE HINDERED, AS LONG AS THE REPUBLICAN GOVERNMENT SHALL SUBSIST."

This intimation of the bishop is extracted from "Annales de l'Association, de la Propagation de la Foi," being a periodical continuation of the "*Lettres Edifiantes*" à Lyons, et à Paris, 1829. As to the case of the "*knocking off of the hat at the bishop's approach*," no doubt the Rev. Mr. Nason *believed* it. For, in the *first* place, there were divers affirmations, not on *Presbyterian authority* merely, that something of the kind actually *did* occur; and, *secondly*, it is notorious, that *in every Catholic country on earth, the man who does not kneel in the street, as the host passes*, will lose not only his *hat*, but perhaps his *head also; for these holy processions*, paying idolatrous worship to a piece of bread, are accompanied by armed men, *to force adoration from every spectator;* and wo to the hapless "heretic" who *cannot* escape through the crowd, and *will not bow down and worship the idol*. Even a *little credulity*, therefore, (supposing the whole story false, into which, however, I intend to inquire,) may be pardoned, when we know, that *Catholics* do the very thing charged on them in Rome, Spain, Portugal, and all the papal states and islands of the American hemisphere.

Bishop England says, (1) "*all who are not in the procession, as the Pope passes—kneel.*" The Pope, having worshipped "*the hidden God,*" as the bishop profanely calls the consecrated wafer—*takes the vessel containing it,* and bareheaded, with incense burning before him, leads on the procession. He says, "NOTHING IS MORE OFFENSIVE TO CATHOLICS, THAN *a transgression of the principle here alluded to;*" viz., "*to kneel as the procession passes, in a decorous, external conformity.*"

I have seen many persons from the West Indies, South America, Spain, and Rome, who *confirm the above statements about being forced to kneel at the point of the bayonet,* or else precipitately retreat before *the approach of the procession.*

It has been a frequent argument of the gentleman during this discussion, that the principles of Presbyterians *led to licentiousness.* Especially has he been loud in thus charging the doctrine of *election.* It did not suffice him, that the Apostle Paul, eighteen centuries ago, met and answered this *heathen* objection, in his *Epistle to the Church of Rome.*

"What shall we say then? Shall we continue in sin, that grace may abound? God forbid. How shall we, that are *dead* to sin, live any longer therein?" (2) "For sin shall not have dominion over you; for ye are not under the law, but under grace. What then? Shall we sin because we are not under the law, but under grace? God forbid. God be thanked ye were the servants of sin; but ye have obeyed from the heart, that form of doctrine which was delivered you. Being then *made free from sin,* ye became the servants of righteousness." (Verses 14, 15, 17, 18.) "Whom He did foreknow, He also did predestinate to be *conformed to the image of his son.*" (Rom. viii. 29.) But Paul's testimony did not *suffice.* The gentleman, in a written paper, thrown in during the discussion, thus said :—

"*Consequently, as individuals, they (Presbyterians) may pay their debts by an act of the legislature, and live in affluence afterwards. They may give to* BIBLE SOCIETIES, *Tract Societies, Sunday School Union, and Missionary Societies,* WHAT BELONGS TO THEIR CREDITORS, *and yet eat well, dress well, sleep well, and feel no remorse.*" And, again; "*The same motives of selfishness, that govern* INDIVIDUALS, *govern also, more or less, all sects and denominations. . . . . The doctrine of Presbyterianism authorizes the remorseless violation of the principles of justice, honesty, truth; and permits that sect to establish its own ascendancy over other sects,* on THEIR RUINS.

(1) Page 64, Ceremonies of the Holy Week.   (2) Chap. VI. v 1—2.

And when they shall have done so, though your property, and reputation, and liberty to worship God according to the dictates of your conscience, should fall a sacrifice to their arts, or sectarian ambition, still they will feel no remorse." These are, indeed, heavy charges—not only against Presbyterians, but against all God's people, who hold the same views, and (I tremble while I say it) *against the word of God.* For these ungodly slanders, I need not say, he brings not a solitary proof. There are but three methods of proof possible in the case.

1. He might refer directly to the *word of God*. *His word*, even Mr. Hughes will allow, contains *no doctrine opposed to good morals, and the well-being of society*. Then, are these Presbyterian doctrines contained in the Bible? This question, however, the gentleman dare not touch. A Papist has no *liberty* to reason on this subject. If you convince him, he is yet not *convinced*. His *rule of faith forbids him to think for himself;* and if he should venture to *reason*, he is guilty of this absurdity, that though neither *reason, nor the Bible, nor any thing else*, but *"his infallible judge of controversies"* is capable of convincing HIM; yet, he expects OTHERS to be open to *reason*, and to be led by *private interpretation*, though *he will not*. The Papist declares, at the outset, that he is *incapable* of being *convinced;* and *rejects* those very means which he tries to use in *convincing others.* He is, therefore, insincere at every step, and cannot honestly reason on the subject; or, if honest, absurdly *inconsistent.*

2. The next method of *proof*, is an appeal to the *whole Presbyterian system.* What *does it say?* Does it not, at large, in the Confession of Faith (1) most abundantly and explicitly declare, *that without holiness, no man shall see the Lord; that repentance, regeneration, good works, and growth in these, and perseverance in them till death, is the end and effect of the decrees of God; that love to God,* and *love to man, are binding on all,* and that *none are, or can be, saved without it.* It is true, we do not think with Papists, that there is *any saving merit in good works,* and WE prefer to let GOD ELECT; they prefer the POPE *to do it;* and say, that none can be saved, who *reject their faith, and are not subject to their Pope.* We prefer to let *God* fix the *terms of salvation;* and believe, as he hath said, *"that whosoever shall call on the name of the Lord, shall be saved,"* even if it be from the bosom of the fallen Church of Rome.

But the gentleman says we have a *"hidden sense"* in our *standards*, differing from our *avowed* principles. But *"secreta monita"* belong to him and his Jesuit brethren! And it was

---

(1) Chap. III., section 3; Chap. X., Chap. XII.; XIII. *Of Sanctification;* Chap. XIV., Chap. XV. Of Repentance unto Life; XVI. *Of Good Works*, to name no more.

"*from our standards*" that he pledged himself to *prove our opposition to liberty.* Here they are. No *torture* can make them prove that our doctrines advocate or sustain licentiousness, dishonesty, &c., &c. You see, gentlemen, how *utterly* he has failed; and you must be struck (by contrast) with the abundant testimony produced on the other side.

3. *The other, and only other conceivable method of proof is from facts.* And here I have called in vain for proof, that "*our doctrine authorizes the remorseless violation of justice, holiness, and truth.*" Where has he laid his hand on one fact, or one page of history to prove it? I know we *are at best unworthy;* and that, *compared with God's holy standard, we come very far short.* But, compared *with other denominations* of our brethren, above all, comparing *Presbyterian* with *papal* countries—or *Presbyterian* with *papal* clergy—or Presbyterian with *papal laity,* who will venture to say that *papal doctrines* have produced better, or as *good effects* on the public, or on the personal character and morals, as *Presbyterian?* The gentleman himself has not ventured to say *it,* much less to attempt the *proof of it.*

Now, I admit, that any *system of doctrine,* which *necessarily leads to licentiousness,* or that *habitually* produces, or *even permits* and *connives* at the sins charged on us by the gentleman, is false, wicked, offensive to God, contrary to the Bible, and destructive of society, as well as of the souls of men. I join issue with the gentleman on this ground, and am willing by it to stand or fall. Perhaps he may say my opinion of Calvinism is *partial. I own I love it.* But we adduced Swift, (*Episcopalian,*) Dryden, (*Papist,*) Bancroft, (*Unitarian,*) testifying to its direct and mighty influence in promoting *liberty.* The gentleman *passed* by Dryden, and charged *the rest* with *partiality.* But we will add other witnesses. *Bishop Burnet* (does the gentleman *know him?* he was a moderate Arminian,) says,—"A Calvinist is taught, *by his opinions,* to think *meanly of himself,* [how *unlike* the picture drawn by Mr. Hughes!] and *to ascribe the honour of all to God;* which lays in him a deep *foundation for humility:* he is also much inclined to *secret prayer,* and to a *fixed dependence* on God."

The article *Predestination,* in the *Encyclopedia Britannica,* said to be written by an able foreign lawyer, tell us,—"There is one remark which we feel ourselves bound in justice to make, *although it appears* to us *somewhat singular.* It is this: that from the earliest ages down to our own days, if we consider the character of the ancient stoics, the Jewish Essenes, the MODERN CALVINISTS and Jansenists, when compared with that of their antagonists, the Epicureans, the Sadducees, the Arminians, and the JESUITS, we shall find that they *have excelled, in no small degree,* in the practice of the most *rigid and respectable virtues;* and have been the *highest honour of their own ages,* and the best *models for imitation for every succeeding age."* This surely is no measured praise; and yet, that it is from one who was *no Calvinist*, appears, not only from the above remark on *"the singularity"* of *the fact*, stated by him, but still more, from the following sentence. "At the same time, it must be confessed *that their virtues have in general been rendered unamiable, by a tinge of gloomy and severe austerity."*

Finally. *"In Letters addressed to a Serious and Humble Inquirer,"* &c., by the Rev Edward Cooper, Rector of Hampstall Ridwane, (a distinguished Episcopal clergyman of England, and no CALVINIST,) it is thus written: "Among *no denomination* or *description of professing Christians, is there to be found a larger portion of humble, pious, and devoted servants of God, persons of a truly Christian spirit, zealous of good works, and exemplary in every duty and relation of life, than among those who hold the Calvinistic tenets.* I am sure that your *observation and your candour will fully justify this statement.* And, therefore, *so far this system is to be judged of by its* ACTUAL EFFECTS, I think, that on a candid reconsideration of the subject, you will be induced to abandon your objection, and to admit, that it was founded on *an erroneous* and *partial view of the subject."* The *objection* which he was exposing, is the same urged by Mr. Hughes—*"the immoral tendency of the system."* He says, *"*WHERE *is the tendency of this doctrine to make* its followers *slothful,* or *confident, negligent of the means of grace,* or *inattentive to moral and relative duties ?"* He also calls it *"a caluminated system."* It has been so from the days of the Apostle Paul, down to our times. But if the gentleman will appeal to history; *to facts;* go to *Calvinistic* New England; to *Cavinistic* Scotland; to *Calvinistic* Holland; or to *American Calvinists;* and compare them with the *glory* of popery anywhere, in any age! *This is* the test. Let us appeal to it. Agreeing with the gentleman, that any *system whose tendency is immoral,* is *ruinous to society,* and to *all its blessings, civil and religious,* I go hand in hand with him, into his own boasted religion. And I will take my examples from the *era of the Reformation, after the world had made a fair trial of popery for ages; when* Rome had "extinguished in their own blood" the Albigenses and Waldenses; and when PROTESTANTS, properly so called, arose to REFORM, and to RESIST. I will also go not to *Protestant,* but to *papal writers*—who can be supposed to have no *"prejudices"* against the "Catholic Church," and whose testimony shall decide the question.

In our late Controversy, several references were made to the *" Consilium,"* or "Letter of Advice," given to Paul the III. by four cardinals and five prelates, appointed by him for counselling him, on the state of the Roman Catholic Church. My Reverend friend seemed exceedingly reluctant to *touch* this state paper from

Rome; or to permit the American people to *hear* of it. Copious extracts from it, were left almost unnoticed by him, and for this plain reason, that the *less* said about this extraordinary document the *better*. But it is an American principle to examine every subject. This too, is the fearless, open-faced spirit of universal truth. It is needful for *Rome*, but not for Christianity, to *cover up*. *Rome* suffers from free inquiry; *truth* and freedom suffer without it. As it is very possible that my learned and *candid* friend may deny the authority, and even existence, of this document, a few words by way of preface may not be out of place. Pope Paul III. appointed the nine dignitaries of the church, whose names are subscribed to the paper, to give him their advice, as to the state of the church, and the best method of reforming it. This they did with such plainness that he did not venture to carry their suggestions into effect; though he so far approved them as to publish their letter. Its disclosures were of such a character that the Protestants soon republished it in various languages. In Germany, Sturmius published it in Latin, with a preface; and Luther gave it to the world in German "accompanied (says the learned M'Crie in his work on the Reformation in Italy, p. 115,) with animadversions, in which among other satirical remarks, he says that the cardinals contented themselves with removing the small *twigs*, while they allowed the *trunk* of corruption to remain unmolested; and like the Pharisees of old, *strained at gnats and swallowed camels*. To set this before the eyes of the readers, he prefixed to the book a print, in which the Pope is represented as seated on a high throne surrounded by the cardinals, who hold in their hands, long poles with foxes' tails fixed to them like brooms, with which they sweep the room."

Pallavicini, the papal historian of the Council of Trent (Lib. III. Sec. 59,) complains that the Pope, in this production, *exposes* the church. He writes as follows : "...... By ordering a reformation of morals, he acknowledged the existence of corruptions, and countenanced the distracting speeches which heretics circulated among the vulgar."

Cardinal Quirini refers to this document (in his Diatriba De Gestis Pauli III.) *in proof* that Paul *wished to reform the church.* He tells us it was printed at Rome by Paul III. A.D. 1538. Wolfius (in his Leo. Memorial. Tom. ii. p. 398—449.) inserts this Consilium, or "Advice of the Bishop," at length, with a Preface by Vergerio. It was also reprinted by Schelhorn, with a letter to Cardinal Quirini. (See M'Crie's Italy, pages 114—120.)

It is a singular fact, that Caraffa, one of these nine advisers, *afterward*, when he became Pope Paul IV. actually put his *own joint production* into the PROHIBITORY INDEX, as a condemned book! Another Pope once said, when *taxed* with a *change* in his views, after his elevation, "*since I have risen higher, I see better."* On this principle ought we not to recommend Brother Hughes for speedy and high promotion at Rome?

The following translation of the Letter of Advice, was made by the Rev. Dr. Claggett of the Established Church of Great Britain, and may be seen with his able Preface in "The Preservative against Popery," vol. 1st.

So much for the history of this document. As to its *charater and meaning,* we ask no more than a faithful perusal of it, to convince any honest man that such a church *cannot be infallible:* Or if this be infallibility—from such *perfection* good Lord deliver us! Let it be borne in mind that this paper is Roman Catholic testimony.

" *The advice given to* POPE PAUL THE THIRD, *by four Cardinals, and five other Prelates, whose names are underwritten, in order to the amendment of the state of the Church.*

" Most blessed Father, we are so unable to express that mighty thanks the whole body of the Church is bound to pay to Almighty God, who has in these times raised up you to be the Supreme Bishop and Pastor of his flock, and gives you likewise that mind which you have, that we have no hope so much as to conceive how great they are. For that spirit of God, by which, as the prophet speaks, the heavens are made firm, has decreed, *as we cannot but see, by your hand to support the church, now that she is not only leaning, but just falling headlong into ruin; nay, to advance her to her ancient eminence, and to restore her to her former beauty.*

" It is no uncertain conjecture of this purpose of God, which we are enabled to make, whom your holiness called to you and required, that without any regard had to you, or to any one else, we should signify to you *what those abuses are, and most grievous distempers wherewith the Church of God, and especially the court of Rome, has for a long time been affected, whereby also it has come to pass, that these pestilent diseases growing to their height by little and little, the Church, as we see, is upon the very brink of ruin.* And *because your holiness* (being taught by the Divine Spirit, who, as St. *Austin* says, does without noise of words speak in the heart) *very well understands this to be the original of these mischiefs; that some Popes, your predecessors, having itching ears, as says the apostle Paul, heaped up teachers after their own lusts, not to learn from them what they ought to do, but that they should take pains and employ their wit to find out ways how it might be lawful for them to do what they pleased:* to which we may add, that as the *shadow* follows the body, so *flattery follows greatness,* and truth can hardly find any way to *the ears of princes;* hence it has come to pass, that there have been doctors ever ready to maintain, that all benefices *being the Pope's* and *the Lord having a right to sell what is his own, it must necessarily follow, that the Pope is not capable of the guilt of simony;* insomuch, that *the Pope's will and pleasure, whatever it be, must needs be the rule for all that he does; which doubtless would end in believing every thing lawful that he had a mind to do.*

"*From this source, as from the Trojan horse, those so many abuses, and such mortal diseases, have broken forth into the Church of God, which have reduced her, as we see, almost to a state of desperation; the fame of these things having come to the ears even of infidels,* (let your holiness believe us, speaking what we know) *who deride Christianity more for this, than for any thing else; so that through ourselves, we must needs say through ourselves, the name of Christ is blasphemed amongst the nations.*

" But to reduce all our thoughts to some certain heads; *since your holiness is both the prince of these provinces, which are the ecclesiastic estate and territory,* and *withal, the governor of the universal Church, and likewise the bishop of Rome;* we have not taken upon ourselves to speak of those things which concern that *principality,* which, by your prudence, is so excellently governed, as we see. We will touch upon these matters only, that belong to the office of the universal pastor, and some also that are proper to the *Roman* bishop.

" First of all then, we think, most blessed Father, according to what *Aristotle* says, in his *Politics,* that, as in every other commonwealth, so in the ecclesiastical government of the Church of *Christ,* it should be esteemed the principal law of all, that laws should be observed as much as is possible; and that it *be not lawful to dispense with the laws,* but for a cause urgent and necessary. But one thing there is of moment next to this, or rather of far greater consequence, as *we think, that it is not lawful for the Pope, who is Christ's vicar, to make any gain to himself of the use of the keys,* of the power of the keys we say, which *Christ* hath committed to him. For this is the commandment of *Christ: Freely ye have received, freely give.*

"And here the first abuse in this kind is, that in the *ordination of clerks, especially of Presbyters, no manner of care and diligence is used, but every where the most uneducated youths, of the vilest parentage, set out with nothing but evil manners, are admitted to holy orders, even to priesthood itself, though that be the character which expresseth Christ more than all others.* From hence grow innumerable scandals; from hence comes *the contempt of the ecclesiastic order;* and *hence it is, that the reverence of God's worship is not only diminished, but well nigh extinguished.*

" Another abuse of a most grievous nature, is in the collation of ecclesiastical benefices, especially with cure of souls, and above all, of bishoprics; the manner having been, that good provision is made for those who have the benefices, but for the flock of *Christ*, and the Church, *none at all.*

"There is another abuse also in the changing of benefices, upon contracts, that are, all of them, *simoniacal*, and in which no regard is had to any thing but gain.

"Again; it is an ancient law established by *Clement*, that *the sons of priests* should not *succeed* their fathers in their benefices; and this, lest the common patrimony of the Church should become a private estate. But, as we hear, this venerable law is dispensed with; and we must not conceal what every prudent person will, by himself, discern to be a great truth, that *no one thing* hath raised more of that *envy* against *the clergy*, from whence so many *seditions* have *already happened*, and *more are at hand*, than *this turning of ecclesiastical profits and revenue from being a common to a private thing. All men* had some *hope before this*, but *now they are reduced to despair, and sharpen their tongues against this holy see.*

"These things being set right, which refer to the *appointment of your ministers*, who are, as it were, the instruments for the *right performing* of God's worship, and the *well-ordering* of the people in a Christian life; we must now come to those things which relate to *the government of Christian people:* as to which matter, most holy father, there is an abuse in the first place to be corrected; and the greatest care is to be taken, that bishops especially, no nor curates, be absent from their churches and parishes, unless for a weighty cause, but keep their residence; but especially the bishops, since they are the *husbands of the Church* committed to their care. For we appeal to God, that *no sight can be more lamentable to a Christian man going through Christendom, than this solitude of the Churches. Almost all the pastors are withdrawn from their flocks, which are, almost every where, entrusted with hirelings.*

"In the orders of the *Religious*, there is another abuse to be corrected, that many of them are so degenerate, that they are grown scandalous, and their examples pernicious to the *Seculars.* We think the *Conventual orders* are to be abolished, not by doing to any man that injury of dispossessing him, *but by forbidding them to admit any more:* for thus, without wronging any one, they *would soon be worn out, and good Religious might be substituted instead of them; but at present, it were best, that all children, who are not yet professed, should be taken from their monasteries.*

"We have already said, most holy father, that it is by no means *lawful to make any gain by the use of the keys*, in which matter the words of Christ stand firm and sure, *Freely ye have received, freely give.* This does not only belong to your holiness to take notice of, but to all who share in this power; and therefore, we desire, that it may be observed by your Legates and *Nuncios:* for, as *the custom which has much prevailed*, dishonours this see, and makes the people clamorous, so the contrary would be exceedingly for the ornament of the one, and for the edification of the other.

"*Christian people are disturbed by another abuse, which concerns Nuns, that are under the care of the Conventual Friars, where, in most monasteries, public sacrileges are committed, to the intolerable scandal of the citizens. Let your holiness deprive the Conventuals of this care, and give it to the ordinaries, or to others, as you shall see cause.*

"There is another abuse in the *collectors for the Holy Ghost,* for *St. Anthony,* and others of this kind, *which put cheats upon rusticks, and simple people, and entangle them in a world of superstition.* These collectors, we think, ought to be taken away.

"We conceive it also to be an abuse, to dispense with the marriage of those *that are in the second degree of consanguinity,* or affinity, unless it be for a weighty reason. Nor should dispensations be granted without other degrees, but where the cause is honest, and *still without money,* unless the parties were married before; in which case, it is lawful to impose a pecuniary punishment, in order to absolution from sin already committed, and to convert it to pious uses, such as your holiness promotes. *For, as where there is no sin in the use of the keys to be done away, no money can be demanded;* so where absolution from sin is desidered, a pecuniary mulct may be laid, and designed for pious uses.

"In the absolution of a simoniacal person, there is another abuse; and 'tis a dismal thing to consider, *that this plague reigns in the Church to that degree, that some are not afraid to be guilty of simony, and to go presently for absolution.—The truth is, they buy their absolution, and so they keep the benefice they bought before.*

"*It has been a custom also to change the wills of testators, who have left a certain sum of money for pious and charitable purposes; which, by the authority of your holiness, is transferred to the heir or the legatee, under pretence of their poverty, &c., and this is gained by money too.*

"And thus, according to our capacity, having summarily described all those things which belong to the duty of a supreme bishop of the Catholic Church; it remains, that we say something *of that* which belongs to the *Roman* bishop.—This city of *Rome* is both the mother of the Church, and mistress of other Churches: wherefore, the worship of God and purity of manners should flourish there most of all.

"*Nay, in this city, whores walk about, as if they were goodly matrons; or they ride upon mules, and are at noon-day followed up and down by men of the best account in the families of cardinals and by clergymen. We see no such degeneracy in any other city, but in this, which is to be an example to all others. These whores live in splendid houses: 'tis a filthy abuse, and ought to be mended.*

" We hope that you are chosen to restore the name of *Christ,* forgotten by the nations, and even by us of the clergy; that hereafter it may live in our hearts, and appear in our actions, to heal our diseases, to reduce the flock of Christ into one sheep-fold, to remove from us that indignation and vengeance of God, which we deserve, which is now ready to fall upon us, which now hangs over our heads.

"*The names of the Cardinals, &c.*

" GASPARD, Cardinal Contarene.
" JOB. PETER, Cardinal Theatine, afterwards Paul IV.
" JAMES, Cardinal Sadolet.
" REGINALD POLE, Cardinal of England.
" FREDERICK, Archbishop of Brundusium.
" JOB. MATTHEW GIBET, Bishop of Verona.
" GREGORY CORTESE, Abbot of St. George at Venice.
" FRIAR THOMAS, Master of the Sacred Palace.
" There should be another to make nine."

Now here is a picture of *the papal church* by *papal authority,* after it had ruled the world for ages. We have necessarily omitted perhaps one half of its contents, from the extreme length of the *document.* But let any impartial mind survey this scene of a church in ruins, with the head and the members, the ministry and the monasteries *rotten* at the heart, and all tending to ruin, on the testimony of many of their own prelates! What does this history say? Does it not show the need *of 'a reformation?* And, if the gentleman's argument be true, as we allow, that doctrines which *lead to immorality* are *ruinous* and anti-social doctrines, then, what must those doctrines be which produce, or even tolerate, such corruptions? It is but reasoning from *effect* to *cause.* "*By their fruits ye shall know them,*" saith our Lord. Here they are in loathsome profusion.

If my hearers will now advert to all that I have said of the *doctrines* of *indulgences,* of *purgatory,* of *penance,* of *priestly pardon of sins,* of *auricular confession,* of *celibacy,* to name no more, they will be able clearly to discern the natural, the necessary *causes* of these *tremendous effects* on morals and social *order.*

Before I close I must notice some of the gentleman's impertinences, which come out at the close, like *dregs,* from an exhausted mind, and a choleric spirit.

He says my "*quotation of his language* (about the Jesuits) *is not to be depended on."* I spurn his reflections; and appeal to his documents. He said I paid him an unintended *"compliment"* by calling him a Jesuit. Moreover, he has been their *eulogist* uniformly, in *both* my controversies with him. In the *first*,(1) Mr. Hughes says of the Jesuits:—*"In my opinion religion and science suffered by the suppression of the Jesuits; and that both are gainers by their restoration."* Is not this *praise?* And, in the *light* of my *previous abundant exposure of their terrific doctrines*, it is praise most disgraceful to the author.

He said, at the same *place*, "THE INQUISITION MAY HAVE BEEN A GOOD THING *abused."* It is to trifle with Heaven, and insult all men, but *inquisitors*, to say so. Is not this being its "apologist?" If it should result that I misquote his words, now that they are written words, the gentleman must remember that if words be changed *after* I quote them, it is no fault of mine. If they be not changed, my quotations will be found *literal*, when I profess them so. Sometimes it is necessary to give the substance—a page of *trash* in a *sentence*. I try to be a faithful *chymist*.

Dr. *Miller* is still kept up before the public. Mr. Hughes reminds me of a *fop* I once knew, whose chief business seemed to be to convince the *little world* that he was *intimate* with the *great world*. Mr. Hughes may be assured that *Dr. Cook*, and the other *kitchen*-scribblers who unite with him in calumniating Dr. Miller, have not destroyed an hour of his rest. The only *emotion* which Dr. Miller and many others feel, in contemplating these men, (who dishonour, by being in it, a much valued Christian Church) is, *wonder* that they do not go *all the way* to *popery;* like the newly "converted Burlington brother," who has relieved himself of inconsistency, wife, children, and all *"other big and little responsibilities,"* as Fanny Wright called such *ungodly encumbrances*, by joining himself to you.

The gentleman is mistaken about my "altering my tone." He *falsely* charged me with unkindness to *"poor" emigrants.* I replied, "we fear not the *virtuous* poor. *Rich, or poor, if they be Jesuits, priests, or their tools, we do fear them.*

I regret that my allusion to the *"convent"* makes the gentleman expose *himself.* My defence is in the *proof* already given, that, in other days (2) *monastic institutions were very brothels.* If the Boston mob were mistaken in the opinion, I cannot help it. I asserted no more than that they did so think.

The retreat of Mr. Hughes before Daniel Webster, and the other authorities cited by me, is *characteristic*. His forces, like the *Roman* quincunx, retain their *shape*, though they may *shift*

---

(1) See Letter XXXI.
(2) See the same subject, called *"sacrilege,"* exposed by the *nine bishops* and *cardinals* quoted in this speech.

their position. He now retreats, blustering against me. I called for his authority for saying that the Sunday School Union declared "*their desire to become the dictators of the consciences of thousands of immortal beings.*" This the *gentleman quoted, with appropriate marks, and underscored,* as from the documents of *the Society.* I called for the reference. He has *withheld it.* I now demand it again—the *year* and the *page* of the *report containing it;* and, if not produced, I will expose the gentleman.

In reply to his question, *How the rich Protestants are to be bought up by monies sent from such poor Catholic countries abroad?* I answer. The *Catholic Church* is *rich.* The *pope and priesthood are rich.* The *emperor of Austria is rich.* The *monastic houses are rich.* The *Jesuits are rich.* The *people* are poor, and oppressed too. The *church* and the *pope,* the *Austrian* monarch, and the propaganda, and the Leopold Foundation, *they* send the *money* and the *men.* Does the answer satisfy?

In regard to "*Mr. Smith,*" his *papal* vouchers and *recommendations* falsify Mr. Hughes's attack. Gentlemen, you perhaps recollect the fable of the *fox* and the *grapes.* The *grapes,* which were out of his *reach,* were *sour.* As soon as a man leaves popery he is not "*worth having;*" yet they catch only the *off-scourings* of *Protestantism*—half crazy women, who want homes; *romantic, disappointed* old maids, and men who have sunk into contempt in Protestant pulpits. So far popery *drains usefully.* You are welcome to all you have, or may yet have.

It is *ominous* to see the priest of Rome assail "*the continental Congress.*" He is most wise to forbear *meeting* these statements. It is easy to *assert* or *deny.* Now, here is that venerable body publicly declaring that "THE CATHOLIC RELIGION HAS DELUGED ENGLAND WITH BLOOD." A priest of Rome denies it. Which is the more WEIGHTY, DISINTERESTED PARTY?—which most devoted to *American liberty?* Yet it was to warn England against popery in North America that the paragraph which so sorely wounds the "man of sin" was drafted.

P.S Why has the gentleman so strangely forgotten John Wesley's argument? Let us hear from him on that subject.

"*Is the Presbyterian Religion, in any or in all its principles or doctrines, opposed to civil or religious liberty?*"

AFFIRMATIVE IV.—MR. HUGHES.

I HAD occasion, Mr. President, to point out to the attention of this meeting and the public, the efforts of the gentleman, to accomplish, by the help of prejudice, what he knows he cannot accomplish by the use of *legitimate* weapons, sound argument, and sober reasoning. When these are fairly twisted out of his hands, and turned against him, he stoops to avail himself of every abusive epithet, that may render his opponent odious in the estimation of those for whom alone he seems to speak and write—the bigoted, the prejudiced, the ignorant. "Papist," "Emissaries of the Pope," "Foreigner," "Jesuit,"—these are his last and safest resource. I showed him, that a *similar mode* of refutation was employed against Christ, by those who called him a "Samaritan," and said "he had a devil." In other words, I showed him, that *abuse* is *not argument*. I refer the reader to the passage; and, if it appears, that I did NOT "compare myself to Jesus Christ," NOR him to "the murderers of our Master," it will follow, that in charging me with having done this, he "BEARS FALSE WITNESS AGAINST HIS NEIGHBOUR." Is it not so? I refer to the passage.

He next returns to the "PREDESTINATION." He admits, that the burning of Huss was "foreordained" by God; and yet, charges on the council, as a crime, that it did not OPPOSE and DEFEAT what God had thus "foreordained!!!" But, I refer to the argument, *as stated in my last speech*, and ask the reader to say whether the gentleman has not completely *evaded it*. He cannot meet it. A doctrine which has decided, that "*from all eternity*, God has FOREORDAINED WHATSOEVER COMES TO PASS," takes away *all* liberty, civil, religious, and personal. There are no two ways of it. The thing is plain, and cannot be denied. Either the doctrine is false, or else there is no liberty. Man, *according to that principle*, is a machine; and conscience, a mockery. I wish the gentleman to go back to my last speech, and attempt to show error in the reasoning by which I established this consequence. That he has not done so, I take as a proof, that he feels the thing to be impossible. His attempt to prove the doctrine by texts of Scripture, shows, that I stated it fairly—and this is enough. If the question were of the TRUTH of the doctrine, and not of its bearing on civil and religious liberty, I should follow him, and expose his perversion of the sacred writings, when he quotes *them* in support of the blasphemy, that makes God first "*foreordain*" the sin, and then punish the sinner for having done that which HE COULD NOT AVOID DOING!!

I had stated, that (except, perhaps, the Congregationalists) "the high-toned Presbyterians were the *only* denomination that had not become ashamed of the avowal of this doctrine." He does not meet the statement; and yet, by a slight *shifting of terms*, he affects to have refuted it. He says, the "twelve CREEDS of the original Reformers," and the "Episcopalian ARTICLES" have it. But had I denied this? Did I assert, that "CREEDS and ARTICLES" —parchment, are capable of becoming "ashamed?" I said, those "DENOMINATIONS" had become ashamed to avow the doctrine of predestination, as avowed by the high-toned Presbyterians. Has the gentleman refuted the statement? Not a word of it. He slides the question from the "denomination" spoken of, into the "CREEDS and ARTICLES;" and this he calls "proof."

He charges me with having said, that "except the Calvinistic Baptists, the Baptists are not Calvinists." The gentleman, himself, is entitled to the merit of so silly an assertion. I know, as well as he, that NONE of the Baptists are "Calvinists." The branch of that denomination, which holds the doctrine of "foreordination, is called, from this circumstance, "Calvinistic Baptists;" and I stated what the gentleman has not denied, that all the *other sections* of that denomination had become ashamed of the avowal of that doctrine. When he *invents* a witty statement, and puts it forth as mine, it becomes proper, that I should disclaim it, and let him enjoy the advantages of his wit.

That St. Augustine ever taught the doctrine, that "*God has, from all eternity, foreordained* WHATSOEVER *to pass,*" is what I positively deny. And now, let the gentleman "expose me," as he promised. To assert it, is a libel on his character. The doctrine implicitly accuses God, as being the *author* of sin; and it is a libel on the character of the Scriptures to say, that *they* inculcate any such impious tenet.

I said, that by his creed, he is bound to "REMOVE, *according to his place and calling*, ALL FALSE WORSHIP, and all the monuments of idolatry;" and that, by the AMERICAN CONSTITUTION he is bound to leave them where they are. If he *obeys* his country, he *disobeys* God. Can he obey both? Impossible. So long as the Presbyterians abstain from "REMOVING ALL FALSE WORSHIP," so long do they continue in the VIOLATION *of one of God's commandments*, as may be seen in the Confession of Faith. I ask the gentleman whether this is not the fact? I ask, "*on Presbyterian principles,*" how he can get over it? He "thinks" this is the "twelfth time" the question has been put;

—well; let him *answer it*, and I promise I shall not afflict him with it afterwards. But let him meet it fairly and fully. Will he tell us how Presbyterians can obey GOD by "removing false worship;" and obey the CONSTITUTION by NOT *removing* it, but minding their own business?

I quoted from the Confession, the doctrine, that the "MAGISTRATES" OF THIS REPUBLIC are bound to be "NURSING FATHERS" to the Church. I have quoted from the same Confession of Faith the *meaning* of "the Church." I showed, that to belong to "the Church," it was necessary to "PROFESS" the "TRUE RELIGION;" and that to "profess the true religion," it was necessary to ADMIT THE CONFESSION OF FAITH, "as containing the summary of the doctrines, taught in the Holy Scriptures." So that by the Confession of Faith, the Presbyterian Church is the *baby* to which the "magistrates" are to become "NURSING FATHERS." Has the gentleman denied this? Has he met the argument? Supposing the Catholics held such a doctrine; supposing they maintained, that the magistrates' duty is to be "NURSING FATHERS" to the Church, as *they* understand it; how loudly would the country ring with denunciations against them! Yet here is the doctrine AVOWED by the Presbyterian creed; and its ministers pretend, that they are only anxious, forsooth, that all denominations should be equally protected!

The gentleman says, "WE hold, that not only the Presbyterians, but all, every where, who *love the Lord* are of Christ's Church." Now, this is something like charity. But he forgets, that he and a few others, at Pittsburg, EXCOMMUNICATED THE WHOLE CATHOLIC WORLD, both of the present and of past generations, as being NO PART *of the Church of Christ*. Now, he tells us, that *if* they "loved the Lord," they *were* "of Christ's Church." Why, then, did he not *postpone* their excommunication, until he should be certain whether they "loved the Lord," or not? But in making the "love of the Lord" the criterion of "Christ's Church," has he stated the PRESBYTERIAN DOCTRINE? Not he, indeed. The universal designation, in the CONFESSION OF FAITH, is not those "who love the Lord," but those who "PROFESS THE TRUE RELIGION, TOGETHER WITH THEIR CHILDREN." (1) The SYNOD OF YORK may meet again, and before the period of its meeting, I advise the gentleman to RETRACT HIS NEW DEFINITION, and to return to the "standards." Otherwise, *his* orthodoxy may become a subject of investigation.

He says, "we (Presbyterians) believe a part of the true Church *lay hid* in the Church of Rome, at the occurrence of the reformation." "*A part* lay hid;" then, the inference is, that since it was "HID," he cannot know any thing respecting it. But the *other* parts, that were *not* "hid"—does the gentleman know any thing

(1) See page iii. ... 176, 346.

of them either ? He testifies to what was *invisible*, "hid,"—and acknowledges, that the other "part," or "parts" of the true Church which were *not* invisible, were nowhere to be found !! In fact, the Church was visible *then*, as it is now.

The quotation, which the gentleman has adduced from the Catholic Telegraph, as evidence of Catholic sentiment respecting this government, is every way discreditable to him, as a logician, and as a friend of truth. As a logician, because, if the writer of it had been a Catholic of the United States, still it would be illogical and unjust to make the *whole body* of the Catholics accountable for his assertions and views. As a lover of truth, for in this character he knew, or ought to have known, that it was an *article copied from a Canadian paper*, the Advocate, and published to show the handle which the disgraceful proceedings, in the destruction of the convent at Boston, were giving to the *enemies of republican institutions.* If the gentleman did not know this, he was culpably ignorant; and he must excuse me for saying what all honest men will admit, that his culpable ignorance is no excuse for the calumnies with which he is attempting to blacken the character of the Catholics of the country. When, therefore, he says, it was the language of a "papal journal," the Catholic Telegraph, he says what is destitute of truth. It was *copied* into that paper, from a foreign journal, as similar articles were copied into most of our secular papers, without being the language or the sentiments of the editors.

As for Bishop England's sentiments, on the propriety of laymen not interfering in the government of the Church, they are such as he has a right, in the exercise of his own judgment, to entertain and express. With us, doctrines are not made up, as with Presbyterians, from the gatherings of the opinions of the people. They are *tenets of revelation ;* they are held and taught as such, and the votes of the people cannot make them *true* or *false*. They were revealed to be *taught* and *believed*, and not to be *"coughed down"* in such assemblies as the late Synod of York.

When the gentleman represents Bishop England, as having *"disgraced himself by his open defence of the inquisition,"* he states, or assumes against that calumniated prelate, a charge which is utterly false. He did, what I have done myself, in the former part of this Discussion ;—he instructed the popular ignorance of those Protestants, who supposed,—from the prejudices instilled into them by false teaching from the pulpits, and false statements in books,—that the inquisition was a portion of the Catholic religion. He proved, that it was no such thing. The charge of "defending the inquisition," deserves the same appellation by which the Protestant editor of Cincinnati characterized the calumny, published in all the Presbyterian papers, and *never corrected* in any, about " HATS OFF GENTLEMEN, THE BISHOP'S COMING "—he called it an "impudent lie." But I shall not so designate this charge against Bishop England. I shall only say, it is unfounded in truth.

The quotation from Pallavicini is not to be found in the reference given. The gentleman could not understand it, if he saw it. Let him, therefore, get some one who *can* give the reference correctly. In the meantime, it purports to be "*The advice given to Paul III. by* FOUR *cardinals, and* FIVE *other prelates, whose names are written under, in order to the amendment of the state of the Church.*" And yet, though there are "four" and "five" names "*under-written*" in the document, the translator, when he has given "eight" names, says, with much simplicity, there *should be* another to make nine!!" But, besides this, Raynaldi, in reference to this document, states, positively, that it was *vitiated* in the marginal notes, put by both Sturmius and Luther. Supposing, however, that it is precisely what the gentleman represents, it only proves the solicitude of its authors, to see men brought back to the purity and holiness of Catholic morals; and certainly does not prove, that the doctrines of the Presbyterian religion are *not* opposed to civil and religious liberty.

The gentleman, in pretending to meet my argument on the subject of predestination, represents me as charging on Presbyterians DISHONESTY AND IMMORALITY. Here, again, I am constrained to advise the meeting, that his statement is not to be depended on. Whoever will take the trouble to examine the passage, as it stands in my speech, will discover, that I showed simply the consequences naturally flowing from the doctrine of "God's decrees," as stated in the Confession of Faith; by which, men are "foreordained" from all eternity to everlasting life, or everlasting death, in such a manner, that neither their *good works*, nor their *evil actions* can, in the least, alter or affect their eternal destiny. This is the doctrine of Presbyterianism—the gentleman cannot deny it. As *a necessary* "*consequence*" *of this doctrine*, I stated, that Presbyterians "*may*" commit every immoral act to which selfish or sectarian ambition prompts them. He represents me, as *charging them* with actually doing these immoral acts; and it is in this, that he "*bears false witness against his neighbour,*" and makes the statement which is not to be depended on. Yet, it is a fact, that is sustained by the general experience of mankind, that the *more* "religious" Presbyterian individuals become, the more diminished is the confidence which persons of other denominations are willing to place in their integrity, as regards matters of this world generally. Those who before were frank, sincere, generous, charitable, and every thing that man has a right to expect from his fellow men in the social relations of life, become,—from the moment they are deeply indoctrinated in the Confession of Faith,—more or less gloomy, morose, illiberal, uncharitable, (except to saints like themselves,) and with regard to *the rest of mankind,* infinitely pharisaical. In general, however, the worst of them are greatly better than their creed. Common sense, the opinions of mankind, and the inextinguishable sympathies of human nature, work out in practice, and defeat the irresponsible licentiousness, that is authorized by a doctrine, which teaches, that all men will be saved or damned by a "DECREE," fixed from all eternity, and which neither good works nor bad works have any power to alter. All things are "FOREORDAINED." This is enough. It brings the matter to this point, that whenever a crime is committed, it could not be avoided by the agent, who was acting under the ETERNAL DECREE OF OMNIPOTENCE.

The gentleman wishes me to charge the Presbyterians directly with the immoralities, *thus* authorized, in the doctrine of their creed. Then, he would say, that *I* was a calumniator, and HE would be the defender, of their character. I charge not their character; and his certificates from Bancroft and Burnet are, to my mind, extremely ridiculous. The argument does not require me to show what Presbyterians *are,* but what their creed makes it of no importance in the future life for them *to have been.*

He asks me whether I know who Burnet was? I answer yes. He was the husband of a Presbyterian *wife*—the son of a Presbyterian *mother*. He was an Episcopalian in *head,* for he wore a bishop's mitre, and received a bishop's *revenue*. But he was, probably, and in *my opinion,* decidedly, a Presbyterian in heart. He was a faithless historian, who published, as HISTORY, says Sir James Macintosh, "the evidence *on one side* thus raked together by him AS A PURVEYING ADVOCATE," against the legitimacy and claims of the Prince of Wales to the throne of England. When the "evidence" "raked together," expressly and avowedly *for that purpose,* was found to be *unnecessary,* he published it as HISTORY. (1)

And now, since I have shown, that I know who Burnet was, and who "Usher" was, I must beg leave to cite, by way of certificate, for the morality of Presbyterians, the testimony, not of a Unitarian, or a Papist, or a moderate Arminian, but of the whole Church of Scotland, met in General Assembly. Let the gentleman and the audience not say, that Mr. Hughes is slandering the Presbyterian denomination—the witnesses are the United Fathers of the Church itself. In the preamble to an act of the Assembly, passed in the year 1578, it is set forth, that "THE GENERAL ASSEMBLY OF THE KIRK FINDING UNIVERSAL CORRUPTION OF THE WHOLE ESTATES OF THE BODY OF THE REALM, THE GREAT COLDNESS AND SLACKNESS IN RELIGION IN THE GREATEST PART OF THE PROFESSORS OF THE SAME, WITH THE DAILY INCREASE OF ALL KIND OF FEARFUL SINS AND. ENORMITIES, AS INCESTS,

(1) Macintosh's History of Revolution, p. 617.

ADULTERIES, MURDERS, (COMMITTED IN EDINBURGH AND STIRLING,) CURSED SACRILEGE, UNGODLY SEDITION AND DIVISION WITHIN THE BOWELS OF THE REALM, WITH ALL MANNER OF DISORDERED AND UNGODLY LIVING," &c. &c.

In the year 1648, about seventy years after this, the General Assembly again testify to the state of Presbyterian morality in Scotland; and state, that "IGNORANCE OF GOD, AND OF HIS SON, JESUS CHRIST, PREVAILED EXCEEDINGLY IN THE LAND; THAT IT WERE IMPOSSIBLE TO RECKON UP ALL THE ABOMINATIONS THAT WERE IN THE LAND; AND THAT THE BLASPHEMING OF THE NAME OF GOD, SWEARING BY THE CREATURES, PROFANATION OF THE LORD'S DAY, UNCLEANLINESS, EXCESS AND RIOTING, VANITY OF APPAREL, LYING AND DECEIT, RAILING AND CURSING, ARBITRARY AND UNCONTROLLED OPPRESSION, AND GRINDING THE FACES OF THE POOR BY LANDLORDS AND OTHERS IN PLACE AND POWER, WERE BECOME ORDINARY AND COMMON SINS." (1)

The testimony of the associate synod, as late as the year 1778, is of similar import. "A GENERAL UNBELIEF OF REVEALED RELIGION (PREVAILS) AMONG THE HIGHER ORDERS OF OUR COUNTRYMEN, WHICH HATH, BY A NECESSARY CONSEQUENCE PRODUCED, IN VAST NUMBERS, AN ABSOLUTE INDIFFERENCE AS TO WHAT THEY BELIEVE, EITHER CONCERNING TRUTH OR DUTY, ANY FARTHER THAN IT MAY COMPORT WITH THEIR WORLDLY VIEWS." (2)

Then, speaking not of the "higher orders," but of the "country generally," they lament it as *now*, "THROUGH THE PREVALENCE OF INFIDELITY, IGNORANCE, LUXURY, AND VENALITY SO MUCH DESPOILED OF ALL RELIGION, AND FEELING THE WANT OF IT." (3)

If we go back to the first congregation of Presbyterians in Scotland, those who murdered Cardinal Beaton and their associates, including their preachers, John Rough and John Knox, we shall find, that the picture of morals was nearly uniform from first to last. Buchanan, a Presbyterian himself, tells us that, after having exercised on the cardinal, what Fox, in his lying book of Martyrs, blasphemously calls not only the "judgment," but the "WORK" of God, "THEY MADE A VERY BAD USE OF THIS RESPITE, WHICH THIS TEMPORARY ACCOMMODATION PROCURED THEM; AND THAT, NOTWITHSTANDING THE ADMONITIONS OF KNOX, THEY SPENT THEIR TIME IN WHOREDOM AND ADULTERY, AND ALL THE VICES OF IDLENESS." (4)

Take in connexion with this state of public morals, the hypocritical sanctimoniousness which made them so tender of "God's honour," that, whilst these crimes were flagrant and universal

---

(1) Acknowledgement of Sins.
(2) Warning, p. 54.
(3) Ibid, p. 64.
(4) Guthrie's History of Scotland, V. p. 397.

among themselves, they were passing laws, making it death for the Catholic to have "HEARD OR SAID MASS THREE TIMES"!!! They whine over their own flagrant violations of the law of God, whilst, by way of appeasing Heaven, they twist the rope, or whet the sword of death against the Catholic for an act of religious worship "according to the dictates of his conscience," and performed too, it may be, with closed and bolted doors, or in the cave of the mountains. Sir, the gentleman must be profoundly ignorant of the history of his system, or he never would have pushed himself forward on public notice as the advocate of civil and religious liberty, and that, too, in the name of Presbyterianism, above all others' creeds!! He must have supposed that I was as unacquainted with it as himself, or he never would have forced himself on my attention, seeing that, if I did not spurn his advances, I, at least, shrank from his importunate approaches. Let him now leave off borrowing "certificates" of character from Bancroft and Burnet; and make himself acquainted with history—with the testimony of the Presbyterian fathers; and if he can refute it, let him do so. If he cannot—let him acknowledge, that, whilst Bancroft, a Unitarian, had nothing to say of the Presbyterians, except that they were a little "gloomy" or so, the friends, yea the fathers of the Church, have quite a different tale to tell.

But the question, after all, is not whether Presbyterians are, or are not, less moral than other denominations. I am willing to admit that they are as moral as others; and that, as regards the "outside of the platter," the reading of the Bible, the keeping of the Sabbath, and the censuring of their neighbours for not being, and in the same way, as good as themselves;—the saints among the Presbyterians, male and female, are the strictest moralists that have appeared in the world—since the days of the Pharisees. But the question is, what *motive* for holiness is held forth; what *ability* to be virtuous is recognised in the Presbyterian creed? Men, in that system, are saved by ELECTION, and DAMNED by predestination; and their works, GOOD or BAD, were "foreordained" from all eternity. Where is the MOTIVE to MORALITY in this system; where is the freedom of human agency, necessary to a *moral* action, recognised? No where. EVERY THING is eternally, omnipotently, immutably "foreordained." Then where is freedom? Let the gentleman answer this. I shudder at the consequences of this doctrine, in relation to the attributes of the good and just Deity. And no wonder, when I see Calvin advancing, as a doctrine of Christianity, that it is not absurd to assign the same CRIME (suppose murder) to GOD, to SATAN, and TO MAN. (1) When I see him refuting, or attempting to refute those who maintain, that God only *permits* the existence of evil, and the commission of crime, and asserting, that he (God) positively WILLS

---

(1) Institutes, Lib. 2. Chap. IV.

and ordains the commission of CRIMES, so as to be called the "AUTHOR OF THEM."

"*Et jam satis apertè ostendi*, DEUM VOCARI OMNIUM EORUM (CRIMINUM) AUCTOREM, *quæ isti censores volunt otioso tantum ejus permissu contingere.*"

"*I have shown already, with sufficient clearness,*" says he, "THAT GOD IS CALLED THE AUTHOR OF THOSE (crimes,) *which these censors will have, as happening* ONLY *by his indolent permission.*" (1)

It is no pleasure to me, sir, to make these exhibitions of what it must be painful to the feelings of Presbyterians to read, but even they cannot justly censure me, for spreading out a doctrinal principle of their religion, which, if applied in practice, would sap the foundations of public and private virtue. When Presbyterian ministers have relinquished the preaching of "*peace* and *good will* among men," and not content with enjoying the rights of conscience, themselves, are endeavouring to deprive their Roman Catholic fellow-citizens of that sacred right, by firing the passions of the multitude—the ignorant multitude, into the belief, that by destroying our property, as well as our character, they would be doing a service to God and to their country—it is time to advise the *true* lovers of civil and religious liberty, of the principles of doctrine by which they are actuated. Let them only succeed to remove *one* tile from the sacred edifice of religious freedom, whose vaulted roof is ample enough to protect all, and as time rolls on, not a stone upon a stone will remain, down to its deepest foundation.

Here are two principles which are enough to move the world. The one, that their salvation being dependent on the DECREE of God, cannot be *secured* nor *aided* by VIRTUE—(if it can, let the gentleman say so)—cannot be *defeated* or *jeoparded* by crime—if it can, again, let him say so.

The other principle is, that they avow it as an obligation imposed on *them* by Almighty God, to "REMOVE ALL FALSE WORSHIP, AND ALL MONUMENTS" OF WHAT they are arrogantly pleased to call "IDOLATRY;" and this "ACCORDING TO EACH ONE'S PLACE AND CALLING." Not only Catholic Churches and Convents, but "ALL FALSE WORSHIP." In this *supposed* commandment, (for God never made a commandment for Presbyterians, which he did not make equally for all denominations,) is to be found the solution of that restlessness, that turbulence and domineering, which has stood forth in the uniform history of the Presbyterians, as a moral problem exciting the curiosity of those who were unacquainted with the doctrinal principle from which it emanated. Suppose *each* denomination were to make for itself such an obligation, and then say, that God had imposed it, what would be

(1) Institutes, Lib. 1, Chap. XVIII., Sec. 3.

the consequence, on the hypothesis, that ALL should try, as all are bound, *to keep the commandments of God?*

The gentleman is much annoyed by the uniform language of intolerance and presumption, found in all the Confessions of Faith, of the Calvinistic Churches, as exhibited in my last speech. Those doctrines unequivocally stated in their standards, if reduced to practice, would not leave another denomination in the land. And in this, they are not a particle more inimical to civil and religious liberty, than the present Confession, the single clause making it their duty, imposed by God himself, to "REMOVE ALL FALSE WORSHIP," even in the United States, being equivalent to all the tyranny over conscience, expressed in the the creeds of other times, and other countries. I refer the reader to those documents, and request him to consider what consequences they would lead to, if reduced to practice.

The gentleman's only defence is, that some passages in those creeds have been left out of the American Confession; as I never failed to mention. To this defence I have to make a few observations in reply, which will show that it is perfectly nugatory. 1st. The difference is only *in words*, the doctrine, as I have shown, being *substantially* the same in all. 2d. The OMISSION of a few phrases in the genuine and original Confessions of Faith, which would have *alarmed* the friends of civil and religious freedom in this country, by their naked arrogance, is no proof that the *doctrine expressed* by them has been *rejected* or *condemned* as *heretical*. The gentleman, indeed, has said that they were heretical in religion as well as in politics. But he has given no proof. You may imagine how hard he is pressed, when he throws all Presbyterians overboard, as believers in a HERETICAL DOCTRINE, except those of the United States, since the Revolution. And yet the same doctrine for which he condemns them, is substantially and unequivocally expressed in their creed at the present day, as I have already established. According to him, the Calvins, the Knoxes, the Lightfoots, the whole ASSEMBLY OF WESTMINSTER, that *framed the standards*, were all, in so much, heretics. Now it is a pity, that after such a generous *immolation* of Presbyterian fathers, still his argument should fail. Why? Because the Presbyterian Church in this country, regards those Presbyterian Churches of other times and countries, whose creeds I quoted in my last speech, AS SOUND IN THE FAITH. As such, they hold communion with them, proving thereby, that the Presbyterians of this country have NOT *condemned* those creeds, although their persecuting clauses are not expressed *in print*, as fully as they had been before the American Revolution. This the gentleman will not venture to deny, and his admission of it is fatal to his defence. But again, when ministers of those churches are admitted into the Presbyterian Church, *in this country*, are they required to renounce and condemn those doctrines which are *omitted* in the present republican standard? THEY ARE NOT. This is equally fatal to the gentleman's defence. And let him not affect to tell us any more that the doctrines of the Presbyterians have been reformed since the Revolution; these facts prove that on the doctrine of intolerance, the Presbyterians of the United States have *condemned* nothing in those Confessions of Faith of England, Scotland, Geneva, Holland, or elsewhere, which I quoted in my last speech. And yet, in opposition to these facts, the gentleman has given up, and virtually denounced as heretics, those who are regarded by the Presbyterian Church *now*, and in this *country*, as sound and orthodox, whilst they are known to hold the doctrines which he says have been rejected!! Had I not reason, therefore, to say, that whenever a man stands forth to defend or advocate civil and religious liberty, or the rights of conscience, and at the same time professes belief in the *Presbyterian religion*, he attempts to reconcile contradiction, and renders himself necessarily and supremely ridiculous.

The feature which was essentially wanting to the argument against the Catholic Church, is the fact, that persecution was *enjoined by doctrine*. That Catholic states, and Catholic writers of great eminence, have advocated principles adverse to liberty of conscience, is not disputed. That other Catholic states and writers have supported opposite principles, is what the gentleman will not venture to deny. But, on the other side, this is not the case. All the blood that has been shed by Presbyterians, has been shed on a principle of doctrine. This constitutes the difference. I do not say, that the Presbyterians are persecutors in this country; but I do say, that in this, they act in opposition to their doctrine, as stated in all their Confessions of Faith—including the one that obliges them to remove "ALL FALSE WORSHIP."

We shall now see the effects of these doctrines in countries in which they have been reduced to practice. Calvin is the father and founder of the Presbyterian religion. He is one of the great reformers. His praise is in all the Churches. His doctrine on this subject is what is found in the Confessions of Faith;—his conduct, in practising that doctrine, shall be the evidence of its *friendship* to civil and religious liberty. I shall content myself with stating a few principal facts, omitting many circumstances calculated to heighten the atrocity of the proceedings. I shall quote also from *Protestant* historians.

A man of the name of GRUET, in Geneva, for exercising liberty of conscience, and calling Calvin the "new Pope," was put to death in 1550. (1) Sebastian Castalio, master of the public school of Geneva, for using the liberty of thought and speech against Calvin's "unconditional predestination," was deposed from his office, and banished from the city. (2) Jerome Bolsec,

---

(1) Mosheim, vol. ii. p. 125.   (2) Ibid.

for differing in opinion from Calvin, was imprisoned first, and afterwards sent into banishment. (1) Jacque de Bourgoyne, a nobleman, to "avoid Calvin's vengeance," says Mosheim, for having endeavoured to save Bolsec, removed from Geneva, and passed the remainder of his days in rural retreat. (2) Who understood CALVINISM better than CALVIN? And his *practice* is the best commentary on the second commandment, which obliges all Presbyterians, by the commandment of God, to "REMOVE ALL FALSE WORSHIP." Calvin fulfilled this commandment, by "removing" the "false worshippers," which amounts to the same. These instances of persecution and death for conscience' sake, are generally lost sight of in magnitude of the horror with which the mind is filled by the execution of SERVETUS, and its circumstances. I admit, that he was a heretic, but in this he was only like Calvin himself. It was this man's misfortune to have detected and exposed several mistakes and errors in Calvin's Institutes, which inspired this Pope of Geneva with such hatred, that he declared, writing to Viret and Farel, that "if ever this heretic (SERVETUS) should fall into his hands, he would order it so, that it should cost him his life." It is to be borne in mind, that Servetus was *not in any manner* subject to the laws of Geneva, either civil or religious. But, passing on his way as a traveller, he was about to cross the lake to Zurich, and whilst waiting for a boat, was betrayed to Calvin, who had him arrested and thrown into prison. This was on a Sunday, when it was unlawful to arrest any one, except for a capital crime. But Calvin, in opposition to the laws of God, the laws of the state, the rights of nations, and the voice of human nature, had him seized on the spot. His situation is described by a Protestant historian in the following words: "*Far from his own country, fallen into the hands of cruel strangers, all under the influence of Calvin, his avowed enemy, who bore him a mortal hatred; stript of all his property; confined in a damp prison, and neglected till he was almost eaten up with vermin, denied an advocate, and loaded with every indignity that barbarity could invent.* (3) The fate of SERVETUS was, that he was burned to death by Calvin's procurement, on the 27th of October, 1553. Such is the practice of the Calvanistic doctrine, in regard to heretics, as exemplified in the life of its author, Calvin himself. To show that his cruel heart never felt the sting of remorse for this murder, which was, of course, "foreordained" in the "decrees of God," he wrote a book entitled, "A FAITHFUL ACCOUNT OF THE ERRORS OF MICHAEL SERVETUS, IN WHICH IT IS PROVED, THAT HERETICS OUGHT TO BE RESTRAINED WITH THE SWORD." Not only this; in his letter to the Marques de Poet, dated September 30th, 1561, he says, "*Honour, glory, and*

(1) Mosheim, vol. ii. p. 125.   (2) P. 126.
(3) Robinson's Eccles. Researches, p. 340.

riches shall be the reward of your pains: but, above all, do not fail to rid the country of those zealous scoundrels, who stir up the country to revolt AGAINST US. SUCH MONSTERS SHOULD BE EXTERMINATED, AS I HAVE EXTERMINATED MICHAEL SERVETUS, THE SPANIARD."

Such was the man, by whom the Presbyterian religion was founded. And in every country in which that religion has prevailed, and become supreme in political power, its *doctrines* have sanctioned persecution, and its hands have been stained with blood. I state this fact on the faith of history, and if the gentleman can point out a single exception, I shall acknowledge, that in one instance the statement is incorrect.

Let us begin with the Calvinistic cantons of Switzerland. If the doctrines of the Calvinists had authorized the persecution of *only Catholics*, its advocates might claim sympathy from the other Protestant denominations. But the fact is, that all sects were alike to it. It claimed the right to dictate to men's consciences; and wo be to those who were not prepared to fall down and worship its arrogant pretensions to infallibility. In the Cantons of Switzerland, it punished with *fine*, such of its own citizens as should exercise the rights of conscience in embracing the *Baptist* religion. Baptists who were not citizens, were "BANISHED WITH THE EXPRESS THREAT, THAT IF THEY RETURNED THEY SHOULD BE DROWNED TOGETHER WITH THEIR LEADERS."(1) In the Canton of Zurich, it was decreed that not only the Baptists themselves, but those who *protected* them, should be PUT TO DEATH. Those who would not inform against them, were CONDEMNED AS PERJURERS to IMPRISONMENT AND EXILE. "*De punir de mort, soit les Anabaptistes, soit ceux qui les protegeroient: et d'emprisonner, et de banner même, comme des parjures, ceux qui ne les deceleroient pas.*"(2) Some of these wretched Baptists having returned to the country, were actually PUT TO DEATH BY DROWNING, "*a cause de leur opiniatrete, on les noya.*"(3) In Berne, the punishment against the Baptists was, that the men should be BEHEADED, and the WOMEN DROWNED. In 1566, Gentillis was beheaded at Berne, for judging for himself, in opposition to Calvinistic infallibility. And as late as 1633, ANTHONY, a minister at Geneva, WAS BURNED TO DEATH for the same crime. (4) This is the effectual fulfilment of the second commandment, "removing all false worship." This is the practical exemplification of the doctrine that turns the magistrates into "nursing fathers to the church." It is remarkable, that whilst in Holland they put the heretics to death by the *block*; in Geneva by the *stake*; in New England by *hanging*; they selected *drowning* for the Baptists

(1) Ruchets' Hist. of Refor. in Switzerland. vol.1. p. 556.
(2) Idem, vol. iii. p. 99.   (3) Idem, vol. iv. p. 218.
(4) Priestley's Church Hist. vol. iii. p. 359.

in Switzerland, as if they would *pun* on the supposed heresy of their victims, by the manner of their execution.

The second saint in the Presbyterian Calendar, is JOHN KNOX. He was what may be termed, *legate à latere*, to the "Pope of Geneva." He was the principal framer of Presbyterian doctrine and discipline in Scotland, and, like his master, he held these "tenets of faith," which made it *his duty* to be a man of blood. This is not the place to enter on the conduct or character of Cardinal Beaton, who is by no means regarded either as a saint or a martyr in the Catholic Church. He was a man who fell by hands of assassins; and John Knox, according to Doctor Heylin, characterizes that cold-blooded assassination as a "GODLY ACT."

Of course, according to the Confession of Faith, this assassination was one of those things which God had "foreordained" in his "eternal decrees." This Knox's understanding of the doctrine of the Presbyterian religion is clear, not only from his calling the murder of Beaton a "godly act," but also from those principles which he laid down as universal tenets of faith.

"YE ARE BOUND TO REMOVE FROM HONOUR, AND TO PUNISH WITH DEATH (*if the crime so require*) SUCH AS DECEIVE THE PEOPLE, OR DEFRAUD THEM OF THAT FOOD OF THEIR SOULS, I MEAN GOD'S LIVELY WORD." (1)

"NONE PROVOKING THE PEOPLE TO IDOLATRY OUGHT TO BE EXEMPTED FROM THE PUNISHMENT OF DEATH." (2)

"THE PUNISHMENT OF SUCH CRIMES AS ARE IDOLATRY, BLASPHEMY, AND OTHERS THAT TOUCH THE MAJESTY OF GOD, DOTH NOT APPERTAIN TO THE KINGS AND CHIEF RULERS ONLY—BUT TO THE WHOLE BODY OF THE PEOPLE, AND TO EVERY MEMBER OF THE SAME." (3)

"IT IS NOT ONLY LAWFUL TO PUNISH TO THE DEATH SUCH AS LABOUR TO SUBVERT THE TRUE RELIGION, BUT THE MAGISTRATES AND PEOPLE ARE BOUND SO TO DO, UNLESS THEY WILL PROVOKE THE WRATH OF GOD AGAINST THEMSELVES." (4)

"INTIMATION WAS MADE TO OTHERS, AS TO THE ABBOT OF CORRAGNEL, THE PARSON OF SANGHAR, AND SUCH, THAT THEY SHOULD NEITHER COMPLAIN TO THE QUEEN NOR COUNCIL, BUT SHOULD EXECUTE THE PUNISHMENT THAT GOD HAS APPOINTED TO IDOLATERS IN HIS WORD, WHEREVER THEY SHOULD BE FOUND." (5)

Here we see the true origin and meaning of the Confession of Faith, touching the duty of the "magistrates" as "nursing fathers" to the church. Here we see the true and original meaning of the texts of Scripture, still preserved in the Confession of Faith, directing the reader to those punishments which "God had appointed to idolaters in the old law." Here we see, not only the magistrates, but the people instructed, in the name of the insulted

(1) Appeal to Knox's Hist. of Reform. p. 10. (2) Idem, p. 21.
(3) Idem, p. 22.   (4) Idem, p. 25.   (5) Knox's Hist., p. 352.

God, that not only they may, but that they "ARE BOUND" to murder idolaters, blasphemers, and such as by "false worship" do touch the divine Majesty. Here we see the true meaning and origin of the Presbyterian second commandment, about "detesting and opposing all false worship, and, according to each one's place and calling, removing it and all the monuments of idolatry." Here we see the meaning of those texts which we find even in the republican edition of the Westminster Confession, in which the Presbyterian denomination claims the authority of God "to smite the seven nations stronger and mightier than they, and to show no mercy to them." (1) And yet the gentleman is, or affects to be, ignorant of the meaning of those passages in his creed, which I have pointed out as opposed to civil and religious liberty. These evidences from Geneva and Scotland show how the Presbyterian religion came to have followers, and by what kind of arguments it maintained itself. They show what reason HOUSTON had to say that it made but little progress until the "magistrates," "according to their place and calling," became "nursing fathers," and set about "removing all false worship and all the monuments of idolatry." I say nothing of the arrogance of this creed, which, founded, as it avowedly is, on *private opinion*, would dare to pronounce as a settled question, that the religion of the Roman Catholics is "idolatry," and that of all other denominations "false worship"—and would claim for its own members, the impudent right to "remove" them.

I beg, sir, the attention of this meeting to the operation of the doctrine here stated, and which the gentleman does not deny to be that of the Presbyterian creed. I have already exhibited the reasons why it was in perfect accordance with the Presbyterian religion for Dr. Ely to aim at what he innocently called a "CHRISTIAN PARTY" in politics; and why, good man, he would prefer a "sound Presbyterian" for his chief magistrate. Whenever that project shall be realized, the sleeping doctrines of the second commandment will awake into action and effect. And here it is that the seemingly unmeaning clause, "according to each one's place and calling," will explain itself in irremediable works of destruction to civil and religious liberty. Does the gentleman say that this is Mr. Hughes's gratuitous assertion? Then let the operation of the doctrine, when it was reduced to practice, be its interpreter.

We have already seen John Knox, the founder of Presbyterianism in Scotland, "the man of God," proclaiming that the people and magistrates were bound to put to death such as they might consider to be guilty of blasphemy, heresy, or idolatry." After commencing by that "godly act," the assassination of Cardinal Beaton, the progress of Calvinism in Scotland was traced by that of sedition, violence, devastation and plunder. But once

(1) Deut. vii.

fairly established on the ruins of a religion that had been introduced by peace and persuasion, we shall see the operation of its doctrines. There was a "Christian party in politics, and the chief magistrate a sound Presbyterian;" they were all bound to "remove all false worship, and all the monuments of idolatry—each according to his place and calling."

I shall quote from Lord Kames's Abridgement of the Statute Law, an abstract, as published in the Scotch Magazine for October, 1778.

In 1581 it was enacted (1) "THAT ALL PROFESSED PAPISTS BE OBLIGED TO LEAVE THE KINGDOM WITHIN A LIMITED TIME, UNLESS THEY WILL SUBSCRIBE THE CONFESSION OF FAITH; AND THAT NONE SELL OR DISPERSE POPISH BOOKS UNDER THE PAIN OF BANISHMENT AND CONFISCATION OF MOVEABLES." Is not this a beautiful specimen of the Presbyterian system, "according to each one's place and calling?" Here is the amiable practice of the doctrine which lies dormant in the Confession of Faith, since the declaration of American Independence. But why, dormant? Because the genius of civil and religious freedom would not tolerate its blasphemous tyranny over thought and conscience.

Again, in 1587, it was enacted, (2) "THAT PROFESSED JESUITS AND SEMINARY PRIESTS, FOUND IN ANY PART OF THE REALM, SHALL BE APPREHENDED, PURSUED, AND INCUR THE PAIN OF DEATH AND CONFISCATION OF MOVEABLES;—THAT WHOEVER WILLINGLY AND WITTINGLY RECEIPTS AND SUPPLIES ANY OF THEM FOR THE SPACE OF THREE DAYS AND THREE NIGHTS TOGETHER, OR SEVERALLY AT THREE TIMES, SHALL INCUR THE TINSEL OF THEIR LIFE-RENTS. THAT ALL SAYERS AND HEARERS OF MASS, ALL WHO REFUSE TO RESORT TO THE PREACHING OF GOD'S WORD, AND ALL WHO SHALL, BY REASONING, OR DISPERSING OF BOOKS OR LETTERS, ENDEAVOUR TO PERSUADE ANY OF HIS MAJESTY'S SUBJECTS TO DECLINE FROM THE PROFESSION OF THE TRUE RELIGION, SHALL INCUR THE TINSEL OF THEIR MOVEABLES AND OF THEIR LIFE-RENT."

In 1593, (3) it was enacted "THAT THE RECEIPTERS AFORESAID SHOULD, FOR THE FIRST FAULT, LOSE THEIR MOVEABLES, THEIR LIFE-RENT FOR THE SECOND, AND FOR THE THIRD, INCUR THE PAIN OF TREASON." We all know what that was.

An act passed in the year 1587, (4) ordered "*Papistical* BOOKS *to be searched for and destroyed by the magistrates of burghs, with concourse of the minister; and those who import the same to be punished in their persons and goods, at the king's will.*"

"*The saying of mass, receipting of Jesuits, seminary priests, trafficking papists, against the king's majesty and religion, professed within the realm, declared to infer the* PAIN OF TREASON, *both against the Jesuits, mass-priests, trafficking papists*

(1) Chap. 106. (2) Idem, 24. (3) Idem, 168. (4) Idem, 25.

and the receipters of them; but in case of satisfaction given to the king and kirk, the receipters not to be liable." (1)

By acts passed in the years 1594, ch. 196, and in 1607, ch. 1, it was enacted, "THAT ALL WILFUL HEARERS OF MASS and concealers of the same, be CAPITALLY punished, and their goods and gear escheated to the king's use."

"Presbyteries appointed to summon before them all papists, and those suspected of papistry, in order to satisfy the kirk, and if they compear not, or refuse to give satisfaction, they are to be dilated to the privy council; who must direct letters, charging the said papists, and those suspected of papistry, to appear before them, and to produce sufficient certificates of due satisfaction given to the kirk, under the PAIN OF REBELLION, and of being PUT TO THE HORN: and if they fail therein that they be denounced, and both their single and life-rent escheat belong to the king. And whosoever receipts, supplies or entertains such persons after denunciation aforesaid, shall also incur the penalty of single or life-rent escheat." (2)

Here we see the doctrine of the gentleman's second commandment—after denouncing penalties against those who should dare to exercise *liberty of thought* or conscience—going to extinguish the feelings of human nature, by involving those who should show them hospitality or kindness, in the same or kindred punishments.

In the year 1600 (3) it was enacted that "*the statutes made against Jesuits, seminary priests, sayers and hearers of mass, and their receipters, should be put in due execution; with the following explanation:—That the former acts shall be extended against* THE HEARERS AND SAYERS OF MASS, *without exception. That every person who* HARBOURS *a Jesuit, seminary priest, &c., shall be subjected to the penalties of the former statutes, as wilfully incurring the same, after being warned by public intimation.*"

"A PREMIUM of five hundred marks was ordained by an act, passed in 1700,(4) *for* DISCOVERING *and* SEIZING *any priest*, Jesuit, or trafficking papist that may be convicted."

These are beautiful specimens of liberty of conscience, as understood by Presbyterians under the second commandment of the Decalogue.

In 1700,(5) it was enacted, "*If a man is held and* REPUTED *to be a Jesuit, priest, or trafficking papist; or if it be made out that he has changed his name or surname,* EITHER OF THESE CIRCUMSTANCES, *with his refusing to purge himself of popery, shall be a sufficient cause for the privy council to banish him*

---

(1) Acts passed in 1592, ch. 122; in 1607, ch. 1; and in 1601, ch. 8.
(2) Act of 1594, ch. 197.   (3) Chap. 18.   (4) Idem, 3.
(5) Idem, 3.

forth of the realm, never to return, under pain of DEATH, being a papist."

In other cases, even under pagans, a man was presumed innocent until he was *proved* guilty. *Here,* he was condemned, if he did not prove his innocence, under pain of BANISHMENT and DEATH. And what was the crime? It was the crime of worshipping God, according to the dictate of his conscience!! These instances are enough to prove the practical operation of the second commandment. But they prove more: they show that, without the reasoning powers, the convincing influence, the persuasive eloquence of DEATH-INFLICTING LAWS, the Presbyterians could not have induced the Scotch people to abandon the religion that had civilized them, for the blasphemous doctrine of blind predestination, and the tyrannical dogma, authorizing Calvinists to oppress the thoughts and consciences of other men—" according to each one's place and calling."

The doctrines of Calvinism were no less fruitful on this side of the Atlantic, than they were in Scotland, England, and on the continent of Europe. The Puritans had been themselves the victims of Protestant persecution, and one would suppose, that their own sufferings for conscience' sake, should have taught them mercy towards others. But *their* conduct alone, after their arrival on these shores, is sufficient to show that pure Calvinism and gentle mercy, can never amalgamate in the human breast.

The gentleman will, no doubt, try to *disown* the Puritans, as he has denied all his religious forefathers, down to the last amendment of the Confession of Faith. But it will not do. In every point relating to the duty of the " magistrates as nursing fathers," in every point involving the question of civil and religious liberty, their doctrines were identically the same. NEAL, in his History of the Puritans, tells us, vol. iii. p. 155, that from the meeting of the Westminster Assembly, the " *name* of Puritans was to be sunk," and that of " Presbyterians" substituted. This shows that down to that period the two appellations were common in England. So that the Puritans of New England were English Presbyterians, who had left the country before the meeting of the Westminster divines. Their Church government was *different* from that of Presbyterians, but their *doctrine* was on these subjects the same. They, too, held it as a tenet of faith, that they were bound to " remove, according to each one's place and calling, all false worship, and all the monuments of idolatry." And their history shows the practice to which this doctrine leads. In the United States, since the civil government has guaranteed that the civil and religious rights of all shall be equal, this doctrine is harmless, because it is impracticable. It is still, however, declared to be a commandment of God, and it is possible that, as soon as the Constitution will permit, the saints will return to the observance of it.

But when it reigned predominant among the Puritans of New

England, what were its effects on men who were guilty of *attempting to think for themselves*, or of worshipping Almighty God, according to the dictates of their own conscience? They were "IMPRISONMENT," "FINING," CONFISCATION OF GOODS," "BANISHING," "UNMERCIFUL SCOURGING," "BURNING WITH HOT IRONS," "CUTTING OFF EARS," and "DESTROYING LIFE BY THE IGNOMINIOUS GALLOWS." Here, again, we shall take Protestant authority, that of SEWEL, in his History of the Quakers. Now if there ever was a denomination entiled to be tolerated, it was this. *Their* errors, above those of *all other sects*, were purely errors of the mind, exclusively matters between themselves and God. In all the relations of life, their demeanour was that of meekness, simplicity, integrity, and peace. They appeared with none of that evangelical pugnacity with which Presbyterianism fought its way into the places of power, and overthrew old tyrannies, to establish young tyrannies on their ruins. And yet the stripes which persecution had inflicted on the Puritans, were scarcely healed, when they themselves began to wield the lash against the inoffensive Quakers. "These detestable scenes of more than savage barbarity, says a Protestant writer, began in the month called July, 1656. Mary Fisher, and Ann Austin, having arrived in the road before Boston, the Deputy Governor Bellingham, had them brought on shore, and committed to prison as Quakers. They were stript naked under pretence of knowing whether they were witches; and in this search, (says Sewel,) they were so barbarously misused, that modesty forbids to mention it. After about five weeks' imprisonment, they were sent back to Old England, THEIR BEDS AND BIBLES BEING TAKEN BY THE JAILOR FOR HIS FEES." (1)

"Scarce a month after, eight others of those called Quakers, came; they were locked up in the same manner as the former; and after about eleven weeks' stay, they were sent back. John Endicot bid them 'TAKE HEED THAT YE BREAK NOT OUR ECCLESIASTICAL LAWS, FOR THEN YE ARE SURE TO STRETCH BY THE HALTER.'"

"Then a law was made to prohibit all masters of ships from bringing any Quakers into that jurisdiction. Nicholas Upsal, a member of the Church, and a man of unblameable character, for *speaking against such proceedings*, was fined twenty-three pounds, and IMPRISONED *also, for not coming to Church;* next they banished him out of their jurisdiction; and though a weakly old man, yet he was forced to depart in the winter. Nicholas afterwards, met with an INDIAN Prince, who having understood how he had been used, offered to make him a warm house; and further said, 'WHAT A GOD HAVE THE ENGLISH, WHO DEAL SO WITH ONE ANOTHER ABOUT THEIR GOD!'" (2)

(1) Sewel's History, p. 157.   (2) Idem, pp. 168, 169.

"The following year, 1657, Anne Burden, and Mary Dyer, were imprisoned at Boston; and Mary Clark, *for warning these persecutors to desist from their iniquity*, was unmercifully rewarded with TWENTY STRIPES OF A THREE-CORDED WHIP, ON HER NAKED BACK, and detained in prison about three months, in the winter season. The cords of these whips were commonly as thick as a man's little finger, having each some knots at the end."

"Christopher Holder, and John Copeland, WERE WHIPT AT BOSTON, the same year, each thirty stripes, with a knotted whip of three cords, the hangman measuring his ground and fetching the strokes with all the force he could, which so cruelly cut their flesh, that a woman seeing it, fell down for dead. Then they were locked up in prison, and kept three days *without food*, or so much as a drink of water, and detained in prison for nine weeks, in the cold winter season, without fire, bed, or straw."

"Lawrence and Cassandra Southick, and their son Josiah, being carried to Boston, were all of them, notwithstanding the old age of the two, sent to the House of Correction, and WHIPT *with cords*, as those before, in the coldest season of the year, and had taken from them to the value of four pounds ten shillings, *for not coming to Church*."

"In the year 1658, a law was made, which besides imposing *heavy penalties* and imprisonments, extended to working in the House of Correction, SEVERE WHIPPING, CUTTING OFF EARS, and BORING THROUGH THEIR TONGUES WITH A RED HOT IRON, whether male or female, and such like inhuman barbarities." (1)

"The same year William Brend, and William Leddra, came to Newberry; thence they were carried to Boston to the House of Correction, to work there; but they, unwilling to submit thereto, were kept *five days without any food*, and then *beaten twenty strokes with a three-corded whip*."

"Next they were put into irons, *neck and heels, so close together, that there was no more room left between, than for the lock that fastened them* and kept in that situation sixteen hours, and then brought to the mill to work; but Brend refusing, was beaten by the inhuman jailor, with a pitched rope, more than a hundred strokes, till his flesh was bruised into a jelly, his body turned cold, and for some time he had neither seeing, feeling, nor hearing." (2)

The parson, John Norton, was heard to say, "WILLIAM BREND ENDEAVOURED TO BEAT OUR GOSPEL ORDINANCES BLACK AND BLUE, IF THEN HE BE BEATEN BLACK AND BLUE, IT IS BUT JUST UPON HIM; *and I will appear in the behalf of him that did so*." (3)

(1) Sewel's History, p. 191.   (2) Idem, pp. 190, 192.
(3) Idem, pp. 193, 194.

"In the same year, John Copeland, Christopher Holder, and John Rous, were taken up, and in a private manner, HAD THEIR RIGHT EARS CUT OFF BY AUTHORITY, and, as if these inhuman barbarities were not sufficient, John Norton, and other parsons, petitioned for a law to banish the Quakers ON PAIN OF DEATH. The petition was granted October 20th, 1658, by the Court of Boston. A short extract of the law is as follows:

"Whereas, there is a pernicious sect, (commonly called Quakers,) do take upon them to change and alter the received laudable customs of our nation, and also to destroy the order of the Churches, by DENYING ALL ESTABLISHED FORMS OF WORSHIP; for prevention thereof, this Court doth order and enact, that every person or persons being convicted to be of the sect of the Quakers, shall be sentenced to be BANISHED, UPON PAIN OF DEATH." (1)

"Daniel and Provided Southick, son and daughter to Lawrence and Cassandra, *not frequenting the assemblies of such a persecuting generation*, were fined ten pounds, though it was well known they had no estate, their parents being already brought to poverty by their rapacious persecutors. To get this money, the General Court at Boston issued out an order, by which the treasurers of the several counties were empowered to SELL THE SAID PERSONS to ANY OF THE ENGLISH NATION, at VIRGINIA, or BARBADOES, *to answer the said fines*."

"William Maslon, at Hampton, was fined *ten pounds for two books found in his house; five pounds for not frequenting their Church, and three pounds besides, as due to the parson;* for which fine, he had taken from him what amounted to more than *twenty pounds*. Not long after, above a thousand pounds were taken from some, only because they had separated themselves from 'the PERSECUTING CHURCH." (2)

"Thomas Prince, Governor of Plymouth, was heard to say, *that in his conscience, the Quakers were such a people as deserved to be destroyed, they, their wives and children, their houses and lands, without pity or mercy*. Humphrey Norton, at New Haven, for being a Quaker, WAS SEVERELY WHIPT, and *burnt in the hand with the letter H, to signify Heretic*."

"The unjust and bloody sentence of DEATH was executed upon William Robinson, and Marmaduke Stevenson, the 27th October, 1659. When they were come near the gallows, the parson (Wilson,) tauntingly said to Robinson, 'SHALL SUCH JACKS AS YOU COME IN BEFORE AUTHORITY WITH THEIR HATS ON?' to which Robinson replied, '*Mind you, mind you, it is for the* NOT *putting off the hat, we are put to death!*'" (3)

"The persons that were hanged were barbarously used, even

(1) Sewel's Hist. p. 218.   (2) Idem, p. 219.   (3) Idem, p. 226.

their shirts were ripped off with a knife, and their naked bodies cast into a hole that was dug, without any covering, and parson Wilson makes a ballad on them. On the 31st of the third month, 1660, Mary Dyer was SENTENCED TO DEATH by Endicot, and the next day EXECUTED. William Leddra returned to Boston, was cast into an open prison, and locked in chains day and night, in a very cold winter, and was SENTENCED TO DEATH, and EXECUTED on the 14th of the 1st month, 1661." (1)

"Many, both men and women, were stript naked from the waist and upward, tied to the cart-tail, and SCOURGED in the most brutal and barbarous manner, while the parsons who were the principal instigators to such more than savage meanness, were pleased in nothing better than in the exercise of such anti-Christian and diabolical cruelties."

"Peter Pearson, and Judith Brown, being stript to the waist, were fastened to a cart-tail, and WHIPT through the town of Boston. Also, Josiah Southick was *stript*, and led through the streets of Boston, at the cart-tail, and vehemently SCOURGED by the hangman. The same day he was WHIPT at ROXBURY, and the next morning at DEDHAM. The whip used for these cruel executions, was not of whip-cord, but *of dried guts; and each string with three knots at the end.*" (2)

"December 22d, 1662. At Dover, Anne Coleman, Mary Tomkins, and Alice Ambrose, were sentenced to be *fastened to the cart-tail*, and whipt on their *naked backs*, through eleven towns, a distance of nearly eighty miles. Then, in a very cold day, the deputy, Walden, at Dover, caused these women to be stript naked, from the middle upward, and tied to a cart, and then WHIPT THEM, WHILE THE PARSON LOOKED ON AND LAUGHED AT IT. Two of their friends testified against Walden's cruelty, for which THEY *were put in the stocks.*"

"The women were carried to HAMPTON, and there whipt; from thence to SALISBURY, and *again whipt*. William Barefoot at length obtained the warrant from the constable, and let them go: THE PARSON ADVISING TO THE CONTRARY. Not long after these women returned to Dover, and were again seized, *while in meeting*, and barbarously dragged about at the instigation of (a man *falsely called*) HATE-EVIL NUTWELL, A RULING ELDER."

"The barbarity of their persecutors, on this occasion, exceeds description; being seized in meeting, while on their knees in prayer, they were dragged by their arms nearly a mile through a deep snow, across fields and over stumps, by which they were much bruised. The next day they were barbarously dragged down a steep hill to the water side, and threatened with drowning; and one of them was actually plunged into the water, when a sudden shower obliged them to retreat: at length, after much abuse,

(1) Sewel's History, p. 254.   (2) Idem, pp. 272, 324.

these poor victims of ORTHODOX BARBARITY were turned out of doors at midnight, and with their clothes wet and frozen, were obliged to suffer the inclemency of a very severe winter's night.

"Afterwards, Anne Coleman, and four of her friends, were whipt through Salem, Boston, and Dedham, by order of Hawthorn, the magistrate. Anne Coleman was a little, weakly woman; Bellingham encouraging the executioner while she was fastening to the cart at Dedham, he laid on so severely, that, with the knot of the whip, he split the nipple of her breast, which so tortured her, that it almost took away her life."

Here there was no pretext, no motive but the commandment enjoining the obligation to remove "all false worship," "according to each one's place and calling;" the governor ordering the sentence as a good "nursing father," the hangman executing it, and the parson looking on. There was no crime charged but the crime of *thought*, and its expression.

These are the points of the question, which it is important for the gentleman to clear up. I have shown that the barbarities, here and throughout this speech, enumerated, were founded on the very principles of doctrine still extant in the Confession of Faith. I have shown that those who have interpreted that principle as I have done, were not only orthodox Presbyterians, but the fathers, and founders, and authoritative expounders of the Presbyterian doctrine. Can the gentleman answer these arguments? He may say, as he has said before, that since the Revolution Presbyterians have not put Baptists, or Catholics, or Socinians, or Quakers, or Episcopalians, or Arminians, to death for "idolatry," or "false worship." But this is still the argument, that *because* a man has not committed robbery since he has been confined in prison, *therefore* he is an honest man. Since the Revolution, the thing was impracticable. And hence it is that whilst I have invariably referred to the Confession of Faith for the DOCTRINE, I have referred to countries where it had "fair play," to show its *practice* and effect. The *doctrine* is the text; the *practice* is the commentary. That the practice is founded on the doctrine, no man, who has common sense to estimate the meaning of what is called a "principle," will for a moment deny. It is a principle of faith and morals, that what God has commanded we are bound to do. Now, the Presbyterian religion teaches its votaries that God has commanded them to "REMOVE ALL FALSE WORSHIP." Not simple to preach and pray, that all false worship *may be* removed, but directly and absolutely to "REMOVE IT." Here, then, thanks be to Heaven, the Constitution will not allow them to keep this commandment. Suppose the Constitution would not allow them to keep holy the Sabbath day. And supposing they were to yield obedience to the Constitution, and, by profaning the Sabbath day, disobey God—their condition would not be one whit different from what it is. It makes no matter *which* of the commandments the Constitution obliges them *to* violate. But the effect of the doctrine is to be looked for in countries where the civil constitution puts no obstacle in the way of its observance.

The gentleman tries many an expedient to sink the question in debate, and substitute irrelevant matter in all the majesty of wildness, incoherency, and confusion. He cannot answer my arguments; and yet it would look bad if he were to remain silent. Hence, he flounders away in his own peculiar strain, about popes, and all those things which, as he knows, I have already cleared up under the proper head, in the former question.

It is almost too late for the gentleman to affect that his quotations can be always depended on, when I have proved the contrary, in instances which he has not ventured to take up. He always *makes a charge* of this kind for himself, when he wishes to disprove it, but those which I *specify,* he passes over.

I have said all that is necessary in regard to the Jesuits, in the former question. I have proved, by Protestant writers, that most of the popular prejudices, which pass for history among a certain class of Protestants, are the calumnies of the primitive Calvinists.

The gentleman will have it that I wish to be acquainted with Doctor Miller. I have already stated that the fact is not so. He is surprised that Doctor Cook, of Kentucky, because he *exposed* the *vicious citation of authors* found in the writings of the Princeton professor, did not become a Catholic. It appears that even that exposure has not "disturbed one hour of Doctor Miller's rest." This is precisely what might be expected of those who believe in "foreordination."

The allusion to Mr. Ansley, of Burlington, who is engaged in the peaceable pursuits of his avocations, living with his wife and children, and labouring for them, is no inapt illustration of the intolerant and slanderous spirit with which Calvinism imbues its votaries. Pray, what has he to do with the question; has he written a book; has he appeared in any public capacity, which could warrant the introduction of his name? And yet, because he has exercised that liberty of conscience, for which the gentleman affects to be zealous, his private character is attacked. But the attack betrays the meanness that would insinuate, without the courage to assert, and being founded on falsehood, reflects its infamy back upon its source.

I am not surprised that the gentleman touches lightly on the heartless language in which he seemed to exult, in his last speech, over the labours of the mob in burning the Convent. He says, "if the mob were mistaken, he cannot help it." Indeed! And pray what are he and his associates, "according to their place and calling," doing, but trying to lead the mob of the whole country, wherever it can be found, into the same mistake, that they, (the mob,) "according to THEIR place and calling," may "remove the monuments of idolatry" in the same way? The Presbyterian second commandment requires that it should do so. The religion of the Christian world, for fifteen hundred years before Calvin baptized his opinions in the blood of SERVETUS, is to be called after that period, "monuments of idolatry," by a set of men who are quarrelling among themselves on almost every article of Revelation? And because *they* call it by this name, they inculcate that the people are bound to "REMOVE it."

I have already given the reference which the gentleman calls for, respecting the "dictation to consciences of THOUSANDS of IMMORTAL beings." If he has not the book, as appears, I shall loan it to him. And now let him tell us what was meant by it. Let him say, whether it was not in strict accordance with Presbyterian duty, "according to *each* one's PLACE and CALLING." If Daniel Webster had known the facts, which Doctor Ely's zeal for Presbyterian ascendancy brought before the public notice, his good sense and sound patriotism would have induced him to form the same judgment, which was entertained at Harrisburg, in regard to the whole proceeding. I convicted the gentleman, in relation to it, of having calumniated my character, by making charges against me which were FALSE and INJURIOUS. I refer the reader, for proof of this, to my last speech. He says, I "retreated before Daniel Webster." Not at all, sir; the gentleman himself had made assertions unfounded in fact, and I fastened them on him. I care for TRUTH more than for him or Daniel Webster, with whom, by the way, I was not at issue.

The gentleman talks of insulting the American people, and he has the simplicity to believe that he and his associates do not offer a deeper insult; do not convey an insinuation of greater baseness, than could be done by even an enemy to the national character;—when they insinuate that the "Pope and priesthood, and the Emperor of Austria, are rich enough to buy the American people out of their religious principles!! That nothing but the vigilance of Brutus, Doctor Brownlee, and Mr. Breckinridge has saved the American people from selling themselves, body and soul, to the Pope and the Emperor of Austria!! This is the hardest cut of all.

With regard to "Mr. Smith," I have only to say, that he belongs to that class, of whom Dean Swift said significantly, "*when the Pope weeds his garden, I wish he would not throw his* NETTLES *over our wall.*"

The gentlemen says, that "popery drains usefully," in receiving from Protestantism a few worthless proselytes, unworthy to be retained. If he is sincere in this remark, he refutes those mock apprehensions, by which he and his colleagues are labouring to stir up the people, and break the harmonies of society, on the plea that popery is making such wonderful progress, and that, were it not for them, the Emperor of Austria would buy out Protestantism root and branch.

When he represents me as "ASSAILING the Continental Congress," I have again to caution the reader, that his statement is not to be depended on. Does the gentleman suppose that nobody is acquainted with the "History of England," and that an *opinion* expressed by any body of men, however respectable, is to be taken for proof—when the facts are known to the world which disprove it?

Does not every one know that, since the Reformation, so called, the Catholics of England, Scotland, and Ireland, have been ground to the earth, by the millstone of oppression, intolerance, and persecution? Can the gentleman be ignorant of this? Or does he thrust himself on the discussion, with the simplicity of a child, who knows no other reason for things only because "father says so?" The "paragraph" is justly qualified, when he tells us it was "DRAFTED." Now, history is not "drafted," and this constitutes the difference. It is truly amusing, to hear the gentleman calling for "Wesley's argument," which I have answered by showing, that it was founded on a false assumption. But the predicament in which he finds himself, with regard to the defence of Presbyterianism, must account to the reader, for the wanderings of his memory, and the confusion of his thoughts. The man who acknowledges that God has commanded him to "REMOVE ALL FALSE WORSHIP," has an awkward and difficult part to sustain, when he affects to support the Constitution of the country which FORBIDS HIM TO KEEP THAT COMMANDMENT. I hope, therefore, the audience will make allowance for the gentleman's situation.

"*Is the Presbyterian Religion, in any or in all its principles or doctrines, opposed to civil or religious liberty?*"

NEGATIVE IV.—MR. BRECKINRIDGE.

Mr. President :—

As the gentleman professes to act under the guidance of a living oracle, and an infallible interpreter of the word of God, I will thank him very much for an interpretation in his next speech of the following passage, "*Yet Michael, the archangel, when contending with the devil disputed about the body of Moses, durst not bring against him a railing accusation, but said the Lord rebuke thee.*"(1) His interpretation, if just, will answer his ill-bred and unfounded calumnies, and excuse, yea, I must suppose, commend to this society the pity and silence with which I can pass them by, rejoicing that we are in an age, and in a land, where the TERROR (*with* the *power*) of the priesthood of Rome has *ceased*.

He has charged me with "*shifting the terms*" of the sweeping denial which he made as to the extent of "Calvinism" in the world. He says, I had stated, "that (except perhaps, the Congregationalists) the high-toned Presbyterians were the only denomination that had not become ashamed of the avowal of the doctrine. He does not meet the statement, and yet by a slight shifting of the terms, he affects to have refuted it. He says, 'the twelve creeds of the original reformers,' and 'the Episcopalian articles' have it. But had I denied this? Did I assert that 'creeds and articles'—parchment, are capable of becoming ashamed?" The gentleman's memory is *short*, and he forgets that *litero scripta manet*. In his second speech, night seventh, he thus spoke :—"The *only* denomination I know who have not become ashamed of the avowal of this article, are the high-toned Presbyterians. I *defy the proof* that it is held by the other denominations whom he has mentioned." Here you see

I. He has *shifted his* terms most uncandidly; for in his last speech he *excepts*, with a "perhaps," the Congregationalists, who compose the *mass* of *New* England, and nearly the half of the evangelical Christians of *Old* England. But in the *other*, he

(1) Jude, 9 verse.

excepted *no* denomination; thus *shifting the terms* of his own speech.

II. He flatly contradicts himself. In his last speech, as quoted above, he says he only said that other denominations were *ashamed of* the doctrine. This is *implying* that though they *hold* it, they are not *honest* enough to *avow* it ! But on the last night he said expressly, "I DEFY THE PROOF THAT IT (the doctrine) IS HELD BY THE OTHER DENOMINATIONS WHOM HE HAS MENTIONED." Here he says "*held*," not merely "*ashamed of*." Such tricks are worthy of a Jesuit. It was *his call* for *proof* which led me to quote at large from the *articles* of the Episcopal church, and to refer to other creeds. He shows extreme and impertinent ignorance when he says, "I know, as well as he does, that NONE of the Baptists are *Calvinists;*" whereas, the *majority* of the *Baptists* in Great Britain and America are *decidedly Calvinistic.*

I shall *remember* his denial that Augustine held, "that God from all eternity foreordained whatsoever comes to pass ;" and his knowledge or his candour must suffer not a little in my next reply.

The gentleman asks how I can obey *both* the American Constitution, which *forbids* me *to touch the* "*monuments of idolatry,*" and *our confession,* which commands me "*to remove them ?*" I have answered the question before, by showing that we mean in the confession *no force,* but *truth, moral influence, argument, the press, the Bible, &c. &c.* For example, the fifty Catholics who were converted to Protestantism in Baltimore last year, by *truth,* not *force,* were delivered from the *idolatry of Rome;* ceased to worship a consecrated wafer; ceased to worship saints and angels. Thus we *largely removed the monuments of idolatry.* I know it is not a *pleasant* business to Mr. Hughes. But we cannot help that. Yet if he will show anything *unconstitutional* in all this, except that it violates the *constitution* of the Church of Rome (whose *health* is already not a little impaired by the free discussions going on in America), we will feel ourselves much obliged to him.

As to the article from the "Catholic Telegraph," I pass by the insolent and ill-bred remarks of the gentleman on it. I now challenge the gentleman to prove one word he has said (of the *intention* of the extract) to be true. Till then he stands my calumniator, and the uncandid vindicator of *Catholic enmity to American institutions.* I call on the gentleman distinctly to *prove* what he has said on this subject, or else to disclaim it with proper apology and explanation.

The arguments of our popish advocate have a very *one-sided* way of advancing toward their object. Let us illustrate this. In my last speech I gave long extracts from Bishop England's published letter, attacking directly our republican institutions. Yet the gentleman says *not one* word about it! So also of my Lord Bishop Flagel. I showed by extracts from his communications from *Kentucky to Rome*, that he directly declares that religion cannot be spread among *the Western Indians* "WHILST OUR REPUBLICAN GOVERNMENT SHALL SUBSIST." Yet the gentleman, like his brother Levite of old, *passes by on the other side.* Yet he pays high regard to an article in a newspaper of which he fancied, or he hoped he could, *without detection*, charge me with the perversion. But now, while I recall him to the defence or renunciation of the two above-named *American* (what a contradiction in terms) *Catholic prelates*, I charge him with mis-stating the intention of the extract from the *Catholic Telegraph*, and call on him to *prove* his statements to be true, or *confess* them false.

The gentleman's TWO STEREOTYPE ARGUMENTS appear once more—I think for the thirteenth time. One is, THE DOCTRINE OF ETERNAL DECREES *of God* is destructive of moral, and, therefore, of civil liberty. This argument has already been so much laughed at by the community since the champion of popery first used it in this debate, and so often answered by me, that I should really be ashamed to go over it again, for fear of fatiguing my hearers and future readers. But it may relieve the dry tedium of his *hum drum* repetition of this stale matter, if he would tell us what are the TRUE NEWS of this subject. He attacks the principles of the *Protestants of the Reformation era*, and of the great body of evangelical Protestants *now*. But he gives no other system in its stead. Let us now hear how *he* reconciles the *divine government with moral liberty*. I have showed that the Council of Trent in *one* instance, clearly recognized the doctrine of *election*, and in *another*, shunned giving *any* explanation. Now, until the gentleman gives us a *better* system, and clears up the charges against his *own*, as *acknowledging* what *he condemns* in *ours*, we must hold him responsible as either unpardonably ignorant, or still *worse*. I call on him, then, explicitly, and with no more evasion, to tell us what the Roman Catholic Church does believe on "the decrees," and "election," and if he will tell us, I here pledge myself to prove either that he *falsifies his creed*, or else that the very same objections lie against it which he has charged against *ours*. As to *the other stereotype* argument, concerning the "monuments of idolatry," I can only say, I believe that every creature in this house, not excepting Mr. Hughes, feels fully persuaded that it has been again and again refuted. Yet I do not wonder that his deepest sympathies are kindled for his *gods*. In India it was once wittily said, "*if one would pray against idolatry he must ask God that it may not rain.*" *The Hindoos worship even the things that grow out of the ground.* So of the Church of Rome. She manufactures gods; *she makes priests, and they make gods.* It was said of the *old* Romans, that they had 130,000 gods. But the *new Roman priests* find one in every shrine, and every saint, and every angel, and every image, and every relic, and every consecrated wafer, and, in short, in every *priest*. No wonder that the *priests*, therefore, cry out for their *idols*. As did the *shrine-dealers* at Ephesus, and for the same reason (viz. lest the *gain* of the *craft should suffer*) so do the *priests*. They cry aloud *"great is Diana of the Ephesians."* But the day of their doom is at hand. American Catholics are year by year getting more and more weaned from Rome, and opening their eyes to *priestcraft;* and if we can only for an age, escape the contagion of that foreign infusion which is pouring upon us in Jesuit priests, and the most degraded emissions from papal Europe, I have no doubt, that we shall find the enlightened *Catholics* of America renouncing Rome.

It is curious enough to observe, how the gentleman, by a turn of humour, would put aside the *famous letter* to Paul III. I ask the gentleman to *deny its genuineness,* if he *dares.* He knows too well *what it is,* and on what *proof* it *rests.* Nor does it show the solicitude of the Pope to purify the church. For he never *attempted it,* though the letter called *for it so loudly.* Its *disclosures* show that the Catholic Church was terribly corrupt in her *head and members,* and that the *system leads to such effects.* But *the gentleman has admitted that such a system is destructive of liberty and of society. Therefore on his own principles, I have proved that his own system is destructive of liberty and of society.*

As to the changes which have been *made in our confession* on the subject of *religious liberty,* we have proved that they were *made before* the *American Revolution,* and *by* the patriots who helped to effect it; and *for* the *same* reason that they sought *it,* viz.: the *love of liberty, full and entire—civil and religious.* Mr. Hughes has again and again admitted this change; and yet he *now* says that *" the difference is only in words."* Here, as usual, he contradicts himself, and makes fools of the American people; for he had said the *change* was to *adapt* our *confession* to the *new order* of things. But can the American people be *gulled* with a *change* in a *few words,* when the *thing* remains *the same?* So he seems to intimate. The gentleman's appeal to the civil government of the cantons of Switzerland, and to the *witch stories of* New England *is well.* It shows that he has *nothing against us*—that he is writing against *time*—that he feels it his *task* to make out a speech. And this interprets why he rejected the stenographer's report, and why he was so zealous to go to Mexico. Yes; when we complete this debate, I am well persuaded that those enlightened Catholics who have looked for *a manly, honest defence* of the system which they have been taught was *true,* will look with wonder and deep mortification through these pages, and find them filled with *vulgarity, trash, and tales,* merely thrown in to cloud the discussion and divert the attention. They will say *" Why did he not* REFUTE *as well as* DENY? *Why did he talk about* WITCHES *in New England, when he had promised to show that 'Presbyterian doctrines are opposed to liberty?'* And why did *he pass by unnoticed, unexplained, unanswered, page after page professing to be proof that Catholic doctrines are at war with the civil and religious freedom of man?"*

But these are *"reasons of state"* unto which the "laity must not aspire to look. The gentleman says *"he has already given the reference which I called for"* in the *report of the American Sunday School Union.* I pronounce it utterly false, and now once more demand it—*page, year,* and *report.* His defence of the Burlington brother is *ominous.* He says that he is *"living with his wife and children, and labouring for them."* For his coarse abuse I pardon him. His pen is truly *vulgar.* His tongue, when started in scandal, is *original* and *at home,* as if it were a familiar and favourite business. And this a father confessor to refined and lovely women!!! He breaks forth upon one, like the *"moving bog"* of which I lately read an account, which, though covered at the surface with *luxuriant green,* was no sooner disrupted by some disturbing force, than it broke forth into a dark and slimy stream, which poured its filthy current through field and brooks, and the habitations of men; spreading one dark veil of pollution over the whole face of nature.

But no wonder he starts with conscious wincing at the touch. The cry of the orphan robbed of its father, may yet come up against him before God. The detestable system which can licence brothels in Rome, and tear families asunder in America with fanatical excess, and a degrading superstition that dries up the heart of man, shall not pass unexposed in this land. Nor shall this case stop with the *gentleman's denial,* and exparte testimony. He is *too nearly* involved in this matter to be permitted by an indignant community to be a witness, unless it be as *states-evidence,* and preceeded by *confession* in the ear, not of a priest, but of *the American people.* The gentleman shall hear of this again.

When he charges Calvin with making God the *author of sin,* he *falsified the author with his eyes open.* And now, if he will only give in his next speech, the *context,* and the *passages of Scripture* which Calvin was expounding in meeting the *objections* of Cavillers, I will prove my assertion and charge made in the last sentence.

In the oral debate, and in this repetition of it in *manuscript,* the gentleman has often and very impertinently attacked me on my *"quotations."* You know, gentlemen, how *very numerous* they have been. Of course where he passes them by in silence as he has done with many scores of them) it is *admitting* the *truth* of the *proof,* and the *fairness* of the *method* of *citation.* But I am not satisfied with this *negative* way of conviction. I now, therefore, take up and expose his *positive* charges against me. As his *slanders* are *repeated,* and his last speech really *presents nothing* to be *replied to,* I will here present a paper read by me during the oral debate, which painfully exposes him and his system, but which duty requires me to exhibit.

Reply to the paper thrown into the oral discussion by the Rev. J. Hughes, in which he charges his opponent with divers calumnies against the Church of Rome.

When this pompous and slanderous paper was presented, the Rev. Mr. Hughes was *nominally defending* the Roman Catholic religion. But having, during a succession of three nights, to the surprise of his friends and the compassion of his protestant hearers, utterly failed to meet any of the many facts and arguments brought forward to expose the hostility of his church to civil and religious liberty, he proved and owned himself defeated by a *personal attack* on his opponent, which could have no connexion with the question in debate. He dragged into view the matters of a former controversy, and tried, though in vain, to save his *cause* by blackening the *character* of his adversary when he could not meet his *arguments*—thus illustrating the maxim of the Jesuits, that "*the end justifies the means.*" I promised in due time to expose this paper and its author. Having already given up one of my evenings (devoted to the attack of his doctrines) to *personal defence*, in answer to his *personal* attack, and the gentleman still continuing to call replies, and to press these personalities, it is due to the cause and to myself, to reply in this form before this discussion closes.

1st. He charges me with *calumniating* his church, for saying in a former published controversy, *that according to the Council of Constance, Roman Catholics are not bound to keep faith with heretics.* During that controversy, and again during this debate, I proved the truth of this weighty charge.

Here follows the proof. From the XIX Session of said Council I produced, read, and translated to this assembly (the gentleman then making no reply) the following passage, viz:—*That a safe conduct granted by an emperor or other secular prince to heretics, or those charged with heresy, cannot hinder the competent and ecclesiastical judge from enquiring into the errors of such persons, nor from proceeding in other ways against them, nor from punishing them as much as justice shall require, if they obstinately refuse to recant their errors, although they may have come to the place of judgment depending on said safe conduct, and would not have come otherwise* (etiam si de salvo conductu confissi, ad locum venerint judicii, alias non venturi); *nor is the person promising the safe conduct, bound by it after having done what he could.* (1)

That no faith is to be kept with heretics is so established a doctrine of the Church of Rome that it is heretical to deny it. This principle is taught by such Roman Catholic writers as Bailly, Simanca, Aquinas, Cresswell, Bernard, Cornelio, the Jesuits generally, the Parisian University, and by Popes Gregory IX., Urban

---

(1) See Actæ Ecclesia, tom. i. p. 1669; see also l'Enfant's His. of Coun. Constance, p. 335.

VI., Paul IV., Paul V., Innocent X. to name no others; also by the provincial Councils of Rome, Lateran and Diamper; and also by the general Councils of Lateran Fourth, Lyons, Pisa, and Basil, as well as the Council of Constance. The Councils of Basil and Trent contradict the Rev. Mr. Hughes, and admit the fact about the Council of Constance, in the safe conduct which they granted to the Bohemians and Germans. The Council of Trent in the safe conduct given to the Germans, on the 14th day of May, 1562, thus speaks; added to this, *excluding all fraud and stratagem*, this council promises in good and true faith, that it will seek no occasion either publicly or secretly, by any authority, power, right, statute, privilege of law, or of canons, or of any councils whatsoever, especially the Councils of CONSTANCE and Siena, in whatever form of words expressed, to prejudice in any way the security of this public faith. (1) It was on this admitted principle of the Church of Rome that the powerful and yet unanswered argument of Westley proved that no consistent Roman Catholic, or in other words, none who had not renounced, *ex animo*, this principle of true communion, can be a true citizen of a Protestant government. Multitudes, we rejoice to know, do renounce it. But where we ask does the calumny now lie? For additional proof we refer to Thuanus, iii. 524. Father Paul lib. i. 28, and Labbeus, Alexander, and Cruileb on the Council of Constance.

2d. I am charged by the Rev. gentleman with saying, "that according to the Sixteenth Canon of the Third Council of Lateran, an oath contrary to ecclesiastical utility is perjury, not an oath," and whereas the said canon now produced in the original contains no such doctrine, therefore the charge is FALSE and INJURIOUS as above."

Ans. It is very possible that the gentleman's abridgement of the Book of Councils may not contain this offensive article. But we have the best authority for its existence, viz. Pithon, p. 110. Labbeus, 13 vol. p. 426. Guibert, 3 vol. 504 p. (2) The following are the words of the Holy Council, "Non juramenta, sed perjuria potius sunt dicenda, quae contra utilitatem, ecclesiasticum attentantur." And if more proof is wanting, that this trifling with the sacredness of oaths is an avowed and practical principle of the popes, councils, and Church of Rome, we refer the gentleman to what we have said above in the first head.

3d. The Rev. gentleman thus charges me: "that the Fourth Council of Lateran, A. D. 1215, third canon, freed the subjects of such sovereigns as embraced heresy from their fealty; (Mr. B. same page,) whereas the original canon now produced contains no such doctrine, therefore the charge is again FALSE and INJURIOUS as before."

(1) See Degrees of Coun. Trent. sess. 18. p. 247. Lyons 1624.
(2) See Edgar's Variations of Popery, 278 page.

Proof. Binnius, in his Book of Councils, 8th vol. 807 p. and Labbeus, 13th vol. 934 p. as cited by Edgar, expressly confirm my statement. But we need go no farther than the original canon itself, which has been read in full to this assembly to prove the truth of our assertion. It is as follows: "But if the *temporal lord*, being required and warned by the church, shall neglect to *purge his territory of this heretical filth*, let him by the metropolitan and comprovincial bishops be tied by the bond of excommunication; and if he scorn to satisfy within a year, *let that be signified to the Pope, that he may denounce his vassal, thenceforth absolved from his fidelity,* (or allegiance) *and may expose his country to be seized on by Catholics, who exterminating the heretics, may possess it without any contradiction*, and may keep it in the purity of faith, saving the right of the principle lord, so be it he himself put no obstacle hereto, nor impose any impediment; the same law notwithstanding being kept about them that have no principal lords."

Here then, in express words, and in the very canon itself, is my whole statement affirmed, and the gentleman's confident assertion directly falsified. Not only is this true, but it is matter of history that popes almost without number have absolved subjects from their oath of allegiance to their sovereigns. Thus Gregory in 1078 absolved all from their fidelity who were bound by oath to persons excommunicated, and this he professed to do by apostolical authority. Eos qui excommunicatis fidelitate aut sacramento constricti sunt, apostolica auctoritate a sacramento absolvimus. (1) "*We absolve those who are bound by oath or fidelity to excommunicated persons from said oath, by apostolical authority.*" Clement, in 1306 freed Edward, king of England, from a public oath which he had made to the people to confirm the MAGNA CHARTA. See also what is said under the first head in regard to other popes, provincial and general councils, which have sanctioned the same infamous principle.

4th. I am charged as follows: "That whereas Mr. B. has accused Bellarmine of saying that if the Pope should err in commanding vices and prohibiting virtues, the church would be bound to believe vices to be virtues and virtues to be vices. And whereas Bellarmine has been referred to as maintaining this doctrine, (2) and whereas Bellarmine teaches no such doctrine, but the reverse, therefore this is false and injurious to Catholics."

Proof. I insist that I have fairly represented the sentiment of Bellarmine. Bellarmine is attempting to prove that the Pope is *infallible*, and he pursues this train of argument.

1. The church is bound by conscience to believe the Pope.
2. If the Pope were not infallible, he might command vices and prohibit virtues.

(1) Pithon, 260 page. (2) Mr. B. ibid. p. 19.

8. If the Pope should err in commanding vices and prohibiting virtues, the church would be bound to believe vices to be good, and virtues to be bad.

Mr. Hughes says, "in the former controversy, you stated that it is a principle of Catholics, 'that if the Pope were to command vice and prohibit virtue, he is to be obeyed.'" I answer, *I never stated it is a principle of Catholics*, but merely said *"Bellarmine says."* That I quoted Bellarmine fairly, I appeal to the original quoted by Mr. Hughes. Bellarmine as much asserts the third of these propositions, as he does the first and second. His reasoning reminds me of the following little incident in the Roman History. After the death of Tiberius Gracchus, one Blosius who had taken part with him against the Senate, came to the consul to sue for mercy. His plea was "that he had entertained so high a regard for Gracchus, that he thought he ought to do whatever Gracchus desired." "What," said the consul, "if Gracchus had wished you to set fire to the capitol, would you have thought yourself bound in friendship to have complied with his wishes?" "He would never have wished it," answered Blosius, "but if he had I certainly should have obeyed him." The historian adds, "*nefaria est ista vox.*" "*This is an impious sentiment.*" And so will every man of sense, and honesty, say of the similar sentiment of Bellarmine.

Now to put this matter beyond all doubt, the same Bellarmine in his work against Barklay, c. 13. says, "*In bono sensu, Christus dedit* Petro *potestatem faciendi de peccato non peccatum ; et de non peccato peccatum.*" "In a good sense, Christ gave to Peter power to make that which is sin, to be no sin ; and that which is no sin, to be sin ;" and he infers, that the Pope as Peter's successor has power to do the same. Now can any one conceive how *sin can be made no sin, and no sin be made sin* in A GOOD sense! Is it not the very sense which we have given in the *other* passage ? It is reserved to the morality of Rome to make sin *good*, and virtue, *vice*.

5th. The Rev. gentleman charges me with calumniating the Roman Church, when I assert, that she has suppressed that part of the first commandment (second) which forbids idolatry.

In answer to this, I reply, first, That on a previous evening of this debate, such abundant proofs were given of the truth of this charge, that they need not be repeated here. Second, The copy which I produced from a public library in New York, fully sustained my assertion, which was, that it *gave only four words* of the portion against idolatry, and closed with an expressive et cætera: and whereas, Mr. H. states that said copy contained the whole commandment, we positively deny the truth of the statement; for it was apparent on examination that *many pages* from the place where it *ought to have been* written in full, it was given in *broken fragments*, and not *only the sense*, but the *words*, as much as possible, kept out of view. Third, The fact that he exhibited some copies of one edition, which contained it in full, only proves, that they print *different editions* for *different latitudes.* For it will abundantly appear under the next head, how the priesthood of the same communion, can fraudulently pervert the *Latin* and the *English* of that *same book.*

6th. I am charged with calumniating the translators of this catechism, in two specifications, 1st, for asserting that the translation of Donovan, and that called the Dublin edition, materially differ. In reply, I have only to refer to Cramp's Text Book of Popery, page 380, for a glaring confirmation of this charge. 2d specification, I am charged with slandering the English translation (which is Donovan's) now in use in this country, by accusing it of *manifold frauds* upon the Latin text. The proofs of these frauds I did *not* derive from the Text Book of Popery, but collated the *translation* with the *original*, in the hearing of this assembly. *This translation be it known is sanctioned and recommended by the Rev. gentleman, and all his brethren in America, as faithful and true.* Now I assert that it is *basely a false one.* On page 244 of that translation one whole sentence, *not* in the latin, beginning with these words, "Perfect contrition it is true," &c. *is forged and interpolated.*

In page 97 of the Translation, there are twelve lines of the Latin struck out. These are from Ambrose, who says, "*Christ is the Rock,*" and that Christ conferred his peculiar titles on *the twelve disciples. Why* this is dropped is very clear! But the *forgery* stops not here. The words of the compilers of the catechism, *written many ages after Ambrose died, are put into his mouth,* and he is made to talk like a thorough-paced papist, by leaving in the words—"St. Ambrose saith," and then *erasing* all he had said, and making him father a long paragraph *composed in the 16th century, on the power of the popes !* Is this less than infamous? As we have already given many more specimens of this corrupt translation, we need not now enlarge; but I here challenge Mr. Hughes to meet me on this book before any number of Latin scholars, and I will convict this shameful edition of twenty deliberate and glaring frauds which have been evidently committed with design. And yet the gentleman has ventured to charge me with calumny when I expose these enormities.

But these frauds do not stop with poor St. Ambrose, nor are they confined to the translators of the catechism. By the authority, not only of popes, but of *infallible* councils, a regular warfare has been carried on for ages against all free enquiry; all writers not friendly to Rome have been denounced; Roman Catholic writers have been purged of *unwelcome truths;* they have poisoned the fountains of antiquity; they have dared to prune and correct the writings of the fathers, and *even ventured to lay their correcting and sacrilegious hands on the Word of God.* The prohibitory and expurgatory indexes of Rome are living monuments of these daring frauds.

A copy of one of these works, making a large volume, is now in my possession, and has been already exhibited by me to this assembly.

I. *Specification.—Modern writers pruned and altered.* In the year 1595,(1) Clement VIII, in his catalogue of prohibited books, published a decree, of which the following is an extract. In libris Catholicorum recentiorum, qui post annum Christianæ salutis— 1515, conscripti sint, si id quod corrigendum occurrit, paucis demptis, aut additis emendari posse videatur, id correctores faciendum curent; sin minus, omnino deleatur. *"In the books of modern Catholics, written since the year of our Lord, 1515, if any thing should occur worthy of correction, and it can be done by striking out or putting in a few things, let the correctors have it done; but if not, let it be wholly erased."* The year 1515 marks the rise of Luther! Hence the Pope fixed on that era for his special vigilance over the press!

II. *Specification.—The Fathers corrupted.* If any one wishes to be fully informed on this subject, let him examine James's Treatise on this subject. (2)

a. The sixth canon of the Apostles. "Let not a bishop, a priest, in any sort upon pretence of *religion*, forsake his own wife. But if he chance to do so, let him be excommunicated; or if he continue, let him be degraded."

It has thus been forged by Roman Catholic hands—"or if he continue *in his error*, let him be degraded." The true passage means—if he *continue* to *forsake* his wife, he is to be degraded. The forgery *makes* it mean, that if he *continue* to *keep his wife* he is to be degraded. This is the way the celibacy of the priesthood is *proved.* We have already showed how it is *compensated* by *concubines, &c. &c.*

b. Thirty-second Canon of the Council of Agatha it is written, *"Let a clergyman presume to sue no man before a temporal judge,"* &c. But it has been forged to mean the very opposite by changing *clericus* into *clericum,* and *nullum* into *nullus.* Then it reads *"Let no man presume to sue a clergyman before a secular judge!"* Thus Bellarmine uses it; and in his controversy with Barklay, page 279, tries to excuse it. This passage shows not only a *fraud,* but a fraud to *exalt* the *priesthood,* and put down the *laity.*

c. The Fourth Council of Carthage—(3) "Let no woman, though she be a religious woman or learned, in presence of men presume so far as to baptize any." This is the true passage. But to magnify *baptism* and the *priesthood,* baptism is made necessary to salvation, even to the dying infant. Hence they needed a plan to apply it in all cases. But this passage is in their way; so there

(1) See Campbell's Lectures Ecc. Hist. p. 349.
(2) No. 3507 of the Philadelphia Library Company.
(3) Chap. 99, 100.

has been *added* to it these words—*unless it be in case of necessity.* This forgery opens the door for *nurses* to *baptize infants.*

d. St. Ambrose (1)—"They have not Peter's inheritance which have not Peter's (fidem) *faith.*" Gratian corrupted this into "Peter's (*sedem*) *chair!*"

e. Chrysostom (2)—"It (the seed of the woman) shall bruise thy head." To honour the Virgin Mary, it is forged to read "*she* shall bruise thy head."

f. Preface to the Council of Ephesus. The true reading is this, "In which Council presided the blessed Cyril, formerly Bishop of Alexandria," &c. It is thus forged, to *prop the papacy*, "In which Council *instead of the blessed Celestine the Pope*, presided the blessed St. Cyril!" James gives no less than fifty specimens of this *pruning* and *corrupting* of the Fathers and Councils in the first few centuries.

g. Finally, the Rev. Mr. Hughes himself, in our late controversy cited Tertullian (3) to prove the *primacy* of Rome and the *supremacy* of the Pope; and made it seem to be really so, by garbling the author, and applying all he said to Rome *alone.* Whereas, the *full* passage which I published in parallel lines with his *elliptical* extract, declares that CORINTH, PHILIPPI, THESSALONICA, and EPHESUS were *all* APOSTOLICAL CHAIRS, AS WELL AS ROME!!

III. *Specification.*—*The holy word of God itself has been* CORRUPTED *with wanton profaneness by the Church of Rome.* Out of a crowd of examples we give a few.

a. The Vulgate Bible and the English translation of it sanctify the forgery on Chrysostom cited above, (4) "*she* shall bruise thy head," i. e. the Virgin Mary, we suppose—instead of "*it*," *thy seed, i. e.* CHRIST.

b. Hebrews xi. 21, "Jacob *worshipped* the TOP of *his staff*"— in support of the worship of images. Whereas the true rendering is "worshipped on (that is, leaning on) the top of his staff!"

c. Luke xiii. 3, "Verily, verily, I say unto you, unless ye *do penance*, ye shall all likewise perish." Whereas, the true meaning is, *unless ye repent;* which we need not say is a thing wholly different from doing penance in the Church of Rome.

d. Immediately after the revocation of the Edict of Nantes, 1685, a duly prepared version of the New Testament in the French tongue was extensively circulated for the conversion of Protestants. Mr. Butler in his "Book of the Roman Catholic Church," thus writes—"At the revocation of the Edict of Nantes, *fifty thousand copies* of a French translation of the New Testament were, *at the recommendation of* BOSSUET, distributed among the converted Protestants, by *order of Louis XIV.*" Now, let us examine the

---

(1) Lib. 1. de Poenit. cap. vi. tom. 4.
(2) 17 Homily on Genesis, chap. iii. v. 15.
(3) See page 74 of Whetham's edition.
(4) On Gen. iii. 15.

character of this translation, of whose dissemination the author so much boasts; and which was issued under such high authority. Acts, xiii. 2, the true passage is, "As they ministered unto the Lord," &c. The Bordeaux translation has it, "As they *sacrificed unto the Lord the sacrifice of mass.*" 1 Cor. iii. 15, "If any man's work shall be burned, he shall suffer loss; but he himself shall be saved; yet so as by fire." The Roman Catholic version interpolates the words "of purgatory," so as to make it read, "*He shall be saved by the fire of purgatory.*" 1 Tim. iv. 1, "In the latter times some shall depart from the faith." The Roman Catholic version forges the word "Roman," making it read, "*shall depart from the Roman faith.*" Such frauds and forgeries on the sacred text itself, discover the desperate extremities and reckless spirit of a system, which, in order to carry its own ends, dares to pollute even the sacred fountain of divine truth. (1) Here, then, is my answer to the gentleman's charge of calumny. Let heaven and earth judge between us.

7th. He charges me with calumny for saying "that Catholics call the Pope God." I said in the late controversy that the *Pope called himself* God. On a previous evening however in this debate, I fully proved out of the mouth of the Rev. gentleman's own translator and friend, that the Pope *did* call himself God. Not only so, but it was also shown at the same time, that the Pope was worshipped at Rome as God, and that the titles and attributes of God had been conferred on him by STANDARD WRITERS in the Church of Rome; and with the sanction of councils themselves.

8th. The Rev. gentleman charges me with calumniating his church by asserting that its doctrines are opposed to civil and religious liberty. This charge I have made good by the unanswered and accumulating arguments of the whole debate—to which in general I now refer. But he specifies the Twenty-seventh Canon of the third Lateran, which I adduced, and says it is inadequate proof in itself, and that I *suppressed* a part of it. He says, "*and whereas said canon is no part of the Catholic religion.*" Strange! Does he renounce it, or *de*nounce it? Is it not as much a part of his religion as the directions in our confession of faith about *opposing false religions* and *removing* the *monument of idolatry* are a part of ours? It is *discipline* with him to *remove millions of men* out of the world—but it is *doctrine* with us to remove only the *monuments* of idolatry?

Again. He says this canon was "*a special regulation for a particular case, made in concurrence with the civil power from which alone it could derive its authority.*" But *who* made it? He acknowledges that it was *made with the civil power from which it derived its authority*; and made *by the council!* Then he owns that such a union of Church and state may be made as that the church may *derive authority to raise an army and put*

(1) See Rev. xxii. 18, 19.

multitudes of men to death, sack their towns, and make slaves of them; for a part of the decree published by me is this, "AND LET IT BE FREELY PERMITTED TO PRINCES TO REDUCE MEN OF SUCH STAMP TO SLAVERY." This too is done by *the representative church;* and that church in said decree says, *" We inhibit them" (who fail to take up arms at the call of the Bishop) from a participation of the body and blood of the Lord*—and on the contrary, those who *take* up arms were *" received into the protection of the church,"* and large indulgences were granted to them *by* the church. Here then the gentleman owns that if the state will give the church *power,* she may, as *she did, enslave, fight, curse,* and *kill men;* may reward those *who do,* and excommunicate those who do not *help* her to do these things. *Is not this church and state?* Is not this opposing civil and religious liberty? He says *" it is discipline!"* verily! But does the Roman doctrine *tolerate such discipline?* Does it forbid it? Does it not enforce it? What matter to the persons put to death, whether you call the sword *discipline* or *doctrine?* And what if the government of the United States should give "anthority" to the Pope to destroy us *heretics?* Would it be right? certainly; as the *council did, and as the defender of it says!*

But again he says, "Mr. B. *suppressed the section* which enumerates the crimes of the sects referred to, and thereby deceives his readers by making it appear that the punishment was for speculative errors in doctrine, and not for their crimes against society and the state." He falsely charges me with suppressing. I followed Faber, and he gave all that was necessary (making one page) to prove the persecution of the Roman Catholic Church. But see his reasoning. The church has a *right* to punish; *even to death, men who are guilty of crimes against society and states.* This he admits. This is the very point. I say she has not. What has she to do with *punishing crimes against society and the states, with temporal* pains and penalties!! It matters little whether the church *persecute* for *opinions,* or for *crimes.* It was not for *crimes,* but for *opinions* that the Church of Rome put these poor people to death. But *admit* all the *crimes that are charged.* Does the gentleman say that for *them* his church can *punish men temporally.* Yes this is the *plea.* LET MY COUNTRY HEAR, and PAUSE, and THINK!

9th. Charge of calumny is this—*that I quoted a bull for the extermination of heretics,* which is not preserved at Rome. The copy of the bull (in translation) was then, and is now in my possession. I have sent to England for the original. The gentleman *knows* there is such a bull. He knows too that Popes suppress bulls when they are found to injure them. He may *not* know that even the infamous Bulla in Cœna Domini, (which he told us lately he never saw)—but which all the papal world besides *knows*—which for centuries has sent all mankind to hell but papists, and which he is bound in virtue of holy obedience to read *during lent* every year; I say he may not know that this bull is *not printed* in the Bullarium Magnum.

10th. Calumny, I am charged with a long catalogue of sins against the Third Canon of Fourth Lateran. This canon I read and expounded at large on a former evening. As to the charges of *garbling this canon*, the falsification of the gentleman's charges will also be found in the debate of a former evening, to which I refer this assembly.

As to the matter of the *decree itself*, he says, Mr. B. asserted, "that according to this canon, sovereigns may be deposed, and their subjects released from their allegiance when they become heretics, and that they are to be excommunicated when they neglect to exterminate heretics from their land." He again denies that this is *doctrine*. This is too shallow an artifice to deceive a school boy. He admits it is "doctrine so far as it condemns all heresies in the *abstract*." Well, and what if it condemns heresy in the *concrete;* that is in the *persons of men?* Is it doctrine no more? Is a decree condemning a book, *doctrine;* and the same decree condemning a *man* for holding the *doctrine* in the book discipline? One is *doctrine;* the other is *doctrine* and *discipline*. Is it doctrine to condemn a *book* to the *flames*, and discipline to *condemn a man to them?* Now this decree condemned the DOCTRINES OF MILLIONS, AND THEIR PERSONS TOO! It is the most bloody document I ever read. Mr. Hughes admits that it absolves the subjects of *inferior* lords from allegiance! Yet denies that it does those of lords who were *chief*. But is not the *principle* the same? Is it not persecution, tyranny, and usurpation not to be borne or defended?

Again the decree embraces "*secular powers whatsoever offices they are in?* Does *this exclude any high or low?* It says, "*saving the right of the principal lord;*" but with this sweeping *proviso*, "*if so be he himself put no obstacle thereto, nor oppose any impediment!*" Yet Mr. Hughes has the hardihood to deny that the *sovereigns* or principal lords are embraced in the decree. This cruel, persecuting canon, pays its *bloody soldiery* with heavenly gifts for exterminating heretics. It excommunicates all the *friends* of the heretics; it makes the heretic *intestate, infamous,* and *deprives him of all civil and religious rights;* if a clergyman he is deposed: and twice a year if necessary every prelate is to make the *circuit* of his territory to search for heretics: and *compel* the *whole neighbourhood to swear to inform on heretics*, and those who refuse to *swear*, or swearing *neglect* to inform, are to be reputed heretics; and Bishops are put under *canonical vengeance* if they refuse to act. Did Draco's laws equal these? Does the police of Constantinople *probe and detail* in such detail, and such *ubiquity* as this? And yet this no persecution! Not *opposed* to all sorts of liberty, or if opposed, not *doctrine!* God save our country from a system, which, with honied doctrines and smooth words, may by discipline *bathe the land in blood!*

11th, and lastly. The gentleman has on divers occasions charged me with calumniating the Church of Rome by exaggerated accounts of the number of lives which have been destroyed by her agency, authority, or influence. Now as our chief object was to establish principles, we have confined ourselves for the most part to the discussion of principles; and having abundantly proved that persecution, even to death, *is a principle of the Church of Rome, upon which she has acted for ages*, the amount of blood she has shed in carrying out these principles is a *second* question. The blood which she has shed is a fearful standing *commentary* on her principles; and she has shed enough to *float a man of war!*

Specifications.—1. The crusades for liberating the Holy Land *originated with* and were encouraged and impelled *by* the popes and the priesthood, and Councils of the Church of Rome. These continued for about two centuries, under the significant title of "*the Holy War*," with no less than *eight* expeditions, and the slaughter on both sides of several millions of men. These were sanctioned and urged by Popes Gregory VII., Martin II., Innocent III., &c. In vol. ii. p. 309, of the Acta Ecclesiæ, we have a long decree of the Fourth Council of Lateran, headed "*Expedition for the recovery of the Holy Land.*" This decree *ordains a Christian army*; gives *great indulgences to the cross-bearers*; yea, even a *plenary pardon to them of all their sins*, and *increase of eternal joy in the rewards of the just*, and *adding appropriate and most holy curses upon all those who should in any way hinder the success of these bloody expeditions*. Several millions of Europeans and Asiatics were the *victims* of *these Holy Wars*; and the guilt of their blood is charged to the *Church of Rome*.

2. The persecutions against the Albigenses, Waldenses, and Wickliffites were commissioned by *holy* councils, *preached* up and *pressed* on by the *bulls* of *popes*, and the *ministry* of bishops, inquisitors, &c., and from age to age, carried out on the most *bloody principles* of *persecution* by the Church of Rome. It is impossible to compute the multitudes, not only of men, but of women and children, slaughtered in these crusades. Bruys (1) estimates that 100,000 Albigenses fell in one day. Mezerai and Velly compute the number slain in storming the city of Beziers at 60,000. (2)

The Rev. Mr. Hughes thinks these massacres may be *justified*, because, as he says, the *victims* were not *innocent* victims, but wicked men, and the enemies of society. We are thankful for his candour though he meant it for a *defence*. He speaks in this the spirit and language of his church; for it is a matter of history, that

(1) Vol. iii. p. 139.
(2) See Edgar, p. 252. See also on these crusades, Thuanus, Allx's History of the Waldenses and Albigenses, Jones's Hist. of the same. Mosheim's Ecclesiastical History, as well as Bruys, Meserai and Velly, passim.

the provincial Councils of Toledo, Oxford, Tours, Avignon, Labaur, Montpelier, Narbonne, Albly, and Tolosa, *sanctioned the sanguinary spirit of persecution*, and not only so, but the general Councils of the Four Laterans of Constance and Sienna did the same. (1)

3. The history of the Holy Inquisition, which we have proved on a previous occasion, to have the Pope for its head, infallible authority for its cruelties, and the whole world for its field. Even the Rev. Mr. Hughes has said it was a good institution abused; the Bishop of Aire justifies it for putting guilty victims (that is, Protestants) to death; Bellarmine not only justifies but recommends it, and says, that by this and other means, (2) almost an infinite number of heretics were burned or otherwise put to death by the Church; and he instances Donatists, Manichæans, and Albigenses, who were routed and annihilated by arms. Devoti also honestly defends the Inquisition. Now, in Spain alone, according to the history of I. A. Llorente, secretary to the Inquisition, in a little more than two centuries the victims of the Inquisition, burned or otherwise punished, were no less than 341,057. The horrors of this infamous tribunal we will not attempt to describe; its secrets will never be known until the great day of revelation. The number of its victims in various forms and lands, while it ruled the nations with a rod of iron, must indeed have been fearfully great.

4. The massacre of St. Bartholomew's day, the revocation of the Edict of Nantes, the massacre in cold blood of the Protestants of Ireland, the sanguinary persecutions by the Duke of Alva in Holland, where Father Paul says (3) 50,000 were hanged, beheaded, buried alive, and burned in a short time; the destruction of the Wickliffites, Lollards, and Culdees; the persecutions of Bohemia; the suppression, by force, of the reformation in Italy and Spain; and the millions massacred by Catholics in South America; make a picture of *wickedness* on the one hand, and *woe* on the other, which no created mind can adequately describe or ever conceive. Add to this, that for centuries the potentates of Europe, by the *mixture* of church and state, under a theocracy, of which the Pope was God, were held bound by oath to exterminate and destroy in their dominions all heretics and dissenters from the Church of Rome. In the Cementines (4) there is a long chapter, headed— "*Oaths of fidelity which the Roman Emperors take to the Pope of Rome,*" which fully confirms what we have just said. Now, consider in connexion with this the *millions* slaughtered by the kings and emperors of Europe under the obligation of these oaths against heretics and dissenters from Rome, and then add all these

---

(1) See Dupin, Labbeus, Crabbe, Binnius, Alexander, Bruys, Guibert, and Crotty.
(2) Book ii. chap 22 and 23, on the Laity.
(3) Page 387.   (4) Book ii. tit. 9.

parts together, and you have some imperfect idea of the *butcheries of Holy Mother Church*.

I cannot close this article without indulging myself and my hearers with an extract from the Rev. Mr. Hughes's Ninth Letter of the late Controversy; in which it will be seen at a glance, that he advances principles which will go to justify all the great persecutions of the Church of Rome: principles which vest the civil and religious rights of men in the power of a *despot* or of a *majority;* principles which will justify the Roman Catholics whenever they get the *majority* in this country in shaping the government of the state and the church so as to take *away all constitutional liberty from both;* principles too, which he advanced in defending the persecuting Canon of Fourth Lateran. "*It is to be observed in the first place that this Council was* held at a time when the *feudal system* was in full operation. A council was as it were the *general congress* of Christendom, in which states and sovereigns were represented for the purpose of conferring together on *such matters* as concerned the general welfare. These *secular* representatives had nothing to do with the *definitions of doctrines or morals; and the infallibility of the church had nothing to do* WITH ANY THING ELSE. Still it was deemed the *most convenient time and place* for sovereigns and states to adopt such means, in *conjunction with the clergy,* as might protect the *altar and the throne,* or as the *exigencies* of the period required. The social picture, *mingled theocracy and civil policy of the puritan settlements in New England, presents but a diminutive analogy,* when the pilgrim fathers and their immediate successors (not to speak of other things *far more serious*) would hardly ring the town-house bell unless they found a text of *scripture for it.*" Here, mark that the gentleman owns the fact of "a *theocracy*" in that day of *Rome's supreme dominion* over men's souls and bodies. You remember how he *attacked* lately, and *denounced the persecutions* of New England, and read long extracts against them. He *rightly condemned them*—but here, he is *off his guard,* and on the same principles *defends Rome.* Now, if Rome was *right* against the *Albigenses,* was *New England wrong?* If New England and Rome were *alike* in this, how can he *condemn New England?* Let the logic of Rome explain it! Again (same page) he writes—"So it was in the temporal regulations adopted by the *commingled representatives of church and state at the General Council of Lateran.* Had they NOT THE RIGHT, I *would ask,* AS THE MAJORITY by a MILLION TO ONE, to take measures for the common welfare? The doctrine of Christ teaches submission to the 'powers that be.' Consequences such as you *predicted* of the *Bible Society in Russia,* have *always* followed the footsteps of fanaticism. Had not then the CATHOLIC kings, and CATHOLIC barons, and CATHOLIC *vassals* and all the *orders* of *feudalism* in CATHOLIC EUROPE, the RIGHT by VIRTUE of their MAJORITY to take PRECAUTIONS AGAINST *such*

CONSEQUENCES? NO REPUBLICAN, I should think, would deny it!" Thus, we see, how he denies all *constitutional, original, imprescriptible rights, and* GIVES TO THE POWERS *that be,* to an *autocrat,* or a *majority,* the right to stop the circulation of the Bible, or to destroy the minority, if their own interest depends on it, and yet talks about *republican*—and about rights! His principle clearly is, that *minorities have no rights.* How this *coincides* with the more candid Bellarmine! (1) "When the question is, whether heretics, thieves, and other wicked men are to be EXTIRPATED it is always to be considered, according to the purpose of the Lord, whether it can be done without injury of the *good,* (Catholics) and if indeed it can be done, THEN WITHOUT DOUBT THEY ARE TO BE EXTIRPATED; but if it cannot be done, because they are not sufficiently known, and there is danger of injuring the innocent *instead of the guilty;* OR THEY BE STRONGER THAN WE, and THERE IS DANGER IF WE MEET THEM IN BATTLE THAT MORE MAY FALL AMONG US THAN AMONG THEM, in such case we should be quiet."

(1) Vol. III. chap. 22, de Laicis.

"*Is the Presbyterian Religion, in any or in all its principles or doctrines, opposed to civil or religious liberty?*"

AFFIRMATIVE V.—MR. HUGHES.

MR. PRESIDENT:—

You have heard what the gentleman has put forth, and it would be difficult to find, in our language, a *single word* expressive enough to convey an idea of its character. It is, if I may borrow a term from the Spanish, an "olla-podrida." It is like the variegated robe with which *parental* fondness clothed the patriarchal boy; and the *variety* of its colours furnishes intrinsic evidence, that *patriarchal hands* have been employed in patching it up. But whatever it *is*, you all know what it is NOT—an answer to my speech. And, far from complaining that the gentleman has invoked the aid of friendship in his extremity, I am delighted that he has friends, and that they have sense enough *not to attempt* a refutation of my arguments. The propositions of my last speech, therefore, are tacitly admitted *as unanswerable*. Not a single exception taken at my authorities—not a single attempt to disprove the correctness of my reasoning. I confess that of a train of argument, founded on facts, which exhibited the doctrines of the "CONFESSION OF FAITH" as authorizing and leading to bloodshed, in every country in which the civil constitution did not restrain its intolerance, (as in the United States now,) I did expect that there would be some attempt at refutation. But the reverse is the case; and it proves that the wisdom of older men cannot extricate the Presbyterian religion from the *predicament*, into which it has been brought by the imprudence of the gentleman. There it sticks; and, *until history can be blotted out from the memory of men*, there it will continue, undefended and indefensible; from the indelible charge of having shed the blood of men, for conscience' sake, and that on a principle of doctrine—which is still retained in its public creed.

He mistook his subject when he promised to defend it. Talents superior to his, would be shipwrecked in the undertaking. *His* talents lie in another way; his *forte* is the "ABUSE OF POPERY." This discussion will have taught him more of Presbyterian history than he ever knew before; and, I trust, he will have gleaned from the improvement of his knowledge, the wholesome moral of the old adage, "*that men of* GLASS *ought not to throw stones.*"

He assigns as a reason why he does not attempt to meet my arguments, that "he has answered them already." Sir, a grosser imposition never was attempted on sectarian credulity. Examine his speeches from beginning to end, and tell me WHERE, or WHEN he has answered them! To my quotations from history, showing the unextinguishable intolerance of Presbyterians, he has opposed his ASSERTIONS. Do you call that an answer? To the Protestant and Presbyterian authorities quoted by me to prove their doctrines and deeds of blood, in every country under heaven, that was scourged with their political ascendancy, he opposes "certificates" of Bancroft, or somebody else, setting forth that they were a pretty good kind of people. Do you call that an answer? I prove by testimony that he does not dispute, that the Quakers and other "pestilent heretics," as they were called, were cropped of their EARS, scourged at the cart-tail, and hanged on the gallows, for having exercised liberty of conscience, in opposition to Calvinism, in New England—and he calls this evidence, "witch" stories! Now is this an answer? I show him that the Baptists were put to death by the Presbyterians of Switzerland—and he says, *Oh, that was in Switzerland, but* WE *have not done so, in this* COUNTRY, *since the* REVOLUTION. Do you call that an answer? I show him that in Scotland, the Presbyterians made it death for the Catholic to have worshipped "three times," ACCORDING TO THE DICTATES OF HIS OWN CONSCIENCE; and to this he replies, that his Scotch ancestors were not sound in the faith. Is this an answer? I show that his church holds communion with ALL THOSE CHURCHES—that SHE RECEIVES THEIR MINISTERS—*that some of those ministers are the very men who are stirring up religious discord in the republic now*, and to all this he answers NOTHING. And why does he answer nothing? Because he has nothing to say in reply. The same principles of Presbyterian doctrine which authorized the use of the AXE, and the STAKE, and the HALTER, in other countries, have *never been condemned*—have never been considered as a *departure from orthodoxy* by the Presbyterians of the United States, either since the revolution or before. The gentleman, therefore, must not *pretend* that he has answered these arguments, when he has not. The claim of his creed to the political support of the MAGISTRATES as "nursing fathers to the church"—the pretended COMMANDMENT OF GOD TO "REMOVE ALL FALSE WORSHIP"—contain enough of the DOCTRINE of persecution to authorize the same tragical barbarities which they produced elsewhere. They point out the END which the Presbyterians are bound by their "TENETS OF FAITH" to aim at—and all *scruple* as to the *means* by which this end is to be accomplished, are sufficiently taken away by the doctrine, that God has *unchangeably* "FOREORDAINED WHATSOEVER COMES TO PASS."

And before I proceed to develope still further the radical intolerance and tyranny of this doctrine, I must make a few observations to show the unreasonableness of the gentleman's *attempt to decoy me away from the subject of debate*. He introduces matter which is *out of order*—foreign to the question, and belonging to the *former part* of this discussion. If I turn aside to notice his assertions, (for they are nothing more,) it is manifest that I cannot perform the operation which he finds so painful, viz., the dissection of Presbyterianism. This is what he hopes to defeat. I show him that the arguments by which the DOCTRINE of his church authorized its members to refute all heresies and false worship, were the faggot, and the block, and the halter. And, in order to withdraw the eyes of the public from the contemplation of *this horrible truth*, he says, "why does not Mr. Hughes answer this, and this — the "crusades," the "Inquisition," "St. Bartholomew," "licensed brothels at Rome," "mutilations and forgeries of authors," &c. &c. &c. &c. &c. I reply that my reason for not answering them *now*, is, first, because so far as they are *falsely said to have been* EVIDENCES OF THE DOCTRINES *of the Catholic religion*, I have answered them already, under their proper head, in the former question; to which I refer the audience and the reader. I reply secondly, that they do not belong to *this question*, and that my time and space are *sacred to Presbyterianism*. These are sufficient to show that the gentleman's *ruse de guerre*, to decoy me from exposing the reasons why Presbyterians ought to be ashamed to speak of *"civil and religious liberty,"* is an artifice of which a generous antagonist would feel discredited by stooping to avail himself. Lest, however, the course he has pursued should be construed illogically, and an inference drawn that the case does not warrant, I submit the following remarks and proposal.

1. The crusades had for their object to arrest the progress of the sworn enemies of the Christian name. The *learned* Protestants who have written on the subject, even Southey and James, have acknowledged that the POLITICAL SALVATION of Europe was secured by them. James declares that they were as "JUST AS ANY WARS THAT EVER WERE UNDERTAKEN."

2. The Albigenses were *public enemies of the state and of society by* THEIR CRIMES. They were put down by the civil power, with the permission and the recommendation of the clergy—not as heretics, but as heretics WHO COMMITTED SUCH PUBLIC DISORDERS AS NO GOVERNMENT COULD TOLERATE. Catholics, guilty of the same crimes, would have been put down in the same way.

3. The Hugonot wars in France were wars for political ascendancy. The doctrines of Calvin had taught his disciples that sooner than *his gospel* should not triumph in POLITICS, as well as religion, they might turn *their arms against their country* and their king. They did so, but they did not succeed. It was *they*

who are responsible for the blood that was shed during those melancholy days. Treachery and treason, conspiracy and assassination had been employed *by them*, to accomplish their purpose. And, though treachery was employed against them, *no principle of the Catholic religion was ever adduced to sanction the proceeding of St. Bartholomew.* It was attempted to be justified on the plea, that it was precisely the stratagem *which the Hugonots themselves had intended to employ.*

4. The altering of books is introduced, for what purpose the gentleman alone can tell. The only reason I can imagine, is, to cover the use he has attempted to make of the spurious document, ascribed to Innocent VIII. He says the bull "In Cœna Domini" is not in the Bullarium Magnum. This is simply *untrue.*-- It is found in Vol. III., p. 282. Down to the pretended Reformation there was NO MOTIVE *to alter books*, since *all* were Catholics. *After that*, it would have been USELESS AND ABSURD—*since the Protestants would know the fact.* The *true reason*, therefore, was to guard against the errors which the new religionists were ever zealous to foist into the *republication of Catholic works.* The Scriptures, the Fathers, the Ecclesiastical Writers, were all to be "*reformed*" by those sly alterations, *which changed the meaning of the author, and yet preserved the title of the book.* We have instances in our own day, to prove that the *art* has not been lost or forgotten by Presbyterians. The Sunday School Union—and the American Bible Society, in sending a MUTILATED Spanish Bible to the South Americans with a "*lying title page,*" are cases directly in point.

5. As to charges of "CALUMNIES," to which he pretends *now* to give a REPLY, I shall briefly show how much his "reply" is worth. 1. What *is* his reply? It is only a REPETITION *of the calumnies themselves.* 2. He quotes, when he quotes at all, a *garbled word*, or sentence, and adduces it as evidence, *not of its meaning* IN THE ORIGINAL, *but of the malicious meaning which* CALUMNY has ascribed to it—just as the devil quoted Scripture, to suit his purpose. Let the gentleman not say that I compare him to the devil—I only *borrow an illustration.* 3. But what settles the matter is, that when *I* made out the calumnies, I had the ORIGINAL TEXT AND CONTEXT *spread out on the table.* Then was the time for a man who had a literary reputation either at stake or in prospect, to have felt *laudably indignant* at the charge, and bent over the page, which would *convict* or *acquit him.* Did he do this? Not at all. I specified calumny after calumny; pointed to the books, not Crampt's "Text Book of Popery," not Dr. Miller's ribaldrous "History of Popery," but the ORIGINAL BOOKS, *which calumniators dread;* I challenged him to the open page; I *taunted him* with a prediction *that he would wait* to avail himself of the *absence of the books* to which he referred—but all in vain! A candid man

would have said, "let me see the originals—I am glad you have brought them here, and *marked the references*, for I have always been taught to believe those statements; and I have no wish to aid in the perpetuation of calumnies, if they are such. I shall see for myself, and not depend on FABER any more." Was there any thing of this? Not at all. He said something about his character, and promised, "with the *permission* of God," to reply to the charges—in the absence, as we now see, of the *only witnesses* that could convict or acquit him—the ORIGINAL DOCUMENTS. Here was the test.

But he shall not escape with this. The calumnies which I charged and proved, may be seen under the former head. I have still the original works in my library. And I propose that two interpreters, one a Catholic, appointed by me; the other a Presbyterian, appointed by Mr. Breckinridge, shall appoint, by agreement, a *third*, neither a Catholic nor Presbyterian; and let these, as a tribunal, decide, *by appeal to the original documents*. I propose next to enter into a bond, with security, to pay one hundred dollars to whoever may claim it, for every case in which I do not succeed to *convict the gentleman of the calumnies alleged by me against him;* provided that he or any of his friends will enter into a 'like obligation, of paying one hundred dollars for every instance in which I shall convict him. The forfeit to be given in such charity as either party may choose.

This will test the measure of confidence which he has in his pretended "reply." This will test how far his friends are sincerely disposed to believe that his statements "are to be depended on." This will test whether the conscience of Presbyterianism is as ready to sacrifice *money*, as it is to immolate *truth*. To this test I challenge the gentleman.

Before I enter on the continuation of the general argument, I must go over the small points of the gentleman's speech. I had said, that the only denomination of Protestants who had not become "ashamed" of Calvin's absolute "decrees," were the high-toned Presbyterians, and "*perhaps*" the Congregationalists of New England. I defied the proof, that it was "held" by the other denominations. He *does not give the proof*, but says, that inasmuch I said "*they were ashamed of*," in *one* sentence, and "*they held*," in the other, I have contradicted myself!! He *says so*. But, surely, there is no contradiction. The Lutherans, Episcopalians, General Baptists, Methodists, Swedenborgians, Moravians, Unitarians, and the other denominations of Protestants that I am acquainted with, are "*ashamed of it*," and do not "*hold* it." I said that "none of the Baptists were *Calvinists*." This, he says, "SHOWS MY EXTREME AND IMPERTINENT IGNORANCE;" for, he adds, the majority in Great Britain are "decidedly *Calvinistic*. And, therefore, being Calvinistic, they are *Calvinists!!* Now the Calvinists of Switzerland tied the Baptists back to back, and DROWNED

THEM FOR HERESY—a sufficient proof that I was not "*ignorant*" when I said that none of the Baptists are "*Calvinists.*"

I have too much respect for the moral sense of the age, not to believe and *hope,* that the *gentleman himself* would be "ashamed" of its avowal. Would he not be ashamed to go into a Christian pulpit, and proclaim that the crimes and villanies of the day, and the drunkenness and debaucheries of the night, were all " FOREORDAINED " by God ? Would he not be "ashamed" to say, after Calvin, that the incest of Absolom is set down in Scripture as "GOD'S OWN WORK?" "*Absolon incesto coitu patris torum polluens, detestabile scelus perpetrat;* DEUS TAMEN HOC SUUM OPUS PRONUNCIAT." (1) Would he not be "ashamed" to say, with the father of his religion, that " *God directs whatever is perpetrated by men,* OR EVEN BY THE DEVIL HIMSELF?" " *Ergo quidquid agitent homines vel Satan ipse, Deus tamen clavum tenet* "—literally, "*God holds the keys.*" (2)

The gentleman says, that "*force*" is not intended by the commandment which obliges Presbyterians "*to remove all false worship, and all the monuments of idolatry.*" He ought to know that the uniform practice of his Church explains what was intended by this commandment. *In Geneva it meant* "FORCE,"— in *France,* "FORCE,"— in *Scotland, England,* and *Ireland,* "FORCE,"—in *the Low Countries,* "FORCE,"—in *New England,* "FORCE;"—and if, in this country, it means "*moral influence,*" the fact teaches us to be grateful to Heaven for having given us a *government which compels the Presbyterians to break one of God's commandments, and* DESIST FROM THE USE OF " FORCE " *in removing what* THEY, in the plenitude of arrogance, think proper to designate as "*false worship.*" The article was framed, as it now stands, by the Creed-makers of Westminster, when the *political power,* legislative, executive, and judiciary, was in the hands of Presbyterians, and the gentleman must be extremely ignorant of the history of those times, if he supposes that it was not *framed expressly to sanction the employment of* "*force,*" *in establishing Presbyterian* " *uniformity*" *throughout the three kingdoms.* It was the very rock on which they split. For, if the indomitable intolerance of Calvinism had permitted them to comply with the petitions of the *Independents,* to grant an "*indulgence to* TENDER CONSCIENCES," their power would not have been so short-lived. But nothing short of the "REMOVAL" of all "FALSE WORSHIP" would satisfy their thirst for absolute religious domination. This we have seen already in my last speech, and it shall be more fully shown in the present.

The gentleman wants me to show the "*intention*" of the Editor of the Catholic Telegraph, in copying the article from a foreign paper, animadverting on the affair in Boston. It is enough

(1) Inst. c. 18. § 1.   (2) Ibid.

that I have proved him and his colleagues guilty of *calumny*, when they charged the *authorship* of that article on the Catholic editor himself, and on this assumption of THEIR OWN CALUMNY, would charge its sentiments on the whole Catholic body of the United States. Bishop England and Bishop Flaget had a perfect right to say what they have said, and the man who can extract a *bad meaning from it*, must be one who measures his neighbour's thoughts by the dark standard of his own bosom.

He says he has answered the doctrine of the "decrees" of Calvinism so often, that he would be "*ashamed to go over it again*"—"it *would fatigue his hearers and future readers*. On the contrary, it is so pleasant a doctrine, that they would *never* get tired of it. A doctrine that tells them that all the crimes they ever have committed, or will commit, were "FOREORDAINED" by God, cannot be repeated too often. The passions will exult in it. But if the gentleman would only ONCE *attempt* to answer my arguments, showing its dangerous bearings on civil and religious liberty, his doing so would constitute a variety in his reply, precious as a spice of life. He says, that in this I attack the principle of the "Protestant Reformation era." But why is not he able to defend it, since the *other Protestants generally* have become "ashamed of its avowal."

He says, the "DAY OF OUR DOOM IS AT HAND." This is strong; and considering that the gentleman is in the secrets of the anti-Catholic crusaders, this is SIGNIFICANT language. The "*day* of our doom" may be destined in the "decrees" of Calvin, to come in the "*night*," as was the case with the Convent at Boston. As to "priestcraft," the *odium* of the term may belong to us—the GAIN belongs to the parsons. The "*craft*" is theirs. The American Catholics are much obliged to the gentleman for calling them "*enlightened*." I showed, in my last speech, that what the gentleman calls a "change" in the Confession of Faith, is only an "omission," and that an *omission* is no condemnation, no contradiction. Otherwise, the gospels of the four Evangelists would be in contradiction with each other. The gentleman, unable to meet my arguments, asks a question:—"*But*," says he, "*can the American people be* GULLED *with a change in a few words, when the thing remains the same?*" To this, I reply, I hope not. The American people are not so easily "*gulled*." The fate of the "Sunday Mail petitions," at Washington,—and of the Sunday School Union bill, at Harrisburg, a few years ago, should have taught Presbyterians that the American people are not to be "*gulled* by the change of a few words when THE THING REMAINS THE SAME."

The gentleman is very much afflicted for the *disappointment* which Catholics will feel on reading *my part* of this discussion. I would advise him to husband his sympathies—he will have occasion for them elsewhere. He will have to carry on the "*contro-*

versy by himself," for many a day, before he will have repaired its effects, even to his own satisfaction, much less to that of his orthodox brethren.

I promised, in my last speech, to loan him the book, printed under Doctor Ely's direction, which contains all my former quotations from the proceedings of the Sunday School Union. I had told all about it before. When I had done this, I said I had given the "reference." He says, in his usual polite and veracious style, that this is "UTTERLY FALSE." Let the public judge. But least he should have any pretext for evading it, I tell him that the Preface to the Catalogue of Sunday School Books, for the year 1826, contains the avowal of "DICTATION TO THE SOULS OF THOUSANDS OF IMMORTAL BEINGS." Let the gentleman meet it.

As to Mr. Ansley, *not having an opportunity to defend himself*, the gentleman's attack on his private character is as cruel and heartless a proceeding as it is possible to imagine. The gentleman returns to it, as to a labour of love. *Insinuation* is the safest channel for slander, and the gentleman ought to have left it to those base spirits that take delight in blackening character, without risking the responsibility of being accusers. Until he think proper to *speak out*, I can only say, and I say it with the most undisguised contempt for the insinuation, that " I recognise in it the meanness that would insinuate, without the *courage* to assert," and that so far as it is supposed to relate to myself, it is founded on FALSEHOOD, and must reflect its infamy back on its origin. I hope the gentleman will *speak out* the next time.

He says, I "falsified Calvin with my eyes open." I answer, the statement is not to be depended on. I quoted Calvin's own words, and the audience are to judge whether they "make God the author of sin." If they do not, I am at a loss to know what they mean. But let the audience and the public judge. The gentleman lays down a canon of criticism on the subject of "quotations" which is not orthodox. He says, that when "*I pass his quotations by in silence, it is admitting the* TRUTH *of the* PROOF *and the fairness of the method of citation.*" I caution the *audience* against any such *absurd inference*. I may pass by his "quotations in silence"—1st. Because, if, in every case, I were to stop to correct the want of "*truth,*" or unfairness in the "method of citation," I should lose the whole *time,* and fill up the *space,* that are sacred to something more important than the exposure of faithless citation. 2d. The falsity of the quotation, whether in substance or method, *may be unimportant.* 3d. I may discover, that *faithless though it be,* yet it does not prove the point for which he adduced it. Here are three sufficient reasons why I should pass many of his "quotations by in silence." I have exposed *a few* as a sample, and I believe that the usual rule is to place but little reliance on an author who has corrupted, even in a *single instance,* the testimony of those whom he brings forward as vouchers. The gentleman's inference would require me to prove that he *never* quotes without perverting. This I did not say. But I do say, that in no single instance have I examined his quotations, without being painfully convinced that they were *perverted*, either in altering the *text*, or in perverting the *author's* meaning, and sometimes in both.

In reference to the Catechism of the Council of Trent, the gentleman, after charging a great many frauds on the translation, not one of which he ventures to prove by *citation*, closes with these words, "*but I here challenge Mr. Hughes to meet me before any number of Latin scholars, and I will convict this shameful edition of twenty* DELIBERATE *and glaring* FRAUDS *which have been* EVIDENTLY *committed with* DESIGN.*"* I accept the challenge, and refer it to the tribunal for examining the gentleman's *calumnies*. I shall enter into obligations to pay, by my securities, one hundred dollars for every instance in which he will have succeeded to prove his proposition; provided, he will oblige himself to forfeit a similar sum for every instance in which he will have failed to prove it. Let him name the day when he is willing and ready to enter into these obligations. If he does not, the public will see that he has no confidence in the truth of his proposition. I pronounce it utterly untrue.

The gentleman assumes, in his attempt to vindicate his suppression of a part of the twenty-seventh Canon of the Third Lateran, that I admit the Church had a right to punish the Albigenses " for their crimes." I admitted no such thing : it is his own *perversion of my language*. It is false *in history,* that *the Church punished them for their crimes*. They were punished by their governments for their outrages on society. The Church excommunicated them; and their crimes drew on them their chatisement and suppression. Had not the States which they *disturbed* a right to reduce them ? Had not France its king, and Germany its emperor, and every state in Europe its *civil government.* Supposing that CATHOLICS had leagued together for the destruction of social order, and the commission of crime, as the Albigenses did; supposing they had committed, on "churches and monasteries, virgins and widows, all sexes and ages," those outrages which the gentleman, after Faber, thought it prudent to suppress and conceal, would not the States have a right to reduce them to order, or exterminate them, and would not the authorities of the Church have a right to encourage them to do so? But what would have been lawful on account of their crimes, *if they had been Catholics*, becomes quite otherwise from the moment that their *crimes were sanctified* by the merits of their heresy. Because they were *Albigenses*, the gentleman seems to infer that it was persecution to arrest them in their career of destruction, until they had desolated the whole land " after the manner of pagans," as they were doing. They were the public enemies of society by their crimes

—for this the gentleman admits they ought to be punished. But they were the *enemies of the Catholic religion*, and had assailed, *by violence*, its churches, monasteries, &c., and for this they ought to have been protected, and the Pope, at least, ought not to have encouraged any measures against them!! But, he says, it was at least "discipline," of the Church. No, sir, it was not even discipline. It was a *special* direction for a *special* case. The Synod of York has directed an anti-popery sermon to be preached every year; and this order, or direction, is neither doctrine nor discipline. The direction given at the Council of Lateran, was, in its principle, like that given at the Synod of York. It is neither doctrine nor discipline. If the Catholics had been acquainted with the Presbyterian second commandment, it would not have been necessary to *wait* for the public crimes of the Albigenses. Their "FALSE WORSHIP" alone would have given a sufficient plea to *obey God*, and "REMOVE THEM." This may suggest the difference between doctrine and no doctrine.

He says that I am "bound in virtue of holy obedience, to read the bull In Cœna Domini, *during Lent*, every year." Here, again, he deceives his readers by the assertion. His statement is positively false. I proved, under the former head, that that bull was never admitted in many Catholic countries, and that by a rescript of the Pope himself, it was suppressed throughout the whole world, except in Rome itself. Proof and reasoning are lost on such an opponent, but not, I trust, on the meeting and the public. Finally, he says *"the Church has shed blood enough to float a man of war."* This is quite a moderate *figure*. It used to be "oceans" of blood. I maintain, that not so much as one drop of human blood was ever shed by virtue of any tenet of FAITH or MORALS *in the Catholic religion;* and the gentleman, however bold in his assertions, has been signally defeated in his attempts to prove the contrary. The Catholics have shed blood like the professors of other creeds, but never, like the Presbyterians, *by virtue of one of God's commandments*. Whenever the gentleman ventured on *facts* to prove his assertion, he was found *minus habens*. Now he has recourse to OPINIONS. *He thinks* that *all* the blood shed in the crusades, is chargeable to the Church; the Saracens, like the Albigenses, were innocent lambs. *Wiser* and *more learned* PROTESTANTS, have pronounced that the Crusades were JUST WARS. If so, the gentleman's "man of war," will be *aground*.

Next the *Inquisition*. *He thinks*, that the Church is accountable for the blood shed by the Inquisition. Now every man that knows the history of the countries in which it existed, knows that so far as the shedding of blood was a part of the Inquisition, it was ENTIRELY, AND AVOWEDLY, a *political* and not an *ecclesiastical* tribunal. So that this must be subtracted from the element on which the gentleman would float his "man of war."

Next *the Massacre of St. Bartholomew. He thinks*, that the Church is accountable for this. I have proved the contrary in the former question. The wars in Ireland made the Catholics bleed, and not the protestants, except in the wicked *retaliation of despair.* Let the gentleman read the Vindiciæ Hibernicæ of Mr. Carey, and he will make a profitable addition to his stock of knowledge. As to the rest, the gentleman might as well hold the Church responsible for the blood that was shed at the battle of Waterloo.

Charge, then, all the blood which the gentleman has collected with so much *assertion*, and so little sense or authority, from the CIVIL or FOREIGN WARS, in which *Catholics throughout the world* may have been engaged, each portion to its *proper account*, where HISTORY places it, and the "man of war," which he thought to set "afloat," will be found "high and dry." He has fallen into that *fallacy of logic*, which is sometimes termed *"non causa pro causa,"* assigning *effects* to *one cause*; which belong to another. But as he is bold in *assertion*, and fallacious in logic, so is he fervent in declamation. He looks at the picture drawn from *imagination*, and addressed to *imagination;* and in order to show what patriots he and Doctor Brownlee are, he seems to say, "*Oh, my countrymen, the Catholic Church is guilty of all the blood that was ever shed. Do not, I beseech you, after all the trouble we have had to get money from you, for tracts, and Bibles, and missionaries, and education societies, do not, I pray you, sell yourselves to the Pope. Then our occupation would be gone. Look at this picture* of a ' man of war.' "

The gentleman has said, with his usual regard for truth, that "*Mr. Hughes thinks that these* MASSACRES *may be* JUSTIFIED, *because, as he says, the victims of them were not innocent but wicked men, and the enemies of Society.*" Just for curiosity, I shall number the untruths contained in this short sentence, Mr. Hughes *never* thought or said, that men might be "*massacred*," for being "*wicked men*," (first untruth.) Mr. Hughes *never* thought or said that "*these* massacres" might be "justified," *at all*, (second untruth.) Mr. Hughes *never* thought or said, that *any massacre* might be "justified," on *any plea* (third untruth.) Now if I have, I bind myself to apologize publicly for the language I have used. If I have not, the gentleman owes a triple apology; one *to my character, another to truth*, and the third to *that commandment of God, which says, "thou shalt not bear false witness against thy neighbour*," and which seems to be a dead letter, if at all, in the Presbyterian Catechism.

He says again that I "*own the fact of a theocracy in that day of Rome's supreme dominion over men's souls and bodies.*" Now there is not a word of truth in this assertion. I pointed to the real *Calvinistic* "theocracy" of the early "puritans" in New England, as presenting a "diminutive *analogy*" of the social condition of Europe, at the period of the Fourth Lateran Council. The inference that, therefore, I *own* a theocracy in the Catholic religion, is both illogical in reasoning, and false in assertion. From this *false* assertion, the gentleman draws other inferences intended to prove I care not what; but proving in effect, that Mr. Hughes is, *like his Church*, as wicked as *barefaced calumny* can make him. I am surprised that the gentleman has not more pity on his own reputation; he exposes himself palpably and unmercifully. After having quoted the passage from my letters, showing that the Catholic States of Europe had a right "TO TAKE MEASURES FOR THE COMMON WELFARE," to suppress sedition, and maintain order and subordination in society, he adds, "THUS WE SEE HOW HE (Mr. Hughes,) DENIES ALL CONSTITUTIONAL, ORIGINAL, IMPRESCRIPTIBLE RIGHTS," (not true,) AND GIVES TO THE POWERS THAT BE, TO AN AUTOCRAT, OR A MAJORITY, THE RIGHT TO STOP THE CIRCULATION OF THE BIBLE," (not exactly true,) "*or to destroy the minority, if their own interest depends on it.*" (Utterly and entirely false.) All that I said was, that society has a right to suppress heretics, or no heretics, *who undertake to overthrow the government*. The gentleman had said, that this would have been accomplished in Russia, if the OPERATIONS OF THE BIBLE SOCIETY *had not been arrested;* and I observed in reply, that the Emperor did what *any man would do in his circumstances;* he put down the Bible Society, and we have Mr. Breckinridge's authority for stating, that if he had not done so, he would have "TO LOSE HIS CROWN." (1)

But it is not only in *misrepresentations* of my statements, and *false* inductions, but in direct and *positive matters of fact*, that the gentleman does injury to truth. For instance, he says the Confession of Faith was amended "BEFORE THE AMERICAN REVOLUTION." Now it was amended so far as *printing* is concerned, in the first General Assembly, in 1789, just thirteen years after the Declaration of Independence!! How then could it have been "*before*," as the gentleman has said with *emphasis*. It was not even *before* the *Constitution*.

The question returns then, how can Presbyterians obey God, who *commands them to* "REMOVE ALL FALSE WORSHIP;" and yet obey the Constitutions, which enjoin on them to *disobey God?* This is the point which I cannot get the gentleman to meet, or clear up. He says that he has answered this question before, by showing that WE (Presbyterians,) mean in the CONFESSION, NO FORCE; but *truth, moral influence, argument, the press, the Bible, &c. &c.* This is sophistry which can deceive but few. For, the *meaning* of the "Confession," was determined by *those who drew it up,* nearly two hundred years ago.

(1) See Letters, viii. ix.

The object of the doctrine was to *impose* the solemn league and covenant on all men, and establish "*uniformity*" of religion throughout the three kingdoms. How? By PENAL LAWS, *sanctioning the use of every kind of punishment, from the* STOCKS *to the gallows and the block.* Its meaning has been determined by acts of Parliament, by ejecting the EPISCOPAL CLERGY from their livings, by "REMOVING," VIOLENTLY, every monument of *Catholic piety* from the *Episcopal Churches.* Was this "*moral influence?*" The gentleman need not tell us what "*he*" means in the Confession. Its meaning was written in the blood of the Catholics, Episcopalians, Baptists, Arminians, Quakers, &c., before, long before, he was born. Its meaning is a *settled point*, a "ruled case," and I am astonished that the gentleman should have exposed his knowledge of history, so far as to talk of "moral influence," in connection with the propagation of Calvinism. How was it propagated? I say BY FORCE, and I challenge contradiction. It was a tyrant from its cradle, and before it was ten years of age, it had abolished the "mass," and drowned the Baptists in the same canton. How did it propagate itself, in Geneva? BY FORCE. In France? BY FORCE. In Scotland? BY FORCE. In Holland? BY FORCE. In England? BY FORCE. In Ireland? BY FORCE. How did it preach itself into political power in those countries? It began by LIBELS, and ended by PITCHED BATTLES. The *exordium* of its sermon was *sedition;* — the *peroration, fixed bayonets.* Will the gentleman deny this? He need not; all this is public, notorious, palpable matter of history. But after it had *succeeded* in establishing itself BY FORCE, did it then employ *only* "moral influence?" In answer to this question, I refer the reader to my last speech, and he will see that it employed the influence of the block and the gibbet, for the purpose of "REMOVING ALL FALSE WORSHIP." The American Constitution abridged the *practical* part of the creed, on this subject. But since then, (like Samson in the recovery of his strength,) its *hair has grown out*, its locks have become thick and bushy, and, *impatient of the* "PHILISTINES" by whom it is surrounded, it begins to FEEL that it is NOW strong enough to "*carry away the pillars*" of *the Constitution;*—and judging by the fiery zeal of the gentleman and his colleagues, it is almost *blind* enough to make the attempt. ("*The Presbyterians alone,*" says Dr. Ely, "*could bring a half a million of voters into the field.*")

But so long as the Constitution lasts, the Presbyterian *doctrine* cannot have FAIR PLAY. The magistrates cannot, *conveniently*, be "ITS NURSING FATHERS." But take it where they *were faithful* to the "nursling;" let us see it in the low countries, according to the testimony of one of *its own ministers,* for I like to use its *friends* as *witnesses against it.*

We have seen the fruits of the doctrine about the "REMOVING

OF ALL FALSE WORSHIP," as they ripened in Geneva, Scotland, and New England. Let us see whether they were less bitter in the Low Countries. I shall quote from the "*History of the Reformation, in and about the Low Countries, by the Rev. Gerard Brandt*"—himself a Presbyterian minister, but not a "high-toned Calvinist." In describing the "moral influence," by which Calvinism established itself at Antwerp in 1566, his narrative reminds one of the "*removing*" *process* at Boston—the fulfilling of the second commandment.

"Strada adds, that they (the Calvinists) laid hands on the sacramental bread, or mass-wafers, *trampling them under their feet.* The consecrated chalices they filled with the wine they found in the churches, and drank to one another's health. They smeared their shoes with the holy oil, defiled the church garments with ordure, and, *daubing the books with butter, threw them into the fire:* some of the images and pictures were kicked up and down; others they thrust through with swords, or chopped off their heads with axes; upon others they put on armour, and then tilted against them with spears, javelins, &c. out of wantonness, till the images fell down, and then mocked and jeared them."(1) Was not this *Calvinistic* " moral influence ?"

It may be well to inform the audience that what is called the "*Reformed Religion*" in these extracts is the pure Calvinistic doctrine—held by the Presbyterian Church in the United States. It was introduced at Dort, in 1572, in the following truly *evangelical* manner, converting the Catholics by the pure " moral influence" of persuasion.

"The first sermon preached by the Reformed was under a lime-tree in the Klevenniers Doel, where the shooting-house now stands; but that did not last long, nor would they be so contented. In a little time, *the images were thrown out of the churches, the altars broken down, and the Reformed Religion was publicly exercised.* But, in a certain Journal written at that time, we find that the images in the monastery of the Austin Fryers were broken down on the 26th of July, and that on the *next day* the first sermon was preached there. The Baguines were *forced to fly*, for the troopers brought their horses into their nunneries." (2)

Again, at Utrecht, in 1580, about fourteen years after Calvinism had established itself by the persuasive " moral influence" of the *musket*, the magistrates began to "*nurse*" it :—

"It fared yet worse with the papists at Utrect; for, upon the 18th of June, there was published an order in that city (of which the occasion is not mentioned) forbidding, in the name of the stadtholder and magistrates, the exercise of the Romish religion to all priests, or ordained persons, and their adherents, of that communion, within the said city or liberties thereof, *upon*

(1) Vol. i. p. 193. (2) Idem, p. 297.

forfeiture of their benefices and offices, if they had any, *or the sum of ten gilders;* and this order was to be in force till the stadtholder and states should otherwise direct."(1)

From these extracts the gentleman will learn how Presbyterians, "according to each one's place and calling," are bound to *" remove all false worship, and all the monuments of idolatry."* We have seen that "force" has always and every where been employed for that purpose. In 1581 the following ordinance was published in Amsterdam, by the prime "nursing father."

"On the say day there likewise appeared a placard, in the name of the prince of Orange, as to whom the supreme administration of affairs had been yielded up; in which, not only the printing and selling all manner of scandalous, abuseful, and seditious books and pamphlets, new ballads and songs, without the leave of the magistracy, and name of the publisher, were prohibited, but also, *the exercise of the Romish religion, and the holding either public or private conventicles, on the penalty of a hundred gilders; nevertheless, says the same placard, it is not our intention to impose any burthen, or make inquisition into any man's conscience. The wearing ecclesiastical habits, and keeping schools, without previous examination and permission, were likewise forbidden to all papists."* (2)

The ministers of Calvinism, after having appropriated to their own use the ecclesiastical as well as secular property of the Catholics, by the violences and tyranny here mentioned, came to a decision, in 1588, that not only the Catholic faith should be excluded, but that the exercise of all other religions, but their own, should be prohibited.(3) Burgomaster Hoost, in endeavouring to instil some feelings of humanity into the persecuting soul of this desperate religion, uses an argument which I submit to the gentleman's consideration.

"Particularly," says he, "it is very strange that those who so strenuously maintain the doctrine of predestination, should thus insist on PERSECUTION, OR FORCING OF CONSCIENCES; for, if their doctrine be true, no man can avoid that to which he is ordained."(4)

To show that their doctrine binds them, *in conscience,* to hinder any other worship but their own, the following testimony from their writings will be sufficient.

"Since experience has shown how prejudicial it has been to the church of God, *to tolerate the Anabaptists,* in the free exercise of their schismatical opinions, after the public dispute with -them, just as if there was no difference between the *pure doctrine of the true church* and *their heterodox notions; the ministers,* therefore, of God's word belonging to this province, intreat the

(1) Page 375. (2) Brandt, vol. i. p. 383.
(3) Idem, vol. i. p. 424. (4) Page 470.

deputies of the states to provide some remedy for this *evil*, so as it may be most for the benefit of God's church and the discharge of their *consciences*." (1)

The following testimony shows plainly the nature of the doctrine touching the duty of the civil magistrates to be "*nursing fathers*" to the *church*.

"But God works by instruments or such officers as he has set over the people. Those officers are your lordships, whom God has appointed as supreme moderators and governors under him, in all cases relating to his church. The right which belonged to the Christian magistrate in these matters, who was to take care that the word of God were duly preached, and all scandal or offence removed, was taken away from him by *the Pope; but restored* in some places by the *Reformation*." (2)

Having removed the Catholic, and prevented the Baptist religion, BY FORCE, one would have expected that these Calvinists would tolerate each other. But no. Some of them becoming "ashamed" of Calvin's doctrine about absolute "PREDESTINATION," were PERSECUTED, for exercising their own judgment and the rights of conscience in reference to that tenet, with a cruelty and obstinacy without a parallel. These were called ARMINIANS or REMONSTRANTS, and their persecutors GOMARISTS or CONTRA-REMONSTRANTS. From the moment that these Arminians ventured to think for themselves, the cunning treachery and intolerance of pure, unadulterated Calvinism, such as the gentleman professes, marked them out for vengeance and destruction. How did they begin? By their usual weapon, *slander*. They covered them with calumny, as has been done in Boston, and then employed the mob and the magistrate, alternately, to hunt them down.

"The Remonstrants were (as they themselves complained) through the many SLANDERS *raised against them* in those times, rendered so odious to the common people, and to the vilest of the mob especially, that they could hardly walk the streets without being called Arminians, and other reproachful names, and pointed at as they passed. Many *cried out aloud that they held a correspondence with the Spaniards and Jesuits;* that they received *bribes and pensions from them*, and would have betrayed their country to them, if they had not been hindered. Many suffered themselves to be persuaded, or else made themselves believe (for when once hatred has got possession of a man's heart, he deceives himself as easily as he does others) that their doctrines were mere blasphemy; that God, according to them, had decreed one man (or even one child) from the womb of his mother, to eternal damnation, and another to salvation." (3)

In every age of Calvinism, a pretended zeal for their country,

(1) Page 474.   (2) Vol. II. p. 58.   (3) Idem, p. 427.

and against popery, has been and is the "*premonitory symptom*" of *persecution*. The same cry was raised every where, when they wished a pretext to practice their intolerant second commandment. Accordingly, when in 1618 the Remonstrants wished to heal the division, the Calvinists, says Brandt,

"In order to put this *separation* actually in practice, they *have, by their preaching and discourses,* instilled very ill opinions of the said Remonstrants *into the common people, accusing them* of promoting novelties, describing them by *heretical nick-names,* and *reporting* that they endeavoured to INTRODUCE POPERY, and *to betray the country to Spain.*" (1) Again, still—

"During the course of these affairs and disputes, several people dispersed *libels and scandulous papers,* daily, but without any name to them, with *design to render their adversaries odious.* But it will not be unuseful to set before our reader what the Heer Grotius thought of this kind of proceeding and its consequences. 'If there be any thing,' says he, 'unbecoming a Christian, it is the violating any *man's good name by pasquils and libels.* This, by the Roman or civil law, was forbidden, on pain of death, and justly so, since every man, by such means, has it in his power to *blacken his neighbour,* without his being able to obtain a legal remedy; because his adversary is concealed, who also lies the more boldly, as knowing he cannot be obliged to prove his assertions. How much some of the contra-Remonstrant clergy, and others of their persuasion, have found their account in this way of proceeding, their works will show: in divers of whose books, the nobility and the magistracy of the towns, as well in general as in particular, are painted with the most odious colours.'" (3)

By this it seems that such writings as those of Miss Reed, Brutus, and the "Foreign Conspiracy," are *old* Presbyterian tricks. In fact, when we look at the libels with which the Calvinistic press is teeming, one might almost imagine that Brandt was drawing a picture of them after what is now their conduct and character.

"*The general strife was, who should write and* CALUMNIATE *most*. All the streets and market places rang with the songs and ballads made upon the prisoners, especially upon Oldenbarnevelt, whom every one curst, sentenced, and condemned, with his abettors. The most satyrical papers appeared *without any name* to them. Among the rest, one was entitled The Golden Legion of the New St. John: another, The Golden Bellows of the Spanish Knave; in which the advocate is charged with taking money of the Spaniards; a third, The Theatre of the Arminians, composed in doggrel rhimes, with several other pasquinades of the like kind, too many to be mustered up here. Great numbers

(1) Vol. ii. p. 448.   (2) Page 339.

of satyrical prints and cuts were made in reproach to them; such as, for instance, that called the *Arminian Dung Cart;* the *Arminians'* LAST WILL; and the *Sieve of Justice:* all of them *ridiculing* and exposing the Remonstrants, the past administration, the discharging the warders, the change of the magistrates, and, in a word, representing every incident with the utmost SPITE and RANCOUR."(1)

The gentleman has told us that it was the mob of Boston, mistaking the Convent for what the *slanders of Calvinism* had made of it, destroyed it. But he ought to know that this also is an old trick. The Calvinists in the Arminian controversy had recourse to it for a similar purpose. On one occasion, in 1617, the mob were instigated to fall on the Remonstrant *heretics,* their names being known and their houses marked. Brandt speaks of these outrages as follows:—

"The damage that was done him, as Bishop himself declared, amounted to above five thousand gilders, besides a quantity of books that belonged to other persons, which were partly recovered. His wife, getting out of the house at last, and being pursued by part of the mob, who, with great rage, threatened to murder her, sheltered herself in a house on the Heer Graft; but, not being able to stay there, she climbed over the garden wall of the burgomaster Gerard Jacob Witsen, where she fell, and was taken up senseless; but she was carried into the house with great tenderness, and proper means were used to bring her to herself: when she was recovered, says the burgomaster, 'Well, neighbour, how came you in this condition?' Upon which, being still under great disorder, she burst out into into these words:—'*Ah! sir, this is the fruit of your minister's sermons, who enrage and exasperate the people thus against us!*' "

Among those who stood looking on, and applauding the fury of the mob, there was one, who hearing their insolence blamed, made answer very angrily:—*It were pity but your house and five-and-twenty more were treated in like manner.* Another cried:—*There is no harm done: they have their deserts. If four or five of them had had their heads cleft in the meeting-house, it would have been well done.* Another said:—*What has been done by the boys we are ready to take upon ourselves.* And another:—GOD HAS INSPIRED THESE CHILDREN TO ACT THUS; *he has revealed it to them, that the Arminians seek to enslave the country to the Spaniards, and makes use of those lads to prevent it.*"(2)

It is worthy of remark, that in the whole Controversy, the crime of the Arminians was the EXERCISE OF THE RIGHTS OF CONSCIENCE. As far back as the year 1600, they had avowed their purpose of requiring the magistrate, "according to his place

(1) Vol. ii. p. 566.   (2) Page 295.

and calling," to "remove all false worship," but that of Calvin. Here are the words of Brandt.

"The following year, (1601,) endeavours were *renewed* to persuade the magistrates at Sneek, in Freesland, that NO OTHER SECTS ought to be allowed the liberty of religion, besides the Reformed. And Beza's Discourse, of PUNISHING HERETICS, was translated from the Latin into the Low-Dutch language, and published with a *dedication and recommendation of it to the magistrates*, by Goswin Geldorp, and John Bogerman, ministers of the said town. In the Preface, (which also related what had passed the year before, between the ministers of Sneek and the Anabaptists,) there were the following expressions: '*That God had made it a duty incumbent on the magistrates to defend the true religion*, and OPPOSE THE FALSE WITH ALL THEIR MIGHT. It was, they said, a *poisonous* notion; that the Government ought not to trouble itself about religion, but to leave the ministers to propagate it by themselves as well as they could, by ecclesiastical methods. And yet, as pernicious as such an opinion was, it was very agreeable to many, who found their account in a political, (as they termed it) *but unchristian and unlawful peace*, whereby every man, according to them, was to be *allowed the free exercise of his religion;* to the end, forsooth, that no discord might arise between countrymen and fellow-citizens. This, said they, is 'MAKING PEACE WITH SATAN.' They likewise maintained, 'THAT THERE OUGHT TO BE BUT ONE RELIGION ALLOWED.' And as for that objection, that this would be lording it over men's consciences, they replied, 'That this was the means to *restore to God*, to whom it belonged, the dominion of consciences, *according to his command;* seeing they only attempted to execute the Divine COMMANDS, BY DIVINE METHODS.'(1) Accordingly, by way of '*moral influence*,' as the gentleman tells us, 'On the seventh of September, the magistrates of Gronnigen published a new order, by toll of bell, concerning religious matters; in which was said: THAT THEY PROHIBITED THE EXERCISE OF ALL OTHER RELIGIONS, BESIDES THE REFORMED. So that whoever should presume to RENT HIS HOUSE OR GROUND, TO THE ANABAPTISTS, OR PAPISTS, OR ANY OTHER SECTS, contrary to the ecclesiastical laws of their city, for the use of their meetings or ministers, should forfeit, for every such offence, the sum of *ten dollars*, as should likewise the persons that PRESUMED TO PREACH THERE, or *else be confined to bread and water, for the space of fourteen days*. And if they offended the *third* time, they were to be banished from the city, and the jurisdiction thereof. And all the people that *were found at such meetings*, should forfeit, for each offence,

(1) Vol. ii. p. 8.

two dollars. Whoever was discovered to re-baptise any person, should forfeit twenty dollars, and upon a second conviction, be put to *bread and water*, and condemned as above. *Unbaptized children should be incapable of inheriting.* None should be admitted to any public or private office, BUT UPON SOLEMN OATHS. He that refused to take an oath, should be *punished* according to law. All that lived with women in concubinage, and without lawful marriage, should be punished as whoremongers, if they did not marry, according to the ecclesiastical laws, within the space of a month. Whoever married incestuously, or within the forbidden degrees, or suffered themselves to be joined in matrimony, OUT OF THE REFORMED CHURCH, should not enjoy any advantage thereof, nor inherit any estate, NEITHER SHOULD THEIR CHILDREN BE LEGITIMATE: besides all which, they should be *punished* according as the case deserved." (1)

The bitter experience which the Baptists had of Calvinism, taught them to regret the absence of the Catholic rule, under which, as they stated, "they lived quietly, and were connived at." But it was not the Catholics and Baptists alone, that had reason to complain, under this spiritual and temporal despotism of Calvinism. The Lutherans, and the moderate party called Remonstrants, had equal reason to exchange sympathies. No matter by what name the *"false worship"* was called, the conscience of the orthodox was oppressed with remorse for the violation of God's second commandment, until it was "removed" by the "nursing fathers" of the Church, "according to their place and calling." The offence which Lutheranism gave to their "tender consciences," may be gathered from the following statement in Brandt; speaking of one of their assemblies held 1600, he says:

"In this assembly, there were likewise some resolutions taken in prejudice of the Lutherans. It appeared (as the Journal of the said Synod has it,) that the Martinists, Ubiquitarians, Flaccians, and such like sectaries, were much increased in the country, discovering great animosities, and freely venting their reproaches against the Reformed Church. *The Deputies of the South Holland Synod consulted those of the North about what course should be taken, and it was resolved, That the ministers should lay before the magistrates an account of the places where the Lutherans met*, WITH REASONS FOR SUPPRESSING THE CONVENTICLES, AND PUTTING A STOP TO THE RAILINGS OF THOSE PEOPLE......... What was afterwards resolved by the Court of Justice against the Lutherans, *as also the fresh attempts of the Clergy*, may be gathered from what is recorded in the books of the States, and their committees concerning it, the sum of which is as follows:

(1) Page 9.

"There appeared at the Assembly of the Lords, the States of Holland, Arnoldus Cornelius, and Bernardus la Faille, ministers of Delft, and the Hague, *as deputed by the Synod*, in order to acquaint them that they had been frequently intreated by those of the Church and magistracy of Woerden, to represent to the Lords the States, *the scandal* which was occasioned to *good and sincere minds*, by the *too public exercise of religion*, performed by those who, indeed, called themselves of the Augsburg Confession, but who were not so; forasmuch as our religion, which is styled the Reformed, has a great conformity to it in the matter of the Lord's Supper, and in other points. They therefore prayed, that the resolution or sentence formed by the court against one of their preachers, MIGHT BE PUT IN EXECUTION; and those of the aforesaid Confession, living within the said town of Woerden, BE PROHIBITED to receive any other minister in his stead, and BE HINDERED, as far as possible, from *exercising that religion*. The said deputies moreover alleged, that there ought likewise some care to be taken in other towns, where the said religion was also practised, particularly at Amsterdam, and Rotterdam; to the end that the religion which *alone is publicly allowed in the United Provinces*, (as being the TRUE Christian religion,) might be the better maintained, and *all offence removed;* requesting the due attention of the States, to these matters." (1)

The magistrates, less intolerant than the ministers, allowed the exercise of the Lutheran religion in *that particular instance*, on the following humiliating condition :—

"That the designs of the States had always been, and still were, to force no man's conscience; and, accordingly, that he, the said Glaserus, should be *connived at*, in proceeding with all peaceableness, discretion, and *good manners*, to teach and preach in his Conventicle, at Woerden, as formerly." (2)

But their intolerance towards other sects is not to be wondered at, when we see the extent and malice of their persecutions against their own brethren, the Remonstrants. These denied Calvin's doctrine of eternal, immutable, and absolute predestination, with its appendages, and for THIS, they were *calumniated, suspended, deprived, expelled from their Churches, banished from the country, imprisoned*, or *put to death*, by the intolerant orthodoxy of "high-toned Calvinism." The Synod of Dort decided against the Arminians and in favour of the Gomarists. The real merits of the dispute may be understood from the manner in which Gomarus himself met the Arminian argument, which was then, and is now, and will be to eternity, unanswered and unanswerable.

"Nobody, said he, maintains that God absolutely decreed to reprobate men without sin; but as he decreed the *end*, so he like-

(1) Page 15.   (2) Page 16.

wise did the *means;* that is, HE PREDESTINED HIM TO SIN, AS THE ONLY MEANS OF DEATH." (1) The audience may judge from this, of the merits of the case.

"It happened one time," says Brandt, (speaking of a Remonstrant,) "that walking on the beach at Horne, he met with two ministers, who having a mind to joke with him, said Robert, you seem very pensive, what is the matter with you? He replied, 'tis true, brethren, I was considering *who is the author of Sin.* They: Who do you hold to be the author of sin? He: When sin was first committed, the man laid it upon the woman, and the woman accused the serpent; but the serpent was at that time young, and stupid, and silent; *but now he is grown old and daring, and comes to the* SYNOD OF DORT, *and says, that God is the author of sin.*" (2).

The spirit which actuated that Synod, may be understood from the following extract from Brandt:

"It was likewise reported, that the late President Bogerman, having had a long conference with a great man at the Hague, soon after the breaking up of the Synod, should, upon his return, say with much pleasure, to a friend of his at Leyden, *God be praised, we shall have but one religion in all the Provinces: we will first* EXTIRPATE THE ARMINIANS, AND THEN ALL THE OTHER SECTS MUST COME TO THE CHURCH, OR FLY THE COUNTRY. Other hot-headed zealots cried, We shall now bring matters to such a pass, in a short time, that people *will give money to see an Arminian.* These were the first fruits of those bitter seeds, as the Remonstrants thought, which Bogerman had been sowing seventeen years before, in the Preface to Beza's little tract, *about putting heretics to death.* They were also of opinion, that this placard was partly the effect of the furious zeal of divers of the Synodical members, who hardly talked of any thing else *but of using the secular arm; of rooting out the tares or weeds, by the authority of the civil magistrates; of banishing the Five Articles, and the teachers of them, out of the land; of forbidding the Remonstrants to preach or write.* This was the view, they thought, of the Synodical request, as contained in the sentence of the Remonstrants, *That their High Mightinesses would not suffer* ANY OTHER *doctrine than that of the Synod,* to be publicly taught in their dominions, and cause the decrees of the said Synod to be firmly and perpetually maintained. This opinion, therefore, that the Synod was the great and principal occasion of making such a placard, very much increased the aversion which some had conceived against that body." (3)

These points were carried out into fearful practice. To hold any office in the church or state, to be a schoolmaster, or even an

(1) Brandt, vol. iii. p. 103.   (2) P. 424.   (3) P. 402, 403.

organist, it was necessary to swear a belief in the horrible doctrine which had been approved by the Synod.

"As for the schools, it was agreed that *since all the schoolmasters were required to sign the Confession, and Catechism*, and some also the Canons of Dort, which tended to implant Calvinism in the youth; therefore, those of the clergy that ministered in the country, should take care to warn parents not to send their children to Calvinistical masters, but rather to let them be taught at home, or to act in that matter according to the liberty that should be granted to the Mennonites, or other sects." (1)

The following case is recorded of an ORGANIST, and shows the zeal of the Calvinists to "remove all false worship :"—

"This man was likewise summoned to sign the Formulary of the National Synod; but he earnestly entreated the magistrates, that they would not require it of him. He said, That *his art* had nothing common with the one or the other doctrine: that indeed *he played* in the Church, but did *not preach* there. But this would not avail him; and as they insisted on his subscribing, he burst out at last into these expressions: '*Gentlemen, I can't possibly subscribe the canons*, BUT IF YOU PLEASE TO SET THEM TO TUNES, I AM READY TO PLAY THEM IN THE CHURCH, ON MY ORGAN: in this manner I will serve you with all my heart. Playing the canons to any tune, is agreeable enough to my profession, but subscribing them is against my conscience.' This, his bantering offer, was more displeasing to the magistrates than his serious refusal; insomuch that *neither his art, nor the interposition of his friends*, could prevent his being turned out." (2)

But they first turned the Remonstrants out of their Churches, and then would not allow them to meet for worship, even in the open air. It was demanded by the Calvinists, that:—

"The placards against forbidden meetings, might be revised and enforced in such manner, that those who frequented such meetings *might forfeit their upper garments;* and those who went armed, their weapons; and that they might be obliged to depart, or else be fallen upon wherever they were; and that all those who *corresponded or conversed with any of the exiled persons, should pay a pecuniary fine of six hundred gilders*, and likewise forfeit such offices or employments as they held; and in case they could not answer the said fine of six hundred gilders, they should be sent away into banishment, or suffer other arbitrary punishments." (3)

"On the 16th of February, they (the Remonstrants) held another meeting, likewise out of town, at the house of the Bloomersdyke, but before the sermon was half over, the Dykegrave Dune fell upon them furiously, with a number of soldiers. They who could not save themselves by a timely flight, were plundered. The women

(1) Page 23.   (2) Page 474.   (3) Page 177.

were stript even to their under-petticoats, and the men were robbed of their cloaks, and what money they had about them. The soldiers attacked them, as if they had to do with the common enemy; and some were even dragged along the fields by the hair of their heads. The soldiers seized a young woman, one of which supported her body, whilst the other dragged her all uncovered, by the legs, along the rugged ice, just as a sledge is drawn. In short, they used the poor girl so cruelly, that she died of it soon after." (1)

Thus, sir, we see that in Holland the doctrines of the Presbyterian religion sprang up into the same cruel system of persecution which marked its progress and its presence in those countries of which I spoke in my last speech. The creed of the Synod of Dort is the creed of the Dutch Reformed Calvinists in this country; and its libellous, turbulent, intolerant, persecuting spirit is appropriately represented by one, and, as far as I know, by *only* one of its ministers in the United States, DR. BROWNLEE. The gentleman calls him "*his gallant colleague.*" He is exactly what the case required—a foreigner, a scion of *Scotch* bigotry, grafted on the stock of Dutch *Calvinism*. The saintly communion between these "gallant colleagues," proves that in DOCTRINE there is no difference between their creeds. Besides this, the Westminster Assembly (that made the gentleman's faith, to save him the trouble of looking for it in the Bible) approved of the decision of the Synod of Dort on the doctrines in question. So that, were it not for the protection of equal religious right secured by the AMERICAN CONSTITUTION, the same causes would produce the same effects, *here*, which they never failed to produce *elsewhere*. The gentleman has said that the Confession does not mean "FORCE, *but truth, moral influence, argument, the press, the Bible,*" &c. Sir, a greater imposition on credulity never was attempted. There is NO HISTORICAL EVIDENCE to sustain the assertion; and the whole history of Calvinism, in its beginning, and middle, and end, (by losing the *power* to persecute,) establishes its *refutation*. NO FORCE!!! Read, sir, its seditions and rebellions—read its penal laws and persecutions, and you will blush for its cruelties, as well as for the ignorance that could assert that it does not mean "FORCE." Can the gentleman tell me of ONE SINGLE COUNTRY, in which it was established by any *other means?* I answer, NOT ONE; and I challenge contradiction *with proof.* He cannot show one. Can he tell me of ONE SINGLE COUNTRY, in which, having obtained the political ascendancy, it did *not* employ "FORCE," to crush the *liberty of conscience, speaking, preaching, printing,* in all those who were not prepared to *think*, and *speak*, and *preach*, and *print* in accordance with (or at least not against) its tyrannical dogmas?

(1) Page 231.

Not one, sir, *on the face of the earth!* If he can, let him name it, and I pledge myself to expose the imposition. Let the gentleman, then, reserve such assertions for the Presbyterian pulpit, or those edifying assemblies of which we had a specimen last winter, in Mr. M'Calla's church. Let him hazard them, where he speaks to those who know no better; but let him not venture on them in my presence, at the risk of exposure by history such as he has now received. I return to the point.

The DOCTRINE of the Presbyterian religion, in these United States, the same as in Geneva, Scotland, and Holland, requires, by a commandment of God, that its votaries should, "ACCORDING TO EACH ONE'S PLACE AND CALLING, REMOVE ALL FALSE WORSHIP, AND ALL THE MONUMENTS OF IDOLATRY." But ALL worship besides their own, being founded on *heretical doctrine*, is "FALSE;" therefore they are bound BY THEIR DOCTRINE to remove it. Q. E. D. He says that this is to be done by "moral influence;" and such an acknowledgment from a minister of CALVIN'S religion, is the highest tribute of praise that ever was bestowed indirectly on the American Constitution, which will not tolerate the employment of "force." Yet the Presbyterian Church still retains the warrant from God, under which their fathers employed it: although the Constitution forbids the execution of the heavenly mandate. Which of these will eventually triumph over the other, time only will determine. The pretext *now* is to put down *popery*. But this is the pretext under which they put down the Episcopalians in England, the Arminians in Holland, and the Catholics every where. Of their persecutions of the Catholics in Holland, I have said but little, but there is one single case recorded, which is enough to show how infinite is the barbarity of a doctrine which could so demonize the human heart. It is related by Brandt, a Reformed minister, who was no friend to the Catholics. I shall give it in his own words:—

"There happened something in North Holland about this time, which will appear *a bloody spot in our history:* 'Divers popish housekeepers were, at the instigation of Sonoy, very inhumanly treated by an extraordinary tribunal, or court of judicature, in order to discover a *supposed plot, upon the forced and improbable evidence of certain felons*, who all of them RECANTED *their accusation at the point of death.* One of the said papists, named Koppe Cornelison, was TORTURED TO DEATH; his son Nanning was stretched on the rack *two or three-and-twenty times*, with *new-invented cruelties*, notwithstanding he attested his innocency every time he was taken down; and, at *last*, WAS QUARTERED—HIS HEART WAS TORN OUT OF HIS BODY. A little before his death, when he ought to have *been allowed* some time to think of heaven, and the condition of his soul, the judges gave him SWEET WINE, TO CONFOUND HIS SPEECH AND UNDERSTANDING, which he, through faintness and thirst, greedily swallowed; however, it did not *so far deprive him of sense*, but that, when he mounted the scaffold, he again declared his innocence. But the minister, Jurian Eppeson, under *pretence of strengthening him with arguments from Scripture*, interrupted him with *noise and clamour;* reproving him for denying the crime, and affirming that he had owned it before. Upon which the patient cited him to appear before the tribunal of God within three days, or, as others say, within four or five. The said minister returned home, after the execution of Nanning, much troubled in his mind, continually complaining of the summons given him, and taking his bed, became *a corpse within the time limited.* In like manner Peter Nanningson was most cruelly tortured no less *than four or five-and-twenty times upon the rack;* and after him John Jeromson and Peter Ellertson, both of them popish burghers of Horn, were apprehended upon *the extorted confession* of Nanning, and being carried to prison, the latter of them was racked four times in two days.' "(1)

Sir, you sicken at the narrative; and no wonder. Not satisfied with destroying life, they aim at the DESTRUCTION of the SOUL. They try to make him drunk on the brink of eternity, in order to extort from drunkenness the worthless confirmation of their own slanders—and then ply him with texts of SCRIPTURE!!! But why not? Had not God "FOREORDAINED WHATSOEVER COMES TO PASS?" Of course the "racking," and "sweet wine," and all were "foreordained," and consequently these saints were only carrying out God's decree.

The duplicity which stands so uniformly prominent in the schemes of Presbyterians for the attainment of their political ends, can be explained only on the doctrine of "foreordination." We have seen how they persecuted the Lutherans in Holland, and yet, when it seemed likely to serve their purpose, they wished to unite with them, just as Dr. Ely was willing to unite with Baptists, Episcopalians, Arminians, Lutherans, &c. to form a "Christian party in politics," and place "sound Presbyterians" in places of political trust, where they might be "nursing fathers" to the church, "according to each one's place and calling." The object of all such unions tendered by them, was most accurately described by the Lutherans of Germany, nearly two hundred years ago. Brandt has recorded the occasion, and the issue of it:—

"Before this," says he, "the Reformed had several times offered peace and brotherhood to the Lutherans; but now the condemning and persecuting the Remonstrants had so far cut off all hopes of such a wholesome union, that the Theological Faculty at Wittenburg, in Saxony, published a book this year, under the title of 'A Faithful Warning to all the Lutheran Christians in Bohemia, Moravia, Silesia, and other countries thereunto belonging, carefully

(1) Vol. L p. 316.

to abstain from the erroneous and highly pernicious Calvinistical religion.' In which book they endeavoured to expose the *scandalous and fraudulent dealings*, which, as they said, the Calvinists used, and had used for several years, in offering spiritual fraternity so often to the Lutherans, adding as follows:

" What good there is to be expected from such brethren, may easily be gathered from *the Synod of Dort*, and their proceedings. The Calvinists had several disputes with the Arminians, particularly about the article of grace or election, in which the latter *defended our opinion*, and the former *that of Calvin*. In this controversy the Calvinists at length showed so much heat, that, by a hasty decree of that synod, they condemned the Arminians and their doctrines, *without allowing* them to make any defence, DEPRIVING THEM OF THE EXERCISE OF THEIR RELIGION, and BANISHING their most eminent ministers from their country for ever. Was not that a very *brotherly proceeding?* If they thus treated such who differed from them in a *little more than one article*, viz: that of election or *predestination*, what must *we expect*, who differ from them in so many? Men of sense may easily discover what they would be at. They labour now to get the BRACHIUM SECULARE, THE CIVIL MAGISTRATE ON THEIR SIDE, and to bring such as are of *their opinions* into the best offices. If this succeeds, we shall soon see a general synod called in Germany, those of the Calvinistical religion *presiding and having the direction of all affairs*, judging them according to their own pleasure, not once hearing us, or allowing us to sit in the same synod, but, *as was done at Dort*, rashly censuring our doctrine as *false, hindering the exercise of it*, and driving away the Lutheran ministers, and, unless God prevents it, *totally extirpating our religion*. We conclude from all this, that their offers of *fraternal communion* are not *sincere*, but are only designed as a feint, till they can gather strength and courage to possess themselves of *our churches*. And, if a prince of *their persuasion*, should in time be raised to the imperial dignity, such a spirit as they are of would be sufficient to involve us in blood and destruction, and we poor Lutherans should be butchered like sheep by these our worthy brethren : for with them, *'tis a principle of* RELIGION THAT HERETICS OUGHT TO BE ROOTED OUT BY FORCE; and THAT NONE BUT THE TRUE RELIGION SHOULD BE TOLERATED *in a well-governed state*, as CALVIN, BEZA, and several others of their leaders maintain. From hence they will infer, that the *Lutherans are heretics;* to wit, Nestorians, Eutychians, Pelagians, &c.; *therefore this will be followed by a bloody decree: the Lutherans ought to be extirpated with the sword*. This will be the final determination of our Calvinistical brethren; such good are we to expect from them. 'Tis an Æsopical brotherhood which they offer to us, that is to say, such peace and amity as the wolf offered to the sheep, the better to seize and devour them. Let no man then be *imposed upon* by the amicable name of brotherhood: 'tis under this specious pretence, that they are seeking our destruction; and whoever joins himself to these Calvinists, becomes partaker of all that deceit which *they conceal, and all the vile intrigues which they have chiefly levelled at the Lutheran churches.*" (1)

This extract shows that the doctrine of "removing all false worship" is no new discovery in the Presbyterian creed. The Lutherans knew it, and knew its meaning from their own observation, which the history of their religion ever since has only served to confirm.

Let me now sum up the argument. If I have stated the truth, (and if I have not I beg the gentleman to point out the instance,) the following conclusions are clearly and logically established: 1. That the Presbyterians have scaled the places of political power in every country where their religion has been established, not by "moral influence," but by *sedition, libels, force, violence and bloodshed.* 2. That they established that religion, wherever the government which they attempted to overthrow did not take strong and timely measures for its own safety. 3. That when in political power, they persecuted IN EVERY CASE, and in every degree of the principle, from the imposition of fine, to the shedding of blood. 4. That their persecutions have been founded on, and justified by, the doctrines of their religion. 5. That they constituted themselves the guardians of God's honour, and the avengers of the insult offered to Him by what they arrogantly term "FALSE WORSHIP," and "idolatry." And, 6. That, therefore, their doctrine is opposed, 1st. "To RELIGIOUS LIBERTY," which is the "*right of every man to worship Almighty God, according to the dictates of his own conscience, without injuring or invading the rights of others;*"—and, 2d. That it is opposed to "CIVIL LIBERTY," by which we understand *the absolute rights of the individual, restrained only for the purpose of order in society.* Now I maintain that these positions have been established by the united attestation of facts that cannot be denied, and of reasoning, that cannot be refuted. The gentleman will *say* that they have not been established. But he will take special care to avoid meeting the question. The public must decide.

The gentleman boasts that Presbyterians have not persecuted in the United States. Granted. But I give the glory of their forbearance to the provisions of the Constitution; the better spirit of other denominations; the liberality of the age; or any thing else—rather than the doctrine which makes it of divine obligation for Presbyterians to "REMOVE ALL FALSE WORSHIP,

(1) Pages 330, 331.

AND ALL THE MONUMENTS OF IDOLATRY." The duties of the citizen, and of the sectarian, are in direct conflict. The act of "removing," which is obedience to God, is disobedience to the laws. The act of obedience to the laws, is, like the violation of the Sabbath, an act of disobedience to God, according to *Presbyterian doctrine.*

"*Is the Presbyterian Religion, in any or in all its principles or doctrines, opposed to civil or religious liberty?*"

NEGATIVE V.—MR. BRECKINRIDGE.

Mr. President :—

If scandal be argument, or exultation be victory, or joy at notoriety and exposure be the tests of a good cause, then we must yield the palm to the prince of Jesuits.

The man who challenges the whole Presbyterian Church, cannot it is true, confess himself defeated by one of the feeblest of her sons, without supernumerary shame. And therefore it is not to be wondered at that he covers his wounds by the *argumentum ad verecundiam* which he tries to draw from the charge that his opponent has *aid*. Heaven and truth are aid enough for our cause. David's sling, and David's stone, with David's God, are enough for the vaunting Goliath of the Philistines without the aid of Saul's armour, or "*of patriarchal hands.*" Yet it is a reluctant tribute paid to my arguments that the foe in the field cries out "that the patriarch's hands" are upon him!

The complaint that *my* arguments are "like Joseph's coat," is only an unconscious condemnation of his *own*. *He is leading in the attack*. *I* follow as *respondent*. When he was beaten on the papal question, he gave *vituperation*, and *personal* assaults instead of the *defence* of his cause. At that time, he charged me with tacitly confessing myself personally indefensible, because I pursued the *line* of my discussion, and paid but little attention to his abuse. I then arrested the *argument* to meet the *calumniator:* how effectually the public must judge. I had no sooner renewed the argument, than he resorted again to calumny. I then resolved to reduce my reply and exposure of his personalities into one body, and that body was introduced into my last speech. If it be of "*many colours,*" it was in exposure of a *chameleon*. If not bathed in *blood* like Joseph's coat, it is not the fault of *Joseph's* envious and enraged pursuer. He had charged me with no less than ELEVEN CALUMNIES; and that too while he was *professing* to defend his church against the charge of enmity to civil and religious liberty. The 1st calumny he charged me with was, for saying that his church did not keep faith with heretics; 2d, that she trifled with oaths, if against her interests; 3d, that she absolved subjects from allegiance to heretics; 4th, that I had slandered Bellarmine; 5th, about the second commandment; 6th, about the translation of the Trentine Catechism; 7th, about calling the Pope God; 8th, &c. &c. (see the particulars at large in my last speech.) Most of these charges against me were drawn from a *former* controversy. In replying to his *digressions* could *I fail to digress?* He abused me first, because I would not follow him. Now he ridicules me for doing it. "Olla Podrida!" The *muck-rake* is for "chopt straw;" as well as the *etherial sword* for the *old serpent.* If I stoop to such company, I must answer to its calls. Of that company I confess to you, gentlemen, I have often been heartily ashamed; and if there be a point on which I have really been at a loss in this discussion, it is to reconcile these *two* proverbs of Solomon (in my replies to Mr. Hughes's abundantly coarse and virulent abuse), viz. "*Answer not a fool according to his folly, lest thou also be like unto him. Answer a fool according to his folly, lest he be wise in his own conceit.*" (1) I have surely failed of preventing the *latter evil,* as all the gentleman says of *himself* will readily attest; and I fear at each step lest in seeking to correct the latter I should incur the former. If the gentleman will give me a good example, or in my despair of that a good interpretation of this difficult duty, I will follow the one and adopt the other, as a sincere disciple *quoad hoc.*

The exultation of the gentleman, that my reply to his last speech contained no notice of his *reasonings* and *facts,* is a fit illustration of what I have just said. If I had gone once more over the repeated replies to his stale arguments, if such they may be called, he would have said "chopt straw"—a very *pastoral* and frequent figure with our gentle shepherd. I forbore to *reiterate.* He cries out that I *concede* every thing. The argument from "*decrees of God!*" The "*monuments of idolatry.*" They have "*perished in the using.*" The witch-stories of New England! Do they prove that the doctrines of Presbyterians are opposed to liberty? I might have filled pages in reply with the incantations of papal baptism, or the *hocus pocus* and legerdemain of priestly transubstantiation, in which witch-craft and jugglery are enthroned on the sacraments of Jesus Christ; and he who rejects them, *dies the death,* if popery be true.

And then as to the persecutions of European Presbyterians, I have owned that they *did in a degree practice them; and that they were to be condemned*—and I *united* with the gentleman to *condemn* them. I have gone farther, I have said again and again that almost the whole Christian world had gone astray on the subject of civil and especially of *religious* liberty; in persecuting each other; in establishing religion as a part of the civil code; by intolerance; and mutual oppression: but that American Pro-

(1) Proverbs, xxvi. 4, 5.

testants have adopted a far different system; and *among them, Presbyterians, the objects of his malignant attacks.* But he says, owning that we *have changed*, you were forced to do it by the American Revolution. Well, admit, for the sake of argument, that such was the *cause.* Here however is the *excellent effect.* Now the Church of Rome *first* persecuted; and persecuted *most;* she first *united* church and state—she first made heresy a *civil* offence—she still upholds the union of church and state, wherever she can, as in Spain, Portugal, Austria, South America, and in Rome herself, where the head of the church is head of the state, *ex officio,* and elected to it by *priests* of the Church of Rome; and none but a *priest* of that church, *elected by priests* of that church, can be *Prince of Rome!* The Church of Rome says she *cannot* change, and *will not* change; and she *does not* change in this respect. Now here is the mighty difference. We *have* changed; not merely every practice, but every tenet, that allowed a state establishment of religion. We cannot accept an establishment if it were offered to us. Our avowed published doctrines forbid it; and though the gentleman says very kindly we are hypocrites in all this, still such are our standards. They declare "that it is the duty of the civil magistrate to protect the church of our common Lord, without giving the preference to any denomination of Christians above the rest, *in such a manner that all ecclesiastical persons whatever, shall enjoy the full, free, and unquestioned liberty of discharging every* part of their sacred functions, without violence or dangers." (1) Now I have often called, and called in vain for one such sentence in the voluminous standards of Rome. So far from this, her CATECHISM, BINDING on all the faithful, says, "*Yet it is not to be denied but that they* [heretics and schismatics] *are in the power of the church, as those who may be judged by her, punished and condemned with an anathema;*" and they are compared to "*deserters from an army.*" Chap. x. § 9. Here is direct and universal dominion claimed over all "*heretics and schismatics,*" as all we Protestants are in Rome's view. And again, "*But of them who obeyed not the priests, it is written, 'He that will be proud, and refuse to obey the commandment of the priest, who ministereth at that time to the Lord thy God, by the decree of the Judge that man shall die'*" (2)—This is on the 5th commandment, § 20., in answer to the question, "*With what punishment shall they be visited who break this commandment?*" Here the priesthood is enthroned by the standards of the Roman Church in supreme dominion over life and death itself, and the adduced authority of the word of God is given in proof of the doctrine of the *priest's power.* Here we see the true contrast between our standards and those of Rome.

(1) Confession of Faith, c. xxii. § 3.
(2) Deuteronomy xvii. 12.

But still more; *our* standards say, "God alone is the Lord of conscience :—the rights of private judgment in all matters that respect religion are universal and unalienable : they (Presbyterians) do not even wish to see any religious constitution aided by the civil power, further than may be necessary for protection and security, and at the same time be equal and common to all others." (1) Now if Mr. Hughes will show me this same principle in any part of his standards, I will give up the question. Has your church in any of her standards, ever avowed it? Does not that very Pope to whom Mr. Hughes is bound by a *feudal* oath, and who is head of the Catholic Church *now* while I speak, by force of arms sit a king over millions of men, and support (by the spiritual authority, and temporal, *blended* in his own person) a *religious establishment?* And does the Pope violate any one doctrine of popery in doing all this? Not one! But a religion which can receive or tolerate such an establishment, is opposed to civil and religious liberty, and treads both in the dust. This the Roman Catholic religion does; and this the Presbyterian religion cannot receive or tolerate. Here is a fair and direct *contrast*. Let the gentleman reply. To accept an establishment we must *change :* to reject it, *Catholicity must change*. Is it not so? It must be seen then very clearly how little I have to do with the Presbyterians of Holland, or any others, in this question, save *American Presbyterians;* and how much on the contrary, in an *unchanged church*, Mr. H. has to do with the popery of Europe and Rome, which is *one with his popery in all respects*. This unchangeable unity is thus expressed by Francis Plowden, Esq., a champion of Romanism. "If any one says or pretends to insinuate, that modern Catholics differ in *one iota from their predecessors*, he is either deceived himself, or he wishes to deceive others—*Semper eadem* (ALWAYS THE SAME) is not less emphatically descriptive of our *religion*, than of our *jurisprudence*." No! always the same! The same in the twelfth and in the nineteenth century! The same in Rome and America! *Here again* we call on the gentleman to say, does his religion *forbid* an *establishment?* Has it not an establishment now at Rome, in the person of the head of his church? Then it might without a change *in an iota* have one here, if it could, if it dare! Then it is *opposed* to civil and religious liberty !

In the progress of my arguments in the affirmative, I entered the INTERIOR of the Church of Rome, and proved that she *oppressed* her *own subjects*, as well as *persecuted* "*the heretics and schismatics who were deserters*," and *without her communion*.

It will be directly in place to revert to the points then stated, and contrast the doctrines of the Presbyterian Church with those of Rome, under the respective heads.

(1) Form of Government, b. i. c. i. § 1.

1st. As to Baptism. *What do the standards* of the Church of Rome say?

It was proved from the canons of the Council of Trent, on the first night, that *force is to be applied to compel* children baptized in their infancy to *lead Christian lives when they grow up.* This *was* further proved by the comments of *standard writers,* though (of course) *denied* by Mr. Hughes. For example Dens's Theology, adopted formally by the Catholic Prelates of Ireland, since 1808, cited in my third speech, first night, where the author *quotes the very proof given by me,* and uses the very *word* adopted by the Holy Council, to prove what I affirm, viz. "this also obtains in the case of those who have been baptized in their infancy, as the Council of Trent teaches, sess. 7. can. 14. and the Fourth Council of Toledo, canon 55, that even those who by force, or necessity, adopted the faith, should be forced (cogantur) to hold it." But Mr. Hughes denied that this word in the use of the infallible council, meant any thing but *spiritual* force. Dens, however, is more honest, for he says, "*Unbelievers who have been baptized, as heretics, and apostates generally, and also baptized schismatics, can be compelled by corporal punishment to return to the Catholic faith, and the unity of the Church.*"

"The reason is that they *by baptism are made subjects of the church, and therefore the church has jurisdiction over them, and the power of compelling them by the ordained means to obedience,* to fulfil the obligations contracted in their baptism." I must say again, here is an *honest* Roman! Let those believe Mr. Hughes's denial who are ignorant of the force of language, and the history of the Church of Rome, abd of his motives to *cover up* and to *forget* in this free land, and *enquiring age.* The Rev. Blanco White, once a priest of the "Catholic" Church in Spain, now a member of the Episcopal Church of Great Britain, calls *baptism* in the Church of Rome, "AN INDELIBLE BRAND OF SLAVERY."

Now let us turn to this sacrament in the Presbyterian Church. I invite the gentleman's scrutiny. It will repay our search; it will furnish the contrast in strong relief. Here amidst our institutions, sacraments, and doctrines, is the place to find our views of religious liberty. Why does the gentleman go to the *Netherlands,* when here are our *standards,* almost *untouched?* Two POINTS have been tortured, and repeated twelve or thirteen times to make them speak *against liberty—but in vain.* Here is *the volume,* replete with a *whole system of doctrine!* Why does he shun its hundreds of pages crowded with doctrines proved by appeals to the word of God, not by *Nightingale* or *Brandt,* but by Paul and Matthew and James and John, and by their and our Lord! Now on the sacrament of baptism let him turn over these pages and show me *one word* like *force,* and I will yield up the question in debate. In the 9th chap. *Directory for Worship,* is this section, which is so strongly in contrast with the *papal system* on the same subject, that it shall speak for itself. "Children born within the pale of the visible church and dedicated to God in *baptism* are under the inspection and government of the church, and are to be taught to read and repeat the catechism, the apostle's creed, and the Lord's prayer. They are to be taught to pray, to abhor sin, to fear God, and obey the Lord Jesus Christ. *And when they come to years of discretion, if they be free from scandal, appear sober and steady, and to have sufficient knowledge to discern the Lord's body, they ought to be informed that it is their duty and their privilege to come to the Lord's supper.*" In the Papal Church, baptism, which is a *brand of slavery for life*, is at the same time made *absolutely necessary to salvation;* so that none can be saved *without* it; no, not even the *dying infant;* and those babes who die without it, are forever lost. Thus they drive men into slavery by the fears of eternal damnation. So they believe; and hence, shocking to relate, not only are *nurses* and *physicians*, and the laity at large authorized to administer this sacrament, but if a mother be giving birth to a dying infant, the *priest* will interpose to baptize the babe amidst the awful and, to such men, unapproachable scenes of parturition, and hold the mother suspended between life and death, in order to administer this popish rite and carry out this shocking doctrine. The gentleman may affect to be horrified by the allusion. I put him on his honour to deny or confess, 1st, Whether such be not the *literal fact?* 2d, Whether he has not himself been an *actor* in such scenes? And now let him deny it in the face of the parties in this community who may test the truth of the statement, by an appeal to their own memories!

In contrast with all this, our standards say, (1) "Although it be a great sin to contemn or neglect this ordinance, yet grace and salvation are not so inseparably annexed unto it, that no person can be regenerated or saved without it; or that all that are baptized are undoubtedly regenerated." We *drive* no man to it. We bind no man forcibly by it. We impair not human liberty, or divine truth by our doctrine, discipline, or practice.

2d. We showed at large that AURICULAR CONFESSION, which is *required* in the Roman Church, in *order to salvation*, is in the highest sense an INVASION of personal liberty; and besides being unspeakably corrupting to the *priest*, and absolutely destructive of good morals among multitudes of *the people*, endangers the safety of states, putting alike the rulers and the subjects in the power of the priesthood. By this system of (as it were) omnipresent, and all-knowing espionage, the priests ever *have* ruled, and while it prevails *ever will rule* the state, and corrupt the laity. They know every man's, every woman's, every ruler's secrets. The *directory* for self-examination in the Book of Devotion put forth under the sanction of the Catholic priesthood of America, and now in use in

(1) Con. Faith, chap. xxviii § 5.

this city, is enough of itself forever to *ruin* the system of which it is a part in the eyes of the American people. And the decrees on confession by the Council of Trent, require all the circumstances and particulars of sins to be laid open to the priest. Hence the horrible Spanish book which I exhibited to the audience, asks *females* whether they have *criminal attachments* to any of the *priests?* and if so, to which of the *priests?* And what if she should reply—*to you?*

If incessant and unspeakable evils do not occur, it is a *standing miracle*. *History* shows that this papal *sacrament is a sink of debauchery;* and destructive of all sorts of *human liberty*.

Now here is a point of *decisive contrast*. We ask the gentleman to show us anything in the Presbyterian Church at all corresponding to this enormous evil. Show me the *confessional;* show me this fearful police over men's souls: show me *hundreds of priests* who know every man's, woman's, child's secrets, and can act accordingly; can at a glance look through and through the wants, lusts, plans, desires, resources, of a whole community; show me these things in any *Presbyterian* or any *Protestant* Church.

3d. I showed how the Church of Rome had interfered directly with the liberty of the *press*, the *liberty* of *buying* and *reading*, and *the liberty of thought*. This was done *on system;* by general councils; and is extended even to the *rule of faith and the word of God*. The infallible Council of Trent had by its constituted organ denounced so many books, and among them the word of God in the vernacular tongues of the nations (without a written permission to read it), that the mere *list of names* filled a volume, which I exhibited to the society! That another large volume was filled with a list of *erasures* and *expurgations* of books, especially those which have been written *since the Reformation*, and that the present reigning pope *denounces the liberty of the press*, and the *freedom of religion*.

Now will the gentleman show me any such feature in the Presbyterian or the Protestant Churches of the United States? He has often charged Protestantism with *variations*, and our *rule of faith* with *defects* and various evils, *but never with oppressing* the conscience, restricting the freedom of the mind, *staying* the right of private judgment, laying its rude hand on the press, and even on the free use of the word of God. It is true, he has abused the Synod of Philadelphia for *suspending* Mr. Barnes, and tried to flatter the prejudices of those who think Mr. Barnes was *wronged*. But will he please to show us *the Presbyterian act*, forbidding any man to print, sell, or read Mr. Barnes' work under pain of fines, loss of the edition, and the discipline of the church in its severest forms? The *act denounced the errors of the book*, and *applied ecclesiastical censure to the author*. But how was it with Huss, Jerome of Prague, John Rodgers, and the immense multitude of the martyrs of the *truth* butchered by the Church of Rome? The entire discussion of *the rule of faith* in our late controversy, on the part of Mr. Hughes, went to show the *consolidated character of his church;* its full and formal unity *every where and always;* and the uniformity of its doctrines, the perfection of its rule in producing uniformity, the binding authority of that rule, &c. &c., and in contrast with *it the utter and hopeless division of Protestants;* the number of their sects and parties—even the *thousand and one;* the varieties of their *opinions* on every possible subject touching the revelation of God; and in a word the hopeless distractions and dissimilitudes of *protestantism*. *Now* the gentleman sees what the *drift* of his *reasoning* was THEN. But he *flinches* too late. We remember, though he *wishes* us to forget, that by his own showing his is the only church in America in which perfect *uniformity prevails;* and whose members all speak one language and breathe one *spirit.* The agitated and heterogeneous mass of protestantism can never feel, *think,* or act together; though each of the thousand and one sects were ever so well disposed to govern the nation. But let *Papists* once *prevail;* let their yearly accessions from abroad raise them to a majority; and let them *play off the Protestants* one party *against another,* so as to divide and rule them, and *where, where on the gentleman's own showing, were the security of our freedom?* The *majority* has a right to rule, though it be to establish popery! And a papal majority never divides, changes, or recedes.

Such is the operation of the "Catholic rule of faith." Whereas the *Presbyterian* and Protestant rule, even *"the Bible" in the hands of the people, is the great preservative against priestcraft and fatal consolidation.* We beg the gentleman to examine this *contrast* of his own sketching, and *report* to us, in reply.

4th. In nothing does this contrast appear more striking, than on the *subject,* or as Mr. Hughes would say, the *sacrament* of marriage.

With American Protestants, including Presbyterians, this is no *sacrament;* but a divine institution coeval with the creation of man. It is an institution, accompanied by divine sanctions; but *not peculiar to the church.* Our standards, say, (1) "It is proper that every commonwealth, for the good of society, make laws to regulate marriage; *which all citizens are bound to obey.*" With us a civil magistrate may solemnize marriage, and the civil law has certain important relations to the institution.

But how is it in the Church of Rome? It is enthroned as a *sacrament, under the exclusive regulation of the priesthood;* and no man can *marry* without his *act,* and *" intention,"* and *interposition;* and unless his *intention* be right when he officiates, the solemnization is void, and the contract void, and the issue illegiti-

(1) Directory for Worship, chap. ii. p. 441.

mate, and the seed of all persons not married by a Roman priest is illegitimate; and a Roman priest is forbidden to marry those who are not *baptized* persons. It is indeed expressly said, (1) "*without the presence of the parish priest, or some other priest commissioned by him, or by the ordinary, and that of two or three witnesses, there can be no marriage.*" In a word, under the Gospel, none but *Catholic priests can marry.* Hence this great civil right being tortured into a sacrament, and subordinated to the church, none can marry without her consent and act; and she can dispense even to the second degree, so as to allow brother and sister to marry, for reasons of state; or she can put even *barriers* in the way which none dare to pass over. Here is *slavery.* Here is making matrimony, as well as life's *opening,* and life's *close,* and all the way *through* life, a sort of *fluent sacrament,* so that one is dependent on the priest for *every thing,* great, good, and to be desired, now or forever. They keep *the keys of the treasury, and of life and of death. They keep the great seals;* this *Cerberus* must have his *sop* from every traveller *into,* or *through,* or *out* of the world.

There is another aspect of this subject which has very special interest, and is little thought of in our country. It is very ably presented in the following paper which I have lately met with, published in the heart of Pennsylvania, and which I desire to present for the gentleman's special consideration, adding that I have the work in my possession from which the writer quotes.

"An opinion prevails extensively that a man's sentiments and professions upon the subject of religion should not be made a matter of objection against his elevation to office. It is undoubtedly a very delicate subject—and if such objections should come in vogue at all, it would be difficult, if not impossible, to restrain them within proper bounds. Yet every voter at the polls must and will act upon such motives as seem best to him, and hence it is that the public press has a most weighty and responsible duty to perform, in conveying to the citizens at large correct impressions upon all topics connected with our forms of government.

"The opinion to which we have reference is a deduction from the grand principles of Protestantism—namely, that all men have a right to worship God according to the dictates of their own consciences. This is certainly true; and the Roman Catholic has as much right to worship God in his way as any of the various sects of Protestants have to worship in their way. No man can rightfully be coerced by human law, in matters of conscience, whether he be a Protestant, Catholic, Jew, Mahometan or Pagan. The only power which can be lawfully brought to bear upon him, is the power of the word or the power of persuasion. This is

---

(1) See Catechism of the Council of Trent, p. 313.

Protestantism. It forms the *only* religious article in the constitution, and no man who loves his country can wish to expunge it from our political or religious creed. But does it follow from this, that a man's opinions are of no consequence to the public? Is it not important that sound and just opinions upon all subjects touching our social condition, should be entertained by every citizen, and especially by those citizens who aspire to places of trust? Does it follow because one man has not the right to persecute another for his opinions, that he is in duty bound to take no note of them at the ballot box? To a certain extent our constitution does take notice of *religious opinions,* notwithstanding it declares the right of private opinion. There is a provision which declares that no man who believes in the being of a God, and a state of future rewards and punishments shall be disqualified from holding any office of trust on account of his religious sentiments. Now the meaning of this is, that although every man has a right to enjoy his opinions, yet certain opinions are necessary to make him worthy of high public trusts. In practice too, it is not unfrequent that candidates for public office are called upon for their sentiments upon political subjects. This proceeds upon the ground that their principles, which are comparatively a matter of no importance in private life, become a matter of public concern when they are candidates for places of public trust. It is generally supposed, however, that the religious belief and principles of a man, (excepting certain fundamental articles indispensable to the very idea of that accountability which is implied by an oath,) can have no very close connection with temporal and secular trusts and duties, and no instance has occurred in this country in which a man's *religious* creed has been the subject of direct and public enquiry. This opinion is more correct in relation to any of the Protestant sects than to the Roman Catholics. In that system much passes under the name of religion which mainly concerns the temporal and political condition of men. Our people are not generally aware of this, because they are not attentive to follow out principles to their consequences. Take for example the different views entertained by Protestants and Catholics upon the subject of "MARRIAGE." The former hold it to be a *civil contract,* but of a very peculiar and solemn character; the latter hold it to be a *sacrament.* Now most persons among us suppose this to be a mere theological difference, depending upon metaphysical or scholastic distinction, and one which may be disregarded by the politician, because it can have no political results. No doubt, many among us would think it a very idle objection to a candidate for public office, that he believes marriage to be a sacrament, which can rightly be performed only by a priest of the Roman Catholic Church. What more idle, they would say, than to make such a dogma, a turning point in deciding upon the fitness of a candidate for office? It is not however a difference of opinion, so entirely destitute of consequences, as will appear from the following facts.

"During the ascendancy of Napoleon Buonaparte in France, the Catholic clergy, who had been ejected from the sees and cures by the revolution, were re-established under certain conditions by a treaty (or concordat, as it was called) between the Pope and the French government. This treaty was published in 1802. Pius VII., then Pope, was for a time very grateful. He declared publicly, that next to God, he owed every thing to Napoleon Buonaparte; but shortly afterwards he began to complain of certain laws which the French government had made, and among others the laws relating to marriage. In 1807 a cardinal was sent from Rome to Paris, to negociate about these difficulties. Afterwards discussions were continued at Rome, in which the obstinacy of the Court of Rome, in considering as null and void all marriages solemnized according to the civil code, was signally manifested. The doctrine of the Pope and of his clergy was, that no real or valid marriage *could* exist except by the intervention of a Catholic priest. Still the French code, or parts of it, became more and more extended in Europe, and was introduced into different countries to a greater or lesser extent, and the Court of Rome, in order to counteract the effect of it, despatched instructions, as they were called, exhibiting in bold relief the unsocial and immoral doctrine of that church upon the subject of marriage.

"The following are extracts from a letter of instruction destined for Poland, no longer ago than 1808, where, by law, an attempt had been made to reconcile the sacramental benediction, (as it was called,) with the civil nature of the marriage contract.

"'Such a transaction, (says the Pope's letter) proposed by a Catholic prelate to a royal minister, upon a subject so sacred, considered in its principles, in its consequences, in its whole tenor, leads directly to the result, which modern sectaries have proposed to themselves, namely to make Catholics and bishops, *and even* the Pope himself, confess that the power of governing men is indivisible. * * * * * * * For a Catholic bishop to acknowledge in Catholic marriages, civil publications, civil contracts, civil divorces, civil judgments prescribed by the civil law, is to grant to the prince a power over the sacraments and over ecclesiastical discipline. It is to admit that he can alter the form and the rites—can derogate from the canons—can violate ecclesiastical liberty—can trouble consciences—that he has, by way of consequence, an absolute authority over things and causes purely ecclesiastical—essentially privileged, and dependent on the power of the keys—which is as much as to say that he can put his hand to the censer and make his laws prevail over the laws of the church. Either the bishop should have *dissembled* and *tolerated* a disorder imposed by irresistible force, or if he would say any thing, he should have informed the royal minister that the regulations of the code, so far as they respect marriage, cannot be applied to Catholic marriages in Catholic countries.'

"If we survey the history of nations, we shall not find a single example of a Catholic prince, imposing or suffering to be imposed on his subjects, the obligation to publish and declare their marriage, and to discuss the validity or nullity of it before the judge of the district. A large field would have been opened for the bishop to show the royal minister that in a country where the Catholic religion is that of the state—in a country governed by a Catholic prince, the laws of the civil code relative to marriage cannot be applied to Catholics, nor the observation of them be required without a great scandal—that it would be an attempt, unheard of —and a manifest revolt, against the laws of the church—a novelty leading to error and schism. If these pastoral remonstrances had proved useless, the bishops should have committed their cause and that of the church into the hands of God and continued to teach well the flock committed to their care. * * * * * *

"1st. That there is no marriage, if it is not contracted in the form which the church has established to render it valid.

"2d. That marriage once contracted according to the forms of the church, there is no power on earth which can sunder its tie.

"3d. That it remains indissoluble notwithstanding adultery, and the inconveniences of cohabitation.

"4th. That in case of a doubtful marriage, it belongs to the church alone to judge of its validity or invalidity, so that every other judgment emanating from any other power whatever is incompetent and incapable of authorizing a divorce and of rendering it lawful.

"5th. That a marriage to which there is no canonical impediment is good and valid, and consequently is indissoluble, *whatever impediment the lay power may unduly impose without the consent and approbation of the Universal Church or of its supreme head, the Roman Pontiff.*

"6th. That on the other hand, *every marriage contracted notwithstanding* a canonical impediment—(though abrogated abusively by the sovereign) ought to be holden as entirely null and of no effect—and that *every Catholic is bound in conscience to regard such a marriage as null until it shall be validated by a lawful dispensation granted by the Church, if indeed the impediment which renders it null may be removed by a dispensation.*

"The Bishop of Warsaw had said that the regulations of the code civil relative to marriage did not present any difficulty—that they ordered nothing contrary to the laws of God and of the church and consequently that every one was bound to conform to it. In reply to this judicious reflection the Court of Rome answered in these terms.

"'Is not the article which declares that persons divorced shall not intermarry again, opposed to the laws of God and of the church, &c. &c.—and to say all in one word, is it not an offence to God and to the church, to make laws which subvert ecclesiastical discipline in a matter so delicate?' The Court of Rome then declares that it is an error to regard marriage as a civil contract, '*above all since under the evangelical law it has been elevated to the dignity of a sacrament—and has thereby become a sacred thing independent, as respects its nature and validity, of every species of profane law. And it is so true that the nature and validity of marriage, particularly under the gospel, is independent of every civil contract established by the civil laws, that the Council of Trent declared null every marriage contracted without the solemn forms which it prescribed, and this the Council could not have done, if marriage partook of the nature of two contracts, * * * * * * which depend upon two distinct powers—the one civil and dependant on the civil laws for its validity—the other religious and dependant on the laws of the church.*'

"From the foregoing extracts the reader perceives that however he may regard the *difference* between the doctrine of Protestants and Catholics on the subject of marriage, the *Church of Rome holds the distinction to be all important.* Every considerate man will admit, that of all contracts *marriage is the strictest,* the *most necessary,* and that *which commends itself most seriously to the attention of the civil power.* It is the contract which more than any other *constitutes and perpetuates society.* Upon such a *subject the duties of the Legislator are too grave to be surrendered to a foreign priest*—or to an *assembly of our own priests. Yet every devout Catholic holds that marriage is a sacrament, and the foregoing are some of the inferences resulting from that position.*

"Here then is one illustration of the manner in which a man's religious principles may affect his civil conduct, not as a private citizen merely, but as a legislator and as a public officer. *A man who would send to Rome, or the vicar-general of the Pope in this country, for a dispensation from a canonical impediment to marriage, does so, of course, under the belief that marriage is a sacrament and not a civil contract, and of course, that his marriage though according to the civil law would without a dispensation be null and his issue illegitimate. If he would not do so, but rely on the civil power to declare what marriages are lawful, he would be deemed a schismatic and the subject of ecclesiastical censure and excommunication.* The question may now be put whether a man, who believes in the papal doctrine, that marriage is a sacrament, is not by his own conscience disqualified from holding any public office of trust in a Protestant country?"

There is one respect in which this gentleman excels any other I have ever known.—It is in making something of nothing. *Ex nihilo nihil fit* can no longer be stated by philosophers as an indisputable axiom. Not the spider who will *spin out* his interminable web from the *materials furnished by one poor fly;* not the lean *liver* who decocts his profuse *soups* of *bones* can make a richer use of *nothing* than our self-complacent, unblushing disciple of Loyola. Truly sir, I admit that there is no answering "*these arguments.*" He may weave his spider web and wind his horn of triumph, and still his speeches must be *unanswerable,* while there is nothing in *them to answer.* Such are the first *pages* of the last speech. As might have been expected, his declamation is not only empty but *false.* Thus he says the Quakers were cropped in England by "*Calvinists.*" Now does he mean to say this was by *Presbyterians?* Then it is wholly, wholly *false.* If by *others,* then it is wholly *irrelevant.* His want of candour is as unwise as it is unjust and unlovely. Take for example the *two cases of which* he has made so much, as given by Brandt. Admit it all to be true! as well as the cropping of the poor Quakers!—what then? He infers that Presbyterian *doctrine* is *persecuting doctrine.* Let it be allowed to be so. I turn him to the CATHOLIC HISTORIAN, Father Paul, (1) where he tells us that "FROM THE EDICT OF CHARLES UNTIL THE TIME OF THE PEACE, (in the very same land where the *two men* were put to death,) "there *were hanged, beheaded, buried, and burned to the number of* FIFTY THOUSAND" of the Protestants!!! And now will he say it was *persecution* for Presbyterians to put *two men* to death, and no persecution for *Catholics* to put 50,000? Truly he undervalues the lives of heretics even *more* than the Pope his master, if two Catholics outweigh 50,000 Presbyterians! Now will he say it was only *discipline* to slaughter *Protestants* but *doctrine* to kill even two *papists?* Grotius, whom Mr. H. has often referred to, says these martyrs to liberty and truth in the low countries amounted to 100,000. Yet, after all, the secret sting of Popery was the loss of the nation, and its full final identification with the Protestant cause. For as it often is, persecution made the church of Christ to *grow;* in spite of *anti-christ* and the *Man of sin,* the Reformation reclaimed Holland from papal domination.

The *malignity* of the last speech of the gentleman is so great, that I can only explain it by the efficacy of my *illustrations and authorities.* A gentleman and a Christian cannot answer *malignity* any more than a logician can *reply to gasconade and empty declamation.* Here then I must also pass by the spleen and abuse and ill-bred taunts and vulgarity I meet. I cannot stoop either to *gamble* with the gentleman as he proposes. I know *Protestant money* is popular at St. John's; and that Bishop England thinks well of a *game of cards,* as Mr. Hughes does of a *wager.* When I exhibited Baronius, to the confusion of his audacious misrepresentation in the late controversy, and *claimed* the offered $500—

---

(1) History of Council of Trent, page 387, book v.

how did he meet the pledge? The self-confident air with which he holds forth his $100—resembles the last stake of a desperate gamester. But while I cannot gamble even with a *priest* of Rome, a candidate for the *ring and staff*, lest his "*great swelling words should deceive the unwary*," I will give him some *distinct examples* from the catechism of the Council of Trent, in proof of the truth of my proposition, and to show how empty and uncandid the gentleman's grandiloquence is. The proposal was this—"*But I here challenge Mr. Hughes to meet me before any number of Latin scholars, and I will convict this shameful edition*" (of the English translation of the catechism of the Council of Trent, printed in this country and approved by Mr. Hughes,) "of twenty deliberate and glaring frauds, which have been evidently committed with design." He says of this charge: "*I pronounce it utterly untrue.*" Now for the proof. The translator says in his preface, "*the phraseology of the work is consecrated by ecclesiastical usage.* Whilst, therefore, he has endeavoured to preserve the *spirit*, he has been unwilling to *lose sight of the letter*—studious to avoid a servile exactness, he has not felt himself at liberty to indulge the *freedom of paraphrase:* anxious to *transfuse* into the *copy* the *spirit* of the *original* he has been no less anxious to render it an *express image of that original.*" These are *fair promises*, and pompous pledges.

The first step of the learned "professor," (and he is in the papal college of Maynooth, specially dedicated to the training of a *priesthood*) is wholly to *omit* the Pope's Bull which accompanies the original, and ushered it into the world. The reason for this it is not hard to understand.

I. *Example, is an omission.*

Original Latin.	Our "holy" translator gives the following only:—	A full translation:—
Nam per sacramenta solum si eorum forma servatur peccata remitti possunt: aliter vero nullum jus a peccatis solvendi ecclesiæ datum est: ex quo sequitur tum sacerdotes, tum sacramenta ad peccata condonanda, veluti instrumenta valere, quibus Christus Dominus auctor ipse, et largitor salutis, remissionem peccatorum et justitiam in nobis efficit.	"And sins can be forgiven only through the sacraments, when duly administered. The church has received no power otherwise to remit sin."	By the sacraments only, so that the form of them be kept, sins may be forgiven; but otherwise there is no power of absolving from sin given to the church; whence it follows that the priests, as well as the sacraments, are as it were instruments to the forgiveness of sins by which Christ our Lord, who is the very author and giver of salvation, works in us forgiveness of sins and righteousness.

Here all that part in *italics* is OMITTED. Why that was selected is very plain, for that makes the *priests* not only *means* of *good*, but "*as it were*" *instruments of pardon of sin—a sort of sacraments!* Such profanity he might well be ashamed of; yet his shame should be at the *doctrine*; and his honour and honesty should have given a fair, full *translation.* (1)

II. *Example, is an interpolation.*

Original Latin.	True translation.	Donovan's corruption of the text, defended by Mr. Hughes.
Quod quidem non minus verà de illo etiam homine sacerdos pronunciat qui prius ardentissimæ contritionis vi, accedente tamen confessionis voto, peccatorum veniam adeo consecutus sit. Adduntur præteria complures preces, non quidem ad forman necessariæ, sed ut ea removeantur, quæ sacramenti vim et efficientiam, illius culpa cui administratur, impedire possent. (2)	This (the form of absolution) the priest may pronounce no less truly concerning that man also, who by virtue of a most ardent contrition—yet so as that he has the wish of confession—has obtained from God the pardon of his sins. Many prayers also accompany the form, not because they are deemed necessary, but in order to remove every obstacle which the unworthiness of the penitent may oppose to the power and efficacy of the sacrament.	"This form is not less true, when pronounced by the priest over him who by means of perfect contrition has already obtained the pardon of his sins. *Perfect contrition it is true reconciles the sinner to God, but his justification is not to be ascribed to perfect contrition alone, independently of the desire which it includes of receiving the sacrament of penance.* Many prayers accompany the form, not because they are deemed necessary, but in order to remove every obstacle which the unworthiness of the penitent may oppose to the efficacy of the sacrament.

Here one whole sentence, (that in italics,) *is an entire forgery* to which there is not one corresponding word in the original Latin! *This is adapting the system to the latitude.* He who reads this will better understand what I said in my last speech about the *liberties taken with the Fathers and the Bible in the Church of Rome.*

III. *My third example is a compound of several kinds of iniquities.*—This is the most flagrant, and deliberate act of fraud I have ever seen practised on any author, *living or dead.* The

(1) See Donovan's Translation, 108 page; and the original Latin, p. 75, § 6.
(2) See Latin edition, p. 177. English, pages 241-2.

compilers are here introducing St. Ambrose as authority on the question of the supremacy of the Pope. They extract some twelve lines from that father, and then proceed to add their own *doctrine of the necessity of a visible head to the church on earth.* This translator, advocated by Mr. Hughes OMITS EVERY WORD OF AMBROSE'S extract; and, *retaining his name, puts* the language of the catechists into his mouth, and makes him *father* what was written many, yes, very many centuries *after his death,* and lo, he speaks the language of a thorough-paced papist!!!

Original Latin.

Postremo sanctus Ambrosius ait: "Magna sunt enim Dei munera, qui non solum nobis quæ nostra fuerant reparavit, verum etiam quæ sunt propria concessit: [deinde paucis interjectis sequitur.] Magna autem Christi gratia qui omnia prope vocabula sua discipulis ipsis donavit."— [This father then gives quotations of eight or nine portions of the Bible, to prove the above proposition, viz: *that our Lord bestowed his title on his disciples;* all these are suppressed by the translator, and the following words put into his mouth.] "Si quis objiciat ecclesiam uno capite et sponso Jesu Christo contentam præterea nullum requirere, in promptu responsio est, &c. . . . . Sic ecclesiæ quam ipse intimo spiritu regit hominem suæ potestatis vicarium, et ministrum præfecit, nam cum visibili capite egeat ita salvator noster Petrum universi fidelium generis caput et pastorem constituit," &c.

Translation and true connexion.

Lastly St. Ambrose saith: "Great indeed are the gifts of God, who not only restored to us what had been ours, but even conferred on us what was peculiar to himself: [then after adding a few things he proceeds.] *How great was the grace of Christ, who bestowed nearly all his titles on his disciples."* [Here the quotations from Scripture are introduced, and the extract from Ambrose CLOSES. BY HIM ALL THE DISCIPLES OF CHRIST ARE MADE EQUAL SHARERS IN THESE PECULIAR AND GRACIOUS TITLES. But the translator suppresses that passage, and puts up Peter alone as bearing Christ's titles. This is base fraud.] "If any should object that the church is content with one spouse and one head, Jesus Christ, and requires no other, the answer is obvious, &c. . . . . *So He,* (Jesus,) has placed *over his church which he governs by his invisible spirit,* a man to be his vicar, and the minister of his power; for a visible church requires a visible head, and therefore does our Saviour appoint Peter head and pastor of all the faithful."

By the above fraud, 13 *lines of Ambrose are expunged; and* 12 *lines of the catechism are put into his mouth* and reported as his—being entirely different words, and composed 1200 years after Ambrose died.

A glance at the above will convince any honest man that this is *base work.* Now I gave this book, only as one of many, (including the "Catholic" Fathers, as they are called, and the word of God itself,) in which frauds had been committed on the sacredness of the press, and works *altered* by omissions, forgeries, variations, and false connexions of terms—by the members and head of the Roman Church. Of all the cases given, Mr

Hughes has noticed this *alone*. And now I ask directly whether these are *frauds* or not? Does Mr. H. any longer defend this translator? And now let me ask Mr. H. to lay aside the Jesuit *for once*, and meet these proofs; and as he says my proposition about this translation "*is untrue,*" I require him to prove it, or to confess that *he* has made a *false* statement. If he vindicates the translator, or if he does not now *condemn* him before the public, he becomes *the partaker of his guilt;* if he remains *silent*, it will be a confession of guilt and confusion too. When he shall have met these *three examples*, like an honest man, then we will produce more, and refer the *whole* book to the *proper arbitration*.

And as to the *arbitration* of all undisputed points, I shall rejoice, at the close of this discussion, to refer all the *points* as to the *meaning of words* in the *dead languages, as to the facts about which we are at issue* (or may be before the debate closes) to fit referees. And among other things, the question *to whom* is to be charged the failure to publish the *report* of the stenographer; and why it is that Mr. Hughes can *bet* hundreds of dollars, and yet at no time *pay one cent* toward the expences of the report of the debate, while it was at his instance, said report was laid aside; and thus the *means* of paying the reporter for the time, made unavailing!!

If the gentleman will look into the new edition of Buck's Theological Dictionary, at the close of the book, he will find an article on "the Baptists," drawn up by a distinguished clergyman of this city belonging to that denomination, in which if he has any desire to correct his false statements about the proportion of *Calvinists*, he will find room to regret his rudeness, and to be ashamed of his ignorance; or if he requires it, I will cite it in the next reply.

As to the article in the "Catholic Telegraph," the "*intention,*" as a Catholic priest ought to know, determines the *whole question*. Was not that *intention* to favour the *sentiment* of the article which denounced our *American system as a failure?* If so, then my use of it was the fair and the *only fair* one. Mr. Hughes denies that such *was his intention*, on him then lies the duty of *proof*. He is well aware that he cannot make it good. Hence his silence as to *proof* and his impertinence as to *abuse*.

"The doom" of popery is not pronounced by *me*, but by *God*, who hath said prophetically, "Babylon has fallen, has fallen;" and "that man of sin, whose coming is after the working of satan with all power, and signs, and lying wonders, and with all deceivableness of unrighteousness; whom the Lord *shall* consume with the spirit of his mouth, *and destroy with the brightness of his coming.*" *This* is the doom I speak of. It *has been* working since the morning star of the reformation arose. It *is working* in

Spain, in Portugal, in France, even in Rome; and its signs are seen in the spread of the gospel, in the progress of liberty and truth, and in the desperation of the disciples and defenders of Rome, "*whose wrath is great because they see that their time is short.*"

When the gentleman charges me with suppressing a part of a canon, "*after Faber,*" he gives me *good defence* before honest men, by the very *manner* of attack, for surely the name and example of "Faber" are good, against the name and the renown of *John Hughes.*

As to "*nursing fathers.*" The Presbyterian Church, responding to the American Constitution, which is but a republication of Bible liberty, says *it is the duty of the civil magistrate to protect all denominations, giving the preference to none;* and cites, in proof, the prophet Isaiah who predicts this *protection* to the then persecuted church. Now I call on the gentleman to say what *his church thinks* the duty of *the civil magistrate* on this subject ought to be? I have told him during the unanswered arguments of many addresses, *what it is;* viz. "*to purge his territory of heretical filth,*" "to exterminate heretics;" and, if "being warned, he shall refuse, let it be told the pope, that he may absolve his subjects from their allegiance, and give the territory to those who will keep it free from heretics."

As to the American Sunday School Union. If ever there was an institution in which sectarian domination was impossible, it is this. It is one of the most expressive and unanswerable proofs of the spirit of Mr. Hughes, and of his church, that he attacks such institutions as *that which unites many denominations of Christians, to send out the Bible without note or comment to the whole world ; and which has already caused the Bible to be translated into one hundred and fifty-five languages of the earth!* And that institution, which is even *without price,* teaching *God's word* on *God's day to millions of children in Europe, Asia, Africa, and America;* and which at the *cost of one mass* or *one prayer for a soul in purgatory,* will teach a child *for five years, and dismiss him at the close with a New Testament in his hand..* For *twenty-five cents can all this be done;* the tuition is gratis, by the best heads and hearts of America: [Theodore Frelinghuysen is one of these teachers; and how much of John Hughes's slander think you it would take to stain the fair lawn of his "*detestable Calvinism ?*"] and then twelve and a half for spelling books and reading primers, and twelve and a half cents for the Testament, and *then the whole solicited* by the Sunday School Union, from the American people indiscriminately, save the *Catholics* (they never give to such institutions; and like them as little as their *rubicund* priests do the temperance society), and when solicited, given to the printers and binders of school books and Bibles for the books which are gratuitously bestowed on the poor children! Yes! these are the noble institutions which *foreign Jesuits* fear, hate, and assail in vain.

This man charged the American Sunday School Union with saying, in *one of its reports*, that the purpose of the institution was to " *dictate to the souls of thousands of immortal beings.*" I called for the *proof!* And instead of referring to the report, he talks of some preface to one of the catalogues of books published by the union ! Now I ask him to cite the *whole passage:* to say if it be a report of the society; and if they announce on their own authority, the principle charged on them! Let Mr. Hughes reply.

It is laughable to see the gentleman *apply* his *huge Americanism* and his *heroic love* of liberty to specific cases. He says, for example, " the Synod of York (of Philadelphia *at* York) has directed an anti-popery sermon to be preached every year, *and this order or direction is neither doctrine nor discipline. The direction given at the Council of Lateran,* (which was to destroy the heretics, depose rulers who countenanced them, &c. &c. See the dreadful canon given in full in my second speech, first night) was in its principle like that given at the Synod of York" (*at* York). It was neither doctrine nor discipline.

But what if the Synod had said, "every man who will not receive and believe the doctrines of that sermon *ought to be put to death?*" What then? Would that be *doctrine?* No! Would it be discipline? No! What then? a nullity? Yes! But query, Can a church pass such a resolution without *holding* doctrines and pursuing a *course* unfriendly *to liberty* of *conscience,* and to *civil rights?* I ask is there any thing in the Roman Catholic doctrine which the *persecuting canon of the Lateran Council violates?* Our standards are replete with explicit doctrines *against persecution.* If *the gentleman has one, yes one such,* I do beg him to show it. Now a religion which can allow persecution; whose *infallible council* can *order it;* and yet say it is " neither *doctrine* nor *discipline" to do it,* nor yet AGAINST its doctrine or discipline, has confessed *guilty* to all that we have charged on it. Yet this Mr. Hughes has said !

He says he has exposed "a few (of my quotations) as samples." Pray will the gentleman give *us one?* I exposed the way the Church of Rome corrupted the *Bible* in my last speech? Is that *one* sample? I see—the gentleman is *silent* about that. I exposed the way in which Catholics corrupted the *text* of the *fathers.* The gentleman is silent about that. Is that a *sample* of my false quotations? Ah, gentlemen! the *good* Samaritan did not pass by on the *other* side! It was the *priest* that did so!

The charge of "falsehood" is a matter of course with Mr. Hughes! But when he can put by my side Faber, and Dr. Miller, and the American confederation, and the Bible Society, and the Sunday School Union, and stand himself with " the lewd fellows" who make the mobs, and then after *hearing their crimes suppress them, under the seal of confession,* while he joins their cry against the wise and the good! I say, gentlemen, if Mr. Hughes were to *praise me,* I should feel it a duty at once to begin the work of self-examination!

As to the Synod of Dort, you observe what he says (extracted from its *fierce enemy*) is given by him only with "IT IS RE-PORTED;" a fine foundation truly for pages of calumny. But the "*viper bites the file.*"

I would ask Mr. Hughes to tell me in his next, *when* and *where* the *Presbyterians* had the political and civil power in their hands? When he does this, then it will be time enough to look at his foul-mouthed calumnies. What a heart must that be, which can vent such a spirit? Query? Can any man sit and hear the *confessions* of all the crimes of all sorts of bad men, for *half* a century, and keep a heart cleaner than a common sewer?

The whole of his attack on the church of Holland is exposed *by one word,* in the very extract which he gives from Brandt (vol. 1st. p. 316), when the author says, that what he relates was done "*by an extraordinary tribunal or court of judicature?*" Mr. Hughes would induce his hearers to suppose that all this was the *act* of the *church!*

He says, in reference to the persecuting canon of the great Lateran council—"All that he said was that *society* has a right to suppress heretics, or no heretics, who undertake to overthrow the government."—Very true. But, Mr. Hughes, 1st. These *heretics* were under a foreign government; and not under the Pope's *civil* government? Or do you mean *ecclesiastical* government? That was in *all* these lands! Do you mean that? 2d. The Council of Lateran which met at Rome did not represent "*society,*" but "the Holy Catholic Church!" What had the Pope to do with "*society?*" Suppose the general assembly of the Presbyterian church should say, "*society,*" i. e. "the general assembly," has a right to suppress, (by a crusade of several hundred thousand men,) heretics or no heretics, who undertake to overthrow the (American) "government?" What, I ask had the "Council" to do with the duties of civil "society" in *foreign lands?* or even in Italy, where the Pope is an usurper placed and kept on the backs of the people by Austrian bayonets—while his minions in America, cry out for *liberty, liberty!* Let Mr. Hughes say, first, whether or not the Pope has a right to be a civil Potentate in Rome, from God or man? Is he a legitimate ruler or a tyrant? Settle that question, and then talk of liberty!! As to "*moral influence,*" I need not repeat. Once Mr. Hughes said "we had changed our creed to *suit* the *American Constitution;* I replied, *very well.* Whatever the *cause,* you admit the *fact* of the *change.* And I said, *do you only change too,* and then we will shake hands over our blessed constitution. But, no! Rome never changes! *Now,* the gentleman implies that there is no change in us; that it *still means force*, by a sort of *mystic sense* like the secreta monita of the Jesuits; or like the *consecrated bread*, it is bread to Protestants; to Priests it is "*God, and Christ, very Christ—bones, &c. &c.*"

The gentleman says, "THE INQUISITION WAS ENTIRELY AND AVOWEDLY A POLITICAL AND NOT AN ECCLESIASTICAL INSTITUTION." I am sorry to say he *knows* the reverse to be true; and I have only to refer the reader to what I have already said on that subject, on the Catholic question. *Devoti*, says, (see my long citation from him,) "THE CONGREGATION OF CARDINALS AT ROME INSTITUTED BY THE POPE, IN WHICH THE POPE PRESIDES, IS THE HEAD OF ALL INQUISITORS OVER THE WHOLE WORLD; TO IT THEY ALL REFER THEIR MORE DIFFICULT MATTERS; AND ITS AUTHORITY IS FINAL. IT IS RIGHTLY AND WISELY ORDERED THAT THE POPE'S POWER AND OFFICE SUSTAIN THIS INSTITUTION. FOR HE IS THE CENTRE OF UNITY AND HEAD OF THE CHURCH; AND TO HIM CHRIST HAS COMMITTED PLENARY POWER, TO FEED, TEACH, RULE, AND GOVERN ALL CHRISTIANS."

Now either the Pope is *political head* of all countries where the inquisition has been established, or else it is a religious, and *ecclesiastical* institution. But, gentlemen, I predict that Mr. Hughes will *pass this by* in his *next* speech. And here it is curious to see the gentleman's intermitting conscience and sensibility.

For *one* Catholic *priest's cruel* (and so it was cruel) execution, "he *sickens at the narrative*." But the historian of the *Spanish* inquisition alone tells us that there were, from 1481 to 1812 (only 331 years) 341,021 victims, of whom 31,912 *were burnt to death*. (1)

So of *Servetus*. How Mr. Hughes *groans* in holy pity over that poor, persecuted, injured man! So he was injured; and Calvin, and the Genevese sinned against God and the liberty of Servetus. But Servetus had *run* away from the Catholics of *Vienne*, who only did not *burn him* because they could not *catch him*. And then the Huguenots, and the Albigenses, and the Turks. Why! Why! Historians say "the crusades were *just* wars,"—"they were heretics threatening to overthrow the government." But what had the Pope to do with carrying on wars? What with the military defence of the state? This is to confess all; yes all.

As to the Bulla in Coena, &c. I am glad the gentleman admits it exists. Once *he had never seen it in his life*. Now he stoutly cries out "it is in the *Bullarium Magnum*." I am glad to hear it; and with great pleasure acknowledge that I was *mistaken* in saying it was *not*. It was *only* the *first editions* of *it that* were not there printed. It was for ages growing "*bigger and badder*,"

(1) See Llorente, already quoted.

as one of the gentleman's fellow-men once said of a lesser evil, and the Bullarium contains the form finished out.

As to poor Mr. Ansley, I pity him, and wish him well, especially if he will take care of his family—and I shall think the better of Father Hughes, if he will add his influence to effect or aid in that duty.

The following dignified and sensible letter from Bishop Doane on the subject is my reply to the scurrility and abuse of Mr. Hughes. If Mr. H. deem it satisfactory, very well—I prefer not to publish it, out of respect to the feelings of all the parties. If not satisfactory to Mr. H., then I hereby add it to this speech as a part thereof, for which act I have in the letter the permission of the Right Rev. gentleman.

Burlington, N. J. Feb. 16, 1836.

Rev. Sir—Your letter of the 8th arrived here in my absence. I embrace the earliest leisure moment since my return to reply The case of Mr. Ansley, to which you allude, has been a very painful one, and has indirectly caused me great perplexity. Mr. Ansley was never received as a minister of the Protestant Episcopal Church in the United States. He came to me a stranger and poor, and so engaged my sympathies. As he did not bring letters to me I have never recommended him to the patronage of others. Long before he gave any symptoms of a tendency to Romanism, I saw that his mind was unsettled, and I have since learned that he has been at times insane. I regard him as partially deranged at this time, though competent to pursue his business as a teacher. Of course his adhesion to the Church of Rome is no loss to Protestantism and no gain to her. His strange conduct to his family I account for on the same ground. It is true that he is living with his family. It is not true that he has as yet contributed to their support since they came to him. It is true that both to his wife and children he has been unkind in many ways, and has been unjust to obtain from her articles of separation. It is very probable that a vague hope of being a Roman priest may have had some influence in inducing him to pursue this course. But I have no ground for supposing that he has been encouraged by Mr. Hughes or any other person to pursue this course, or indeed to expect that under any circumstances they would admit him to the priesthood. It should be stated that immediately after the first paroxysm of insanity, which I think was in 1832, he became prejudiced against his wife—though, so far as I can learn, without the slightest reason.

I have thus stated the material facts in the case, as they appear to me. You are at liberty to use the statement as you please. Badly as I think of the papal system, and anxious as I am that its inroads in our country should be resisted, the case of Mr. Ansley has not seemed to me of much importance. An amiable man, of not very strong mind, and very imperfect education in theology, naturally recluse in his disposition and inclined to enthusiasm, he appears to have sunk under the pressure of misfortune into a state of mental alienation, such as had befallen his father before him. Recovering in part, and under some degree of censure in his own church, he seems to have found in the Romish system, elements congenial with the morbid state of his mind and heart, and to have embraced it with an eagerness amounting to desperation. In two or three conversations which I had with him before his final decision, I saw clearly that he knew nothing of the argument—that to reason with him was to twist a rope of sand—and that he was yielding to an impulse which seemed like what we are told of fascination.

I have reason to believe that his accession to the Romish ranks was regarded by them as a triumph. I have reason to believe that it is now regarded by them in a very different light. I have only to wish that since he has chosen them, and they have received him, they would now take him and take care of him. His helpless family have been taken care of by the Christian benevolence of the community; perplexing and painful as his course has been, I cannot but regard him as an object of pity.

Believe me, very truly and respectfully, yours,

G. W. DOANE.

Finally, let me state in a word what has often been said before, that in *other ages, and other countries,* after the days of Constantine, *papists and Protestants* held principles and exercised discipline opposed, in a greater or less *measure to liberty, both civil and religious.* The *Protestants were in the amount of this, as one to one hundred, to the papists. The Reformation was the beginning of a glorious emancipation. Liberty, civil and religious,* has been gradually developing ever since, until it has been matured and restored to Apostolic and Bible grounds in America. *All other sects not professing to be infallible have adopted American principles;* among them *Presbyterians.* But *popery,* as already proved, did once *persecute in fact;* did so on *principle;* and *was* sustained in it by *its discipline.* Popery is the same it ever was. It *will not change.* Therefore it is still as ever opposed to liberty, civil and religious. If discipline is so, many of its doctrines are so. *Hence* it is peaceable, because it has not the *power.* Hence too the former persecutions of Presbyterians, which we unite to condemn, prove nothing to this question; whereas those of *Catholics do much.*

"Is the Presbyterian Religion, in any or in all its principles or doctrines, opposed to civil or religious liberty?"

AFFIRMATIVE VI.—MR. HUGHES.

MR. PRESIDENT :—

You and the audience have seen verified the prediction of my last speech, that Presbyterianism is slow to sacrifice money, whilst it immolates truth by the hecatomb. I had proposed to place at the disposal of charity, one hundred dollars for every instance in which I should have *failed* to convict the gentleman of the calumnies specified in my former speech, requiring that he, or his friends, if they have any confidence in his statement, should forfeit a similar sum, for a similar purpose, as often as I should have convicted him. He dreads this appeal to the *purse*. He knows he should suffer by it, and he shrinks from the test, as Achilles would from the course of an arrow aimed at his heel. He is scrupulous all at once; and he would not be guilty of "gambling," forsooth! Sir, it is no gambling; it is only a *tax*, which I proposed to levy on FALSEHOOD, for the benefit of charity. This question, therefore, is doubly SETTLED; first, by his shrinking from the original documents, and secondly, by his refusal to maintain his assertions at the risk of his purse. *I* always take the precaution to make myself certain of the truth of my statements, when history is in question; and it is thus that I am supported by that confidence which truth alone can inspire. The gentleman, unfortunately for himself, takes ignorant and faithless *partizan guides*, and hence it is that he appears confounded whenever the *original fountains* of history are consulted on these popular calumnies. Hence too, his confidence forsakes him, whenever he is brought up to the trying alternative, of having to *prove*, or having to pay.

My reference to "patriarchial" assistance was not, as he supposes, in compliment to the ability of his speech. But it was to take away the plea on which the feebleness of his arguments has sometimes been accounted for, by those who say that Presbyterianism suffers through his incompetency, rather than from the weakness of the cause itself. This cannot now be said, if, as we have reason to believe, his speeches have the advantage of being revised and amended, at head-quarters. In this way they furnish the best answer to my arguments, that can be furnished, by even the lions of Presbyterianism; and these answers consist in a dexterous evasion of those arguments. The evidences of Presbyterian intolerance, tyranny, and cruelty, seem to have taken them all by surprise. They find them rising up from every country under the sun, where their system existed, and had power to persecute. They find that not only Catholics, but men of all other religions, that ventured to worship Almighty God, "according to the dictates of their own consciences," were the victims of their persecution. They find all this undeniable. And hence it is, that I have had occasion to admire that discretion which has prompted the gentleman to abstain from every attempt to grapple with facts and arguments, which a "lion" of his Church could not overthrow.

The gentleman does well, therefore, to reconcile the "proverbs of Solomon," since he cannot "reconcile" the doctrines of his Church with "civil and religious liberty."

Of what he calls European persecutions, by Presbyterians, he says he "has owned that they did *in a degree* practice them." Now I have proved that they practiced them in EVERY "degree," from the pecuniary fine, to the block, and the stake, and the gibbet; both in Europe and America. I have proved that there is no instance in the records of history, in which they did *not* practice them. I have proved that, by their Confessions of Faith, they were bound to practice them:—that they held the obligation as a "tenet revealed by the Almighty," and that their second commandment, *now*, and in *this country*, (requiring *them* to "REMOVE ALL FALSE WORSHIP,") binds them still to practice them, "according to each one's place and calling." So long as their conscience allows them to continue in the *violation* of that divine precept, so long "false worships" may be left unremoved. He then goes on to tell us, what "he has said again and again." Sir, the question is not what *he* has said. But the question is what his Church has said. For this I refer to the Confessions of Faith, as exhibited in a former speech. Has the General Assembly ever condemned those Confessions? Has it refused communion with the sister Churches that hold them? Has it required that ministers, coming from those Churches, should *renounce* any portion of those Confessions? No such thing. Then, it approves them all; and the gentleman cannot deny it. Consequently, so far as the creed of Presbyterians in this country is concerned, it contains the essence of all the "degrees" of persecution, that was ever practised by its sister Churches in Europe. It requires only a free stage, and *fearless* interpreters.

He refers to the fact, that the "toleration of a false religion" is no longer printed in the Confession of Faith, as a "SIN;" to prove that Presbyterians have changed their persecuting doctrines since the Constitution. This is a sophistry; for it is essentially sinful

to tolerate what God, as they hold, commands them to "REMOVE."
The Catholic doctrine *never* taught that such toleration was *sinful*; and therefore, *it* never could change. We have seen, under the former question, that Catholic nations have been the first to grant this toleration, and never have they been reproached by their Church for it, as if it were sinful, or against any doctrine. This settles that question. The gentleman does not meet the difficulty, by quoting those parts of his standards which instruct the magistrates as to their duties. Their duties flow from the Constitution, and are determined by it, much more wisely than by the Presbyterian General Assembly. He says, that in order to "accept a civil establishment, the Presbyterian doctrine must change." To this I answer, that even if it were true, nothing is easier than this "change." But so far from its being necessary to change, in order to a union with the state, I maintain that its doctrine is expressly adapted for that union: and that the Confession of Faith is completely "out of joint," till it be accepted or secured. This I shall establish in the course of the present speech.

The doctrines of the Catholic Church, on the subject of baptism, marriage, &c., the gentleman *could* learn, if he would only read our Catechisms; but I cannot lose my time, just now, in giving him the instruction of which his remarks on these subjects prove him to stand so much in need. The gentleman, on the subject of baptism, puts two questions, in which he betrays again the meanness that would insinuate, the safeguard of the slanderer, and the cowardice that shrinks from the responsibility of direct honest assertion. If he means to *assert*, I fling his statement back on him; and challenge him to produce his testimony. If he asks for information, I tell him I have too much contempt for the grossness that could give *public utterance* to such a question, and too much respect for myself, to give it any reply. Baptism, marriage, confession, and all the other portions of the Catholic religion, may be called by any *nickname*, which he or Blanco White thinks proper to apply; but they constitute the points in which Catholics exercise their liberty of conscience; and *for this* they are persecuted by the fanatics, of whom the gentleman is a fit representative.

As to the liberty of the press, there can be no *doctrines* in the Catholic religion on that subject, more than on chemistry. But it may have been necessary to take precautions against its abuse, and this is all that the Church has ever done. All sects oppose the liberty of the press, by endeavouring to exclude such publications as expose their real or supposed errors. The writings of Catholics, and the Scriptures of Unitarians, find no favour with Presbyterians. The people of the South, in a particular crisis of society, find it absolutely necessary to check the circulation of the inflammatory publications with which they are inundated. Yet, it does not follow, that the Constitution or its principles are hostile to the liberty of the press. As little so is the Catholic religion, whatever regulations may have been made to restrain its abuse. The principles laid down in the Controversy, respecting the DOCTRINES of the Catholic religion, are maintained still. They admit of no change. They are as old as Christianity, and as universal as the Church. And as the gentleman has been unable to discover among them, any principles or tenets opposed to civil and religious liberty, it follows that such tenets cannot now, or at any future time, be incorporated with them. Laws having a persecuting tendency have been repealed in Catholic countries, and can be repealed where it has not already been done, without any violation of doctrine, without any breaking of the second commandment. These *laws* are what the gentleman, ignorantly perhaps, but certainly *falsely*, calls Catholic doctrines. This has been abundantly proved throughout the present discussion. If I had allowed him to exalt the facts or the follies, or the vices of other times, to the rank of Catholic doctrines, then his argument would have been good. But the question was *exclusively* on the doctrines:—and the doctrines were restricted exclusively to those "tenets of faith and morals, which Catholics hold as having been revealed by Almighty God."

Now let the gentleman boast of the changeableness of doctrine in the Presbyterian Church. And if they have changed, as he asserts, let the next General Assembly break communion with those *sister Presbyteries* in Europe, in whose Confessions of Faith the principle of intolerance is *avowed* as a DOCTRINE. It is avowed in the Church to which Doctor Brownlee belongs. Let them condemn it as an error in DOCTRINE. If they do not, it is their own; and the gentleman makes himself ridiculous, when he denies it. Let them revise *their own* Confession of Faith, and purge out the old leaven of Scotch and English Presbyterian intolerance, with which it is leavened. Let them receive ministers from Europe, where the gentleman acknowledges the intolerance of their doctrine, not as brethren of the same faith, but as converts from another religion, who must first renounce their *errors*, before they can be admitted into the communion and ministry of American Presbyterianism. When this is done, then let them talk of having renounced the errors of their forefathers, and European brethren, but not before. The assertions of a *change* of doctrine, so long as there are these, and a hundred other similar FACTS, to disprove it, must pass for absolutely less than nothing. They are unproved, unsupported, and in direct opposition to the testimony of FACTS.

The Catholics hold marriage to be a sacrament, which cannot be rightly administered, except in the presence of the parish priest. But this is only where the discipline of the Council of Trent is established, which it is not, in this country. Now, whether it were received or not, cannot in the least affect the civil rights of any one. We look on *Protestant marriages*, whether by the magistrate, or parson, to be as sacred and binding, as they do themselves. But they are not Catholic marriages, nor do we regard them as conferring the sacrament. We hold that the legislature or civil government, for sufficient reasons, may grant a divorce, but we hold that the parties divorced are not, therefore, at liberty to marry or violate their conjugal fidelity, until the death of one or the other. Here, the Presbyterian doctrine is more *accommodating*. It allows the husband or wife "in case of such wilful desertion, as can in no wise be remedied by the civil magistrate," to sue out a bill of divorce and MARRY AGAIN. This, the gentleman may call "liberty;" to me it seems to be licentiousness. But at any rate, we have seen that the *sister* Presbyterian Church of Holland, required that all children, whose parents were not married by THEIR CALVINISTIC MINISTERS, should be made ILLEGITIMATE BY LAW! And with the Church of Holland the Presbyterian Church in America holds communion! The gentleman seems to have forgotten all these things.

He acknowledges that he "cannot answer my arguments," and assigns as the reason, that there is "nothing to answer." On that point I leave the public to decide.

Having "nothing to answer," therefore, as he supposes, he has recourse to his old theme, the "abuse of popery." He tells us what Father Paul said. Every man acquainted with the character of Father Paul, Protestant and Catholic, knows him to have been "a Lutheran in a monk's dress." In his history of the Council of Trent, Cardinal Pallavicini pointed out and proved no less than three hundred and sixty-four falsehoods. *Such* a writer is the very authority that suits the gentleman. Dupin and Thuanus belong to the same class. But even Father Paul does not say that Protestants were put to death exclusively for exercising the rights of conscience. They attacked the doctrines of the Catholic Church, and, in doing so, in those times and countries, they attacked the religion of the people at large, *and the laws of the state.* The progress of their doctrine was synonymous with that of civil broils, sedition, rebellion, or revolution, as the gentleman may think proper to call it. They fought their doctrines into supremacy. The Catholics had the *pretext* of self-preservation for those acts which are called persecution. But when the Presbyterians persecuted they had no such *pretext.* They did it on doctrine, as the guardians of their own upstart infallibility, and the avengers of God's insulted majesty. They hanged the Quakers, *because they were Quakers,* and not because they were seditious or enemies to the state. They drowned the Baptists, *because* they deemed it, *in conscience,* a duty to rebaptize, and not because they were traitors. They made it DEATH for the Catholics to have "said or heard mass three times," *because* they exercised the right of conscience in worshipping God according to the liturgy of the Christian Church for fifteen hundred years, rather than according to the worship set up by the murderers of Servetus and of Cardinal Beaton. The exercise of the rights of conscience between man and his God, was the ONLY GROUND on which Presbyterians persecuted to death. But the persecutions by Catholics were on many other grounds, which show that mere liberty of conscience was not the exclusive plea. At the origin of the Reformation so called, the Catholics were in *possession.* This is important. The reformers possessed nothing. Liberty of conscience was, as the gentleman has himself defined it, the "*right of every man to worship God according to the dictates of his own conscience,* WITHOUT INJURING OR INVADING THE RIGHTS OF OTHERS." Now there is no instance on record in which the reformers respected *this* qualification. They claimed liberty of conscience; but the universal attestation of history is, that, under this term, they meant liberty of usurpation on the rights of others in church and state. They had nothing—they claimed to possess themselves of what belonged to others. They claimed it, they prayed for it, they preached for it, they intrigued for it, they fought for it. The martyrs of Presbyterianism, therefore, are men who fell in this struggle for domination, between those who *claimed by possession,* and those who *claimed by usurpation.* In such a case the persecution was by the usurpers, and not by the possessors. But there was no such extenuation for the persecutions of Catholics, Episcopalians, Baptists, Lutherans, Quakers, &c. whom the Presbyterians persecuted. They "invaded," they "injured" no man's *rights.* They simply wished to worship God according to the dictates of their own conscience. For *this,* and for this ALONE, they were, as we have seen, burnt, or hanged, or drowned, or whipt at the cart-tail by the Presbyterians. And why should it not be so, since God has commanded the Presbyterians, according to their book of doctrine, to "*remove* ALL FALSE WORSHIP."

Again, the Presbyterian religion was unknown in the world for fifteen hundred years after the origin of the Christian religion. If there was a Christian religion on the earth, during all that time, it was the Catholic religion. At length a few obscure individuals cry out hoarsely, that this Catholic—this Christian religion of fifteen centuries, was the church, not of Christ, but of Anti-Christ! In other words, that Christ had no church on earth; and therefore, they would make a church for him. They gave no proof that they had been appointed for this purpose—no miracles—no commission—no *extraordinary* sanctity—no motives of credibility like those that accompanied the founding of the first church, and therefore the true church. Now, until this period, Presbyterians *never persecuted;* inasmuch as, until this period, Presbyterians did not exist. Until this period the crimes and vices of Christians were those of Catholics — of men whose.

wicked lives were in open violation of the holy religion which they professed. But then, the glory of all the zeal, patience, purity and holiness, that had adorned the *Christian* name, belonged also to the Catholic Church.

We pass to another consideration. The Presbyterians having *existed* only within the last three hundred years, have been as disproportioned to the Catholics in point of *numbers* as in point of *time*. Their greatest numbers at any time, did not exceed fifteen or twenty millions. Those of the Catholics are now from a hundred and eighty to two hundred millions. Besides this, the Presbyterians have had civil power only for a short time. And it is only when a denomination has civil power, that it can show the workings of its doctrine. We have seen what were those of Presbyterianism. Not a single exception on record—not a single case in which their *doctrines* did not drive them to persecute others when they had the power! I have called on the gentleman repeatedly to name a single kingdom, or canton, or city, or village, in which the civil power belonged to Presbyterians, and they did not use it for persecution. He has not been able to name one! Not so much as ONE!!! Now, supposing they had been as *numerous* as the Catholics—supposing they had been as long in possession of civil power—and had carried out their *doctrines*, as they have done according to their *numbers* and *opportunities* within the short period of their existence, I ask whether, by this time, there would be another denomination of Christians left in existence? Would they not have "*removed all false worship?*" And especially, if, after having been established for centuries in their possession, they had been attacked by upstart and unheard of religionists, as the Catholics were at the Reformation—would they consider it persecution to have refused giving up their churches—their castles—their towns—their government—to men who wielded every concession for the destruction of those from whom it had been obtained? If to have "heard or said mass three times"—to have said "thee and thou"—to have administered baptism by *immersion*, were crimes worthy of DEATH, as we have seen in the history of Presbyterianism, what would it have been, if, having the same *civil power and numerical strength*, which the Catholics had at the time of the Reformation, individuals had arisen to pervert the Scriptures, and prove, by the perversion, that the Presbyterians were Anti-Christs, and proclaim that every blow which was struck for their *destruction*, was a blow against the apocolyptic beast? Why, sir, judging from what Presbyterians have done, during the *short period* of their *existence*, the *paucity of their numbers*, and the few opportunities they have had to persecute, it is not too much to infer that, had they occupied, in *all respects*, the position which the Catholics held at the origin of the Reformation, the advocates of what, in that case, would be the "false worship," would have been chopped up into mince-meat. No man who overlooks these circumstances can form a correct estimate of the extent to which the *doctrines* of Presbyterianism are imbued with the PRINCIPLE and ESSENCE of persecution.

The gentleman, instead of meeting these arguments, turns aside to criticise Donovan's Translation of the Trentine Catechism. I shall not follow him, unless he or his friends have confidence enough in his statements, to sacrifice their purse, to the same extent to which I charge him with having immolated truth. His episodes have no connexion with the subject, even if they were not the assumption of what is false. They are taken from Cramp, who, like Mr. Breckinridge, *begins* and *ends* his quotations in the middle of sentences;—changes the punctuation, and stops at the commencement of the portion that would refute him. The commission of frauds on the word of God is begging the question. *I* say it is the Protestant version that is corrupt; the gentleman says it is the Catholic. Who shall decide? Let those who existed before the origin of the dispute—the *impartial* witnesses—decide. Then, I shall prove the corruption of the Protestant version. It is they who have *changed*, not we. But who corrupted the Bible of the Bishop of Segovia? Who put a falsehood, known, deliberate, intentional falsehood, on the title-page of that Bible whereby to deceive the South Americans? Who gave this corrupting example to American morals? Who gave such a sacrilegious instance to prove that the "end justifies the means?" The Bible Society!! Why is the gentleman silent on that subject? It is far more important than the pretended discrepancy between two translations of the Council of Trent Catechism.

The stenographer should have been engaged by the Society. For three nights there *was none*. The report of the other nine nights did not profess to give the WORDS, but the SUBSTANCE of my arguments. I preferred the words; and did not choose that my arguments should receive their *cast* from a Presbyterian *mould*. When the gentleman proposed to compensate the stenographer by a public contribution, I regarded the proceeding as an insult both to the stenographer and the Society that was supposed to have employed him. If the Society was unable to pay him, from the proceeds of the Discussion, I proposed to pay him half, if the gentleman would pay the other half. But to impose an eleemosynary tax on the audience, to pay the stenographer, was an insult to the Society which they should have repelled promptly and indignantly. *These are the reasons* why I have not contributed, and shall not contribute to any charity collection for the stenographer.

As to the number of *Calvinistic* Baptists, the gentleman may cite any authority he pleases. When, also, in regard to the "intention" of the editor of the Catholic Telegraph, he says it was bad, *he* must prove what he says; and it is not for me, as he pretends, to prove the contrary. To a *gratuitous* assertion, the laws of reasoning authorize us to oppose a gratuitous denial. The onus probandi rests with him.

Respecting the "doom" with which he threatened Catholics in his former speech, he now says that it was "NOT PRONOUNCED BY HIM, BUT BY GOD;" and he incontinently falls into a fit of the apocolyptic mania, which has qualified so many of his predecessors for the Bedlam. Scaliger says of Calvin that he was *wise* for not having written on the Apocalypse,

<small>Sapuit Calvinus quia non scripsit in Apocalypsin.</small>

The ravings, to which this mania has driven those who have been affected with it, are as numerous and extravagant as the vagaries of the human mind, in its most disordered condition. I shall give only one specimen, from the writings of an English divine, who is considered sane notwithstanding.

"He convinced himself that the name of the beast was Lateinos, and that Lateinos must signify the Latin Church. The proof is curious. Lateinos, he contends, is derived from the Hebrew monosyllable LAT, which means to cover or conceal. Now the Latin Church, in the celebration of the mass, conceals some of the prayers from the people, by ordering them to be pronounced with a low voice: therefore the Latin Church is Lateinos, the beast in the Apocalypse. Moreover, the head of the Latin Church resides in the palace of the Lateran, a name derived from the same monosyllable LAT: and the Lateran palace is situated in the country anciently called Latium, an appellation also derived from the same monosyllable LAT: and Latium is a province of that part of Europe called Italy, which also derives its name from the same monosyllable LAT. Be not startled, gentle reader; apocalyptic maniacs can, with equal facility, read backwards or forwards; and Mr. Sharp informs us, that, if we read Italy backwards, we shall have Ylati, in the midst of which is the same Hebrew monosyllable LAT. Naviget anticyram!"

I proved that the gentleman, *following Faber*, falsified the documents to which he referred. He refers to the matter in a tone which seems to intimate, that it is more honourable to corrupt citations with Faber, than give them honestly with Mr. Hughes. With men of such *easy principles* of literary honour it is humiliating to have to contend. With men who are unwilling or incompetent to consult history at the *original fountains*, but who have to take information at *second hand*, without knowing what is true from what is false—with such men controversy and discussion give disgust, and no laurels. Yet such men are the fittest to maintain the position which the gentleman occupies.

As to the "nursing fathers," the gentleman, after various fruitless attempts to explain it as meaning nothing at all, at length takes the true interpretation, and refers to the Prophecies of Isaiah to prove it should be so. Now this is precisely the doctrine of his church; and the arguments by which I showed its dangerous and unfriendly bearing on liberty of conscience and the rights of other denominations—remain unanswered and untouched.

He lauds the Sunday School Union with eulogy, which *may be* deserved, or at least needed; but neither does he touch or meet *my arguments*, on that subject. He represents me as among those who "fear, hate, and assail it in vain." The charge is false and futile. Of its merits or demerits, I have not spoken. I have commented *on its own published documents*, in which was avowed the plan to ALTER BOOKS, and YET KEEP THEIR TITLES, TO CHANGE THE IDEAS OF AUTHORS, TO EDUCATE A POLITICAL INFLUENCE, WHICH IN "TEN, OR AT MOST, TWENTY YEARS," WAS TO WIELD OR CONTROL THE DESTINIES OF THIS COUNTRY, AND IN A WORD "TO DICTATE TO THE SOULS OF THOUSANDS OF IMMORTAL BEINGS." What I attacked, the gentleman does not reply to; what I did *not* attack, he defends. And here let me observe, once for all, that Mr. Frelinghuysen, Mr. Sergeant, Mr. Ralston, Mr. Henry, and the other names which the gentleman has paraded in this discussion, as if they stood in need of vindication, had never been attacked by me. I beg those gentlemen, if they should ever see this Discussion, to be assured that I entertain as much respect for their character, as the gentleman can do; and too much to suppose for a moment, that *they* would ever sanction the grasping ambition of the pretensions which I have censured in the Sunday School Union, or the impressing of a falsehood on the title-page of a Bible, in order to deceive the Spaniards, as has been done by the Bible Society. I wish them to know that it is the gentleman, and not I, that has brought their names forward, *to cover those proceedings over with the mantle of their respectability*. The "PREFACE" was as much by the authority of the Sunday School, as if it had been a "REPORT." He had said it was "false." What does he say now? Does he meet it? Does he justify it? Does he condemn it? NEITHER. There it is, and he has not a word to reply to it.

He refers again to the Synod at York, and Mr. Barnes's case. In all my reading of Synods, either Catholic, or Protestant, I never saw more of the spirit of tyranny over conscience, and of persecution, than was in that case exhibited by the majority. If the power had been as the will seems to have been, Mr. Barnes would have fared no better than the fifteen deputies of the Arminians, who, *after having been invited to the Presbyterian Synod of Dort*, were, on the condemnation of their supposed errors, seized, imprisoned, and hurried into banishment, without being allowed to take leave of their families; as is related by Brandt. If the orthodox brethren at York had had the "nursing fathers" at their command, as they had in Holland, there was spirit enough in the Synod, to treat Mr. Barnes and his friends in the same way. Here was liberty of conscience! Here was the principle of not keeping faith with heretics, fully and authoritatively acted on. First, invite the Arminians to the Synod, then seize their persons and send them into exile, *for being Arminians, and for no other crime.*

The Secreta Monita, of which the gentleman has spoken, is known to every scholar in Europe to be spurious. Even in the British Parliament, it was denounced by as great a bigot as need be, Leslie Foster, as a FORGERY. This very character, or rather merit, in the eyes of bigots every where, may have been the cause of its publication recently in Princeton. Such a work comes appropriately from such a quarter.

Of the Inquisition I have said, that so far as it is an ecclesiastical concern, the principle of it is common to all Churches having orthodox creeds; it is only another name for that spirit of heresy-hunting, with which old Presbyterianism is so thoroughly imbued. So far as it was a tribunal for the dispensation of temporal punishment, it was "ENTIRELY AND AVOWEDLY A POLITICAL AND NOT AN ECCLESIASTICAL INSTITUTION." This account corresponds perfectly with that of Devoti; it is founded in history and truth, as the gentleman is culpably ignorant if he does not know. There is no subject of history on which there is so much ignorance and misinformation abroad, as on the Inquisition. I neither defend nor approve of it. But the very feature, which was most objectionable in it, that which made it so terrible, and left no data for those who would be its historians, was its SECRECY. It tried men for other crimes besides heresy, crimes which were punishable with death in all countries. But of its *victims,* there is no evidence that it kept any record, whilst its secrecy warrants the belief that it did not. Llorentte, and those who have written on it, drew on their imaginations just like Miss Monk, in describing the Convent at Montreal. But besides, those writers were ministering to that morbid appetite, which feasts on the *pretended disclosures* of proceedings which they know to have been conducted in SECRECY. Hence, even the British Critic, an English PROTESTANT REVIEW, says of the work of Llorentte, that "*although it might be too much to say, that the* WHOLE *is false, yet that there can be no more than a weak tincture of truth,* LARGELY DASHED AND BREWED WITH LIES."

With regard to Mr. Ansley, the event has justified my prediction; that "so far as I was concerned at least, the gentleman's insinuations were founded on falsehood, and must recoil upon their source." So it is proven by Bishop Doane's letter. Of that document, the gentleman may make what use he thinks proper. I wash my hands of all proceedings, having for their object to expose the domestic concerns of any family. To the gentleman alone, must belong the undivided glory of this *magnanimous* achievement. He breaks in on the domestic sanctuary of a family, with which he has nothing to do; he hears the gossip of disagreement between husband and wife; *he writes for more*, he knows nothing of the cause, and yet with a heartlessness and indelicacy, which must plant a wound in the breast of a father like himself, and a wife like his own, and children *who have committed no fault*, he blazons these sacred topics in a book!! All to inflict a wound on Popery! And yet he fails. Mr. Ansley had been a Protestant minister; and of his own accord, in the exercise of his rights of conscience, he became a Catholic. This was his crime. Supposing I were to make the manner in which Mr. Breckinridge treats his wife and family the subject of a scandulous dissertation in this Discussion; what would he say? What would the public say? And yet the domestic sanctuary of every man is, or ought to be, as inviolable and as sacred as his. I would not be the author of what he has said on this subject, as he has said it, for all the exchequer of his Church.

I shall now turn to the prosecution of my argument.

We have seen that on the continent of Europe, in Great Britain, Ireland, and New England, that is, in every country in which they existed, Presbyterians persecuted all other denominations when they had the civil power to do so. There is no exception. This they did, as appears by all their CONFESSIONS to which I refer, as quoted in a former speech, on a principle of doctrine. The gentleman began his defence, by disowning and denouncing those European Presbyterians, as unsound in the faith, and as holding errors which *his Church, in this country, since the formation of the Federal Constitution,* has rejected and condemned. I have proved the contrary by FACTS, that are uncontroverted and uncontrovertible, viz: that his Church HOLDS COMMUNION with those sister Churches of Europe; and receives their ministers, not as *converts*, but as brethren *of the* SAME FAITH. Consequently, his Church has not seen any error in the doctrinal intolerance of those foreign Presbyterian creeds. This, therefore, settles *that* question.

He has said, that when Presbyterians teach that God has given them a divine commission to "REMOVE ALL FALSE WORSHIP," the phrase does not mean *force*. Its meaning can be determined only by the intention or understanding of those who framed the creed. Did they mean that this doctrine should be understood to authorize employment of coercion by the state? I answer, that they did; and I shall proceed to prove it.—The Presbyterians had the power of the state, during the whole time of the session of that Assembly, by whom the Confession of Faith was drawn up. They had an opportunity of *proving what it meant,* on the subject of conscience, toleration, &c. Doctor Lightfoot informed the House of Commons, on this subject, that "certainly the devil in the conscience might be, yea, must be bound by the civil magistrate." (1)

In order to show its meaning, we have the fact, that in 1645, they published an ordinance, forbidding the use of the EPISCOPAL COMMON PRAYER-BOOK, not only in places of "public worship," but also "IN ANY PRIVATE PLACE OR FAMILY," under the penalties of "FINES AND IMPRISONMENT."(2) This is what was meant by "removing all *false worship.*" In the same year, they made Lawrence Clarkson, a Baptist, renounce his error of baptizing adult persons, for which exercise of the rights of conscience they had kept him for *six months in a dungeon.*(3) In January of the next year, the "Presbyterian ministers," says Neal, ... " prevailed with the Lord Mayor, and Court of Aldermen, to join with them in presenting to Parliament, an Address,"—" FOR A SPEEDY SETTLEMENT OF CHURCH GOVERNMENT, ACCORDING TO THE COVENANT, AND THAT NO TOLERATION MIGHT BE GIVEN TO POPERY, PRELACY, SUPERSTITION, HERESY, PROFANENESS, OR ANY THING CONTRARY TO SOUND DOCTRINE, AND THAT ALL PRIVATE ASSEMBLIES MIGHT BE RESTRAINED."(4) They held that "toleration was, and would be a root of gall and bitterness;" that it was "soul-poison;" "a sword in the hands of a madman;" "a city of refuge in men's conscience, for the devil to fly to."(5) "The whole Scots' nation," demanded of the Parliament of England, that the civil sanction might be added to support the Westminster creed, "AS THE DIVINES HAD ADVISED;" and what that advice was, may be gathered from the fact, that they conclude with the hope " THAT THE PIETY AND WISDOM OF THE HONOURABLE HOUSES, WILL NEVER ADMIT TOLERATION OF ANY SECTS OR SCHISMS, CONTRARY TO OUR SOLEMN LEAGUE AND COVENANT."(6) Again we find them complaining, that "congregations were ALLOWED" to judge for themselves, in matters of religion, and beseeching Parliament, " *that all separate congregations may be suppressed; that all such separatists, who conform not to the public discipline, may be declared against; that no person disaffected to the Presbyterial government set forth by Parliament, may be employed in any place of public trust,*" &c.(7) They presented a petition to the king at Newcastle, in which among other laws for the grinding of conscience, they required that the Episcopal religion should be utterly abolished *by law*, and that a law should be passed to sanction the kidnapping of Catholic children, in order to educate them "in the Protestant religion."(8) In another petition to the Parliament, they entreat that "ALL SEPARATE CONGREGATIONS, THE VERY NURSERIES OF DAMNABLE HERE-

(1) Crosby, vol. i. p. 176. (2) Neal's Hist. of Pur., vol. iii. p. 171.
(3) Crosby. (4) Neal, vol. iii. p. 291.
(5) Ibid. p. 313. (6) Ibid. p. 314.
(7) Ibid. p. 329. (8) Ibid. p. 332.

TICS, MAY BE SUPPRESSED; AND THAT AN ORDINANCE BE MADE FOR THE EXEMPLARY PUNISHMENT OF HERETICS, AND SCHISMATICS," &c.(1) The Parliament, "*to satisfy the petitioners*," says Neal, declared their resolution to proceed against "*all such ministers, and others, as shall* PUBLISH, or MAINTAIN BY PREACHING, WRITING, PRINTING, or *any other way, anything against, or in derogation of Church government,*" (Presbyterianism.) (2) The celebrated Edwards, in the Preface to his *Gangræna*, lays down the principle and meaning of the commandment about "REMOVING ALL FALSE WORSHIP," which is still in the gentleman's Confession of Faith. " Now," says he, addressing the civil rulers, "A CONNIVANCE AT, AND SUFFERING WITHOUT PUNISHMENT, SUCH 'FALSE DOCTRINES,' AND DISORDERS, PROVOKES GOD TO SEND JUDGMENTS. A TOLERATION DOTH ECLIPSE THE GLORY OF THE MOST EXCELLENT REFORMATION, AND MAKES THESE SINS TO BE THE SINS OF THE LEGISLATURE THAT COUNTENANCES THEM. A MAGISTRATE SHOULD USE COERCIVE POWER TO PUNISH AND SUPPRESS EVILS, AS APPEARS FROM THE EXAMPLE OF ELI."(3) Among the charges to prove the necessity for persecution, he mentions that one of the Independents had the *impiety* to pray "*two or three times, that Parliament might give liberty to tender consciences.*"(4) When the Parliament was in danger from the growing strength of the army, the Scotch Presbyterians being invoked by their English brethren, "*published a declaration, in the name of the kirk, and whole kingdom, wherein they engage, by a* SOLEMN OATH, to establish the Presbyterian government in England," . . . . . and declare against "all toleration and liberty of conscience."(5)

The Scotch Commissioners in London were remonstrating, in the name of their National Church, against the introduction of a " sinful and ungodly toleration in the matters of religion," whilst the whole body of the English Presbyterian clergy, in their official papers, protested against the schemes of Cromwell's party, and solemnly declared, " that they detested and abhorred toleration." " My judgment," said Baxter, a man noted in his day for moderation, " I have always freely made known. I abhor unlimited liberty or toleration of all." " Toleration," said Edwards, another distinguished divine, " will make the kingdom a chaos, a Babel, another Amsterdam, a Jordan, an Egypt, a Babylon. Toleration is the grand work of the Devil, his master-piece, and chief engine to uphold his tottering kingdom. It is a most compendious, ready, sure way to destroy all religion, lay all waste, and bring in all evil. It is a most transcendent, catholic, and fundamental evil. As original sin is the fundamental sin, having the

(1) Neal, vol. iii. p. 364.   (2) Ibid.
(3) Ibid. Append.   (4) Ibid.
(5) Ibid. p. 400.

seed and spawn of all sins in it, so toleration hath all errors in it, and all evils." (1)

These, and many other authorities that might be adduced, prove unanswerably the meaning of the Presbyterian commandment, as it was understood by the Westminster Assembly, that drew it up. The meaning, therefore, in their minds, was simply this—that it was the duty of those who had the civil power, "according to each one's place and calling," to support the Presbyterian Church alone, and to make penal laws, and execute them too, against all those who, in the exercise of their judgment, should adopt, or maintain, any other religion or mode of worship under the "much abused name of liberty of conscience." The gentleman may say, that Presbyterians, *in this country, since the Constitution*, have given that commandment a new *interpretation;* but he must have been extremely unacquainted with the times, history, and circumstances of that doctrine as first promulgated, when he ventured to say that meant *only* "moral influence, the press, preaching, the Bible," &c. It meant FINES, PRISONS, and DEATH. Under its original and TRUE "meaning," Catholics, Episcopalians, Baptists, Quakers and others were to be punished by whatever laws and penalties the "ordinance of magistracy" might find *necessary* for the "REMOVAL OF ALL FALSE WORSHIP AND ALL THE MONUMENTS OF IDOLATRY." Does the gentleman deny this? Here is the proof. In 1648, "the Presbyterian members," says Neal ....."finding they had the superiority in the house, *resumed their courage,* and took the opportunity of discovering their PRINCIPLES and SPIRIT...." How did they discover their principles and spirit? By passing a law against heretics, as they called them, but in reality for the carrying out of the second commandment, as it still stands in the American Presbyterian Confession of Faith. It was passed on the 2d of May, 1648: and ordains *"that all persons who shall willingly* MAINTAIN, PUBLISH, *or* DEFEND, *by* PREACHING *or* WRITING, *the following heresies with obstinacy, shall, upon complaint, and proof, by the oaths of two witnesses, before two justices of the peace, or confession of the party, be committed to prison,* WITHOUT BAIL *or* MAINPRIZE, *till the next gaol delivery; and in case the indictment shall then be found, and the party upon his trial shall not abjure his said error, and his defence and maintenance of the same,* HE SHALL SUFFER THE PAINS OF DEATH, AS IN CASE OF FELONY, WITHOUT BENEFIT OF CLERGY...." This was evidence of zeal against "ALL FALSE RELIGION." You observe, sir, the inhuman features of this law, independent of the "pains of death without benefit of clergy." 1. The oaths of "two witnesses" were sufficient. 2. The exercise of the rights of conscience was deemed, *like murder,* too grievous a crime to admit of "bail or mainprize." 3. It did not allow even the pri-

(1) Verplank's Discourses, pp. 23, 24.

vilege of JURY. 4. Neither did it allow the *liberty of appeal.* Presbyterian Legislators,—Presbyterian witnesses,—Presbyterian judges,—Presbyterian hangmen,—having first the "commandment of God," and next the "law of the land," were thus doubly bound, "*according to each one's place and calling,* (mind that,) *to remove all false worship and all the monuments of idolatry.*" The gentleman may say that no one suffered under this Presbyterian law. But this is easily accounted for. Cromwell drove these spiritual despots from power, before they had an opportunity of putting it in execution. It is the only act of his life for which posterity have reason to be grateful to that profound hypocrite— who was himself a disciple of the Presbyterian school, and did honour to the tuition. But supposing that the Presbyterians had remained in power, and it were our misfortune to live under their mild, tolerant, and liberty-loving principles, what then would be the fact? Why the fact would be, that the UNITARIANS, UNIVERSALISTS, SWEDENBORGIANS, DEISTS, and all those who come under the denominations of INFIDELS would be, ipso facto, under sentence of "DEATH WITHOUT BENEFIT OF CLERGY!"—A murderer, even then would be allowed a clergyman on the scaffold, or at the gallows, but a heretic of the above description should die "without benefit of clergy." By the same "ordinance" the DUNGEON was provided for another class of heretics—which class embraces in the actual state of the religious world, all CATHOLICS, all EPISCOPALIANS, all METHODISTS, all BAPTISTS, and all OTHER DENOMINATIONS, present and future, *except predestinarian Presbyterians.* Does the gentleman venture to deny this? Let him consult the ordinance in Neal, (Vol. iii. p. 484–5,) and the list of errors specifically enumerated as constituting the "false worship" against which the ordinance was levelled, "according to each one's place and calling." I give the gentleman chapter and verse, day and date, for my facts. Neither do I draw my authorities from Tristam Shandy, or renegades from his religion. The writings of the most respectable Protestant, and even Presbyterian ministers and fathers are the fountains from which I derive my testimony of facts, and facts too that should make a Presbyterian BLUSH, whenever any one, (*forgetting who is present,*) happens to mention the words "liberty of conscience."

He may say that this was an act of Parliament;—for which his doctrine is not responsible. Such an assertion would be a fallacy. His doctrine obliges "ALL its members," and each, "*according to his place and calling*"—" to remove false worship." So that a member of Parliament then, or a member of Congress now, is bound to use his *official,* as well as personal, influence to secure this end. The Constitution clothes him with power to be used exclusively in support of the provisions contained in that bill of rights. Hence he is bound, not only *not* to "remove, but to protect, and consequently, *in so much,* preserve "all false religions and all the monuments of idolatry." And yet he professes a creed, the doctrines of which oblige him, by a COMMANDMENT OF GOD, not only to remove them, but even to use his *official* power and influence for that purpose—"ACCORDING TO HIS PLACE AND CALLING." Is there no contradiction here? Is he faithful to the Constitution?—Then he is a traitor to his creed, by disobeying what it commands. Is he true to his creed?—Does he labour, "*according to his place and calling,*" to "remove" all those religions, which the Presbyterian Catechism, Book of Doctrines, arrogantly denominates "false worships?" Then he is a dangerous man to be entrusted with the rights of a free people, who claim to worship Almighty God according to the dictates of their conscience. The members of Parliament, therefore, in passing the above ordinance, were only obeying the commandment of God, as PRESBYTERIANS, "according to their place and calling." But again, it is remarkable that this inhuman law was passed while the Confession of Faith drawn up by the divines of Westminster, *was actually under consideration in the House of Commons*, by whom it was approved on the twentieth of the following month. Not only this, but during the whole session of the Assembly there was a perpetual "billing and cooing" between them and the houses of Parliament; the divines instructing the legislators to make laws against heretics and heresies; and the legislators instructing the divines to make doctrines, by which Presbyterianism might be uppermost, with its iron heel on the necks of all other denominations.

From all this, therefore, the meaning of the second commandment, as expounded by the known and professed intolerance of *those who made it*, is clear, and undeniable. The gentleman did wrong to deny it. He should have known something of its history, and not have put me to the trouble of unfolding it. If the meaning of a book is to be determined by the meaning of *its authors*, then this doctrine of the Westminster Confession of Faith, was *knowingly* and *intentionally* framed to secure spiritual domination to the sect of Presbyterians, and to crush and persecute all other denominations by means of the civil sword and the power of the magistrate. God, who puts limits to the wickedness of men, permitted them to remain in power just long enough to show, by the above ordinance, that their principles should make them a terror to mankind. And when they had prepared their engine of cruelty, to make *legal slaughter* for the vindication of his honour and the true religion, as extensive as their civil domination, he transferred to other hands the sword on which they had seized by usurpation, and of which they were preparing to make such bloody use.

The only question remaining is, whether the Presbyterians in *this age*, and in *this country*, are at liberty to *interpret* their standard of doctrine differently from the sense and meaning intended by the Westminster divines. I say they are NOT. And for the proof I refer to the whole reasoning on which it is attempted to justify the condemnation of Mr. Barnes. His crime (if crime it be) has consisted exclusively in his giving a new interpretation to the Confession of Faith. Therefore, the *true*, ORTHODOX meaning of the Presbyterian doctrines, is the meaning in which they were held by the WESTMINSTER ASSEMBLY—what that was, we have seen above, in the ordinance to which I have referred;—and now, sir, I leave it to you, to this audience, and to the public at large, to say whether this doctrine is not opposed to both civil and religious liberty.

If Presbyterians had the power to carry it out, and *were faithful to what they profess to regard as one of God's commandments*, I ask you whether this doctrine would not be fatal to all that we understand by "rights of conscience." Whilst these Presbyterians were thus making arrangements to lord it over men's souls, and bodies, and property, in England, what was going on in Ireland? What were the officers of this Parliament doing in that ill-fated country? They were not only making it *lawful* to commit murder and assassination, but the murderer and the assassin, in presenting a human head at their council of blood, received as a PENSION the reward which was appointed for killing a WOLF!! (1)

It is true, that the murderer was required to swear that it was the head of a "Catholic priest"—and if he swore that oath, no matter whose head it was, he received his wages! Thus, the conditions of the service were so regulated that the premium was an incentive to murder and perjury at the same time! And the man holding and glorying in the doctrines of the men under whom and by whom *these scenes of horror and blood* made the earth sick—that man pushes himself forward, to make a fuss about "civil and religious liberty!" Let him read the history of his church. We have seen what it was in Switzerland, the Low Countries, Scotland, and every other country where Presbyterians possessed civil power. We have seen what it was in England, *by the very men who made the gentleman's Confession of Faith*, and what it would have been, if that country had continued to be cursed much longer with their spiritual and temporal domination and despotism. In the midst of all this, in their hypocritical confessions of sins, they never failed to ask pardon of Heaven for the sin of "TOLERATION!!" And whilst they were themselves under penal disabilities for conscience' sake — whilst they were petitioning for their *own rights* of conscience, they never failed to represent, as one of their greatest grievances, that *the penal laws were not enforced rigorously enough against the Catholics*. They held that God was angry with *them*, for the culpable mercy of the government in not torturing the Catholics with the rigorous

(1) Curry's Review of the Civil Wars in Ireland, vol. ii. p. 11.

execution of the persecuting laws. These laws I have given a brief outline of, in my last speech on the former question, to which I refer.

The gentleman has told you that all this has been changed in this country. The CONSTITUTION has indeed changed the *working* of the system—but it did not change the principle of its doctrine. We have seen what that principle is, as it respects "false worship." The General Assembly holds, even at this day, communion with the establishment and intolerance of the Scotch Creed, and the Dutch Confession. And this fact proves what the gentleman, with great perseverance, but with fatal forgetfulness of history and facts, has attempted to deny. The creed of the Dutch Reformed Church, of which Dr. Brownlee is minister, teaches, in this country and AGAINST THE CONSTITUTION, that it is the "office" of the MAGISTRATES to take measures whereby to "REMOVE and PREVENT ALL IDOLATRY and FALSE WORSHIP."

From what has been said, it is manifest that the assertion made by the gentleman, viz., that in order "to accept a civil establishment the Presbyterian doctrine must change," is, like a great many of his assertions—*not to be depended on*. It is not only in opposition to the bonds of communion between his Church in this country, and the sister churches that are "civilly established" in Europe, but it is in opposition to his Confession of Faith, in which he is instructed to pray for that very establishment, under the article—"THY KINGDOM COME." At page 309 of the Confession, the Presbyterians are instructed to pray that "the church..... *may be countenanced and* MAINTAINED *by the civil magistrate*." The same Book of Doctrines decides (page 3) that "the Church" is composed of those "who profess the true religion;" and it decides also, as a matter of course, that the "true religion" is the Presbyterian religion. Therefore it is manifest that the Presbyterian Church not only does *not* refuse, but actually PRAYS for, and aspires to, "a civil establishment." For what else but a "civil establishment" does it mean when it claims to be not only "countenanced," but *MAINTAINED*, by the "CIVIL MAGISTRATE?" That the gentleman should be ignorant of the history of his Church did not surprise me; but that he should be ignorant of its very doctrines, actually and openly professed in the CONFESSION OF FAITH, is more than I expected. If he was not ignorant of it, how can we account for his saying that "in order to accept a civil establishment, the Presbyterian doctrine must change?" His own Catechism refutes him, and shows, as well by its doctrine, as its history, that it *was made expressly for a "civil establishment,"* and is essentially "out of joint" till it shall be "MAINTAINED BY THE CIVIL MAGISTRATE."

Now, sir, is this constitutional? Here is the doctrine, ready to produce the same effects *here*, that it has done in all other countries. I have pointed out some of those effects. Let the gentleman himself meditate on the facts and arguments that have been adduced. I do not ask him to *answer them;* he has already, and from the beginning, had the good sense not to expose himself by attempting to refute them. But I wish him to *meditate* on them. And to assist him, let him bear in mind the following considerations:—1. That John Calvin was the founder of his religion. 2. That it was propagated, not by peace and persuasion, but by tumult and riot in the various countries in which it prevailed. 3. That it preached and fought its way into civil power, by invading the rights of others. 4. That when in power, it *persecuted in every instance without exception.* 5. That all other denominations of Protestants were the victims of its persecution, as well as Catholics. 6. That it made "ex post factum" laws EXPRESSLY FOR THE PURPOSE OF PERSECUTING. 7. That its members were, at all times, comparatively few. 8. And its enjoyment of the civil sword limited to *brief periods.* 9. That it had itself suffered for conscience' sake, and should have learnt *mercy* from experience. 10. That notwithstanding all these adverse circumstances, it *shed the blood of man,* and made laws for shedding it in torrents, in every country where it had power to make and execute them. 11. That it *justified* all these atrocities on the plea *that God had authorized,* nay, commanded it, "to remove all false religions, and all the monuments of" what it was impudently pleased to nickname "idolatry"—meaning thereby the religion of the great society of Christians of all nations from the time of the apostles to the present day. Let him meditate on it, in connexion with *these circumstances,* and it will appear that "eye hath not seen, nor ear heard, neither hath it entered into the heart of man to conceive," (so far as the civil and religious rights are concerned) any thing more intolerant, tyrannical, persecuting, bloodthirsty and remorseless, than the dark spirit which John Calvin and John Knox breathed, as the living soul, into the Presbyterian doctrines. Let the gentleman meditate upon the facts—in Switzerland, France, the Netherlands, Scotland, England, Ireland and America.

The hurry of arrangement, and the disorder and confusion by which the gentleman has laboured to keep the *real question* out of view, have necessarily prevented me from doing entire justice to a subject, on which too little is understood. But this I say, that the man, who, in the name of human nature, and the Christian religion, and civil and religious liberty, should write a regular history of Presbyterianism, especially of its persecuting doctrines, would render an incalculable service to his country. He would open the eyes of thousands; he would tear away the mask of hypocrisy under which Presbyterian ambition is now, and has been for years, labouring for a political predominancy, whereby to control this nation from north to south, and from east to west. Finding the stoppage of the Sunday mail too knotty a block for their entering-wedge, they have changed their tactics, but not their object. They think that by using the NO POPERY cry, as a feeler, they have discovered the "soft place" in the head of public opinion, and are trying to hunt down the Catholics to the tune of "hurra for religious liberty." It will not do, sir. Most of the other denominations in this country, are satisfied to enjoy their own liberty of conscience, without invading that sacred right in the person of their neighbours, even though these should be Catholics. Not so the true blue Presbyterian. He professes a creed whose doctrine of absolute election removes all apprehension *for his own sins*, but leaves him to feel remorse for *all* the sins of *all* his neighbours. Now I owe it to truth and candour to state my conviction, that there are hundreds and thousands of Presbyterians who are utterly unacquainted with the hereditary and inherent intolerance of their creed—who would be among the first to resist the spirit of those doctrines, as exemplified in the sectarian and political aspirations of some of their own ministers. Men who, as Americans, feel humbled at the fact that there is in their country enough of the spirit of persecution, to destroy the property and endanger the lives of defenceless ladies, for no other crime, *except that of worshipping Almighty God according to the dictates of their conscience!* But the gentleman is not of the number; his associates, Dr. Brownlee & Co. are not to be numbered with those *real* friends of civil and religious liberty.

I must now notice some of the miscellaneous matter of his speech. And, 1. HIS PERSONALITY AND ABUSE. After having expended every epithet of contempt—"Jesuit," "Papist," "Foreigner," &c. &c. he winds up with the charge of "malignity." I am not surprised at all this; it is a part of the system which he represents. During ten years that I have resided in this city, I have had intercourse with society of all denominations; I have preached nearly every Sunday during that time, oftentimes on controversy, when hundreds of Protestants were present, and I venture to assert that I have not done one action or used one expression, in the pulpit or out of it, to warrant the charge of "malignity." I have wounded no man's feelings; I have ridiculed no man's religion; I have injured no man's character. I have the consolation to believe, therefore, that in the community where I am known, the charge of "malignity" will recoil on its author, and not affect me. I am proud to believe, and have reason to believe, that, though a Catholic and a priest, I stand as high in public, even Protestant estimation, as the gentleman himself. The secret of his accusation is, that, having forced himself on my notice, and compelled me to enter into an oral disputation, I have taught him a few facts respecting his religion, as well as mine, with which he was unacquainted before. Not only this, I established arguments on the basis of those facts, which he is unable to answer. This was very "malignant" to be sure. He says I directed all my "malignant attacks against the Presbyterian religion." Certainly: what had I to do with any other? But greater men than I have been honoured with this species of Calvinistic argument. The appellation of "HOGS," was among the gentlest that Calvin himself could bestow on his theological or literary antagonists. About the time of the Westminster Assembly, the Episcopalians of England were known in the vocabulary of the Presbyterians as the "MALIGNANTS," or the "MALIGNANT FACTION." When John Wesley ventured to preach a sermon on "free grace," in opposition to Calvin's decrees, Mr. Toplady, a worthy son of Geneva, described him, as "hatching blasphemy"—"having a forehead PETRIFIED, and IMPERVIOUS TO A BLUSH"—a "shameless traducer."(1) But the best of the joke is, that he charges me with being personal and abusive!! It is true that I have had to prove his assertions false, continually, and to expose his vitiated citation of authors, as well as his bad reasoning. Now he ought not to mistake *this* for abuse. The *fault* was his, mine was the *duty*. It is true, that I have sometimes retorted, but with milder words, and perhaps more point.

2. MORALITY. He *assumes* that Protestant countries are more moral than Catholic countries. Is this the fact? In the first place we have the testimony of the Reformers themselves, showing that those who embraced the new doctrines became *less moral* than they had been. Luther says, "*we see that, through the malice of the devil, men are now more avaricious, more cruel, more disorderly, more insolent, and much more wicked than they were under popery.*"(2) Musculus says, "*If any one wish to see a multitude of knaves, disturbers of the public peace, &c. let him go to a city where the gospel is preached in its purity.*"(3) ..... The testimony of *all* the other Reformers, as they are called, is to the same effect. Secondly, their *doctrine* was adverse to morals. The Scripture says we are saved by *faith*, but this was not sufficient, and they accordingly corrupted the text by inserting "faith ALONE." Thirdly, the decrees of the Presbyterian religion, setting forth, that God has "FOREORDAINED WHATSOEVER COMES TO PASS," is fatal to morals—by establishing the doctrine that the crimes of the wicked were "foreordained," as well as the virtues of the good. Hence the gentleman is flying in the face of his own decrees, whenever he blames immorality. Fourthly, the gentleman's estimate of morality in Catholic countries is not founded on observation; not on criminal statistics; not on impartial history, but on books written in the spirit of MRS. TROLLOPE, and MISS REED, and MISS MARIA

(1) See Fletcher's Checks, vol. 4. p. 71. (2) In Postil. Dom. part 1.
(3) Musc. Dom. i. Adv.

MONK, combined. Fifthly; it is not fair to compare the profligate portions of society in Catholic countries, with the religious portions of Protestant lands. But, comparing each class with its corresponding class, it will be found that the Catholics have more piety, and are of a more amiable character; that they have more sanctity, with less sanctimoniousness. Finally, that knavery, intellectual immorality, the general system of swindling, which in the large cities of Protestant countries is reduced to the precision of a science, are almost unknown in Catholic countries. The corruption of the heart is the same every where; but, in confirmation of the remark I have just made, it is to be observed that Protestant countries are distinguished by two vices—crimes in particular which were unknown among CHRISTIANS before the Reformation, and are still almost unknown in Catholic countries— FORGERY and SUICIDE. The Calvinists of Holland, rather than lose the trade of Japan, submit to a ceremony which is understood by those who require a compliance, to *be a renunciation of Christ and his religion* — viz., "trampling on the cross." The Catholics gave up the trade, and suffered death rather than comply with it.

3. COMPARATIVE WEALTH. Here the gentleman furnishes no proof. But he forgets some important facts. For instance, that in Protestant countries, the disciples of Calvin, at least, appropriated to themselves the *property* as well as the power of the Catholics, whom they dispossessed of both. So it was in Scotland and England; heretics and idolaters had no right to property. Hence, the *wealth*, and *estates*, and *church property* of Catholics, were seized upon as a ready stock in trade for the saints to commence with. Ireland remained Catholic, and the soil was taken THREE DIFFERENT TIMES from its owners, to enrich the exchequer of Protestant cupidity. I refer to the penal laws cited in my last speech on the former question, to show that the poverty and ignorance of the Irish are the EFFECTS *of Protestant persecution*. Plunder was made lawful, in order to crush them. Education was made *criminal* by the laws, until, within a few years. They preserved their integrity, their religion, and were *robbed of every thing* besides. Their mental independence, with their poverty, is more honourable than the ill-gotten wealth and infamy that cling to their oppressors. The gentleman, therefore, has been unfortunate in his allusion to the wealth of Protestant countries— especially so far as England, Scotland and Ireland are concerned. He ought to have let that subject rest.

4. CELIBACY OF THE PRIESTS AND NUNS. The manner in which the whole class of writers to which the gentleman belongs, treat this topic, and mix it up with imputations of lewdness, betrays the diseased state of their own imaginations, and reminds one of the food and the feast of the hyena. These uxorious parsons, who study the DAUGHTERS of the Church, in-

stead of "the FATHERS"—who, in times of pestilence, take refuge behind the breast-work of their wives and children, and leave their dying members, body and soul, to be taken care of by the sisters of charity and priests, these are the men who, when pestilence has departed, turn round to taunt us with celibacy, and argue as if *they* held the indulgence of lewdness to be a necessity of human nature, and the virtue of chastity to be impossible! On what data do they build such a conclusion? It must be either on innate depravity, or else on experience among their own people. But in neither case is it good reasoning to make the conclusion *general*, when the premises are only *particular*. At all events, the gospel of Christ makes chastity an obligation; and there is no reason why it should be more difficult for priests and nuns, than for UNMARRIED PERSONS GENERALLY, OF BOTH SEXES, AND OF ALL DENOMINATIONS. The reputation of all these, therefore, is wounded by the shafts of base suspicion which the parsons aim at the priests and nuns alone. They would not allow their wives and daughters to go to confession. What does this prove? It proves that, from whatever source *they* may have derived their vile estimate of human nature, they have no confidence in the virtue of their wives and daughters, any more than in that of the priests! But the gentleman says, that indelicate questions are asked. I say, the assertion is FALSE. The priest, who should so far forget the sacredness of his ministry as to abuse the confidence of the confessional, is, by the laws of the Church, DEGRADED FROM OFFICE FOR LIFE. And, in Catholic countries, is doomed to PERPETUAL IMPRISONMENT ON BREAD AND WATER. Is there any such protection against the abuse of nightly and anxious-meetings, among the parsons? I believe not. Finally, who is the blameless parson among them, to whom we cannot oppose as blameless a priest? And who is the bad priest to whom we cannot oppose a worse parson? Their wives have not been able to shield them, in all cases, from either the imputation or the guilt of crime. And among them the instances are as numerous as among us. For that class of parsons who treat the subject of celibacy as the gentleman has done, these remarks are deemed sufficient—to the more dignified ministers of the Protestant churches of every denomination they are not intended to apply.

5. HIS CONTRADICTIONS. To enumerate these in detail, would take up more space than can be spared. At one time, Catholics wanted only power and numbers to destroy the Protestants, root and branch; at another, when they possessed all power and numbers, they were not able to put down the Reformers! At one time, we are charged with having exalted matrimony to the rank of a sacrament; at another, we are charged with treating it contemptuously! At one time, the Church is accused for not punishing the real or pretended vices of the clergy, and removing the scandals given; at another, she is accused of tyranny

for having made laws *expressly for this purpose!* Now, the Pope is represented as commanding the world, and our liberties are gone if he only raise his little finger; and now, he is a powerless old man, supported on his throne only by Austrian bayonets! Thus it is, that in the logical analysis of the gentleman's argument, we discover the bane and antidote. One portion of his assertions refutes the other; and the only difficulty is, to know when he is serious, or which side to believe. He is as contradictory in the matter of his defence, as in that of his attack. Now, he is an orthodox Presbyterian, professing to have received a command to "REMOVE ALL FALSE. WORSHIPS;" and now he is a flaming *patriot,* anxious only to preserve them! He seems to be operated on alternately by the contradictory principles of his creed, and of his country; and his benevolent nature, like Mahomet's coffin, is suspended between them, with the additional circumstance, that he oscillates from one side to the other, as the necessities of his argument may require.

6. CHARACTER OF HIS TESTIMONIES. These may be divided into—OPINIONS and FACTS. *His opinions* may pass for what they are worth. When he shall have lived longer, and read more, and enlarged his intercourse with the world, he may see reason to change his opinions, and say, with the Apostle, "*when I was a child, I thought as a child, I spoke as a child.*" As for *his facts* in argument, they are generally the *opinions* of bigoted Protestants, or *discarded and condemned Catholic writers.* Of the former description, it will be sufficent to mention BANCROFT, BURNET, FABER, CRAMP, BLANCO WHITE, ("Tristam Shandy,") et id genus omne. Of the latter, Dupin, Pascal,.(a Jansenist,) Thuanus, Father Paul, and the Abbe De Pradt. Renegades, apostates,—enemies in disguise, whose works have been REFUTED by *Catholic writers.* That he should have been correctly informed on the Catholic religion, was not to be expected. He would learn our principles from our enemies alone; but as to *our own* approved expositions of doctrine, I hazard but little in saying, that he never read sixty pages of them in his life, except in the mind and spirit which prompt the Deist to read the Bible. The consequence is, that he is profoundly ignorant of the doctrines which he professes to understand and discuss. I shall take any child over six years, that has been instructed in the Catechism, and if that child's answers to twelve questions, on the points disputed between Catholics and Protestants, are not found to be more correct, true, precise, and *theological, than the gentleman's answers to the same questions,*—I shall be ready to make him an apology. Religion among Protestants is not so much a question of *correct knowledge* and TRUTH, as a business OF PARTY; and hence it is, that to multitudes prejudiced by this party feeling, the word "papist," or some other epithet of abuse, is more conclusive, from the lips of a PARSON, than would be a demonstration of

Euclid, submitted by a Catholic priest. No syllogism could make Presbyterians half so orthodox as Dr. Miller's simple story about the "crabs in black velvet." These circumstances account for the ignorance, or rather *false information*, with which the gentleman and his associates attack the Catholic religion; they know the travesty of our faith, and when they destroy this by ribaldry, it is only the creature of their own brain that perishes. Our faith remains untouched as before.

FINALLY.—HIS ASSERTIONS THAT PRESBYTERIANS HAVE NOT PERSECUTED IN THIS COUNTRY. This is true, so far as *life* and *property* are concerned. But so far as REPUTATION, CHARACTER, and GOOD NAME could be destroyed, invaded, or injured by base falsehoods, slanders and calumnies, invented, circulated, and patronised *by Presbyterians*, a more subtle and cruel persecution has never been waged than they have, for the last few years, carried on against their Catholic fellow-citizens. The fate of the Convent at Boston, shows that the transition from the blackening of character to the destruction of property, and the risk of life, is easy and natural. They first bear false witness against the Convent, and then burn it down, *on the strength of their own calumnious testimony*. Is not this persecution? Doctor Beecher and his associates first fire the passions of the people, and the falsehoods which those preachers propagate in the name of the living God, acting on the minds of ignorant and credulous followers, place the torch in the hands of the midnight incendiaries. Property has been destroyed—lives have been jeoparded—by the spirit of Presbyterian persecution in the United States, and in the nineteenth century—*for no other crime save that of worshipping God, according to the dictates of conscience!!*

The instruments of obedience to the second commandment, for "removing this monument of idolatry," searched among the ruins,—they even did not spare the *sepulchre*, in the hope of discovering something to sustain their slanders. They found nothing. But not dismayed, the spirit of lying and slander which had taken possession of them, became emboldened by the scene of desolation which it had produced. It attempted to blacken and destroy the character of the Catholics, by new slanders. They had dungeons for the inquisition under their churches,—and one of these propagators of "false witness against their neighbour," directs his brother bigots, in case of his sudden disappearance, to look for his body *under the Catholic churches*. So that, in case the fanatic should commit suicide, or hide for six weeks, he expects that the Catholic churches are to be destroyed, in order to find, or, at least, search for his remains. Foreign conspiracies were invented, and charged on the Catholics;—an old trick in the tactics of Presbyterian persecution. They knew both of these charges to be *false*. There was no evidence to sustain either;

and the rule is, that men are to be held *innocent* until they are *proved* guilty. The story about having knocked down a senator, was proven by the Cincinnati papers, to have been "AN IMPUDENT LIE." Still it is *consecrated in their writings,* as if it had not been a slander. Book after book has been published—slander after slander has been repeated,—but yet nothing proved against the Catholics. In general, these charges are vague, and not made directly against individuals by name. They thus shun the legal consequences of their defamation. But, in some instances, this "hunger and thirst" for calumnies against "popery" have betrayed individuals into very unpleasant circumstances, from which they have had to extricate themselves by a *humiliating* process. Let me give an instance.

From the Christian Herald, January 8, 1836.

THE AMENDE HONORABLE.—Having, in the Christian Herald, of the 11th of July, published a paragraph which seemed to insinuate a charge of improper conduct on the part of the Rev. John O'Reilly, during his absence in the summer from this city, I do hereby declare that I had no intention to injure the character of this gentleman, and, for the satisfaction of him and his friends, and repair any injury he may have sustained from that article, I do hereby declare my belief that said rumours were unfounded. Given under my hand, January 1, 1836.

T. D. BAIRD.

This, I should say, is a humiliating business for a Presbyterian MINISTER. But even this was not sufficient. He had to make another attempt to repair the injury to character.

From the same, of January 22, 1836.

Having, in the Christian Herald, of the 8th instant, published some hasty remarks upon the controversy existing between the Rev. John O'Reilly and myself, I hereby acknowledge that they were made under a misconception, and calculated to convey an erroneous impression concerning the condition on which Mr. O'Reilly agreed that all legal proceedings should cease, and the suit be withdrawn, which conditions were as follows,—viz., that I should publish the explanation, and pay all expenses.

T. D. BAIRD.

But to enumerate all the instances in which they have attempted to blacken the character of Catholics by slander, would be endless. And it is a fact, of which Catholics may be proud, that the issue in every charge, has eventuated not in the establishment of the accusation, but in fixing, silently, the brand and seal of the slanderer on their accusers. Generally, indeed, the tales of fiction set forth by these men and women, Miss Reed, Doctor

Brownlee, poor, fallen, Mr. Smith, the gentleman himself, and the last ally in the holy cause, Miss Maria Monk, are so incredible, or so stupid;—so extravagant, or so indecent;—that to sober and reflecting minds, they betray only the depraved zeal of their authors, and the weakness of the cause, which is reduced to the necessity of employing such base means of support. Miss Reed is now quite eclipsed; and at present the contest is between Mr. Smith, and the Rev. Mrs. Hoyte, alias Miss Monk. The business of simple lying against the Catholics, had been exhausted; and hence, in the more recent publications, scenes of the lowest and vilest debauchery, with a suitable sprinkling of murders, and infantcide, are presented with such clumsy grossness, that *even* the Journal of Commerce could not swallow them. The character of the writer was infamous; but that circumstance made her the more appropriate to the vocation, whereunto she had been called by the parsonhood. The dirtier the implement, the fitter for the work which they have to carry on. The plan of a conspiracy is laid, the mother of an illegitimate child is selected, and the victim of their own depravity is made the instrument by which it is intended to destroy the reputation of a whole community. Was anything ever conceived more black, more dastardly, more diabolical? An attempt is made to bribe the mother of the unfortunate woman to join in the conspiracy, and to support it by PERJURY. The following is an extract of the AFFIDAVIT, in which she disclosed the attempt that had been made to corrupt her veracity, by these unprincipled hypocrites : . . . . " The next day Mr. Hoyte came in with an elderly man, Dr. Judge Turner, of St. Albans. They demanded to see the child, which I produced. Mr. Hoyte demanded if I had discovered the mother; I said not. She must be found, said he; she has taken away a shawl and a bonnet belonging to a servant girl at Goodenough's; he would not pay for them, *she had cost him too much already;* that his things were kept at the hotel on that account: being afraid that this might more deeply involve my daughter, I offered my own shawl to replace the one taken; Mr. Hoyte first took it, but afterwards returned it to me on my promise that I would pay for the shawl and bonnet. In the course of the day, Mrs. Tarbert found my daughter, but she would not come to my house; she sent the bonnet and shawl, which were returned to the owner, who had lent them to my daughter to assist her in procuring her escape from Mr. Hoyte, at the hotel. Early on the afternoon of the same day, Mr. Hoyte came to my house with the same old man, wishing me to make all my efforts to find the girl, in the meantime speaking very bitterly against the Catholics, the Priests, and the Nuns; mentioning that my daughter had been in the Nunnery, where she had been ill-treated. I denied that my daughter had ever been in a Nunnery, that when she was about eight years of age, she went to a day-school; at that time came in two other persons, whom Mr. Hoyte introduced; one was the Rev. Mr. Brewster. I do not recollect the other reverence's name. *They all requested me, in the most pressing terms, to try to make it out that my daughter had been in the Nunnery; and that she had some connexion with the Priests of the Seminary, of which Nunneries and Priests he spoke in the most outrageous terms; said, that should I make it out, myself, my daughter, and child, would be protected for life.* I expected to get rid of their importunities, in relating the melancholy circumstances by which my daughter was frequently deranged in her head, and told them, that when at the age of about seven years, she broke a slate-pencil in her head; that since that time her mental faculties were deranged, and by times much more so than at other times, but that she was far from being an idiot; that she could make the most ridiculous, but most plausible stories; and that as to the history that she had been in a Nunnery, it was a fabrication, for she never was in a Nunnery; that at one time I wished to obtain a place in a Nunnery for her, that I had employed the influence of Mrs. De Montenach, of Dr. Nelson, and of our pastor, the Rev. Mr. Esson, but without success. *I told them notwithstanding I was a Protestant, and did not like the Roman Catholic religion—like all other respectable Protestants, I held the Priests of the Seminary and the Nuns of Montreal in veneration, as the most pious and charitable persons I ever knew."* (1)

Here, sir, is a scene of complicated depravity, for which it would be difficult to find a parallel. The only one I can remember equal to it, is that in which Brandt tells, of one of the Catholic victims of Presbyterian persecution in Holland, to whom they gave sweet wine, in order to make him drunk in the agonies of death, on the rack.

Persecution advances by degrees, and it is a fact as well established in history, as the burning of Servetus by Calvin, that Presbyterians, as they persecuted to death in every country where they had power, so in every case, the first degree of that persecution was, in the thick, black, gross, and unmeasured calumnies which they heaped on the character of their intended victims. At an early period of their history in France, Maimburg, quoted by Bayle, (2) says, their libels against the Jesuits, the clergy and government of France, already amounted to TEN VOLUMES, which were filled, says he, with "*all that detraction and the blackest malignity have ever invented, of* SUPPOSED CRIMES, *atrocious invectives and calumny, spread out brutally, and without judgment or taste. . . . .*" Bayle, though himself educated a Calvinist, confirms the truth of this statement. Chalmers tells us, that the Presbyterians accomplished the destruction of the unfortunate Queen of Scots, by the same means. (3) The same

(1) Extract from Mrs. Monk's oath. (2) Avis Aux Ref. vol. ii. p. 586.
(3) Chalmer's Life of Mary, vol. ii. p. 9.

means of CALUMNY AND SLANDER, were employed for the destruction of the ARMINIANS, in Holland; and the Episcopalians in England; as we see in Brandt and Neal, passim. To their CALUMNIES we trace, on the most respectable testimony, the origin of the wicked principles which ignorance has so long and so falsely attributed to the Jesuits. These calumnies were echoed in the clamours and writings of the infidels and Jansenists, of the last century, and from these again, the Calvinists and others, now derive only new editions of their own old slanders. The bishops of France, when called upon, gave the true character of the Jesuits in their answer to the king, who had submitted this subject of inquiry.

"Article II. How the Jesuits behave in the instructions, and in their own conduct, with regard to their instructions, and in their own conduct, with regard to certain opinions which strike at the safety of the king's person; as likewise, with regard to the received doctrines of the clergy of France, contained in the declaration of the year 1682; and in general, with regard to their opinions on the other side of the Alps." Here is their testimony:—

"Our history informs us, that, in the infancy of the society in France, the CALVINISTS used their utmost endeavour to hinder the growth of a body of men, raised on purpose to oppose their errors, and to stop the spreading contagion: to this end, they dispersed into all parts a multitude of pamphlets, in which the Jesuits were arraigned as professing a doctrine inconsistent with the safety of his majesty's sacred person; *being well assured, that the imputation of so atrocious a crime was the shortest and securest way to bring about their ruin.* These libels soon raised a prejudice against the Jesuits, in the minds of all those who had any interest in opposing their establishment in France, and some communities even joined in the impeachment. The crimes which are *now laid to their charge*, in the numberless writings that swarm in all parts of your majesty's dominions, are no other than those which were MALICIOUSLY FORGED, and *published above one hundred and fifty years ago.* It is not from such LIBELS as THESE, that we are to form a just idea, or rational judgment, of the Jesuits' doctrine or behaviour: such wild and groundless accusations did not deserve our attention, and the little notice we took of them, may be a convincing proof to your majesty, of the Jesuits' innocence." (1)

In England, during their civil wars, the same course of circulating the most *absurd and stupid calumnies* was systematically pursued, as we learn from the testimony of Protestant writers. Bishop Warburton tells us "*they* (the Presbyterians,) *preached and fought for the King's destruction; and fasted and*

(1) Judgment of the Bishops of France, concerning the doctrine, the government, the conduct, and usefulness of the French Jesuits. Appendix.

prayed for his preservation, WHEN THEY HAD BROUGHT HIM TO THE FOOT OF THE SCAFFOLD." But their calumnies never ceased. At times, the Catholics were solemnly denounced as "the sowers of discord between the king and his faithful commons." (1) This day, whole fleets of foreign Papists were created upon the coasts; the next day, the ordinary equipage of a Catholic nobleman was magnified into a Popish army; viz: the Earl of Bristol's. (2) Now the nation was terrified with the report of "AN ARMY UNDER GROUND." (3) Then the inhabitants of London were frightened with the intelligence of a new gunpowder plot for "BLOWING UP THE RIVER THAMES, AND DROWNING THAT FAITHFUL PROTESTANT CITY." (4) At last one Beale, a tailor, at Cripplegate, was introduced to the House of Commons, by no less a man than the celebrated John Hampden, (5) who averred, that "*walking in the fields near a bank, he overheard from the opposite side of it, the particulars of a plot, concerted by the Priests and other Papists, for one hundred and eight assassins to murder one hundred and eight leading members of Parliament, at the rate of ten pounds for every lord, and of forty shillings for every commoner, so murdered.*" (6) To show the bigotry of the first men in the nation, at that time, against the Catholics, it will be sufficient to mention, that upon this very deposition of the Cripplegate tailor, stuffed with other circumstances equally absurd, and unsupported by any collateral evidence, (7) the House of Commons proceeded to the most violent measures against them; and, under pretence of greater security, ordered the train-bands and militia of the kingdom to be in readiness, and to be placed under the command of that real traitor the Earl of Essex. (8)

The Episcopal clergy fared no better. Heylin tells us, ... "they could find no other title for the Archbishop of *Canterbury*, than *Belzebub of Canterbury, Pope of Lambeth,* the *Canterbury Caiphas, Esau, a monstrous anti-Christian Pope, a most bloody opposer of God's saints, a very anti-Christian beast, a most vile and cursed tyrant.* They tell us further of this humble and meek spirited man, that *no Bishop ever had such an aspiring and ambitious mind, as he; no, not Cardinal Wolsey: None so proud as he; no, not Stephen Gardiner of Winchester: None so tyrannical as he; no, not Bonner, the butcher of London.* In general, he tells us both of him, and the rest of the bishops, That they are *unlawful, unnatural, false, bastardly governors of the Church, the Ordinances of the Devil, petty Popes, petty antiChrists, incarnate devils, Bishops of the devil, cogging, cozening*

---

(1) Remonstr. of Parl. an. 1641. (2) Nalson's Collections, Pref. p. 76. (3) Exam. of Neal's Hist. of Puritans, by Grey, vol. ii, p. 260. (4) Ibid. vol. ii. p. 260. (5) Clarendon's Hist. of Rebellion. (6) Nalson's Col. vol. ii. p. 646, &c. (7) Ibid. p. 647. (8) Ibid.

knaves, and will lie like dogs. That they are *proud, popish, presumptuous, profane, paltry, pestilent, pernicious Prelates, and usurpers; enemies of God, and the most pestilent enemies of the State; and, that the worst Puritan in* England *is an honester man than the best Lord Bishop in Christendom."* (1)

In fact, this was the spirit of their founders. They adopted from the cradle the motto,

Calumniare audacter, semper aliquid adhærebit.

The Rev. Mr. Whitaker, a clergyman of the English Episcopal Church, tells us of Knox, (and gives facts to prove it,) "that he was an original genius in lying, ... that he felt his mind impregnated with a peculiar portion of that spirit of falsehood, which is so largely possessed by the father of lies." (2) Of Buchanan, another Scotch Presbyterian Reformer, Whitaker tells us, ... "that he became equally devoid of principle, and of shame, ready for any FABRICATION of falsehood, and capable of any operation in villany."(3) The testimony of Doctor Stewart is to the same effect. (4)

In fine, this learned Protestant author, Whitaker, whose subject introduced him to all the sources of information, says, "FORGERY, *I blush for the honour of Protestantism, while I write, seems to have been* PECULIAR *to the Reformed. I look in vain for one of these accursed outrages of imposition among the disciples of Popery."* (5)

I now take leave of the subject. Nothing but necessity could have induced me to enter into this discussion. My apology to my friends, both Catholics and Protestants, is, that a system of ferocious denunciation had been organized, for the purpose of destroying the civil and religious rights of Catholics, and thus depriving them of those constitutional privileges which, in common with the patriots of other denominations, they bled to purchase. This system was under the direction of the gentleman, and a few Presbyterian ministers, FOREIGNERS; of whom, Dr. Brownlee may be regarded as chief. These men, if they pursue their measures of intolerance, disorganizing the harmonies of society, and propagating religious bigotry, instead of charity, peace, and goodwill among men, will bring disgrace on even the Presbyterian name. This is the opinion of the more sober and rational portion of their own members. I am aware that, in ordinary circumstances, it is not for the Catholic priest, the minister of a religion whose principles have been promulged throughout the world for eighteen hundred years, to enter into dispute with the unsettled advocate of

---

(1) Dr. Heylin's Hist. of Pres.   (2) Vindication of Mary, vol. ii. p. 22.
(3) Vindic. of Mary, ibid.   (4) Hist. of Scotl. vol. ii. p. 245.
(5) Vol. ii. p. 2.

turbulence and fanaticism, no matter by what name he may be called. But when a Presbyterian minister, the ripeness of combined ignorance and bigotry, steps forward in the name of liberty and God, to show reasons why their followers should fire the convents, and churches, and property of Catholics, it is time to put the lovers of peace and order on their guard. It is time that the people should know something of Presbyterian, as well as Catholic history. If the gentleman had been a Baptist, I should have let him pass on. If he had been a Methodist, I should have said nothing. If he had been a Quaker, I should have heard his professions of zeal for "civil and religious liberty," in silence.

The principles of Roger Williams, and of William Penn, would have disarmed resentment. Whether it is owing to the pacific principles of these denominations, or to the fact that, never having possessed civil power, they never had the strong temptation to persecute, it is certainly true that neither the Friends, nor the Baptists, nor the Methodists have ever been guilty of persecution for conscience' sake. Their robes are as yet unstained with this crime—and they are unwise in this age of the world, if they do not continue to preserve them as they are. But for a disciple of Presbyterianism to make himself conspicuous—and stand forth to talk of the rights of conscience, whilst the mantle of Calvinism, with which he covers himself, is stained and purple with the blood of men of every creed, and of every country where it could be shed;—this was too much. When the gentleman assumed this position, and pressed himself importunately on my notice, when he knew that I was averse to disputation, then I felt it due to the public to administer to him the rebuke of history, which ignorance had so wantonly provoked. My only wish is, that he and his brethren, who have more zeal than discretion, may preserve these testimonies of history, which establish the character of his creed, and labour to correct the ugliness and deformity of its features, instead of attempting to break the innocent MIRROR, for reflecting them truly.

I have established my arguments by the most respectable authorities, generally Presbyterians and Protestants. I have, I trust,' attacked no other denomination of Christians, and I can say with truth, that towards men of all denominations I cherish feelings of benevolence, charity, and good will. It was painful to me to have spoken of Presbyterians, among whom I have the pleasure to number many friends, as I have done. But Mr. Breckinridge imposed it on me as a duty to say the truth—and I have done so. I would rather, however, be employed in soothing, than exciting, even by necessity, the feelings of religious prejudice and bigotry on either side. Men have but a short time to live in this world, and why should they, and especially they who minister, embitter the cup of human existence? Let Presbyterians worship God, according to the dictates of their conscience, let Catholics do the same. But let neither be engaged in the unholy work of sowing discord among brethren, or in rupturing the ties of harmony which bind all citizens into, at least, social union. Blessed are the peace-makers, for they shall be called the children of God. Whose children can they be, who are destroyers of peace and sowers of discord?

If I have spoken of individuals not immediately connected with this discussion, I have done so only in relation to their *published writings;*—and never have I touched their private character or history. In this regard, therefore, I trust that I have violated no rule of propriety. I have left eave-droppers and tattlers, to those who may need, and can employ them. Finally, the gentleman has the closing speech—and I shall have no opportunity to expose it. If he can bring forward argument to show that the Presbyterian religion is not as intolerant and as persecuting as its doctrines and history have proved it to be, I shall be happy to read them. But if, instead of this, he shall elope from "THE QUESTION," and relapse into the abuse of popery, he will thereby furnish the best evidence that, on both questions, he has signally and triumphantly FAILED.

"*Is the Presbyterian Religion, in any or in all its principles or doctrines, opposed to civil or religious liberty?*"

NEGATIVE VI.—MR. BRECKINRIDGE.

MR. PRESIDENT :—

AT the close of the *oral* debate, I predicted that Mr. Hughes would *never permit* the publication of our Discussion. One of his own followers in this city has truly said, that Mr. Hughes has made such statements in the debate, that he *never* will agree to its publication. We have now a practical demonstration of the truth of the statement. The Discussion is little more than half *finished;* yet I have received his *last piece,* containing his farewell to me, to the public, and to the defence of his deserted cause. He has avowed his determination to write no more to the publishing committee and to the Society ; and has even gone so far as to require that the society should peremptorily close the debate, and stop me, as well as *connive* at his retreat! All this has been done, too, after his solemn public promise to write the debate anew, if the society and I would agree to lay aside the stenographer's report. The society, however, with much unanimity, and after long patience, resolved (on the last evening) that the portion of the debate now finished should be published, and then the disputants, or either of them, might go on, under the sanction of the society, to finish the questions at issue. Mr. Hughes has behaved in so extraordinary a way, that his retreat from the discussion is in fact the settlement of the question; and its history deserves to be preserved, as illustrative of the acts of a Jesuit to shun the light; and the desperation of a cause, which, with all his talents and learning, he cannot defend. I therefore incorporate one of my letters to the society, written on the occasion of his refusing to proceed, as a brief explanation of the state of the case. And in confirmation of what is said in it, I appeal to *the members of the society, and to the records of the institution.*

Philadelphia, March 29th, 1836.

TO THE PRESIDENT OF THE YOUNG MEN'S
LITERARY AND DEBATING SOCIETY.

SIR,

HAVING been informed, that the young gentlemen of the Society have delayed the final decision of the painful question now pending, in regard to the publication of the debate, until this evening, I take the liberty of making an additional communication through you to the Society.

As no little time has passed since the debate began, and many changes have taken place in our arrangements, a rapid retrospect of the circumstances may not now be amiss. The following facts will not be disputed, it is supposed, by any member of the Society; or if disputed, are capable of ample proof.

1. Mr. Hughes *refused*, on the third night, to proceed without a *reporter*—yet *he* afterwards rejected the *reporter's work*.

2. Mr. Hughes selected the present method of preparing the debate for the press; and he pledged himself to complete it in this way; and he proposed no *limits* or *terms* at the *commencement* of this plan of preparation: on the contrary, he found fault with the former Publishing Committee for seeking to restrict him; and a new committee was appointed by the Society to carry the new plan into effect.

3. The Society did thus and otherwise sanction the present plan, and agree to carry it into effect. And it was on the faith of Mr. Hughes's pledge, and theirs, that I gave up the stenographer's report, and adopted Mr. Hughes's plan. And it was on the faith of the same united pledge, that the debate should be completed, *sold*, and published, that I advanced a considerable sum of money to pay the Society's debt to the reporter.

4. Mr. Hughes first set the example of *enlarging* the form of the original debate; for when the first Publishing Committee opposed his *additions* to the report of the stenographer, he said he was to be the judge of how much or how little should be added. Acting on this principle, we began, *afterward*, to rewrite the whole, each having full liberty. When, therefore, Mr. Hughes complains of the dilation of the Discussion, he should remember that he is not only the *sharer*, but *author* of the practice.

5. Though more matter has been *written* than was *spoken* on the same number of nights, yet a considerable portion of the topics, presented in the oral debate, have, as yet, not been touched in the manuscript; as, for example, the *supremacy of the Pope*; the *doctrine of the Roman priesthood*; the *order of the Jesuits*; the *monastic institutions*; the *immoral tendency of the system of popery*; the *Inquisition*; the *papal conspiracy abroad against the liberties of our country, are all yet to be examined, and were all gone over in the debate*. This, Mr. Hughes well knows. Yet he seeks now to stop short, and exclude all that yet remains. Besides all this, there are allusions in the discussion of the second general question, to the discussion of the first, which *first* will not appear, if we arrest the debate here. How absurd will this appear; and to me, how palpably unjust? Mr. Hughes, contrary to the order of the debate, contrived to alternate, very absurdly, one speech on one question, and one speech on the other. And

now we have each question half discussed; yet he insists on publishing *now*, and publishing *no more!*

In view of all these facts, I can hardly think it possible for your honourable body to do such violence to my rights, as *now* to force a close of the Discussion on me. Being, however, unfeignedly anxious to bring every part of the Discussion, as speedily as possible, before the American people, I have conceded much to the wishes of others, as will be seen in my last letter, to which I respectfully refer the Society.

That there may be no room left to complain of my terms, I here add, to the proposals of that communication, the following, viz:—

As Mr. Hughes *refuses* to go farther in the debate, let it be agreed, that, *for this reason*, we will *now* publish *four nights* of the manuscript debate: let me then complete my argument on the papal question, and publish it under the sanction of the Society, accompanied by an explicit avowal of the fact, that Mr. Hughes declines to pursue the Discussion. I will publish the second part at my own risk, and ask no more than what is stated above. If Mr. Hughes asks more, his country must see why; and his best friends must blush for him, when he shall not only abruptly, and after all his pledges, withdraw from the Controversy, but even seek to silence me midway the question.

I feel well assured, sir, that the honourable young gentlemen, of all names and sects, over whom you preside, will esteem my wishes reasonable; and will unite to sustain me in my obvious rights.

But if not, then I must appeal to the American public; and reverting to the alternative, the painful alternative, stated in my former letter, I must seek shelter from injustice, before a larger and better tribunal, who love liberty, who will do justice; and before whom, if God give me help, I am resolved to spread out the *whole of the debate*, and the history, as well as the matter of it, if my stipulated rights should now be so seriously invaded.

With full confidence in the candour and justice of the Society,
I remain, dear sir, very respectfully,
Your friend and fellow-citizen,
JOHN BRECKINRIDGE.

P. S. I understand it has been alleged, that, inasmuch as I called on the audience to aid in paying the fees of the stenographer, at the close of the debate, therefore, he was confessedly *my* reporter. It is well known, as I then avowed, that the *reason* of the call was the *poverty* of the *Society*, (which had no funds,) and the pressing wants of the reporter, who expected to leave the city the next morning. Besides, it is fully known, that, for three nights, the Committee had failed to get a reporter; and Mr. Hughes *refused* to proceed *without* one. Then, at the request of the Committee, I wrote for Mr. Stansbury—the faithful reporter of the American Congress for some dozen years. And yet, after all, Mr. Hughes *rejects* his *reports*. *Then*, when we yield to his wishes, give up the reporter's manuscript, and begin, at his request, to write *anew*, he proceeds but *half* way through; when lo, again, and of a sudden, without consultation, or agreement with the other parties, he *resolves to stop*. Will the Society sustain such a course? It was on the faith of Mr. Hughes's repeated pledge, to complete the debate, and on the faith of the Society's pledge, to cause it to be completed, and sold, and published, that I advanced money to pay the debt of the Society. Will the Society now permit, nay, aid in a continuance to defeat the publication?

J. B.

Since the Society adopted the last course so firmly, Mr. Hughes has so far come to terms, as to allow *me* to proceed, though he *retreats himself*. Men do not *commonly retreat* from the *victory* of their *cause*. I exceedingly regret his retiring so pertinaciously. *But the way is open (and I hereby make it known) to any respectable, accredited priest of the Church of Rome, who will take the place of his absent friend, while I go over the ground which he traversed in the debate, but forsakes at the press.*

It becomes my duty now to reply, so far as any reply is called for, to his *last speech* (now before me) on the *Presbyterian question*.

And really I hardly know what order to observe in this reply. Despair and fury, abuse, flight and confusion "fluctuate through his pages in unknown agitation." He seems to have felt it was his *last*. *It is the confusion of retreat*. I had as well take it up by the order of pages and paragraphs—for there is surely no other *line* of argument. It is the order of confusion and of final rout.

1. First, then, as to his "*bet*." Though I declined *it*, I accepted his *reference*, and I am now prepared to fulfil my promise, in St. John's Church, the day after he shall preach the eulogy of the Neapolitan queen, if he pleases: viz., to show the forgeries and frauds by *addition*, *erasure* and *perversion* in twenty places in Donevan's Translation of *that very Catechism* which Mr. Hughes recommends to his flock, and is the standard of the Romish Church! And what does Mr. Hughes say in reply? Why that I got the facts from *Cramp*. But still, are they facts? He dare not deny them *again*. I got them fresh from the *fountains*, and will confront him with them, if he will name the day and the place. He asks, what have these charges to do with the question? I reply, much. He *once denied* them. Besides, they prove that Roman Catholic writers are, as a body, unless they *be laymen*, not to be trusted. They commit forgeries on their own books; and on the *word of God*. Thus they *are not to be*

& usted. I refer to my fourth speech on the *second question* (the last but one) for a crowd of *unnoticed proofs* of this *awful fact.*

2. The charge, that we hold communion with *European Presbyterian Churches which hold persecuting doctrines*, is pressed by Mr. H. with much triumph—to prove that we hold the *same doctrines ourselves.* I had often said that the American Presbyterians had rejected and expunged several clauses *from the Westminster Confession of Faith which were intolerant,* and I proved the fact that they made this change *before the adoption of the American Constitution,* which shows that it was a matter of *choice,* and not of *force,* (as Mr. Hughes *once* said). Mr. Hughes replies, that we have fellowship with those who hold these persecuting doctrines, to prove that we at *heart approve* them, though we *profess* to have *renounced* them. He says—*"And if they have changed, as he asserts, let the next General Assembly break communion with those sister Presbyteries in Europe, in whose Confessions of Faith the principle of intolerance is avowed as a doctrine."* Now, the truth is, Mr. Hughes, ignorantly I would fain hope, has entirely *falsified* the *facts.* We hold no such communion with any such churches. The Church of Scotland has an establishment, and *retains* the intolerant *doctrine.* The consequence is we have no communion with her. The Irish Church (the Synod of Ulster) receives the *regium donum.* We have no reciprocation with her; of which we have had a notable illustration in the person of our late delegate to the British churches. He went as a *delegate from* the General Assembly of our church to the *Congregational Churches of England and Wales*—but not to the *Scotch*—not to the *Irish Presbyterian Church.* So much for the *historical verity of the gentleman.*

But now for his argument. Is he *honest* in the use of it? Is it good, where the facts support it? He says it is. Then it settles the question between us. For is he not in full and direct *communion with the Church of Rome, which has an establishment?* Is not the American papal (what a contradiction in terms!) church under the Pope? And is not the Pope head of an *established church,* and *a temporal prince also?* And has not Mr. Hughes boasted that the papal church is the *same* and *one* all over the *world*—in *Spain,* and *Austria,* and every where? And are not the churches in these empires *intolerant,* and *exclusive,* and, by his own confession, *persecuting?* Yet he has fellowship with them all! Priests from them all pass into direct connexion with the American Catholics! They are received *ad eundem* at St. John's! Yea, and the bishops of this diocese, and bishops of every diocese, in *this country,* hold their *offices* directly from the Pope, a *foreign prince,* and the *head* of a *state establishment!* This I say then settles the question, by Mr. Hughes's own showing. For he says of us, *"Let them condemn it (intolerance) as an error in doctrine. If they do not—it is their own; and the gentleman makes himself ridiculous when he denies it."*

I will add, that the Reformed Dutch Church has explicitly denounced the doctrine of intolerance; and I have the *public act* of her Synod containing it in my possession. Here is another *slip* in the gentleman's statements.

3. The gentleman *affects* to be much shocked at my allusion to the horrific practice of *ante-natum* baptisms. It is indeed a *shocking subject.* But if such things are too shocking to *tell*, how shocking to *do?* If the gentleman will only publicly deny, 1. That, by their doctrine, unbaptized *infants* cannot be saved: 2. That they do not practice in his Church such baptisms: 3. And that he *never* did *himself perform such a baptism*, I will give the public such proof as shall make him blush—or publicly apologise for my statement.

4. AS TO MARRIAGE. Mr. Hughes has entirely evaded the argument contained in my last speech. To it, without repeating, I refer the reader. How amazing, that he can leave untouched such a *body of facts!* He says " *Catholics* hold marriage to be a sacrament, which cannot be rightly administered except in the presence of a parish priest. But this is only where the discipline of the Council of Trent is received, which it is not in this country." The latter clause is not only gratuitous, but a mere fiction. On page 313 of Donevan's Translation of the Council of Trent's Catechism, it is said expressly, ... " *Without the presence of the parish priest, or of some other priest commissioned by him or by the ordinary, and that of two or three witnesses, there can be no marriage.*" Now does this say one word about *"the receiving of the discipline of the Council of Trent?"* Not one word. Mr. Hughes well knows that by his *doctrines* every marriage in Christendom is *illegitimated* that has not been performed by a Catholic priest! And when he says, "whether it were received or not it cannot affect the *civil right of any one*," he passed by the *point* of the question. We know, thank God, that his holding our children *illegitimate*, and our civil contracts *void*, does not make them so. But the question is, whether any man that thinks so is a fit person to represent our rights, or make our laws, in state and national legislatures? Does not every man who believes marriage to be a sacrament subject that relation necessarily to the Church and Pope of Rome, and reject all right or fitness of the civil power to judge of the lawfulness of marriage? And would not Mr. Hughes treat any Catholic holding the reverse of this as a schismatic, and the subject of discipline? And, then, can any man, with these views, conscientiously hold an office of trust in a Protestant country? I rejoice that *some* of our best citizens are *Catholics.* But it is little more than *nominal* with those who have intelligence, and they are, day by day,

becoming more and more *Protestant by the power of truth and public opinion*. And this controversy has made Mr. Hughes, by necessity, more of a *Protestant* than the Pope will like. I am sure if this Discussion should reach Rome, *in time*, he will get the *rod* rather than the *staff*.

5. He says—"*All sects oppose the liberty of the press, by endeavouring to exclude such publications as expose their real or supposed errors.*" This is most surprising! But is this the same thing with saying, "*If any one shall presume to read or possess the Bible without a written permission of a bishop or inquisitor, he shall not receive absolution until he shall have first delivered up such Bible to the ordinary?*" Is the *effort*, by *persuasion*, to *discourage* the use of a *bad book*, or one we *think bad*, the same thing as forbidding *reading or printing*, under pains and penalties of body and soul? One is *papal*, the other is *Protestant* treatment of the *press!* and not only the *press* in general, but even the *holy word of God*. Turretine (Bened.) has said, "There is no place of mercy left to the Book of God. Men fly from the Gospel, in the Italian or Spanish tongue, faster than they would run from the plague of pestilence."

6. The gentleman's principles will leak out. He says, "They [the *Protestants* at the era of the Reformation] *attacked* the doctrines of the Catholic Church, and, in doing so, in those times, and countries, they attacked the religion of the people at large, and the laws of the state." Now, at this period, the Roman Church had every thing in its power. So it had been for ages. There had been a full opportunity to try its principles. All (he says) were *Catholics*. And he exults that, though this was so, they shed so little blood. He forgets "*the almost infinite number*" of poor heretics, whom Bellarmine tells us the church had put to death. *After* they were extirpated, the church ceased to *kill*. "*Solitudinem faciunt, pacem appellant.*" But as they possessed *all the power*, so they acted out *their principles*. And what were they? As the gentleman says, "*they had possession!*" And how did they exercise their power? Why, as he says, "*the Catholic religion was the law of the state.*" Yes; of every state on earth in their power. I challenge the example of one *state* in the world, for the ages of their dominion, where they did not *establish their religion by law* where *they had the power*. And will they not do the same here if they ever become able? The gentleman says, they *change not*. Their *system* has worked so for AGES, and EVERYWHERE, with not *one exception*, *not one*, for *ages on ages!* Is not its very genius, essence, and nature, intolerance and domination? But the strange part is to come. He pleads their *usurped power* as *a reason* for its *continued exercise;* and even as making its exercise *lawful!* "At the origin of the Reformation, so called, the *Catholics were in possession*. This is important. The *Reformers possessed nothing* . . . . . . They

had nothing—they claimed to possess themselves of the rights of others." "Had nothing!" Had they not their *bodies*, their *souls*, their *country*, their *rights*, their Bible? "*Had nothing.*" No! "*They claimed to possess themselves of the rights of others ;*" that is, they claimed that the *Catholic religion should cease to be the "law of the state"*—so that they should not be denied liberty of thought, worship, printing, and discussion. But, as the gentleman more than intimates, "*these were the rights of others.*" This was the very language of the papists at the diet of *Spires* in 1529! It was for LIBERTY the Reformers contended. It was *liberty* that the *diet refused them ; liberty of worship,* and of *discussion,* "*as it would interfere with the rights of others ;*" that is, of the *Catholics,* "who had *possession*," as Mr. Hughes, repeating the language of that day, has said. It is an ever-memorable fact, that the *name* of PROTESTANT was then and there acquired by the illustrious men who PROTESTED AGAINST TYRANNY—*in reference to their religious and civil rights.* The *doctrinal* question was incidental. It was LIBERTY they sought, and against oppression they PROTESTED.

It may be as well here, as elsewhere, to say, that the boasted toleration of the papal colony of *Maryland* is, in a great measure, an empty name. For, in the first place, they well knew, from the strong *Protestant* power prevailing in the parent country, and from the very terms of the *grant, popery* could never be established by law in any colony of the British crown. Again, it was *only toleration—not true liberty.* And still, again, *Unitarians were put to death by law.*(1) Now, was this *liberty?* Is this ground of boast? When Mr. Hughes accuses Presbyterians of murdering "Quakers," and drowning "Baptists," I can only say, that he falsifies history, and slanders their good name. And while we mourn over the ill-judged and guilty persecutions of New England, in that day of the dawning of freedom, it ill becomes that man, whose "*frock of office*" has descended to him on a sea of blood, (innocent blood, shed by his Church,) to stand up and mouth the heavens, about the intolerances of a few peeled and scattered Puritans, who had learned from Rome the *spirit* of intolerance, and whose sins in that way, compared with those of Rome, making every allowance for disparity of numbers, and of duration, were about as *one* to *one million.* Rome is estimated, by impartial historians, to have caused the extinction of about 60,000,000 of our race. Rome has put to death more *men,* by her crusades, inquisitions, &c., than all Protestant christendom combined, have *shed drops* of human blood for the same guilty cause; and papal Rome has *far, far* outdone *pagan* Rome in the work of persecution and inhuman butchery.

7. He says, the Presbyterians have existed for only three

---

(1) See Langford, pp. 27–32.

hundred years; and that, if, with their spirit, they had held the world as long as the Catholics have, they would have butchered the *race*.

That Presbyterians have, *in former days, persecuted,* and been intolerant, I have *already* acknowledged. That papists hate them, I do not wonder, especially *Calvin,* and the brave Hollanders, and the indomitable Scotch, English, and Irish Presbyterians. Well do the papists remember *their love of liberty.* They cannot forget or forgive it. Dryden has said all in a word —he too a *Catholic.*

> " *So presbytery and its pestilential zeal,*
> *Can only flourish in a* COMMON WEAL—
> *In fenny Holland, and in fruitful Tweed,*
> *And like the first, the last effects to be,*
> *Drawn to the dregs of a democracy."*

Admitting, for the sake of argument, that Presbyterianism, which is as old as the Gospel of Christ, has existed only *three hundred* years, and that it arose at the era of the Reformation, has it not been prominent among the struggles for liberty ever since? Has it not been persecuted most dreadfully by Catholics, and by Episcopalians; and again and again? Does the gentleman pretend to say that they have *ever*—yes, *ever* begun the work of intolerance? Tell me where! Tell me when! Has he forgotten the scenes of the Low Countries; the bloody tragedies of Scotland, acted out first by Catholics, and then by Episcopalians? Has he forgotten the butcheries of Ireland, and the persecutions in Virginia? Is the name of *Huguenot* erased from his *pretermitting* memory? Has he forgot that he has already said, that Presbyterians never had "*Cæsar*" in their power but once? Yet now he asks me to show him *when* they had the *civil power* ("Cæsar") in their hands, and did not persecute? *He knows the Church never had the power.* He knows the acts he charges on *the Church* are falsely charged by *him* on *her:* that they were acts of *Parliaments;* and conscious of the glaring falsehood, he anticipates detection by *admitting* it. He knows that the cases he cites, even admitting all said to be true, (a great stretch of charity to a Jesuit,) that they were *acts of self-defence,* or of *retaliation.* He also knows that I have freely and fully condemned every persecuting act of *Presbyterians and Protestants;* and that, (as I have proved,) the intolerant articles, *two in number,* contained in the Westminster Confession of Faith, were voluntarily and unanimously erased *before* the adoption of the American Constitution; and that the terms of our *Confession are full, various, and clear,* on the whole subject—not merely of *toleration,* but *of protection* of all religions—*all having equal rights.* He insists, that when we say "kings should be nursing fathers" of the Church of our common Lord, we mean a state establishment of Presbyterianism.

I do not wonder that he *involuntarily* enforces his *right of interpretation*. But right glad are we, that we are not in Rome,—or we might have some of those *knotty arguments* which appeal to the *quivering flesh*, and those *stone-dead, knock-down arguments* of which *Baxter speaks*. Being in America, where *persuasion* is the only *force*, and discussion the only *way*, we must claim to tell what our creed is *ourselves*. And as Mr. Hughes has tried *discussion* from the press, and then left it, *half-complete;* (1) has then tried the *rostrum*, and still refused to abide by its reports;(2) and finally has fled the field *midway* the *manuscript* preparation of his debate, we must do the best we can *alone*, and on the *Protestant and American plan of argument*.

And now, as to the three hundred years of our *acknowledged* existence, where has *liberty* been found? where science? where enterprise, commerce, order, and public prosperity? Has it been in Italy? In Spain? In Catholic Germany? In Catholic Ireland? Has England, has Holland, has Scotland, have the United States of America, been *Catholic* since the Reformation? No! Protestant! Have these States been *Presbyterian?* In them Presbyterians have *abounded*. Have these States been famed for what was eminent in all that can bless and exalt a nation? *Confessedly foremost!* Let Mr. Hughes deny it if he can. He will not pretend to do it.

But reverse the scene. Go to Spain now. There the *priests especially*, the *monks* and *Jesuits*, are ranged with Don Carlos against the party that is struggling for *liberty and light*. Go see the *monasteries*, how, in the judgment of the *people*, (they, too, called *Catholic*,) are demolished by *thousands* as *the sinks of corruption*, as *castles* of despotism, as the *strong holds* of priestly domination?

Or will you survey Portugal? There you see the Pope denouncing, by public appeal, the reformation of *Don Pedro*, and giving the power of his arm to the monster Miguel. Hear him denounce the new government for daring *to interfere*, in its own territory, for the regulation of the priesthood!

Go to Italy, and see the Pope a public despot, his throne resting on the *parks* of Austrian artillery; *collecting his taxes* in the name of the *fisherman*, as the successor of Peter and vicar of Jesus; *one day blessing the horses and the asses of the city* in the name of the holy Trinity, to keep off evil spirits and pestilence; the next, cursing liberty in the name of God, and sending a *bishop's ring to John Hughes*, or a cardinal's hat to John, Bishop of Charleston.

There is one point in this Discussion, of very great consequence, which Mr. Hughes has continually endeavoured to keep

---

(1) See the former Controversy.
(2) See our correspondence on the subject.

out of view. It is this: that *American Protestants differ on the whole question of civil and religious liberty, very widely from European Protestants; whereas, Catholics being subject to an European head, and being one and unchangeable, are the same here as in Rome, and the same now as they were at the Reformation of Luther.*

I therefore never did, and never would, undertake to defend our ancestry in those things which were intolerant; but have, with all true American Protestants, rejected and reprobated those things. Hence, gentlemen, I have often, very often, when I knew Mr. Hughes was slandering European Presbyterians, passed on, since that was not the question; and since I knew full well that he wished by that means to call *me off from the true question,* which *is American Presbyterianism.* If I had followed him through his distortions of the history of European *Protestants* (for half the cases he has adduced were not *Presbyterian* at all) I should have had no time left to exhibit the great principles involved in the Discussion, nor to illustrate the grounds on which *American Presbyterians rest their system.*

Now it is well known that American *Episcopalians* are not chargeable with the *persecutions of their British ancestry;* and, if I mistake not, they have formally and explicitly renounced the doctrine of *intolerance,* and *of establishments.* Suppose, then, that John Hughes, in the superlativeness of his impudence, should approach the venerated father of the American Episcopal Church, Bishop White, and should say to him — "Sir, besides being a *heretic,* whom I denounce as such every time I recite the regular services of our mass-house, as incapable of salvation, while out of the true faith, I charge you with being an enemy to liberty, because your Episcopal fathers *persecuted* and even *burned* Catholics and *Presbyterians,* and because you are an Episcopalian!" But the meek and venerable man replies—"Sir, you ought to know that American Episcopalians have, in their public formularies and standards, condemned all intolerance, and all religious establishments, as anti-*Christian,* and anti-*American.*" The ill-bred Jesuit might say, as he is very much accustomed to do, "*Sir, you lie,*"—" you are not sincere—your creed *used* to mean very differently—and, under it, you may still persecute, and have an establishment, and oppress *Irish* and *all other Catholics.*" Just so he has said of Presbyterians.

But reverse the case. How is it with you, Mr. Hughes? Have you *renounced the intolerant doctrines of European papists?* Mr. Hughes—*The Holy Catholic Church, and its faith, without which none can be saved—never changes.* Have you renounced the doctrine of *church and state, as now illustrated and enforced in every country on earth where Catholics have the power, and as now sustained in the person of the Pope, your lord and master?* Mr. Hughes—*All Catholics, every where, are one people.* We *receive our doctrines and offices from the holy father, the Pope, who is the head of the universal church, and centre of unity.*

Such, then, is the true state of the question; and, until American Catholics *renounce the Pope, and his system, and give up the doctrine of an infallible, unchangeable church,* it is clear that they *must* hold, as they now do, anti-American doctrines. We have abundantly proved this already. We desire to leave it very prominently in the view of every reader of this Discussion.

8. As to the American Bible Society. The gentleman knows how fully I exposed his slanders, during the late *oral* debate. Now he *flies* the course *before* we reach that stage of the question; and yet asks why I am *silent* about it. All I need *now* say is, that the whole gross and abusive attack on that noble institution is founded on this fact, that the *American Bible Society* has omitted the *fabulous and uninspired Apocrypha —* which, of course, appears on the face of every Bible; as the *omitted parts* make about *a hundred and sixty* chapters, it can *hardly be called* a "*fraud.*"

9. *As to Faber.* I meant to say that *Faber's* name was above the charge of *ignorance* and *fraud;* and that, as Mr. Hughes had done me the honour to put me with him " in the same condemnation," I merely remarked, that I should be quite as likely to be *believed* on Faber's testimony, as *disbelieved* on Mr. Hughes's. But it is not only Hughes against *Faber;* it is Hughes against *truth.* Not one word, or one syllable, on that whole subject, as uttered by Mr. Hughes, *is true.*

10. As to the Sunday School Union. He finds he has unhappily met, in its *noble halls,* as it diffuses to millions the bread of life, such men as Alexander Henry, and John Sergeant, and Daniel Webster, and Theodore Frelinghuysen, and Robert Ralston. No wonder he starts back; and hides his dagger; and refuses his support to his original assertions. Strange! and yet *not* strange, when we remember who, and where he is, and what he has been doing.

11. Calvin had too much to do with the *direct exposure of anti-Christ,* as he *rose to view before him,* to have much leisure or need to trace his features in the Apocalypse. But perhaps the gentleman does not *know* (for the Fifth Lateran Council, in its eleventh session, forbade its priests to preach concerning the coming of anti-Christ, especially to fix the time of it) that Pastorini (Dr. Walmsly, a Catholic minister) had admitted that *Rome* is to be the *seat of anti-Christ.* This is yielding the whole question. For, either the Pope is he, or else, if anti-Christ is to supplant the Pope from being head of "the *true church,"* then the true church will have *failed.* Certain it is, that anti-Christ and the Pope cannot both reign in Rome, except as they are one; and they are so near akin that it will require a *dispensation* to allow their *nuptials.*

12. Poor Mr. Ansley! I named him not—*at first*. On the contrary, my allusion to him was anonymous—for those reasons of delicacy which Mr. Hughes *affects to feel*. It was Mr. Hughes who dragged his *name to light*. It was in St. John's (I learned) that this man renounced *Protestantism;* and under the direct auspices of Mr. Hughes. The reason for naming such cases, is, that the direct *effect*, and even *requirement*, of popery is that *priests should have no wives*. Hence, before a married man can enter the priesthood of Rome, he must *leave his wife, as a wife forever—whether she will or not*. Hence it is the asylum of so many villains, who grow weary of *one wife*—but may *keep twenty concubines*. It is an anti-social and abominable doctrine, a disgrace to the church and all its priesthood. And it is high time, indeed, that the *holy wrath* and *pure benevolence* and *papal delicacy of a renegado Jesuit*, should burn against me because I intimate that the doctrine of celibacy parts husbands from wives, and beggars helpless babes—when the same Jesuit is seeking, far and near, to spread this very doctrine, and these very effects; and exults, like a hungry tiger, when he can thus prey upon the credulity or domestic misery of some fanatical Protestant! I spurn, before the universe, the hypocrisy and baseness of such a system, and feel it to be my duty, my privilege, and my joy, to hold up such infamous principles and practices to the detestation of mankind. And if the gentleman will go to Burlington, N. J., he will there find a full confirmation of all that I have said, in the *honest indignation* of a *thousand bosoms*.

And I hereby publish the dignified letter of Bishop Doane, because Mr. Hughes's impertinence makes it a duty, and the Bishop kindly allows it. I pity Mr. Ansley. May God teach him his duty to his family, and *the great sin of deserting "the wife of his youth."*

13. Next we have Mr. BARNES and the SYNOD OF PHILADELPHIA, and Mr. Hughes, good man, with his crocodile tears! How he wonders at oppression! The inquisitors would not do so! No! What unheard of cruelty! It far exceeds the burning of John Huss and Jerome of Prague! The massacre of St. Bartholomew's night did not equal it! I hardly think Mr. Barnes will bottle Mr. Hughes's tears, or thank him for the manner of his notice. However that may be, if Mr. Hughes had read the trial he would have known my views of it; and whatever his views of it, this is certain, Mr. Barnes had a trial offered to him in the Synod, and refused. He then appealed to a higher court, and to it the case goes. He had already been tried in a court below. But how did the priest in Wilmington (Del.) a few years ago fare, whose sin I will not *shock* Mr. Hughes's ears by reciting? Did he get a trial? No! Did the church in this country cover his sin? Oh yes! It was *indelicate* to publish it; and too cruel to *try him*. He was chased to Rome by a wily prelacy which well knows

how to hide *iniquity*, and to *oppress the weak*. The Pope would have saved the Synod all this vast round of trouble, trial, appeal and discussion, by cutting the *knot* and the *neck* at the same blow.

14. His reasoning on our *prayers*, is truly farcical. We are enjoined he says by our confession to pray *"that the church may be countenanced and maintained by the civil magistrate."* But the same book he says declares, that the church is composed of those who profess the true religion. And *Presbyterianism is the true religion. Therefore we pray for an establishment!* I know no better proof of the *barrenness* of his field of argument than such logic. This is the secret of his late *retreat*. He was run out of matter. But let us look at the best he has to give. In the first place, we pray that God would bless and maintain, and cause the civil magistrate to maintain and countenance, *all Christian churches*. There is not one word in the *Confession of Faith like the assertion*, that we *alone* are the true church. On the contrary it is expressly and repeatedly declared, (as already proved) that we are only one branch of the *universal church*. The *Jews* and *Catholics* are the only *bigots* on *this subject*. It is a part of Mr. Hughes's creed *"that out of the true Catholic faith none can be saved."* Not so with us. Yet on this false statement of his, turns his *profound argument*. Again, when we pray that the civil magistrate may do so, it is but saying in other words, so far as *American Churches are concerned, Oh, Lord, perpetuate the American Constitution* which protects thy people in their unalienable rights, and which is the peculiar foe of anti-Christian and papal domination over the consciences of thy creatures!!! But I am ashamed to stoop to such petty and puerile trifling. Yet he believes this to be *profound*, and if I had passed it by, it might have been trumpeted as *unanswerable*.

15. As to MARIA MONK, I have not named her. It seems *some of the holy fathers liked her better than* Mr. Hughes does. I never *rest great principles on insulated cases*. But surely it is very *needless* for any body TO INVENT *stories* about NUNNERIES and MONASTERIES, while they are now demolishing them by THOUSANDS in *Spain*, &c. for THEIR CORRUPTIONS and OPPOSITION to the best interests of states; and when the blackest page of history is that which *records their character*. But more of this hereafter. I remark again, if MARIA MONK *be false* it is *now* easy to show it, and so, to do it, as to identify the *propagators* of the forgery. For I find in the *"Protestant Vindicator"* of *this week*, the FOLLOWING CHALLENGE, which I commend to Mr. Hughes's chivalry, and love to his church and her institutions.

"*Challenge*.—The Roman Prelates and Priests of Montreal; Messrs. Conroy, Quarter, and Schneller, of New York; Messrs. Fenwick and Byrne of Boston; Mr. Hughes of Philadelphia; the Arch Prelate of Baltimore, and his subordinate Priests; and Cardinal England of Charleston, with all other Roman Priests, and every Nun, from Baffin's bay to the gulf of Mexico, are hereby challenged to meet an investigation of the truth of Maria Monk's 'Awful Disclosures,' before an impartial assembly, over which shall preside seven gentlemen; three to be selected by the Roman Priests, three by the Executive Committee of the New York Protestant Association, and the seventh as Chairman, to be chosen by the six.

"An eligible place in New York shall be appointed, and the regulations for the decorum and order of the meetings, with all the other arrangements, shall be made by the above gentlemen.

"All communications upon this subject from any of the Roman Priests or Nuns, either individually or as delegates for their superiors, addressed to the *Corresponding Secretary of the New York Protestant Association*, No. 142 Nassau street, New York, will be promptly answered."

Now as Mr. *Hughes is expressly named*, let him meet the call like a man; or henceforth keep *still* at St. John's.

The previous remarks exhaust the little argument there is to be found in the last speech of Mr. Hughes, which he discharged retreating. For his *large assertions* there needs no rebutter. For his *little arguments*, of many heads, I refer to the whole past discussion, as a full reply.

And now, before I close this article, it becomes my duty, in a brief (and it must be very brief) way to present to the public, a view of the field of argument over which we passed in the debate, and which he has left *undefended*, and avowed *indefensible*, by his abrupt and irrevocable withdrawal.

After completing the argument as given *for substance* in the previous discussion, I proceeded next to show, that while the papal system is so decisively opposed to the civil, and especially the religious liberty of others, out of the communion of "*the church*," it has bound its own subjects with a series of *bonds*, which make it the most severe and compacted hierarchy on earth. A real "*Catholic*" is another name for *a slave for life*. The system is so constructed in its doctrines, institutions, and discipline, as to receive a man into *bondage* when he *comes into the world;* to *lead him through life in bondage;* and send him out of the world bound hand and foot, dependent on priestly *acts* and *intentions whether* he be saved or lost, and whether if he get into purgatory and not into hell, he shall stay there a long or a short time, before he *rises* to Heaven! In another part of this discussion we have exposed the *bondage* of *papal baptism, papal matrimony,* and the *papal rule of faith*. We now propose to examine the *bonds themselves*. An illustration of the system supported by them is very important—*in proof that the Roman Church is the enemy of liberty*.

I. THE CREED AND OATH OF PIUS.—In the year 1564, (after the final rising of the Council of Trent,) Pius IV. issued a *creed* containing a summary of the doctrines decreed by that

Council—which was received universally in the Roman Catholic Church; and this creed, being intended to publish and enforce, the decrees of that Council—is accompanied by an oath under whose sanction it is to be adopted. The Bull of Pius IV. which promulgated this creed required *all doctors, and teachers, and heads of universities to profess it;* and no election or promotion was to be considered valid without its adoption. Another bull required all heads of cathedrals, monastic institutions, and the military orders, to profess this creed. Persons also received into the communion of the church "*from without*," are bound to adopt this creed. Dr. Milner in his "*End of Controversies*," chap. XVI. says "The same creeds, viz. the Apostle's creed, the Nicene creed, the Athanasian creed, AND THE CREED OF POPE PIUS IV. DRAWN UP IN CONFORMITY *with the definitions of the Council of Trent*, ARE EVERY WHERE RECITED AND PROFESSED, *to the* STRICT LETTER, &c. But the universal reception and binding authority of this document will hardly be denied. What then are its contents? After a *profession of faith*—after the form of the Apostle's and Nicene creed, there is an addition of some *twelve new articles as* foreign to the Apostle's creed as to Christian truth. They are as follows:

1. I most firmly admit and embrace apostolical and ecclesiastical *traditions,* and all other observances and constitutions of the same church.

2. I also admit the sacred Scriptures according *to the sense which the holy mother church has held and does hold, to whom it belongs to judge of the true sense and interpretation* of the holy Scriptures; nor will I ever *take or interpret them otherwise than according to the unanimous consent of the fathers.*" The first adopts all the *trash of Roman traditions;* the second binds the mind never to think for itself in religion, and adopts the impossible test of *unanimity among the fathers.*

3. The third article is, "I profess also that there are truly and properly seven sacraments of the new law, instituted by Jesus Christ, and for the salvation of mankind, though not all for every one: to wit, *Baptism, confirmation, eucharist, penance, extreme unction, orders, and matrimony, and that they confer grace.*

4. The fourth adopts the definitions of the "*Holy Council of Trent*"—on original sin, and justification, by the latter of which, among other things, it is declared that "*without the sacrament of Baptism, which is the sacrament of faith, no one can ever obtain justification,*" hanging thus the saving of the soul on the arm of the *priest.*

5. Adopts the horrible doctrine of *transubstantiation and the mass;* "*that in the mass there is offered to God a true, proper, and propitiatory sacrifice for the living and the dead*"—making every priest a sacrificer of Jesus Christ; and thus again hanging salvation directly on *his act and his alone;* for while in extreme cases, laymen *may baptize; none in the universe,* who is not

a *"Catholic" priest*, may or can *transubstantiate* the *wafer*, or offer up *the sacrifice of mass, and to this they are bound by oath.*

6. Adopts the doctrine of purgatory, that is *temporary* punishment after death; which is the way to heaven for the *faithful*. (*Heretics all go to hell*, as the XII. Article will presently declare,) and this again, is made to depend on *acts* of men on earth, the *acts* of the *priest*. "*The souls detained therein are helped by the suffrages of the faithful.*" By this is meant the prayers (*well paid for*) of the living, offered *through the priests* for the *souls of the dead, to get them out of purgatory;* so that for the soul of his father, his wife, or his child, lying in all the horrors of purgatory, he must employ the priest's *official services, and pay him for them, in order to deliver that* soul from torment!!

Could there be a more *enriching*, or a more *binding* doctrine than this? Hence a distinguished public man said to a friend of mine in this city, while the former Controversy was going on, "*The doctrine of purgatory gives the Catholic priests great advantage over the Protestants.*" It truly does! We have no such *mines of wealth for the priesthood, and bond of slavery for the people.*

7 & 8. Adopt and profess the heathen doctrine of worshipping (for it is no less,) *saints* and their *relics; the images of Christ, of the "Virgin Mother of God,"* and *of other saints; yet this is binding on all.*

9. *Professes faith in the power of indulgences.* "I *also affirm that the power of indulgences was left by Christ in the church, and that the use of them is most wholesome to a Christian people.*" They have been well called "*bills of exchange on purgatory.*" They are dispensed by the *Pope, through the priests.* Being "a bundle of licenses to commit sin," they are *popular;* being *sold* they are very *profitable*, and depending on *the foreign* will of the Pope, they give to his "*keys*" (with which he professes to unlock an infinite *treasury of merits of the whole papal pantheon,* not only the *merits of our Lord,* but of *all saints,*) an unbounded power over the people.

10. "*I acknowledge the Holy Catholic, Apostolic, Roman Church for the mother and mistress of all churches; and I promise true obedience to the Bishop of Rome, successor to St. Peter prince of the Apostles and vicar of Jesus Christ.*" "THE MISTRESS OF ALL CHURCHES." What an epithet for *a Christian church!* And then this direct allegiance to the pope. Is *it less than slavery?*

11. "*I likewise undoubtedly receive and profess all other things delivered, defined, and declared by the sacred canons of general Councils.*" Here is a universal adoption of all the persecuting canons, and all the profane, civil, and *immoral* legislation of all the general Councils. "*And particularly the holy council of Trent,*" the *worst and last of all.* Yet every priest is bound on oath to receive, "*all things defined, delivered, and declared*" by that conventicle!

"*And I condemn, reject, and anathematize all things contrary thereto, and all heresies which the church has condemned, rejected, and anathematized.*" Here, by wholesale, they curse over all *their* curses, and in the *gross*, affirm, *known* or *unknown*, their direful persecutions.

12. "*This true Catholic faith, without which no man can be saved, which I at present freely profess and truly hold, the same I will take care as far as in me lies, shall be most constantly held and confessed by me*, whole and unviolated, with God's assistance, to the last breath of life; and by all my subjects, or those the care of whom in my office belongs to me, shall be held, taught and preached. I, THE SAME N, PROMISE, VOW, AND SWEAR; SO HELP ME GOD, AND THESE HOLY GOSPELS." *This is peculiarly the priest's article.* He is the SLAVE of the POPE, and a PARISH POPE TO THE PEOPLE.

(1) He swears that there *is no salvation* to those who hold not this creed; as for example, PURGATORY, SUPREMACY OF THE POPE, INDULGENCES, IMAGE AND SAINT WORSHIP, TRANSUBSTANTIATION, TRADITIONS OF ROME, &c. &c. Was there ever such *exclusiveness*, such intolerance, and yet sustained by AN OATH! (2) He swears to do all, for life, that he can, without ever restricting himself to what is *right*, to spread this system among those *under his care*, or subject to him! Then will *Protestants*, who know this, ever trust their children to " Catholic" priests? Either they will "do all that in them lies" to make " Catholics" of their children, or else they are *perjured;* for they *swear to do this.* (3) And consider the *bonds* under which this oath brings the conscience and creed of every Roman priest upon earth! Bound by *oath* to the *Pope* and to the *peculiar and exclusive doctrines* of the church; bound by *oath* to receive all the tyrannic and persecuting decrees of all the General Councils, and to seek by all means in their reach the diffusion of these anti-liberal principles!!

The last named of these articles, as taken by the *priests*, differs somewhat from the form usually adopted for the profession of the *laity.* That for the laity, however, explicitly declares that "*without this true Catholic faith none can be saved.*"

And now who can look at this *juramentum* "oath," and *professio fidei*, "*profession of faith,*" without distinctly perceiving how the whole church is bound up in *bonds* to the fearful hierarchy of Rome, by the creed of *Pius* IV.

11. *But we pass to consider next, the* EPISCOPAL OATH OF ALLEGIANCE TO THE POPE.—This oath, like the Bulla in Cœna Domini was *crescent*, augmenting its size and strictness with the gradual rise of popery in the world. The earliest form adopted, consisted of *seven particulars*, which are still found in the Corpus Juris Canonici, (the body of the canon law,) in the Decret. of Greg. IX. l. ii. title 24. It is much more simple, and less rigid than that afterwards used, given in full, in the Roman Pontifical, and ex-

tracted from it into Barrow's *unanswered* Treatise on *Supremacy.* This is exactly a *feudal oath,* and binds every Roman Catholic bishop on earth to the foot of the papal throne. It is as follows: "I, N, elect of the church of N, will henceforward be faithful *and obedient* to St. Peter the Apostle, and to the holy Roman Church and to *our Lord,* the lord N, pope N, and to his successors canonically coming in. I will neither advise, *consent,* or *do any thing* that they may lose life or member, or that their persons may be seized, or *hands anywise laid upon them, or any injuries offered to them under any pretence whatever.* The counsel which they shall entrust me withal, by themselves, their *messengers,* or letters, I will not knowingly reveal to any to their prejudice. I will *help them to defend and to keep the Roman papacy;* and the ROYALTIES OF ST. PETER, *saving* my order, *against all men.* The legate of the apostolical see, going and coming, I will honourably treat and help in his necessities. THE RIGHTS, HONOURS, PRIVILEGES, AND AUTHORITY OF THE HOLY ROMAN CHURCH OF OUR LORD THE POPE, *and his foresaid successors, I will endeavour to preserve, defend, increase, and advance. I will not be in any counsel, action, or treaty in which shall be plotted against our said lord, and the Romish Church, any thing to the hurt or prejudice of their persons, right, honour, state, or power; and if I shall know any such thing to be treated or agitated by any whatsoever, I will hinder it to my power, and as soon as I can, will signify it to our said lord, or to some other by whom it may come to his knowledge. The rules of the holy fathers, the apostolic decrees, ordinances, or disposals, reservations, provisions, and mandates, I will observe with all my might, and cause to be observed by others.* HERETICS, SCHISMATICS, AND REBELS TO OUR SAID LORD, OR HIS FORESAID SUCCESSORS, I WILL TO MY POWER PERSECUTE AND OPPOSE. I will come to a council when I am called, unless I am hindered by a canonical impediment. I WILL BY MYSELF IN PERSON VISIT THE THRESHOLD OF THE APOSTLES EVERY THREE YEARS, AND GIVE AN ACCOUNT TO OUR LORD AND HIS FORESAID SUCCESSORS OF ALL MY PASTORAL OFFICE, *and of all things anywise belonging to the state of my church, to the discipline of my clergy and people, and lastly to the salvation of souls committed to my trust; and will in like manner humbly receive and diligently execute the apostolic commands. And if I be detained by a lawful impediment, I will perform all the things aforesaid by a certain messenger, hitherto specially impowered, a member of my chapter, or some other in ecclesiastical dignity, or else having a parsonage; or in default of these, by a priest of the diocese, or in default of one of the clergy,* [of the diocese,] *by some other secular or regular priest of approved integrity and religion, fully instructed in all things above mentioned. And such impediment I will make out by lawful proofs, to be transmitted by the foresaid messenger to the cardinal proponent, of the holy Roman church, in the congregation of the sacred council. The possessions belonging to my table, I will neither sell, nor give away, nor mortgage, nor grant anew in fee, nor anywise alienate, no not even with the consent of the chapter of my church, without consulting the Roman pontiff. And if I shall make any alienation, I will thereby incur the penalties contained in a certain constitution, put forth about this matter.* So HELP ME GOD AND THESE HOLY GOSPELS."

This is a COMPLETE FEUDAL OATH. No man can take it to the Pope and be the *consistent* citizen of his *own* country—or the *free* citizen of any country. How can any Catholic bishop maintain this oath to the Pope, and be an *honest* citizen of the United States? The reader will please remember that *under these bonds*, in the memorable contest between the Pope and the *Republic of Venice*, the Jesuits *all turned traitors and went over to the Pope.*

But we have not room to comment; and it is not necessary. It speaks for itself.

III. Another topic (which Mr. Hughes has *excluded* by abruptly stopping) which was presented in the debate, was that the doctrines of *supremacy* and *of the priesthood, made the people the bond-slaves of the priesthood.*

The doctrine of supremacy in the words of the council of Florence is this: "*That the apostolic chair, and Roman high priest, doth hold a primacy over the universal church; and that the Roman high priest is the successor of St. Peter, the prince of apostles, the true heir-tenant of Christ, and the head of the church; that he is the father and doctor of all Christians; and that unto him in St. Peter, full power is committed to feed and direct the Catholic Church under Christ; according as is contained in the acts of general councils and in the holy canons.*"

And Leo X. (approved by the Lateran Council at the very era of the Reformation), "*Christ before his departure from the world, did in solidity of the rock, institute Peter and his successors to be his lieutenants, to whom it* IS SO NECESSARY TO OBEY, THAT HE WHO DOTH NOT OBEY MUST DIE THE DEATH."

The doctrine of the priesthood makes a POPE for every *parish;* as that of supremacy makes a *God on earth* of the *head-pope.* The *pope* grinds the *priesthood,* and they grind the *people.* In the Catechism of the Council of Trent it is thus written, (1) "*In the minister* of God who sits in the tribunal of penance, as his legitimate judge, he (the penitent) venerates the power and person of our Lord Jesus Christ." This is blasphemy. Again, (2) "THEY HOLD THE PLACE, AND POWER AND AUTHORITY OF GOD ON EARTH." Again, (3) "*The power of consecrating and offering the body and blood of our Lord, and of remitting sins, with which the priesthood of the new law is invested, is such as cannot be comprehended by the human mind, still less can it be equalled by, or assimilated to any thing on earth.*" Every priest is in *fact a God.* Hence he controls our elections—raises or allays a mob by the waving of his hand (among his own people)—forgives sins,

(1, Donovan's Trans. page 342.   (2) Page 283.   (3) Same page.

admits men to heaven, lets them out of purgatory, &c. &c.! What awful unearthly power! To strike such a man is *death*, where the Catholic religion is *established!* But who *believing* this would *dare* to strike or offend him? The men among the Catholics who are *worst*, often fear the *priest* most, on the principles by which some of the Eastern nations worship the devil, because of his *power* and *willingness to do them harm*. Besides all this, no *act of his* is valid unless he *intends* to make it so. Such is the *doctrine of intention.* Hence *to displease him is ruin* to his poor people. And again, *once a priest always a priest.* They cannot take away his office. The sacrament of orders *impresses an indelible character.* And hence they teach and hold that however wicked a priest may be, yet he is to be venerated as a *priest* of Christ! Thus it is written: (1) "AND OF THIS THE FAITHFUL ARE FREQUENTLY TO BE REMINDED, IN ORDER TO BE CONVINCED, THAT WERE EVEN THE LIVES OF HER MINISTERS DEBASED BY CRIME, THEY ARE STILL WITHIN HER PALE, AND THEREFORE LOSE NO PART OF THE POWER WITH WHICH HER MINISTRY INVESTS THEM." Here is a shelter for every knave and debauchee; and here is sustaining the power, influence, and authority of the priesthood, to the last dregs of human, papal, priestly crime.

All these facts Mr. Hughes has *once* tried to meet; but failing, *now wisely* shuts the debate. All must see why he does so.

In the late debate, I proved at large, on the *authority* of the *French Parliament,* and of *Catholic writers,* THAT THE ORDER OF THE JESUITS, *who are the pope's great propagandists,* cannot, and never did prevail in any country, without destroying *its liberties,* and *its morals.* Mr. Hughes shuns enquiry on this topic, by withdrawing from the discussion before it is *reached in writing,* having been defeated on it in the *oral* debate, and having then rejected the stenographer's report. Mr. Hughes is the apologist, nay the eulogist of the *Jesuits.* The *secreta monita,* which Mr. Hughes well knows, rest on *good proof,* are not our *only,* or our chief proof, as those who heard the debate will testify.

But we are not allowed to introduce this subject here. Mr. Hughes refuses to allow me to proceed—refuses to proceed himself. He will withhold what he has written, if I add more to the *present amount before* it is put to press.

NUNNERIES. We proved in the oral debate, that they had *uniformly* been *prisons* to the *inmates,* and *generally brothels* for the priests; that every nation almost of Europe which had tried them, had been sorely injured by them in vital respects, especially by the astonishing immoralities which they systematically propagated among *females and priests.*

And this was done on the authority of Catholic writers of different ages. In Spain and Portugal, which though *late,* are at *last* awaking from the long slumber of slaves under the papal yoke, these nurseries of *popery and of pollution* are perishing

(1) Catechism, 94, 95.

before the wild fury of an injured and outraged people. If the *disclosures* of *the secrets* of the *nunneries* in our continent be *not* true, I can only say that they are most *faithful* reports of the history of the same institutions, in other ages, and in other lands. Let any man read what Erasmus, what De Ricci, what the Bishop of Sultsburg, and the Bishops of Bononia, *all Catholic writers,* say of these institutions, (which Mr. Hughes defends, and is continually attempting to honour and multiply) and he must arise from their perusal deeply convinced that *their friend* is his *country's enemy.*

But Mr. *Hughes declines to discuss this topic also.*

AND THE INQUISITION. Mr. Hughes its apologist! In America! In the 19th century! It is enough! Yet he declines discussing the question when he sees it coming, and retreats shutting the door by which he is pursued.

We proved the fact of *the conspiracy among foreign papists against the liberties of our country;* showing at the same time that popery is a *political,* much more than a *religious institution.* Mr. Hughes refuses to have it published, or at least he declines to meet the proof from the press, after having heard it in the debate.

The immoralities of the papal system show it to be the "*man of sin.*" The dreadful tendency of the doctrines of *indulgences, priestly absolution,* and *confession in secret* to a *priest;* and the *impurities* even of their *very books* of devotion, were exhibited at large in the debate. He *shunned* them *then,* he *flies* from them now. A *Spanish book* used in confession in South America, and "*The Christian's Guide to Heaven,*" issued under the sanction of Bishop Kenrick, have in them the most reprehensible matter. From the latter I give a specimen of the questions for self-examination, in preparation for confession to a priest. I blush to record it! But how else shall we expose it? They who print it, circulate it, use it, have themselves denounced the exposure of it? On page 82, it says, "*consult the table of sins to help your memory.*" In this table, under the sixth commandment, is the following paragraph. "Committed adultery, fornication or incest. Procured pollution in one's self or others. Wanton words, looks, or gestures. Lascivious dressing, colours, or painting. Lewd company. Lascivious balls, or revellings. Dishonest looks. Unchaste songs. Kissing, or unchaste discourses. Took carnal pleasure by touching myself, or others of either sex. Showed your skin or some naked part of your body to entice others. Eat hot meats, or drank hot wine to procure or excite lusts."

Is not this the *vocabulary* of a *brothel?* What but a Roman Catholic Priest, "could have had the pollution to conceive it, or the audacity to give it in a book of devotions; to prepare a female to meet him at confession? When I first read this infamous passage it struck me as possible that it may have been given for *private* use. It were horrible even then. But not so. The same book in the same connexion adds, "If you have any thing upon your conscience which you have a *particular difficulty in confessing, cease not with prayers and tears to importune your Heavenly Father* to assist you in this regard, till he gives you the grace to *overcome that difficulty.* Let it (*your confession*) be *entire as to the kind and number of your sins;* and such circumstances as quite change the nature of your sins, or notoriously aggravate it." This drags the *whole heart,* and all its *details* to light. The fifth chapter also of the Council of Trent, *On Confession, commands* the *most secret kind of mortal sins to be confessed, as indispensable to their forgiveness.*

Now can such a system fail to ruin any *heart,* or church, or country in which it prevails, and then too as a part of *religion?* If this be *religion,* what must the *rest be?* I beg pardon of my country for the record of this loathsome matter. But I felt that I should have to ask a still deeper pardon for *suppressing it.*

Finally, I reviewed the CANON LAW, which is binding upon all Catholics, which is a *depository of the papal system,* as an *active, organized mass;* and from it, at large, I proved the tyranny of Rome; her enmity to liberty; her persecuting spirit; and her total and ruthless bigotry and intolerance.

It was and is in vain to call Mr. Hughes to its defence.

Now from all these sources of proof, we showed the enmity of the *system* of popery to *civil* and especially *religious* liberty.

These several heads have been *excluded* from this *volume of the Discussion* by Mr. Hughes's determination not to admit them, though every member of the society knows that they were in succession produced, and dwelt on in the *oral* debate. This recapitulation of them is designed to show to the public how large the sources of proof are; how limited the discussion about to be put to press is; how inadequate a view it gives of the subject as traversed on the rostrum; *who* abridged it thus; and *why* he has done it.

And now at the close of these remarks, it becomes my duty to make the following suggestions.

1. That I always distinguish between the *priesthood* and the *laity* of the Church of Rome. The *priesthood* make the hierarchy and are the seat of power, oppression, darkness, and pollution. I respect unfeignedly many of the *laity,* whom I esteem it my happiness to know. The intelligent members of that communion in the United States have been and are fast verging to protestantism. They are strictly speaking only *semi-papal;* and one happy effect of these discussions, as I have good reason to know, has already been to open many eyes to the true character of popery. For example, when Mr. Hughes (as in the late discussion), backed by Bishop Kenrick, *took off,* by a public disclaimer, the papal prohibition (*recorded in the rules of the index*) to read controversies with heretics, thousands of Catholics availed themselves of that permission to *read the Discussion.* And so as to the *reading of the Bible.* In this way therefore, Mr. Hughes's *denial of the doctrines* and *discipline* of his church, is (though reversely) producing the

best effects for the truth, though on his part, in a most unenviable way. For as he is ashamed of many features of his system, and denies them, it is death to it by *suicide;* instead of *destruction* in the field of manly argument. The result will be the same.

2. It is an A'merican and a Bible principle to *examine* every thing. If there be any thing in *Presbyterianism* that shall prove *wrong* in itself or *opposed to liberty* we desire to know it—and to renounce it. We profess not to be unchangeable, or infallible. We invite enquiry. But I think it will appear very plain that Mr. Hughes has found *little in us against liberty*. Hence he ran to *Europe*. There we did not largely follow him; for it was *aside* from the question. We agreed with him that our fathers were in some things *wrong*, and in others *intolerant*. Most of his statements were *false*, as we have occasionally *proved;* and may more fully do *hereafter*. But we were determined to press the real question, and leave his scandal to refute itself.

3. Catholic priests in America are so ill-bred, that it seems impossible to debate with them as *gentlemen*. Nothing but the great interest at stake would ever have induced me to debate with Mr. Hughes after I discovered how reckless and unamiable a man he was. Yet I feel it to be my duty thus publicly to say that I deeply regret my having occasionally expressed myself with improper severity towards him. I expect to meet him before a *higher bar* than that of the American people, which is surely the first of *earthly tribunals*. It is with some humble consciousness of the integrity of my purpose, and a deep impression of the value and glory of the truth, that I review my intercourse with Mr. Hughes.

4. It is my purpose, if heaven permit, to pursue this question to its legitimate close; and at my leisure, exhibit those features of the discussion which have been suppressed by Mr. Hughes.

Finally, I dedicate my imperfect attempts to defend the great cause of *American liberty* to the youth of our beloved country, *whose breasts*, as has been no less truly than beautifully said by one of our greatest statesmen — *are the shrine of freedom*. To them, under God, our liberties are committed.

May it be an imperishable deposit.

THE END.

WE, the undersigned, Committee on Publication, after having carefully examined this work, do certify that it is a true copy of the manuscript of the Discussion as placed in our hands by the Rev. gentlemen for publication.

THOMAS BROWN, M. D
WILLIAM DICKSON.

www.ingramcontent.com/pod-product-compliance
Lightning Source LLC
Chambersburg PA
CBHW031945290426
44108CB00011B/684